Lawrenceville Press

A Guide to Microsoft®
Office 2000 Professional

for Windows® 98

Bruce Presley
Beth Brown
Elaine Malfas
Vickie Grassman

**All orders including educational, Canadian, foreign,
FPO, and APO may be placed by contacting:**

Lawrenceville Press, Inc.
P.O. Box 704
Pennington, NJ   08534-0704
(609) 737-1148
(609) 737-8564 fax

This text is available in hardcover and softcover editions.

16 15 14 13 12 11 10 9 8 7 6 5 4 3 2 1

We believe the best way to introduce students to computing is with an applications course that gives them considerable "hands-on" computer experience. This objective is best accomplished with an applications software package such as Microsoft Office 2000, which teaches students to use and integrate data between word processor, spreadsheet, database, presentation, and desktop publishing applications. A well-rounded applications course should include discussion of the Internet as well as discussions about the roles computers play in modern society, and a brief history of computers. Learning the vocabulary of computing is also important. These goals are accomplished by this text. The emphasis of this text is on the concepts of computing and problem solving so that students learn how computer applications can be applied to a wide range of problems. The text is written to be used either in a one or two term course by students with little or no previous computer experience.

Design and Features

Format Each chapter contains numerous examples and screen captures to help students visualize new concepts. Important commands are listed on the first page of each chapter. Office 2000 menus are displayed in the margins for easy reference.

Objectives An outline of the significant topics that will be covered is presented at the beginning of each chapter.

History of Computers Before learning to use the applications software, Chapter One introduces students to a brief history of computers and the vocabulary needed to understand concepts presented in later chapters.

Concepts of Applications The first chapter of each application begins with an introductory section that describes the application and its uses. In this way, students are taught the purpose of the application without being overly concerned with the specific software. If the student then goes on to use another software package, he or she will fully understand the general concepts behind the application.

Hands-on Practices In the applications chapters each new concept is presented, discussed, and then followed by a "hands-on" practice which requires the student to test newly learned skills using the computer. The practices also serve as excellent reference guides to review applications commands. Answers to all the practices are included in the *Teacher's Resource Package*.

Chapter Summaries Each chapter concludes with a summary that briefly discusses the concepts covered in the chapter.

Vocabulary Sections At the end of each chapter is a listing of new terms and definitions. A separate section lists Office 2000 commands and buttons.

Review Questions Numerous review questions are keyed to each section of the chapter, providing immediate reinforcement of new concepts. Answers to all review questions are included in the *Teacher's Resource Package*.

Exercises Each application chapter includes a set of exercises of varying difficulty, making it appropriate for students with a wide range of abilities. Answers to all exercises are included in the *Teacher's Resource Package*.

Internet Chapters One and Eighteen introduce students to the Internet and the World Wide Web and discuss how to research a topic on the Web.

Ethical Implications Because computers play such an important role in modern society, Chapter Eighteen discusses the social and ethical implications of living in a computerized society.

Computer Related Careers It is hoped that many students will become interested in careers in computing based upon their experience in this course. A section in Chapter Eighteen outlines different computer careers and the educational requirements needed to pursue them.

Appendices Office 2000 keyboard shortcuts, available functions, customizing forms and reports in Design view, and keyboarding skills are presented in appendices at the end of the text.

Teacher's Resource Package

When used with this text, the Lawrenceville Press *Teacher's Resource Package* provides all the additional material required to offer students an excellent introductory computer applications course. These materials place a strong emphasis on developing the student's problem-solving skills. The Package divides each of the chapters in the text into lessons that contain the following features:

- **Assignments** Suggested reading and problem assignments.

- **Teaching Notes** Helpful information that we and our reviewers have learned from classroom experience.

- **Discussion Topics** Additional material that supplements the text and can be used in leading classroom discussions.

- **Worksheets** Problems that supplement the exercises in the text by providing additional reinforcement of concepts.

- **Quizzes** A short quiz that tests recently learned skills.

In addition to the material in the lessons, other features are included in each chapter:

- **Tests** Two sets of comprehensive tests for each chapter as well as a midterm and final examination. Each test consists of multiple choice questions and "hands-on" problems that are solved using the computer. A full set of answers and a grading key are also included.

- **Review Question answers** Complete answers for the review questions presented in the text.

A master CD, included with the Package, contains the following files:

- **Data files** All files the student needs to complete the practices and exercises in the text. These files allow students to work with large amounts of data without having to type it into the computer. Also included are the files needed to complete the worksheets, quizzes, and tests in the Package.

- **Power Point Presentations** Slides that present topics and graphics from the chapter.

- **Tests** The tests are also provided in Word files so that they can be edited.

- **Answer files** Answers to the practices, exercises, worksheets, quizzes, and tests.

Student data diskettes that contain the files needed to complete the practices and exercises can easily be made by following the directions in the Teacher's Resource Package Introduction. Student CDs are also available for purchase in packs of 10.

As an added feature, the Package is contained in a 3-ring binder. This not only enables pages to be removed for duplication, but also allows the instructor to keep notes in the Package.

A Guide to Microsoft Office 2000 Professional

Previous editions of our applications texts have established them as leaders in their field, with more than two million students having been introduced to computing using our "hands-on" approach. With this new edition, we have made significant improvements over our earlier applications texts. These improvements are based on the many comments we received, a survey of instructors who are teaching the text, and our own classroom experience.

This text presents material for the word processor, spreadsheet, and database in introductory, intermediate, and advanced chapters making the text appropriate for students at a variety of levels. The integration of data between applications is covered in two chapters. The presentation application and desktop publishing application are discussed in two chapters. Other chapters introduce the Internet, the World Wide Web, and discuss search techniques. Additional topics include the Windows 98 operating system, history of computers, telecommunications, and e-mail.

A Guide to Microsoft Office 2000 Professional is available in hardcover and softcover editions. The softcover edition has an improved sewn lay-flat binding, which keeps the text open at any page and gives the book additional strength.

As classroom instructors, we know the importance of using a well written and logically organized text. With this edition we believe that we have produced the finest introductory computer applications text and Teacher's Resource Package available.

Acknowledgments

The authors are especially grateful to the many instructors and their students who classroom test our texts as they are being written. Their comments and suggestions have been invaluable.

We thank Rick May of Courier Book Companies, Inc. who supervised the printing of this text. The line drawings were created by John Gandour.

The success of this and many of our other texts is due to the efforts of Heidi Crane, Vice President of Marketing at Lawrenceville Press. She has developed the promotional material which has been so well received by instructors around the world, and coordinated the comprehensive customer survey which led to many of the refinements in this edition. Joseph DuPree and Christina Albanesius run our Customer Relations Department and handle the many thousands of orders we receive in a friendly and efficient manner. Richard Guarascio and Michael Porter are responsible for the excellent service Lawrenceville Press offers in shipping orders.

Melissa Kinzer, the newest member of our staff, created many of the screen captures and contributed to the vocabulary, review questions, and index.

We also thank our colleague Nanette Hert. She has offered valuable suggestions on ways in which this text could be improved as well as editing the text and exercises.

Finally, we would like to thank our students, for whom and with whom this text was written. Their candid evaluation of each lesson and their refusal to accept anything less than perfect clarity in explanation have been the driving force behind the creation of *A Guide Microsoft Office 2000 Professional*.

About the Authors

Bruce W. Presley, a graduate of Yale University, taught computer science and physics at The Lawrenceville School in Lawrenceville, New Jersey for twenty-four years where he served as the director of the Karl Corby Computer and Mathematics Center. Mr. Presley was a member of the founding committee of the Advanced Placement Computer Science examination and served as a consultant to the College Entrance Examination Board. Author of more than thirty computer texts, Mr. Presley is president of Lawrenceville Press and teaches computer applications.

Beth A. Brown, a Computer Science graduate of Florida Atlantic University, is director of development at Lawrenceville Press where she has coauthored a number of applications and programming texts and their Teacher's Resource Packages. Ms. Brown currently teaches computer applications and computer programming.

Elaine Malfas is a graduate of Hartwick College and earned her M.S. degree in Technical Communication from Rensselaer Polytechnic Institute. Ms. Malfas has coauthored several computer texts and their accompanying Teacher's Resource Packages. Currently Ms. Malfas teaches computer applications and desktop publishing.

Vickie Grassman is a Computer Information Systems graduate of Florida Atlantic University. Ms. Grassman has coauthored several application texts and their accompanying Teacher's Resource Packages. Ms. Grassman currently teaches computer applications.

Table of Contents

Chapter Three - Introducing the Word Processor

Chapter Four - Formatting Documents

Chapter Five - Word Processor Features

Chapter Six - Advanced Word Processor Features

Chapter Seven - Introducing the Spreadsheet

Chapter Eight - Spreadsheet Techniques

Chapter Nine - Worksheets and Charts

Chapter Ten - Advanced Spreadsheet Techniques

Chapter Eleven - Integrating the Word Processor and Spreadsheet

Chapter Twelve - Introducing the Relational Database

Chapter Thirteen - Relational Database Techniques

Chapter Fourteen - Relational Database Reports and Advanced Database Techniques

Chapter Fifteen - Integrating the Database with the Word Processor and Spreadsheet

Chapter Sixteen - Making Presentations with PowerPoint

Chapter Seventeen - Desktop Publishing with Publisher

Chapter Eighteen - The Internet and the Social and Ethical Implications of Computers

Appendix A - Microsoft Office Keyboard Shortcuts and Functions

Appendix B - Creating Customized Forms and Reports

Appendix C - Keyboarding Skills

A Guide to Microsoft Office 2000 Professional

Chapter One
Introducing the Computer

Chapter One Objectives

After completing this chapter you will be able to:
1. Discuss the history of computers.
2. Define what a computer is.
3. Describe the components of a personal computer.
4. Understand how computers work.
5. Describe what software and hardware are.
6. Describe common storage and peripheral devices.
7. Understand telecommunications.
8. Describe networks and network services.
9. Describe the Internet and the World Wide Web.

This chapter discusses the history of computers and how they process and store data. Networks and important social and ethical issues relating to computers are also discussed.

1.1 Mechanical Devices

Pascaline

One of the earliest mechanical calculating devices was the *Pascaline*, invented in 1642 by the French philosopher and mathematician Blaise Pascal. The Pascaline was a complicated set of gears that operated similarly to a clock. It was designed to only perform addition. Unfortunately, due to manufacturing problems, Pascal never got the device to work properly.

Blaise Pascal
1623 – 1662

The Pascaline was a mechanical calculating device invented by Blaise Pascal in 1642

Stepped Reckoner

Later in the 17th century Gottfried Wilhelm von Leibniz, a famous mathematician, invented a device that was supposed to be able to add and subtract, as well as multiply, divide, and calculate square roots. His device, the *Stepped Reckoner*, included a cylindrical wheel called the *Leibniz wheel* and a moveable carriage that was used to enter the number of digits in the multiplicand. However, because of mechanically unreliable parts, the device tended to jam and malfunction.

Gottfried Wilhelm
von Leibniz
1646 – 1716

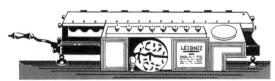

The Stepped Reckoner was another early attempt at creating a mechanical calculating device

Difference Engine

In 1822 Charles Babbage began work on the *Difference Engine*. His hope was that this device would calculate numbers to the 20th place and then print them at 44 digits per minute. The original purpose of this machine was to produce tables of numbers that would be used by ships' navigators. At the time, navigation tables were often highly inaccurate due to calculation errors. In fact, a number of ships were known to have been lost at sea because of these errors. Although never built, the ideas for the Difference Engine lead to the design of Babbage's Analytical Engine.

Analytical Engine

The *Analytical Engine*, designed around 1833, was supposed to perform a variety of calculations by following a set of instructions, or program, stored on punched cards. During processing, the Analytical Engine was planned to store information in a memory unit that would allow it to make decisions and then carry out instructions based on those decisions. For example, when comparing two numbers, it could be programmed to determine which was larger and then follow an appropriate set of instructions. The Analytical Engine was also never built, but its design served as a model for the modern computer.

The History of Punched Cards

In 1810 Joseph Jacquard, a French weaver, used cards with holes punched in them to store weaving instructions for his looms. As the cards passed through the loom in sequence, needles passed through the holes and then picked up threads of the correct color or texture. By rearranging the cards, a weaver could change the pattern being woven without stopping the machine to change threads.

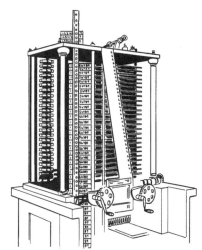

Babbage's Analytical Engine was designed as a calculating machine that used punched cards to store information

Charles Babbage
1792 – 1871

Ada Byron
1815 – 1852

Babbage's chief collaborator on the Analytical Engine was Ada Byron, Countess of Lovelace, the daughter of Lord Byron. Interested in mathematics, Lady Byron was a sponsor of the Analytical Engine and one of the first people to realize its power and significance. She also wrote of its achievements in order to gain support for it. Ada Byron is often called the first programmer because she wrote a program based on the design of the Analytical Engine.

Babbage had hoped that the Analytical Engine would be able to think. Ada Byron, however, said that the Engine could never "originate anything," meaning that she did not believe that a machine, no matter how powerful, could think. To this day her statement about computing machines remains true.

1.2 Electro-Mechanical Devices

By the end of the 19th century, U.S. Census officials were concerned about the time it took to tabulate the continuously increasing number of Americans. This counting was done every 10 years, as required by the Constitution. However, the Census of 1880 took nine years to compile which made the figures out of date by the time they were published.

Hollerith's tabulating machine

In response to a contest sponsored by the U.S. Census Bureau, Herman Hollerith invented a tabulating machine that used electricity rather than mechanical gears. Holes representing information to be tabulated were punched in cards, with the location of each hole representing a specific piece of information (male, female, age, etc.). The cards were then inserted into the machine and metal pins used to open and close electrical circuits. If a circuit was closed, a counter was increased by one.

Herman Hollerith
1860 – 1929

Based on the success of his tabulating machine, Herman Hollerith started the Tabulating Machine Company in 1896. In 1924, the company was taken over by International Business Machines (IBM).

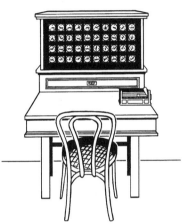

Herman Hollerith's tabulating machine, invented for the Census of 1890, used electricity instead of gears to perform calculations

Hollerith's machine was immensely successful. The general count of the population, then 63 million, took only six weeks to calculate. Although the full statistical analysis took seven years, it was still an improvement over the nine years it took to compile the previous census.

Mark I

In 1944, the *Mark I* was completed by a team from International Business Machines (IBM) and Harvard University under the leadership of Howard Aiken. The Mark I used mechanical telephone relay switches to store information and accepted data on punched cards. Because it could not make decisions about the data it processed, the Mark I was not a computer but instead a highly sophisticated calculator. Nevertheless, it was impressive in size, measuring over 51 feet in length and weighing 5 tons. It also had over 750,000 parts, many of them moving mechanical parts which made the Mark I not only huge but unreliable.

Howard Aiken
1900 – 1973

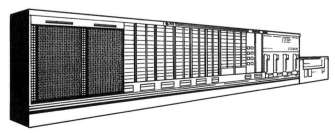

The Mark 1 was over 51 feet long and weighed over 5 tons

1.3 First Generation Computers

*John Atanasoff
1903 – 1995*

*Clifford Berry
1918 – 1963*

The first electronic computer was built between 1939 and 1942 at Iowa State University by John Atanasoff, a math and physics professor, and Clifford Berry, a graduate student. The *Atanasoff-Berry Computer* (ABC) used the binary number system of 1s and 0s that is still used in computers today. It contained hundreds of vacuum tubes and stored numbers for calculations by electronically burning holes in sheets of paper. The output of calculations was displayed on an odometer type of device.

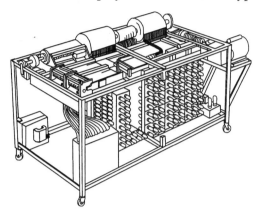

The Atanasoff-Berry Computer used the binary number system used in computers today

The patent application for the ABC was not handled properly, and it was not until almost 50 years later that Atanasoff received full credit for his invention. In 1990, he was awarded the Presidential Medal of Technology for his pioneering work. A working replica of the ABC was unveiled at the Smithsonian in Washington, D.C. on October 9, 1997.

ENIAC

*John Mauchly
1907 – 1980*

*J. Presper Eckert
1919 – 1995*

In June 1943, John Mauchly and J. Presper Eckert began work on the *ENIAC* (Electronic Numerical Integration and Calculator). It was originally a secret military project which began during World War II to calculate the trajectory of artillery shells. Built at the University of Pennsylvania, it was not finished until 1946, after the war had ended. But the great effort put into the ENIAC was not wasted. In one of its first demonstrations, ENIAC was given a problem that would have taken a team of mathematicians three days to solve. It solved the problem in twenty seconds.

The ENIAC was originally a secret military project

A Guide to Microsoft Office 2000 Professional

The ENIAC weighed 30 tons and occupied 1500 square feet, the same area taken up by the average three bedroom house. It contained over 17,000 vacuum tubes, which consumed huge amounts of electricity and produced a tremendous amount of heat requiring special fans to cool the room.

computer

The ABC and the ENIAC are first generation computers because they mark the beginning of the computer era. A *computer* is an electronic machine that accepts data, processes it according to instructions, and provides the results as new data. Most importantly, a computer can make simple decisions and comparisons.

1.4 The Stored Program Computer

The ABC and ENIAC required wire pulling, replugging, and switch flipping to change their instructions. A breakthrough in the architectural design of first generation computers came as a result of separate publications by Alan Turing and John von Neumann, both mathematicians with the idea of the stored program.

Alan Turing
1912 – 1954

program

In the late 30s and 40s, Alan Turing developed the idea of a "universal machine." He envisioned a computer that could perform many different tasks by simply changing a program rather than by changing electronic components. A *program* is a list of instructions written in a special language that the computer understands.

CPU

In 1945, John von Neumann presented his idea of the stored program concept. The stored program computer would store computer instructions in a *CPU* (central processing unit). The CPU consisted of different elements used to control all the functions of the computer electronically so that it would not be necessary to flip switches or pull wires to change instructions.

John
von Neumann
1903 – 1957

EDVAC
EDSAC

Together with Mauchly and Eckert, von Neumann designed and built the *EDVAC* (Electronic Discrete Variable Automatic Computer) and the *EDSAC* (Electronic Delay Storage Automatic Computer). These computers were designed to solve many different problems by simply entering new instructions that were stored on paper tape. The instructions were in *machine language*, which consists of 0s and 1s to represent the status of a switch (0 for off and 1 for on).

machine language

UNIVAC

The third computer to employ the stored program concept was the *UNIVAC* (UNIVersal Automatic Computer) built by Mauchly and Eckert. The first UNIVAC was sold to the U.S. Census Bureau in 1951.

These first generation computers continued to use many vacuum tubes which made them large and expensive. They were so expensive to purchase and run that only the largest corporations and the U.S. government could afford them. Their ability to perform up to 1,000 calculations per second, however, made them popular.

1.5 Second Generation Computers

transistor

In 1947, William Shockley, John Bardeen, and Walter Brittain of Bell Laboratories invented the *transistor* for which they were awarded the 1956 Nobel Prize in physics. The invention of the transistor made computers smaller and less expensive and increased calculating speeds to up to 10,000 calculations per second.

John Bardeen,
William Shockley,
and Walter Brittain

One transistor (on right) replaced many tubes, making computers smaller, less expensive, and more reliable

Model 650

In the early 1960s, IBM introduced the first medium-sized computer named the *Model 650*. It was expensive, but it was much smaller than first generation computers and still capable of handling the flood of paperwork produced by many government agencies and businesses. Such organizations provided a ready market for the 650, making it popular in spite of its cost.

Second generation computers also saw a change in the way data was stored. Punched cards were replaced by magnetic tape and high speed reel-to-reel tape machines. Using magnetic tape gave computers the ability to *read* (access) and *write* (store) data quickly and reliably.

read, write

1.6 High-Level Programming Languages

Second generation computers had more capabilities than first generation computers and were more widely used by business people. This lead to the need for *high-level programming languages* that had English-like instructions and were easier to use than machine language. In 1957, John Backus and a team of researchers completed *FORTRAN* (FORmula TRANslator), a programming language with intuitive commands such as READ and WRITE.

One of the most widely used high-level programming languages has been COBOL, designed by Grace Murray Hopper, a Commodore in the Navy at the time. *COBOL* (COmmon Business Oriented Language) was first developed by the Department of Defense in 1959 to provide a common language for use on all computers. The Department of Defense (DOD) also developed Ada, named after the first programmer, Ada Byron.

Developed in the 1960s by John Kemeny and Thomas Kurtz at Dartmouth University, BASIC was another widely used programming language. *BASIC* (Beginner's All-Purpose Symbolic Instruction Code) has evolved to Visual Basic, which is widely used today for Windows programming.

Grace Murray Hopper
1906 – 1992

While working on the Mark II at Harvard University, Rear Admiral Dr. Grace Murray Hopper found the first computer bug when a moth flew into the circuitry causing an electrical short. While removing the dead moth, she said that the program would be running again after the computer had been "debugged."

A Guide to Microsoft Office 2000 Professional

1.7 Third Generation Computers

The replacement of transistors by *integrated circuits* (ICs) began the third generation of computers. In 1961, Jack Kilby and Robert Noyce, working independently, developed the IC, sometimes called a *chip*. One IC could replace hundreds of transistors, giving computers tremendous speed to process information at a rate of millions of calculations per second.

ICs are silicon wafers with intricate circuits etched into their surfaces and then coated with a metallic oxide that fills in the etched circuit patterns. This enables the chips to conduct electricity along the many paths of their circuits. The silicon wafers are then housed in special plastic cases that have metal pins. The pins allow the chips to be plugged into circuit boards that have wiring printed on them.

A typical chip is about 0.5" wide by 1.5" long

In 1964, the IBM *System 360* was one of the first computers to use integrated circuits and was so popular with businesses that IBM had difficulty keeping up with the demand. Computers had come down in size and price to such a point that smaller organizations such as universities and hospitals could now afford them.

Robert Noyce
1927 – 1990

Noyce developed the integrated circuit while working for Fairchild Semiconductor. In 1968, he left Fairchild to form the company now known as Intel Corporation.

1.8 Mainframes

A *mainframe* is a large computer system that is usually used for multi-user applications. The IBM System 360 was one of the first mainframes available. They are used by large corporations, banks, government agencies, and universities. Mainframes can calculate a large payroll, keep the records for a bank, handle the reservations for an airline, or store student information for a university—tasks that require the storage and processing of huge amounts of information.

Jack S. Kilby
1923 –

Kilby, working for Texas Instruments, developed the first integrated circuit. To demonstrate this new technology, he invented the first electronic hand-held calculator. It was small enough to fit in a coat pocket, yet as powerful as the large desktop models of the time.

Mainframe computers are large and set up in their own rooms

Most people using mainframes communicate with them using *terminals*. A terminal consists of a keyboard for data input, and a monitor for viewing output. The terminal is connected by wires to the computer, which may be located on a different floor or a building a few blocks away. Some mainframes have hundreds of terminals attached.

1.9 Fourth Generation Computers

Marcian Hoff
1937 –

Stephen Wozniak
1950 –

Steve Jobs
1955 –

In 1970, Marcian Hoff, an engineer at Intel Corporation, invented the *microprocessor*, an entire CPU on a single chip. The replacement of several larger components by one microprocessor made possible the fourth generation of computers.

The small microprocessor made it possible to build a computer called a *microcomputer* that fits on a desktop. The first of these was the Altair built in 1975. In 1976, Stephen Wozniak and Steven Jobs designed and built the first Apple computer.

Advances in technology made microcomputers inexpensive and therefore available to many people. Because of these advances almost anyone could own a machine that had more computing power and was faster and more reliable than either the ENIAC or UNIVAC. As a comparison, if the cost of a sports car had dropped as quickly as that of a computer, a new Porsche would now cost about one dollar.

1.10 The Personal Computer

Microcomputers, often called *personal computers* or *PCs*, fit on a desktop. Modern PCs have computing power and storage capacity that rival older mainframes. The computer you will use is a microcomputer:

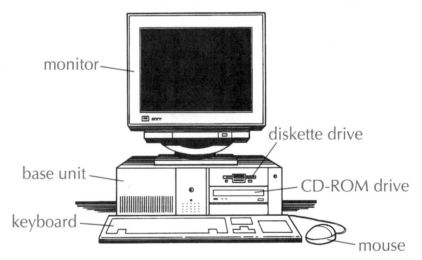

A PC combines a keyboard, monitor, external drives, and a mouse in a desktop-sized package

Microcomputers contain four types of *hardware* components:

1. **Input Devices:** devices from which the computer can accept data. A keyboard, CD-ROM drive, disk drive, and a mouse are all examples of input devices.

2. **Memory:** ICs inside the base unit where data can be stored electronically.

3. **CPU (Central Processing Unit):** an IC inside the base unit that processes data and controls the flow of data between the computer's other units. It is here that the computer makes decisions.

Apple Computer, Inc.

In 1976, two computer enthusiasts, Stephen Wozniak and Steve Jobs, built the Apple personal computer and marketed it to other computer enthusiasts. The original design and production of the Apple took place in Jobs' garage. The initial success of the Apple lead to the Apple II and later the Apple Macintosh.

The Macintosh set new standards for ease of computer use with its graphical user interface that includes icons, windows, pull-down menus, and a mouse.

A Guide to Microsoft Office 2000 Professional

4. **Output Devices:** devices that display or store processed data. Monitors and printers are the most common visual output devices. The hard disk, which is inside the base unit, and the diskette and CD-ROM are the most common storage output devices.

The diagram below illustrates the direction that data flows between the separate components of a computer:

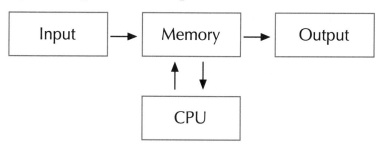

Notice that all information flows through the CPU. Because one of the tasks of the CPU is to control the order in which tasks are completed, it is often referred to as the "brain" of the computer. However, this comparison with the human brain has an important flaw. The CPU only executes tasks according to the instructions it has been given; it cannot think for itself.

software

Microcomputers require software to perform tasks. *Software* is instructions stored as electronic data that tells the computer what to do. *Operating system software* is run automatically when the computer is turned on and enables the user to communicate with the computer by using input devices such as the mouse and keyboard. *Applications software* is written by programmers to perform a specific task, such as a word processor.

1.11 Memory: ROM and RAM

Computers have two types of memory contained on chips, *ROM* and *RAM.* Read Only Memory, or ROM, contains the most basic operating instructions for the computer. The data in ROM is a permanent part of the computer and cannot be changed. The instructions in ROM enable the computer to complete simple jobs such as placing a character on the screen or checking the keyboard to see if any keys have been pressed.

Random Access Memory, or RAM, is temporary memory where data and instructions can be stored. Data stored here can be changed or erased. When the computer is first turned on, this part of memory is empty and, when turned off, any data it contains is lost. Because RAM storage is temporary, computers have auxiliary data storage devices. Before turning the computer off, the data in RAM can be saved to a floppy diskette or the hard disk so that it can be used again at a later time.

1.12 The CPU

The CPU (Central Processing Unit) directs the processing of information throughout the computer. It can only follow instructions that it gets from ROM or from a program in RAM.

A CPU chip measures about 2" by 2"

Within the CPU is the *ALU* (Arithmetic Logic Unit), which can perform arithmetic and logic operations. The ALU is so fast that the time needed to carry out a single addition is measured in *nanoseconds* (billionths of a second). The ALU can also compare numbers to determine whether a number is greater than, less than, or equal to another number. This ability is the basis of the computer's decision-making power.

How does the computer perform calculations?

How does the computer subtract, multiply, or divide numbers if the ALU can only perform arithmetic and compare numbers? The ALU does this by turning problems like multiplication and division into addition problems. This would seem to be a very inefficient way of doing things, but it works because the ALU calculates so fast. For example, to solve the problem 5×2, the computer adds five twos, $2 + 2 + 2 + 2 + 2$, to calculate the answer, 10.

1.13 Bits and Bytes

binary

The electrical circuits on an IC have one of two states, off or on. Therefore, the *binary number system* (base 2), which uses only two digits (0 and 1), was adopted for use in computers. To represent numbers and letters, a code was developed with eight binary digits grouped together to represent a single number or letter. Each 0 or 1 in the binary code is called a *bit* (BInary digiT) and an 8-bit unit is called a *byte*.

bit, byte

ASCII

In order to allow computers to interchange information, the American Standard Code for Information Interchange, or *ASCII*, was developed. In this code, each letter of the alphabet, both uppercase and lowercase, and each symbol, digit, and special control function used by the computer is assigned a number. The ASCII representation of the letters in the name JIM are 74, 73, 77. Both the decimal and binary code representations of those numbers are shown below:

Letter	Decimal	Binary code
J	74	01001010
I	73	01001001
M	77	01001101

memory size

MB

GB

K

The size of memory in a computer is measured in bytes. For example, a computer might have 16 MB of RAM. In computers and electronics *MB* stands for *megabytes* where mega represents 2^{20} or 1,048,576 bytes and *GB* stands for *gigabytes*, which is 2^{30} or 1,073,741,820 bytes. Bytes are sometimes described as *kilobytes*, for example 256K. The *K* comes from the word *kilo* and represents 2^{10} or 1,024. Therefore, 64K of memory is really 64 × 2^{10} which equals 65,536 bytes.

1.14 Storage Devices

Computers include devices for long-term storage. The capacity of these storage devices is measured in bytes, just as memory, and ranges from 1.44 MB to many gigabytes. Most PCs have three drives: a *diskette drive*, a *CD drive*, and a *hard disk drive*. The diskette and CD (compact disc) drives are accessible from outside the base unit, and the hard disk is completely contained inside the base unit. All three drives use a different kind of storage media:

diskette   CD   hard disk

Data can be stored on diskette, CD, or hard disk (internal)

diskette   Sometimes called a floppy disk, *diskettes* are made of a mylar (thin polyester film) disk that is coated with magnetic material and then loosely *CD*   encased in hard plastic. Each diskette has a capacity of 1.44 MB. *CDs* are made of a mylar disk with a reflective coating that is sealed in clear, hard plastic. Each CD can store over 650 MB of data, equal to the storage capacity of over 470 diskettes. CD drives can be CD-ROM (compact disc *CD-RW, hard disk*   read only memory) or *CD-RW* (compact disc read write). *Hard disks* are made of an aluminum disk coated with a magnetic material. Unlike diskettes and CDs, hard disks are permanently installed inside a hard disk drive. Each hard drive may have multiple disks inside, and therefore have large storage capacities of many gigabytes.

Other storage devices, some of which are becoming standard in PCs, are:

Storage Device	Capacity	Description
DVD-ROM drive	4.7 GB	Reads data, audio, and video from a digital versatile disc (similar to a CD). It can also read traditional CDs.
DVD-RAM drive	5.2 GB	Reads and writes data to a digital versatile disc.
Iomega Zip drive	250 MB	Reads and writes data to a disk almost as small as a diskette
Iomega Jaz drive	2 GB	Reads and writes data to a disk almost as small as a diskette
SuperDisk drive	120 MB	Reads and writes data to a disk similar to a floppy diskette. It can also read and write to floppy diskettes.
tape drive	7 GB	Stores data on magnetic tape sealed in a cartridge.
removable hard drive	230 MB	Reads and writes data to a disk constructed like diskettes but larger.

hard disk array

Completely external to the PC is the *hard disk array*. Enormous amounts of data can be made transportable using hard disk arrays. These are towers of several hard drives (not just large diskettes as in the removable hard drives) that combine to equal 72 GB or more. Each hard drive can be removed from the tower and transported to another array tower.

1.15 Peripheral Devices

A PC becomes much more versatile when other devices such as printers and scanners are used with it. Such devices are sometimes called *peripheral devices* because they are attached to the computer.

laser printer

Two commonly used types of printers are laser and inkjet. A *laser printer* uses a beam of light and toner to generate characters and graphics on

ink jet printer

paper. *Toner* is a fine powder that fuses to paper when heated . An *inkjet printer* uses an ink cartridge to place very small dots of ink onto paper to create characters and graphics. Inkjet printers are less expensive than laser printers and can be used to inexpensively generate full-color images and text. Laser printers, however, can generate images that are of higher resolution and quality than the images generated by an inkjet printer. Color laser printers are also available, but are relatively expensive.

scanner

Another common peripheral device is the scanner. A *scanner* uses a beam of light to create a digital image from artwork such as photos and drawings. The digitized image can then be incorporated into a document.

1.16 Telecommunications

Telecommunications is the transmitting and receiving of data over telephone lines with the use of a modem. With the use of communications software, a *modem* converts a computer's binary data into tones that can be transmitted over phone lines. To receive data, a modem converts the tones from the phone line into binary data. This process involves what is called signal <u>mo</u>dulation and <u>dem</u>odulation, hence the name modem. Modems are used so that two computers can communicate directly with each other.

Modems can be "external" (outside the computer) or "internal" (within the base unit)

The rate at which data is transmitted is measured in *bits per second* (bps). The most common modem rates are 33.6K and 56K bps.

telecommuting

Telecommuting is the use of telecommunications to work at home rather than in the office. For example, writers and news reporters can write their stories at home on a word processor and then transmit the documents to their office. As another example, financial consultants, accountants, and travel agents can easily access databases from home rather than driving to an office.

1.17 Networks

Businesses, universities, and other organizations often network their computers. A *network* allows computers to exchange data and to share applications software and devices, such as printers. Two common network technologies are LAN (Local Area Network), used to connect devices within a building or on a campus, and WAN (Wide Area Network) which is used to connect computers over long distances.

LAN
network interface card

In a *LAN*, the base unit of computers and other devices each contain a circuit board called a *network interface card*. A cable then plugs into the network interface card to connect one device to another to form the LAN:

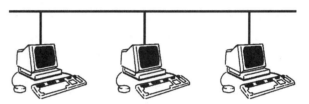

Networked computers can share files and send messages

WAN

In a *WAN*, each site uses a dedicated computer to send and receive data that is then communicated to the computers on the network. For example, a WAN that interconnects computers in New York, Miami, and Paris requires three dedicated computers, one for each site. The dedicated computers are then connected through network cards and modems to computers at each site to form a WAN.

The most widely accessed network is the *Internet*, a worldwide network that is not controlled by any one organization. Many organizations link their networks to the Internet. Individuals can get access to the Internet through telecommunications and an Internet service provider or an online service. An *Internet service provider* (ISP) offers access to the Internet for a fee. An *online service*, for example America Online, offers access to the Internet as well as other services also for a fee.

The Internet is viewed as a large network where the computers in this network are either servers or clients that communicate using software called *TCP/IP*. A *server* computer, often called an *Internet site*, provides information. A *client* computer accesses servers to request information. The client-server structure of the Internet is called *interactive* because the information accessed is a result of selections made. For example, when you connect to the Internet, your computer becomes a client. You can then interact with the Internet by selecting the information you wish to receive.

An *intranet* is a network that also uses TCP/IP software but is used by a single organization and is not accessible from the outside.

History of the Internet

The Internet was originally a United States research project at the Advanced Research Projects Agency (ARPA). ARPA had a network called ARPANET that researchers used to communicate with each other as they developed TCP/IP (Transmission Control Protocol/Internet Protocol). TCP/IP is the protocol software that is the basis for the way computers on the Internet communicate.

When the TCP/IP software was ready in 1983, the ARPANET and a few outside sites were connected using the new software to form the Internet. Today the Internet includes millions of computers worldwide.

1.18 Network Services

e-mail

One widely used feature of the Internet is e-mail. *E-mail*, which means *Electronic mail*, allows an individual with an e-mail account to send messages to another person with an e-mail account. E-mail can be received in a matter of seconds, even if the recipient is located half way around the world.

To be able to send and receive e-mail over the Internet, your computer must be connected either through a network or a modem to the Internet and you must have your own unique address, such as jdoe@xyz.com. The first part of the address is the username, which refers to the person who has the e-mail account. The part after the @ symbol indicates the domain name, which is discussed later in the chapter. Note that e-mail addresses do not contain spaces.

BBS

A *bulletin board service*, sometimes referred to as a *BBS*, allows a user to participate in a discussion group. There are thousands of bulletin board services with topics ranging from accounting to zoology. Businesses often maintain a bulletin board service for their employees only. Other bulletin board services allow any network user to join.

netnews
newsgroup
article

Network News, sometimes referred to as *netnews* is a popular BBS available on the Internet. This system uses the term *newsgroup* to refer to an individual bulletin board, and *article* refers to the message posted to the newsgroup. Members of a newsgroup must check for new articles and can post (send) articles regarding the topic of discussion.

listserv

mailing list

Internet users can also join a listserv. A *listserv* is basically a discussion group that uses e-mail to send messages. *LISTSERV* is a program that maintains the *mailing list*, a list of e-mails addresses, of the users who subscribe to a particular listserv. When a user posts a message to a listserv, every user who subscribes to the listserv receives a copy of the message.

1.19 Using a Network

netiquette

Network users are assigned a user name and password to log on to the network. This enables networks to identify who has permission to log on to a network. It also enables networks to allow employees to have different levels of access, which allows for security and privacy. When using networks, a certain etiquette referred to as *netiquette* should be followed:

- Do not attempt to access the account of another user without authorization.

- Do not post messages or send e-mail under another person's name or user name.

- Be careful when giving personal information such as your address and phone number over the Internet.

- Use appropriate subject matter and language, and be considerate of other people's beliefs and opinions. This is especially important when posting messages that will be sent to every user on the network.

1.20 The World Wide Web

Web
Web site

The most popular way to interact with the Internet is through the World Wide Web (WWW), also called the *Web*. An Internet site can have thousands of *Web sites*, and each Web site is composed of either one document or a group of documents called *pages*. What makes the Web useful is that each site can present information in the form of text, graphics, and sound. The Web is aptly named because Web pages can have *hyperlinks*, which are links to either another portion of the current page, other pages at the Web site, or other Web sites.

hyperlink

Web browser
URL

A client that is accessing a Web site needs both a Web browser and a Uniform Resource Locator (URL). A *Web browser* is software that displays the graphics, text, and sound of the Web site. A *URL* is an address that tells the Web browser what Web site to go to. For example, to access the latest news at Cable News Network's (CNN) Web site you need to know the URL:

http://www.cnn.com

The first part of the URL, http, is the protocol used to transfer data over the Internet. There are a number of different protocols, but in this text we will discuss only the *http protocol* which stands for HyperText Transfer Protocol. URL addresses do not contain spaces. The two forward slashes following the colon separate the protocol from the domain name, in this case www.cnn.com. The *domain name* is the server name on the Internet. A domain name can give many clues about the organization running the server. In the example URL above, www indicates a Web site, cnn represents the company's name, and com is an identifier which indicates that it is a commercial organization. Other identifiers include:

Identifier	Meaning
com	commercial organization
edu	educational institution
gov	government facility
mil	US military facility
net	networking organization
org	nonprofit organization
ca	Canada
us	United States

Internet Explorer

A popular Web browser is Internet Explorer. Chapter Eighteen explains how to use Internet Explorer and how to find information on the Web.

History of the Web

The Web came into existence in 1980 when Tim Berners-Lee, a consultant for CERN in Europe, wrote a program that allowed special links between arbitrary computers on the Internet. With the new program, data could be transmitted and received over the Internet in the form of text, graphics, and sound from locations called sites. The Web has now grown to include millions of Internet sites.

1.21 The Software Revolution

The development of applications that have general uses, such as the word processor, lead to a software revolution. As more computers were sold, more applications were developed.

In this text, the Microsoft Office package will be used. It includes five common applications: word processing, spreadsheet, database, desktop publishing, and presentation graphics.

Word processors allow the user to insert and delete text, correct mistakes, move text, and perform numerous other functions all on the computer screen.

Spreadsheets primarily store numeric data which can then be used in calculations. Spreadsheets are useful for preparing financial calculations. The primary advantage of a spreadsheet is its ability to automatically update the calculations should the data it stores be changed.

Databases store and manipulate large quantities of data. A database can store the names, addresses, grades and extracurricular activities for all of the students in a school. Data can be added or deleted and printed reports produced.

Desktop publishing allows text and graphics to be placed on a page and manipulated until the layout appears as desired.

Presentation graphics allows the user to combine text and graphics to create professional looking material to use in an electronic slide show.

Chapter Summary

history of computers
The earliest computing devices were mechanical, requiring gears, wheels and levers, and were often unreliable. The advent of electricity brought about electro-mechanical machines, and later first generation computers that used vacuum tubes and were capable of performing thousands of calculations per minute. The architectural design of computers changed with the idea of a machine that could perform many different tasks by simply changing its program. With the development of the transistor came second generation computers that were much smaller and faster. Programming languages were developed so programmers could write English-like instructions. Third generation computers used integrated circuits. Fourth generation computers, the modern microcomputers of today, include an entire CPU on a single chip.

personal computers
All PCs have several hardware components: (1) input devices (keyboard, mouse, drives) for entering data and commands, (2) memory for storing commands and data, (3) a central processing unit for controlling the operations of the computer, and (4) output devices (monitor, printer, drives) for viewing and storing the processed information. PCs also require operating system software and applications software.

RAM
ROM
storage devices
Memory is contained on ICs and comes in two forms, RAM, which can be erased and used over, and ROM, which is permanent. Because the contents of RAM are lost when the computer's power is turned off, storage devices such as diskettes, CD-ROMs, and hard disks are used to store data.

CPU
ALU
A CPU directs the processing of information throughout the computer. Within the CPU is the ALU, which is the basis of the computer's decision-making power.

binary
bit
byte
ASCII
memory size
Because the electrical circuits of an IC have one of two states, off or on, the binary number system is used to represent the two states: 0 for off and 1 for on. Each 0 or 1 in a binary code is called a bit. The computer uses binary digits grouped into bytes to express all information. The ASCII code is used to translate numbers, letters, and symbols into a one byte binary code. The size of memory is measured in bytes, usually in MB or GB.

A Guide to Microsoft Office 2000 Professional

peripheral devices

Peripheral devices are devices such as scanners and printers that are attached to a PC. Two commonly used types of printers are laser and inkjet. A scanner uses a beam of light to create a digital image from artwork.

LAN
WAN

Internet

intranet

Networks allow computers to exchange data and to share applications software and devices. Two common network technologies are LAN (Local Area Network) and WAN (Wide Area Network). A LAN is used to connect devices within a building. A WAN is used to connect devices over a very long distance. The most widely accessed network is the Internet. Computers on the Internet communicate with TCP/IP software. For those who do not have Internet access through an organization's network, individual access can be purchased through an Internet service provider or an online service. An intranet is a network that is used by a single organization and is not accessed from the outside.

telecommunications
telecommuting

Telecommunications is the transmitting and receiving of data over telephone lines with the use of a modem. Telecommuting is the use of telecommunications to work at home rather than in an office.

network services
netiquette

Users of a network are usually assigned an account that consists of a user name and secret password to log on to the network. E-mail, bulletin board service, and listservs are common services on a network. Netiquette is the etiquette that should be used when using a network.

World Wide Web

The most popular way to interact with the Internet is through the World Wide Web. A client that is accessing a Web site needs both a Web browser and a URL (Uniform Resource Locator).

software revolution

The development of applications that have general uses, such as the word processor, lead to a software revolution. As more computers were sold, more applications were developed. You will be using Microsoft Office to introduce you to word processor, spreadsheet, database desktop publishing and presentation graphics applications.

Vocabulary

ALU (Arithmetic Logic Unit) The part of the CPU that handles arithmetic and logic operations.

Applications software Commercially produced programs written to perform specific tasks.

Article A message posted to a newsgroup.

ASCII (American Standard Code for Information Interchange) The code used for representing characters in the computer.

Base 2 See Binary number system.

Base unit Unit where the CPU, memory, and internal hard disk drive is housed.

BASIC A high-level computer language developed by John Kemeny and Thomas Kurtz.

BBS (bulletin board service) A network service that allows a user to participate in a discussion group.

Binary number system Number system used by modern computers—uses only digits 0 and 1.

Bit (BInary digiT) A single 0 or 1 in the binary code.

Bits per second The rate at which data is transmitted.

Byte A group of 8 bits.

CD Disc made of mylar with a reflective coating that is sealed in clear, hard plastic.

CD-ROM drive Drive accessible from outside the base unit. Used to read the data on a CD.

CD-RW drive Drive accessible from outside the base unit. Used to read and write data on a CD.

Chip See Integrated circuit.

Client A computer accessing the Internet to request information.

COBOL A high-level programming language designed by Grace Murray Hopper.

Computer An electronic machine that accepts data, processes it according to instructions, and provides the results as new data.

CPU (Central Processing Unit) An IC inside the base unit that processes data and controls the flow of data between the computer's other units.

Data Information either entered into or produced by the computer.

Database An application that stores and manipulates large quantities of data.

Desktop publishing An application that allows text and graphics to be placed on a page and manipulated until the layout appears as desired.

Diskette Sometimes called a floppy disk. Made of mylar coated with a magnetic material and then loosely encased in hard plastic.

Diskette drive Drive accessible from outside the base unit. Used to read and write data to a diskette.

Domain name A server name on the Internet.

DVD A digital versatile disc similar to a CD, that stores 4.7 to 5.2 GB of data. Used in a DVD-ROM or DVD-RAM drive.

DVD-RAM drive Drive accessible from outside the base unit. Used to read and write data to a DVD (digital versatile disc).

DVD-ROM drive Drive accessible from outside the base unit. Used to read data from a DVD (digital versatile disc).

E-mail (electronic mail) A message sent over a network to another user on the network.

FORTRAN A high-level programming language developed by John Backus.

GB (gigabyte) Measurement of computer memory capacity. 1,073,741,820 bytes.

Hardware Physical devices that make up the computer.

Hard disk Made of aluminum coated with a magnetic material. Permanently installed inside the hard disk drive.

Hard disk array A tower of several hard drives where each drive can be removed and transported to another array.

Hard disk drive Drive completely enclosed in the base unit. Used to read and write to disks within the hard drive.

High-level programming language A programming language that uses English-like instructions.

HTTP (HyperText Transfer Protocol) The protocol used by Web sites to transfer data over the Internet.

Hyperlink Links to either another portion of the current page, other pages at the Web site, or other Web sites.

Inkjet printer A printer that uses an ink cartridge to place very small dots of ink onto paper to create characters and graphics.

Input Data used by the computer.

IC (Integrated Circuit) Also called a chip. A silicon wafer with intricate circuits etched into its surface and then coated with a metallic oxide that fills in the etched circuit patterns.

Interactive Where the information received is a result of the selections made.

Internet A worldwide computer network.

Internet service provider (ISP) A company that offers access to the Internet for a fee.

Internet site See server.

Intranet A network that uses TCP/IP software, but is not accessible from outside the organization using the network.

Jaz disk A disk, almost as small as a diskette, that stores 2 GB of data. Used in a Jaz drive.

Jaz drive Drive used to read and write data to a Jaz disk.

K (kilobyte) Measurement of computer memory capacity. 1,024 bytes.

Keyboard Device resembling a typewriter used to input data into a computer.

Laser printer A printer that uses a beam of light and toner to generate characters and graphics on paper.

Listserv A discussion group that uses e-mail to send messages.

Local Area Network (LAN) A network that interconnects computers within a local area.

Machine language Instructions in binary code (0s and 1s).

Mailing list A list of e-mail addresses.

Mainframe Computer system that is usually used for multi-user applications.

MB (megabyte) Measurement of computer memory capacity. 1,048,576 bytes.

Memory ICs in the base unit where data can be stored electronically.

Microcomputer A computer that fits on a desktop and uses a microprocessor.

Microprocessor An entire CPU on a single chip.

Modem Device that converts binary data into tones and tones back into binary data so that computer data can be sent over telephone lines.

Monitor Used to display computer output.

Mouse An input device from which the computer can accept information.

Nanosecond One billionth of a second.

Netiquette The etiquette that should be followed when using a network.

Netnews see Network News.

Network Allows computers to exchange data and to share applications software and devices.

Network interface card A circuit board that goes into the base unit of a computer for networking.

Network News A BBS available on the Internet.

Newsgroup An individual bulletin board.

Online service A company that offers access to the Internet as well as other services for a fee.

Operating system software Software that allows the user to communicate with the computer.

Output Data produced by a computer program.

PC (Personal Computer) A small computer employing a microprocessor. See also microcomputer.

Peripheral device A device attached to a PC.

Presentation graphics An application that allows the user to combine text and graphics to create professional looking material to use in an electronic slide show presentation.

Printer An output device.

Program List of instructions written in a special language that the computer understands.

RAM (Random Access Memory) Temporary memory where data and instruction can be stored.

Read Accessing data from a storage medium.

Removable hard drive Drive used to read and write data to a removable disk.

ROM (Read Only Memory) Data that is a permanent part of the computer and cannot be changed.

Scanner Uses a beam of light to create a digital image from artwork.

Server A computer on the network of the Internet that provides information.

Software Instructions stored as electronic data that tells the computer what to do.

Spreadsheet An application that is used to primarily store numeric data which can then be used in calculations.

SuperDisk A disk, very similar to a floppy diskette, that stores 120 MB of data. Used in a SuperDisk drive.

SuperDisk drive Drive used to read and write data to a SuperDisk.

Tape drive Drive used to read and write data to a magnetic tape.

TCP/IP Software that is the base of the Internet.

Telecommunications Transmitting and receiving computer data over telephone lines with the use of a modem.

Telecommuting Using telecommunications to work at home.

Terminal A keyboard and monitor used to communicate with a mainframe.

Toner A fine powder that fuses to paper when heated. Used in laser printers.

Transistor An electronic device that replaced the vacuum tube making computers smaller and less expensive and increasing calculating speeds.

Uniform Resource Locator (URL) An address that tells a Web browser which Web site to access.

Web See World Wide Web.

Web browser Software that is used to display the graphics, sound, and text of Web sites.

Web page Information at a Web site that can include graphics, text, and links to other Web sites or pages.

Web site A location on the WWW where information is presented in Web pages using graphics, text, and sound.

Wide Area Network (WAN) A network that interconnects computers over a long distance.

Word processor An application that allows the user to insert and delete text, correct mistakes, move text, and perform numerous other functions all on the computer screen.

World Wide Web (WWW) Computers on the Internet that transmit text, graphics, and sound using special software.

Write Storing data on a storage medium.

Zip disk A disk, almost as small as a diskette, that stores 250 MB of data. Used in a Zip drive.

Zip drive Drive used to read and write data to a Zip disk.

A Guide to Microsoft Office 2000 Professional

Review Questions

Sections 1.1 — 1.4

1. Briefly describe the Pascaline and explain what mathematical operations it was designed to perform.

2. a) What mathematical operations was the Stepped Reckoner supposed to perform?
   b) Why was it unreliable?

3. What did Ada Byron mean when she said that the Analytical Engine could never "originate anything"?

4. a) For what purpose did Herman Hollerith invent his tabulating machine?
   b) What were punched cards used for in the tabulating machine?

5. Why wasn't the Mark 1 considered a computer?

6. What number system did the Atanasoff-Berry Computer use?

7. For what purpose was the ENIAC originally designed?

8. What is a computer?

9. In what way did Alan Turning and John von Neumann improve upon the design of the ENIAC?

10. a) What is a program?
    b) What is machine language?
    c) List the first three computers designed to use a stored program.

Sections 1.5 — 1.9

11. Why was the invention of the transistor important to the development of computers?

12. How did the use of magnetic tape improve the performance of computers?

13. a) What is a high-level programming language?
    b) Who designed COBOL?
    c) List three high-level programming languages.

14. Explain what integrated circuits are and why they have been important in the development of computers.

15. a) What is a mainframe?
    b) What is the usual way for a person to communicate with a mainframe?

16. Why was the invention of the microprocessor important to the development of computers?

17. List some of the advantages of a microcomputer compared with the ENIAC or UNIVAC.

Sections 1.10 — 1.15

18. What are input and output devices used for?

19. Describe the flow of data between the components of a computer.

20. In what way was the design of Babbage's Analytical Engine similar to the modern computer?

21. a) What is the difference between ROM and RAM?
    b) How is each affected by turning off the computer?

22. Explain what a CPU does.

23. Why was the binary number system adopted for use in computers?

24. Explain what a bit and a byte are.

25. Why was ASCII developed?

26. a) How many bytes of data can 32 MB of RAM store?
    b) How many bytes of data can a 3 GB hard drive store?

27. a) Describe the diskette drive, CD-ROM drive, and hard disk drive and the storage media they use.
    b) List three other storage devices used with a PC.

28. What is the difference between a laser printer and a ink jet printer?

29. What is telecommunications?

30. a) What does a modem do?
    b) What is a modem used for?

31. What is telecommuting?

32. a) What is a network?
    b) What is a LAN?
    c) What is a WAN?

33. What is the Internet?

34. What does the phrase "the Internet is interactive" mean? Give an example.

35. List three network services and describe them.

36. a) What is netiquette?
    b) List the four netiquette guidelines described in the chapter.

37. What is the World Wide Web?

38. a) What is a Uniform Resource Locator?
    b) Give an example of a URL.
    c) What does the http in a URL indicate?

39. What is a Web browser?

40. List and describe the applications you will be learning using Microsoft Office.

Shut Down

Format

Copy Disk

Programs

Details

Folder

Rename

Copy Here

Move Here

Create Shortcut(s) Here

Restore

Empty Recycle Bin

Help

Files or Folders

Chapter Two Objectives

After completing this chapter you will be able to:

1. Define what an operating system is.
2. Use the mouse as an input device.
3. Understand the features of the Windows 98 GUI.
4. Manipulate a window.
5. Understand the features of a dialog box.
6. Understand how to use and properly handle diskettes.
7. Start an application.
8. Use My Computer and Windows Explorer to view files and folders.
9. Format, copy, write protect, and backup a diskette.
10. Copy, move, delete, and rename files and folders.
11. Create folders and shortcuts.
12. Recover deleted files.
13. Use online help and find files.

The History of PC Operating Systems

With the development of personal computers (PC) in the early 70s came the need for PC operating systems (OS). In 1973, Gary Kildall, founder of Digital Research, Inc., developed CP/M (Computer Program for Microcomputers). CP/M became the leading OS with sales peaking in 1981. In early 1981, IBM negotiated with Microsoft Corporation to develop an OS for its new personal computer. Microsoft developed MS-DOS (Microsoft Disk Operating System), which became the leading OS and contributed to the huge success of the IBM PC.

In 1985, Microsoft developed the Microsoft Windows graphical user interface in an effort to create a more user-friendly interface. Microsoft introduced a new GUI OS called Windows 98 in 1998.

William H. Gates III
1955 –

In 1975, while a freshman at Harvard University, Bill Gates and his friend Paul Allen created a Basic language interpreter for the Altair computer. With the success of Basic for the Altair, Gates and Allen founded the Microsoft Corporation in 1977. The huge success of Microsoft began in 1981 when Gates developed MS-DOS (Microsoft Disk Operating System) for the new IBM-PC. Today Microsoft is known for its Windows operating system, Office application software package, and many programming languages, such as Visual Basic.

T his chapter introduces Windows 98, the operating system used to run the applications in the Microsoft Office package. How to use the mouse, windows, and dialog boxes are discussed. Proper handling and formatting of a diskette, and making backups of files are also introduced.

2.1 Operating Systems

All microcomputers run software that allow the user to communicate with the computer using the keyboard and mouse. This software is called the *disk operating system* (DOS). When the computer is turned on, the operating system software is automatically loaded into the computer's memory from the computer's hard disk in a process called *booting*.

A widely used operating system is *Windows 98*, which has a *graphical user interface*, or GUI (pronounced "gooey"). A GUI displays pictures called icons on the computer screen. *Icons* are used to perform various tasks.

Through the use of Windows 98, multitasking is possible. *Multitasking* allows for more than one application to run at the same time. For example, with Windows 98 both word processor and spreadsheet applications can run simultaneously. Windows 98 also supplies applications and tools that allow you to easily work with the operating system.

2.2 Applications Software

Applications software is written by professional programmers to perform a specific application or task. Most applications created for use with Windows 98 have interfaces with similar features. The *interface* of an application is the way it looks on the screen and the way in which a user provides input to the application. For example, two elements of Windows 98 applications are dialog boxes and windows. A *dialog box* allows the user to choose and enter information that is needed to complete an action, and a *window* is the area on the screen that contains an open application or document. A *document* is the material that you create using an application and a document stored on disk is called a *file*.

2.3 Using the Mouse

The computer comes equipped with an input device called a *mouse*, which is used to perform a variety of tasks. A mouse has two or three buttons and looks similar to:

The mouse

mouse pointer

When the mouse is in use, the *mouse pointer* is displayed on the screen. One common shape of the mouse pointer is an arrow:

The mouse pointer

The mouse pointer may change shape depending on the current operation being performed. For example, an hourglass shape ( ) is displayed when the computer is performing a task and cannot accept additional input at that time.

moving the mouse pointer

Sliding the mouse on the top of a desk causes the mouse pointer to move on the screen. Slide the mouse to the left and the mouse pointer moves to the left; slide the mouse to the right and the mouse pointer moves to the right.

pointing

Moving the mouse to place the mouse pointer on an icon or other object is called *pointing*. In this text, when we say to point to an object on the screen, we mean to move the mouse until the mouse pointer is placed on the object.

selecting

clicking

An object on the computer screen can be *selected* by pointing to it and pressing the left mouse button and releasing it quickly. This type of selection is called *clicking*. When we say to select, or click on, an item, we mean to point to it and then press and release the left mouse button.

right-clicking

Right-clicking is pressing the right mouse button and releasing it quickly. Pointing to an object on the screen and then right-clicking displays a list of commands that are related to that object.

double-clicking

A special form of clicking is double-clicking. As the name implies, *double-clicking* means to point to an object and press the left mouse button twice in rapid succession.

dragging

The last mouse technique is called *dragging*. When we say to drag, we mean to press and hold the left mouse button while moving the mouse. In some cases, an object can be moved by dragging it. When we say to drag an object, we mean to point to it and then hold down the left mouse button while moving the mouse. When the object is in the desired location, release the mouse button. At times, dragging using the *right* mouse button is necessary. The results of dragging with the right mouse button can be very different from dragging with the left mouse button. Unless specified, always use the left mouse button when dragging.

2.4 The Windows 98 GUI

The *Windows 98 GUI* contains features that allow you to easily use the operating system and applications software. When Windows 98 is running, the computer screen is referred to as the *Desktop*. The Desktop's three most important features are the Start button, Taskbar, and icons:

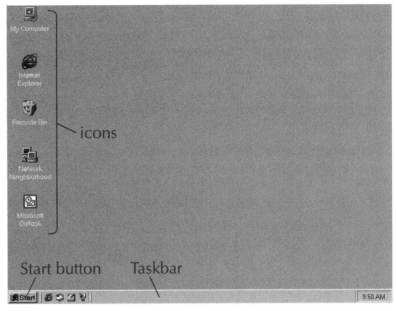

Your Desktop may appear different depending on the properties selected for your computer

Clicking on the Start button displays a list of commands:

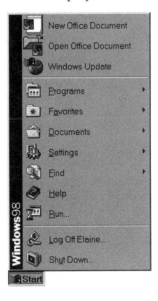

command *Commands* perform specific tasks and actions. Note the Shut Down command. This command should always be selected before you turn off the computer.

The *Taskbar* displays the names of every open program. Clicking on a program name on the Taskbar displays or minimizes that program's window. The Taskbar allows you to easily switch between open programs.

The icons displayed on the Desktop are used to represent files and programs. Icons are double-clicked to perform tasks and run programs.

Practice 1

In this practice you will view the Windows 98 Desktop, locate the Start button, and view the Start menu.

1) BOOT THE COMPUTER

a. Turn on the computer and the monitor. After a few seconds, the computer automatically loads Windows 98.

b. After Windows 98 is booted, the Welcome to Windows 98 dialog box may appear. If the dialog box appears, first point to the Close button (☒) in the upper-right corner of the dialog box by moving the mouse until the mouse pointer is on it. Next, click on the Close button by pressing the left mouse button once. The dialog box is removed from the Desktop.

2) IDENTIFY THE PARTS OF THE DESKTOP

a. Identify the icons on the Desktop. How many icons appear on the Desktop?

b. Locate the Taskbar on the Desktop. Are there any open programs?

c. Locate the Start button and point to it.

3) VIEW THE START MENU

a. Click once on the Start button. Commands are displayed. Note how some of the commands have an arrow (▸).

b. Point to Programs. The names of the applications available on your computer are displayed.

c. Click once anywhere outside the list to remove the list of commands.

2.5 Using Windows

Applications, as well as most documents, are displayed in their own windows. All windows have similar features:

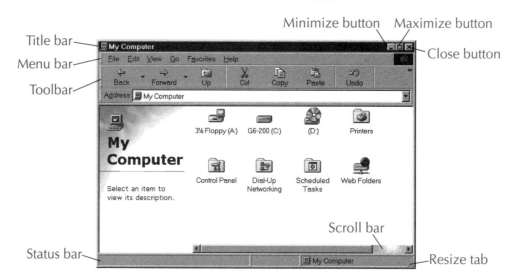

- **Title bar** displays the name of the application or document.

- **Menu bar** displays the names of pull-down menus that contain commands.

- **Toolbar** contains shortcuts for commonly used actions.

A Guide to Microsoft Office 2000 Professional

- **Status bar** displays information about the application or document.
- **Minimize button** (🔲) reduces an application's window to its name on the Taskbar.
- **Maximize button** (🔲) expands the window to fill the screen.
- **Restore button** (🔲) is displayed instead of the Maximize button when a window has been maximized. Clicking on this button restores the window to its previous size.
- **Close button** (✖) closes a document window or ends the application and removes the window from the screen.
- **Scroll bar** is used to bring the unseen parts of the document into view.
- **Resize tab** is dragged to resize the window. The mouse pointer is displayed as a double-headed arrow (↖) when pointing to the Resize tab. A window can also be resized by pointing to any window border to display a double-headed arrow and then dragging the mouse pointer.

moving a window   A window can be moved by dragging its Title bar.

Practice 2

In this practice you will minimize, maximize, and restore a window. The Windows 98 Desktop should still be displayed from the last practice.

1) DISPLAY A WINDOW

a. On the Windows 98 Desktop, double-click on the My Computer icon. The My Computer window is displayed.
b. Locate the features of the window.

2) MANIPULATE THE WINDOW

a. If the window is maximized, click on the Restore button (🔲) to decrease the size of the window, otherwise click on the Maximize button (🔲).
b. Click on the minimize button (🔲). The window is reduced to the My Computer button on the Taskbar.
c. On the Taskbar, click on the My Computer button. The window is again displayed.
d. Click on the Restore or Maximize button. The window is returned to its original size.

3) CLOSE THE WINDOW

Click on the Close button (✖). The window is removed from the screen and the My Computer application is closed.

2.6 Using Dialog Boxes

A dialog box is used to supply the information needed to execute a command. Dialog boxes may have several options:

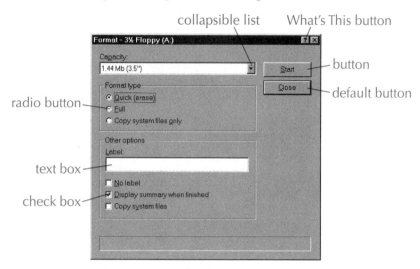

The Format dialog box contains typical dialog box features

- **Button** initiates an action when clicked.

- **Text box** is used to type information that may be needed by a command.

- **Check box** is used to select an option; usually any number of check box options may be selected at the same time.

- **Radio button**, also called *option button*, is used to select an option; usually only one of a set of radio buttons may be selected at a time.

- **Collapsible list**, also called *box* or *drop-down list* displays a list of options to choose from by clicking on the down arrow ().

- **Default option** is an entry or option that has already been selected for you. For example, the Close button in the Format dialog box is the default button and has a solid outline. If no other options are selected, the default options are used when the *Enter key* is pressed.

- **What's This button** () is used to display information about the dialog box options. Clicking on the What's This button displays the ⟨? mouse pointer. Clicking the question mouse pointer on an option in the dialog box displays information about that option.

- **Close button** removes a dialog box without applying any options. A Cancel button is sometimes displayed instead of Close. A dialog box can also be removed by pressing the *Escape key*.

It is possible to select dialog box options without using the mouse. Each option in a dialog box has an underlined letter. Pressing and holding the *Alt key* and then pressing the underlined letter selects that option. For example, pressing Alt+S when the Format dialog box is displayed selects the Start button. Pressing the *Tab key* makes the next option in the dialog box active.

2.7 Using Diskettes

Files are often stored on a diskette. Handling diskettes carefully is important because they store documents in a magnetic format that is vulnerable to dirt and heat. Observing the following rules will help to ensure that your diskettes give you trouble-free service:

1. Keep diskettes away from electrical and magnetic devices such as computer monitors, television sets, speakers, and any type of magnet.

2. Do not expose diskettes to either extreme cold or heat.

3. Store diskettes away from dust, dirt, and moisture.

4. Never touch the diskette's magnetic surface, as doing so can damage it and destroy valuable data.

2.8 My Computer

My Computer

My Computer is an application that comes with Windows 98 and is used to view and organize files and folders. Double-clicking on the My Computer icon on the Windows 98 Desktop displays a window with icons representing the hardware components of your computer:

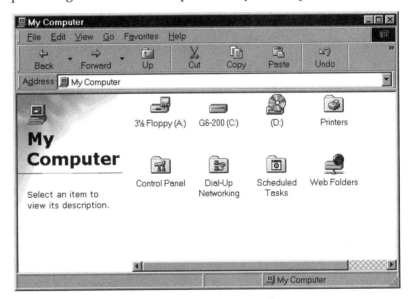

The My Computer window

Double-clicking on one of the drive icons displays the files and folders stored on that disk drive in another window. *Folders* ( ) are used to store and organize related files. For example, double-clicking on the (C:) drive icon displays the contents of the (C:) drive. Then, double-clicking on the My Documents folder displays the contents of that folder:

Folders

Folders can contain other folders. For example, you could create a folder with the name "Spring 2001" that stores all files related to your classes for the 2001 spring semester. Additionally, you could have subfolders for each class that semester stored in the Spring 2001 folder.

Navigating the My Computer Window

On the Toolbar are three buttons to help navigate through folders. The Back button returns you to the previously displayed folder. Clicking on the Forward button displays the next folder in a previously displayed sequence of folders. Clicking on the Up button displays the folder one level up.

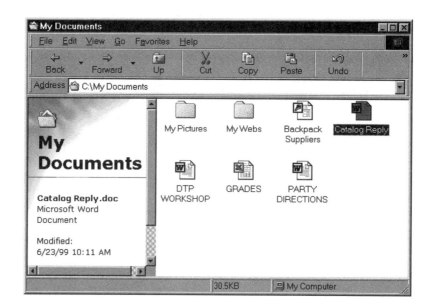

The My Computer window is set up similar to a Web page. Clicking on an icon in the right pane displays information about the selected item in the left pane, as shown in the example above.

Double-clicking on the Printers icon displays available printers. Double-clicking on one of the available printers while you are printing a document displays a window with the status of your print job.

My Computer is also used to format a diskette and copy a diskette as discussed in the next two sections.

2.9 Formatting a Diskette

A new diskette may need to be formatted before it can be used. *Formatting* a diskette prepares it to receive data. The steps for formatting a diskette are:

1. Double-click on the My Computer icon. A window is displayed.

2. Place the diskette to be formatted into drive A:

3. Right-click on the 3½ Floppy (A:) icon. A menu is displayed:

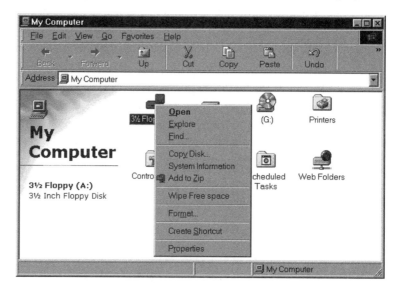

4. Click on the For<u>m</u>at command. The Format dialog box is displayed:

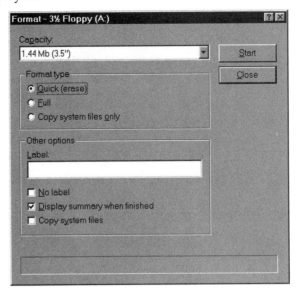

5. Select the Start button.

6. If a dialog box appears saying the diskette cannot be quick formatted, select the OK button to accept full format. The formatting process may take a few seconds.

7. Select the Close button to remove the Format Results dialog box and then select Close to remove the Format dialog box.

2.10 Copying a Diskette

The entire contents of a diskette may be copied to another diskette. The steps for copying a diskette are:

1. Double-click on the My Computer icon. A window is displayed.

2. Right-click on the 3½ Floppy (A:) icon. A menu is displayed.

3. Click on the Cop<u>y</u> Disk command. The Copy Disk dialog box is displayed:

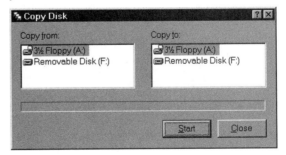

4. Click on the appropriate drive icons in the Copy from and Copy to sections if they are not already selected.

5. Place the diskette to be copied from (source diskette) into the drive and then select the Start button.

6. When prompted, place the diskette that will be copied to (destination diskette) into the drive and then select the OK button.

7. Select the Close button to remove the Copy Disk dialog box when copying is complete.

write protecting a diskette

Because any data on the destination diskette is overwritten when using the Copy Disk command, it is a good idea to *write protect* the source diskette so that it is not accidently used as the destination diskette. To write protect a diskette, turn to the back side of the diskette and slide the write protect tab upward. The write protect tab is located in the upper-left corner on the back of the diskette:

write protect tab

This diskette is write protected because the write protect tab has been pushed up

making backups

A *backup* is a copy of a file or diskette. Although it is easy to create backups of a file or diskette, many people do not take the time to do so. However, the few minutes it takes to backup a file could save hours if the file is damaged or deleted and must be recreated.

It is important to keep backup diskettes in a different location than the original copies. That way, the chances of both copies being destroyed are low. For example, if you keep your data diskettes in the computer lab, keep the backup copies at home. Businesses often store their backup copies in special fireproof safes, in safe deposit boxes at a bank, or with a company that provides off-site storage for computer data.

Practice 3

In this practice you will format a diskette. The following instructions assume that the 3½ floppy diskette drive is the A: drive and that you have a diskette for formatting. Note that any data that is on the diskette will be lost.

1) OPEN MY COMPUTER

Double-click on the My Computer icon. The My Computer window is displayed.

2) FORMAT A DISKETTE

a. Place the diskette into drive A:.
b. Right-click once on the 3½ Floppy (A:) icon.
c. Click on the Format command. A dialog box is displayed. Note the different options in the dialog box.
   1. Select the Start button.
   2. If a dialog box appears saying the diskette cannot be quick formatted, select the OK button to accept full format. It may take a few seconds to format the diskette.
   3. Select the Close button. The Format Results dialog box is removed.
   4. Select the Close button. The Format dialog box is removed.

3) CLOSE THE MY COMPUTER WINDOW

Click on the Close button (![X]). The My Computer window is removed.

4) REMOVE THE DISKETTE FROM THE DRIVE

2.11 Starting an Application

An application is started by first clicking on the Start button on the Windows 98 Taskbar and then pointing to Programs to display a menu of the applications available on your computer. Pointing to a command that has an arrow (▸) displays a group of related items.

The Start button is used to start an application

Clicking on the application in the menu starts the application and displays the application in a window.

2.12 Windows Explorer

Windows Explorer is an application that comes with Windows 98 and is used to view and organize files and folders. Windows Explorer is similar to My Computer in that it shows the contents of the computer, but it is different because it shows the hierarchy of the folders.

Clicking on the Start button, pointing to the Programs command, and then selecting Windows Explorer starts Windows Explorer and displays the Exploring window:

disk drives

folders

files

The Windows 98 Exploring window

The Exploring window is divided into two panes. The left pane displays a list of all the Folders stored on the computer and the computer's hardware components, which are represented by icons and their corresponding names. The right pane of the Exploring window displays the contents of whichever folder is selected on the left pane, as indicated on the Address bar.

The folders and files displayed in the right pane can be displayed in different ways. It is helpful to display information about a file or folder such as the size, type, and the date it was last modified, as in the example on the previous page. This can be done by clicking on View in the Menu bar and then clicking on the Details command.

Notice how there are plus signs (+) and minus signs (–) to the left of the folder icons in the left pane. If a folder has a plus sign next to it, this indicates subfolders within that folder. Clicking on a plus sign displays these subfolders and changes the plus sign to a minus sign. Clicking on the minus sign will hide the subfolders and change the minus sign back to a plus sign.

Practice 4

In this practice you will use Windows Explorer to view the files and folders in the computer.

1) OPEN WINDOWS EXPLORER

    a. On the Windows 98 Taskbar, click the Start button.
    b. Point to the Programs command and then click on the Windows Explorer command. The Exploring window is displayed. Note the two panes of the window and their contents.

2) VIEW THE FILES AND FOLDERS

    a. If not already done, select the My Computer icon in the left pane of the Exploring window. Note how all the available hardware is displayed in the right pane of the window.
    b. In the left pane, click on the (C:) drive icon. Note that the contents of the (C:) drive is displayed in the right pane.
    c. Navigate through the contents of the computer by clicking on different folders and subfolders displayed in the left pane.

A Guide to Microsoft Office 2000 Professional

2.13 File and Folder Management Using My Computer

The My Computer application simplifies the tasks of copying, moving, creating, and deleting files and folders. *Copying* a file leaves the original file in its present location and places an exact copy in a new location. *Moving* a file removes it from its present location and places it in a new location.

copying a file

The steps for copying a file are:

1. Select the file to copy by clicking once on its icon.
2. Click on the Copy button on the Toolbar.
3. Double-click on the destination folder to open it
4. Click on the Paste button on the Toolbar.

moving a file

A file can be moved from one location to another location by using the same steps for copying a file, substituting the Cut button for the Copy button.

copying & moving a folder

Folders can also be copied and moved using the steps listed previously. When copying or moving folders, all of the subfolders and files are also copied or moved.

creating a folder

A new folder can be created by first opening the existing folder or disk drive that is to contain the new folder. Clicking on File in the Menu bar, pointing to the New command and then clicking on Folder displays a new folder icon with the text "New Folder." The folder can then be renamed following the steps described below.

renaming a file or folder

Renaming a file or folder replaces an existing name with a new name. A file or folder can be renamed by first right-clicking on its icon and then selecting the Rename command from the displayed menu. A new name can then be typed and Enter pressed. Files and folders can have names up to 255 characters including spaces. Some special characters, such as \ / : * ? " < >, are not allowed.

creating a read-only file

A file can be made read-only to prevent it from being altered. A *read-only* file cannot have changes made to it. This means that any edits made to the file cannot be retained. A file is made read-only by selecting the file and then clicking on the Properties button on the Toolbar, which displays a dialog box. Selecting the Read-only check box in the Properties dialog box and selecting OK makes the file read-only.

deleting a file or folder

A file or folder can be deleted by selecting it and then pressing the Delete key or clicking on the Delete button on the Toolbar. Windows 98 will then display a warning asking you if you are sure you want to delete the file or folder.

2.14 File and Folder Management Using Windows Explorer

The Exploring window also allows you to copy, move, create, and delete files and folders using the same methods discussed in the previous section. Files and folders can also be copied or moved using a method called *drag and drop*.

drag and drop

copying & moving a file

A file can be copied or moved from one location to another location by using the right mouse button to drag the file's icon to the destination folder. When the mouse button is released a menu is displayed. Clicking on the Copy Here command in the menu copies the file to the new location. Clicking on the Move Here command in the menu moves the file to the new location.

copying & moving a folder

Folders can also be copied and moved using the drag and drop methods described above. When copying or moving folders, all of the subfolders and files are also copied or moved.

creating a shortcut

A *shortcut* is an icon on the Desktop that when double-clicked will display a file or start a program. A shortcut to a file or program can be created by dragging the icon which represents the desired file or program to the Desktop using the right mouse button. After releasing the right mouse button, clicking on the Create Shortcut(s) Here command from the displayed menu creates the shortcut. When dragging an icon from the Exploring window to the Desktop, part of the Desktop needs to be displayed. Therefore, you may need to resize the Exploring window to display a portion of the Desktop.

Practice 5

In this practice you will create a folder, copy a file, rename a file, and make the file read-only. The following instructions assume that the 3½ floppy diskette drive is the (A:) drive and that you have a diskette containing files. The Exploring window should still be displayed from the last practice.

1) CREATE A FOLDER

a. Insert a diskette with files into the (A:) drive.
b. In the left pane, click on the 3½ Floppy (A:) icon. Any files on the diskette appear in the right pane.
c. On the Menu bar, click on the File menu, then point to New, and from the submenu click on the Folder command. A new folder icon with the highlighted name "New Folder" is displayed in the right pane.
d. Type the name Temporary to replace the default name and press Enter. The diskette in the (A:) drive now contains a folder.

2) COPY A FILE

a. The files stored on the diskette should still be displayed in the right pane. If not, click on the 3½ Floppy (A:) icon.
b. Using the right mouse button, drag a file's icon to the Temporary folder you created in the step above.
c. Release the mouse button when the Temporary folder icon is highlighted. From the displayed menu, click on the Copy Here command.
d. A copy of the file now exists in the Temporary folder on the diskette in the (A:) drive.

3) CREATE A READ-ONLY FILE

    a. In the left pane, click on the plus sign (+) next to the 3½ Floppy (A:) icon. Any subfolders are displayed.

    b. In the left pane, click on the Temporary folder icon. The file copied in the last step is displayed in the right pane.

    c. In the right pane, click on the file's icon to select it.

    d. On the Toolbar, click on the Properties button. A dialog box is displayed.

        1. At the top of the dialog box, select the General tab if it is not already displayed.

        2. Click on the check box next to the Read-only option.

        3. Select the OK button. The file is now read-only and no editing changes may be saved.

4) RENAME THE COPIED FILE

    a. In the right pane, right-click on the file's icon. A menu is displayed.

    b. Select the Rename command from the displayed menu. The name is highlighted and a blinking cursor is displayed.

    c. Enter a new name for the file and then press Enter.

    d. A dialog box is displayed asking if you want to rename the read-only file. Select the Yes button.

5) CLOSE THE EXPLORING WINDOW

2.15 Recovering Deleted Files

Recycle Bin

When a file is deleted it is not removed from the hard disk, instead it is moved to the *Recycle Bin*. Therefore, deleted files can be recovered. A file can be recovered by double-clicking the Recycle Bin icon on the Desktop to display the recently deleted files. Selecting the file to be recovered and then clicking on the Restore command after clicking on the File menu recovers the file.

Because deleted files are stored in the Recycle Bin, the deleted files are still taking up space on the computer's hard disk. If you want to permanently delete the files to have more space on the hard disk, right-click on the Recycle Bin icon and then click on the Empty Recycle Bin command. Windows 98 will ask if you want to delete the files. Selecting the Yes button will permanently delete the files stored in the Recycle Bin and free up space on the computer's hard disk. It is important to note that Windows 98 automatically empties the Recycle Bin periodically. Therefore, it is not always possible to recover a deleted file.

2.16 Using Online Help

Windows 98 online help

Online help can be used to explore the features of Windows 98. Clicking on the Help command after clicking on the Start button displays the Windows Help window:

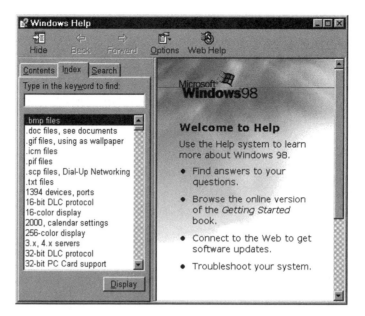

Selecting the Index tab allows you to either type a word to search for or select from a list of topics. After entering or selecting the topic, selecting the Display button shows information pertaining to the topic.

application online help

Online help can also be used to explore the features of an application and help answer questions you might have. Most Windows 98 based applications have a Help menu. Commands from this menu can be used to display information using a dialog box similar to the one shown above.

2.17 Finding Files

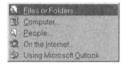

At times you may not know which folder a file is in, or you may only know partial information about a file's name. When this occurs, the Find command can be used to locate a file. Clicking on the Start button, pointing to the Find command, and then clicking on the Files or Folders command displays the Find window:

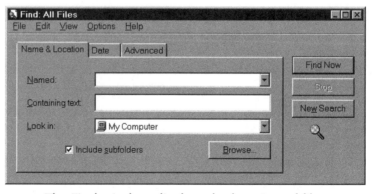

The Find window displays the location of files

If the complete name of a file is known but not the location, the location can be found by typing the complete name in the Named entry box, clicking on the Look in collapsible list and selecting the appropriate drive, and then selecting the Find Now button. This searches the contents of the computer and then displays the location of the file.

If only the partial name of a file is known, the location can be found by using an asterisk (*) in place of the unknown characters. For example, suppose the location of a file that included "Lisa" in the file name is unknown and the rest of the file name is also unknown. Entering *Lisa* in the Named entry box and then selecting the Find Now button will display the location of all the files that contain "Lisa" as part of the file name. The asterisk (*) is used to represent unknown characters.

It is also possible to find a file when the entire name is unknown, if some of the text contained in the file is known. For example, a word processor file with an unknown file name that contains the text "March 17, 2001 Meeting Agenda" can be located by entering the text in the Containing text entry box and then selecting the Find Now button. This will display a list of all the files containing the text "March 17, 2001 Meeting Agenda".

Practice 6

In this practice you will use the Windows 98 online help to find information on how to create folders. You will also use the Find command to find a file. The diskette used in the previous practice should still be in the (A:) drive.

1) *START ONLINE HELP*

 a. Click once on the Start button.
 b. Click on the Help command. The Windows Help window is displayed.
 c. Click on the Index tab if it is not already displayed.

2) *VIEW INFORMATION ON FOLDERS*

 a. Type Folders in the entry box. A list of help topics is displayed.
 b. Click on the "creating" option in the list and then select the Display button. The steps on how to create a new folder is displayed in the window.

3) *CLOSE ONLINE HELP*

 Click on the Close button (🗙) to remove the window.

4) *FIND A FILE*

 a. Click once on the Start button.
 b. Point to the Find command, and then click on the Files or Folders command.
 c. Click on the Name & Location tab if the Named entry box is not already displayed.
 d. Type read* in the Named entry box.
 e. In the Look in collapsible list, click on the down-arrow (▼) and select the (C:) drive if it is not already selected.
 f. Click on the Find Now button. The contents of the hard drive are searched, and the location of any file that begins with read is displayed.
 g. Click on the Close button (🗙). The Find window is removed.

Chapter Summary

This chapter introduced the Windows 98 operating system and some of its applications. Windows 98 is a disk operating system with a graphical user interface.

A mouse is an input device used to select an object on the screen by pointing to the object and then pressing the left mouse button once (clicking). Some objects are selected by double-clicking which is pressing the button twice in rapid succession. Dragging is the technique of holding down the mouse button while moving the mouse. In some instances it may be necessary to use the right mouse button instead of the left mouse button, but only when specifically stated to do so.

Once Windows 98 is loaded, the Windows 98 Desktop is displayed. The Start button is used to start an application. The Taskbar, at the bottom of the Desktop, displays a button for each open program. This allows you to easily switch between open programs. The icons on the Desktop represent items in the computer.

Applications and documents are usually displayed in their own windows. An application is written by professional programmers to perform a specific task. A document is the material that you create using an application and is called a file when saved to disk. All windows have similar features such as a Menu bar and the Minimize, Maximize, Restore, and Close buttons.

Dialog boxes are used to supply information needed to execute an action. Common elements found in dialog boxes are buttons, text boxes, check boxes, radio buttons, and collapsible lists. A default option is an entry or option that has already been selected. If no other options are selected, the default options are used when the Enter key is pressed. The Alt key can be used to select options and the Tab key to make the next option active.

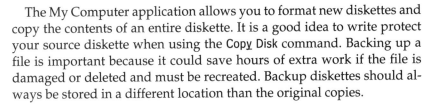

Files are often stored on diskette in a magnetic format. Diskettes should always be handled carefully to avoid problems.

My Computer

The My Computer application allows you to format new diskettes and copy the contents of an entire diskette. It is a good idea to write protect your source diskette when using the Copy Disk command. Backing up a file is important because it could save hours of extra work if the file is damaged or deleted and must be recreated. Backup diskettes should always be stored in a different location than the original copies.

My Computer and Windows Explorer can be used to navigate through the files and folders stored in the computer. Folders are used to store and organize related files. Files and folders can be copied and moved using buttons on the Toolbar or using a method called drag and drop. Folders are created using the Folder command from the New submenu of the File menu. Read-only files cannot have changes made to them. Files and folders can also be deleted and renamed. Shortcuts can be created on the Desktop to display a file or start a program.

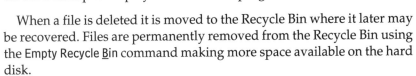

Recycle Bin

When a file is deleted it is moved to the Recycle Bin where it later may be recovered. Files are permanently removed from the Recycle Bin using the Empty Recycle Bin command making more space available on the hard disk.

Windows 98 online help and the Find command provides information about Windows 98 features, and locates files on the computer, respectively.

Vocabulary

Alt key Used to select a dialog box option.

Applications software Software written by professional programmers to perform a specific task.

Backup A copy of a file or diskette.

Booting The process by which Windows 98 is loaded into the computer's memory from the hard disk.

Box See collapsible list.

Button A dialog box option that initiates an action when clicked.

Check box A dialog box option used to select an option.

Clicking Placing the mouse pointer on an object and quickly pressing and releasing the left mouse button once.

Collapsible list A dialog box option that displays a list of options to choose from by clicking on the down-arrow.

Commands Perform specific tasks and actions.

Copying Leaves the original file or folder in its present location and places an exact copy in a new location.

Default A typical entry or option that has already been selected for you.

Desktop The computer screen that displays the Start button, Taskbar, and icons.

Dialog box Allows information to be entered that is needed to complete an action.

Disk Operating System Software that allows the user to communicate with the computer using the keyboard and mouse.

Document The material that you create using an application.

Double-clicking Placing the mouse pointer on an object and pressing the left mouse button twice in rapid succession.

Drag and drop A method of copying or moving objects by dragging them to a new location.

Dragging Holding down the left mouse button while moving the mouse.

Drop-down list See collapsible list.

Enter key Accepts a highlighted menu command or selected dialog box options.

Escape key Cancels the current operation.

File A document that is stored on disk.

Folder Organizes and stores related files.

Formatting Preparing a diskette to receive data.

GUI (Graphical User Interface) A program that uses icons that perform specific tasks.

Icon A picture on the screen that is used to run programs and perform tasks.

Interface The way an application looks on the screen and the way in which a user provides input to the application.

Menu bar A horizontal bar located at the top of an application's window that displays the names of pull-down menus that contain commands.

Mouse Input device that is used to move the mouse pointer and perform a variety of tasks.

Mouse pointer A shape displayed on the screen when the mouse is in use.

Moving Removes a file or folder from its present location and places it in a new location.

Multitasking A feature of Windows 98 which allows more than one application to run at the same time.

My Computer A Windows 98 application used to view and organize files and folders, format a diskette, and copy a diskette.

Pointing Moving the mouse to place the mouse pointer on an icon or other object located on the screen.

Radio button A dialog box option used to select an option from a group of options.

Read-only A file that cannot be changed.

Recycle Bin Stores deleted files for a period of time so that they may be recovered.

Renaming Replacing an existing file or folder name with a new name.

Resize tab Located in the lower-right corner of a window and used to change the size of a window.

Right-clicking Placing the mouse pointer on an object and quickly pressing and releasing the right mouse button once.

Scroll bar Used to bring the unseen parts of a document into view.

Selecting Clicking on an object on the screen.

Shortcut An icon on the Desktop used to display a file or start a program when double-clicked.

Start button When clicked, displays a list of commands from which applications can be run.

Status bar Located at the bottom of a window and displays information about the application or document.

Tab key Selects the next option in a dialog box.

Taskbar Displays a button for each open program.

Text box A dialog box option that accepts typed information that may be needed by a command.

Title bar Located at the top of a window and displays the name of the application or document.

Toolbar Located at the top of a window and contains shortcuts for commonly used actions.

Window The area of the screen that contains an open program or document.

Windows Explorer A Windows 98 applications program used to view and organize files and folders stored in the computer.

Windows 98 An operating system that uses a graphical user interface.

Write protect Moving the write protect tab on a diskette so it cannot receive data.

Windows 98 Commands and Buttons

⊠ **Close button**   Removes the current document window from the screen, closes an application, or removes a dialog box. Found in the upper-right corner of a window or dialog box.

Copy button   Copies a file or folder from one location to another location. Found on the My Computer and Windows Explorer Toolbars.

Cop**y** Disk **command**   Copies the contents from one diskette to another diskette. Displayed after right-clicking on the (A:) drive icon in the My Computer window.

Copy Here **command**   Copies a file or folder from one location to another location. Displayed when dragging a file or folder with the right mouse button.

Create **S**hortcut(s) Here **command**   Creates a shortcut. Displayed after releasing the right mouse button when dragging a file or folder's icon.

Cut button   Moves a file or folder from one location to another location. Found on the My Computer and Windows Explorer Toolbars.

Delete button   Deletes a file or folder. Found on the My Computer and Windows Explorer Toolbars.

Details **command**   Displays a file or folder's size, type, and the date it was last modified. Found in the **V**iew menu in the My Computer and Exploring window.

Empty Recycle **B**in **command**   Permanently deletes the contents of the Recycle Bin and frees up hard disk space. Displayed after right-clicking on the Recycle Bin icon on the Desktop.

Files or Folders **command**   Locates files in the computer. Found in the **F**ind submenu in the Start menu.

Folder **command**   Creates a new folder in the currently selected folder or disk drive. Found in the **N**ew submenu in the **F**ile menu.

For**m**at **command**   Formats a diskette. Displayed after right-clicking on the (A:) drive icon in the My Computer window.

Help **command**   Displays information about Windows 98. Found in the Start menu.

▣ **Maximize button**   Expands the window to fill the screen. Found in the upper-right corner of a window.

▬ **Minimize button**   Reduces an application's window to its name on the Taskbar. Found in the upper-right corner of a window.

Move Here **command**   Moves a file or folder to a new location. Displayed when dragging a file or folder with the right mouse button.

Paste button   Used to copy and move a file or folder from one location to another location. Found on the My Computer and Windows Explorer Toolbars.

Programs **command**   Displays a menu of the application available on your computer.

Rena**m**e **command**   Highlights a file or folder's name so it can be changed. Found in the Start menu.

▣**Restore button**   Restores a window to its previous size. Found in the upper-right corner of a window when the window has been maximized.

R**e**store **command**   Recovers a deleted File. Found in the File menu in the Recycle Bin window.

Sh**u**t Down **command**   Should be selected before turning off the computer. Found in the Start menu.

▣ **What's This button**   Display information about a dialog box option. Found in the upper-right corner of a dialog box.

Review Questions

1. a) What is a disk operating system?
    b) What is a GUI?
    c) What is applications software?

2. a) What is a mouse?
    b) What is pointing?
    c) What is double-clicking?

3. List the steps required to drag an object.

4. a) What is the Desktop?
    b) What does the Taskbar allow you to do?
    c) What do icons represent?

5. List the features found in a window and describe them.

6. a) What is a dialog box used for?
    b) Name four options available in a dialog box and describe their purpose.

Sections 2.7 — 2.10

7. a) Why is it important to take good care of a diskette?
    b) What should be avoided when handling or storing a diskette?

8. a) What is My computer and what is it used for?
    b) What is a folder used for?

9. List the steps required to format a diskette.

10. a) What command is used to duplicate the entire contents of one diskette to another diskette?
    b) What happens to the original data on a diskette when it is used as a destination diskette?

11. List the steps required to write protect a diskette.

12. a) Why should backups of data be created?
    b) Why is it important to keep backup diskettes in a different location than the originals?

Sections 2.11 — 2.17

13. List the step required to start Windows Explorer.

14. a) What is Windows Explorer used for?
    b) Explain what is displayed in the Exploring window.

15. a) What is the difference between copying and moving a file?
    b) What happens to a folder's subfolders and files when the folder is moved?

16. List the steps required to copy a file using My Computer.

17. List the steps required to create a subfolder named Letters in the My Documents folder.

18. Can changes be made to a read-only file?

19. List the steps required to move a file using the drag and drop method.

20. What is the Recycle Bin used for?

21. a) List the steps required to display information on diskettes in the Windows 98 online help.
    b) What menu in an application can be used to help answer questions you might have?

22. Why would an asterisk (*) be used with the Find command?

23. List the steps required to find the location of a file named Harold Pinter Thesis.

New Office Document

Hide the <u>O</u>ffice Assistant

Show the <u>O</u>ffice Assistant

<u>S</u>ave

<u>C</u>lose

E<u>x</u>it

Open Office Document

<u>O</u>pen

<u>P</u>rint

<u>P</u>rint Layout

<u>N</u>ormal

<u>Z</u>oom

Chapter Three Objectives

After completing this chapter you will be able to:

1. Describe a word processor.
2. Explain why the word processor is ideal for producing a variety of different documents.
3. Create a new word processor document.
4. Identify the different parts of the document window.
5. Use the word processor to enter and modify text.
6. Display menus and select commands.
7. Save a document.
8. Understand automatic spelling and grammar checking.
9. Use the toolbars.
10. Show formatting marks and identify them.
11. Close a document and exit Word.
12. Open a previously saved document.
13. Print a document.
14. Change how a document is viewed.
15. Scroll to view a document.

The History of the Word Processor

In 1964, the term *word processor* was invented by IBM as a way to market the Selectric typewriter which could record words on a magnetic tape. The recording capability meant that revisions could be made to text without having to retype the entire document. Wang Laboratories and others soon surpassed IBM with their own versions of a dedicated word processor which by this time included magnetic diskettes for storage and display screens for viewing the document before printing. With the development of the PC in the early 70s came the development of word processor application software. The first word processor application was Easy-Writer developed by John Draper for the Apple II computer. When the IBM PC was introduced in 1981, a version of EasyWriter was written for it as well. Another popular word processor for the PC was WordStar, developed by Rob Barnaby and Seymour Rubenstein. The cost of the PC was much less than a stand-alone word processor making the word processor obsolete. Today there are many word processor applications available.

This chapter introduces Microsoft Word, a powerful word processor used to create printed and online documents.

3.1 What is a Word Processor?

A *word processor* is an application that is used to produce easy to read, professional-looking documents, such as letters, résumés, and research papers. It is a powerful tool that can be used to make changes to (edit) and modify the look of (format) a document. Documents can be saved and then recalled later to make changes or to print a copy.

When editing a document, only those words requiring changes need to be retyped. Words, phrases, and paragraphs can be easily moved, copied, changed, or deleted. Text can be copied from one document to another so that lengthy paragraphs or several pages of text can be included in another document without having to retype them. With a word processor, a document can be viewed on the monitor as it will appear when printed.

Using the Programs Menu

Another way to start an Office application is by selecting the application from the **Programs** menu, found in the **Start** menu.

3.2 Creating a New Word Document

Microsoft Word is the word processor application in the Microsoft Office package. Office applications can be accessed using commands in the **Start** menu on the Windows Taskbar:

Creating New Documents

If Word has already been started, the <u>N</u>ew command from the <u>F</u>ile menu (see Section 3.7) can be used to display the New dialog box.

Another way to create a new document when Word is already started is by clicking on the New Blank Document button () on the Standard Toolbar.

Selecting the New Office Document command displays the New Office Document dialog box:

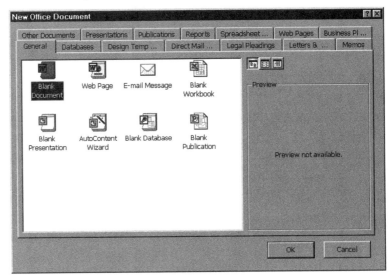

A new document is created using the New Office Document dialog box

Blank Document

Clicking on the Blank Document icon and then selecting the OK button starts Word and creates a new, empty word processor document. There are several features of Word that will be important as you learn to use this application:

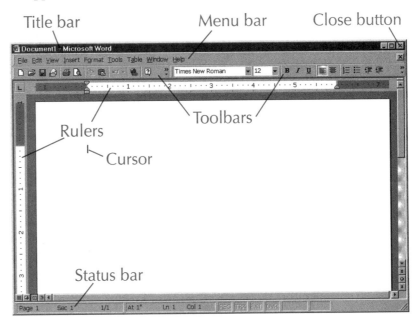

- **Menu bar** contains the names of pull-down *menus* which contain commands that will be discussed later.

- **Toolbars** contain shortcuts for commonly used actions.

- **Title bar** displays the name and type of document. The name Document1 is used temporarily until you name the document.

- **Rulers** contain markings for measuring and are used to format text, which is discussed later.

- **Cursor** is a blinking vertical line that indicates where the next character typed will be placed. In a new document the cursor is in the upper-left corner.

- **Close button** closes the open document or application.

- **Status bar** displays information about the pages in a document.

3.3 The Assistant

When Word is started, a small animated character called an *Assistant* appears. The default Assistant is named Clippit. The purpose of the Assistant is to provide help and suggestions as you use any of the Microsoft Office applications. For example, a light bulb appears when the Assistant has a helpful tip:

Clicking once on the light bulb displays the helpful tip:

The tip can be removed from the screen by clicking on the OK button.

The Assistant can also be used to find helpful information. Clicking once anywhere on the Assistant displays the following:

Typing a question and then selecting the Search button displays a list of topics to choose from. Selecting a topic displays the Microsoft Word Help window next to the document window:

Close button

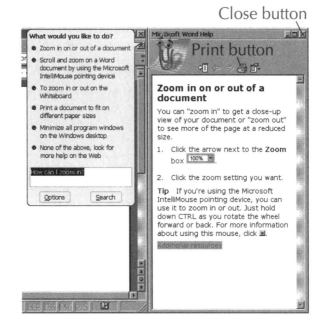

The topic can be printed by clicking on the Print button (). Clicking on the Close button (⊠) closes the Help window.

The Assistant can be removed by selecting the Hide the Office Assistant command from the Help menu. The Assistant can be displayed again by selecting the Show the Office Assistant command from the Help menu or by clicking on the Microsoft Word Help button (?) on the Standard Toolbar.

Practice 1

In this practice you will create a new word processor document in Microsoft Word.

1) CREATE A NEW WORD PROCESSOR DOCUMENT

    a. On the Taskbar, click on the Start button. A menu is displayed.

    b. Click on New Office Document. A dialog box is displayed.

        1. Click on the Blank Document icon and then select OK. Word starts and a new, empty word processor document is created. Note the Menu bar, Toolbars, Title bar, and other features.

2) VIEW THE ASSISTANT

    a. Click once on the Assistant. A small window is displayed next to the Assistant. A question could be typed in this window when help is needed.

    b. Press the Esc key. The window next to the Assistant is removed.

3.4 Using the Keyboard with Word

The keyboard is used to enter text in a document. There are also keys on the keyboard that are used to perform other specific actions, such as moving the cursor or deleting text:

The keyboard

The cursor can be moved, without erasing or entering text, using the *arrow keys*, also called the *cursor control keys*. These keys can only be used to move the cursor within existing text. Pressing an arrow key once moves the cursor either up or down one line, or one character to the left or right. The arrow keys are *repeat keys*, meaning that the cursor will continue to move as long as an arrow key is held down.

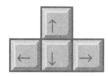

The *Control key* (marked Ctrl) can be used with the arrow keys to move the cursor in the document. Pressing Ctrl+left arrow moves the cursor to the beginning of the word to its left. Similarly, pressing Ctrl+right arrow moves the cursor to the beginning of the word to its right.

Pressing the *Home key* or *End key* moves the cursor to the beginning of the line of text or the end of the line, respectively.

The *Delete key* is used to erase the character directly to the right of the cursor. When a character is deleted, the characters to its right are moved over to fill the gap. The Delete key is not the same as the right-arrow key, which moves the cursor but does not erase characters.

The *Backspace key* (sometimes marked with just an arrow) is used to erase the character directly to the left of the cursor. Any characters to the right are automatically moved to fill the gap left by the deleted character. The Backspace key should not be confused with the left-arrow key, which only moves the cursor and does not erase characters.

The *Escape key* (marked Esc) is used to cancel (escape from) the current operation. The specific effect that pressing the Escape key will have depends on the operation being performed.

The *Enter key* is used to end a paragraph or to terminate a line of text. When Enter is pressed, the current paragraph is ended and the cursor moves to the next line, creating a new paragraph.

3.5 Editing Text in a Document

editing

Once text has been entered in a document, it may be *edited*, or changed, as needed. One possible edit is to add text. The arrow keys are used to move the cursor to where new text is to appear, and then the new text is typed. Any text to the right of the new text is moved to make room.

I-Beam pointer

insertion point

The mouse can be used to move the cursor. When the mouse pointer is moved into a document, it changes from an arrow shape to the text pointer or *I-Beam pointer* (I). Clicking the I-Beam pointer in text moves the cursor to that position. This is a helpful technique when working with long documents. This technique is sometimes called creating an *insertion point* because it is used to place the cursor.

3.6 Word Wrap

As text is typed in a document, Word automatically determines if the next word will fit on the end of the current line or if it must go on the next line. This process is called *word wrap*.

The effects of word wrap can be seen when deleting or inserting text. When new text is added to a line, any words to the right are moved over, and those words that do not fit are moved to the next line. There may be a "domino" effect as words in the rest of the document move from one line to the next. Similarly, when text is deleted, words are moved up from the lines below.

Because of word wrap, the Enter key should be used only to end a paragraph. For example, to end a paragraph and insert a blank line before the next paragraph, Enter is pressed twice. Pressing Enter once ends the paragraph and moves the cursor to the beginning of the next line. Pressing Enter again creates a blank line and a new paragraph.

Practice 2

In this practice you will enter text into a document and then edit it by using the arrow and Delete keys. A new document should be displayed from the last practice.

1) *TYPE A LINE OF TEXT INTO THE DOCUMENT*

Carefully type the following line. Hold down the Shift key to generate the capital letter and the colon(:):

Dear camper:

Do not press the Enter key.

2) *MOVE THE CURSOR WITHOUT ERASING ANY TEXT*

Move the cursor to the right of the letter m by pressing the left-arrow key four times.

3) *DELETE THE LETTER "m"*

Press the Backspace key once. Note how the text per: has moved over to fill the area where the letter m appeared. The document now displays Dear caper:.

4) *INSERT A CHARACTER*

Press the M key. An m is inserted, and the text Dear camper: is again displayed.

5) *MOVE THE CURSOR AND CREATE NEW PARAGRAPHS*

a. Press the right-arrow key until the cursor is to the right of the colon. Press the right-arrow key again a few times. Word does not allow the cursor to move beyond the text, and the assistant may offer a helpful tip. Ignore the Assistant for now.

b. Press Enter twice. The Dear camper: paragraph is ended, a blank line created, and a new paragraph is created.

6) ENTER THE REST OF THE LETTER

Type the following text, pressing the Enter key as indicated (↵) and allowing the rest of the text to word wrap. Use the Delete and arrow keys to correct any typing errors:

> Thank you for your request. Enclosed you will find our catalog of really good camping gear, a pamphlet about our guided canoe trips, and a price list. Reservations are required for guided canoe trips. Please call us soon if you have any questions. ↵
> ↵
> Sincerely,↵
> ↵
> ↵
> ↵
> Quentin Lee↵
> Mud Lake Outfitters

Check – Your document should look similar to:

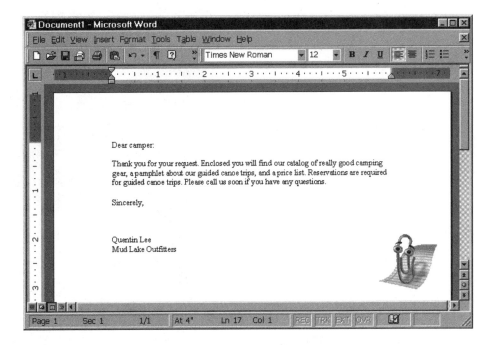

7) MOVE THE CURSOR AND DELETE TWO WORDS

a. Move the mouse so that the pointer is in the document. The I-Beam pointer is now displayed.
b. Place the I-Beam pointer on the word really in the first sentence of the letter.
c. Click the left mouse button. The cursor is moved to the position of the I-Beam pointer.
d. Press Ctrl+right arrow. The cursor is moved to the beginning of the word good.
e. Press Ctrl+right arrow again. The cursor is moved to the beginning of the word camping.
f. Press the Backspace key until the words really good are deleted. Be sure to leave only one space between of and camping.

8) EDIT THE LETTER

Insert new text and use the Delete and arrow keys as necessary to make the following changes:
1. Change the word pamphlet to brochure
2. Insert a space and the words feel free to after the word Please
3. Remove the word soon and a space, leaving one space between us and if.

<u>Check</u> – Your document should look similar to:

Dear camper:

Thank you for your request. Enclosed you will find our catalog of camping gear, a brochure about our guided canoe trips, and a price list. Reservations are required for guided canoe trips. Please feel free to call us if you have any questions.

Sincerely,

Quentin Lee
Mud Lake Outfitters

3.7 Using Menus

At the top of the document window is the Menu bar. Each word on the bar is the name of a pull-down menu from which different commands can be selected. Clicking once on a menu name displays the commands of that menu. For example, clicking on the word <u>F</u>ile displays its menu:

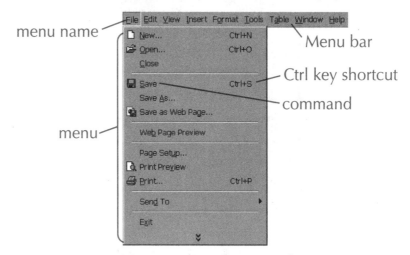

Menus are lists of commands

Pointing to a command on the menu highlights it. Highlighted commands are shown in reversed text (white letters on a dark background). Clicking on the highlighted command selects it. In the practices of this text, we denote selecting a command from a menu using the → symbol. For example, <u>F</u>ile → <u>S</u>ave indicates that the <u>S</u>ave command should be selected from the <u>F</u>ile menu.

Clicking outside a displayed menu or pressing the Escape key removes the menu.

 The arrows (❯) at the bottom of the menu indicate that there are more commands available in the menu. Pointing to the arrows expands the menu to display more commands. Word remembers which commands have been selected and displays the most commonly used commands in the unexpanded menu.

Some commands have an ellipsis (…) after the command name (<u>N</u>ew and <u>O</u>pen are examples in the menu above). This means that a dialog box will appear when this command is selected. Dialog boxes were explained in Section 2.6. Other commands may be displayed in dimmed text, indicating that they cannot be selected at this time.

A Guide to Microsoft Office 2000 Professional

Menus may also be displayed using the keyboard. Note that one letter in each of the menu names is underlined. Pressing and holding the Alt key while pressing the underlined letter once displays that menu. For example, holding down the Alt key and pressing the F key once displays the File menu. In this text, we denote this sequence of keystrokes as Alt+F. Commands can be selected in a similar way. When the menu is displayed, pressing the key that corresponds to the command's underlined letter selects the command. For example, the Save command is selected from the File menu by first pressing Alt+F to display the menu, and then pressing the S key. This sequence is written as Alt+F S.

Some commands have a Ctrl key shortcut listed next to them in the menu. These shortcuts can be used to select a command without displaying a menu. For example Ctrl+S is listed next to the Save command in the File menu, which indicates that pressing and holding down the Ctrl key and pressing the S key once selects the Save command.

3.8 Saving a Document

A new document is stored in the computer's memory until it is *saved*. When a document is saved, a copy of what is currently stored in the computer's memory is placed on the computer's internal hard disk or on a diskette. The computer still retains the document in memory so that now there are two copies—one in memory that is displayed on the screen and one saved on disk. Once a document has been saved, it can later be loaded into memory for further editing or printing. Note that the computer's memory can only store data if the computer is on.

Documents saved on disk are called *files* and must be given names to identify them. *File names* can be up to 255 characters long and can contain uppercase and lowercase letters, numbers, and spaces. Colons (:), asterisks (*), question marks (?), and some other special characters may not be used. Examples of valid file names are Notes, CHAPTER 5, and 2nd Memo. It is important to give a file a name that describes what it contains. For example, a file containing a letter to your friend Greta is better named Greta Letter or Letter to Greta rather than just Letter.

A document is saved by selecting the Save command from the File menu. The Save As dialog box is displayed the first time a document is saved:

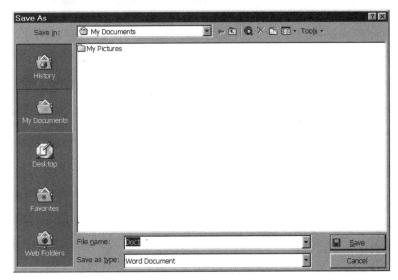

Why Save Often?

Saving a document often when working on it helps to prevent its accidental loss. An interruption in power can wipe everything out of the computer's memory. Just bumping the power cord may cause the memory to be erased. Therefore, saving a document as often as possible is a good practice. Saving before attempting to print is also important because a problem involving the printer could cause the most recent changes in a document to be lost.

Selecting the appropriate folder from the **Save** in collapsible list indicates where your file will be saved. Typing a descriptive name in the **File name** entry box and selecting the **Save** button places a copy of the document on disk using the name you supplied.

overwrites

Note that any editing changes made to a previously saved file are not stored unless the file is saved again, which *overwrites* the original copy on disk.

Practice 3

In this practice you will save the document created in Practices 1 and 2 using the name Catalog Reply. The document should be displayed from the last practice.

1) REMOVE THE ASSISTANT

    a. On the Menu bar, click on the word <u>H</u>elp. The <u>H</u>elp menu is displayed.
    b. Point to the Hide the <u>O</u>ffice Assistant command in the displayed menu. The command is highlighted in the menu.
    c. Click on Hide the <u>O</u>ffice Assistant to select the command. The Assistant is removed.

Note: the remaining practices in this text assume that the Assistant does not appear in the document window.

2) SELECT THE SAVE COMMAND FROM THE FILE MENU

Select <u>F</u>ile → <u>S</u>ave. Since this is the first time the document is saved, Word displays a dialog box that prompts you to enter a file name for the document.

    1. The text in the File name entry box should be highlighted. Type Catalog Reply to replace the existing text:

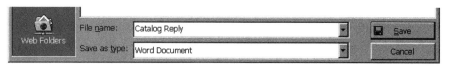

    2. In the Save in collapsible list, select the appropriate folder.
    3. Click on the Save button. A copy of the file in memory is stored on the hard disk using the name Catalog Reply. Note that the file name Catalog Reply is now displayed in the Title bar.

3.9 Automatic Spelling and Grammar Checking

One useful feature of a word processor is its ability to spell check. Spelling is checked by comparing the words in a document to those in a dictionary file. In Word, spelling is automatically checked as words are typed. If a word is spelled incorrectly or is not in the dictionary file, a red wavy line appears below it:

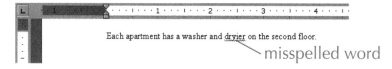

A misspelled word can be corrected by first right-clicking on it to display a menu of suggested words, then clicking on the correct spelling:

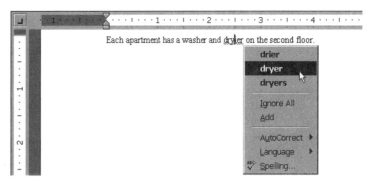

Clicking the right mouse button displays suggested spellings

Right-Clicking on a Misspelled Word

Make sure that the pointer is on the misspelled word when you right-click, or a different menu may appear. Pressing the Esc key removes the menu from the window.

Because the dictionary file does not contain every word in the English language, a wavy red line may appear below a correctly spelled word, such as a proper name. When this happens, the wavy line can be ignored. Selecting the Ignore All command in the menu removes the red wavy line from all of the occurrences of the word in the document.

Word also has a grammar checker that displays a green wavy line below a word, phrase, or sentence when a possible grammar problem is detected:

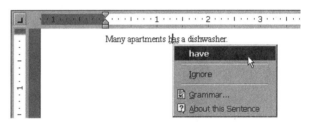

Right-clicking on the green wavy line displays suggested corrections.

A green wavy line might appear below an acceptable sentence. When this happens, the wavy line can be ignored. Selecting the Ignore command in the menu removes the green wavy line.

3.10 Using the Toolbars

The Standard Toolbar and the Formatting Toolbar are displayed next to each other in Word. Both toolbars contain buttons that represent different actions:

Save button

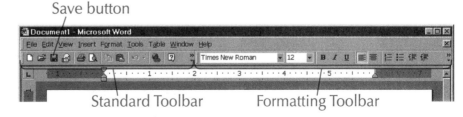

Standard Toolbar   Formatting Toolbar

The *Standard Toolbar* is used to execute commonly performed actions, such as saving a document. The *Formatting Toolbar* is used for formatting text, which is discussed in Chapter Four. Clicking on the arrows () at the far right of each toolbar expands the toolbar to display more buttons. Word remembers which buttons have been selected and displays the most commonly used ones in the unexpanded toolbar.

screen tip   Clicking on a button performs an action. Pointing to a button (not clicking) displays a *screen tip* which describes the action that button will perform:

Screen tips describe the action performed by a button

   Clicking on the Save button () saves a document. If the document is new and has not yet been named the Save As dialog box is displayed. Other buttons will be discussed when their corresponding actions are introduced.

Practice 4

In this practice you will edit the Catalog Reply document and correct any misspellings. The Catalog Reply document should be displayed from the last practice.

1) EDIT THE DOCUMENT

   a. Place the cursor at the beginning of the word Dear at the top of the document.
   b. Type Joyce Rollins and press Enter.
   c. Type 42 Thimble Roawd and press Enter. Note the red wavy line under Roawd, indicating that Word cannot find it in the dictionary.
   d. Type Weston, MO 66018 and press Enter.
   e. Press Enter again to create a blank line between the address and the greeting of the letter.

2) CORRECT THE MISSPELLED WORD

Move the pointer to Roawd and click the right mouse button. A menu is displayed with the word Road as one of the suggested spellings. Correct the spelling by clicking on Road in the menu. Word makes the correction and the address now reads 42 Thimble Road.

Check – Your document should look similar to:

Joyce Rollins
42 Thimble Road
Weston, MO 66018

Dear camper:

Thank you for your request. Enclosed you will find our catalog of camping gear, a brochure about our guided canoe trips, and a price list. Reservations are required for guided canoe trips. Please feel free to call us if you have any questions.

Sincerely,

Quentin Lee

3) USE THE TOOLBAR TO SAVE THE MODIFIED CATALOG REPLY

   a. Point (do not click) to a button on the Standard Toolbar and hold the position for a few seconds. Note the screen tip describing the action of the button.
   b. Point to the Save button (), and then click once. The modified Catalog Reply is saved on disk, overwriting the old version.

3.11 Showing Formatting Marks

Characters such as spaces, tabs (discussed later), and paragraph markers are not normally displayed, but can be displayed in the document window as special symbols. These symbols are called *formatting marks* and do not appear on the paper when a document is printed:

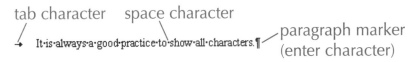

tab character   space character

paragraph marker
(enter character)

It·is·always·a·good·practice·to·show·all·characters.¶

It is much easier to edit a document when these characters are visible. Formatting marks are displayed by clicking on the Show/Hide ¶ button (¶) on the Formatting Toolbar. Clicking on the Show/Hide ¶ button again hides the formatting marks. It is always a good practice to display formatting marks, especially when editing text.

3.12 Closing a Document and Exiting Word

When you are finished working on a document, it should be saved and then closed. *Closing a document* means that its window is removed from the screen and it is no longer in the computer's memory. A document is closed by selecting the Close command (Ctrl+N) from the File menu. If you attempt to close a document that has been edited but not saved, Word warns you with a message:

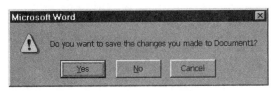

If you want to save the changes before closing, select the Yes button. If you want to close the document without saving the edited version, select the No button. The Cancel button reverses the Close command and returns the cursor to the document.

Why Close Documents?

Closing a document prevents accidental changes and frees computer memory. A document can be quickly closed by clicking on its Close button () in the upper-right corner of its window.

When you are finished working with Word, it should be exited properly so that documents in memory are not damaged or lost. *Exiting Word* means that its window is removed from the screen and the program is no longer in the computer's memory. Word is exited by selecting the Exit command from the File menu. If you have created a new file or made changes to a previously saved document, Word displays the same warning dialog box as when closing a document.

Practice 5

In this practice you will display formatting marks, close Catalog Reply to remove it from memory and then exit Word. The Catalog Reply document should be displayed from the last practice.

1) SHOW FORMATTING MARKS

On the Standard Toolbar, click on the Show/Hide ¶ button (¶) if formatting marks are not already displayed. You may need to click on the arrows (») at the far right of the toolbar to display the button.

<u>Check</u> – Your document should look similar to:

```
Joyce·Rollins¶
42·Thimble·Road¶
Weston,·MO·66018¶
¶
Dear·camper:¶
¶
Thank·you·for·your·request.·Enclosed·you·will·find·our·catalog·of·camping·gear,·a·
brochure·about·our·guided·canoe·tips,·and·a·price·list.·Reservations·are·required·for·
guided·canoe·trips.·Please·feel·free·to·call·us·if·you·have·any·questions.¶
¶
Sincerely,¶
¶
¶
¶
Quentin·Lee¶
Mud·Lake·Outfitters¶
```

2) CLOSE THE DOCUMENT

Select File → Close. The document no longer appears in the window. If a warning dialog box is displayed, select Yes to save the changes and close the document.

3) PROPERLY EXIT WORD

Select File → Exit. The document window is removed from the screen.

3.13 Opening a Document

A saved file that has been closed must be loaded from disk to the computer's memory before it can be edited. This process is called *opening a file*. A file is opened by selecting the Open Office Document command from the Start menu, which displays the Open Office Document dialog box:

The file names of saved documents are displayed in the Open Office Document dialog box

Selecting the appropriate folder from the Look in collapsible list displays a list of file names. Clicking on the desired file name and selecting the Open button starts Word, transfers a copy of the document to the computer's memory, and displays it in the document window.

Another way to open an existing document is to select the Open command (Ctrl+O) from the File menu or the Open button () on the Standard Toolbar. However, the File menu and toolbars are available only when Word is running, not after it has been exited.

3.14 Printing a Document

A document is printed by selecting the Print command (Ctrl+P) from the File menu to display the Print dialog box. Your dialog box may be different depending on the printer you are using:

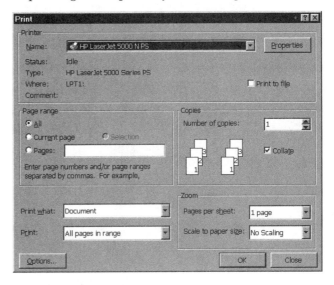

Because the default values are most commonly used, you will usually just select the OK button to begin printing. If more than one copy of the document is to be printed, type the number required in the Number of copies entry box and then select OK. If only certain pages are to be printed, select the Pages option and enter the desired page numbers, separated by commas, in the entry box before selecting OK.

 The Print button (🖨) on the Standard Toolbar may also be used to print a document. However, clicking on this button does not display the Print dialog box. Instead, one copy of the document is printed using the default settings.

How Documents Are Printed

A document is printed by sending a copy from the computer's memory to the printer. To do this, the computer must be connected to a printer and the printer must be turned on and be online.

Practice 6

In this practice the Catalog Reply document will be opened, edited, saved, and then printed.

1) OPEN CATALOG REPLY

    a. On the Taskbar, click on the Start button. A menu is displayed.
    b. Select the Open Office Document command. A dialog box is displayed.
        1. In the Look in collapsible list, select the appropriate folder.
        2. Click on Catalog Reply.
        3. Select the Open button. Word is started, a copy of Catalog Reply is transferred to the computer's memory, and the document is displayed in a window.

2) EDIT THE DOCUMENT

    Change the greeting of the letter from Dear camper: to Dear outdoor enthusiast:.

3) SAVE, PRINT, AND THEN CLOSE THE MODIFIED CATALOG REPLY

a. Select <u>F</u>ile → <u>S</u>ave. The document is saved.

b. Select <u>F</u>ile → <u>P</u>rint. A dialog box is displayed.

    1. Note that the **Number of copies** option is 1. Select **OK** to print one copy of Catalog Reply.

c. Select <u>F</u>ile → <u>C</u>lose. Catalog Reply is removed from the window.

3.15 Changing Views

There are several different ways to view a document in its window. The view can be changed by selecting commands from the <u>V</u>iew menu. In *Print Layout* view, the document appears on separate pages, just as it will when printed:

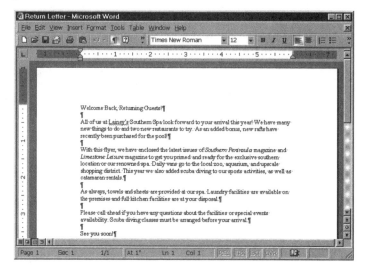

In *Normal* view, the separate pages of the document are not displayed, just the text, with dotted lines representing where pages end:

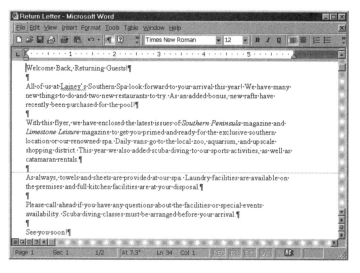

A Guide to Microsoft Office 2000 Professional

The magnification of a displayed document can also be changed. Selecting the <u>Z</u>oom command from the <u>V</u>iew menu displays the Zoom dialog box:

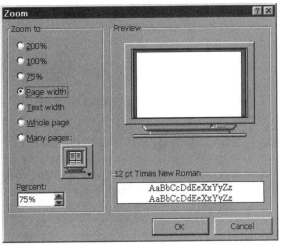

The magnification of a document can be changed in the Zoom dialog box

The Zoom to options affect how big or small the document appears in the document window.

3.16 Screen Scroll

Most documents are too long to be entirely displayed in the window. Bringing hidden parts of a document into view is called *screen scroll*. The scroll bars on the right side and bottom of the document window are used to scroll a document:

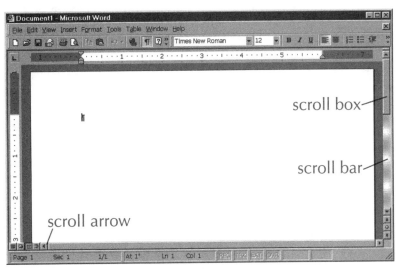

The scroll bars, arrows, and boxes are used to move through a document

There are several ways to move a document in the window:

* clicking once on the down *scroll arrow* moves the document up one line, and clicking once on the up scroll arrow moves it down one line.

The View Buttons

Four buttons in the lower-left corner of the Word window can be used to quickly change views:

Clicking once on either the Normal view button (▤), Web layout view button (▣), Print layout view (▤), or Outline view (▥) button changes the appearance of the document in the window.

The Browse Buttons

The Browse buttons, located below the vertical scroll bar, can be used to scroll through a document. The Select Browse Object button (▣) is used to select how the document will be browsed, for example by page. The Previous (▲) and Next (▼) buttons then scroll the document by page, similar to the Page Up and Page Down keys.

- dragging the *scroll box* moves the document in larger increments. For example, dragging the scroll box to the middle of the scroll bar displays the middle of the document.

- clicking directly on the *scroll bar* above or below the scroll box scrolls the document by one screen towards the top or bottom of the document, respectively.

Any text scrolled off the screen is not lost, it is just not displayed at that time. Note that the cursor does not move within the document when the scroll bars are used.

   The keyboard can be used to scroll a document by pressing the Page Up or Page Down keys. These keys scroll the document one window towards the top or bottom of the document. The cursor can be moved quickly to the first character in a document by pressing Ctrl+Home, or to the last character by pressing Ctrl+End.

Practice 7

In this practice a document will be scrolled and the cursor moved by using the mouse. A previously created Word document named SCROLL will be used. Each line in SCROLL is numbered to help demonstrate screen scroll.

1) OPEN SCROLL

Select File → Open. A dialog box is displayed.
1. In the Look in collapsible list, select the appropriate folder.
2. Click on SCROLL.
3. Select the Open button. A copy of SCROLL is transferred to the computer's memory, and the document is displayed in a window.

2) CHANGE VIEWS AND MAGNIFICATION

a. Display the View menu. Note that Print Layout view is selected, indicating that the document is displayed in that view.
b. Select Zoom. A dialog box is displayed.
  1. Select the Whole page option, then select OK. The size of the displayed document is changed so that the edges of the page can be seen.
c. Select View → Normal. The document is now displayed in Normal view, without the page edges displayed.

3) MOVE THE CURSOR TO THE BOTTOM OF THE SCREEN

Press the down-arrow key until the cursor is on the last line of text currently displayed in the document.

4) SCROLL DOWN TEN LINES USING THE SCROLL ARROW

Click the pointer on the down scroll arrow (▼) in the vertical scroll bar ten times. Note that each time the down-arrow is selected, a line scrolls off the top of the screen, and the next line in the document appears from the bottom.

5) PLACE THE CURSOR IN THE LAST LINE IN THE DOCUMENT

a. Point to the scroll box in the vertical scroll bar.
b. Drag the scroll box to the bottom of the scroll bar and release the mouse button. The last line of the document, paragraph 80, is displayed.
c. Move the I-Beam pointer into the text of paragraph 80 and click the left mouse button to place the cursor.

6) SCROLL TO THE FIRST LINE IN THE DOCUMENT

    a. Click on the up arrow in the vertical scroll bar and hold down the button. The screen will scroll as long as the button is held down. Note how the scroll box moves in the bar as the screen scrolls. Also note that the cursor does not move as the document is being scrolled.

    b. When paragraph 1 is displayed, release the mouse button.

7) EXIT WORD

    Select File → Exit. SCROLL is closed and the document window is removed from the screen.

Chapter Summary

This chapter introduced the word processor, which can be used to produce professional-looking documents quickly and efficiently. Microsoft Word is the word processor application in the Microsoft Office package. Text in word processor documents can be changed easily. Documents can be saved and later reopened to edit or print a copy.

Blank
Document

A new document is created by selecting the New Office Document command from the Start menu on the Windows Taskbar, which displays a dialog box. Selecting the Blank Document icon and then OK creates a new document.

At the top of the document window is the Menu bar that contains the names of pull-down menus. The menu's commands are displayed by clicking on the menu name, and a command is selected by clicking on it. Below the Menu bar are the Standard and Formatting Toolbars which contain buttons that can be clicked to perform an action. In the center of the window is the document which contains the cursor. At the bottom of the window is the Status bar which displays information such as the number of pages in the document.

Word contains an animated Assistant that displays helpful tips and allows you to search for help topics. The Assistant can be removed from the window by selecting the Hide the Office Assistant command from the Help menu.

Cursor control keys, also called arrow keys, are used to move the cursor through the document without changing any text. The Home and End keys move the cursor to the beginning or end of the line, respectively. The Backspace key is used to remove the character to the left of the cursor, and the Delete key erases the character directly to the right. The Escape key cancels the current operation, and the Enter key is used to end a paragraph.

editing

I-Beam pointer

Once text has been entered in a document, it may be edited, or changed, as needed. When the mouse pointer is moved into a document, it changes from an arrow shape to the text pointer or I-Beam pointer ($\mathcal{I}$). Clicking the I-Beam pointer in text moves the cursor to that position.

Word automatically determines if the next word will fit on the end of the current line or if it must go on the next line. This process is called word wrap.

Clicking once on a menu name in the Menu bar displays some of the commands in that menu. Pointing to the arrows at the bottom of the menu expands the menu to display more commands. In a menu, selecting a command name that is followed by an ellipsis (...) will display a dialog box where information is entered. A command can also be selected using the Alt key or Ctrl key.

A document can be saved to disk by selecting the Save command from the File menu. When saved, a document is given a name of up to 255 characters to identify it. Each file name must be unique.

When text is typed into a document, Word automatically checks the spelling using a dictionary file. If the spelling is not found, a red wavy line appears under the word. A menu of suggested spellings can be displayed by right-clicking on the misspelled word. Word also checks grammar and indicates a possible grammar problem with a green wavy line.

The Standard and Formatting Toolbars contain buttons that represent different actions such as Save. Pointing to a button (not clicking) displays a screen tip which describes the action that button will perform. Clicking on a button performs the action. Clicking on the arrows at the far right of each toolbar expands the toolbar to display more buttons.

 When editing text in a document, formatting marks should be displayed by clicking on the Show/Hide ¶ button on the Standard Toolbar.

To remove a file from the computer's memory, it must be closed using the Close command from the File menu. Previously created files can be opened by selecting the Open command. The Exit command from the File menu is used to properly exit Word.

To avoid losing a file, it should be saved before printing. A document is printed using the Print command from the File menu.

Commands in the View menu affect how the document appears in the document window. Print Layout view displays the document on separate pages, as it will appear when printed. Normal view displays only the text in the document, with dotted lines indicating where pages end. The Zoom command displays a dialog box of options that affect the magnification of the displayed document.

Bringing hidden parts of a document into view is called screen scroll. The scroll bars below and on the right of the document window are used to scroll through a document. The Page Up and Page Down keys can also be used to scroll a document, as well as Ctrl+Home and Ctrl+End.

This chapter discussed the commands and procedures necessary to produce a word processor document. The major steps in producing such a document are:

1. Display the word processor document by either creating a new one or opening a previously created document.

2. Enter text or edit the document.

3. Save the document.

4. Print the document if desired.

5. Close the document.

6. Exit Word properly.

Vocabulary

Assistant An animated character that offers helpful tips and allows you to search for help topics.

Alt key Used to select commands from a menu.

Arrow keys Four keys that move the cursor up, down, right, and left in the window without changing any text.

Backspace key Used to erase the character directly to the left of the cursor.

Close button Closes the document or application.

Closing a document The process of removing a document from the computer's memory and from the screen.

Ctrl key Used with the arrow keys to move the cursor. Also used to select commands from a menu.

Cursor A blinking vertical line in the document that indicates where the next characters typed will be placed.

Cursor control keys See Arrow keys.

Delete key Erases the character directly to the right of the cursor.

Editing Changing the contents of a document once text has been entered.

End key Moves the cursor to the end of the current line of text.

Enter key Used to end a paragraph or to terminate a line of text.

Escape key Cancels (escapes from) the current operation.

Exiting Word The process of removing the Word application from the computer's memory and from the screen.

File A document that is stored on disk.

File name A unique name for a file stored on disk.

Formatting marks Characters that are displayed in the document window as special symbols but do not appear on paper when a document is printed.

Formatting Toolbar A toolbar that provides shortcuts to commonly performed text formatting actions.

Home key Moves the cursor to the beginning of the current line of text.

I-Beam pointer The shape of the mouse pointer when it is moved into a document.

Insertion point The position of the cursor.

Menu A list of commands.

Menu bar A horizontal bar below the Title bar that contains the names of available menus.

Microsoft Word The word processor application in the Microsoft Office package.

Normal view Displays only the text in the document, with dotted lines representing where each page ends.

Print Layout view Displays the document on separate pages, just as it will appear when printed.

Opening a file The process of transferring a saved file from disk to the computer's memory and displaying it in a window.

Overwrite When a saved file is replaced with an edited version of the file.

Repeat key A key that repeats its action when held down, such as an arrow key.

Rulers Markings along the top and left side of the document window that are used for measuring.

Saving a document The process of storing a copy of a document that is currently in the computer's memory on a disk.

Screen scroll Bringing hidden parts of a document into view.

Screen tip A description of the action that a button on the Toolbar will perform.

Scroll arrows Used to move a document one line at a time.

Scroll bars Used to move a document one screen up or down.

Scroll box Used to move a document in large increments.

Standard Toolbar A toolbar that provides shortcuts to commonly performed actions.

Status bar Displays information about the pages in a document.

Title bar A bar at the top of the window used to display the file name and type of a document.

Toolbar A bar that contains shortcuts to commonly performed actions.

Word processor Computer application that is used to produce documents.

Word wrap The process Word uses to determine whether a word will fit on the current line or must go on the next line.

Word Commands and Buttons

Close **command** Removes a document from the window and the computer's memory. Found in the File menu.

Exit **command** Removes the Word application from the computer's memory and from the screen. Found in the File menu.

Hide the Office Assistant **command** Removes the Assistant from the screen. Found in the Help menu.

New Office Document **command** Displays the New Office Document dialog box. Found in the Start menu.

Normal **command** Changes the view of a document to Normal view. Found in the View menu.

Open **command** Displays a dialog box that allows the user to open an existing document. Found in the File menu. The Open button (⬚) can be used instead of the command.

Open Office Document **command** Opens an existing document. Found in the Start menu.

Print **command** Displays a dialog box that allows the user to print a document. Found in the File menu. The Print button (⬚) on the Standard Toolbar can be used instead of the command.

Print Layout **command** Changes the view of a document to Print Layout view. Found in the View menu.

Save **command** Displays a dialog box that allows the user to transfer a document from the computer's memory to disk. Found in the File menu. The Save button (⬚) on the Standard Toolbar can be used instead of the command.

¶ **Show/Hide ¶ button** Displays formatting marks such as spaces and paragraph markers. Found on the Standard Toolbar.

Show the Office Assistant **command** Displays the Assistant. Found in the Help menu. The Microsoft Word Help button (⬚) on the Standard Toolbar can be used instead of the command.

Zoom **command** Displays a dialog box with options that affect the magnification of the displayed document. Found in the View menu.

Review Questions

1. List two reasons to use a word processor.

2. Name three different types of organizations that could benefit from using word processors. Explain how each would benefit.

3. How is a new word processor document created from the Windows Desktop?

4. What is displayed in the Title bar of the document window?

5. What is the cursor?

6. a) What is the Assistant?
   b) What is the purpose of the Assistant?
   c) How is the Assistant removed from the document window?

7. What are each of the following keys used for?
   a) Escape key
   b) Delete key
   c) Backspace key

8. How may the cursor be moved down 3 lines and then 10 places to the right without affecting text?

9. What does pressing the Enter key do when typing text in the word processor?

10. What is the difference between pressing the Backspace key four times and the left-arrow key four times when the cursor is located in the middle of a line of text?

11. List the steps required to change the word sea to ocean in the sentence:

    Dolphins live in the sea.

12. What is the shape of the mouse pointer when the pointer is in a document?

13. How can the mouse be used to move the cursor?

14. What is word wrap?

Sections 3.7 — 3.12

15. a) How is a menu displayed?
    b) How can a menu be removed from the screen without selecting a command?

16. List three reasons why it is important to save a word processor document.

17. a) What is a file?
    b) Why is a file given a name?
    c) What are the restrictions to consider when deciding on a new file name?

18. When a file is saved where does it go? Is it removed from the computer's memory?

19. If a previously saved file is edited, will the changes be automatically made to the file on disk, or must the file be saved again?

20. What does it mean when a red wavy line appears under a word in the document?

21. List the steps required to display and then select a suggested spelling for a misspelled word.

22. What are the Toolbars used for?

23. How can a document be saved without using the Save command from the File menu?

24. a) What are formatting marks?
    b) How can formatting marks be displayed in a document?

25. a) What happens to a file when it is closed? Is it automatically saved?
    b) Why is it important to close a file when you are finished working with it?

26. a) Why is it important to exit Word properly?
    b) List the steps required to exit Word starting from the document window so that the document being worked on is saved.

Sections 3.13 — 3.16

27. List the steps required to transfer a previously saved file from disk into the computer's memory.

28. What menu and command is used to print a document?

29. a) How does a document appear in Print Layout view?
    b) How does a document appear in Normal view?
    c) How can you change the magnification of a displayed document?

30. a) What is screen scroll?
    b) Describe two ways to scroll through a document.

31. Describe how to use only the mouse to scroll to the end of a document and place the cursor in the last sentence.

32. What is the quickest way to move the cursor from the last sentence of a document to the first character in the document?

A Guide to Microsoft Office 2000 Professional

Exercises

Exercise 1 ——————————————— Ceramics Info Request

You need a letter requesting information sent to your friend.

a) In a new document create the following letter, allowing Word to wrap the text:

September 22, 2001

Ms. Marcia Paloma
Periwinkle Ceramics
Big Pine Lane
Sunport, FL 33568

Dear Ms. Paloma:

I am excited about taking the introductory ceramics class. I look forward to making several projects this spring. My friend would also like to enroll in your ceramics program. Please send information to the following address:

Kaitlin Pruitt
44 Simple Lane
Plain City, FL 33101

Thank you very much.

Sincerely,

Student Name

Be sure there are five blank lines below the date and three blank lines below the closing Sincerely.

b) Check the document on screen for errors and misspellings and make any corrections.

c) Save the document naming it Ceramics Info Request and print a copy.

d) Make the following changes to the letter:

- Change the word introductory to advanced in the first sentence.
- Change the words enroll in to look into in the third sentence.
- Change the words Student Name to your name.

e) Save the modified Ceramics Info Request and print a copy.

You have been asked to write a thank you letter to Mrs. Kristine LeBon for her donation.

a) In a new document create the following letter, allowing Word to wrap the text:

January 21, 2001

Mrs. Kristine LeBon
17 North Main St.
Reedsburg, GA 04459

Dear Kristine:

I am writing to thank you for your very generous donation to the Sarah Bernstein Memorial Library. We are always appreciative of donations, both monetary and otherwise.

As you are well aware, our library has needed new carpeting for several years now. The old rugs were an ugly avocado color. The new carpeting not only looks beautiful, but will also help keep the environmental conditions good for books.

Thanks again from the gang at the Sarah Bernstein Memorial Library.

Sincerely,

Chris Warheit
Library Assistant

Be sure there are five blank lines below the date and three blank lines below the closing Sincerely.

b) Check the document on screen for errors and misspellings and make any corrections.

c) Save the letter naming it Donation Thanks.

d) Make the following changes:

- Delete the word very in the first sentence of the first paragraph.
- Add the following sentence to the end of the first paragraph: Your donation was truly a welcome surprise.
- Delete the sentence The old rugs were an ugly avocado color. in the second paragraph.
- Change good for books to favorable for printed materials at the end of the second paragraph.
- Change the gang to all of us in the third paragraph.
- Change the words Chris Warheit to your name.

e) Save the modified Donation Thanks and print a copy.

Exercise 3 ———————————————— Entertainment Review

The local newspaper has an opening for an entertainment critic. In a new document create a half-page review of the last movie, concert, play, art show, or similar event that you attended. Check the document on screen for errors and misspellings and make any corrections. Save the document naming it Entertainment Review and print a copy.

Exercise 4 ———————————————— Vacation

In a new document create a one-page description of your last vacation. Describe where you went, how you traveled, what you saw and did. Check the document on screen for errors and misspellings and make any corrections. Save the document naming it Vacation and print a copy.

Exercise 5 ———————————————— Geology Schedule

You have enrolled in an independent study of the geologic eras of the earth and your instructor wants a schedule of topics and due dates for your research papers.

a) In a new document create the following memorandum, substituting your name for Student Name and allowing Word to wrap the text:

MEMORANDUM

TO: Dr. Janet Sung, Geology Department
FROM: Student Name
DATE: January 15, 2001
SUBJECT: Geologic eras topics and due dates

The following schedule outlines the research paper topics and due dates for my independent study on the geologic eras of the earth:

Topic Due Date
Precambrian 1/29
Paleozoic 2/12
Mesozoic 2/26
Cenozoic 3/12

One week before each due date I will submit an outline containing a specific topic and a list of sources for each paper.

b) Check the document on screen for errors and misspellings and make any corrections.

c) Save the document naming it Geology Schedule and print a copy.

Exercise 6 ———————————————— Things To Do

In a new document create a list of eight things you want to do on the weekends. Include the title Things To Do at the top of the page. Make sure there is a blank line separating the title from the list. Check the document on screen for errors and misspellings and make any corrections. Save the document naming it Things To Do and print a copy.

Exercise 7 ——————————————————————— PROPOSAL

Dr. Ellie Peterson and Dr. Jeremy Prow are studying coral reefs off the coast of Florida. They have used the word processor to create a funding proposal for their coral research.

 a) Open PROPOSAL and make the following changes:

 - Edit the heading so it reads A PROPOSAL FOR CORAL RESEARCH at the top of the page.
 - Change the word basic to complete in the first sentence of the first paragraph under the Summary subheading.
 - Change the word accomplish to complete in the last sentence of the same paragraph.
 - Delete the phrase state of the art in the first sentence of the second paragraph under the Purpose and Description subheading.

 b) Check the document on screen for errors and misspellings and make any corrections.

 c) Save the modified PROPOSAL.

 d) Use the following steps to print only page 1:

 1. Select File → Print.
 2. In the Pages entry box type 1.
 3. Select OK to print only the first page of this multi-page document.

Exercise 8 ——————————————————————— Journal

A word processor can be used to keep a journal. In a new document create a one-page journal entry describing what you did last week. Add your plans for the upcoming weekend. Check the document on screen for errors and misspellings and make any corrections. Save the document naming it Journal and print a copy.

Exercise 9 ——————————————————————— Grand Opening

You have opened a retail store. Your store could sell jewelry, clothing, sporting goods, or anything else you wish.

 a) In a new document create a flyer that will be sent to prospective customers announcing your grand opening. Be sure to include the name, address, and phone number of your store, as well as a list of some of the special items you will be selling. Also include the date and time of the grand opening.

 b) Check the document on screen for errors and misspellings and make any corrections.

 c) Save the document naming it Grand Opening.

 d) Your promotions manager suggested having a special sale at the grand opening. At the very top of the flyer add the title 20% OFF EVERYTHING! Save the modified Grand Opening and print a copy.

The sports editor for your college newspaper would like you to write an essay on karate.

a) In a new document create the following essay, allowing Word to wrap the text:

Karate has become very popular among people of all ages. Karate is a form of martial arts that often improves overall physical and mental health. Learning self defense is one of the main reasons people study karate. It may also improve a person's self-esteem and teaches physical and mental discipline. Students often find that it helps them stay focused, and as a result improves their grades.

A typical karate class has four parts. Class begins with stretching and calisthenics. This is important because each person needs to be flexible and have stamina when doing karate. Next, drills on fundamental karate skills are performed. These drills are followed by a kata, which is a choreographed floor exercise. Classes are concluded with free sparring.

b) Check the document on screen for errors and misspellings and make any corrections.

c) Save the document naming it Karate.

d) Make the following changes:

- Delete the word overall in the second sentence of the first paragraph.
- Change the word performed to conducted in the fourth sentence of the second paragraph.
- Add the sentence Karate cannot only improve your physical and mental health but it is also fun to do. at the end of the second paragraph.

e) Save the modified Karate and print a copy.

You have been asked to write an article for a newsletter about an environmental issue.

a) In a new document create the following article, allowing Word to wrap the text:

Lawn Sprinklers

We all know that fresh water is essential to our survival. Fresh water is needed to cook our meals, to drink, and to bathe. Many people do not realize that fresh water is a natural resource that needs to be used wisely. Although most of the earth is covered in water, only a very small percentage of that water is fresh water suitable for consumption.

One way you can help to conserve fresh water is to use lawn sprinklers efficiently. Lawn sprinklers should be set to run only during early morning and late evening hours when the sun is not hot. Running sprinklers in the middle of the day leads to much of the water evaporating and not being absorbed into the ground. Also, when nature's sprinklers (rain) are on, make sure your sprinklers are not.

If each of us does a little, we can do a lot to conserve our fresh water supply.

b) Check the document on screen for errors and misspellings and make any corrections.

c) Save the document naming it Water Conservation and print a copy.

Exercise 12 —————————————————————————— Ten Years

In a new document create a two or three paragraph essay on "What I will be doing 10 years from now." Check the document on screen for errors and misspellings and make any corrections. Save the document naming it Ten Years and print a copy.

Exercise 13 —————————————————————————— Campsite Request

You need a letter to request camping space for your club's annual camping trip.

a) In a new document create the following letter, allowing Word to wrap the text:

Student Name
1655 Jacaranda Blvd.
Plainfield, NC 28031
February 19, 2001

Ursula Verde
Birch Tree Campground
RR1
Clewiston, SC 02618

Dear Ursula:

I am writing to request a reservation for the annual Prairie Dog Wilderness Club camping trip. Last year we needed more room! Therefore, I would like to reserve eight tent sites in the remote camping area of your campgrounds. We will be arriving on June 9 and leaving on June 17. Enclosed is a check for $300 as a deposit. We look forward to camping!

Sincerely,

Student Name

Be sure there are five blank lines below the date and three blank lines below the closing Sincerely.

b) Check the document on screen for errors and misspellings and make any corrections.

c) Save the document naming it Campsite Request.

d) Make the following changes:

- Change the date to the current date.
- Change the words Student Name to your name at the beginning and the end of the letter.
- Add another paragraph requesting brochures for the area attractions.

e) Save the modified Campsite Request and print a copy.

Print Pre<u>v</u>iew

<u>U</u>ndo

Select A<u>l</u>l

<u>F</u>ont

<u>P</u>aragraph

Page Set<u>u</u>p

<u>H</u>eader and Footer

<u>B</u>reak

<u>T</u>abs

Chapter Four Objectives

After completing this chapter you will be able to:

1. Print preview a document.
2. Reverse or repeat the effects of the last command using the Undo and Redo commands.
3. Select and delete blocks of text.
4. Apply character formats, such as different fonts and sizes.
5. Apply paragraph formats, such as alignment and line spacing.
6. Apply page formats, such as margins and headers and footers.
7. Add a header and footer to a document.
8. Insert page numbers into headers and footers.
9. Insert manual page breaks.
10. Position text using tabs and tab stops.

Chapter Three introduced the commands necessary to create, edit, save, and print word processor documents. This chapter covers formatting options that improve the appearance and readability of documents. These formatting options are used to change:

- the look of characters with formats such as bold, underline, italic, and different fonts and sizes.

- the way paragraphs appear using alignment, line spacing, tabs, and tab stops.

- the arrangement of text on the page with margins, headers and footers, and pagination.

Other features such as windows and print preview are also discussed.

4.1 Previewing a Document

Selecting the Print Preview command from the File menu allows you to view a document's pages on the screen as they will appear when printed. This enables you to see the effects of formatting without actually having to print the document:

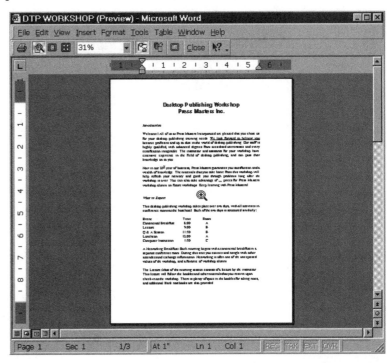

Once in print preview, the document can be viewed in different ways. For a multipage document, pressing the Page Up or Page Down key displays the previous page or next page, respectively. The next or previous page can also be displayed using the vertical scroll bar. When the mouse pointer is moved onto the document, the pointer shape changes to a magnifying glass (). Clicking the magnifying glass on the page zooms in to that portion of the page, allowing you to view formatting in more detail. Clicking again restores the page to full size.

Selecting the Print button (🖨) on the Standard Toolbar prints a copy of the document using the default printer settings. Selecting the Close button or pressing the Esc key returns you to the document window.

A document may also be print previewed by clicking on the Print Preview button (🔍) on the Standard Toolbar.

Practice 1

In this practice you will print preview a document.

1) OPEN DTP WORKSHOP

    a. On the Taskbar, click on the Start button. A menu is displayed.
    b. Select the Open Office Document command. A dialog box is displayed.
        1. In the Look in collapsible list, select the appropriate folder.
        2. Click on DTP WORKSHOP.
        3. Select the Open button. Word is started and DTP WORKSHOP is opened.

2) PRINT PREVIEW DTP WORKSHOP

    a. Select File → Print Preview. The print preview window is displayed with the first page of DTP WORKSHOP.
    b. Move the pointer to the middle of the previewed page. Note that the shape of the pointer has changed to a magnifying glass (🔍).
    c. Click the left mouse button once. Although the document is magnified on the screen, it will not be enlarged when printed.
    d. Click again to return to the default magnification.

3) SCROLL THE DOCUMENT IN PRINT PREVIEW

    a. Click once on the down scroll arrow (▾) in the vertical scroll bar. The second page of DTP WORKSHOP is displayed.
    b. Continue to click on the down scroll arrow until the last page of DTP WORKSHOP is displayed.
    c. Press the Page Up key until page 1 of the document is displayed.
    d. On the Print Preview Toolbar, select Close to return to the document window.

4.2 The Undo Command and the Repeat Command

There may be times when you execute a command or perform an action by mistake. To reverse the effects of the last action, the Undo command (Ctrl+Z) is selected from the Edit menu. There are also some actions that cannot be reversed, such as executing the Print command, because the document has already been printed.

Undoing More Than One Action

Each time you select the Undo command, the previous action is then available to undo. For example, if you typed a word, deleted a character, and then typed another word, the first time you select the Undo command the last word is removed. Selecting the command again undeletes the character, and selecting the Undo command a third time removes the first word you typed.

Be Careful with Highlighted Text

Care must be taken when highlighting text because a highlighted block of text can easily be deleted or moved. When text is highlighted, pressing a key replaces the highlighted block with the typed character. Dragging on a highlighted block displays the ⬉ mouse pointer and moves the highlighted block to the location where the mouse button is released. A more precise way of moving text is discussed in the next chapter.

The Edit menu is a *smart menu* that changes to reflect the current situation. For example, typing text and then displaying the Edit menu shows the Undo Typing command. Selecting the Undo Typing command deletes all text entered since the last action performed.

There may also be times when you execute a command or perform an action and need to do it again. The same action can be performed a second time by selecting either the Redo or the Repeat command (Ctrl+Y) from the Edit menu.

The Undo button (⟲) and the Redo button (⟳) on the Standard Toolbar can also be used to reverse or repeat actions.

4.3 Selecting and Deleting Blocks of Text

In the last chapter, the Backspace key was used to remove text one character at a time. For large amounts of text, this method is too time consuming. Text can be deleted faster by first selecting the text to be removed. *Selected text* is shown highlighted on the screen:

This Friday night at the George Stamos Auditorium will be a command performance by the Ivy Quintet. Tickets are available at the box office for $2.00 for students, faculty and staff, and $7.50 for all others. The box office is open Tuesday through Saturday 8 a.m. to 5 p.m. and Sunday 8 a.m. to noon.¶

The second sentence is selected

Pressing the Backspace key or the Delete key then removes all of the selected text.

The easiest way to select text is by dragging the I-Beam pointer over the desired text to form a *highlighted block*. Anything from a single character to several pages of text can be highlighted. When using this technique, be careful to only include the text to be deleted in the highlight. Also note that pressing a key replaces the highlighted block with the typed character. A highlight can be removed without deleting the text by clicking once anywhere in the document or pressing an arrow key.

There are several other methods for highlighting text:

- Double-clicking on a word highlights it from the first character to the last and includes the space after the word.

- Holding down the Shift key and clicking the mouse in the document highlights the text from the current cursor position to the position where the pointer was clicked.

- Holding down the Shift key and pressing an arrow key highlights from the original cursor position in the direction of the arrow key.

- Moving the mouse pointer to the left of the text (near the left edge of the page) changes the pointer to a right-pointing arrow shape (⬈). Clicking once highlights the line of text to the right of the pointer. Double-clicking highlights the entire paragraph, and triple-clicking highlights the entire document. The right-pointing arrow can also be dragged up or down to highlight multiple lines of text.

- Executing the Select All command (Ctrl+A) from the Edit menu highlights the entire document.

In this practice you will select and delete highlighted blocks of text. The Underline command will be used to restore a deleted block. Open DTP WORKSHOP if it is not already displayed.

1) SELECT TEXT BY DRAGGING

    a. Move the pointer into the paragraph at the top of the document that begins "Welcome!"

    b. Drag the mouse (hold down the left button and move the mouse) several words to the right. Each character the pointer passes over is highlighted.

    c. Release the mouse button. The highlight remains.

2) REMOVE THE HIGHLIGHT

    Click once on any text. The highlight is removed.

3) SELECT A WORD

    a. Move the pointer over a word and double-click. The entire word and any space after it is highlighted.

    b. Press the up-arrow key to remove the highlight.

4) HIGHLIGHT THE ENTIRE DOCUMENT

    a. Select Edit → Select All. All the text in the document is highlighted.

    b. Click once on any text to remove the highlight.

5) HIGHLIGHT A SENTENCE

    a. In the first paragraph of the introduction, place the cursor just to the left of the "T" in "The president of our company…."

    b. Move the I-Beam pointer, **but do not click**, after the space following the period at the end of the sentence. Make sure that the I-Beam pointer is just to the left of "We look…."

    c. Hold down the Shift key and click once. A highlight is created from the current cursor position to the pointer position. Be sure the space after the period is included in the highlight.

6) DELETE THE HIGHLIGHTED BLOCK

    Press the Delete key. All of the highlighted text, the entire sentence, is deleted.

7) DELETE AND RESTORE THE NEXT PARAGRAPH

    a. Move the pointer to the left of the paragraph that begins "All Press Masters…" until the right-pointing arrow shape (⇗) is displayed.

    b. Double-click the mouse. The entire paragraph is highlighted.

    c. Press the Delete key. The paragraph is removed.

    d. Select Edit → Undo Clear. The paragraph is restored.

8) SAVE THE MODIFIED DTP WORKSHOP

    Save the modified DTP WORKSHOP. In future practices, any of these highlighting techniques may be used when you are directed to select blocks of text.

4.4 Formatting Documents

The way text appears on a page is called its *format*. A document's format includes emphasized text such as <u>underlined</u> or **bold** characters. Formatting also includes the placement of text on the page, the size of margins, the alignment of text within margins, and the spacing between lines of text.

In Word, documents are formatted by selecting commands and options. Each formatting option is associated with a specific *level* that describes how the format will affect a document: character, paragraph, or page. *Character formats* affect only the currently highlighted text, which can be a single character, a word, or several sentences. A *paragraph format* affects the entire paragraph that contains the cursor, and only that paragraph. *Page formats* affect the entire document.

4.5 Character Formats - Fonts

A *font* or *typeface* refers to the shape of characters. The letters in this paragraph are shaped differently from the blue letters above in the section title because the characters are formatted in a different font.

The default font in Word is Times New Roman. There are also special fonts such as ZapfDingbats that contain tiny pictures called *dingbats*. There are many fonts to choose from, for example:

Helvetica: ABCDEF abcdef 1234567890

AGaramond: ABCDEF abcdef 1234567890

Bookman: ABCDEF abcdef 1234567890

Courier: ABCDEF abcdef 1234567890

ZapfDingbats: ✿✛•:•❖✤✦ ☞➡✓✔✗✖✗✗✚✒

The font of text is changed by first highlighting the text and then selecting the Font command from the Format menu, which displays a dialog box:

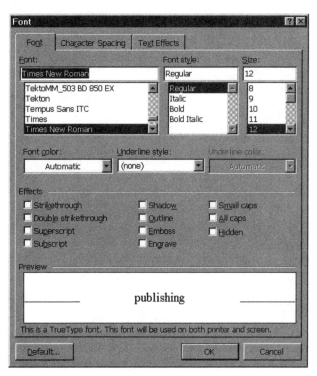

The Font section of the dialog box contains a scrollable list of font names. Selecting the desired font and then OK applies the font to all of the highlighted text.

The Font dialog box can also be displayed by right-clicking on any highlighted text and selecting the Font command from the displayed menu:

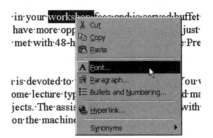

The Font collapsible list on the Formatting Toolbar can be used to change the font of highlighted text. Clicking on the down arrow (▾) displays a list of available fonts. Clicking on the desired font name in the list applies the font to any highlighted text.

4.6 Character Formats - Size

Characters can be displayed in different sizes. The size is measured in *points*, and there are 72 points to an inch. For example:

This is an example of 9 point Helvetica.

This is an example of 10 point Helvetica.

This is an example of 12 point Helvetica.

This is an example of 14 point Helvetica.

This is an example of 18 point Helvetica.

The same dialog box used to change the font of highlighted text is used to change the size. Selecting the Font command from the Format menu displays the dialog box. The Size section contains a scrollable list of sizes to choose from. A size can also be typed into the Size entry box. Selecting OK then applies the formatting to any highlighted text.

The Size collapsible list on the Formatting Toolbar can be used to change the size of highlighted text. Clicking on the down arrow (▾) displays a list of sizes to select from. A size can also be typed into the Size collapsible list, and pressing Enter applies the formatting to the highlighted text.

Text Size

Changing the size of text affects the look of a document and can help distinguish between headings and body text. Body text is usually from 6 to 14 points, while headings are usually from 16 to 72 points.

Practice 3 ✸ ————————————————————————

In this practice you will format text in different fonts and sizes. Open DTP WORKSHOP if it is not already displayed.

1) CHANGE THE FONT OF THE ENTIRE TITLE

    a. Highlight the entire title at the top of the document, "Desktop Publishing Workshop Press Masters Inc."

    b. Select Format → Font. A dialog box is displayed.

        1. Select Helvetica from the scrollable list of Font names.

        2. Select OK. The highlighted text is now formatted as Helvetica.

A Guide to Microsoft Office 2000 Professional

2) INCREASE THE FONT SIZE OF THE ENTIRE TITLE

    a. The title "Desktop Publishing Workshop Press Masters Inc." should still be highlighted.

    b. On the Formatting Toolbar, from the Size collapsible list select 18. The highlighted text is now 18 point.

    c. Click anywhere to remove the highlight.

<u>Check</u> – The title should now be formatted as Helvetica and 18 point:

> Desktop·Publishing·Workshop¶
> Press·Masters·Inc.¶
> ¶
> ¶
> Introduction¶
> ¶
> Welcome!·All·of·us·at·Press·Masters·Incorporated·are·pleased·that·you·chose·us·for·your·
> desktop·publishing·training·needs.·We·look·forward·to·helping·you·become·proficient·

3) SAVE THE MODIFIED DTP WORKSHOP

When to Apply Formats

Any new text inserted in existing formatted text will automatically be given the same format. For example, a character typed between two bold characters is automatically made bold. This leads to a very common error. Suppose you are creating a new document, and after typing a title, you highlight the text and make it bold. When you press Enter and begin to type the next paragraph, it is also bold. In fact, all of the text from this point on will be bold!

This problem can be solved by highlighting everything but the original title and deselecting any applied styles. However, the problem is best avoided by following this simple rule:

Type all of the text for your document first and then go back and apply the desired formatting.

4.7 Character Formats - Style

The way in which a character is emphasized is called its *style*. The most common styles are bold, italic, and underline:

Bold text is printed darker so that words and phrases stand out on a page. It is often used for titles and headings.

Italic text is slanted and is mostly used for emphasis. It is sometimes used for headings.

<u>Underline text</u> is often used in footnotes and endnotes for referring to the title of publications.

Regular text, sometimes called normal text, is the default style. Regular text does not have any emphasis.

The same dialog box used to change the font and size of highlighted text is used to change the style. Selecting the <u>F</u>ont command from the F<u>o</u>rmat menu displays the dialog box. The Font style section contains a list of styles to choose from. Selecting OK then applies the formatting to any highlighted text.

The Bold (**B**), Italic (*I*), and Underline (<u>U</u>) buttons on the Formatting Toolbar can be used to apply character styles to selected text. More than one button can be used on highlighted text to apply multiple styles.

Ctrl key shortcuts can also be used to apply styles to highlighted text:

SHORTCUT	STYLE
Ctrl+B	bold
Ctrl+I	italic
Ctrl+U	underline

Practice 4 —————————————————————————

In this practice you will format text in the bold, italic, and underline styles. Open DTP WORKSHOP if it is not already displayed.

1) *BOLD THE ENTIRE TITLE*

    a. Highlight the entire title at the top of the document, "Desktop Publishing Workshop Press Masters Inc."

    b. Select Format → Font. A dialog box is displayed.

        1. In the Font style section, click on the Bold option.

        2. Select OK. The dialog box is removed and the highlighted text is bold.

    c. Click anywhere to remove the highlight.

2) *FORMAT TEXT USING THE FORMATTING TOOLBAR AND A SHORTCUT*

    a. Highlight the text in the next line, the "Introduction" title.

    b. On the Formatting Toolbar, click on the Italic button (*I*). The highlighted text is shown italic on the screen and the Italic button appears pushed in.

    c. Press Ctrl+B. The highlighted text is both bold and italic on the screen.

    d. Click anywhere to remove the highlight.

3) *ITALICIZE THE REST OF THE TITLES*

    a. Scroll down page 1 until the "What to Expect" title is displayed, and highlight the title.

    b. Right-click on the highlighted "What to Expect." A menu is displayed.

    c. Click on the Font command in the menu. A dialog box is displayed.

        1. In the Font style section, click on the Bold Italic option.

        2. Select OK to apply the style and remove the dialog box.

    d. Click anywhere to remove the highlight.

    e. Scroll through the rest of the document and format the "What to Bring," "Our Computers," and "See You Soon!" titles as bold and italic.

4) *UNDERLINE A SENTENCE IN THE INTRODUCTION*

    a. Scroll to the top of page 1.

    b. Highlight the sentence that starts "We look forward to…." Do not highlight the space after the period.

    c. On the Formatting Toolbar, click on the Underline button (U). The highlighted text is underlined.

    d. Click anywhere to remove the highlight.

5) *REMOVE UNDERLINING FROM PART OF THE SENTENCE*

    a. Place the cursor after the "u" in "you" in the underlined sentence.

    b. Press and hold the Shift key.

    c. While holding down the Shift key, press the right-arrow key. A highlight is created.

    d. Continue to hold the Shift key while pressing the right-arrow key until the remainder of the sentence is highlighted.

    e. On the Formatting Toolbar, click on the Underline button.

    f. Click anywhere to remove the highlight. Only the first six words of the sentence are underlined.

<u>Check</u> – Your document should look similar to:

Desktop·Publishing·Workshop¶
Press·Masters·Inc.¶
¶
¶
Introduction¶
¶
Welcome!·All·of·us·at·Press·Masters·Incorporated·are·pleased·that·you·chose·us·for·your· desktop·publishing·training·needs. ·<u>We·look·forward·to·helping·you</u>·become·proficient· and·up·to·date·in·the·world·of·desktop·publishing. ·Our·staff·is·highly·qualified, ·with· advanced·degrees·from·accredited·universities·and·every·certification·imaginable. ·The·

6) *SAVE AND THEN PRINT THE MODIFIED DTP WORKSHOP*

4.8 Character Formats - Superscripts and Subscripts

Superscript is a format that raises text slightly above the current line and *subscript* moves text slightly below the current line. For example:

In her 5th Avenue boutique, Dina Johannsen sold her designer perfume called "DJ's H_2O."

The "th" after the 5 is a superscript, and the "2" in H_2O is a subscript.

The same dialog box used to change the font, size, and style of highlighted text is used to format superscripts and subscripts. Selecting the Font command from the Format menu displays a dialog box. The Effects section contains the Superscript and Subscript options. Selecting OK then applies the formatting to any highlighted text.

Ctrl key shortcuts can also be used to apply superscript and subscript formatting to highlighted text:

SHORTCUT	STYLE
Ctrl+Shift+=(equal sign)	superscript
Ctrl+=(equal sign)	subscript

Practice 5

In this practice you will format text as superscript and subscript. Open DTP WORKSHOP if it is not already displayed.

1) FORMAT TEXT AS SUPERSCRIPT

    a. In the third paragraph of the introduction, highlight the "th" after the number 20.
    b. Select Format → Font. A dialog box is displayed.
        1. In the Effects section, click on the Superscript check box.
        2. Select OK. The highlighted text is now raised slightly above the surrounding text.

2) FORMAT TEXT AS SUBSCRIPT

    a. In the same paragraph, highlight the word "low" in the sentence that reads "take advantage of low prices…"
    b. Select Format → Font. A dialog box is displayed.
        1. In the Effects section, click on the Subscript check box.
        2. Select OK. The highlighted text is now lowered slightly below the surrounding text.

Check – Your document should look similar to:

Now·in·our·20th·year·of·business,·Press·Masters·guarantees·you·satisfaction·and·a·wealth· of·knowledge.··The·materials·that·you·take·home·from·this·workshop·will·help·refresh· your·memory·and·guide·you·through·problems·long·after·the·workshop·is·over.·You·can· also·take·advantage·of·low·prices·for·Press·Masters·workshop·alumni·on·future·workshops.· Keep·learning·with·Press·Masters!¶

3) SAVE THE MODIFIED DTP WORKSHOP

4.9 Paragraph Formats - Alignment

The *alignment* of text in a paragraph refers to its position relative to the sides of the page: left, centered, right, and justified. For example:

> Left aligned, the default, means that the left edge of a paragraph is straight. The right edge of the paragraph is jagged. This format is most often used in letters and research papers.

> Centered is the alignment most often used for headings and titles in documents. Each line of a centered paragraph is equidistant from the left and right sides of the page.

> Right aligned is the opposite of left aligned. The right edge of a right-aligned paragraph is straight while the left edge of the paragraph is jagged.

> Justified alignment creates straight edges at both sides of a paragraph. This alignment is often used in newspapers and books. Word adjusts the space between words on each line of justified text so that it extends perfectly across the page.

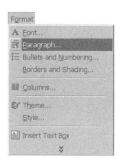

Selecting the Paragraph command from the Format menu displays the Paragraph dialog box, and selecting the Indents and Spacing tab displays the following options:

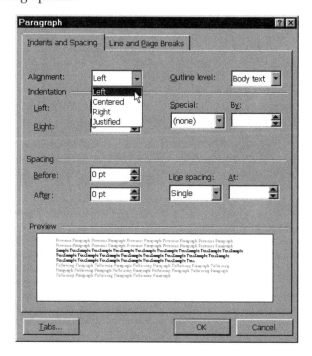

Clicking on the down arrow (▼) next to the Alignment collapsible list displays the options to select from. Selecting the desired alignment and then OK aligns the text in the paragraph that contains the cursor. Multiple paragraphs can be formatted together by highlighting them first, and then applying the desired alignment.

The Paragraph dialog box can also be displayed by right-clicking in any paragraph and selecting the Paragraph command from the displayed menu:

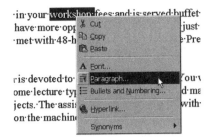

The Align Left (▤), Center (▤), Align Right (▤), and Justify (▤) buttons on the Formatting Toolbar can be used to format a paragraph. Ctrl key shortcuts can also be used to format the alignment of paragraphs:

SHORTCUT	STYLE
Ctrl+L	left align
Ctrl+E	center
Ctrl+R	right align
Ctrl+J	justify

4.10 Paragraph Formats - Line Spacing

The amount of space between lines in a paragraph can be changed. Single spacing places text on each line of the page and double spacing spreads the lines so that there is additional space between each line. Double spacing can make a document more readable, leaving room for written notes between lines. For example:

single spacing

> This paragraph is single spaced. There is only a little space between the lines for notes or comments, but more text fits on each page. Most printed text, including this book, is single spaced.

double spacing

> This paragraph is double spaced. Note how space is left between
>
> each line for notes or comments. Double spacing is used mostly for
>
> academic papers and drafts.

The same dialog box used to change the alignment of paragraphs is used to change the line spacing. Selecting the Paragraph command from the Format menu displays the dialog box. The Line spacing collapsible list contains options to choose from. Selecting OK then applies the formatting to the paragraph that contains the cursor. Multiple paragraphs can be formatted together by highlighting them first, and then applying the desired line spacing.

Like alignment, changing the spacing affects only the paragraph that currently contains the cursor, or all of the paragraphs in a highlighted block. Single spacing is the default in Word.

Paragraph Format Review

Type all the text for your document first. Next, place the cursor in the paragraph to be formatted, select the Paragraph command, and then select the desired option(s).

Ctrl key shortcuts can also be used to format line spacing:

SHORTCUT	STYLE
Ctrl+1	single spacing
Ctrl+2	double spacing

Practice 6

In this practice you will format alignments and spacing in DTP WORKSHOP. Open DTP WORKSHOP if it is not already displayed.

1) CENTER THE FIRST TWO LINES IN THE DOCUMENT

a. Scroll to the top of page 1 if it is not already displayed.
b. Click the I-Beam pointer in the title "Desktop Publishing Workshop" at the top of page 1 to place the cursor.
c. Select Format → Paragraph. A dialog box is displayed.
  1. Click on the down arrow of the Alignment collapsible list. A list of options is displayed.
  2. Select the Centered option.
  3. Select OK. The dialog box is removed and the text is centered.
d. Place the cursor in the next line of the document "Press Masters Inc."
e. On the Formatting Toolbar, click on the Center button (▤). The text is centered.

2) JUSTIFY THE PARAGRAPHS IN THE INTRODUCTION

a. Place the cursor anywhere in the paragraph that begins "Welcome! All of us...."
b. Hold down the Shift key and click in the last paragraph of the introduction, the one that begins "Now in our 20th year...." A highlighted block is created that contains some text from each paragraph in the Introduction.
c. On the Formatting Toolbar, click on the Justify button (▤). All of the highlighted paragraphs are justified.
d. Click anywhere to remove the highlight.

3) DOUBLE SPACE THE SECOND PARAGRAPH OF THE INTRODUCTION

a. Right-click in the second paragraph, the one that begins "All Press Masters workshops...." A menu is displayed.
b. Select the Paragraph command in the menu. A dialog box is displayed.
  1. Click on the down arrow of the Line spacing collapsible list. Line spacing options are displayed.
  2. Select the Double option.
  3. Select OK. The paragraph containing the cursor is double spaced.

Check – Your document should look similar to:

Desktop·Publishing·Workshop¶
Press·Masters·Inc.¶
¶
¶
¶
Introduction¶
¶
Welcome!· All· of· us· at· Press· Masters· Incorporated· are· pleased· that· you· chose· us· for· your· desktop· publishing· training· needs.· We· look· forward· to· helping· you· become· proficient· and· up· to· date· in· the· world· of· desktop· publishing.· Our· staff· is· highly· qualified,· with· advanced· degrees· from· accredited· universities· and· every· certification· imaginable.· The· instructor· and· assistants· for· your· workshop· have· extensive· experience· in· the· field· of· desktop· publishing,· and· can· pass· their· knowledge· on· to· you.¶
¶
All· Press· Masters· workshops· are· organized· with· the· individual· in· mind.· In· addition· to· the·

instructor,· your· workshop· will· have· one· assistant· for· every· five· attendees· during· the·

hands· on· computer· sessions.· As· you· work· on· the· computers,· these· assistants· will· be· right·

there· with· you· to· help· you· and· answer· any· questions· you· may· have.¶

A Guide to Microsoft Office 2000 Professional

4) *DELETE THE DOUBLE-SPACED PARAGRAPH*

    a. Highlight the entire double-spaced paragraph.
    b. Press Delete to delete the paragraph.
    c. Press Delete again so that one blank line separates the two paragraphs in the Introduction.

5) *SAVE THE MODIFIED DTP WORKSHOP*

Templates

Rather than recreating a document with complex formatting over and over again, it can be created once and then saved as a template, enabling duplicates to be created as necessary. Templates are previously created files that include only the basic elements.

Selecting the Save As command from the File menu and then selecting Template from the Save as type collapsible list saves the current document as a template. A template is used by selecting the General tab in the New Office Document dialog box.

4.11 Page Formats - Margins

Margins are shown in Print Layout view as the white region around the text on a page. The default margins in Word for an 8.5 inch by 11 inch page are 1.25 inches for the left and right and 1 inch for the top and bottom:

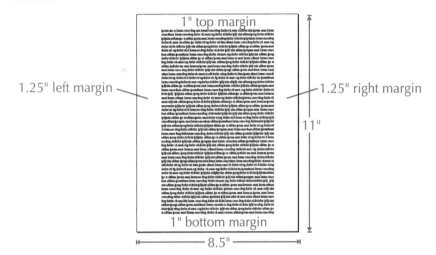

Changes to the margins have an inverse affect on the amount of text that a page can contain. Widening the left and right margins decreases the number of characters that fit on a line and narrowing the same margins increases the line's capacity. Similarly, larger top and bottom margins decrease the number of lines of text a page can contain and smaller top and bottom margins increase the page's capacity.

Selecting the Page Setup command from the File menu displays a dialog box, and selecting the Margins tab displays the following options:

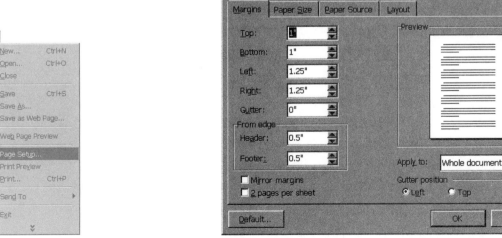

Top, Bottom, Left, and Right margins each have their own entry box. Margins can be changed by typing the desired measurements into the appropriate entry boxes. Selecting OK applies the formatting. For example, the bottom margin is changed to 0.75 inches by first double-clicking on the value in the Bottom entry box, typing 0.75 (the new value), and then selecting OK.

Changing the margins can affect the number of pages in a document. The displayed page and the total number of pages in a document are indicated in the Status bar at the bottom of the document window:

displayed page   total pages

The status bar contains information about the currently displayed page and the total pages

Practice 7

In this practice the margins of DTP WORKSHOP will be changed. Open DTP WORKSHOP if it is not already displayed.

1) CHANGE THE MARGINS

Select File → Page Setup. A dialog box is displayed.

1. Click on the Margins tab if the margin options are not displayed.
2. Triple-click in the Left margin box to highlight the measurement.
3. Type 2.5 to replace the old value.
4. Triple-click in the Right margin box to highlight the measurement.
5. Type 3 to replace the old value.
6. Select OK. The document now has a left margin of 2.5 inches and a right margin of 3 inches. Note how there is more white space on the left and right of the document. Also note the page indicator—there are now 4 pages in the document.

2) PRINT PREVIEW DTP WORKSHOP

a. Print preview the document. Scroll to the first page in the document if it is not already displayed. Note how much more room appears on the left and right of the page because the margins have been increased:

b. Press Esc to return to the document window.

Select <u>F</u>ile → Page Set<u>u</u>p. A dialog box is displayed.

1. Change the Left margin to 1.5.
2. Change the Right margin to 1.5.
3. Select OK. The document now has left and right margins of 1.5 inches.

4) *SAVE THE MODIFIED DTP WORKSHOP*

4.12 Page Formats - Headers and Footers

Documents can be made more informative by including text at the top and bottom of each page, which are the areas called the *header* and *footer*, respectively. Headers and footers are often used to indicate the current page number, the document's file name, the author's name, or the date.

A header or footer can be added to a document by first selecting the <u>H</u>eader and Footer command from the <u>V</u>iew menu. The text is dimmed in the document, the header box is displayed at the top of the page, and the Header and Footer Toolbar is displayed:

The cursor is automatically placed in the header, allowing you to type the desired text. Text in the header can then be formatted using commands and Toolbar buttons like any other text.

The cursor is moved from the header to the footer by clicking on the Switch Between Header and Footer button () on the Header and Footer Toolbar. Each time the button is clicked, Word scrolls the document until the header or footer is visible and places the cursor in it. Once the cursor is in the footer, text can be typed and then formatted. Headers or footers can be removed from a document by highlighting the text and pressing the Delete key.

Clicking on the Close button in the Header and Footer Toolbar removes the Toolbar from the window, dims the header and footer text, and displays the document.

Displaying the Document

Another way to close the Header and Footer Toolbar and display the document is to double-click in the dimmed body text.

An existing header or footer can be edited by double-clicking in the header or footer area.

Text entered in the header or footer is printed on each page of the document. However, it is possible to have the header and footer not printed on the first page but printed on the rest of the pages. Selecting the **Page Setup** command from the **File** menu displays the Page Setup dialog box, and selecting the **Layout** tab displays the following options:

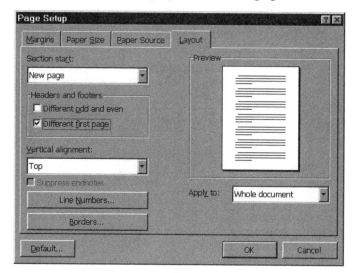

Selecting the **Different first page** option and then **OK** removes the contents from both the header and footer on the first page of the document.

4.13 Adding Page Numbers

Page numbers are helpful in longer documents and can be added to a header or footer by clicking on the Insert Page Number button on the Header and Footer Toolbar:

Insert Page Number button

A page number is inserted at the current cursor position, and can be formatted like any other text. Word will then print the appropriate page number at the top or bottom of every page in the document. A page number can be deleted from a header or footer by highlighting it and pressing the Delete key.

Practice 8

In this practice you will create a header and footer in DTP WORKSHOP. Open DTP WORKSHOP if it is not already displayed.

1) CREATE A HEADER

a. Scroll to the top of page 1 if it is not already displayed.

b. Select **View → Header and Footer**. The text is dimmed and the cursor is placed in the Header box. Note the Header and Footer Toolbar.

c. Type Press Masters Workshop. These words will now appear at the top of every page in the document.
d. Highlight all of the header text.
e. On the Formatting Toolbar, from the Font list select Helvetica. The text in the header is now formatted as Helvetica.
f. With the header text still highlighted, click on the Center button on the Formatting Toolbar. The header text is now centered.

2) CREATE A FOOTER

a. On the Header and Footer Toolbar, click on the Switch Between Header and Footer button ( ). The cursor is placed in the Footer box.
b. Type your name, followed by two spaces.
c. On the Header and Footer Toolbar, click on the Insert Page Number button ( ). The number 1 is inserted at the current cursor position, into the footer.
d. Highlight the page number, then format it as 10 point bold Helvetica using the Formatting Toolbar.
e. On the Header and Footer Toolbar, click on the Close button. The header and footer are now dimmed.

3) PREVIEW THE DOCUMENT

a. Print preview the document. Page 1 of DTP WORKSHOP is displayed. Note the text in the header and the page number in the footer.
b. Scroll to view page 2. Note the page number is a 2.
c. Preview the rest of the document and then return to the document window.

4) REMOVE THE HEADER AND FOOTER FROM THE FIRST PAGE

a. Select File → Page Setup. A dialog box is displayed.
   1. Click on the Layout tab if the layout options are not displayed.
   2. Select the Different first page option.
   3. Select OK. The dialog box is removed from the window and the header and footer are removed from page 1 of the document.
b. Print preview the document. Page 1 of DTP WORKSHOP is displayed. Note that the header and footer are no longer visible on page 1.
c. Scroll to view page 2. Note the header and footer, and that the page number is a 2.
d. Print preview the rest of the document and then return to the document window.

5) SAVE THE MODIFIED DTP WORKSHOP

4.14 Page Formats - Pagination

page breaks

When using Word, it is not necessary to determine how many lines of text will fit each printed page. Word automatically inserts *page breaks* where one page ends and the next begins using a process called *pagination*. As a document is edited, the pagination is automatically updated.

manual page breaks

Manual page breaks can be placed anywhere in a document when a new page should be started before the text on the previous page reaches the bottom. When a manual page break is inserted, a line is displayed with the words "Page Break." Placing the cursor in the text where the new page should start and selecting the Break command from the Insert menu displays a dialog box:

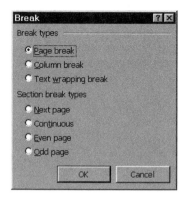

Selecting OK accepts the default option of Page break and inserts a manual page break at the cursor's position.

A page break may also be inserted at the current cursor position by pressing Ctrl+Enter. Manual page breaks can be deleted by placing the cursor to the left of the page break and pressing the Delete key. The document is repaginated and text from the next page is moved up to fill the current page.

Practice 9

In this practice you will insert manual page breaks. Open DTP WORKSHOP if it is not already displayed.

1) INSERT A MANUAL PAGE BREAK

    a. Scroll to the beginning of the document and display formatting marks if they are not already displayed.

    b. Place the cursor just before the "N" in the second paragraph that starts "Now in our 20th year...."

    c. Select Insert → Break. A dialog box is displayed.

        1. Select OK. The default option of Page break is selected and text to the right of the cursor is moved to the next page.

    d. Scroll up to view the top of page 1. A line is displayed with the words "Page Break."

2) PREVIEW DTP WORKSHOP

    a. Print preview the document. Note the blank space at the bottom of page 1 as a result of the manual page break.

    b. Return to the document window.

3) DELETE THE MANUAL PAGE BREAK

    a. Place the cursor just to the left of the page break line.

    b. Press the Delete key. Text from page 2 is moved up to page 1.

4) INSERT TWO MANUAL PAGE BREAKS

    a. Scroll to the bottom of page 1.

    b. Place the cursor just to the left of the words "Questions and Answers."

    c. Select Insert → Break, then select OK. A manual page break is inserted and the text to the right of the cursor is moved to the next page.

    d. Scroll to the bottom of page 2.

    e. Place the cursor just to the left of the title "Our Computers."

    f. Select Insert → Break, then select OK. A manual page break is inserted.

5) SAVE AND CLOSE THE MODIFIED DTP WORKSHOP

A Guide to Microsoft Office 2000 Professional

4.15 Tabs and Tab Stops

Tabs are used to position text within a line. When the Tab key is pressed a tab character is inserted and the cursor and any text to the right are moved over to the position of the next tab stop. *Tab stops* are locations on the Ruler specifying the length of the tab character (how far it moves the cursor).

In Word, default tab stops are located at every half inch and are generally used for indenting text from the margin. For example, when beginning a new paragraph, pressing the Tab key once indents the first line half an inch.

A tab character is deleted the same as any other character by placing the cursor to the left of the tab and pressing the Delete key. Any text is automatically moved to the left to fill the space previously created by the tab.

Practice 10

In this practice you will format a new document and use tabs to indent text.

1) CREATE A NEW DOCUMENT AND ENTER A TITLE

  a. Create a new document.
  b. Type Name's Lunch Specials, using your name instead of Name, and then press Enter three times to add two blank lines after the title.

2) ENTER THE REST OF THE TEXT

  a. Type Choose Any Three Items for $3 and press Enter.
  b. Type the following text, pressing the Tab key as indicated (→) at the beginning of each line and pressing Enter (↵) at the end of each line:

→	Hummus and a Pita ↵
→	Seafood Chowder ↵
→	Garden Salad ↵
→	Falafel ↵
→	Half a Tuna Sandwich ↵
→	Frosted Brownie ↵
→	Fruit Cup

3) FORMAT THE TEXT

  a. Highlight the title "Name's Lunch Specials."
  b. Format the title as 36 point bold Helvetica, center aligned.
  c. Click anywhere to remove the highlight.
  d. Highlight the text "Choose Any Three Items for $3."
  e. Format the text as 24 point bold and italic Helvetica.
  f. Click anywhere to remove the highlight.
  g. Highlight all the text below the title that you just formatted, starting with "Hummus…" and ending at "…Fruit Cup."
  h. Format the text as 24 point Helvetica.
  i. Click anywhere to remove the highlight.

<u>Check</u> – Your document should look similar to:

Donna's·Lunch·Specials¶
¦
·*Choose·Any·Three·Items·for·$3*¶
→ Hummus-and-a-Pita¶
→ Seafood·Chowder¶
→ Garden·Salad¶
→ Falafel¶
→ Half·a·Tuna·Sandwich¶
→ Frosted·Brownie¶
→ Fruit·Cup¶

4) SAVE, PRINT, AND THEN CLOSE THE DOCUMENT

   a. Select <u>F</u>ile → <u>S</u>ave. A dialog box is displayed.
      1. In the File name entry box, type Lunch Specials to replace the existing text.
      2. In the Save in collapsible list, select the appropriate folder.
      3. Select the **Save** button. The document is saved with the name Lunch Specials.
   b. Print a copy of Lunch Specials.
   c. Close Lunch Specials.

4.16 Setting Individual Tab Stops

A common use for tab stops is to create tables of data arranged in columns. Rather than using the default tab stops, new tab stops are usually created at the desired intervals for the table.

A tab stop can be set at any position on the Ruler. When a tab stop is set Word automatically ignores the default stops to the left. That is, setting a tab stop at 1.4 inches automatically removes the default tab stops at 0.5 and 1.0 inches. The default stop at 1.5 inches is not affected.

When the Tab key is pressed, a tab character is inserted and text to the right of the tab is aligned at the next tab stop according to the type of tab stop:

- **Left tab stop** (▟) aligns the beginning of the text at the stop.
- **Right tab stop** (▙) aligns the end of the text at the stop.
- **Center tab stop** (⊥) centers the text equidistant over the stop.
- **Decimal tab stop** (⊥) aligns the decimal point (period character) at the stop.

An example of each tab stop is shown below:

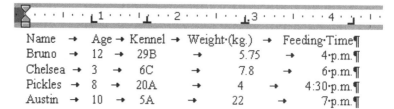

Name	→	Age	→	Kennel	→	Weight·(kg.)	→	Feeding·Time¶
Bruno	→	12	→	29B	→	5.75	→	4·p.m.¶
Chelsea	→	3	→	6C	→	7.8	→	6·p.m.¶
Pickles	→	8	→	20A	→	4	→	4:30·p.m.¶
Austin	→	10	→	5A	→	22	→	7·p.m.¶

Tab stops are indicated by markers on the ruler

Tab stops are set by selecting the <u>T</u>abs command from the F<u>o</u>rmat menu, which displays the following dialog box:

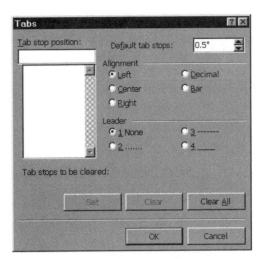

Multiple tab stops can be set at the same time using this dialog box

Tab Leaders

A tab leader is a character that repeats to fill the space spanned by a tab. A tab leader may include characters such as ...., ----, or ___. The dotted pattern is often used for creating a table of contents. The dashes are most commonly used in forms in which blanks must be a specific length. In a multiple choice test, the solid line may be used to represent a blank.

Typing the **Tab stop position**, selecting the appropriate **Alignment**, and then selecting **Set** creates a tab stop at that position. This procedure can be repeated to create as many tab stops as desired. Selecting **OK** removes the dialog box.

The Tabs dialog box can also be displayed by double-clicking on a tab stop on the Ruler or by clicking on the **Tabs** button in the Paragraph dialog box.

A specific tab stop can be removed by selecting it from the **Tab stop position** list in the Tabs dialog box and then selecting **Clear**. A tab stop can also be removed by dragging its marker from the Ruler down into the document. Any text that was aligned at a deleted stop is automatically reformatted.

 Individual tab stops can also be set using the Tab Selection button on the Ruler:

Tab Selection button

Each time you click on the Tab Selection button a different tab stop is displayed. Once the desired tab stop is displayed, clicking once in the Ruler places a tab stop that can then be dragged to the desired location. For example, clicking on the Tab Selection button until the Right tab stop (⌐) is displayed, and then clicking once in the Ruler creates a right tab stop at that location.

Tab stops are a paragraph format like alignment or line spacing. When tab stops are created, they are set for the current paragraph only. This makes it possible for different paragraphs to have different tab stops. As the cursor is moved through the text, the Ruler changes to show the tab stops set for the current paragraph. Like all paragraph formats, tab stops can be applied to a number of paragraphs at the same time by highlighting the paragraphs first and then setting the stops.

Practice 11 ☼ ————————————————————————————

In this practice you will create a table by setting and deleting tab stops. Open DTP WORKSHOP.

1) LOCATE THE TABLE OF DATA IN THE WHAT TO EXPECT SECTION

Scroll to the "What to Expect" section, located at the bottom of page 1 in the document. In this table, there is a single tab between each column: one tab between "Event," "Time," and "Room." However, because tab stops have not yet been set, this table is not easy to read.

2) HIGHLIGHT THE TABLE

a. Place the cursor anywhere in the first line of the table, the one that reads "Event → Time → Room."
b. Drag the mouse slowly down the table. When the highlight is in the last line of the table (Computer Instruction → 1:30 → C), release the button. Any tab stops set now will affect all of the highlighted paragraphs.

3) SET TAB STOPS FOR THE TABLE

Select Format → Tabs. A dialog box is displayed.
       1. In the Tab stop position entry box, type 2.25.
       2. In the Alignment section, select Right.
       3. Select the Set button to create the tab stop.
       4. In the Tab stop position entry box, type 3.
       5. In the Alignment section, select Left.
       6. Select the Set button to create the tab stop.
       7. Select OK. The table is now formatted and is easy to read.

4) DELETE AN EXISTING TAB STOP AND CREATE A NEW TAB STOP

a. Highlight the table if it is not still highlighted.
b. Point to the left tab stop at the 3" mark on the ruler (·⌞·).
c. Drag the tab stop down off of the Ruler. The tab stop is removed.
d. In the upper-left corner of the document, click on the Tab Selection button until the Center tab stop (⊥) is displayed in the button.
e. Click once anywhere in the Ruler. A center tab stop is created.
f. Drag the new tab stop to the 3" mark on the Ruler. The third column is now centered.
g. Click anywhere to remove the highlight.

Check – Your document and Ruler should look similar to:

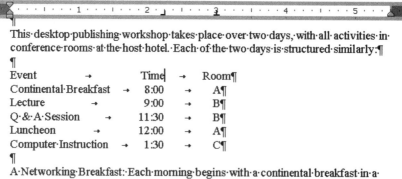

5) SAVE, PRINT, AND THEN CLOSE THE MODIFIED DTP WORKSHOP

    a. Save the modified DTP WORKSHOP.
    b. Print the entire document. Note on the printed copy all of the formatting: headers, footers, paragraph formats, text formats, etc.
    c. Close DTP WORKSHOP.

6) EXIT WORD

Chapter Summary

This chapter introduced the commands necessary to format a word processor document to improve its appearance and readability. A document can be previewed by selecting the Print Preview command. In print preview, a document's pages are displayed on the screen as they will appear when printed.

To reverse the effects of the last action performed, the Undo command from the Edit menu is used. The Repeat or Redo command performs an action again. The Undo and Redo buttons on the Standard Toolbar can be used instead of the commands.

Text can be selected by dragging the I-beam pointer over it to create a highlighted block. When a formatting command is selected, the format is then applied to the block. A highlighted block can be deleted by pressing the Backspace key or Delete key.

The way text appears on a page is called its format. There are three levels that describe how the format will affect the document: character, paragraph, and page. Character formats affect the currently highlighted text, paragraph formats affect the entire paragraph that contains the cursor, and page formats affect the entire document.

The Font command from the Format menu displays the Font dialog box which contains options for changing the style, font, and size of highlighted text. The Font dialog box can also be displayed by right-clicking on highlighted text and selecting the Font command from the menu that appears. Bold and italic styles are common character formats. Text can also be made to appear superscripted or subscripted using options in this dialog box. The Bold, Italic, and Underline buttons on the Formatting Toolbar and Ctrl key shortcuts can also be used to format text.

Selecting the Paragraph command from the Format menu displays the Paragraph dialog box which contains options for changing the alignment and line spacing of a paragraph. This dialog box can also be displayed by right-clicking in any paragraph and selecting the Paragraph command from the menu that appears. A left aligned paragraph has a straight left edge and a right aligned paragraph has a straight right edge. Centered text is equidistant from the left and right sides of the page, and a justified paragraph has straight edges at both sides. The Align Left, Align Right, Center, and Justify buttons on the Formatting Toolbar and Ctrl key shortcuts may also be used to format alignment. Line spacing can be formatted as single spacing or double spacing. When alignment or line spacing is set, it affects the paragraph containing the cursor or all the paragraphs in a highlighted block.

Margins are the white regions shown around text in Print Layout view. The margins for a document can be changed using the Page Setup command from the File menu.

Headers and footers are text displayed at the top or bottom of each page in a document and can be created by selecting the Header and Footer command from the View menu and then entering the text. The cursor is moved from the header to the footer using the Switch Between Header and Footer button on the Header and Footer Toolbar. Page numbers and information such as a title or name can be printed in a header or footer. The current page number can be printed by placing the cursor in the header or footer and selecting the Insert Page Number button on the Header and Footer Toolbar.

manual page breaks

Pagination is the process by which Word determines where one page ends and the next begins. When it is necessary to end the current page, a manual page break can be inserted using the Break command from the Insert menu. Pressing the Delete key removes the page break to the right of the cursor.

Tabs are used to position text within a line. Tab stops are locations specifying the position of the tab character. Different types of tab stops are left, right, center, and decimal. A left tab stop aligns the beginning of the text at the stop. A right tab stop aligns the end of the text at the stop, and a center tab stop centers the text equidistant over the stop. Decimal tab stops align the decimal point (period character) at the stop. Multiple tab stops are set using the Tabs command from the Format menu. Individual tab stops can be set using the Tab Selection button on the Ruler.

Vocabulary

Alignment Position of text in a paragraph relative to the margins. Left, right, centered, or justified.

Block A highlighted section of text that may contain anything from a single character to an entire document. A block can be created by dragging the mouse over the desired text. Any applied formatting affects the currently highlighted text.

Bold text Character format that makes text appear darker. Used for making words or phrases stand out on a page.

Centered alignment Alignment format that positions text evenly between the left and right margins.

Character format A formatting option that affects only the currently highlighted characters.

Collapsible list Displays a list of options to choose from when the down arrow is clicked.

Dingbat A small picture found in some special fonts such as ZapfDingbats.

Double space Formatting a paragraph so that there is a blank line between each line of text.

Font Shape of a set of characters.

Footer Information that is printed at the bottom of each page.

Format The way that text appears on a page, including options such as margins, fonts, emphasized text, and headers and footers.

Header Information that is printed at the top of each page.

Highlighted block Text that has been selected. Highlighting is usually done by dragging or clicking the mouse.

Italic text Character format that makes text appear slanted. Sometimes used for headings.

Justified alignment Paragraph format in which each line of text is made to extend from the left margin to the right by adding extra space between words.

Left alignment Default paragraph format where text is even with the left margin, while the right side is jagged.

Manual page break A page break that is inserted to force text onto the next printed page.

Margin The white region around the text on a page.

Page break The location where one printed page ends and another begins.

Page format A formatting option that affects the entire document.

Pagination Process by which Word determines where one page ends and another begins.

Paragraph alignment How text is printed in relation to the margins: left (default), right, centered, or justified.

Paragraph format A formatting option that affects the paragraph containing the cursor or the highlighted paragraphs.

Point The unit used to measure character size. There are 72 points per inch.

Right alignment Paragraph format where text is set even with the right margin while the left side is ragged.

Selected text Text that is shown highlighted in the document.

Single space The default paragraph format where each line of text is placed so that there is no space in between.

Smart menu A menu that changes to reflect the current situation.

Style The way in which a character is emphasized.

Subscript Text printed slightly below the normal line.

Superscript Text printed slightly above the normal line.

Tab stop A location on the Ruler specifying the position of the tab character.

Tabs Characters used to position text within a line. Used to create tables or to indent the first line of a paragraph.

Typeface Also commonly referred to as font. See font.

Underlined text Character format that puts a line under text. Used to emphasize text.

Word Commands and Buttons

■ Align Left button Left aligns the text in the selected paragraph. Found on the Formatting Toolbar.

■ Align Right button Right aligns the text in the selected paragraph. Found on the Formatting Toolbar.

B Bold button Applies bold formatting to any selected text. Found on the Formatting Toolbar.

Break command Displays a dialog box that allows the user to insert a manual page break at the current cursor position. Found in the Insert menu.

■ Center button Centers the text in the selected paragraph. Found on the Formatting Toolbar.

Font command Displays a dialog box that allows the user to apply character formats. Found in the Format menu.

Header and Footer command Displays the Header and Footer Toolbar and allows the user to enter and format text in the header and footer of a document. Found in the View menu.

I Italic button Applies italic formatting to any selected text. Found on the Formatting Toolbar.

 # Insert Page Number button Inserts a page number at the current cursor position in a header or footer. Found in the Header and Footer Toolbar.

■ Justify button Justifies the text in the selected paragraph. Found on the Formatting Toolbar.

Page Setup command Displays a dialog box that allows the user to apply page formats. Found in the File menu.

Paragraph command Displays a dialog box that allows the user to apply paragraph formats. Found in the Format menu.

Print Preview command Used to view a document as it will appear when printed. Found in the File menu. The Print Preview button (🔍) on the Standard Toolbar can be used instead of the command.

Restore button Button displayed in the upper-right corner of a document window in place of the Maximize button when a window has been maximized. Used to restore a window to its original size.

Select All command Highlights the entire document. Found in the Edit menu.

■ Switch Between Header and Footer button Moves the cursor to either the header or footer box in a document. Found in the Header and Footer Toolbar.

L Tab Selection button Allows the user to select the type of tab stop that will be created by clicking on the Ruler. Found on the Ruler.

Tabs command Displays a dialog box that allows the user to set or clear individual tab stops. Found in the Format menu.

U Underline button Applies underline formatting to any selected text. Found on the Formatting Toolbar.

Undo command Reverses the effects of a command or action. Found in the Edit menu. The Undo button (↺) on the Standard Toolbar can be used instead of the command.

Review Questions

Sections 4.1 — 4.3

1. How can you view each page of a document as it will appear when printed?

2. If you make a mistake in formatting a paragraph, what is a fast method for correcting the error?

3. a) What is meant by a highlighted block?
   b) How can you tell which text is selected?

4. a) List one reason for creating a highlighted block.
   b) List two methods for highlighting an entire paragraph of text.

5. List the steps required to delete the second paragraph in a five paragraph document.

Sections 4.4 — 4.8

6. a) What is a document's format?
   b) Describe the formats (in terms of margins, headers and footers, pagination, and paragraph alignment) used in three publications.

7. List the three formatting levels.

8. a) What does font refer to?
   b) List five fonts available on your computer.

9. a) What is character size measured in?
   b) How many points are there in an inch?

10. List the steps required to bold the first line of text and italicize the second line in a document.

11. After bolding a document title, you discover that you have also accidentally centered and bolded the first two paragraphs. List the steps required to remove these formats from the paragraphs.

12. List the steps required to format the title of a document to bold, 24 point Helvetica.

13. List the steps required to superscript the word up and subscript the word down in the sentence:

    Sea turtles come up for air and then swim down to the bottom.

Sections 4.9 — 4.14

14. a) What is meant by justified text?
    b) List the steps required to justify a paragraph.

15. a) What is meant by centered text?
    b) What type of text is usually centered?

16. a) List the steps required to left align the first paragraph in a document and right align the second paragraph.
    b) Describe how the two paragraphs formatted in part (a) look different.

17. What is the easiest way to justify all of the paragraphs in a document at once?

18. a) What is double spacing?
    b) Why might you want a document to be double spaced?

19. a) List the steps required to double space only the second paragraph in a document that contains five paragraphs.
    b) How can a double spaced paragraph be returned to single spacing?

20. a) What are margins?
    b) What are the default margins in Word?

21. a) List the steps required to change the margins of a document so that the left margin is 2" and the right margin 3".
    b) How long is a line of text after these margins have been set? (Assume an 8.5" x 11" sheet of paper.)

22. a) What is a header?
    b) What is a footer?
    c) What type of information is often included in a header or footer?

23. List the steps required to have Word print the text Proposal in the header and a page number in the footer on each page of a document.

24. a) What is meant by pagination?
    b) How can you create a manual page break?
    c) List the steps required to delete the manual page break set in part (b).

25. a) What are tabs used for?
    b) What is a default tab stop?
    c) What are default tab stops often used for?

26. Explain each of the four types of tab stops:
    a) left
    b) right
    c) center
    d) decimal

27. a) List the steps required to set a center tab stop at 2.25".
    b) How can the tab stop described in part (a) be removed?
    c) How can you tell where tab stops have been set?

28. List the steps required to change a center tab stop at 2.5" to a left tab stop at 3".

Exercises

Exercise 1 — Ceramics Info Request

The request letter created in Chapter Three, Exercise 1 needs to be formatted. Open Ceramics Info Request and complete the following steps:

a) Justify the entire letter.

b) Change the left and right margins to 1.5".

c) Create a left tab stop at 2" for the entire letter.

d) Insert a tab character before the date at the top of the letter, and at the bottom of the letter before the closing ("Sincerely,") and before your name.

e) Check the document on screen for errors and misspellings and make any corrections.

f) Save the modified Ceramics Info Request and print a copy.

Exercise 2 — OPENINGS

The OPENINGS document contains several lines that can be used to start a short story. Open OPENINGS and complete the following steps:

a) Choose one of the lines, delete the rest, then write a short paragraph using the remaining line as the opening line.

b) Justify and double space the paragraph.

c) Create a header with a title for the story center aligned. Bold and increase the size of the title to 18 point.

d) Create a footer with your name right aligned.

e) Check the document on screen for errors and misspellings and make any corrections.

f) Save the modified OPENINGS and print a copy.

Exercise 3 — Entertainment Review

The entertainment review created in Chapter Three, Exercise 3 needs to be formatted. Open Entertainment Review and complete the following steps:

a) Create a bold, center aligned title that has the name of the event you reviewed. There should be a blank line between the title and the first paragraph.

b) Italicize any titles in the review, such as the title of a movie, a song title, etc.

c) Justify the body of the review so that it looks more like a newspaper article.

d) The paper's editors like all submissions to be doubled spaced. Format the body of your review to conform with their wishes.

e) Create a header with the text CRITIC'S CHOICE center aligned.

f) Create a footer with your name right aligned.

g) Check the document on screen for errors and misspellings and make any corrections.

h) Save the modified Entertainment Review and print a copy.

Exercise 4 ———————————————————— TELECOMMUTING

The TELECOMMUTING document contains information on the advantages of telecommuting. Open TELECOMMUTING and complete the following steps:

a) Format the following headings as 14 point, bold, Helvetica, and center aligned:

> "Computers in the Home Office"
> "The Process of Telecommuting"
> "Advantages of Telecommuting"
> "Telecommuting in Coral County"

b) Underline the first sentence of the second paragraph that begins "Telecommuting is possible because…."

c) Justify the first paragraph that begins "Over the past ten years…."

d) Change the left and right margins to 0.75".

e) Insert a page break before the heading "Telecommunicating in Coral County."

f) Create a header with the text TELECOMMUTING center aligned.

g) Create a footer with your name right aligned.

h) Format the table data on page 2 with the following tab stops:

- at 2" create a right tab stop (for the number of people)
- at 3.5" create a right tab stop (for the percentage of population)

i) Format the column titles "Number of People" and "Percentage of Population" with the following tab stops:

- at 1.75" create a center tab stop (for "Number of People")
- at 3.5" create a center tab stop (for "Percentage of Population")

j) Bold the column titles "City," "Number of People," and "Percentage of Population."

k) Italicize the last line in the table that contains the totals.

l) Check the document on screen for errors and misspellings and make any corrections.

m) Save the modified TELECOMMUTING and print a copy.

Exercise 5 ———————————————————— Geology Schedule

The memo created in Chapter Three, Exercise 5 needs to be formatted. Open Geology Schedule and complete the following steps:

a) Format the word "MEMORANDUM" as bold and italic.

b) Bold the words "TO:," "FROM:," "DATE:," and "SUBJECT:." Be sure to include the colon when bolding the words.

c) Double space the paragraphs with "TO:," "FROM:," "DATE:," and "SUBJECT:."

d) Replace the spaces after the colons in the words "TO:," "FROM:," "DATE:," and "SUBJECT:" with a tab.

e) Format the "TO:," "FROM:," "DATE:," and "SUBJECT:" lines of text with a left tab stop at 1".

f) Create a header with the text Independent Study in Geology center aligned.

g) Create a footer with your name right aligned.

h) Edit the data and column titles in the listing of research papers so that there is a single tab between each paper topic and due date. Delete any spaces that were previously used to separate the columns.

i) Format the entire table with a right tab stop at 1.5".

j) Modify the tab stops set in part (i) to a center tab stop at 1.5".

k) Italicize the column titles.

l) Check the document on screen for errors and misspellings and make any corrections.

m) Save the modified Geology Schedule and print a copy.

Exercise 6 ———————————————— WELCOME

The WELCOME document contains a letter for new customers to Nudelman's Gym. Open WELCOME and complete the following steps to the letter:

a) Format the title "Nudelman's Gym" as 18 point, bold, in a different font of your choice, and center aligned.

b) Format all occurrences of "work" in "workout" as superscript and all occurrences of "out" in "workout" as subscript.

c) Change the top and left margins to 2".

d) Justify all the paragraphs of the letter except for the "Nudelman's Gym" title.

e) Create a footer with your name right aligned.

f) Format the entire table at the bottom of the letter with the following tab stops:

- at 1.25" create a left tab stop (for the hours on Monday - Friday)
- at 2.75" create a left tab stop (for the hours on Saturday)
- at 4.25" create a left tab stop (for the hours on Sunday)

g) Format the column titles as bold and italic.

h) Check the document on screen for errors and misspellings and make any corrections.

i) Save the modified WELCOME and print a copy.

Exercise 7 ──────────────────────────── PROPOSAL

The Coral Research Proposal modified in Chapter Three, Exercise 7 needs to be formatted. Open PROPOSAL and complete the following steps:

a) Bold and center align the headings "A PROPOSAL FOR CORAL RESEARCH" and "GROWTH STUDIES OF CORAL ON SOUTH FLORIDA REEFS."

b) Italicize all of the subheadings: "Summary," "Purpose and Description," "Coral," and "Computerized Guide."

c) Change the top and bottom margins to 1.25" and the left and right margins to 1.5".

d) Create a footer with your name and the page number center aligned.

e) Insert a page break before the subheading "Computerized Guide" at the bottom of page 1.

f) Bold, increase the size, and center align the "BUDGET" heading on page 2.

g) Format the list below the "BUDGET" heading with the following tab stops:

- at 0.75" create a left tab stop
- at 4.5" create a decimal tab stop

h) Insert a page break before the subheading "Notes" at the bottom of page 2.

i) Check the document on screen for errors and misspellings and make any corrections.

j) Save the modified PROPOSAL and print a copy.

Exercise 8 ──────────────────────────── Journal

The journal created in Chapter Three, Exercise 8 needs to be formatted. Open Journal and complete the following steps:

a) Format all the text as italic.

b) Justify all the text.

c) Create a footer with your name right aligned.

d) Check the document on screen for errors and misspellings and make any corrections.

e) Save the modified Journal and print a copy.

Exercise 9 ──────────────────────────── Grand Opening

The store flyer created in Chapter Three, Exercise 9 needs to be formatted. Open Grand Opening and complete the following steps:

a) Bold all occurrences of the store's name.

b) Format the "20% OFF EVERYTHING!" title as 36 point. Since this is a flyer, increase the font size of the rest of the text so that the information fills the page.

c) Format appropriate paragraph alignments throughout the flyer.

d) Create a footer with your name right aligned.

e) Check the document on screen for errors and misspellings and make any corrections.

f) Save the modified Grand Opening and print a copy.

Exercise 10 ———————————————————— PRESIDENTS

The PRESIDENTS document contains a list of all the presidents of the United States, which needs formatting with tab stops. Open PRESIDENTS and complete the following steps:

a) Set left tab stops at 0.75" and 4" inches and a right tab stop at 3.5" so that the table appears similar to the following:

Number	President	Years in Office	Party
1.	George Washington	1789-1797	(none)
2.	John Adams	1797-1801	Federalist
3.	Thomas Jefferson	1801-1809	Democratic-Republican
…	…	…	…

b) Save the modified PRESIDENTS.

c) Bold the column titles.

d) Double space the entire table.

e) Create a header with your name center aligned.

f) Create a footer with the page number center aligned.

g) Save the modified PRESIDENTS and print a copy.

Exercise 11 ☼ ———————————————————— Water Conservation

The article created in Chapter Three, Exercise 11 can be improved. Open Water Conservation and complete the following steps:

a) Bold and increase the size of the document's title to 14 point.

b) Enter the text By *your name* under the title, and format it as italic. Insert a blank line below the byline.

c) Justify the text in the body of the article.

d) Change the top and bottom margins to 3".

e) Create a header with the text Environmental Issue center aligned and bold.

f) Create a footer with your name right aligned and italic.

g) Check the document on screen for errors and misspellings and make any corrections.

h) Save the modified Water Conservation and print a copy.

Exercise 12

The local newspaper would like to print the essay created for Chapter Three, Exercise 12. Open Ten Years and complete the following steps:

a) Create a center aligned title that describes your essay.

b) Format the title as 20 point, bold, Helvetica.

c) Insert two blank lines between the title and the first paragraph.

d) Double space the text in the body of the essay.

e) Change the top and bottom margins to 1.5" and the left and right margins to 2".

f) Create a header with your name right aligned.

g) Check the document on screen for errors and misspellings and make any corrections.

h) Save the modified Ten Years and print a copy.

Exercise 13

In a new document create the following table, separating the columns with single tab characters (do not precede the first column with a tab character):

Vitamin	Usage in Body	Common Food Sources
A	skeletal growth, skin	green leafy or yellow vegetables
B1	metabolism of carbohydrates	whole grains, liver
B12	production of proteins	liver, kidney, lean meat
C	resistance to infection	citrus fruits, tomatoes
E	antioxidant	peanut, corn oils

Note: Your table will not look like the one above until tab stops have been set.

a) Save the document naming it Vitamins.

b) Format the entire table with the following tab stops:

- at 1.25" create a left tab stop (for the usage in body)
- at 3.5" create a left tab stop (for the common food sources)

c) Create a bold, center aligned title with the text Vitamins and Their Usage. Insert a blank line between the title and the table.

d) Bold the column titles in the table.

e) Subscript the "1" in "B1" and subscript the "12" in "B12."

f) Change the top and bottom margins to 0.75".

g) Create a footer with your name right aligned.

h) Check the document on screen for errors and misspellings and make any corrections.

i) Save the modified Vitamins and print a copy.

In a new document create the following table, separating the columns with single tab characters (do not precede the first column with a tab character):

Island	Area (km2)	Tallest Peak	Peak Height (m)
Hawaii	6,501	Mauna Kea	4,139
Maui	1,174	Haleakala	3,007
Oahu	979	Kaala	1,208
Kauai	890	Kawaikini	1,573
Molokai	420	Kamakou	1,491
Lanai	225	Lanaihale	1,011
Niihau	118	Paniau	384
Kahoolawe	72	Lua Makika	443

Note: Your table will not look like the one above until tab stops have been set.

a) Save the document naming it Hawaiian Islands.

b) Format the entire table with the following tab stops:

- at 1" create a left tab stop (for the area)
- at 2.5" create a center tab stop (for the tallest peak)
- at 4" create a right tab stop (for the peak height)

c) In the paragraph with the column titles, change the right tab stop at 4" to a center tab stop at 3.75".

d) Bold the column titles in the table.

e) Create a bold, center aligned title with the text The Hawaiian Islands. Insert a blank line between the title and the table.

f) Superscript the "2" in the column title "Area (km2)."

g) Format the entire document as 11 point Helvetica.

h) Create a footer with your name center aligned.

i) Check the document on screen for errors and misspellings and make any corrections.

j) Save the modified Hawaiian Islands and print a copy.

In a new document create the following table, separating the columns with single tab characters (do not precede the first column with a tab character):

Measurement	Units	Symbol	Formula
Area	square meter	m2	m2
Heat	joule	J	N x m
Power	watt	W	J/s
Force	newton	N	kg x m/s2
Pressure	pascal	Pa	N/m2
Velocity	meter per second	m/s	m/s

Note: Your table will not look like the one above until tab stops have been set.

a) Save the document naming it Science Review.

b) Format the entire table with the following tab stops:

- at 1.5" create a left tab stop (for the units)
- at 3.5" create a center tab stop (for the symbol)
- at 5" create a right tab stop (for the formula)

c) Format all occurrences of "2" in the table as superscript.

d) Insert three blank lines after the first table, then create the following table, separating the columns with single tab characters (do <u>not</u> precede the first column with a tab character):

Formula	Name
C2H2	acetylene
H2O	water
K2SO4	potassium sulfate
NH3	ammonia
CH4	methane
C6H6	benzene

Note: Your table will not look like the one above until tab stops have been set.

e) For the entire second table, delete the existing tab stops and format a left tab stop at 1" (for the name).

f) In the second table, format all occurrences of numbers as subscript.

g) At the top of the document, create a bold, center aligned title with the text Science Review Sheet. Insert a blank line between the title and the first table.

h) Bold the column titles in both tables.

i) Change the top margin to 2".

j) Create a header with your name left aligned.

k) Check the document on screen for errors and misspellings and make any corrections.

l) Save the modified Science Review and print a copy.

Advanced
Exercise 16 ———————————————————— Garments

In a new document write a letter to a clothing company. Discuss your favorite garments, colors, and fabrics, and describe what you would like to wear next year. Include a table of at least five lines of text. Format the text as 10 point and a different font. Include a footer with the text From the desk of Name center aligned, using your name for Name. Save the letter naming it Garments and print a copy.

Advanced
Exercise 18 ——————————————————— Using Word

In a new document create an instruction manual that teaches the reader how to write a letter in Word. The document should be at least two pages long. Include a table of at least five lines of text. Format the document as justified with a 1.5" left margin and a 0.75" right margin. Add a header with your name center aligned, and a footer with the page number right aligned. Save the document naming it Using Word and print a copy.

A Guide to Microsoft Office 2000 Professional

Chapter Five
Word Processor Features

<u>C</u>opy

<u>P</u>aste

Cu<u>t</u>

Clipboard

<u>F</u>ind

R<u>e</u>place

<u>T</u>hesaurus

<u>P</u>aragraph

Foot<u>n</u>ote

Date and <u>T</u>ime

<u>W</u>ord Count

<u>C</u>lip art

Columns

Chapter Five Objectives

After completing this chapter you will be able to:

1. Copy and move highlighted blocks of text.
2. Use the Windows Clipboard and the Office Clipboard.
3. Find text using the Find command.
4. Locate text and replace it using the Replace command.
5. Use the thesaurus to suggest synonyms for words.
6. Indent paragraphs.
7. Format hanging indents and first line indents.
8. Format bulleted and numbered lists.
9. Create and edit footnotes.
10. Insert time stamps.
11. Display the number of words in a document.
12. Add a graphic to a document and change the graphic's size.
13. Format a document with columns.

This chapter discusses several word processor features, including commands for moving and copying text. Formatting such as hanging indents, bulleted lists, and columns are also covered.

5.1 Copying and Pasting Text

There are times when text needs to be repeated in a document. Rather than typing the text multiple times, it can be duplicated using the Copy and Paste commands from the Edit menu.

Windows Clipboard

When the Copy command (Ctrl+C) is selected, highlighted text is copied to a special area of memory called the *Windows Clipboard*. The original highlighted text remains. When the Paste command (Ctrl+V) is selected, a copy of the Windows Clipboard contents is placed at the current cursor position. If the cursor is positioned within existing text, any text after the cursor is automatically moved to make room for the pasted text.

The steps for copying text in a document are:

1. Highlight the text to be copied.

2. Select the Copy command. A copy of the highlighted text is placed on the Windows Clipboard.

3. Place the cursor where the text is to be inserted.

4. Select the Paste command. A copy of the highlighted block is placed at the cursor position.

Another way to select the Copy or Paste command is to right-click on the highlighted text and select the appropriate command from the displayed menu.

On the Standard Toolbar, the Copy button () executes the Copy command, and the Paste button () executes the Paste command.

5.2 Moving Text

Text can be moved from one place to another using the Cut and Paste commands. For example, a sentence can be removed from one paragraph and placed in a paragraph on the next page. Text that is cut is removed from the document and placed on the Windows Clipboard. Any text after the cut text is automatically moved to fill the space. The Cut command (Ctrl+X) is different from the Copy command because Copy leaves the original highlighted text, instead of removing it.

The steps for moving text are:

1. Highlight the text to be moved.

2. Select the Cut command. The highlighted text is removed from the screen and placed on the Windows Clipboard.

3. Place the cursor where the moved text is to be inserted.

4. Select the Paste command. The previously cut text is placed at the cursor position.

The Cut command can also be selected from the menu that is displayed by right-clicking on the highlighted text.

 On the Standard Toolbar, the Cut button ( ) executes the Cut command.

Practice 1

In this practice you will use the Cut, Copy, and Paste commands and the Windows Clipboard. Highlighted text will be moved and other text copied.

1) OPEN MOCKINGBIRD MUSIC

Open MOCKINGBIRD MUSIC and display formatting marks if they are not already displayed.

2) HIGHLIGHT THE TEXT TO BE MOVED

In the large paragraph near the top of page 1, highlight the last sentence, the one that begins "Our students have won…." Do not include the paragraph marker in the highlight.

3) MOVE THE HIGHLIGHTED BLOCK OF TEXT

a. Select Edit → Cut. The highlighted text is removed from the screen and placed on the Windows Clipboard.
b. Scroll down to the bottom of the page and place the cursor in the blank paragraph below the "Harps" paragraph.
c. Press Enter to create a new paragraph.
d. Select Edit → Paste. The text is inserted at the cursor position.

4) HIGHLIGHT THE TEXT TO BE COPIED

In the large paragraph near the top of page 1, highlight the last sentence, the one that begins "We take pride…." Do not include the paragraph marker in the highlight.

5) COPY THE HIGHLIGHTED BLOCK OF TEXT

a. On the Standard Toolbar, click on the Copy button ( ).
b. Scroll to the end of the document and place the cursor at the end of the last paragraph, after the exclamation point in "…make us proud!"
c. Type a space.
d. Press Ctrl+V. The sentence is inserted as the last paragraph of the document.
e. Scroll up in the document and note that the original sentence is still there.

6) SAVE AND CLOSE THE MODIFIED MOCKINGBIRD MUSIC

5.3 Using the Office Clipboard

The *Office Clipboard* is a special Clipboard that is available in Microsoft Office programs including Word. The Office Clipboard stores up to 12 different cut or copied items, which can then be pasted individually or all together. Selecting the <u>C</u>opy command from the <u>E</u>dit menu once places a copy of highlighted text on the Windows Clipboard, as discussed in Section 5.1. Selecting the <u>C</u>opy command immediately again activates the Office Clipboard, places a copy of the highlighted text on the Office Clipboard, and displays the Clipboard Toolbar:

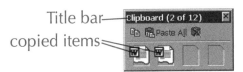

Title bar — copied items

- **Title bar** indicates the number of items currently on the Office Clipboard.
- **Copy button** (📋) selects the <u>C</u>opy command.
- **Paste All button** (📋 Paste All) pastes copies of all the items on the Office Clipboard at the current cursor position.
- **Clear Clipboard button** (📋) removes all the items from the Office Clipboard.

Placing the pointer on a copied item on the Clipboard Toolbar displays a screen tip that contains the first few words of the pasted item. After identifying the item, clicking once on it pastes a copy at the current cursor position. Note that the last item copied is in the last position on the Office Clipboard.

The Clipboard Toolbar can be removed from the document window by clicking on the Close button (⊠). The Clipboard Toolbar can be displayed without copying text by selecting the Clipboard command from the <u>T</u>oolbars submenu in the <u>V</u>iew menu.

Practice 2

In this practice you will use the Office Clipboard to copy and paste text.

1) OPEN PARTY DIRECTIONS

Open PARTY DIRECTIONS and display formatting marks if they are not already displayed.

2) COPY THE FIRST BLOCK OF TEXT AND ACTIVATE THE OFFICE CLIPBOARD

a. Highlight the text in the first two paragraphs of the document, from the title "Directions to Aaron's House" to "…See you there," including the paragraph marker at the end.
b. Select <u>E</u>dit → <u>C</u>opy. The highlighted text is copied to the Windows Clipboard.
c. Select <u>E</u>dit → <u>C</u>opy. The Office Clipboard is activated, the Clipboard Toolbar is displayed, and a copy of the highlighted text is placed on the Office Clipboard. Note: if there is more than one copied item on the Clipboard Toolbar, select the Clear Clipboard button (📋) to delete all the items, then select the Copy button (📋) to place one copy of the highlighted text on the Office Clipboard.

3) COPY ANOTHER BLOCK OF TEXT

a. Highlight the entire "CUT HERE…" paragraph, including the paragraph marker at the end.

b. Select <u>E</u>dit → <u>C</u>opy. A copy of the highlighted text is placed on the Office Clipboard. There are now two items on the Office Clipboard.

4) PASTE BOTH ITEMS AT ONCE

a. Place the cursor at the end of the paragraph that begins "CUT HERE…" and press Enter once to create a new paragraph.

b. Select the Paste All button (Paste All). Copies of both items on the Office Clipboard are placed at the current cursor position.

c. Select the Paste All button again. Copies of both items are again pasted into the document.

d. Select the Paste All button again. A third set of copies is pasted.

5) PASTE A COPY OF THE FIRST BLOCK

a. Move the mouse pointer (but do not click) onto the first item on the Clipboard Toolbar. A screen tip appears with the first few words of the copied text. Your screen tip should begin "Directions to Aaron's House…."

b. Click once on the item. A copy of that copied item is placed in the document at the current cursor position.

<u>Check</u> – Your document should look similar to:

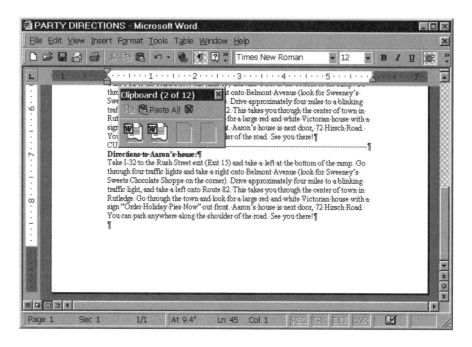

6) CLEAR AND CLOSE THE CLIPBOARD

a. On the Clipboard Toolbar, select the Clear Clipboard button ( ). All of the items on the Office Clipboard are removed.

b. Click on the Close button ( ) to remove the Clipboard Toolbar from the document window.

7) SAVE, PRINT, AND THEN CLOSE THE MODIFIED PARTY DIRECTIONS

5.4 Finding Text in a Document

The Find command is used to scan a document for *search text* that may be a single character, word, or phrase. Selecting the Find command from the Edit menu (Ctrl+F) displays a dialog box where search text is typed:

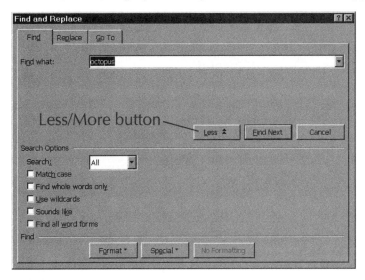

Selecting the Less button reduces the dialog box's size and hides the Search Options. Selecting the More button expands the dialog box again.

In the example above, the word octopus has been entered as the search text. When the Find Next button is selected, Word starts searching from the current cursor position and continues through the document looking for the search text. If a match is found, Word stops searching and highlights the found text. Selecting Find Next continues the search. If the search text is not found, a message similar to the following is displayed:

Word could not find the search text

The Match case option is used when occurrences of search text with the same capitalization are to be found. For example, with the Match case option selected, a search for Cat will not find CAT or cat.

The Find whole words only option is used when occurrences of the search text that are not part of another word are to be found. For example, a search for fin will not only find fin but also finer, stuffing, and muffin unless the Find whole words only check box is selected. The Match case and Find whole words only options can be used together to perform a precise search.

Clicking on the Cancel button ends the search and removes the dialog box.

5.5 Finding Special Characters

Special characters such as tab and paragraph characters can also be located using the Find command. For example, suppose you wish to find occurrences of the word finally that occur at the beginning of a paragraph. Since all (except the first) paragraphs in the document have a paragraph marker before them, a precise search would include a paragraph marker before the word finally. Clicking on the Special button in the Find and Replace dialog box displays a list of special characters:

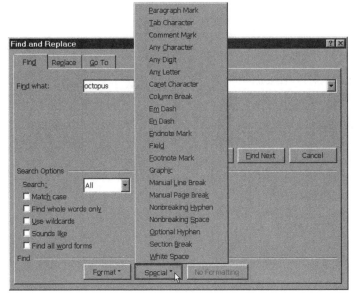

Special characters selected from this list can be included in the search text

Selecting Paragraph Mark from the list inserts ^p in the Find what entry box, and then the rest of the search text can be typed:

This search text will find any occurrence of "finally" at the beginning of a paragraph

Similarly, a tab character can be found by selecting Tab Character from the list. The tab character appears as ^t in the Find what entry box.

Practice 3

In this practice you will search for text and special characters.

1) OPEN DTP WORKSHOP

2) FIND SEARCH TEXT

    a. Make sure that the cursor is at the very beginning of the document.

    b. Select Edit → Find. A dialog box is displayed.

        1. In the Find what entry box, type the word instruction.

        2. Select the Find Next button. The first occurrence of "instruction" is highlighted. Note that the highlighted word starts with a capital "I" even though the search text has a lowercase "i."

        3. Select Find Next to highlight the next occurrence of the search text.

4. Continue to select Find Next until Word displays a message saying that it has finished searching the document. Note that occurrences of both "instruction" and "Instruction" were found.
5. Select OK. The message dialog box is removed.
6. Select Cancel to remove the Find and Replace dialog box. Note that the cursor was returned to the top of the document.

3) MODIFY THE SEARCH TEXT

Select Edit → Find. A dialog box is displayed. The previously entered text instruction is displayed and highlighted in the Find what entry box.
1. Select the More button if the Match case option is not already displayed.
2. Select the Match case option so that only "instruction" with a lowercase "i" will be found.
3. Select Find Next. Note how the found text has a lowercase "i."
4. Select Find Next again. A message is displayed saying that Word has finished searching the document. This is because there are no more occurrences of "instruction" with a lowercase "i" in the document.
5. Select OK. The message dialog box is removed.
6. Select Cancel to remove the dialog box and end the search.

4) SEARCH FOR OCCURRENCES OF "LUNCHEON" AT THE BEGINNING OF A PARAGRAPH

Select Edit → Find. A dialog box is displayed. The previously entered text instruction is displayed and highlighted in the Find what entry box.
1. Select the More button if the Search Options are not already displayed.
2. Select the Special button to display the list of special characters.
3. Click on Paragraph Mark at the top of the list to place the ^p code in the Find what entry box, replacing the highlighted text, then type the word luncheon. This will have Word locate all occurrences of "luncheon" that begin a paragraph. Your dialog box should look similar to:

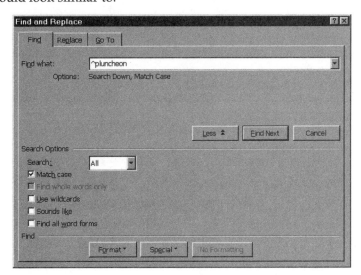

4. Deselect the Match case option so that all occurrences of "luncheon" will be found.
5. Select Find Next to start the search. The first "luncheon" located is in the "What to Expect" list. Note how the paragraph marker in the line above it is also highlighted.
6. Continue to select Find Next until Word displays a message saying that Word has finished searching the document.
7. Select OK and then Cancel to remove the dialog boxes.

5) SAVE THE MODIFIED DTP WORKSHOP

5.6 Replacing Text

The Replace command from the Edit menu (Ctrl+H) is used to locate text and then change it to other text you supply called the *replace text*. This makes it easy to create different versions of a document. For example, after creating and printing a letter requesting information from Mount Pine Ski Resort, the Replace command can be used to change each occurrence of "Mount Pine" to "Livermore Peak" and the new letter printed. "Livermore Peak" can then be changed to another ski resort, and so on, creating several letters.

Selecting the Replace command displays the Find and Replace dialog box with the Replace tab selected:

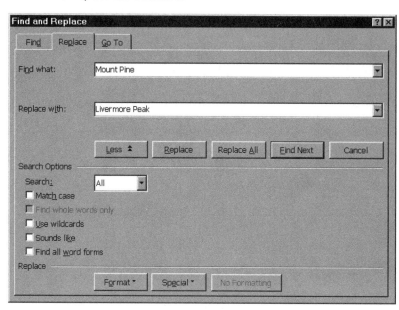

Word will search for "Mount Pine" and replace it with "Livermore Peak"

Selecting Replace starts searching from the current cursor position for the first occurrence of the search text, which is then highlighted. Selecting Replace again changes the highlighted text to the replace text and then finds the next occurrence of the search text. Find Next can be selected to find the next occurrence of the search text without making changes to the highlighted text.

The Replace All button can be selected to automatically replace all occurrences of the search text with the replace text. Using the Replace button instead of the Replace All button is usually preferable because you can verify each replacement before it is made.

Tab and paragraph characters may be used in either the search or replace text. The Find whole words only option is used when occurrences of the search text that are not part of another word are to be replaced. The Match case option is used when only text that has the same capitalization as the search text is to be replaced.

Finding and Replacing Header and Footer Text

When searching for text using either the Find or Replace commands, Word searches the entire document and then looks in the header and footer. If the search text is found in the header or footer, the found text is highlighted and displayed at the bottom of the document window so that it can be edited or replaced.

Capitalization

If the Match case option is not selected when replacing text, Word uses the capitalization of the found text. For example, using puppy as the search text and dog as the replace text, when Word finds an occurrence of Puppy, it replaces it with Dog.

A Guide to Microsoft Office 2000 Professional

5.7 Using the Thesaurus

A *thesaurus* is a collection of *synonyms,* which are words that have similar meanings. Using a thesaurus can help make your writing more interesting. Word contains a thesaurus that can be used to find synonyms for many words and phrases. For example, "chilly" is a synonym for "cool." A list of synonyms can be displayed for a word by highlighting the word and then selecting the Thesaurus command (Shift+F7) from the Language submenu in the Tools menu:

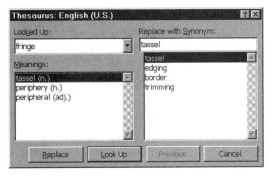

Synonyms are displayed for a selected word or phrase

Because words can have different definitions, Word provides a list of Meanings identified by their parts of speech (adjective, noun, verb, etc.). The Replace with Synonym list corresponds to the highlighted meaning. Clicking on a meaning highlights it and changes the list of synonyms. Clicking on a synonym selects it. Selecting the Replace button replaces the word in the document with the selected synonym.

Synonyms can be displayed for any of the suggested meanings by first highlighting the word in the list and then selecting Look Up. This procedure may be continued for as many words as desired. Selecting Cancel removes the dialog box, leaving the word in the document unchanged.

Like the dictionary, Word uses a file for its thesaurus which does not contain every possible word. If the selected word cannot be found, a dialog box is displayed with an alphabetical list of possible words:

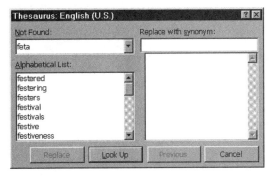

Suggestions are provided when a selected word is not found

Messages like this are usually the result of highlighting a misspelled word.

Note that the thesaurus will only replace the highlighted word or phrase. For example, the word fringe might appear five times in a document, but only the highlighted fringe will be replaced with the selected synonym. Multiple occurrences can be changed using the Replace command.

Synonyms for Phrases

The Word thesaurus can give synonyms for a number of phrases. For example, Word displays anticipate, hope for, and expect as synonyms for the phrase "look forward to."

Practice 4

In this practice you will use the Replace command and the thesaurus. Open DTP WORKSHOP if it is not already displayed.

1) REPLACE ALL OCCURRENCES OF "INSTRUCTOR"

Select Edit → Replace. A dialog box is displayed. The previously entered text ^pluncheon is displayed and highlighted in the Find what entry box.

1. In the Find what entry box, type the word instructor, replacing the highlighted text.
2. In the Replace with entry box, type the word trainer.
3. Select the Replace button. The first occurrence of "instructor" is highlighted.
4. Select Replace. The highlighted text is replaced with "trainer" and the next occurrence of "instructor" is highlighted.
5. For each "instructor" found, click on the Replace button.
6. When a message is displayed that says Word has finished searching the document, select OK.
7. Select Close to remove the dialog box.

2) LOCATE THE WORD TO BE CHANGED

At the top of page 1, highlight the word "pleased" in the first sentence that begins "All of us at Press Masters...."

3) SELECT THE DESIRED SYNONYM AND REPLACE THE WORD

Select Tools → Language → Thesaurus. A dialog box is displayed.

1. In the Replace with Synonym list, select the word "delighted."
2. Select the Replace button. The word "pleased" is replaced with "delighted" and the dialog box is removed.

4) CHANGE THE WORD "FIELD"

a. Highlight the word "field" in the last sentence of that same paragraph, the sentence that begins "The trainer and assistants...."
b. Press Shift+F7 . The Thesaurus dialog box is displayed with several meanings for "field."

1. In the Meanings list, click on the word subject, because the definition of "field" that is being used in the sentence is most similar to "subject." Your dialog box should look similar to:

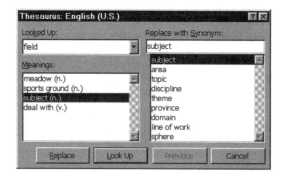

2. Select area from the list of synonyms.
3. Select Replace. The word "field" is replaced by "area."

5) SAVE THE MODIFIED DTP WORKSHOP

5.8 Paragraph Formats - Indents

Margin settings apply to an entire document and cannot change from paragraph to paragraph. However, it is possible to decrease the width of lines of text in a specific paragraph by using *indents*. Indents are often used to set off paragraphs such as a quotation.

The default indents are 0 inches, meaning that lines extend from the left margin to the right margin. Specifying left and right indents causes a paragraph to have a shorter line length:

> This paragraph is not indented. Each line of text extends from the left margin to the right margin.
>
> > This is an indented paragraph. The lines of text are shorter between the left and right margins.

Selecting the <u>P</u>aragraph command from the F<u>o</u>rmat menu displays the Paragraph dialog box. Selecting the Indents and Spacing tab displays the following options:

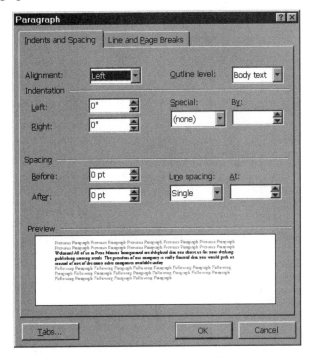

The indent amounts are typed into the Left and the Right entry boxes. For example, to indent a paragraph by 1 inch on both the left and right, type 1 in the Left entry box, 1 in the Right entry box, then select OK.

Setting an indent affects only the paragraph that contains the cursor. Multiple paragraphs can be formatted together by first highlighting them and then applying the indents.

Indents can also be set by dragging markers on the Ruler:

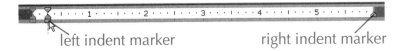

left indent marker   right indent marker

Dragging an indent marker changes the indent for either the paragraph that contains the cursor or for the highlighted block of paragraphs. When an indent marker is dragged, a dotted line appears that helps line up text. This method of changing indents is usually less precise than using the Paragraph command.

Practice 5

In this practice you will indent paragraphs. Open DTP WORKSHOP if it is not already displayed.

1) FORMAT A PARAGRAPH WITH INDENTS

a. If the Ruler is not displayed, select View ➝ Ruler.

b. Scroll to the bottom of page 1 and place the cursor in the paragraph that begins "A Networking Breakfast…." Note the indent markers on the Ruler.

c. Select Format ➝ Paragraph. A dialog box is displayed.

    1. Select the Indents and Spacing tab if those options are not already displayed.

    2. In the Indentation section, enter 0.5 for the Left indent.

    3. Enter 0.75 for the Right indent.

    4. Select OK. The dialog box is removed and the paragraph has left and right indents. Note the positions of the indent markers on the Ruler.

2) CHANGE THE RIGHT INDENT

a. Be sure the cursor is still in the "A Networking Breakfast…." paragraph.

b. On the Ruler, drag the right indent marker to the 5" mark. Note how the right indent of the paragraph changes.

3) FORMAT SEVERAL PARAGRAPHS WITH INDENTS

a. Place the cursor in the next paragraph, the one that begins "The Lecture…."

b. Scroll down until the paragraph that begins "Computer Instruction…" is visible.

c. Hold down the Shift key and click once in the "Computer Instruction…" paragraph. Several paragraphs are included in the highlight.

d. Select Format ➝ Paragraph. A dialog box is displayed.

    1. Select the Indents and Spacing tab if those options are not already displayed.

    2. Enter 0.5 for the Left indent.

    3. Enter 0.5 for the Right indent.

    4. Select OK. The dialog box is removed and the highlighted paragraphs now have left and right indents.

Check – Your document should look similar to:

> Questions·and·Answers·Although·you·are·welcome·to·ask·
> questions·during·the·lecture,·the·question·and·answer·session·
> allows·the·assistants·to·share·their·knowledge,·too.·The·attendees·
> also·sometimes·share·their·ideas,·and·a·good·exchange·often·gets·
> started·that·follows·through·to·the·end·of·the·workshop.¶
> ¶
> Luncheon:·The·luncheon·is·included·in·your·workshop·fees·and·is·
> served·buffet·style·in·a·separate·conference·room.·Here·you·have·
> more·opportunities·to·network·or·just·make·friends.·Special·dietary·
> needs·can·be·met·with·48-hour·advance·notice·at·the·Press·Masters·
> main·office.¶
> ¶
> Computer·Instruction:·The·afternoon·is·devoted·to·time·on·the·
> computers.·You·will·experience·a·mix·of·brief·tutorials,·some·
> lecture-type·instruction,·and·printed·materials·that·will·guide·you·
> through·mini-projects.·The·assistants·will·be·right·there·with·you·to·
> answer·your·questions·and·help·you·on·the·machines.¶
> ¶
> ¶
> ▪ *What·to·Bring*¶
> ¶
> When·you·check-in·at·the·workshop,·you·will·receive·a·package·of·materials·that·
> includes·a·booklet,·handouts,·a·blank·diskette,·and·an·assortment·of·promotional·
> materials·from·various·companies.·You·will·not·need·anything·else·to·complete·
> the·workshop,·but·you·may·want·to·bring·some·other·items·with·you.¶

4) SAVE THE MODIFIED DTP WORKSHOP

A Guide to Microsoft Office 2000 Professional

5.9 Paragraph Formats - Special Indents

hanging indent

A paragraph can be formatted so that the first line is indented differently from the rest of the paragraph. When the first line of a paragraph is farther to the left than the rest of the paragraph it is formatted with a *hanging indent*. A hanging indent is often used for lists, outlines, or bibliography entries in a research paper. Below is a bibliography entry using a hanging indent:

Riggi, Donna. *The Complete Guide to Stocking and Selling Mattresses.* Chicago: Winding Staircase Press, 1993.

A hanging indent is created for the paragraph that contains the cursor by first selecting the Paragraph command from the Format menu. Selecting the Indents and Spacing tab displays those options:

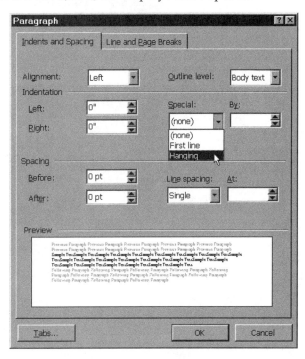

Selecting the Hanging option in the Special collapsible list and then OK formats the paragraph with a 0.5" hanging indent:

The default measurement for a hanging indent is 0.5" and appears in the By entry box. Changing this measurement changes the hanging indent.

A hanging indent can also be created by dragging the hanging indent marker on the Ruler:

—hanging indent marker

first line indent   A paragraph can also be formatted with a *first line indent*, which indents the first line of the paragraph more than the rest of the paragraph. A first line indent is often used for formatting the paragraphs of text in a document. For example, this paragraph that you are reading is formatted with a first line indent.

A first line indent is created for the paragraph that contains the cursor by first selecting the <u>P</u>aragraph command from the <u>F</u>ormat menu and then Indents and Spacing tab to display those options. Selecting the First Line option in the Special collapsible list and then OK formats the paragraph with a 0.5" first line indent (the default). Changing this measurement in the By entry box changes the distance that the first line is indented from the rest of the paragraph. First line indents can also be created by dragging the first line indent marker (▽) on the Ruler.

5.10 Creating Lists

bulleted list   One use for hanging indents is in the creation of *bulleted lists*. In a bulleted list, each item is a separate paragraph formatted with a hanging indent, a tab, and a special character such as a bullet (•). In Word, a bulleted list is created by first highlighting the paragraphs in the list

> There·are·many·things·to·do·at·the·Great·Seas·Resort:¶
> Snorkel·off·the·world·famous·Barracuda·Beach·in·our·ultra·high·
> quality·rental·gear¶
> Dine·in·one·of·our·eight·luxurious·restaurants·including·the·five·
> star·Dixie·Diamond·Steak·House¶
> Lounge·by·one·of·five·luxury·swimming·pools¶
> Shop·in·our·promenade·of·36·stores¶

 and then clicking on the Bullets button (▤) on the Formatting Toolbar:

> There·are·many·things·to·do·at·the·Great·Seas·Resort:¶
> •→Snorkel·off·the·world·famous·Barracuda·Beach·in·our·ultra·
>   high·quality·rental·gear¶
> •→Dine·in·one·of·our·eight·luxurious·restaurants·including·the·
>   five-star·Dixie·Diamond·Steak·House¶
> •→Lounge·by·one·of·five·luxury·swimming·pools¶
> •→Shop·in·our·promenade·of·36·stores¶

Note that Word automatically formats the paragraph with a hanging indent, and adds a tab and a bullet character to each paragraph. The bulleted items can be indented farther by clicking on the Increase Indent button (▤) on the Formatting Toolbar.

numbered list   Bulleted lists are used when each item is equally important. *Numbered lists* show a priority of importance and are used, for example, for the steps in a recipe. Numbered lists are created by first highlighting the paragraphs and then clicking on the Numbering button (▤) on the Formatting Toolbar:

A Guide to Microsoft Office 2000 Professional

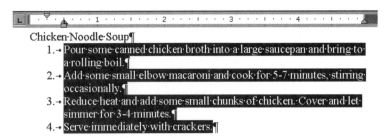

Chicken·Noodle·Soup¶
    1.→Pour·some·canned·chicken·broth·into·a·large·saucepan·and·bring·to·a·rolling·boil.¶
    2.→Add·some·small·elbow·macaroni·and·cook·for·5-7·minutes,·stirring·occasionally.¶
    3.→Reduce·heat·and·add·some·small·chunks·of·chicken.·Cover·and·let·simmer·for·3-4·minutes.¶
    4.→Serve·immediately·with·crackers.¶

Note that Word automatically formats the paragraph with a hanging indent, and adds a number followed by a period and a tab to each paragraph. The numbered items can be indented farther by clicking on the Increase Indent button ( ) on the Formatting Toolbar.

The bullets or numbering formats can be removed from text by highlighting the formatted paragraphs and then deselecting the appropriate button on the Formatting Toolbar.

Practice 6 ☼ ——————————————————————————

In this practice you will create a bulleted list in DTP WORKSHOP and then create a hanging indent in MOCKINGBIRD MUSIC. Open DTP WORKSHOP and display formatting marks if they are not already displayed.

1) FORMAT A BULLETED LIST

    a. Scroll to the middle of page 2 and locate the list of items in the "What to Bring" section.
    b. Highlight all four paragraphs in the list, from "Notepads and pens" to "Sweater or jacket."
    c. On the Formatting Toolbar, click on the Bullets button (▤). The items in the list are formatted with bullets and a hanging indent.

2) SAVE, PRINT, AND THEN CLOSE THE MODIFIED DTP WORKSHOP

3) FORMAT A HANGING INDENT

    a. Open MOCKINGBIRD MUSIC and display formatting marks if they are not already displayed.
    b. Highlight all three paragraphs in the "Lessons Available" section, from "Mondays..." to "...General Percussion."
    c. Select Format → Paragraph. A dialog box is displayed.
        1. Select the Indents and Spacing tab if those options are not already displayed.
        2. In the Special collapsible list, select Hanging.
        3. Select OK. The dialog box is removed and the highlighted paragraphs now have a 0.5" hanging indent.

4) MODIFY THE HANGING INDENT

On the Ruler, drag the hanging indent marker (▲) to the 2" mark. Click anywhere to remove the highlight. Your document and Ruler should look similar to:

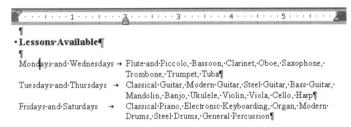

¶
·**Lessons·Available**¶
¶
Mondays·and·Wednesdays → Flute·and·Piccolo,·Bassoon,·Clarinet,·Oboe,·Saxophone,·Trombone,·Trumpet,·Tuba¶
Tuesdays·and·Thursdays → Classical·Guitar,·Modern·Guitar,·Steel·Guitar,·Bass·Guitar,·Mandolin,·Banjo,·Ukulele,·Violin,·Viola,·Cello,·Harp¶
Fridays·and·Saturdays → Classical·Piano,·Electronic·Keyboarding,·Organ,·Modern·Drums,·Steel·Drums,·General·Percussion¶

5) *FORMAT A NUMBERED LIST*

 a. Locate the list in the "Tips on Learning to Play an Instrument" section.
 b. Highlight all five paragraphs in the list, from "Purchase…" to the last "…Practice!"
 c. On the Formatting Toolbar, click on the Numbering button (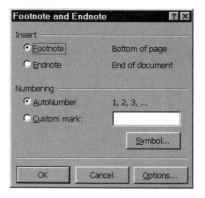). The items in the list are formatted with numbers and a hanging indent.

6) *SAVE, PRINT, AND THEN CLOSE THE MODIFIED MOCKINGBIRD MUSIC*

5.11 Creating Footnotes and Endnotes

Research papers and reports often include *footnotes* to document sources. Selecting the Footnote command from the Insert menu displays the following dialog box:

Footnote and AutoNumber are the default options. Selecting OK inserts a superscripted number at the current cursor position and also adds the same number at the bottom of the page. In Print Layout view, the footnote looks similar to:

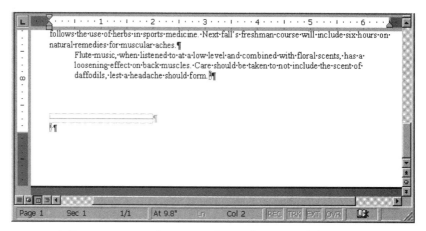

A line separates footnotes from the rest of the text in Print Layout view

In Normal view, an additional window appears at the bottom of the window with the footnote number:

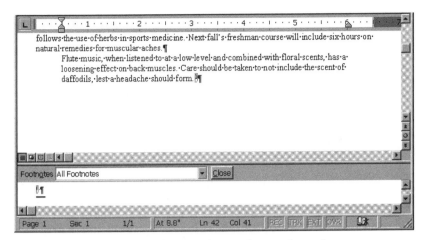

follows·the·use·of·herbs·in·sports·medicine.·Next·fall's·freshman·course·will·include·six·hours·on·
natural·remedies·for·muscular·aches.¶
Flute·music,·when·listened·to·at·a·low·level·and·combined·with·floral·scents,·has·a·
loosening·effect·on·back·muscles.·Care·should·be·taken·to·not·include·the·scent·of·
daffodils,·lest·a·headache·should·form.¶

In Normal view, the window splits to show footnotes

In either view, the cursor is automatically placed to the right of the footnote number so that the footnote can be entered. Footnote text can then be edited and formatted like any other text.

Word sequentially numbers footnotes, and automatically renumbers footnotes when one is moved, copied, or deleted. A footnote can be deleted by deleting the footnote number in the text, which automatically removes the reference from the bottom of the page.

Endnotes appear separately on the last page of a document, and are sometimes used instead of footnotes. Select the Endnote option in the Footnote and Endnote dialog box to create endnotes instead of footnotes.

Practice 7

In this practice you will create a footnote.

1) OPEN DTP WORKSHOP

2) CREATE A FOOTNOTE

   a. At the bottom of page 3, place the cursor at the end of the quote in italics, the paragraph that ends "…since fire was discovered."

   b. Select Insert → Footnote. A dialog box is displayed.

      1. Select OK to accept the defaults. The dialog box is removed, Word inserts a 1 at the current cursor position and the cursor is moved to the bottom of the page where the footnote text may be entered. Note the horizontal line separating the reference from the rest of the text.

3) ENTER THE FOOTNOTE TEXT

   Type the following text:

      Grossman, Lucinda. From Cave Painting to Distance Learning: A Study of Global Educational Systems (Atlanta: Brandenburg Press, 1988) 143.

4) FORMAT THE FOOTNOTE TEXT

   a. Highlight the book title, "From Cave Painting to Distance Learning: A Study of Global Educational Systems."

   b. On the Formatting Toolbar, click on the Italic button. The book title is italicized.

   c. With the cursor in the footnote text, drag the first line indent marker (▽) on the Ruler to the 0.5" mark. The footnote now has a first line indent of 0.5 inches.

<u>Check</u> – The footnote should look similar to:

Grossman, Lucinda. *From Cave Painting to Distance Learning: A Study of Global Educational Systems* (Atlanta: Brandenburg Press, 1988) 143.

5) SAVE, PRINT, AND THEN CLOSE THE MODIFIED DTP WORKSHOP

5.12 Inserting Time Stamps

It is easier to keep track of document revisions when printouts include the time they were printed. A *time stamp* includes the current date and time in a document and is created by first selecting the Date and Time command from the Insert menu to display the Date and Time dialog box:

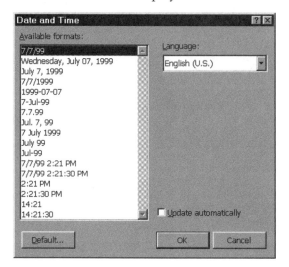

Selecting an Available formats option and then OK places a time stamp at the current cursor position:

Selecting the Update automatically option will insert a time stamp composed of a code instead of characters. When the file is later opened or printed, the code is automatically updated.

The date and time can appear on each page in a document by placing a time stamp in a header or footer. Buttons on the Header and Footer Toolbar can be used as well as the Date and Time command to place time stamps. Clicking on the Insert Date button () or Insert Time button () inserts a date or time stamp at the current cursor position:

Insert Date   Insert Time

Time stamps that are inserted using the Header and Footer Toolbar buttons are updated automatically.

5.13 Displaying Document Information

It can be useful to know the number of pages, words, or characters contained in a document. For example, journalists often *write for space*, which means writing to fill a precise amount of newspaper or publication space. Some student assignments also require a certain number of words. Selecting the Word Count command from the Tools menu displays a dialog box with information about the document:

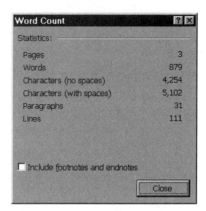

Selecting the Include footnotes and endnotes option will add the footnotes and endnotes to the displayed information. The information for a portion of a document can be displayed by highlighting the desired text before selecting the Word Count command.

Practice 8

In this practice you will add a time stamp to a header and determine the number of words in a document.

1) OPEN MOCKINGBIRD MUSIC

2) INSERT A TIME STAMP IN THE HEADER

a. Select View → Header and Footer. The cursor is placed in the Header box and the Header and Footer Toolbar is displayed.
b. Type the words Printed on and then type a space.
c. Select Insert → Date and Time. A dialog box is displayed.
   1. Click on the date and time format that appears similar to **9/8/99 9:00 AM**.
   2. Select the Update automatically option if it is not already selected.
   3. Select OK. The current date and time is inserted at the cursor position.

3) INSERT A TIME STAMP IN THE FOOTER

a. On the Header and Footer Toolbar, click on the Switch Between Header and Footer button ( ). The cursor is placed in the Footer box.
b. On the Header and Footer Toolbar, click on the Insert Date button ( ). The date is inserted in the footer.
c. On the Header and Footer Toolbar, click on the Close button. The header and footer are now dimmed.

4) DETERMINE THE NUMBER OF WORDS IN THE DOCUMENT

a. Select Tools → Word Count. A dialog box is displayed. How many words are in the document?
b. Select Close. The dialog box is removed.

a. Save the modified MOCKINGBIRD MUSIC.
b. The time stamp will be updated each time the document is opened or printed. Carefully note the current time, especially the minutes.
c. Print a copy of MOCKINGBIRD MUSIC. The header printed at the top of the page reflects the time of printing, not the time the stamp was placed in the header. Also, the time stamp in the document has been updated on the screen.
d. Close MOCKINGBIRD MUSIC.

5.14 Adding Graphics to a Document

clip art

A document that includes graphics is usually more interesting and informative. Because of this, Microsoft Office includes graphics called *clip art*. Selecting the Clip Art command from the Picture submenu in the Insert menu displays the Insert ClipArt dialog box:

Back button (dimmed)

categories

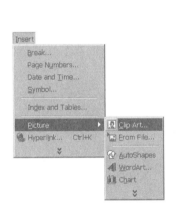

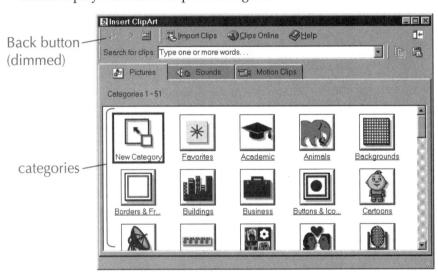

Clicking on a category displays the available clip art graphics in that category. For example, clicking on Animals displays clip art graphics of animals. Clicking on a graphic in a category displays a pop-up menu:

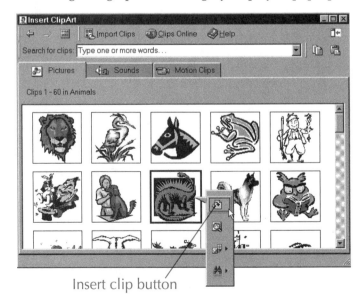

Insert clip button

Clicking on the Insert clip button () in the pop-up menu inserts a copy of the graphic into the document at the current cursor position. The Back button (⬅) in the dialog box can be used to display the categories again. Clicking on the Close button (✖) removes the dialog box.

resizing a graphic

Once a graphic is inserted into a document, clicking once on it selects it and displays handles for resizing:

handle

Graphics can be resized by dragging on a handle

Pointing to a handle changes the pointer to a double-headed arrow shape (↗), and then dragging resizes the graphic. Dragging on the center of the graphic (not a handle) moves it. Wherever the graphic is moved, the text will move to make room. The Cut, Copy, and Paste commands can be used to create copies or move a selected graphic. Pressing the Delete key deletes the selected graphic. Clicking anywhere in the document other than on the graphic deselects it and removes the handles.

In a document, a graphic can have formats applied to the paragraph it is in. For example, a graphic can be centered by placing the cursor in its paragraph and clicking on the Center button on the Formatting Toolbar.

5.15 Creating Columns

Columns are commonly used in newspapers, newsletters, magazines, and other long publications to make lines of text easier to read. A document can be formatted in multiple columns by selecting the Columns command from the Format menu, which displays the Columns dialog box:

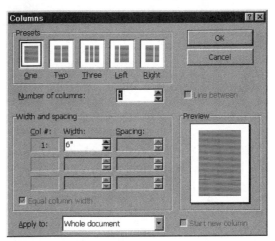

The number of columns per page can be chosen by either selecting one of the Presets options or typing a number in the Number of columns entry box. The Line between option can be selected to include a line between the columns. Selecting OK applies the formatting to the document.

A document can also be formatted with multiple columns using the Columns button ( ) on the Standard Toolbar.

Width and Spacing Options

The Width and spacing options in the Columns dialog box can be used to format columns of different widths, instead of the default equal widths.

Practice 9

In this practice you will insert clip art and format a document with columns.

1) OPEN DTP WORKSHOP

2) FORMAT THE DOCUMENT WITH TWO COLUMNS

    a. At the top of page 1, place the cursor just to the left of "Desktop" in the title of the document if it is not already there.

    b. Select Format ➜ Columns. A dialog box is displayed.

        1. In the Number of columns entry box, type 2.

        2. Select OK. The text in the document is formatted in two columns.

3) INSERT A GRAPHIC

    a. At the top of page 1, place the cursor just to the left of "Desktop" in the title of the document if it is not already there.

    b. Press Enter to create a new paragraph, then press the left arrow key to place the cursor in the blank paragraph.

    c. Select Insert ➜ Picture ➜ Clip Art. A dialog box is displayed.

        1. Click on the Academic category. Graphics that relate to education are displayed.

        2. Click on the first graphic, a stack of three books, to select it. A pop-up menu is displayed.

        3. Click on the Insert clip button (🖼). The graphic is inserted into the document.

        4. Click on the Close button of the dialog box to remove it.

4) RESIZE THE GRAPHIC

    a. If the graphic's handles are not displayed, click once on the graphic to select it.

    b. Move the I-Beam pointer to the handle in the upper-left corner of the graphic. The I-Beam pointer changes to a double-headed arrow shape (↗).

    c. With the double-headed arrow pointer on the handle, drag the handle downward and to the right a little. Note how the dotted lines move with the mouse to indicate the size of the graphic. When the graphic is a little smaller, release the mouse button.

    d. Click anywhere in the document to deselect the graphic.

5) PRINT PAGE ONE

    a. Save DTP WORKSHOP.

    b. Select File ➜ Print. A dialog box is displayed.

        1. Select the Pages option and then type 1 in the Pages entry box.

        2. Select OK. The first page of the document is printed. Note how the text and graphic in the printout resembles that shown on the screen.

6) DELETE THE GRAPHIC AND FORMAT THE DOCUMENT FOR ONE COLUMN

    a. Click once on the graphic to select it.

    b. Press the Delete key. The graphic is removed from the document.

    c. Press the Delete key again. The empty paragraph is removed from the document.

    d. Select Format ➜ Columns. A dialog box is displayed.

        1. In the Presets options, click on the One column option.

        2. Select OK. The text in the document is formatted in one column again.

7) SAVE AND CLOSE THE MODIFIED DTP WORKSHOP

8) EXIT WORD

    A Guide to Microsoft Office 2000 Professional

Chapter Summary

Windows Clipboard

This chapter introduced several word processor features. Highlighted text can be moved or copied using the Copy, Cut, and Paste commands. Buttons on the Standard Toolbar can also be used. When text is Cut or Copied it is placed on the Windows Clipboard.

The Office Clipboard is a special clipboard that stores up to 12 different cut or copied items. The Office Clipboard can be displayed by Selecting the Copy command twice in succession. The Copy button, Paste All button, and Clear Clipboard button on the Clipboard Toolbar are used to manipulate the Office Clipboard items.

The Find command scans a document for a particular combination of characters called search text. The Replace command substitutes the search text with specified replace text. Special characters, such as the tab character, can be used in either the search or replace text. Searches start from the current cursor position.

The Thesaurus command lists synonyms for a highlighted word and then allows you to replace the word with one of the synonyms.

hanging indent

first line indent

Indents are used to decrease the width of the text lines in a paragraph, and are created using the Paragraph command. A hanging indent formats the first line of text in a paragraph to stick out to the left over the rest of the text, and a first line indent formats the first line of text with an indent.

bulleted list
numbered list

Bulleted and numbered lists are created using the Bullets button and Numbering button on the Standard Toolbar. Numbered lists are used when order is important. Items in bulleted or numbered lists can be indented farther by clicking on the Increase Indent button on the Formatting Toolbar.

Footnotes and Endnotes are created using the Footnote command. Word automatically places the appropriate number in the text and at the bottom of the page containing the footnote. When a footnote number is deleted from the text, its corresponding footnote is removed from the bottom of the page and any remaining footnotes are renumbered. Endnotes are created by selecting the Endnote option in the Footnote and Endnote dialog box, and appear on the last page of a document.

The Date and Time command from the Insert menu is used to include a date and time code in a document. The code can be automatically updated whenever the document is printed or previewed. Time stamps can be included in headers and footers using the Insert Date or Insert Time buttons on the Header and Footer Toolbar.

The Word Count command from the Tools menu is used to display a document's information.

clip art

Word provides many different clip art graphics that can be placed in a document using the Clip Art command. A selected graphic can be moved, copied, and resized.

Columns can make a document easier to read and are created using the Columns command, which displays a dialog box allowing the user to select the number of columns and the amount of space between them.

Vocabulary

Bulleted list List created with a hanging indent and a tab character where each item is set off by a special character such as a bullet.

Clip art Graphics used in documents.

Endnote Used to document a source. Appears on the last page of a document.

First line indent First line of a paragraph that is farther to the right than the rest of the paragraph.

Footnote Used to document a source, and is located at the bottom of the page containing the footnoted material.

Hanging indent First line of a paragraph that is farther to the left than the rest of the paragraph.

Indent Paragraph formatting option that decreases the width of text lines.

Numbered list List created with a hanging indent and a tab character where each item is set off by a number that indicates each item's priority in the list.

Office Clipboard Special clipboard available in Microsoft Office programs.

Replace text Text entered by the user that is to take the place of search text.

Search text Text entered by the user that Word looks for in a document.

Synonym A word that has the same or similar meaning as another word.

Thesaurus A collection of synonyms.

Time stamp A marker in a document that automatically displays the current date and/or time when a file is opened or printed.

Windows Clipboard Area in memory where Cut or Copied text is stored.

Write for space Writing to fill a precise amount of newspaper or publication space.

Word Commands and Buttons

⇐ Back button Displays the categories in the Insert ClipArt dialog box. Found in the Insert ClipArt dialog box.

☰ Bullets button Formats a paragraph with a hanging indent and inserts a bullet to create a bulleted item in a list. Found on the Formatting Toolbar.

Clear Clipboard button Removes all items from the Office Clipboard. Found on the Clipboard Toolbar.

Clip Art **command** Displays a dialog box that allows the user to insert clip art into a document at the current cursor position. Found in the Picture submenu in the Insert menu.

Clipboard **command** Displays the Clipboard Toolbar. Found in the Toolbars submenu in the View menu.

Columns **command** Formats a document into multiple columns. Found in the Format menu. The Columns button (▦) on the Standard Toolbar can be used instead of the command.

Copy **command** Places a duplicate of the highlighted text on the Windows or Office Clipboard without removing the text from its original location. Found in the Edit menu. The Copy button (▣) on the Standard Toolbar can be used instead of the command.

Cut **command** Removes highlighted text and places it on the Windows or Office Clipboard. Found in the Edit menu. The Cut button (✂) on the Standard Toolbar can be used instead of the command.

Date and Time **command** Displays a dialog box that allows the user to insert a time stamp at the current cursor position. Found in the Insert menu.

⇥ Increase Indent button Moves an item in a bulleted or numbered list farther to the right. Found on the Formatting Toolbar.

Insert clip button Inserts a copy of the selected graphic at the current cursor position. Found in the pop-up menu displayed when a graphic is selected in the Insert ClipArt dialog box.

Insert Date button Inserts a time stamp in the form of a date at the current cursor position. Found on the Header and Footer Toolbar.

Insert Time button Inserts a time stamp at the current cursor position. Found on the Header and Footer Toolbar.

Find **command** Displays a dialog box that allows the user to scan a document for search text. Found in the Edit menu.

Footnote **command** Displays a dialog box that allows the user to place footnotes or endnotes into a document. Found in the Insert menu.

Numbering button Formats a paragraph with a hanging indent and inserts a number to create a numbered item in a list. Found on the Formatting Toolbar.

Paste All button Pastes copies of all the items on the Office Clipboard at the current cursor position. Found on the Clipboard Toolbar.

Paste **command** Copies text from the Windows Clipboard to the document at the current cursor position. Found in the Edit menu. The Paste button (▣) on the Standard Toolbar can be used instead of the command.

Replace **command** Displays a dialog box that allows the user to search a document for search text and substitute it with replace text. Found in the Edit menu.

Thesaurus **command** Lists words with meanings similar (synonyms) to a highlighted word. Found in the Language submenu in the Tools menu.

Word Count **command** Displays a dialog box with the document's information. Found in the Tools menu.

Review Questions

1. a) What is meant by duplicating text?
    b) List the steps required to copy the second paragraph in a document to a point directly after the fourth paragraph.

2. a) What is meant by moving text?
    b) What is the difference between moving and copying text?

3. a) What happens when the Paste All button on the Clipboard Toolbar is clicked on?
    b) How can you determine which item on the Clipboard Toolbar you would like to paste?
    c) List the steps required to remove all the items from the Clipboard Toolbar and remove the toolbar from the document window.

4. a) What is meant by finding search text?
    b) Give three examples of when you might use the Find command.

5. List the steps required to find each occurrence of Jerome in a document.

6. In a search for the word hat, how can you avoid finding the word that?

7. List the steps required to precisely search for the word The at the beginning of each paragraph.

8. What is replace text?

9. Why is it usually better to use the Replace button repeatedly instead of the Replace All button in the Replace dialog box?

Sections 5.7 — 5.10

10. a) What is a thesaurus?
    b) What is a synonym? Give an example.
    c) List the steps required to have Word list the synonyms for the word house in a document.

11. What is an indent and when might one be used?

12. List the steps required to format a paragraph with half-inch left and right indents.

13. List the steps required to format a paragraph with a hanging indent of 0.25 inches.

14. List the steps required to format a paragraph with a first line indent of 0.5 inches.

15. List the steps required to format three paragraphs as a bulleted list.

16. When would a numbered list be used instead of a bulleted list?

17. List the steps required to format three paragraphs as a numbered list.

Sections 5.11 — 5.15

18. a) What is a footnote used for?
    b) List the steps required to create a footnote in a document.
    c) Where are the footnotes displayed in a document?
    d) How can a footnote be edited?
    e) How can a footnote be deleted?
    f) What happens to the numbers on the other footnotes when one is deleted?

19. a) What is a time stamp and why might it be used?
    b) List two ways to insert a time stamp into a header.

20. What command is used to determine the number of words in a document?

21. List the steps required to add a clip art graphic to a document.

22. a) How can a document be formatted with three columns?
    b) How can a three column document be changed to a two column document?

Exercises

Exercise 1 ——————————————————————————— TAKING TESTS

The TAKING TESTS document gives directions on how to take a test, but the steps are listed out of order. Open TAKING TESTS and complete the following steps:

    a) Use the Cut and Paste commands to place the directions in proper order. Be sure there is a blank line between each step.

    b) Create a header with your name right aligned.

    c) Save the modified TAKING TESTS and print a copy.

Exercise 2 ——————————————————————————— Favorite Quote

Create a new document that contains your favorite quote 40 times, each in a separate paragraph. Hint: consider duplicating a text block with more than 1 line.

    a) In a new paragraph at the end of the document, insert a time stamp that includes the current time.

    b) Create a header with your name right aligned.

    c) Save the document naming it Favorite Quote and print a copy.

Exercise 3   ——————————————————————————— Entertainment Review

The review modified in Chapter Four, Exercise 3 needs to be refined. Open Entertainment Review and complete the following steps:

    a) Create 0.5" left and right indents for the first paragraph of your review.

    b) In the footer, after your name, insert a space and then a time stamp that includes the current date.

    c) In a new paragraph at the end of the document, add a sentence that states the number of words in the document.

    d) Format the document with two columns.

    e) Save the modified Entertainment Review and print a copy.

Exercise 4   ——————————————————————————— TELECOMMUTING

The TELECOMMUTING document modified in Chapter Four, Exercise 4 needs to be refined. Open TELECOMMUTING and complete the following steps:

    a) Create 0.5" left and right indents for the paragraph that begins "…if 10% to 20%…."

b) A footnote needs to be placed after the period ending the quote you just indented. Create the following footnote for the quote, formatting it appropriately:

[1] Effy Oz, *Ethics for the Information Age* (Wm. C. Brown Communications, Inc., 1994).

c) Insert an appropriate clip art graphic in a new paragraph at the top of the document above the heading "Computers in the Home Office." Resize the graphic smaller so that the document prints on two pages.

d) Save the modified TELECOMMUTING and print a copy.

Exercise 5 ——————————————————— CAMPING TIPS

The CAMPING TIPS document contains a list of helpful information on camping. Open CAMPING TIPS and complete the following steps:

a) Use the Find command to locate the word unwind in the document and then use the thesaurus to replace it with a synonym.

b) Format the entire document, except the title, as a numbered list.

c) Format the list of items after the first camping tip as a bulleted list. Use the Increase Indent button on the Formatting Toolbar to indent the entire list farther so that it is a sub-list of the first camping tip.

d) Create a header with your name right aligned.

e) Save the modified CAMPING TIPS and print a copy.

Exercise 6 ——————————————————— Things To Do

The list created in Chapter Three, Exercise 6 needs to be refined. Open Things To Do and complete the following steps:

a) Format the list of eight things you want to do as a numbered list.

b) Create a right aligned header with your name followed by a space and a time stamp that includes the current date and time.

c) Save the modified Things To Do and print a copy.

Exercise 7 ——————————————————— PROPOSAL

The research proposal modified in Chapter Four, Exercise 7 needs to be refined. Open PROPOSAL and complete the following steps:

a) Use the Find command to locate the word greater in the proposal and then use the thesaurus to replace it with a synonym.

b) Replace all occurrences of aging with growth.

c) Format the three numbered stages on page 2 as a numbered list.

d) In a new paragraph at the end of the document, add a sentence to that states how many words are in the document.

e) Save the modified PROPOSAL and print a copy.

Exercise 8 ⚙ ———————————————————— Journal

The journal modified in Chapter Four, Exercise 8 needs to be refined. Open Journal and complete the following steps:

a) In the footer, after your name, insert a space followed by a time stamp that includes the current date and time.

b) Format the document with two columns.

c) Save the modified Journal and print a copy.

Exercise 9 ——————————————————SCIENCE MUSEUM

The SCIENCE MUSEUM document contains information on a museum. Open SCIENCE MUSEUM and complete the following steps:

a) Format the exhibits for each of the five departments in the museum as a bulleted list to make them more readable.

b) Create 0.5" left and right indents for the paragraph that begins "It is my dream that the Sunport Science Museum...."

c) A footnote needs to be placed after the period ending the quote you just indented. Create the following footnote for the quote:

   [1] Elaine Diver, Keynote address, Sunport Science Museum Dedication, Sunport, FL, 15 Feb. 1965.

d) Insert an appropriate clip art graphic below the title and center align it (Hint: format the paragraph containing the graphic as center aligned). Resize the graphic if necessary so that all the information fits on one page.

e) Create a header with your name right aligned.

f) Save the modified SCIENCE MUSEUM and print a copy.

Exercise 10 ⚙ ———————————————————— Karate

The karate essay created in Chapter Three, Exercise 10 needs to be refined. Open Karate and complete the following steps:

a) Make a copy of the second sentence in the first paragraph and place it after the second paragraph. Leave a blank line between the second paragraph and the copied sentence.

b) Format the second paragraph with 0.5" left and right indents.

c) In a new paragraph at the end of the document, add a sentence that states the number of words in the document.

d) Create a header with your name right aligned.

e) Save the modified Karate and print a copy.

Exercise 11 ———————————————————— Water Conservation

The environmental article modified in Chapter Four, Exercise 11 needs to be refined. Open Water Conservation and complete the following steps:

  a) Insert two blank lines after the second paragraph which ends "sprinklers are not," then add the text below, pressing Enter after each line:

> Here are three more easy things you can do to conserve water:
> Don't leave the water running when you are brushing your teeth or washing your hair.
> Only fill the bathtub up half way.
> When you are washing your car, do not leave the hose running while you are not using it.

  b) Format the last three sentences you just entered as a bulleted list.

  c) In a new paragraph at the end of the document, insert an appropriate clip art graphic. Format the paragraph as center aligned.

  d) Format the document as two columns and resize the graphic, if necessary, so that it fits in the second column and the document prints on one page.

  e) Create a header with your name right aligned.

  f) Save the modified Water Conservation and print a copy.

Exercise 12 ———————————————————— SUNPORT CAMPING

The SUNPORT CAMPING document contains a short article on the recent Sunport Camping Symposium. Open SUNPORT CAMPING and complete the following steps:

  a) Use the <u>F</u>ind command to locate the word eat in the article and then use the thesaurus to replace it with a more descriptive word.

  b) Format the symposium specials, starting with "Johnson Cooking" and ending with "The Camp Grounds Company," as a bulleted list.

  c) Italicize the two book titles in the paragraph after the bulleted list.

  d) Footnotes need to be placed after the punctuation marks at the end of each book title. Create the following footnotes, formatting each one appropriately:

> [1] Gordon Washington, *Mountain Streams are Nice But Ponds are Better* (New Haven: Persimmons Publishing, 1994) 133.
> [2] Henrietta Lebon, *Good Dirt Bad Dirt* (Minneapolis: Baked Zucchini Press, 1995) 54.

  e) Create a header with your name right aligned.

  f) Save the modified SUNPORT CAMPING and print a copy.

Exercise 13 ———————————————————— Campsite Request

The letter created in Chapter Three, Exercise 13 needs to be refined. Open Campsite Request and complete the following steps:

  a) Use the <u>F</u>ind command to locate the word arriving in the document and then use the thesaurus to replace it with a synonym.

  b) Replace the date in the letter with a time stamp that includes the current date.

c) Create a header with your name right aligned.

d) Save the modified Campsite Request and print a copy.

Advanced Exercise 14 ———————————————— Web Service

The word processor can be used to make page-sized flyers.

a) In a new document create a flyer that announces your new business called "Indiana Internet Innovations." Include the following information:

- the phone number and fax number of your business (make them up).
- the Internet address of your Web page: http://www.inno.fake.
- a bulleted list of services such as web page design, web page maintenance, custom graphics, and custom forms.
- at least two of the following phrases: You can be on the WEB!, Special Service Packages Available, Now Available, Step Up to the Internet!
- one appropriate clip art graphic

Also include any other text you need.

b) Format all of the text to be at least 18 point. You can use more than one font size, for example format the business name as larger.

c) Format the text with two different fonts and two different paragraph alignments.

d) Save the document naming it Web Service and print a copy.

Advanced Exercise 15 ———————————————— Newsletter

In a new document create a newsletter on any topic. Save the document naming it Newsletter and print a copy when complete. Be sure to check the document on screen for errors and misspellings and make any corrections. Your newsletter should contain the following:

- At least two pages.
- At least four different stories.
- Two advertisements.
- Correct spelling.
- Justified paragraphs.
- Appropriate character formatting. The titles of each article should be bold and in a larger point size than the text of the article. Titles of books, magazines, songs, etc. should be italicized.
- At least one numbered or bulleted list.
- A header with the title of the newsletter.
- A footer with a centered page number.
- At least one table of information. Be sure that tabs and tab stops are used to align the information in the tables.
- At least one footnote.
- At least two clip art graphics.
- Two columns per page.

Page one of an example newsletter could look similar to the following:

Advanced Exercise 16 ———————————————————— Lunch Menu

In a new document create a lunch menu for a restaurant. Your menu should contain the following:

- The name of the restaurant.
- Two columns.
- At least one clip art graphic.
- At least one bulleted or numbered list.
- A header with the name of the restaurant.
- A footer with a message, such as Personal Checks Not Accepted.

Be sure to use tabs and tab stops to align the prices. Format the menu appropriately, using emphasized text and different fonts and sizes. Check the document on screen for errors and misspellings and make any corrections. Save the document naming it Lunch Menu and print a copy.

Advanced Exercise 17 ———————————————————— Basic Resume

In a new document create a résumé for yourself. Your résumé should contain the following:

- Four sections of information with the following titles: Education, Experience, Skills, and Accomplishments.
- At least one bulleted or numbered list.
- A header with your name, address, and phone number.
- A footer with the message References available upon request.

Format the résumé appropriately, using emphasized text, different fonts, different sizes, and tabs and tab stops. Check the document on screen for errors and misspellings and make any corrections. Save the document naming it Basic Resume and print a copy.

Table

Row

Column

Symbol

Hyphenation

Style

Outline

Index and Table

Break

Hyperlink

Envelopes and Labels

Record New Macro

Macros

Chapter Six Objectives

After completing this chapter you will be able to:

1. Create a table structure and enter data.
2. Format a table and the contents of cells.
3. Insert special characters into a document.
4. Hyphenate a document.
5. Apply styles to text and paragraphs.
6. Create an outline using a style.
7. Create a table of contents.
8. Create sections in a document.
9. Format different headers and footers in different sections.
10. Insert section page numbers.
11. Create hyperlinks to the Internet and to another part of the document.
12. Create an e-mail message and send it.
13. E-mail an existing document.
14. Create labels.
15. Record and run macros.

This chapter introduces advanced features of the word processor that are used to organize and format long documents. Creating table structures, labels, and macros are discussed, as well as sending e-mail.

6.1 Using Tables

Tables consist of rows and columns that are used to make information easier to read and understand. Previously, tabs and tab stops were used to arrange information into tables. For example, the information below has been organized into a table using tabs and tab stops:

Element	→	Symbol	→	Atomic·Number	→ Atomic·Mass¶
Calcium	→	Ca	→	20	→ 40.1¶
Gold	→	Au	→	79	→ 197.0¶

However, the same information can be arranged into a *table structure*:

Element□	Symbol□	Atomic·Number□	Atomic·Mass□	□
Calcium□	Ca□	20□	40.1□	□
Gold□	Au□	79□	197.0□	□

A table structure consists of rows and columns

The table structure above has three rows and four columns. *Rows* are horizontal and, in this example, the first row contains the titles. *Columns* are vertical. The intersection of a row and column is called a *cell*. Data is entered in the cells.

cell

inserting a table

A table structure is inserted into a document by first placing the cursor in the desired location and then clicking on the Insert Table button () on the Standard Toolbar. A grid of squares is displayed, with each square representing a cell. Moving the pointer over the squares highlights them. For the table structure shown above, the highlighted squares would appear similar to:

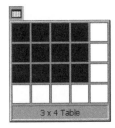

Highlighted squares indicate the table structure's dimensions

When the desired squares are highlighted, clicking once places the table structure at the current cursor position. Data can then be entered into the individual cells.

Table structures can also be inserted into a document by selecting the Table command from the Insert submenu in the Table menu, which displays a dialog box. Entering the desired number of rows and columns and selecting OK inserts a table structure in the document.

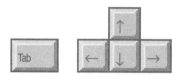

entering data in a table

Data is entered into a cell of a table structure by first clicking the mouse pointer in a cell to place the cursor and then typing the data. Pressing the Tab key moves the cursor to the next cell in the row. If the cursor is in the last cell of a row, pressing the Tab key moves the cursor to the first cell in the next row. The arrow keys can also be used to move the cursor from cell to cell.

6.2 Formatting the Cell Contents in a Table

Formatting the contents of cells in a table can make the information easier to read and understand. Cell formats include the alignment of data in a cell and character formats such as fonts.

alignment

character format

By default, Word left aligns the data in cells. The alignment can be changed by placing the cursor in a cell and then clicking on the desired alignment button on the Formatting Toolbar. Character formats can also be applied to a cell's contents by first highlighting the characters in the cell and then applying the desired formatting options, as described in Chapter Four. An entire cell's contents can be highlighted by moving the pointer to the left edge of a cell until it changes to a solid diagonal pointer shape (◢) and then clicking once.

highlighting rows and columns

In many cases, the same formatting needs to be applied to an entire row or column of cells. To do this, the row or column must first be selected by highlighting it. A row is highlighted by moving the pointer to the left of the row until the right arrow shape (↗) is displayed, and then clicking once. A column is highlighted by moving the pointer to the boundary at the top of the first cell in the column until a solid down arrow (↓) is displayed, and then clicking once. Multiple rows and columns can be selected by dragging the pointer after highlighting the first row or column. Once the desired rows or columns are highlighted, formatting can be applied using options on the Formatting Toolbar, such as the Bold button or the Font collapsible list.

Another method of highlighting rows or columns is to place the cursor in a cell and then select the Row or Column command from the Select submenu in the Table menu.

6.3 Formatting Tables

Formatting the appearance of a table can make the information easier to read and understand. Table formats include the height and width of rows and columns.

changing the height and width of rows and columns

When a table structure is created, Word automatically adjusts the column widths so the table structure stretches from the left margin to the right margin, with each column having the same width. A column's width is changed by dragging the column's right boundary. Moving the pointer to the *boundary*, the line separating the columns, changes the pointer to a double-headed arrow (←||→):

Element□	Symbol□	Atomic·Number□	Atomic·Mass□	□
Calcium□	Ca□	20□	40.1□	□
Gold□	Au□	79□	197.0□	□

Dragging the boundary to the left or right decreases or increases the column's width, respectively.

Row height is changed in a similar manner by dragging the row's boundary. After entering data into a table, double-clicking on a boundary resizes the row or column so that it is just tall or wide enough to display the data entirely.

When text in a cell is formatted with a larger point size, the height of the entire row is increased to accommodate the larger characters. Pressing the Enter key when the cursor is in a cell also increases the row's height, allowing additional paragraphs of text to be entered into a cell. The column widths and the first row's height in the table structure below have been modified:

Element□	Symbol□	Atomic·Number□	Atomic·Mass□	□
Calcium□	Ca□	20□	40.1□	□
Gold□	Au□	79□	197.0□	□

The column widths and the height of the first row in this table structure have been resized

adding a row or column to a table

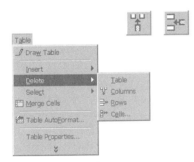

After creating a table structure, you may want to add a row or column to it. When a row is highlighted, the Insert Rows button (⧉) is available on the Standard Toolbar. Selecting this button adds a row above the highlighted row. A column is added to a table structure in a similar manner by selecting the Insert Columns button (⧉), which adds a column to the left of the highlighted column.

A row or column can be deleted by placing the cursor in a cell and then selecting the <u>R</u>ows or <u>C</u>olumns command from the <u>D</u>elete submenu in the T<u>a</u>ble menu. An entire table can be deleted by placing the cursor in any of the cells and then selecting the <u>T</u>able command from the <u>D</u>elete submenu in the T<u>a</u>ble menu.

Practice 1

In this practice you will insert a table structure into a document and format it.

1) OPEN VOLCANOES

This document is a report about volcanoes.

2) INSERT A TABLE STRUCTURE

a. Scroll to the bottom of page 2 and place the cursor in the blank paragraph after the sentence that ends "…the last eruption:"

b. On the Standard Toolbar, click on the Insert Table button (▦). Empty squares are displayed.

c. Move the mouse pointer over the squares until four rows and three columns are highlighted (a 4 x 3 table) and then click the mouse. The table structure is inserted into the document.

3) ENTER DATA INTO THE FIRST ROW

a. Click once in the first cell of the first row to place the cursor if it is not already there.
b. Type Name.
c. Press the Tab key. The cursor is now in the second cell of the first row.
d. Type Country and then press the Tab key. The cursor is now in the third cell of the first row.
e. Type Last Erupted and then press the Tab key. The cursor is now in the first cell of the second row.

4) ENTER THE REMAINING DATA

Follow the procedure in step 3 to enter the remaining rows of data:

Mt. Saint Helens	United States	1980
Mt. Etna	Italy	1992
Mt. Hekla	Iceland	1980

5) FORMAT THE DATA

a. Move the pointer to the top boundary of the third column until the solid down arrow (↓) is displayed and then click once. The column is highlighted.
b. On the Formatting Toolbar, click on the Align Right button (▤). The data is right aligned.
c. Move the pointer to the left of the first row until the right arrow shape (↗) is displayed and then click once. The first row is highlighted.
d. Use options on the Formatting Toolbar to format the highlighted data as 14 point and Bold. Notice that the row height increases.
e. Click anywhere to remove the highlight.

6) FORMAT THE TABLE STRUCTURE

a. Move the pointer to the boundary between the first and second column until the pointer changes to a double-headed arrow shape (◄║►).
b. Drag the boundary to the left until the first column is just slightly wider than the data. Notice that Word automatically changes the column width of the second column so that the table structure still stretches from the left to the right margin.
c. Repeat step 6, parts (a) and (b) for the second and third columns. Now the table structure no longer stretches from the left to the right margin.

7) ADD A COLUMN AND FORMAT IT

a. Highlight the third column.
b. On the Standard Toolbar, click on the Insert Columns button (▥).
c. In the new column, type Height (m) as the column title.
d. Type 2,549 in the second cell, 3,323 in the third cell, and 1,491 in the last cell of the column.
e. Point to the boundary between the third and fourth columns and then double-click the double-headed arrow pointer on the boundary. The column is resized just wide enough to display the data.

Check – Your table should look similar to:

the ground. The exact location of where they come out of is called a vent. A volcano usually has
more than one vent. The following table lists three volcanoes and the date of the last eruption: ¶

Name¤	Country¤	Height (m)¤	Last Erupted¤¤
Mt. Saint Helens¤	United States¤	2,549¤	1980¤¤
Mt. Etna¤	Italy¤	3,323¤	1992¤¤
Mt. Hekla¤	Iceland¤	1,491¤	1980¤¤

8) SAVE THE MODIFIED VOLCANOES

A Guide to Microsoft Office 2000 Professional

6.4 Inserting Special Characters

There are many characters available in Word that do not appear on a key on the keyboard. Some examples of special characters are the bullet (•), copyright symbol (©), and degree symbol (°).

Selecting the Symbol command from the Insert menu displays a dialog box with many special characters. Clicking once on a character enlarges it so that it is easier to view:

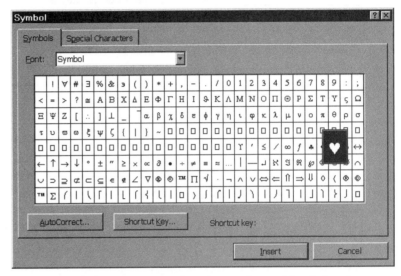

Special characters can be chosen from this dialog box

Selecting the Insert button places the selected character into the document at the current cursor position. Selecting Close removes the dialog box.

The special characters displayed in the dialog box change when a different font is selected from the Font collapsible list. For example, the dialog box above displays special characters for the Symbol font.

6.5 Hyphenating Documents

Hyphenating a document is a process that divides words, if necessary, at the end of lines with a hyphen (-) so that part of a word wraps to the next line. Hyphenation can smooth out very ragged right edges in left-aligned text and can lessen the space between words in justified text.

Once a document is otherwise complete, hyphenation can be performed. Selecting the Hyphenation command from the Language submenu in the Tools menu displays the Hyphenation dialog box:

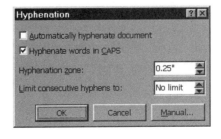

Selecting the Automatically hyphenate document option and then OK hyphenates the entire document. The Hyphenation zone option specifies the amount of space to leave between the last word in a line and the right margin. The smaller the hyphenation zone, the less ragged the right edge will be. The Limit consecutive hyphens to option specifies how many consecutive lines of the text can be hyphenated. Sometimes a word should not be split across two lines, such as a company name that is all uppercase. In this situation, the Hyphenate words in CAPS option should be deselected.

6.6 Applying Built-In Styles

A *built-in style* is a named set of character and paragraph formats. In a new document, several built-in styles are available from the Style collapsible list on the Formatting Toolbar:

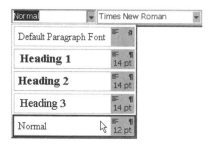

A paragraph with the Normal style applied to it is left-aligned, 12 point Times New Roman. By default, Word applies the Normal style to paragraphs in a document. Other built-in styles and their corresponding formats include:

Style	Formatting
Normal	Times New Roman 12 point left-aligned
Heading 1	**Arial 16 point bold left-aligned**
Heading 2	***Arial 14 point bold italic left-aligned***
Heading 3	**Arial 13 point bold left-aligned**

A built-in style is applied to a paragraph by placing the cursor in the desired paragraph and then selecting the style from the Style collapsible list on the Formatting Toolbar.

Styles help you produce documents with a consistent look. For example, long documents, such as reports, usually contain headings and body text. *headings* *Headings* are titles that separate the paragraphs of *body text* by topic. To *body text* stand out from the body text, headings are often bold and have a larger and different font than the body text.

There are many other built-in styles that are not listed in the Style collapsible list. All the available styles can be viewed by selecting the Style command from the Format menu, which displays the Style dialog box. Selecting All styles in the List option displays all the built-in styles. The selected style's preview and description are displayed in the right side of the dialog box:

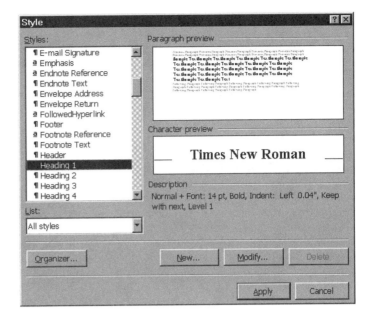

Selecting a style and then the Apply button applies the style to the paragraph containing the cursor. The built-in style is also added to the Style collapsible list for future use.

Practice 2

In this practice you will insert a special character, apply built-in styles to headings and subheadings, and hyphenate a document. Open VOLCANOES if it is not already displayed.

1) INSERT A SPECIAL CHARACTER

   a. Scroll to the top of page 2 until the "Introduction" heading is displayed.
   b. In the second sentence of the paragraph, place the cursor between "2200" and "C."
   c. Select Insert → Symbol. A dialog box is displayed.
      1. Select Symbol from the Font collapsible list if it is not already selected.
      2. Click on the degree character (°), located near the lower-left area of the dialog box. The character is enlarged for better viewing.
      3. Select the Insert button. A degree symbol is placed into the document at the current cursor position.
      4. In the same sentence, place the cursor between "5000" and "C." You may need to drag the Title bar of the Symbol dialog box to move the dialog box out of the way. The degree symbol should still be selected.
      5. Select the Insert button. A degree symbol is inserted.
      6. Select Close. The dialog box is removed.

2) APPLY BUILT-IN STYLES TO THE MAIN HEADINGS

   a. Scroll to the top of page 2 and place the cursor in the "Introduction" heading.
   b. On the Formatting Toolbar, from the Style collapsible list select the Heading 1 style. This style is now applied to the "Introduction" heading.
   c. Place the cursor in the "Volcano Facts" heading.
   d. On the Formatting Toolbar, from the Style collapsible list select the Heading 1 style.
   e. Scroll to the bottom of page 4 and apply the Heading 1 style to the "Conclusion" heading.

3) APPLY BUILT-IN STYLES TO THE SUBHEADINGS

    a. Scroll to the middle of page 2 and place the cursor anywhere in the "Stages of Volcanic Activity" subheading.

    b. On the Formatting Toolbar, from the Style collapsible list select the Heading 2 style.

    c. Scroll through the rest of the document and apply the Heading 2 style to the "Types of Volcanoes" and "Types of Lava Rocks," subheadings.

    d. Scroll to the middle of page 2 and place the cursor in the "Eruption Stage" subheading.

    e. On the Formatting Toolbar, from the Style collapsible list select the Heading 3 style.

    f. Scroll through the rest of the document and apply the Heading 3 style to the "Cooling and Inactive Stage," "Cinder Cones," "Shield Volcanoes," "Composite Volcanoes," "Basalt," "Obsidian," and "Andesite" subheadings.

4) HYPHENATE THE DOCUMENT

    Select Tools → Language → Hyphenation. A dialog box is displayed.

       1. Select the Automatically hyphenate document option.

       2. Select OK. The dialog box is removed and Word hyphenates the document. Scroll through the document and look for hyphenated words.

5) SAVE AND THEN PRINT THE MODIFIED VOLCANOES

6.7 Using Outline View

Outline view allows you to easily see and modify the organization of a document. A document is displayed in Outline view by selecting the Outline command from the View menu. For example, shown below is a document in Print Layout view on the left and the same document in Outline view on the right:

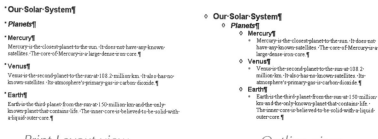

Print Layout view   Outline view

In Outline view, Word uses the built-in styles to determine heading levels and body text. Paragraphs with a Heading style are indented according to their levels where the Heading 1 style is at a higher level than Heading 2. Paragraphs with the Normal style are body text and have the lowest level. The different levels are differentiated by icons:

- **Body text** is indicated by a small square (◘) next to the first line in a paragraph.

- **Headings followed by a paragraph with a lower level** have a plus sign (✚) to the left of the heading.

- **Headings followed by a paragraph with the same level** have a minus sign (◘) to the left of the heading.

A Guide to Microsoft Office 2000 Professional

When a document is displayed in Outline view, the Outlining Toolbar is also displayed:

- **Promote button** (◆) or **Demote button** (➡) applies the next higher or lower level style, respectively, to the paragraph containing the cursor.

- **Demote to Body Text button** (➡) applies the Normal style to the paragraph containing the cursor.

- **Move Up button** (⬆) or **Move Down button** (⬇) moves the paragraph containing the cursor before or after the preceding paragraph, respectively.

- **Expand button** (✚) or **Collapse button** (➖) displays or hides the body text under the heading containing the cursor, respectively.

- **Show Heading buttons** (1 2 3 4 5 6 7) display only those heading levels that correspond to that button number and higher. Text in lower levels is hidden.

- **Show All Headings button** (All) switches between displaying all the heading levels and body text or only headings levels.

moving entire topics   Entire topics can be moved by first clicking once on a heading's plus sign to highlight that heading and any subheading or body text under it. Selecting the Move Up or Move Down button on the Outlining Toolbar moves the highlighted topic.

A document can be printed in Outline view using the Print command or the Print button on the Standard Toolbar. The printout will contain the same headings and body text as displayed on the screen. Selecting the Print Layout command or the Normal command from the View menu displays the document in a different view from Outline view.

Practice 3   ❄ ───────────────────────────────

In this practice you will display a document in Outline view and print the outline. Open VOLCANOES if it is not already displayed.

1) *DISPLAY VOLCANOES IN OUTLINE VIEW*
   a. Scroll to the top of page 2 and place the cursor in the first heading, "Introduction."
   b. Select View → Outline. The document is displayed in Outline view. Note the different levels in the document.

2) *DISPLAY DIFFERENT LEVELS OF HEADINGS*
   a. On the Outlining Toolbar, click on the Show Heading 1 button (1). Only the headings with the Heading 1 style are displayed.
   b. On the Outlining Toolbar, click on the Show Heading 2 button (2). Heading levels 1 and 2 are displayed.
   c. On the Outlining Toolbar, click on the Show Heading 3 button (3). All three heading levels are displayed.

3) MOVE THE "TYPES OF LAVA ROCKS" TOPIC

a. Click on the plus sign (✛) next to the "Types of Lava Rocks" subheading. The subheadings are highlighted.

b. On the Outlining Toolbar, click on the Move Up button (⬆). The highlighted subheadings are moved before the "Composite Volcanoes" subheading.

c. On the Outlining Toolbar, click on the Move Up button three more times. The highlighted subheadings are moved before the Types of Volcanoes heading.

d. On the Outlining Toolbar, click on the Show All Headings button (All). Notice that the text under each subheading also moved.

e. On the Outlining Toolbar, click on the Show Heading 3 button (3).

f. Click anywhere to remove the highlight.

4) SAVE AND THEN PRINT THE DOCUMENT IN OUTLINE VIEW

a. Save the modified VOLCANOES.

b. On the Standard Toolbar, click on the Print button. An outline of the document is printed with only the headings and subheadings displayed.

c. Select View → Print Layout. The document is again displayed in Print Layout view.

d. Save the modified VOLCANOES.

6.8 Creating a Table of Contents

A *table of contents* lists the headings and subheadings of a document and the corresponding page numbers. Word can automatically create a table of contents for a document based on the built-in styles applied to its headings and subheadings. A table of contents is created by first placing the cursor where the table of contents should appear and then selecting the Index and Tables command from the Insert menu. Selecting the Table of Contents tab in the dialog box displays the following options:

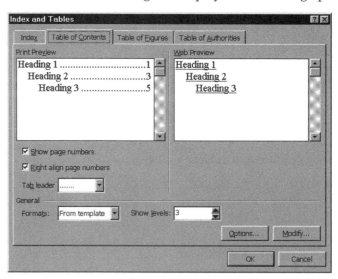

In the Formats collapsible list, the type of table of contents is selected. The Print Preview section displays a sample of what the selected format will look like. Selecting the Show page numbers option includes the corresponding page numbers for headings and the Right align page numbers option aligns the page numbers with the right margin. The Show levels option allows you to specify the number of heading levels you want to include. Selecting OK creates a table of contents for the document and inserts it at the current cursor position.

Each entry in a table of contents created by Word is a hyperlink to the corresponding heading. Pointing to a table of contents entry changes the pointer to a hand shape (). Clicking once scrolls the document to the corresponding heading and places the cursor in it. For example, clicking on the Planets heading in the table of contents shown below places the cursor in the Planets heading:

Our·Solar·System..→..1¶
   Planets...→..1¶
      Mercury..→..1¶
      Venus...→...1¶
      Earth...→...1¶

˙ Our·Solar·System¶

˙ *Planets*¶

˙ Mercury¶
Mercury·is·the·closest·planet·to·the·sun.·It·does·not·have·any·known·
satellites.·The·core·of·Mercury·is·a·large·dense·iron·core.¶

˙ Venus¶
Venus·is·the·second·planet·to·the·sun·at·108.2·million·km.·It·also·has·no·
known·satellites.·Its·atmosphere's·primary·gas·is·carbon·dioxide.¶

updating a table of contents

Word does not automatically update a table of contents when changes are made to a document. A table of contents can be updated by first selecting it by moving the pointer into the margin to the left of the table until the right arrow shape (⇗) is displayed and clicking once. When the table of contents is selected, pressing the F9 key displays the Update Table of Contents dialog box:

F9

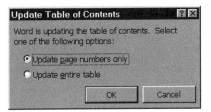

Selecting the Update entire table radio button and then OK tells Word to update any headings and subheadings and their corresponding page numbers in the table of contents.

6.9 Creating Sections in a Document

Long documents, such as reports, often need to have several different page formats. For example, page three of a five page report may need to be formatted to two columns, while the remaining pages need to be formatted with only one column. A document must first be divided into different parts, called *sections*, before more than one page format can be applied.

A document is divided into sections by inserting a *section break*, which is similar to a manual page break. A section break is inserted at the current cursor position by selecting the Break command from the Insert menu, which displays the Break dialog box:

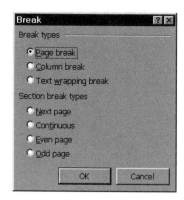

The Next page option inserts a section break at the current cursor position and starts the next section on a new page. The Continuous option inserts a section break at the current cursor position and starts the next section on the same page. Selecting OK inserts the section break.

The Status bar at the bottom of the document window displays what section of the document the cursor is in. When formatting marks are displayed, section breaks are identified by a double line and the type of section break. For example, a Continuous section break was added to the following document:

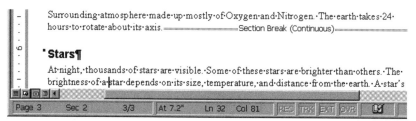

The page indicator on the Status bar shows the cursor is in section (Sec) 2 of the 3 page document

Text that was to the right of the cursor is now in the next section of the document. After a document is divided into sections, any page formats that are applied affect only the section that contains the cursor.

A section break is removed by placing the cursor to the left of the section break and pressing the Delete key.

Practice 4

In this practice you will create a table of contents for VOLCANOES and divide the document into two sections. Open VOLCANOES if it is not already displayed.

1) INSERT A TABLE OF CONTENTS
    a. Scroll to the top of page 2.
    b. Place the cursor in the blank paragraph above the "Introduction" heading.
    c. Type TABLE OF CONTENTS and then press Enter.
    d. Select Insert → Index and Tables. A dialog box is displayed.
        1. Select the Table of Contents tab if the table of contents options are not already displayed.
        2. In the Formats collapsible list, select Formal.
        3. Select OK. A table of contents is inserted at the current cursor position.
    e. Bold and center align the "TABLE OF CONTENTS" title.

A Guide to Microsoft Office 2000 Professional

2) *USE A HYPERLINK IN THE TABLE OF CONTENTS*

Point to the "Obsidian" entry in the table of contents, and click once. The document is scrolled to the Obsidian heading, and the cursor is placed at the beginning of the heading.

3) *INSERT A SECTION BREAK*

a. Scroll down to display the text below the table of contents, and place the cursor before the "I" at the beginning of the "Introduction" heading.
b. Select Insert → Break. A dialog box is displayed.
  1. Select the Next page option.
  2. Select OK. A section break is inserted between page 2 and 3 and the main text of the report is moved to page 3. Note that the Status bar displays Sec 2 because the cursor is currently in section 2 of the document.

4) *SAVE THE MODIFIED VOLCANOES*

6.10 Using Section Headers and Footers

In Chapter Four, headers and footers were added to a document to make it more informative. However, there may be times when you do not want the same header or footer on every page. A document divided into sections can have different headers and footers in each section.

Section headers and footers are created the same way as document headers and footers. However, the header and footer area of each section is denoted with a section number, such as Header -Section 2-. By default, each section header and footer contains the same text as the previous section. For example, if Solar System is entered as the header text in section 1, the header in section 2 automatically contains Solar System:

The header text in section 2 is based on the header text in section 1

A different header or footer can be created for a section by first placing the cursor in the header or footer box then deselecting the Same as Previous button () on the Header and Footer Toolbar. Any existing header or footer text that was used in the previous section's header or footer can then be deleted and the new header or footer text typed.

6.11 Using Section Page Numbers

front matter

body

Different page numbering may be required for different parts of a document. For example, the *front matter* of a formal report usually uses separate page numbering from the body of the report. Front matter is information that comes before the body of a report, such as the title page, table of contents, list of acknowledgments, etc. The *body* of a report contains the information being presented. The front matter is usually numbered with small Roman numerals (i, v, x) and the body is numbered with Arabic numerals (1, 5, 10) starting at 1.

A document that has been divided into sections can have different page numbering formats applied to each section. After placing the cursor in the header or footer of the desired section, deselecting the Same as Previous button on the Header and Footer Toolbar allows the header and footer text and page numbering for that section to be different from the previous section. After a page number is inserted by clicking on the Insert Page Number button () on the Header and Footer Toolbar, its format or the starting number can be changed by clicking on the Format Page Number button () on the Header and Footer Toolbar to display the Page Number Format dialog box:

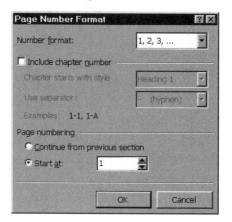

Page number formats and the starting number are set using this dialog box

restarting page numbers

The format of the page number is selected from the Number format collapsible list which includes options for Arabic numerals, Roman numerals, and letters. Page numbering can be started at a number other then the actual page number by selecting the Start at option and then entering the desired beginning number.

Practice 5

In this practice you will insert different page numbers in the footers of section 1 and section 2. Open VOLCANOES if it is not already displayed.

1) INSERT A PAGE NUMBER IN THE FOOTER

    a. At the top of page 2, place the cursor in the "TABLE OF CONTENTS" title.

    b. Select File → Page Setup. A dialog box is displayed.

        1. Click on the Layout tab if the layout options are not displayed.

        2. Select the Different first page option.

        3. Select OK. The title page of the report should not have a page number displayed.

    c. Select View → Header and Footer. The cursor is placed in the header of section 1.

    d. On the Header and Footer Toolbar, click on the Switch Between Header and Footer button (🗐) to place the cursor in the footer of section 1.

    e. On the Header and Footer Toolbar, click on the Insert Page Number button (🔢) to insert the page number in the footer.

    f. On the Formatting Toolbar, click on the Center button. The page number is center aligned.

g. On the Header and Footer Toolbar, click on the Format Page Number button (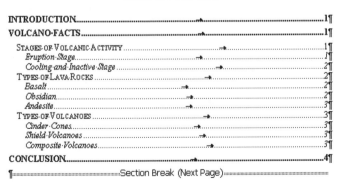). A dialog box is displayed.
    1. In the Number format collapsible list, select i, ii, iii, ... for small Roman numerals.
    2. Select OK. The dialog box is removed.

h. Click on the Close button in the Header and Footer Toolbar.

2) *FORMAT THE PAGE NUMBER IN THE FOOTER OF SECTION 2*

a. Scroll through the document to view the dimmed footer text. Notice that the footer in section 2 on page 3 also contains page numbers. However, the page numbers need to be formatted to start numbering at 1. Also note that the page indicator in the Status bar displays the page number and section number of the cursor location.

b. Place the cursor anywhere in section 2 if it is not already there. The Status bar indicates the section that currently contains the cursor.

c. Select View → Header and Footer. The cursor is placed in the header of section 2.

d. On the Header and Footer Toolbar, click on the Switch Between Header and Footer button ( ) to place the cursor in the footer of section 2.

e. On the Header and Footer Toolbar, click on the Same as Previous button ( ) to deselect it. Now the footer in section 2 will not be the same as the footer in section 1.

f. On the Header and Footer Toolbar, click on the Format Page Number button ( ). A dialog box is displayed.
    1. In the Number format collapsible list select 1, 2, 3 ... for Arabic numbers if it is not already selected.
    2. Select the Start at option. The cursor is placed in the entry box.
    3. Type 1 if it is not already there. The page numbering in section 2 will now start at 1 instead of 3.
    4. Select OK. The dialog box is removed.

g. On the Header and Footer Toolbar, click on the Close button.

h. Print preview the document. Zoom in and note the different page numbers, then close the print preview window.

3) *UPDATE THE TABLE OF CONTENTS*

a. At the top of page 2, move the pointer to the left of the table of contents until the right arrow shape is displayed, and then click once. The entire table of contents is selected.

b. Press the F9 key. A dialog box is displayed.
    1. Select OK to accept the default option of Update page numbers only. The table of contents now shows the correct page numbers.

Check – The table of contents should look similar to:

4) *SAVE, PRINT, AND THEN CLOSE THE MODIFIED VOLCANOES*

6.12 Creating Hyperlinks to the Internet

The general purpose of a document is to communicate information. To help accomplish this, a document can include a hyperlink to a Web page on the Internet:

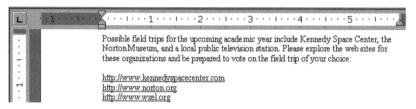

Clicking on a hyperlink in a Word document connects your computer to the Internet and displays the Web page. Note that the computer you are using needs to have Internet access in order to connect to the Internet.

A hyperlink is inserted into a document at the current cursor position by either selecting the Hyperlink command (Ctrl+K) from the Insert menu or clicking on the Insert Hyperlink button ( ) on the Standard Toolbar to display the Insert Hyperlink dialog box:

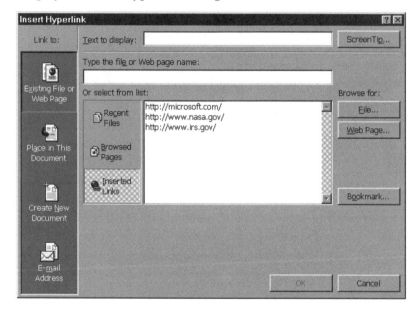

Entering the URL for the Web page in the Type the file or Web page name entry box and selecting OK inserts a hyperlink into the document. The text http:// is automatically added to the beginning of the URL. Hyperlinks are automatically formatted as underlined blue text in a Word document.

On some occasions, you may want a description to appear in the document as the hyperlink instead of the URL. Typing text in the Text to display entry box, in addition to entering a URL in the Type the file or Web page name entry box, will place the text in the document and format it as a hyperlink to the specified URL.

After inserting a hyperlink, pointing to it changes the pointer to a hand shape ( ) which indicates you can click on the hyperlink to connect to that Web page.

6.13 Creating Hyperlinks to Another Part of the Document

Hyperlinks cannot only connect the user to a Web page, but also to another place in the currently opened document. You have already created hyperlinks to another part of a document when you created the table of contents in the VOLCANOES document.

A hyperlink to another part of the open document is inserted at the current cursor position by either selecting the Hyperlink command from the Insert menu or clicking on the Insert Hyperlink button ( ) on the Standard Toolbar to display the Insert Hyperlink dialog box. Selecting the Place in This Document button on the left side of the dialog box displays the current outline for the document:

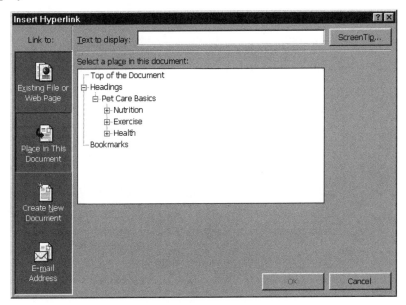

Clicking on the plus or minus signs next to the headings displays other heading levels. Clicking on a heading level places the heading in the Text to display entry box, which can then be changed if desired. Selecting OK inserts a hyperlink to the selected heading.

6.14 Creating Newsletters in Word

Word processors have become very popular for producing newsletters. For example, clubs and organizations often produce monthly newsletters to inform their members of upcoming events and issues.

title area

Newsletters have several common elements. For example, most newsletters have a title area, some text, and graphics. A *title area* is the section at the top of the first page that contains the title, date, and other publication information. The remaining pages of the newsletter are usually formatted in two or three columns with informative headers and footers.

Because the first page of a newsletter contains different page formats then the rest of the document, a newsletter created in Word is divided into sections. The first page is separated into two sections, and the rest of the newsletter is a third section. The first page has a large title area created by entering the publication information in the first section of the document. The second section is for the text on the first page, and the third section is the text on the rest of the pages. Additional sections can be added as needed for different page formats. A table of contents is usually included on the first page.

Practice 6

In this practice you will format the SPACE TRANSMISSIONS document as a newsletter with hyperlinks.

1) OPEN SPACE TRANSMISSIONS

This document already contains text and graphics for the newsletter. The title area has not been created. Display formatting marks if they are not already displayed.

2) CREATE THE TITLE AREA

a. Near the top of page 1, place the cursor in the blank paragraph just above the heading "In This Issue."
b. Select Insert → Break. A dialog box is displayed.
   1. Select the Continuous option.
   2. Select OK. Section 1 of the document is now the title area of the newsletter.

3) FORMAT THE FIRST PAGE FOR TWO COLUMNS

a. Place the cursor in section 2 of the document if it is not already there.
b. Select Format → Columns. A dialog box is displayed.
   1. In the Number of columns entry box, type 2.
   2. Select OK. The first page for the newsletter now has a title area in section 1 and two columns in section 2.

4) FORMAT THE REMAINING PAGES FOR THREE COLUMNS

a. At the top of page 2, insert a Continuous section break right before the heading "Space Exploration Facts."
b. Format section 3 of the document for three columns.

5) SAVE THE MODIFIED SPACE TRANSMISSIONS

6) INSERT A HYPERLINK

a. In the second column of page 2, place the cursor after the sentence ending "NASA's Web site at" that is just before the "Mission to Mars" heading.
b. Press the spacebar once.
c. Select Insert → Hyperlink. A dialog box is displayed.
   1. Click on the Existing File or Web Page button at the left side of the dialog box if it is not already selected.
   2. In the Type the file or Web page name entry box type www.nasa.gov.
   3. Select OK. A hyperlink is added to the document. Note that Word added http:// to the hyperlink.

7) SAVE THE MODIFIED SPACE TRANSMISSIONS

8) DISPLAY NASA'S WEB SITE

a. Move the mouse pointer over the hyperlink you just entered until the hand shape () is displayed and click once. If necessary, ask your instructor for help in connecting to the Internet. After connecting to the Internet, NASA's Web page is displayed.
b. Explore the Web page. When done, close the Web page.

9) PRINT AND THEN CLOSE SPACE TRANSMISSIONS

6.15 Creating an E-Mail Message

E-mail Message

An e-mail message can be sent directly from Word. In the New Document dialog box, selecting the E-mail Message icon and then OK starts Word and displays a new, blank e-mail message:

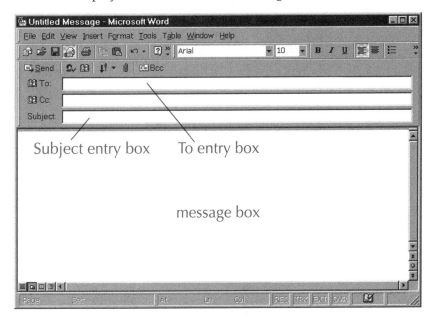

The e-mail address of each recipient is typed in the To entry box separated by semicolons, a description is typed in the Subject entry box, and the message is typed in the message area. The message can be formatted like any other Word document you have created. When the message is complete, clicking on the Send button (Send) connects your computer to the Internet and sends the message.

6.16 E-Mailing an Existing Document

An existing document can be e-mailed from Word. For example, if you were working on a report and needed experts in Utah to review it, you could e-mail the document to them.

An open document can be sent as an e-mail message by first clicking on the E-mail button ( ) on the Standard Toolbar, which displays the address information entry boxes. The e-mail address of each recipient is typed in the To entry box separated by semicolons, and a description is typed in the Subject entry box. Clicking on the Send a Copy button (Send a Copy) connects your computer to the Internet and sends the document as an e-mail message. The address information is removed from the screen and the document remains open and displayed.

Practice 7

In this practice you will create and send an e-mail message, and then send the DTP WORKSHOP document as an e-mail message.

1) CREATE A NEW E-MAIL MESSAGE

    a. On the Taskbar, click on the Start button. A menu is displayed.
    b. Select the New Office Document command. A dialog box is displayed.
        1. Click on the E-mail Message icon and then select OK. A new, empty e-mail message is created. Note the To and Subject entry boxes and the message area.

2) ENTER THE ADDRESS INFORMATION

    a. In the To entry box, type office@lvp.com (the @ sign is created by pressing Shift+2) or an address specified by your instructor.
    b. In the Subject entry box, type Meeting Reminder.

3) ENTER THE MESSAGE

Place the cursor in the message area and type the following text, allowing Word to wrap the text if necessary:

> Greetings to you on this lovely day! How are you? I just wanted to remind you that the next club meeting is on Friday. Hope to see you there!

4) SEND THE MESSAGE

Click on the Send button (⊟ Send). If necessary, ask your instructor for help in connecting to the Internet. The document window is removed and the message is sent.

5) OPEN DTP WORKSHOP

6) SEND THE DOCUMENT AS AN E-MAIL MESSAGE

    a. On the Standard Toolbar, click on the E-mail button (🖹). The address information entry boxes are displayed at the top of the window.
    b. In the To entry box, type office@lvp.com or an address specified by your instructor.
    c. In the Subject entry box, change the existing text to Workshop Information for You.
    d. Click on the Send a Copy button (⊟ Send a Copy). If necessary, ask your instructor for help in connecting to the Internet. After connecting to the Internet, the message is sent.

7) CLOSE DTP WORKSHOP

6.17 Creating Labels

Word allows you to easily print multiple labels that contain the same text. For example, you can create return address labels instead of writing your return address on envelopes.

When printing labels, special adhesive paper with multiple labels to a page is used in the printer. The Avery® brand of adhesive labels is widely used, and the dimensions of many of its labels have been included in Word. Therefore only the Avery product number needs to be selected to create labels in the appropriate format.

Return address labels are created by selecting the Envelopes and Labels command from the Tools menu, which displays a dialog box. Selecting the Labels tab displays the following options:

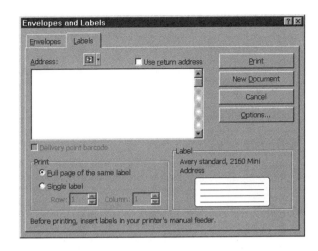

The text for the labels is entered in the large **Address** entry box. Next, clicking on the Options button displays the Label Options dialog box. Selecting the desired Avery label in the Product number list and then OK displays the Envelopes and Labels dialog box again. The labels are now ready to be placed into a document by selecting the New Document button. The labels can then be saved, formatted, and printed.

When the labels are ready to print, remember to insert the special adhesive paper into the printer before printing.

Practice 8

In this practice you will print return address labels on plain paper.

1) CREATE A NEW DOCUMENT

2) CREATE THE RETURN ADDRESS LABELS

Select Tools → Envelopes and Labels. A dialog box is displayed.
1. Select the Labels tab if the labels options are not already displayed.
2. Select the Options button. A dialog box is displayed.
   a. In the Product number list, scroll until 5267 - Return Address is displayed and then select it.
   b. Select OK to return to the labels options.
3. Type your first and last name in the large Address entry box and then press Enter.
4. Type your street address and then press Enter.
5. Type your city, state, and zip (or province and postal code).
6. Select the New Document button. The dialog box is removed, a new document is created, and the labels are displayed in the new document.

3) FORMAT THE LABELS

a. Select Edit → Select All. All of the text in the document is selected.
b. On the Formatting Toolbar, from the Font Size list select 9. All of the text is now 9 point and fits on the small return address labels.

4) SAVE, PRINT, AND CLOSE THE DOCUMENT

a. Save the document naming it My Return Labels.
b. Print a copy on plain paper.
c. Close My Return Labels.

6.18 Recording Macros

When creating documents, you may often repeat a series of steps to create a specific outcome. For example, every week a manager may use a table to display employee work hours. Word allows you to create macros to help automate repetitive tasks. A *macro* is a named series of recorded commands and actions that perform a specific task.

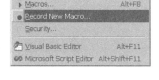

A macro can be recorded in Word by selecting the Record New Macro command from the Macro submenu in the Tools menu, which displays a dialog box:

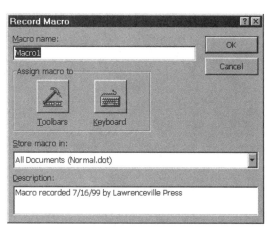

A name for the macro is typed in the Macro name entry box, and a description is typed in the Description entry box. Selecting OK begins the recording and the pointer changes to the shape.

The sequence of steps are recorded by simply selecting the desired commands and options as usual. During recording, the mouse can be used to select the commands and options in dialog boxes but cannot be used in the document. For example, to format bold text as part of the macro, the text must be highlighted using the keyboard and not the mouse.

While a macro is being recorded, the Stop Recording Toolbar ( ) is displayed. Click the Stop Recording button (■) to end recording after all the macro's steps have been performed. The Pause Recording button (‖●) can be clicked to interrupt the recording.

After recording a macro, it can be run by selecting the Macros command (Alt+F8) from the Macro submenu, which displays the Macros dialog box. Selecting the desired macro then the Run button runs the macro.

Macro Names

The name of a macro must begin with a letter, and can have up to 255 total letters, numbers, and underscore characters. Spaces and other punctuation are not allowed.

Practice 9

In this practice you will create a macro that inserts a formatted table structure into a document.

1) CREATE A NEW DOCUMENT

2) CREATE A MACRO

Select Tools → Macro → Record New Macro. A dialog box is displayed.

1. In the Macro name entry box, type TimeTable.
2. In the Description entry box, type Macro that inserts a formatted table structure, replacing the existing text.
3. Select OK to begin recording the steps. The pointer changes to the shape.

3) RECORD STEPS TO CREATE AND FORMAT THE TABLE

    a. Select Table → Insert → Table. A dialog box is displayed.
       1. In the Number of columns entry box, type 7 .
       2. In the Number of rows entry box, type 6.
       3. Select OK. The table structure is inserted and the cursor is in the first cell.
    b. Enter the following text in the first row of cells, using the Tab or arrow keys to move the cursor:

       Employee   Mon   Tue   Wed   Thu   Fri   Sat

    c. Enter the following employee names in the first column, using the down arrow key to move the cursor: Eklund, Lopez, Quinn, Rosen, Sladek.
    d. Using the arrow keys, move the cursor to any cell in the first row. (Do not use the mouse.)
    e. Select Table → Select → Row. The first row is highlighted.
    f. Format the highlighted row as bold and change the font size to 14 point.
    g. Using the arrow keys, place the cursor in the second cell in the second row.
    h. On the Stop Recording Toolbar, click on the Stop Recording button (■).
    i. Close the document without saving it.

4) OPEN EMPLOYEE HOURS

5) RUN THE MACRO

    a. Place the cursor in the second blank paragraph below the sentence that reads "For week starting 2/12."
    b. Select Tools → Macro → Macros. A dialog box is displayed.
       1. Select TimeTable in the Macro name list.
       2. Select Run. A formatted table is inserted into the document.
    c. Place the cursor in the second blank paragraph below the sentence that reads "For week starting 2/19."
    d. Run the TimeTable macro again.

6) SAVE, PRINT, AND THEN CLOSE THE MODIFIED EMPLOYEE HOURS

7) EXIT WORD

6.19 Where can you go from here?

The last four chapters have introduced you to the concepts of word processing. You can now create, edit, format, and print word processor documents. The word processor has other features not discussed in this text which you may want to explore using the online help.

A powerful feature of Word is its ability to integrate information stored in a database with a word processor document to produce personalized form letters. This process is called mail merge and is described in Chapter Fifteen. In addition, Chapter Eleven describes how to integrate spreadsheet data and charts into a document.

There are many different word processor programs available, such as WordPerfect and Works. Because you have learned how to use Word, you will easily be able to learn and use other word processors.

Chapter Summary

This chapter explained how to create table structures and introduced features that help organize and format long documents. Creating labels and macros were also introduced.

inserting a table

entering data in a table

Table structures created by Word can be inserted into a document to help organize information into rows and columns. The Insert Table button is used to insert a table structure at the current cursor position. Data is entered into a table by clicking in a desired cell and then typing the information. The cursor can be moved in the table structure using the Tab or arrow keys. A row, column, or table can be deleted by first highlighting it and then selecting the appropriate command from the Table menu.

character format
alignment
highlighting rows and columns

Character formatting can be applied to the data in the cells of a table structure. The alignment of data in cells can be changed using the alignment buttons on the Formatting Toolbar. Entire rows or columns can be highlighted by moving the pointer to the left of the row or the top of the column and clicking once. Multiple rows and columns can be highlighted by dragging the pointer.

changing the height and width of rows and columns

Column widths can be changed by dragging the right boundary of a column. Row heights can be changed in a similar manner. When the cursor is in a cell, the Insert Rows button can be used to insert a row. When a column is highlighted, the Insert Columns button can be used to insert a column. A row or column can be deleted by placing the cursor in a cell and then selecting the Row or Column command from the Delete submenu in the Table menu.

Special characters can be inserted into a document using the Symbol command from the Insert menu.

Hyphenation is used to smooth out very ragged right edges in left-aligned text and can lessen the space between words in justified text. The Hyphenation command from the Language submenu in the Tools menu is used to hyphenate text in a document.

Built-in styles can be applied to a selected paragraph by selecting a style from the Style collapsible list on the Formatting Toolbar. Headings are titles that separate the paragraphs of body text by topic.

headings
body text

Outline view displays specific heading levels and is used to modify the organization of a document. The different heading levels and body text are identified by indents and icons. Additional buttons on the Outlining Toolbar are displayed in Outline view that allow you to easily apply styles and move paragraphs.

Word can create a table of contents based on the built-in styles applied to a document's headings and subheadings. The Index and Tables command is used to insert a table of contents at the current cursor position. Each entry in a table of contents is a hyperlink to the corresponding heading. The table of contents can be updated after changes have been made to a document by selecting it and pressing the F9 key.

Dividing a document into different sections allows several different page formats to be applied to one document. The Break command is used to insert section breaks into a document. When using different section

A Guide to Microsoft Office 2000 Professional

headers and footers, the Same as Previous button on the Header and Footer Toolbar needs to be deselected. Different page numbering can be applied to the different sections by selecting the Format Page Number button, which displays the Page Number Format dialog box.

A hyperlink to Web pages can be added to a document by selecting the Hyperlink command. Clicking on a hyperlink in a document automatically connects your computer to the Internet and displays a Web page. Hyperlinks can also be added that link to another part of the same document, similar to the hyperlinks in a table of contents.

The advanced features of word processors allow for easy creation of newsletters. The first page of a newsletter contains the title area that contains publication information. Sections are used to format the newsletter with different page formats.

E-mail Message

 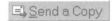

E-mail messages can be created by selecting the E-mail Message icon in the New Document dialog box. After typing the recipient's address in the To entry box and entering the message, clicking on the Send button connects the computer to the Internet and sends the message. An open document can also be sent as an e-mail message by clicking on the E-mail button on the Standard Toolbar, typing the address information, and clicking on the Send a Copy button.

Labels are created using the Envelopes and Labels command. Before printing labels, special adhesive paper needs to be inserted into the printer.

Macros can be useful in automating repetitive tasks. The Record New Macro command is used to record the series of steps needed to complete a task.

Vocabulary

Body The information being presented in a report.

Body text The main paragraphs in a document that present information.

Boundary The lines that separate cells in a table structure.

Built-in style A named set of character and paragraph formats.

Cell The intersection of a row and column in a table structure where data is entered.

Column Vertical cells in a table structure.

F9 key Displays a dialog box that allows the user to update the table of contents.

Front matter The information that comes before the body of a report.

Headings Titles that separate the paragraphs of body text by topic.

Hyphenating Divides a word, when necessary, at the end of a line with a hyphen (-) so part of the word wraps to the next line.

Macro Named series of commands and actions that perform a specific task.

Normal style The 12 point, Times New Roman, left-aligned default style applied to text.

Outline view Allows you to easily view and modify the organization of a document.

Row Horizontal cells in a table structure.

Section break Where one section of a document ends and another begins.

Sections Parts of a document that can contain different page formatting.

Table of contents Lists the headings and subheadings of a document and their corresponding page numbers.

Table structure Rows and columns inserted by Word to help arrange information into a table.

Title area A section at the top of a newsletter that contains information about the publication.

Word Commands and Buttons

Break command Displays a dialog box that allows the user to insert a section break at the current cursor position. Found in the Insert menu.

Collapse button Hides the body text under the heading containing the cursor. Found in the Outlining Toolbar.

Column command Highlights the column containing the cursor in a table structure. Found in the Select submenu in the Table menu.

Columns command Deletes a highlighted column or columns in a table structure. Found in the Delete submenu in the Table menu.

Demote button Applies the next lower level style to the paragraph containing the cursor. Found in the Outlining Toolbar.

Demote to Body Text button Applies the Normal style to the paragraph containing the cursor. Found in the Outlining Toolbar.

E-mail button Allows the user to send the currently open document as an e-mail message. Found on the Standard Toolbar.

Envelopes and Labels command Displays a dialog box that allows the user to create and print labels. Found in the Tools menu.

Expand button Displays the body text under the heading containing the cursor. Found in the Outlining Toolbar.

Format Page Number button Displays a dialog box that allows the user to format the numbering and change the starting number. Found on the Header and Footer Toolbar.

Hyperlink **command** Displays a dialog box that allows the user to insert a hyperlink at the current cursor position. Found in the Insert menu. The Insert Hyperlink button ( ) on the Standard Toolbar can be used instead of the command.

Hyphenation **command** Displays a dialog box that allows the user to hyphenate a document. Found in the Language submenu in the Tools menu.

Index and Tables **command** Displays a dialog box that allows the user to insert a table of contents at the current cursor position. Found in the Insert menu.

Insert Columns button Adds a column to the left of the selected column in a table. Found on the Standard Toolbar when a column is highlighted.

Insert Page Number button Inserts a page number at the current cursor position. Found on the Header and Footer Toolbar.

Insert Rows button Adds a row above the selected row in a table. Found on the Standard Toolbar when a column is highlighted.

Insert Table button Allows the user to insert a table structure at the current cursor position by highlighting the desired number of cells.

Macros **command** Displays a dialog box that allows the user to select and run a macro. Found in the Macro submenu in the Tools menu.

Move Down button Moves the paragraph containing the cursor to after the preceding paragraph. Found in the Outlining Toolbar.

Move Up button Moves the paragraph containing the cursor to before the preceding paragraph. Found in the Outlining Toolbar.

Outline **command** Displays a document in Outline view. Found in the View menu.

Pause Recording button Temporarily stops the recording of steps for a macro. Found on the Stop Recording Toolbar.

Promote button Applies the next higher level style to the paragraph containing the cursor. Found in the Outlining Toolbar.

Record New Macro **command** Displays a dialog box that allows the user to name a macro and begin recording it. Found in the Macro submenu in the Tools menu.

Row **command** Highlights the row containing the cursor in a table structure. Found in the Select submenu in the Table menu.

Rows **command** Deletes a highlighted row or rows in a table structure. Found in the Delete submenu in the Table menu.

Same as Previous button Deselected to allow for different section headers or footers. Found on the Header and Footer Toolbar.

Send a Copy **button** Connects your computer to the Internet and sends the currently open document as an e-mail message.

Send **button** Connects your computer to the Internet and sends an e-mail message.

Show All Headings button Switches between displaying all the heading levels and body text or only heading levels. Found in the Outlining Toolbar.

Show Heading buttons Displays only those heading levels that correspond to that button number and higher. Text in lower levels is hidden. Found in the Outlining Toolbar.

Stop Recording button Ends the recording of a macro after the all the steps have been performed.

Style **command** Displays a dialog box that contain information about all built-in styles. Allows the user to apply a style to the selected paragraph. Found in the Format menu.

Symbol **command** Displays a dialog box that allows the user to insert a special character into a document. Found in the Insert menu.

Table **command** Displays a dialog box that allows the user to insert a table structure by entering the desired number of rows and columns. Found in the Insert submenu in the Table menu.

Review Questions

Sections 6.1 — 6.3

1. a) What are table structures?
    b) What is a cell?

2. List the steps required to insert a table structure with four columns and three rows into a Word document.

3. List two ways to move the cursor in a table structure.

4. List the steps required to right align the data in the first column of a table structure and then bold the data in the first row.

5. a) List the steps required to insert a row between rows three and four of a table structure.
    b) List the steps required to insert a column between column one and two of a table structure.

6. a) List the steps required to increase the width of the second column in a five column table structure.
    b) What happens to the row height when the font size of the data stored in that row is increased?

Sections 6.4 — 6.8

7. List the steps required to insert one bullet character at the beginning of a paragraph.

8. a) What is hyphenation?
    b) What does hyphenation do to justified text?

9. a) What is a built-in style?
    b) What are headings?
    c) What is body text?
    d) What formatting does the Normal style apply to a paragraph?

10. List the steps required to apply the Heading 2 built-in style to a paragraph.

11. What command is used to view all the built-in styles?

12. What is Outline view used for?

13. List three buttons on the Outlining Toolbar and describe what they are used for.

14. a) What does clicking on the plus sign next to a heading do?
    b) How can this be useful?

15. List the steps required to only print the first three heading levels in a document.

16. a) What is a table of contents?
    b) List the steps required to insert a table of contents at the current cursor position.

17. a) What happens to the pointer when it is moved over an entry in the table of contents?
    b) What happens when the entry is clicked on?

Sections 6.9 — 6.11

18. Why would sections be used in report?

19. What is the difference between Next page and Continuous section breaks?

20. List the steps required to insert a Next page section break at the current cursor position.

21. How can a document have Gift Catalog as a header on page 1 and Gift Catalog - Jewelry as a header on page 2?

22. List the steps required to have Roman numeral page numbers in a footer on pages 1 through 4 of a document and Arabic page numbers in a tooter on pages 5 through 7 in the same document.

23. List the steps required to start page numbering at 1 in the second section of a document that actually starts on the third page.

Sections 6.12 — 6.19

24. List the steps required to insert a hyperlink to a Web page at the current cursor position.

25. List the steps required to insert a hyperlink to a heading in the same document at the current cursor position.

26. a) What is the title area of a newsletter?
    b) Why is a newsletter document divided into sections?

A Guide to Microsoft Office 2000 Professional

27. List the steps required to create and send an e-mail message from Word.

28. List the steps required to send the currently open document as an e-mail message.

29. What command is used to create labels?

30. What type of paper is used to print labels?

31. a) Describe a useful macro.
    b) List the steps required to create the macro described in part (a).
    c) List the steps required to run the macro created in part (b).

Exercises

Exercise 1 ————————————————————————————SCIENCE MUSEUM

The SCIENCE MUSEUM document last modified in Chapter Five, Exercise 9 needs a table that displays the hours of operations. Open SCIENCE MUSEUM and complete the following steps:

a) Insert a table structure with three rows and three columns (a 3 x 3 table) in the blank paragraph after the sentence that begins "The hours of operation...."

b) Enter the following data into the table starting in the first cell:

Day	Open	Close
Weekdays	9:00 a.m.	8:00 p.m.
Sunday	12:00 p.m.	5:00 p.m.

c) Bold the text in the first row.

d) Decrease the width of the columns appropriately.

e) Insert a row between the Weekdays and Sunday rows.

f) Enter the following data into the new row:

Saturday   10:00 a.m.   7:00 p.m.

g) Resize the clip art at the top of the document as necessary so that all the information fits on one page.

h) Save the modified SCIENCE MUSEUM and print a copy.

Exercise 2 ———————————————————————————— ELEMENTS

The ELEMENTS document contains information on elements and chemical formulas. Open ELEMENTS and complete the following steps:

a) Insert a table structure with four rows and three columns (a 4 x 3 table) in the blank paragraph after the "Alkali Metals" subheading. Make sure there is a blank line before and after the table.

b) Enter the following data into the table starting in the first cell:

Element	Symbol	Atomic Number
Lithium	Li	3
Sodium	Na	11
Potassium	K	19

c) Insert a table structure with five rows and three columns (a 5 x 3 table) in the blank paragraph after the "Nonmetals" subheading. Make sure there is a blank line before and after the table.

d) Enter the following data into the table starting in the first cell:

Element	Symbol	Atomic Number
Carbon	C	6
Nitrogen	N	7
Oxygen	O	8
Fluorine	F	9

e) Insert a table structure with four rows and three columns (a 4 x 3 table) in the blank paragraph after the "Noble Gases" subheading. Make sure there is a blank line before and after the table.

f) Enter the following data into the table starting in the first cell:

Element	Symbol	Atomic Number
Helium	He	2
Neon	Ne	10
Argon	Ar	18

g) Insert a table structure with four rows and two columns (a 4 x 2 table) in the blank paragraph after the last paragraph in the document. Make sure there are blank lines before and after the table.

h) Enter the following data into the table starting in the first cell:

Compound	Formula
Water	H_2O
Sodium Chloride	NaCl
Ammonia	NH_3

i) Bold and increase the size of the text in the first row of all the tables.

j) Decrease the width of the columns in each table appropriately.

k) Apply the Heading 1 style to the "Elements" and "Chemical Formulas" headings.

l) Apply the Heading 2 style to the "Alkali Metals," "Nonmetals," and "Noble Gases" subheadings.

m) Create a header with your name right aligned.

n) Print a copy of the first and second headings in Outline view.

o) Save the modified ELEMENTS and print a copy in Page Layout view.

Exercise 3 ——————————————————— SOLAR SYSTEM

The SOLAR SYSTEM document contains a report on our solar system. Open SOLAR SYSTEM and complete the following steps:

a) Have Word hyphenate the document.

b) Apply the Heading 1 style to the "Introduction," "Our Solar System," and "Conclusion" headings.

c) Apply the Heading 2 style to the "Planets," "Objects," and "Stars" subheadings.

d) Apply the Heading 3 style to each planet subheading and the "Meteoroids" and "Comets" subheadings.

e) Move the topic "Objects" (including the subheadings and text underneath it) to after the "Stars" subheading and text.

f) Print one copy of the first, second, and third level headings in Outline view.

g) Have Word insert a Formal table of contents before the paragraph marker at the top of page 2. Include a title for the table of contents and format it appropriately.

h) Insert a Next page section break after the table of contents you just inserted.

i) Create a section 1 footer with your name followed by a small Roman numeral page number center aligned. No page number should appear on the first page in section 1.

j) Create a section 2 footer with your name followed by an Arabic page number starting at 1 and center aligned.

k) Update the table of contents to reflect the new page numbering.

l) Save the modified SOLAR SYSTEM and print a copy.

Exercise 4 ——————————————————— DTP WORKSHOP

The DTP WORKSHOP document last modified in the practices of Chapter Five needs formatting applied to different sections. Open DTP WORKSHOP and complete the following steps:

a) Insert a Continuous section break before the heading "Our Computers."

b) Insert a Continuous section break in the blank paragraph before the quote that begins "To seek knowledge…" at the end of the document. The document now contains two sections.

c) Format section 2 as two columns.

d) Save the modified DTP WORKSHOP and print a copy.

Exercise 5 ——————————————————— HONORS HANDOUT

The HONORS HANDOUT document contains information on different honors clubs at Ivy University. Open HONORS HANDOUT and complete the following steps:

a) Insert a table structure with four rows and four columns (a 4 x 4 table) in the blank paragraph after the last sentence under the "Fraternities" subheading. Make sure there is a blank line after the table.

b) Enter the following data into the table starting in the first cell, using the Symbol command to insert the Greek letters into the table:

Name	Greek Letters	College	Members
Delta Epsilon Phi	ΔΕΦ	Business	45
Lambda Pi Sigma	ΛΠΣ	Liberal Arts	56
Xi Psi Zeta	ΞΨΖ	Engineering	34

c) Bold and increase the size of the text in the first row.

d) Decrease the width of the columns appropriately.

e) Apply the Heading 1 style to the "Honors Program," "Honors Societies," and "Honors Classes" headings.

A Guide to Microsoft Office 2000 Professional

f) Apply the Heading 2 style to the "Clubs" and "Fraternities" subheadings.

g) Apply the Heading 3 style to the following subheadings:

Business Honors Society   Delta Epsilon Phi
Honors Computer Club   Lambda Pi Sigma
Science Club of Honors   Xi Psi Zeta

h) Have Word insert a Formal table of contents before the paragraph marker at the top of page 2. Include a title for the table of contents and format it appropriately.

i) Insert a Next page section break after the table of contents you just inserted.

j) Create a section 1 footer with your name followed by a small Roman numeral page number center aligned. No page number should appear on the first page in section 1.

k) Create a section 2 footer with your name followed by an Arabic page number starting at 1 and center aligned.

l) Update the table of contents to reflect the new page numbering.

m) Save the modified HONORS HANDOUT and print a copy.

Exercise 6

Create a new e-mail message with a paragraph in the message area describing your favorite restaurant. Type the text Great Food as the Subject. Send the message to office@lvp.com or to an address specified by your instructor.

Exercise 7 — PROPOSAL

Send the PROPOSAL document last modified in Chapter Five, Exercise 7 as an e-mail message to office@lvp.com or to an address specified by your instructor. Type the text Proposal for Research as the Subject.

Exercise 8

Create a sheet of labels with the appropriate information on each label depending on the type of label you create. Use regular paper to print the labels.

Exercise 9

Documents often require page numbering in the footer. Create a macro that creates a footer similar to Page 1 center aligned. Name the macro PageNumberFooter.

Advanced
Exercise 10 ———————————————————————— My Favorite Recipe

Recipes in a cookbook often appear with different page formats. In a new document enter your favorite recipe. Format the document into three sections as follows:

Section 1: include the name of the recipe, your name, and a clip art graphic

Section 2: list the ingredients for the recipe in the order they will be used, and format the section with two columns

Section 3: a numbered list of the recipe steps

Save the document naming it My Favorite Recipe and print a copy.

Advanced
Exercise 11 ———————————————————— Technology Research

Research a technology topic using the Internet. Write a report based on the information you found. The report should include a title page and table of contents in addition to the body of the report that uses footnotes when appropriate. Use the word processing features you learned in this chapter and previous chapters. Include at least two hyperlinks, and create your own style using the Style dialog box. Save the report naming it Technology Research and print a copy.

Advanced
Exercise 12 ———————————————————— Deluxe Newsletter

Create a four page newsletter using the information presented in Section 6.14. Format the newsletter with at least three different sections and at least two hyperlinks. Save the newsletter naming it Deluxe Newsletter and print a copy.

Advanced
Exercise 13 ———————————————————————————

Create a macro that saves the open document, prints a copy, and then closes the document. Save the macro with an appropriate name and description.

A Guide to Microsoft Office 2000 Professional

All

Print Pre<u>v</u>iew

Page Set<u>u</u>p

C<u>e</u>lls

<u>D</u>own

<u>R</u>ight

Chapter Seven Objectives

After completing this chapter you will be able to:

1. Define what a spreadsheet is.
2. Identify the different parts of the spreadsheet window.
3. Create a spreadsheet and enter data into it.
4. Save, close, and print a spreadsheet.
5. Create headers and footers in a spreadsheet.
6. Change the width of columns.
7. Select cell ranges by highlighting blocks of cells.
8. Format a spreadsheet.
9. Use formulas to perform calculations.
10. Use cell references in formulas.
11. Use the SUM, AVERAGE, and ROUND functions.
12. Enter formulas by pointing.
13. Show the formulas in cells.
14. Copy adjacent cells and formulas.
15. Understand relative cell references.

The History of the Spreadsheet

The earliest double-entry books, used to record business transactions, are from the 14th century. The transactions were recorded using a pencil and paper with the data in rows and columns. This method was essentially unchanged until the introduction of the PC in the 70s. In 1978 Dan Bricklin, a graduate student at the Harvard School of Business, and his friend Bob Frankston, developed the first spreadsheet application software called VisiCalc. VisiCalc, written for the Apple II, was one of the most widely used software products during the 80s and helped change how businesses did business. In 1983, Jonathan Sachs and Mitchell Kapor, founders of Lotus Development Corporation, introduced Lotus 1-2-3 for the IBM PC. Lotus 1-2-3 integrated operations of a spreadsheet with graphics to produce charts, and became one of the most successful application software products of all time. Today, spreadsheet applications are a standard business tool.

$\mathbf{T}$his chapter introduces Microsoft Excel, a powerful spreadsheet application used to store numeric data and perform calculations.

7.1 What is a Spreadsheet?

A *spreadsheet* is rows and columns of data. The term comes from the field of accounting where business activities were tracked on large sheets of paper that spread out to form a "spreadsheet." Today, a spreadsheet application is used to electronically store data. For example, the spreadsheet below keeps track of grades:

	A	B	C	D	E	F
1	Name	Test 1	Test 2	Test 3	Test 4	Student Average
2		9/12/01	10/10/01	11/14/01	12/12/01	
3	Demps, K.	85	73	88	92	84.5
4	McCallister, T.	92	88	85	91	89.0
5	Matos, A.	72	63	67	72	68.5
6	Smith, L.	87	92	85	93	89.3
7	Sun, L.	94	91	93	84	90.5
8	Adams, V.	70	74	80	83	76.8

In the spreadsheet above, rows 3 through 8 store the name and grades for six students. For example, the name Demps, K., the grades 85, 73, 88, 92, and the average 84.5 form a row. Columns B through E each store a title, date, and all of the grades for a single test. For example, the title Test 1, date 9/12/01, and grades from 85 to 70 form a column.

The spreadsheet is set up to make calculations such as student averages. These averages will automatically be recalculated if a grade is changed. These are the primary advantages of a spreadsheet application; the ability to perform calculations on data and to automatically recalculate when changes are made to the data

7.2 Creating a New Excel Spreadsheet

workbook

Blank
Workbook

Microsoft Excel is the spreadsheet application in the Microsoft Office package. In Excel, spreadsheets are called *workbooks*. Selecting the New Office Document command from the Start menu on the Windows Taskbar displays the New Office Document dialog box. Clicking on the Blank Workbook icon and then selecting the OK button starts Excel and creates a new, empty spreadsheet:

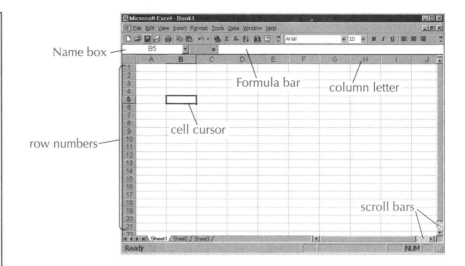

Name box

Formula bar

column letter

cell cursor

row numbers

scroll bars

Creating and Opening a Spreadsheet

If Excel has already been started, the **New** command from the **File** menu can be used to display the New dialog box. The **Open** command from the **File** menu can be used to open an existing spreadsheet.

The New button (⬜) on the Standard Toolbar can also be used to create a new spreadsheet and the Open button (📂) can be used to open an existing spreadsheet when Excel is already stared.

Cell Reference vs. Cell Contents

Each cell is identified by its cell reference, such as A3 or C2, and each cell can contain data, such as the number 5 or the text Paul. This system is similar to mailboxes at the post office where each box (or cell) has a name and can store information. Be careful not to confuse the cell reference with the data it stores.

Formula Bar

If the Formula bar is not displayed, select the **Formula Bar** command from the **View** menu to display it.

- **Columns** are identified by letters at the top of the spreadsheet. In Excel they are lettered from A to Z and then AA to IV for a total of 256 columns. In the spreadsheet above, only columns A through J are displayed.

- **Rows** are identified by numbers down the left side of the spreadsheet. In Excel they are numbered from 1 to 65,536. In the spreadsheet above, only rows 1 through 22 are displayed.

- **Scroll bars** are used to display other rows and columns that are not currently displayed.

- **Cell** is the intersection of a row and column. Each cell can store a single item of data. In the spreadsheet above, the cell in column B row 5 is selected. When a cell is *selected*, its corresponding column letter and row number appear darker then the other column letters and row numbers. Data can be entered into a selected cell only.

- **Cell reference** is the column letter and row number that identifies a single cell. For example, the cell reference of the selected cell above is B5.

- **Cell cursor** is a solid outline that can be moved to select a cell. In the spreadsheet above, the cell cursor is on cell B5.

- **Name box** shows the current location of the cell cursor which in the above spreadsheet is B5.

- **Formula bar** displays the contents of the selected cell.

7.3 Moving the Cell Cursor

 When the mouse pointer is moved onto the spreadsheet, it changes from an arrow shape to a plus sign (✚). Clicking the plus sign on a cell moves the cell cursor to that cell.

scrolling   If the desired cell is not displayed, the scroll bars can be used to bring hidden rows and columns into view. Clicking once on one of the scroll arrows moves the spreadsheet one row or column in the direction of the arrow. Holding the mouse button down on the scroll arrow continues the scroll. Dragging the scroll box moves the rows and columns a greater distance. Note that the cell cursor does not move when the scroll bars are used.

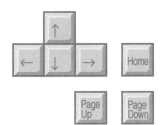

The keyboard can also be used to move the cell cursor. Pressing an arrow key once moves the cell cursor either up or down one row, or one cell to the left or right, automatically scrolling the spreadsheet as necessary. Pressing the Home key moves the cell cursor to the first cell in the row it is in. Pressing the Page Up or Page Down key moves the cell cursor to the cell one screen up or down, respectively.

7.4 Entering Data into a Spreadsheet

labels, values
times/dates

Spreadsheets can store three types of data: labels, values, and times/dates. *Labels* are text and cannot be used in calculations. *Values* are numeric and can be used in calculations. *Times/dates* are either a time, such as 12:10 PM, or a date, such as 6/4/01. A time/date entry may be used in some calculations. In the grade book spreadsheet, student names and titles (such as Demps, K. and Test 1) are labels, a grade (such as 90) is a value, and a date (such as 9/12/01) is a time/date. Labels, values, and times/dates appear differently in spreadsheet cells:

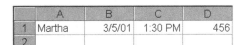

	A	B	C	D
1	Martha	3/5/01	1:30 PM	456
2				

Labels are left aligned and values and times/dates
are right aligned in a cell

Data is entered into a cell by selecting that cell and typing the data. As data is typed, it appears in the cell and on the Formula bar, and the Cancel and Enter buttons are activated:

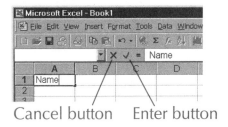

Cancel button   Enter button

Clicking on the *Enter button* (✓) enters the data and leaves the cell cursor on the selected cell. Clicking on the *Cancel button* (✗) cancels data entry and restores the cell's original contents. There are also keys on the keyboard that are used to perform similar actions:

- Pressing the *Enter key* enters the data and then selects the next cell in the column.

- Pressing the *Tab key* enters the data and then selects the next cell in the row.

- Pressing an *arrow key* enters the data and then selects the next cell in the direction of the arrow key.

- Pressing the *Escape key* cancels data entry and restores the cell's original contents.

If a mistake is made when entering data, it can be corrected by selecting the cell and typing the correct data. The new data then replaces any previous data. If the mistake is noticed while typing the data, the Backspace key can be used to delete one character at a time.

Date Interpretation

When entering dates using the MM/DD/YY format, Excel interprets years 00 – 29 as the years 2000 through 2029 and years 30 – 99 as the years 1930 through 1999. The Formula bar always displays the four-digit year even when the cell displays a two-digit year.

Checking the Spelling

The spelling checker can help to ensure accurate spelling of text in a spreadsheet. Text is spell-checked using the Spelling button ( ) on the Standard Toolbar or by pressing the F7 key. Checking begins at the current cell cursor position. Cells that do not contain text are ignored. Highlighting a portion of the spreadsheet (see Section 7.9) before spell checking checks only the highlighted section.

7.5 Editing Cell Contents

Editing in a Cell

Double-clicking on a cell displays a blinking cursor in the cell allowing characters to be entered or deleted.

Selecting a cell and then pressing the F2 key displays a blinking cursor in the cell and the contents can then be edited.

A cell's data can be edited by first selecting the cell to display its contents on the Formula bar. Next, clicking the pointer on the Formula bar displays a blinking cursor allowing characters to be entered or deleted. When the data has been corrected, the Enter button is clicked or the Enter key is pressed.

The contents of a selected cell can be erased by pressing the Delete key. Selecting the All command from the Clear submenu in the Edit menu erases a selected cell's contents and its formatting. If a cell is cleared by mistake, immediately selecting the Undo command (Ctrl+Z) from the Edit menu or the Undo button ( ) on the Standard Toolbar restores the cell's contents. You can undo the last 16 actions performed.

Practice 1

In this practice you will create a grade book spreadsheet.

1) CREATE A NEW SPREADSHEET

    a. On the Taskbar, click on the Start button. A menu is displayed.
    b. Select the New Office Document command. A dialog box is displayed.
        1. Click on the Blank Workbook icon to select it.
        2. Select OK. Excel starts and a new, empty spreadsheet is created.

2) ENTER THE COLUMN TITLES IN ROW 1

    a. Note that the cell cursor is on cell A1. Type Name and then click on the Enter button (✓). Cell A1 now contains the label Name. Note that the Formula bar displays the currently selected cell's contents.
    b. Press the right-arrow key to move the cell cursor to cell B1, then type Test 1.
    c. Press the Tab key. The label is entered and the cell cursor is moved to the next cell in the row, C1.
    d. Type Test 2.
    e. Press the Tab key. The label is entered and the cell cursor is moved to the next cell in the row, D1.
    f. Continue this procedure to place the headings Test 3 in cell D1 and Test 4 in cell E1.

3) ENTER THE TEST DATES

    a. Select cell B2 and type the date 9/12/01. Click on the Enter button. Note that Excel right aligns a date when entered into a cell.
    b. Select cell C2 and type the date 10/10/01. Press the Tab key. The cell cursor is moved to the next cell in the row, D2.
    c. Enter the date 11/14/01 in cell D2 and the date 12/12/01 in cell E2.

4) ENTER THE STUDENT NAMES AND GRADES

Enter the following labels and values starting in cell A3:

Demps, K.	85	73	88	92
McCallister, T.	92	88	85	91
Matos, A.	72	63	67	72
Smith, L.	87	92	85	93
Sun, L.	94	91	93	84
Adams, V.	70	74	80	85

A Guide to Microsoft Office 2000 Professional

5) EDIT A GRADE

a. Select cell E8.
b. On the Formula bar, move the pointer to the right of the number 5 and click once to place the cursor.
c. Press the Backspace key once to delete the number 5.
d. Type a 3 and then press Enter. The grade is now an 83.

Check – Your spreadsheet should look similar to:

	A	B	C	D	E
1	Name	Test 1	Test 2	Test 3	Test 4
2		9/12/01	10/10/01	11/14/01	12/12/01
3	Demps, K.	85	73	88	92
4	McCalliste	92	88	85	91
5	Matos, A.	72	63	67	72
6	Smith, L.	87	92	85	93
7	Sun, L.	94	91	93	84
8	Adams, V.	70	74	80	83

7.6 Saving and Closing a Spreadsheet

Selecting the Save command (Ctrl+S) from the File menu or clicking on the Save button on the Standard Toolbar () saves the spreadsheet. After saving a spreadsheet, it should be closed if no longer needed by using the Close command from the File menu.

7.7 Previewing and Printing a Spreadsheet

The Print Preview command from the File menu or the Print Preview button () on the Standard Toolbar is used to view the spreadsheet as it will appear when printed. A spreadsheet is printed by selecting the Print command (Ctrl+P) from the File menu which displays a dialog box. Selecting the OK button in the dialog box prints the portion of the spreadsheet that contains data. A spreadsheet can also be printed by clicking on the Print button () on the Standard Toolbar. When the Print button is used, the Print dialog box is not displayed and one copy of the spreadsheet is printed using the default settings. You should always save the spreadsheet before printing.

gridlines

row and column headings

Gridlines and row and column headings can make a spreadsheet printout easier to read. *Gridlines* are solid lines that mark off the rows and columns, similar to what appears in Excel. *Row* and *column headings* are the row numbers and column letters. Selecting the Page Setup command from the File menu displays the Page Setup dialog box. Selecting the Sheet tab displays the Gridlines and Row and column headings options. Selecting these options and then OK will display gridlines and row and column headings when the spreadsheet is previewed or printed.

Dotted Lines

After print previewing a spreadsheet, dotted lines appear on the spreadsheet. The dotted lines indicate where one page ends and the next begins. These lines also appear after printing a spreadsheet.

7.8 Creating Headers and Footers

Information such as your name, the date, or the file name can be included in a spreadsheet's header or footer for more informative print-outs. A header or footer is added to a spreadsheet by first selecting the Page Setup command from the File menu, then the Header/Footer tab to display header and footer options:

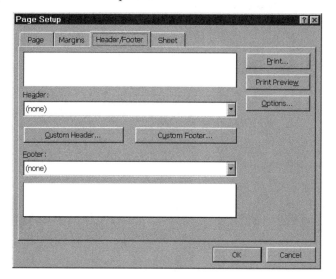

The Header and Footer collapsible lists contain preset options to choose from. Selecting the Custom Header or Custom Footer buttons displays another dialog box where header or footer text can be entered. For example, selecting the Custom Header button displays the following dialog box:

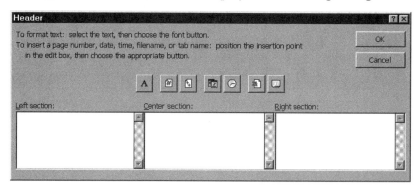

Enter text in the entry boxes to create a header

In the dialog box, text typed in the Left section, Center section, or Right section entry boxes is left, center, or right aligned in the header, respectively. Buttons in the dialog box are used to insert codes at the cursor position:

- Page Number button (#) inserts the current page number.
- Total Pages button ( ) inserts the total number of pages.
- Date button ( ) inserts the current date.
- Time button ( ) inserts the current time.
- File Name button ( ) inserts the filename.

When the spreadsheet is previewed or printed, the codes are replaced with the appropriate information.

Additional Header and Footer Options

The Font button (A) is used to format the text entered in the entry boxes and the Sheet Name button ( ) is used to insert the sheet name. Sheets are discussed in Chapter Nine.

A Guide to Microsoft Office 2000 Professional

Practice 2

In this practice you will add headers and footers to the spreadsheet created in Practice 1 and save it.

1) CREATE A HEADER AND A FOOTER

Select File → Page Setup. A dialog box is displayed.
1. Select the Header/Footer tab if those options are not already displayed.
2. Select the Custom Header button. The Header dialog box is displayed.
   a. Click once in the Center section entry box to place the cursor.
   b. Click on the Date button ( ). The code &[Date] is placed in the box.
   c. Select OK. The dialog box is removed.
3. Select the Custom Footer button. The Footer dialog box is displayed.
   a. Place the cursor in the Right section entry box then type your name.
   b. Select OK. The dialog box is removed.
4. Select OK. The dialog box is removed.

2) PREVIEW THE SPREADSHEET

a. Select File → Print Preview. The print preview window is displayed with the portion of the spreadsheet containing data. Note the header and footer. However, also notice how it is difficult to read the spreadsheet because there are no gridlines or row and column headings.
b. Select Close to return to the spreadsheet window.
c. Select File → Page Setup. A dialog box is displayed.
   1. Select the Sheet tab to display different options.
   2. Select the Gridlines option.
   3. Select the Row and column headings option.
   4. Select OK. The dialog box is removed.
d. On the Standard Toolbar, click on the Print Preview button ( ). Note how much easier the spreadsheet is to read.
e. Select Close to return to the spreadsheet window.

3) SAVE AND THEN PRINT THE SPREADSHEET

a. Select File → Save. A dialog box is displayed.
   1. In the File name entry box, type Grades.
   2. In the Save in collapsible list, select the appropriate folder.
   3. Select Save. The spreadsheet is saved and the dialog box is removed.
b. Select File → Print. A dialog box is displayed.
   1. Select OK to print the spreadsheet. The printout contains only the portion of the spreadsheet that contains data.

Resizing Columns

A column can also be resized by selecting the Width command from the Column submenu in the Format menu. Then in the displays dialog box, type the desired width in the Column width entry box and select OK.

Multiple columns can be resized at once by selecting the columns and then dragging the boundary of one of the columns or selecting the Width command.

7.9 Changing a Column's Width

A column's width can affect the way Excel displays numeric data. If a cell is not wide enough to display its value, scientific notation is used. For example, the value 123456789012 is displayed as 1.23457E+11. Labels are displayed in their entirety until they encounter another cell containing data.

A column's width is changed by dragging the column's right boundary. Pointing to the *boundary*, the bar separating the column letters at the top of the spreadsheet, changes the pointer shape to a double-headed arrow:

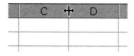

Dragging the boundary changes column C's width

Dragging the boundary to the right increases the width of the column, and dragging to the left decreases the width. Note that the width of single cells cannot be changed, only the width of whole columns can be changed.

Another technique for resizing a column is to double-click on the column's right boundary. This resizes a column so that it is just wide enough to display the data it contains.

7.10 Highlighting Cells

highlighted block

Adjacent spreadsheet cells can be selected together to form a *highlighted block*. A block of cells is highlighted by dragging the pointer from one cell to another:

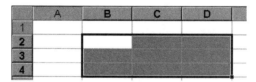

The mouse pointer was placed on cell B2 and then dragged to cell D4 to create this highlighted block

Another way of creating a highlighted block is by first selecting the starting cell, then holding down the Shift key and clicking the mouse pointer on the last cell in the block. An entire row or column can be selected by clicking on the row number or column letter. Clicking on the box above row 1 and to the left of column A selects the entire spreadsheet.

7.11 Formatting Alignments and Fonts

Formatting is usually applied to cells so that the data they contain is easier to understand. Formatting does not change the data stored in a cell, only the way it is displayed.

Unless formatted otherwise, cells containing labels are left aligned, and values and times/dates are right aligned. For this reason, labels and values displayed in the same column do not line up. For example, the test labels and dates in the Grades spreadsheet do not align in the column.

Selecting the C̲ells command from the F̲ormat menu displays the Format Cells dialog box, and selecting the Alignment tab displays alignment options:

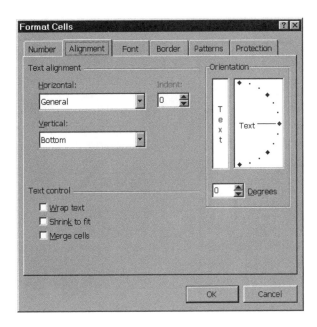

Selecting the Left, Center, or Right option from the Horizontal collapsible list and then OK changes the alignment of the selected cell accordingly. The Align Left (▤), Center (▤), and Align Right (▤) buttons on the Formatting Toolbar can also be used to change the alignment of a selected cell.

Selecting the Font tab in the Format Cells dialog box displays options for changing the font, font style, and size of the data in a selected cell. Font and font size can also be changed by selecting the desired format from the Font and Font Size boxes on the Standard Toolbar. The Bold (**B**), Italic (*I*), and Underline (U) buttons on the Formatting Toolbar can also be used to apply formatting.

7.12 Formatting Numeric Data

A numeric value is automatically formatted if a $, %, or a decimal position is included with the number. For example, entering $45.67 in a cell formats that cell to display any number entered in it with a dollar sign and 2 decimal places. If 34 is then entered in that cell, $34.00 is automatically displayed. Negative amounts will be displayed in red and inside parentheses. Similarly, entering 45% in a cell formats that cell to display any number entered in it with a percent sign and 0 decimal places. If 55.3 is then entered in that cell, 55% is automatically displayed.

Formatting can also be applied to the value in a selected cell by executing the Cells command (Ctrl+1) from the Format menu, which displays the Format Cells dialog box. Selecting the Number tab in the dialog box displays the options shown on the next page:

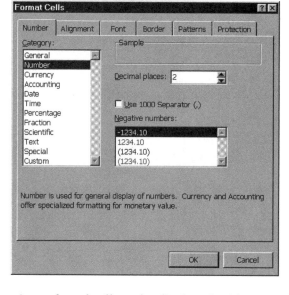

Number

The values in a selected cell can be displayed with a specific number of decimal places by selecting the Number option and then typing the desired number of decimal places in the Decimal places entry box. For large numbers, the Use 1000 Separator (,) option displays the value stored in a cell with separating commas, such as 1,000,000. Pound signs (####) are displayed if a cell is not wide enough to display the formatted number.

Currency

The Currency option displays the value stored in a cell with a dollar sign and two decimal places. The number of decimal places can be changed in the Decimal places entry box. Negative amounts are displayed with a preceding negative sign (–). The Accounting option displays the value stored in a cell with the dollar sign and decimal point lined up in a column. Selecting the $ button on the Formatting Toolbar is the same as selecting the Accounting option.

Percentage

The Percentage option displays the value stored in a cell as a percentage with 2 decimal places. For example, a cell storing the value 0.15 formatted as percent displays 15.00%. The number of decimal places can be changed in the Decimal places entry box. As with the number format, currency and percent do not change the value that is stored in the selected cell, only how that value is displayed. The % button on the Formatting Toolbar formats the value in a cell as a percentage with no decimal places.

Time/date

Time/date values can also be formatted by selecting one of the many Date or Time options in the Format Cells dialog box.

Practice 3

In this practice you will format the Grades spreadsheet. Open Grades if it is not already displayed.

1) BOLD THE NAME LABEL

    a. Select cell A1.
    b. On the Formatting Toolbar, click on the Bold button (**B**). The label is now bold.

2) WIDEN COLUMN A BY DRAGGING

    Note that the label in cell A4 is cut off because the column is too narrow to display it entirely.

    a. Point to the boundary between columns A and B. The pointer changes to a double-headed arrow ().

b. Drag the boundary to the right approximately halfway across column B. Column A should be wide enough to display the entire label in cell A4. If not, drag the column boundary farther to the right.

3) RIGHT ALIGN AND BOLD THE TEST LABELS

a. Drag the pointer from cell B1 to cell E1. Cells B1 through E1 are highlighted as a block.
b. Select Format → Cells. A dialog box is displayed.
1. Select the Alignment tab if the alignment options are not already displayed.
2. In the Horizontal collapsible list, select Right.
3. Select the Font tab. The font options are displayed.
4. In the Font style list, select Bold.
5. Select OK. The labels are right aligned and bold.

4) FORMAT THE DATES

a. Select cell B2.
b. Hold the Shift key down and click on cell E2. Cells B2 through E2 are highlighted as a block.
c. Select Format → Cells. A dialog box is displayed.
1. Select the Number tab. The number formatting options are displayed.
2. Select Date in the Category section if it is not already selected.
3. Scroll the Type list until a date similar to 3/14/1998 is displayed.
4. Click on the date to select it.
5. Select OK. The dates in row 2 now display the full year.

5) SAVE AND CLOSE THE MODIFIED GRADES

What's Displayed in the Formula Bar?

The Formula bar displays the selected cell's actual contents instead of the value displayed in the cell. For example, when the Formula bar shows =2+3 for the selected cell, the cell displays 5. When looking for errors in a spreadsheet, the Formula bar is the first place to start.

Order of Operations Example

What value is displayed when the formula =9+12/3 is evaluated? Is the sum of 9 and 12 divided by 3? If so, the answer is 7. Or is the result of 12 divided by 3 added to 9 to produce 13? Entering the formula in Excel results in 13 being displayed. Division is performed first and then addition because order of operations is followed.

7.13 Using Formulas to Perform Calculations

A primary benefit of using a spreadsheet is its ability to perform calculations using formulas. *Formulas* are mathematical statements used to calculate values. For example, entering the formula =25 * 3 in a cell displays the value 75. Note that every formula in Excel must begin with an equal sign (=).

The following mathematical operators can be used in a formula:

Exponentiation	^
Multiplication	*
Division	/
Addition	+
Subtraction	−

Exponentiation means to raise to a power and is represented by the caret (^) symbol. For example, $2^2 = 4$ and $5^3 = 125$.

Excel evaluates a formula from left to right, using the *order of operations* to indicate the priority of operators. If a formula contains two operators of equal priority, the leftmost operator is used first. The following order of operations is used when a formula is evaluated:

1. Any number raised to a power is calculated first.

    =4+3^2 produces the value 13

<table>
<tr><td>

Remembering the Order of Operations

To remember the order of operations, memorize this simple phrase:

Please
Excuse
My **D**ear
Aunt **S**ally

The initials correspond to the following, in order:

Parenthesis
Exponents
Multiply **D**ivide
Add **S**ubtract

</td></tr>
</table>

2. Calculations involving multiplication and division, which are of equal priority, are performed next.

   =3+5*6/2 produces the value 18

   Here, Excel first multiplies 5 and 6 to get 30, and then divides by 2 to get 15. Finally, 3 is added to 15 to produce 18.

3. Third in the order of operations is addition and subtraction, which are of equal priority.

   =7+4*2 produces the value 15

   Here, Excel first multiplies 4 and 2 to get 8. The final result is computed by adding 7 to 8 to produce 15.

When a formula contains parentheses, whatever operations are within them are performed first. By using parentheses the order of operations can be changed. For example, to add 7 and 4 and then multiply the result by 2, parentheses must be used:

   =(7+4)*2 produces the value 22

Here are other formulas and their results:

Formula	Resulting value
=2*2+3*2	10
=25*8/4	50
=35+12/3	39
=3+5*8+7	50
=(3+5)*(8+7)	120
=3^2*8-4	68
=6+2^2	10
=(6+2)^2	64

Entering an invalid formula in a cell causes Excel to display an error message. For example, a number cannot be divided by zero because the result is mathematically undefined. Therefore, entering =10/0 displays #DIV/0! in the cell. Depending on the error, Excel may display an error dialog box similar to:

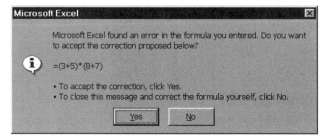

Excel may display a dialog box when an invalid formula has been entered

Selecting **Yes** accepts Excel's correction. Selecting **No** removes the dialog box so that the formula can be corrected.

Practice 4

In this practice you will enter formulas into the cells of a new, empty spreadsheet to perform calculations.

1) CREATE A NEW SPREADSHEET

2) ENTER LABELS

   a. Select cell A1 and enter the label Example Formulas.
   b. Bold the label. Note that the text extends into the next cell.
   c. Double-click on the boundary between columns A and B. Column A is widened just enough to display the label.
   d. Select cell A2 and enter the label Formula.
   e. Select cell B2 and enter the label Result.
   f. Italicize both labels and right align the label in cell B2.

3) ENTER A LABEL AND A FORMULA

   a. Select cell A3.
   b. Type 20/50 and then click on the Enter button. The result is a label because it is not preceded by an equal sign.
   c. Select cell B3.
   d. Type =20/50 and then click on the Enter button. The result 0.4 is displayed. Note that the formula is displayed on the Formula bar, and the result of the formula is shown in the cell:

	A	B	C
	B3 ▼	= =20/50	
1	**Example Formulas**		
2	*Formula*	*Result*	
3	20/50	0.4	

4) ENTER FORMULAS

Enter each of the labels and formulas shown below in the cells indicated. Note the resulting values of the formulas:

In cell		**enter**		**In cell**		**enter**		**to display**	
	A4		20*50		B4		=20*50		1000
	A5		20–50		B5		=20–50		–30
	A6		2+20*5+50		B6		=2+20*5+50		152
	A7		(2+20)*(5+50)		B7		=(2+20)*(5+50)		1210
	A8		20/0		B8		=20/0		#DIV/0!

5) SAVE THE SPREADSHEET

Save the spreadsheet in the appropriate folder naming it Formula Examples.

Circular References

A circular reference occurs when a cell's formula refers to either itself or to another cell whose calculation involves the current cell. For example, placing the formula =B5–C1 in cell B5 creates a circular reference because it is not possible for cell B5 to refer to itself in a formula. Placing =B5–C1 in cell D10 also creates a circular reference if either B5 or C1 contain a formula that refers to D10. When a circular reference is created, Excel alerts you by displaying a dialog box.

7.14 Using Cell References in Formulas

A cell reference may be used in a formula. When Excel evaluates the formula, it uses the cell reference to locate the value needed in the calculation. For example, if cell B3 stores the value 20 and cell C2 stores the value 50:

Formula	**Resulting value**
=B3/C2	0.4
=B3*C2	1000
=B3–C2	–30
=2*B3+5*C2	290
=B3+5*C2+8	278
=B3+5*(C2+8)	310
=(B3+5)*(C2+8)	1450

A formula cannot reference the cell it is stored in. For example, the formulas above cannot be stored in cells B3 or C2 because this would cause an error called a *circular reference*.

Practice 5

In this practice you will enter formulas that contain cell references. Open Formula Examples if it is not already displayed.

1) ENTER A LABEL

    a. Select cell A10 and enter the label Example Formulas with Cell References.
    b. Bold the label.
    c. Select cell A11 and enter the label Formula.
    d. Select cell B11 and enter the label Result.
    e. Italicize both labels and right align the label in cell B11.

2) ENTER VALUES INTO THE SPREADSHEET

    a. Select cell E10 and enter the value 20.
    b. Select cell F10 and enter the value 50.

3) ENTER FORMULAS

    a. Select cell A12.
    b. Type E10/F10 and then click on the Enter button. The result is a label because it is not preceded by an equal sign.
    c. Select cell B12.
    d. Enter the formula =E10/F10. The result 0.4 is displayed.
    e. Enter each of the labels and formulas shown below in the cells indicated. Note the resulting values of the formulas:

In cell		enter		In cell		enter	to display	
In cell	A13	enter	E10*F10	In cell	B13	enter	=E10*F10 **to display**	1000
	A14		E10-F10		B14		=E10–F10	–30
	A15		2+E10*5+F10		B15		=2+E10*5+F10	152
	A16		(2+E10)*(5+F10)		B16		=(2+E10)*(5+F10)	1210
	A17		E10^2+F10^2		B17		=E10^2+F10^2	2900
	A18		(E10+F10)^2		B18		=(E10+F10)^2	4900

4) ENTER A NEW VALUE IN CELL E10

    a. Select cell E10.
    b. Enter 30 to replace the current value. Every formula in the spreadsheet referencing cell E10 is automatically recalculated. A major advantage of using a spreadsheet is that formulas are automatically recalculated when values they reference change.

5) FORMAT CELLS TO DISPLAY ONE DECIMAL PLACE AND COMMAS

    a. Highlight cells B12 through B18.
    b. Select Format → Cells. A dialog box is displayed.
        1. Select the Number tab if the number formatting options are not already displayed.
        2. Select Number in the Category section. Enter 1 in the Decimal places entry box.
        3. Select the Use 1000 Separator (,) option.
        4. Select OK. Note that the values in cells B12 through B18 are displayed with 1 decimal place and commas.

A Guide to Microsoft Office 2000 Professional

Check – Your spreadsheet should look similar to:

	A	B	C	D	E	F
1	Example Formulas					
2	*Formula*	*Result*				
3	20/50	0.4				
4	20*50	1000				
5	20-50	-30				
6	2+20*5+50	152				
7	(2+20)*(5+50)	1210				
8	20/0	#DIV/0!				
9						
10	Example Formulas with Cell References				30	50
11	*Formula*	*Result*				
12	E10/F10	0.6				
13	E10*F10	1,500.0				
14	E10-F10	-20.0				
15	2+E10*5+F10	202.0				
16	(2+E10)*(5+F10)	1,760.0				
17	E10^2+F10^2	3,400.0				
18	(E10+F10)^2	6,400.0				

6) SAVE, PRINT, AND THEN CLOSE THE MODIFIED FORMULA EXAMPLES

   a. Save the modified Formula Examples.
   b. Print a copy of the spreadsheet with gridlines and row and column headings.
   c. Save and close the spreadsheet.

7.15 Using Functions to Perform Calculations

argument

For performing common calculations, Excel includes built-in functions that can be included in a formula. A *function* performs a task that results in a single value. A function requires data, called *arguments*, to perform its task. The arguments of a function are enclosed in parentheses after the function name and are usually cell references. For example, to accomplish the task of adding the values stored in cells A1, B5, and E7 a

SUM

formula that contains the built-in SUM function is used:

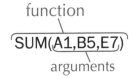

In this example, the values to be summed are stored in nonadjacent cells. Therefore, the SUM arguments are separated by commas.

range

When adjacent cells are the arguments of a function, a *range* of cells may be referenced by typing the first cell reference followed by a colon (:) and then the last cell reference. For example, the formula =SUM(G1:G3) sums the values in cells G1, G2, and G3. Functions are useful because they often make a formula shorter and are less error-prone, especially when a large range of cells is involved.

Arguments

The SUM and AVERAGE functions ignore cells that contain text or are empty when their cell references are included as arguments.

AVERAGE   The AVERAGE function adds the values of the cells in the range and then divides the result by the number of cells in the range. For example, the formula =AVERAGE(C12:C17) sums the values in cells C12, C13, C14, C15, C16, and C17 and then divides the total by 6.

Practice 6

In this practice you will enter formulas to calculate the total and average sales for a candy store.

1) OPEN CANDY SALES

2) FORMAT THE VALUES AS CURRENCY WITH 2 DECIMAL PLACES

    a. Highlight cells B2 through B10. The sales amounts are highlighted as a block.
    b. Select Format → Cells. A dialog box is displayed.
         1. Select the Number tab if the number formatting options are not already displayed.
         2. Select Currency in the Category section.
         3. Type 2 in the Decimal places entry box if it is not already there.
         4. Select OK. The values are displayed as currency with 2 decimal places.

3) USE A FUNCTION TO SUM THE VALUES

    Select cell B11 and enter the formula:

        =SUM(B2:B10)

    The sum $300,632.03 is displayed. Note how the total is also formatted as currency because it is summing values that have already been formatted.

4) ENTER THE FORMULA TO AVERAGE THE VALUES

    Select cell B12 and enter the formula:

        =AVERAGE(B2:B10)

    The average sales, $33,403.56, is displayed in cell B12.

5) SAVE, PRINT, AND THEN CLOSE THE MODIFIED CANDY SALES

7.16 Entering Formulas - Pointing

When typing a formula, cell references can be entered by pointing. *Pointing* is when a formula is typed to where a cell reference should appear and then the mouse pointer is clicked on a cell, which places its reference in the formula. Selecting a block of cells places a range in the formula. Pointing is the best method for entering cell references into a formula because typing errors are avoided.

For example, in the spreadsheet on the next page, =SUM(was typed into cell B5. The range was then entered into the formula by dragging the mouse from cell B2 to cell B4. The colon (:) is automatically inserted by Excel:

A Guide to Microsoft Office 2000 Professional

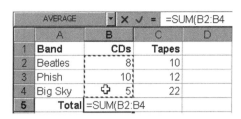

Selecting a block of cells enters its range into a formula

The formula is completed by typing a right parenthesis and clicking on the Enter button or pressing Enter.

7.17 Displaying Formulas

Spreadsheet formulas are displayed at their cell locations by pressing Ctrl+` (the accent mark):

	A	B	C
1	**Band**	**CDs**	**Tapes**
2	Beatles	8	10
3	Phish	10	12
4	Big Sky	5	22
5	**Total**	23	44

Before pressing Ctrl+`

	A	B	C
1	**Band**	**CDs**	**Tapes**
2	Beatles	8	10
3	Phish	10	12
4	Big Sky	5	22
5	**Total**	=SUM(B2:B4)	=SUM(C2:C4)

After pressing Ctrl+`

 The accent key is located above the Tab key on the keyboard. A formula that is longer than the cell width can be displayed in its entirety by increasing the column width.

Printing when formulas are displayed prints the formulas stored in the cells rather than the values. Pressing Ctrl+` again displays values in each cell, although any column widths that were increased remain wider and need to be reformatted.

Practice 7

In this practice you will enter formulas to calculate the average grade on a test and a student's average in the Grades spreadsheet created in Practices 1, 2, and 3.

1) OPEN GRADES

2) USE A FORMULA TO AVERAGE THE GRADES FOR TEST 1

    a. Select cell B9.
    b. Type =AVERAGE(
    c. Highlight cells B3 to B8. Excel enters the cell references for the selected range into the formula.
    d. Type the closing parentheses) and then press Enter. The average for Test 1, 83.33333, is displayed in cell B9.

3) CALCULATE A STUDENT'S TERM AVERAGE

Select cell F3 and use pointing to enter the formula =AVERAGE(B3:E3). The average 84.5 is displayed.

4) ADD TITLE FOR THE NEW INFORMATION

a. Select cell F1 and enter the label Student Average.
b. Format the label as bold and right aligned if it is not already formatted.
c. Resize the column longer so that the label is displayed entirely.
d. Select cell A9 and enter the label Test Average.
e. Format the label as italicized and right aligned.

5) VIEW AND PRINT THE FORMULAS

a. Save the modified Grades.
b. Press Ctrl+` (located above the Tab key).
c. Print a copy of the spreadsheet with gridlines and row and column headings.
d. Press Ctrl+` to again display only the values of each cell.

6) SAVE THE MODIFIED GRADES

7.18 Copying Adjacent Cells

Fill handle

Cell contents can be copied to adjacent cells using the Fill handle. The *Fill handle* is the solid square in the lower-right corner of a selected cell or block of cells:

	A	B	C	D
1	The Cost of Making Pizzas			
2				
3	Ingredients	Cheese	Extra Cheese	Vegetarian
4	Dough	$1.25	$1.25	$1.25
5	Cheese	$1.50	$2.50	$1.50
6	Sauce	$0.50		

Fill handle

The contents of cell B6 can be copied to adjacent cells by dragging the Fill handle

The mouse pointer changes to a cross hairs shape (✚) when placed on the Fill handle. Dragging the Fill handle copies the contents of the selected cell or block of cells to the adjacent cells:

	A	B	C	D
1	The Cost of Making Pizzas			
2				
3	Ingredients	Cheese	Extra Cheese	Vegetarian
4	Dough	$1.25	$1.25	$1.25
5	Cheese	$1.50	$2.50	$1.50
6	Sauce	$0.50	$0.50	$0.50

The Fill handle was dragged from cell B6 to cell D6

Commands from the Fill submenu in the Edit menu can also be used to copy a cell's contents to adjacent highlighted cells. Displaying the Fill submenu from the Edit menu displays the Down and Right commands. The Down command (Ctrl+D) is used if the selected cells are in a column, and the Right command (Ctrl+R) is used if the selected cells are in a row.

Series

If a cell contains a date, time, or a combination of text and a number, then a series is created when the Fill handle is dragged. For example, in the spreadsheet below, cells A1 through A3 were selected and then the Fill handle dragged to cell C3:

	A	B	C
1	Jan	Feb	Mar
2	2:00 PM	3:00 PM	4:00 PM
3	Test 1	Test 2	Test 3

A series of numbers is also created by selecting two cells and then dragging the Fill handle. For example, highlighting a cell that contains 2 and an adjacent cell that contains 4 and then dragging the Fill handle produces a series of even numbers; 6, 8, 10, etc.

A Guide to Microsoft Office 2000 Professional

7.19 Copying Formulas

When a formula is copied, the cell references in the formula are automatically changed relative to the new row or column. For example, in the spreadsheet below, cell B5 contains the formula =SUM(B2:B4). Copying this cell to cell C5 creates the formula =SUM(C2:C4) in cell C5:

| C5 | | ▼ | = | =SUM(C2:C4) |

	A	B	C	D
1	Band	CDs	Tapes	
2	Beatles	8	10	
3	Phish	10	12	
4	Big Sky	5	22	
5	Total	23	44	

relative cell references

Cell references that reflect the row or column they have been copied to are called *relative cell references*.

7.20 The ROUND Function

Rounding vs. Formatting

The ROUND function actually changes the value stored in the cell, while formatting only affects the way the information is displayed.

Excel follows certain rules when rounding numbers. A number with a decimal portion greater than or equal to 0.5 is rounded up and a number with a decimal portion less than 0.5 is rounded down.

A negative number as the second argument of the ROUND function rounds a value to the nearest 10s, 100s, etc. For example =ROUND(72.86,-1) displays 70. The formula =ROUND(72.866,-2) displays 100.

The ROUND function changes a value by rounding it to a specific number of decimal places. For example, to round the value stored in cell C16 to one decimal place, the formula =ROUND(C16,1) is used. If the value stored in C16 is 42.851 the rounded result is 42.9. To round a stored value, the cell reference is used as the first argument of the ROUND function, and the second argument is the number of decimal places that the result is to be rounded.

Often the result of a formula should be rounded. For example, the test averages should be rounded to 2 decimal places in the Grades spreadsheet. This means that the class average on Test 1 would be computed as 83.33, not 83.33333. To round the result of a formula, the formula is the first argument and the desired number of decimal places is the second argument of the ROUND function. For example, Test 1's average can be rounded to 2 places with the formula:

=ROUND(AVERAGE(B3:B8),2)

To round a value to the nearest integer, a 0 is used to indicate no decimal places: =ROUND(AVERAGE(B3:B8),0).

7.21 Exiting Excel

When you are finished working with Excel, it should be exited properly so that any spreadsheets in memory are not damaged or lost. Exiting Excel means that its window is removed from the screen and the program is no longer in the computer's memory. Excel is exited by selecting the Exit command from the File menu. If you have created a new spreadsheet or modified a previously saved spreadsheet, Excel displays a warning dialog box asking if you want to save your spreadsheet.

Practice 8

In this practice you will copy the formulas in the Grades spreadsheet and use the ROUND function. Open Grades if it is not already displayed.

1) COPY A FORMULA USING THE FILL HANDLE

    a. Select cell B9. Note the Fill handle in the lower-right corner of the cell.
    b. Point to the Fill handle of the cell. The mouse pointer changes to cross hairs (**+**).
    c. Drag the Fill handle from cell B9 to cell E9. The formula is copied to cells C9 through E9.
    d. Select cell E9. The formula displayed on the Formula bar shows how the cell references have been automatically changed.

2) COPY ANOTHER FORMULA USING THE FILL HANDLE

    a. Select cell F3.
    b. Drag the Fill handle from cell F3 to cell F8. The formula is copied.

3) ROUND THE AVERAGES TO 2 DECIMAL PLACES

    a. Select cell B9.
    b. On the Formula bar, click the pointer to display the cursor. Move the cursor before the word AVERAGE and type: ROUND(
    c. Move the cursor to the end of the formula and type ,2) so that the formula on the Formula bar is:

        =ROUND(AVERAGE(B3:B8),2)

    Click on the Enter button. The average is now rounded to 2 decimal places, 83.33.

4) ROUND ALL TEST AVERAGES TO 2 DECIMAL PLACES

    a. Select cell B9 if it is not already selected.
    b. Drag the Fill handle from cell B9 to cell E9. The formula is copied.

5) ROUND DEMPS, K.'S AVERAGE TO 1 DECIMAL PLACE

    a. Select cell F3.
    b. On the Formula bar, place the cursor before the word AVERAGE and type: ROUND(
    c. Move the cursor at the end of the formula and type ,1) so that the formula is:

        =ROUND(AVERAGE(B3:E3),1)

    Click on the Enter button. The average is still 84.5.

6) ROUND ALL STUDENT AVERAGES TO 1 DECIMAL PLACE

    a. Select cell F3 if it is not already selected.
    b. Use the Fill handle to copy the formula in cell F3 to cells F4 through F8.

7) FORMAT AVERAGES TO DISPLAY 1 DECIMAL PLACE

    a. Highlight cells F3 through F8 if they are not already selected.
    b. Select Format ➔ Cells. A dialog box is displayed.
        1. Select the Number tab if the number formatting options are not already displayed.
        2. Select Number in the Category section. Enter 1 in the Decimal places entry box.
        3. Select OK. Note that the value in cell F4 is displayed with a trailing zero in order to display the number to 1 decimal place.

Check – Your spreadsheet should look similar to:

	A	B	C	D	E	F
1	Name	Test 1	Test 2	Test 3	Test 4	Student Average
2		9/12/2001	10/10/2001	11/14/2001	12/12/2001	
3	Demps, K.	85	73	88	92	84.5
4	McCallister, T.	92	88	85	91	89.0
5	Matos, A.	72	63	67	72	68.5
6	Smith, L.	87	92	85	93	89.3
7	Sun, L.	94	91	93	84	90.5
8	Adams, V.	70	74	80	83	76.8
9	Test Average	83.33	80.17	83	85.83	

8) SAVE, PRINT, AND THEN CLOSE THE MODIFIED GRADES

a. Save the modified Grades.
b. Display formulas. Resize columns as necessary so all the formulas are displayed entirely.
c. Print the spreadsheet with gridlines and row and column headings.
d. Close the spreadsheet without saving changes.

9) EXIT EXCEL

Chapter Summary

This chapter covered the basics of creating a spreadsheet. A spreadsheet is rows and columns of data. The primary advantage of a computerized spreadsheet is the ability to perform calculations on data, and to recalculate automatically when changes are made to the data.

row and column headings
cell
cell reference
Name box
cell cursor, Formula bar

A new spreadsheet is created by selecting the Blank Workbook icon and then OK in the New Office Document dialog box. In the Excel window, rows are identified by numbers, and columns by letters. A cell is the intersection of a row and column and is identified by its cell reference. For example, D4 is the cell reference of the cell located at column D and row 4. The Name box shows the current location of the cell cursor, and the Formula bar shows the contents of the selected cell.

labels, values
times/dates

Spreadsheet cells can store three types of data: labels, values, and times/dates. Labels are text and cannot be used in calculations. Values are numeric and can be used in calculations. Times/dates are either times (10:30 AM) or calendar dates (9/21/01), and both can be used in certain types of calculations.

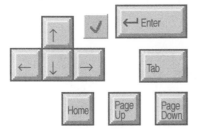

Data is entered into a spreadsheet by moving the cell cursor to a cell, typing the data, and clicking on the Enter button. Pressing the Enter key, Tab key, or arrow key after typing data into a cell enters the data and then moves the cell cursor to an adjacent cell, in a direction depending on which key is pressed. To move through a spreadsheet, the scroll arrows or the Home, Page Up, and Page Down keys can be used.

editing cell contents

deleting cell contents

A cell needs to be selected before it can be edited. Clicking the pointer in the Formula bar displays a blinking cursor, and characters can then be entered or deleted. Pressing the Delete key erases the contents of the selected cell. The All command from the Clear submenu deletes a cell's contents and formatting. Selecting the Undo command from the Edit menu restores the cell's contents.

A spreadsheet is saved or closed by selecting the <u>S</u>ave or <u>C</u>lose command from the <u>F</u>ile menu. It is printed by selecting the <u>P</u>rint command from the <u>F</u>ile menu. The Print Pre<u>v</u>iew command from the <u>F</u>ile menu is used to display the spreadsheet as it will appear when printed. These commands can also be performed by using buttons on the Toolbar.

gridlines
row and column headings
headers and footers

Spreadsheet printouts can be made easier to read by selecting the Gridlines and the Row and column headings options in the Page Setup dialog box. Information can be entered in a spreadsheet's header or footer using the Header/Footer options in the Page Setup dialog box to provide more informative printouts.

changing column width

The width of a column can be changed by dragging its right boundary or double-clicking on the column's right boundary.

highlighted block

Formatting and editing commands can be applied to a highlighted block of cells. A highlighted block of cells is formed by dragging the mouse from one cell to another cell.

formatting cell contents

The C<u>e</u>lls command from the F<u>o</u>rmat menu is used to display the Format Cells dialog box where options can be selected that affect how values are displayed in the cell. Buttons on the Formatting Toolbar can be used to change the alignment, font, font size, and font style of cell contents.

formulas

Formulas are mathematical statements used to calculate values which can be stored in cells. All formulas must begin with an equal sign (=) and may contain cell references. For example, if cell B5 stores the value 12 and cell C8 stores 10, the formula =B5*C8 would display 120.

order of operations

Excel uses an order of operations when evaluating a formula. First it performs exponentiation, then multiplication and division, and finally addition and subtraction. Operations of the same priority are performed from left to right. The order of operations can be changed by using parentheses.

SUM

AVERAGE
ROUND

Excel contains built-in functions that are used to perform common calculations. The formula =SUM(B3:B8) includes the SUM function. The formula's argument, B3:B8, is called a range and defines the cells to be summed. The formula =AVERAGE(C3:C7) averages the values in the cells C3, C4, C5, C6, and C7. The formula =ROUND(C5,2) rounds the value stored in cell C5 to two decimal places. Similarly, the formula =ROUND(AVERAGE(B7:F7),1) rounds the average of the values in the range B7:F7 to one decimal place.

pointing

Cell references can be entered into a formula by using the mouse to click on them. This technique is called pointing. The formulas in a spreadsheet are viewed by pressing Ctrl+`.

Fill handle

relative cell references

The contents of a selected cell or block of cells can be copied to a row or column of adjacent cells by using the Fill handle or the <u>D</u>own and <u>R</u>ight commands from the Fi<u>l</u>l submenu. When this is done, the cell references in the copied formulas automatically change to reflect the new row or column they are in. Cell references that reflect the row or column they have been copied to are called relative cell references.

Vocabulary

Argument Cell references enclosed in parentheses that are used by a function to perform the calculations.

Arrow keys Enters data and then selects the next cell in the direction of the arrow key.

AVERAGE Function that adds the values of the cells in a range and divides the result by the number of cells in the range.

Boundary The bar separating the column letters at the top of the spreadsheet.

Cell Where a row and column intersect. A cell is identified by its column letter and row number, for example C3.

Cell cursor Solid outline around a cell that is used to indicate the selected cell.

Cell reference The column letter and row number used to identify a cell (i.e., B3).

Circular reference An error that occurs when a formula references the cell it is stored in.

Column Vertical line of data identified by a letter.

Column headings The column letter at the top of each column.

Date Data in the form of a calendar date (i.e., 9/5/01).

Enter key Enters data and then selects the next cell in the column.

Escape key Cancels data entry and restores the cell's original contents.

Fill handle Used to copy a cell's contents to adjacent cells.

Formula Mathematical statement used to calculate values. A formula must always begin with an equal sign. For example, =C5+D7+E8 is a formula.

Formula bar Area near the top of the spreadsheet window that displays the contents of the selected cell.

Function Performs common calculations and returns a single value. The formula =SUM(B3:B8) contains a function.

Gridlines Solid lines that mark off the rows and columns in a spreadsheet.

Highlighted block Adjacent spreadsheet cells that have been selected. Formatting commands can be applied to a highlighted block, affecting every cell in the selection.

Label Words or characters stored in a cell that cannot be used in calculations.

Microsoft Excel A spreadsheet application in the Microsoft Office package.

Name box Located near the top of the spreadsheet window. Displays the location of the cell cursor.

Order of operations The rules the computer uses to evaluate the priority of the operators.

Pointing Clicking on a cell to specify its cell reference in a formula.

Range Adjacent cells in a row or column. B3:B8 is a range.

Relative cell reference A cell reference that when copied reflects the row or column it has been copied to.

ROUND Function that changes a value by rounding it to a specific number of decimal places.

Row Horizontal line of data identified by a number.

Row headings The row number at the left of each row.

Scroll bars Used to display columns and rows not currently displayed.

Selected cell The spreadsheet cell containing the cell cursor as indicated by a solid outline.

Spreadsheet Rows and columns of data on which calculations can be performed.

SUM Function that adds the values in a range of cells.

Tab key Enters data and then selects the next cell in the row.

Time Data in the form of a time (i.e., 12:30 PM).

Values Numeric data that can be stored in cells and used in calculations.

Workbook An Excel spreadsheet file.

Excel Commands and Buttons

Align Left button Left aligns the contents of the selected cell(s). Found on the Formatting Toolbar.

Align Right button Right aligns the contents of the selected cell(s). Found on the Formatting Toolbar.

All command Deletes the selected cell's contents and formatting. Found in the Clear submenu in the Edit menu.

Bold button Formats highlighted cell(s) as bold. Found on the Formatting Toolbar

Cancel button Erases the data in the Formula bar and leaves the selected cell unchanged. Found on the Formula bar.

Cells command Displays a dialog box where alignment, font, and number formatting options can be selected. Found in the Format menu.

Center button Centers the contents of the selected cell(s). Found on the Formatting Toolbar.

Close command Removes the spreadsheet from the Excel window and the computer's memory. Found in the File menu.

Down command Copies a cell's contents into the highlighted cells of a column. Found in the Fill submenu in the Edit menu.

Enter button Enters data and leave the cell cursor on the selected cell. Found on the Formula bar.

Font box Displays a list of fonts to choose from. Found on the Formatting Toolbar.

Font Size box Displays a list of font sizes to choose from. Found on the Formatting Toolbar.

Italic button Formats highlighted cell(s) as italic. Found on the Formatting Toolbar.

Print command Displays a dialog box for selecting printing options. Found in the File menu. The Print button ( ) on the Standard Toolbar can be used instead of the command.

Page Setup command Displays a dialog box where options for printing with gridlines and row and column headings and creating a header or footer can be selected. Found in the File menu.

Print Pre**view command** Displays the spreadsheet as it will appear when printed. Found in the File menu. The Print Preview button ( ) on the Standard Toolbar can be used instead of the command.

Right command Copies a cell's contents into the highlighted cells of a row. Found in the Fill submenu in the Edit menu.

Save command Saves a spreadsheet. Found in the File menu. The Save button ( ) on the Standard Toolbar can be used instead of the command.

Underline button Formats highlighted cell(s) as underlined. Found on the Formatting Toolbar.

Review Questions

1. What are the primary advantages of using a spreadsheet application?

2. List the steps required to create a new spreadsheet in Excel.

3. a) What is the difference between a row and a column?
   b) What is a cell?
   c) What is the cell cursor?
   d) What is the Name box?
   e) What information is displayed on the Formula bar?

4. Give an example of a cell reference and the data stored in that cell.

5. a) How can spreadsheet columns that are not displayed be brought into view?
   b) What happens when the Home key is pressed?

6. a) What is the difference between a label and a value entry?
   b) What is a date entry? Give an example.
   c) What is a time entry? Give an example.

7. How many of each of the following types of entries are stored in the Grades spreadsheet shown in Practice 1?
   a) labels
   b) values
   c) dates
   d) times

8. After typing data into a cell what happens when you:
   a) click on the Enter button?
   b) press the Enter key?
   c) press the Tab key?

9. a) What are two ways you can cancel the current data entry into a cell and restore the cell's original contents?
   b) If a mistake has been made entering data into a cell, how can it be corrected?

10. List the steps required to enter the value 65 into cell C4 of a new, empty spreadsheet.

11. If a mistake has been made in a formula how can it be corrected?

12. List two ways that the contents of a cell can be deleted.

Sections 7.6 — 7.12

13. a) List two ways to save a spreadsheet.
    b) What should be done if the spreadsheet has been saved and is no longer needed?

14. List the steps required to view a spreadsheet as it will appear when printed.

15. What options can be selected from the Page Setup dialog box to make a spreadsheet printout easier to read?

16. List the steps required to have your name left aligned and the current date right aligned in the header of a spreadsheet.

17. Is it possible to change the width of only a single cell?

18. List the steps required to increase the width of a column.

19. a) What is a highlighted block?
    b) List two ways to highlight cells B3 through C12.

20. List the steps required to:
    a) format a cell to display a number with 3 decimal places.
    b) bold and right align the contents of a cell.
    c) format a cell to display a value in dollars to 2 decimal places.

Sections 7.13 — 7.14

21. Briefly explain what a formula is and give two examples.

22. a) What is meant by order of operations?
    b) Which operation is performed first?
    c) Which operation is performed last?
    d) How can the order of operations be changed?

23. If a formula contains three operators, all of the same priority, which will be used first?

24. If 10/20 is entered into a cell, Excel considers it a label. How must the entry be changed so that 10 will be divided by 20?

25. What value would be calculated by Excel for each of the following formulas?
    a) =2+7*5+4
    b) =(2+7)*(5+4)
    c) =5+10/5
    d) =(5+10)/5
    e) =2^3+4

26. What value would be calculated by Excel for each of the following formulas if cell C15 stores a value of 16 and cell D8 a value of 4?
    a) =C15*D8
    b) =C15+5+D8
    c) =C15*5+D8
    d) =C15*(5+D8)
    e) =C15/D8

27. Write a formula to calculate:
    a) the product of the values stored in cells A1, B3, and C4.
    b) the sum of the values stored in cells A3, A4, A5, A6, A7, and A8.
    c) the average of the values stored in cells B5, B6, and B7.
    d) the average of the values stored in cells A1, B3, and C4.

Sections 7.15 — 7.21

28. What is the difference between a formula and a function?

29. a) What is meant by a range of cells?
    b) Give an example of a range of cells contained in a row.
    c) Give an example of a range of cells contained in a column.

30. Write a formula that uses a function to calculate the average of the values stored in cells B3, B4, B5, C5, D5, and E5.

31. Write a formula that uses a function to calculate:
    a) the sum of the values stored in cells B4, B5, B6, and B7.
    b) the sum of the values stored in cells B4, C4, D4, and E4.
    c) the average of the values stored in the column of cells D7 to D35.
    d) the average of the values stored in the row of cells F3 to J3.

32. What is usually the best method for entering cell references in a formula?

33. How can the formulas stored in the cells of a spreadsheet be displayed instead of the values they calculate?

34. a) List the steps required to copy the contents of cell A1 into cells A2, A3, A4, and A5 using the Fill handle.
    b) List the steps required to copy the contents of cell C1 into cells D1, E1, and F1 using the Fill command.

35. a) What is a relative cell reference?
    b) List the steps required to copy the formula =AVERAGE(C5:C9) stored in cell C22 into the range of cells D22 to G22 so that the formula correctly calculates the average for each column.

36. What will be displayed in cell A2 if the value stored in cell C5 is 98.345 and the formula =ROUND(C5,2) is stored in cell A2?

37. Using functions, write a formula to calculate:
    a) the sum of the values in cells Exercise 18 ↺ C5, C6, C7, C8, and C9 rounded to 2 decimal places.
    b) the sum of the values in cells B5, C5, D5, and E5 rounded to the nearest integer.
    c) the average of the values in cells A1, A2, A3, B1, B2, and B3 rounded to 1 decimal place.

38. What is the difference between using the ROUND function to display a value with 2 decimal places or formatting a value to display 2 decimal places using the Cells command?

39. List the steps required to Exit Excel.

Exercises

Exercise 1 ——————————————————————— Activity

Spreadsheets can be helpful in personal time management. One way to organize your time is to determine the time you spend on different activities during one week.

a) In a new spreadsheet enter the following labels in row 1 starting in column A: Activity, Sun, Mon, Tue, Wed, Thu, Fri, Sat.

b) Bold all the labels in row 1. Right align all the days of the week labels.

c) Resize the column width of columns B through H so they are just wide enough to display the data entirely.

d) Starting in row 2, enter the appropriate label and number of hours you spend each day of the week on each of the following activities:

- school classes
- athletics
- extracurricular groups and clubs
- studying and doing homework
- eating
- sleeping
- watching television or listening to music
- talking on the phone
- doing housework
- working at a job

Resize column A as necessary to display all the labels entirely. Format all the hours to display 1 decimal place.

e) Save the spreadsheet naming it Activity.

f) Most people's schedules do not account for all 24 hours in a day. Include a row, after the last activity, and enter formulas that use a function to calculate the amount of unaccounted time in your schedule for each day. Include an appropriate label for the unaccounted time.

g) In cell I1, enter the label Total Hours. Enter formulas that use a function to calculate the total hours spent for the week on each activity. Format the total hours as number with 1 decimal place if it is not already formatted.

h) In cell J1, enter the label Avg. Hours. Enter formulas that use a function to calculate the average number of hours spent per day on each activity for the week.

i) Resize columns as necessary so that all the data is displayed entirely.

j) Create a header with your name right aligned.

k) Save the modified Activity and print a copy with gridlines and row and column headings.

l) Execute the appropriate action to display the formulas in the cells instead of values. Resize columns as necessary so that the formulas are completely displayed. Print a copy with gridlines and row and column headings.

The owner of Squeaky Clean Cars wants to use a spreadsheet to keep track of his budgeted and actual expenses.

a)   In a new spreadsheet enter the data as shown below. Resize columns as necessary so that all the data is displayed entirely:

	A	B	C	D
1	Squeaky Clean Cars			
2				
3		June Expenses Budget		
4		Budgeted	Actual	
5	Soap	$35.00	$28.65	
6	Wax	$50.00	$43.45	
7	Vinyl Cleaner	$25.00	$32.75	
8	Window Cleaner	$15.00	$20.50	
9	Sponges and Towels	$10.00	$12.56	

Format the numeric values as currency with 2 decimal places.

b)   Save the spreadsheet naming it Squeaky Clean Cars.

c)   The owner would like to know the difference between what was budgeted and what he actually spent. In cell D4, enter the label Difference. Enter formulas that use cell references to subtract the actual costs from the budgeted costs.

d)   In cell A10, enter the label Total: and right align it. Enter formulas that use a function to total the Budgeted and Actual columns.

e)   Bold the labels in column A and row 3. Italicize and right align the labels in row 4. Resize columns as necessary so that all the data is displayed entirely.

f)   Create a header with your name right aligned.

g)   Save the modified Squeaky Clean Cars and print a copy with gridlines and row and column headings.

h)   Execute the appropriate action to display the formulas in the cells instead of values. Resize columns as necessary so that the formulas are completely displayed. Print a copy with gridlines and row and column headings.

A swim team wants to use a spreadsheet to keep track of the last swim meet's results.

a)   In a new spreadsheet enter the data as shown below. Resize columns as necessary so that all the data is displayed entirely:

	A	B	C	D	E
1	Swimming Event	Floyd	Abby	Eric	Katina
2	100 M Freestyle	2:54:00	2:45:40	2:55:06	2:23:36
3	100 M Breaststroke	3:07:17	3:12:40	2:56:27	3:28:16
4	100 M Butterfly	2:57:15	2:45:12	3:10:36	2:58:56
5	100 M Backstroke	3:00:30	2:45:18	2:55:09	3:12:16
6	200 M Individual Medley	3:56:50	5:25:25	4:34:07	4:24:36
7	400 M Medley Relay	5:34:08	5:45:02	5:46:25	5:51:32

Format the average times with an appearance similar to 13:30:55.

b) Save the spreadsheet naming it Swim Meet.

c) In cell F1, enter the label Avg. Time. Enter formulas that use a function to calculate the average time of each swimming event.

d) Italicize all the labels in row 1. Right align all the swimmers' names and the Avg. Time label in row 1. Resize columns as necessary so that all the data is displayed entirely.

e) Create a header with your name right aligned.

f) Create a footer with the text September 10 Swim Meet Results center aligned.

g) Save the modified Swim Meet and print a copy with gridlines and row and column headings.

h) Execute the appropriate action to display the formulas in the cells instead of values. Resize columns as necessary so that the formulas are completely displayed. Print a copy with gridlines and row and column headings.

Exercise 4 ———————————————————— Student Stats

A local universities' Admissions department wants to create a spreadsheet to keep track of the statistics on the number of undergraduate and graduate students in each college.

a) In a new spreadsheet enter the data as shown below. Resize columns as necessary so that all the data is displayed entirely:

	A	B	C
1	College	Undergraduate	Graduate
2	Business	3098	250
3	Education	1356	189
4	Liberal Arts	2589	180
5	Pharmacy	2398	212
6	Social Science	1586	98

b) Save the spreadsheet naming it Student Stats.

c) In cell A7, enter the label Total: and then right align and italicize it. Enter formulas that use a function to calculate the total number of undergraduate students and the total number of graduate students at the university.

d) In cell A8, enter the label Average: and then right align and italicize it. Enter formulas that use a function to calculate the average number of undergraduate students and the average number of graduate students at the university.

e) Format the numeric values to display commas and 0 decimal places.

f) Bold all the labels in row 1. Right align the Undergraduate and Graduate labels. Resize columns as necessary so that all the data is displayed entirely.

g) Create a header with your name right aligned.

h) Create a footer with the current date center aligned.

i) Save the modified Student Stats and print a copy with gridlines and row and column headings.

j) Execute the appropriate action to display the formulas in the cells instead of values. Resize columns as necessary so that the formulas are completely displayed. Print a copy with gridlines and row and column headings.

The accountant for Coral county has decided to use a spreadsheet for the city hall payroll.

a) In a new spreadsheet enter the data as shown below. Resize columns as necessary so that all the data is displayed entirely.

	A	B	C
1	First Name	Last Name	Salary
2	Sang	Cho	$42,000
3	Jill	Grossman	$25,500
4	Jason	Jones	$26,000
5	Christa	Smith	$28,900
6	Tanya	White	$32,000

Format the salaries as currency with 0 decimal places.

b) Save the spreadsheet naming it Coral Employees.

c) Employees are paid weekly. In cell D1, enter the label Weekly Pay. Enter formulas that use cell references to calculate the weekly pay for each employee. Weekly pay is calculated by dividing the salary by 52 weeks in a year.

d) In cell B7, enter the label Average: and then right align and italicize it. Enter formulas that use a function to calculate the average salary and weekly pay for the employees. Format the average weekly pay as currency with 2 decimal places.

e) Bold all the labels in row 1. Right align the Salary and Weekly Pay labels. Resize columns as necessary so that all the data is displayed entirely.

f) Modify the weekly pay formulas to use a function to round the weekly pay amounts in column D to 0 decimal places (do not round the average weekly pay formula). Note that the average weekly pay also changes because the numbers have been rounded.

g) Create a header with your name right aligned.

h) Save the modified Coral Employees and print a copy with gridlines and row and column headings.

i) Execute the appropriate action to display the formulas in the cells instead of values. Resize columns as necessary so that the formulas are completely displayed. Print a copy with gridlines and row and column headings.

Researchers of a coral reef study want to computerize their scuba diving log.

a) In a new spreadsheet enter the following data starting in cell A1:

Date	Depth (m)	Duration (min)	Water temp (Celsius)	Visibility (m)
5/8/01	10	60	26	10
5/10/01	18	45	25	12
5/11/01	13	50	27	9
5/13/01	27	15	23	10
5/14/01	11	53	28	11

b) Save the spreadsheet naming it Dive Log.

c) In cell A7, enter the label Average: and then right align and italicize it. Enter formulas that use a function to average the depth and duration of all five dives.

d) Modify the average depth and duration formulas to use a function to round the results to 0 decimal places.

e) Right align and italicize the labels in row 1. Resize columns as necessary so that all data is displayed entirely.

f) Create a header with your name right aligned.

g) Save the modified Dive Log and print a copy with gridlines and row and column headings.

h) Execute the appropriate action to display the formulas in the cells instead of values. Resize columns as necessary so that the formulas are completely displayed. Print a copy with gridlines and row and column headings.

Exercise 7 ———————————————————— Pizza Palace

The owner of Pizza Palace wants to use a spreadsheet to keep track of expenses.

a) In a new spreadsheet enter the data as shown below. Resize columns as necessary so that all the data is displayed entirely:

	A	B	C	D
1	Pizza Palace			
2	Expenses per Pizza			
3				
4	Ingredients	Everything	Vegetarian	Cheese
5	Dough	$1.25	$1.25	$1.25
6	Cheese	$1.50	$1.50	$1.50
7	Sauce	$0.50	$0.50	$0.50
8	Pepperoni	$0.75	$0.00	$0.00
9	Sausage	$1.00	$0.00	$0.00
10	Onion	$0.15	$0.15	$0.00
11	Mushroom	$0.35	$0.35	$0.00
12	Green Pepper	$0.40	$0.40	$0.00

Format the costs as currency with 2 decimal places.

b) Save the spreadsheet naming it Pizza Palace.

c) In cell A13, enter the label Cost of Pizza: and then right align and italicize it. Enter formulas that use a function to calculate the total cost of each pizza type.

d) Bold the Pizza Palace and Expenses per Pizza titles.

e) Bold the labels in row 4. Right align the pizza type labels. Resize columns as necessary so that all the data is displayed entirely.

f) Create a header with your name right aligned.

g) Create a footer with the current date center aligned.

h) Save the modified Pizza Palace and print a copy with gridlines and row and column headings.

i) Execute the appropriate action to display the formulas in the cells instead of values. Resize columns as necessary so that the formulas are completely displayed. Print a copy with gridlines and row and column headings.

Exercise 8 ———————————————————— Balance Sheet

A balance sheet lists a company's assets (what they own), liabilities (what they owe), and stockholders' equity (the owners' investments) as of a specific date. The owner of Nudelman's Gym wants to computerize the company's balance sheet.

a) In a new spreadsheet enter the data and apply formatting as shown below:

	A	B	C	D	E	F
1			Nudelman's Gym			
2			Balance Sheet			
3			Month Ended Jan 31, 2001			
4						
5	Assets:			Liabilities:		
6		Cash	$12,000		Accounts Payable	$75,987
7		Accounts Receivable	$15,000	Stockholder's Equity:		
8		Gym Equipment	$45,000		Stockholder's Equity	$95,003
9		Office Computers	$98,990			
10						
11		Total Assets:		Total Liabilities and Stockholder's Equity:		

b) Save the spreadsheet naming it Balance Sheet.

c) In cell C11, enter a formula that uses a function to calculates the total assets.

d) In cell F11, enter a formula that uses cell references to calculates the total liabilities and stockholder's equity.

e) Create a header with your name right aligned.

f) Save the modified Balance Sheet and print a copy with gridlines and row and column headings.

g) Execute the appropriate action to display the formulas in the cells instead of values. Resize columns as necessary so that the formulas are completely displayed. Print a copy with gridlines and row and column headings.

Exercise 9 ———————————————————— Temp Conversion

The local university's Meteorology department wants to use a spreadsheet to convert Fahrenheit temperatures to the equivalent Celsius temperatures.

a) In a new spreadsheet enter the data and apply formatting as shown below. In cell E3 enter the formula =5/9*(B3–32) to convert the Fahrenheit temperature stored in cell B3 to degrees Celsius:

	A	B	C	D	E
1	Temperature Conversion				
2					
3	Fahrenheit Temp:	20		Celsius Temp:	-6.66667

b) Save the spreadsheet naming it Temp Conversion.

c) Modify the formula in cell E3 to use a function to round the results to 0 decimal places.

d) Enter the following Fahrenheit temperatures in cell B3, one at a time: 0, 32, and 80. What Celsius temperature does each of these convert to?

e) In row 5, have the spreadsheet convert temperatures from a Celsius temperature entered in cell B5 to a Fahrenheit temperature displayed in cell E5. Use 26 for the Celsius temperature. Include appropriate labels. The formula needed for converting from degrees Celsius to Fahrenheit is =9/5*B5+32. Use a function to round the result to 0 decimal places. Resize columns as necessary so that all the data is displayed entirely.

f) Enter the following Celsius temperatures in cell B5, one at a time: 0, 12, and –21. What Fahrenheit temperature does each of these convert to?

g) Create a header with your name right aligned.

h) Save the modified Temp Conversion and print a copy with gridlines and row and column headings.

i) Execute the appropriate action to display the formulas in the cells instead of values. Resize columns as necessary so that the formulas are completely displayed. Print a copy with gridlines and row and column headings.

Exercise 10 ————————————————— Upgrade Costs

A technology coordinator needs projections for computer related costs through the year 2005. Years 2000 and 2001 have already been established.

a) In a new spreadsheet enter the following data starting in cell A1:

Year	Hardware	Software	Training
2000	$15,750	$5,500	$2,500
2001	$0	$8,000	$2,500

Format the costs as currency with 0 decimal places.

b) Save the spreadsheet naming it Upgrade Costs.

c) Hardware is upgraded every other year with an expected 15% increase over the last upgrade and software costs are expected to increase 7% each year starting in 2002. The training budget is $2,500 per year. Enter formulas that use cell references to calculate the costs for years 2002 through 2005.

d) Use a function to round the formulas for the hardware and software costs to 0 decimal places. Format all of the numeric values as currency with 0 decimal places.

e) Format the labels in row 1 as right aligned and bold. Resize columns as necessary so that all the data is displayed entirely.

f) Create a header with your name right aligned.

g) Save the modified Upgrade Costs and print a copy with gridlines and row and column headings.

h) Execute the appropriate action to display the formulas in the cells instead of values. Resize columns as necessary so that the formulas are completely displayed. Print a copy with gridlines and row and column headings.

Spreadsheets can help you keep track of your class grades. You are to create a spreadsheet of your grades in this class for the chapters you have covered so far. This exercise assumes assignments are graded using a point system (i.e., reviews are worth 20 points, tests are worth 100 points)

a) In a new spreadsheet enter your points for the practices, review questions, exercises, and tests. Also, enter the total points possible for each chapter. Include appropriate labels and proper formatting as shown below. Your spreadsheet will have different data but should look similar to:

	A	B	C	D	E	F	G
1		Ch 1	Ch 2	Ch 3	Ch 4	Ch 5	Ch 6
2	Practices	None	25	25	30	27	25
3	Review Questions	20	15	20	20	18	20
4	Exercises	None	None	50	45	43	47
5	Test	91	89	85	94	85	90
6	Possible Points	120	150	200	200	200	200

b) Save the spreadsheet naming it Class Scores.

c) In cell H1, enter the label Total Points. Enter formulas that use cell references to calculate the total points you earned for the practices, review questions, exercises, and tests. Also calculate the total points possible.

d) Resize columns as necessary so that all the data is displayed entirely.

e) In cell A8, enter the label Current Grade and then right align, bold, and italicize it. In cell B8, enter a formula that uses cell references and a function to calculate your grade. Your grade is calculated by dividing the total points you earned by the total points possible. Format your current grade as a percentage with 0 decimal places and bold.

f) Create a header with your name right alined.

g) Create a footer with the text Computer Class Grades center aligned.

h) Save the modified Class Scores and print a copy with gridlines and row and column headings.

i) Execute the appropriate action to display the formulas in the cells instead of values. Resize columns as necessary so that the formulas are completely displayed. Print a copy with gridlines and row and column headings.

Spreadsheets can be helpful in personal financial management. One way to organize your finances is to use a spreadsheet as a checkbook register.

a) In a new spreadsheet enter the data and apply formatting as shown below:

	A	B	C	D	E
1	Date	Transaction	Description	Expenses	Income
2	1-Feb-2001	Opening Deposit			$200.00
3	5-Feb-2001	Coral Gas	Gas for car	$20.00	
4	8-Feb-2001	Deposit	Paycheck		$100.00
5	10-Feb-2001	Sally's Diner	Dinner out	$15.35	
6	15-Feb-2001	Coral Square Cinema	Movie	$6.75	
7	16-Feb-2001	Deposit	Birthday check		$25.00
8	18-Feb-2001	Book Palace	Magazines	$15.98	
9	19-Feb-2001	Full Belly	Dinner out	$10.50	
10	22-Feb-2001	Coral Square Mall	Lunch out	$5.75	
11	24-Feb-2001	Coral Gas	Gas for car	$15.00	
12	26-Feb-2001	Deposit	Paycheck		$100.00

b) Save the spreadsheet naming it Checkbook.

c) In cell F1, enter the label Balance and right align and bold it if it is not already formatted.

d) In column F, enter formulas that use cell references to calculate the balance after each transaction. To calculate the balance, subtract the expense from the previous balance and add the income to the previous balance.

e) In cell C13, enter the label Total: and then right align and bold it. Enter formulas that use a function to calculate the total expenses and total income for the month.

f) Create a header with your name right aligned.

g) Create a footer with the text Personal Finances center aligned.

h) Save the modified Checkbook and print a copy with gridlines and row and column headings.

i) Execute the appropriate action to display the formulas in the cells instead of values. Resize columns as necessary so that the formulas are completely displayed. Print a copy with gridlines and row and column headings.

An income statement lists a company's revenues (money they earn), expenses (money they pay out), and net income/loss (revenues minus expenses) for a specific time period. Fluffy Bakery is a small home business that uses a spreadsheet to produce an income statement.

a) In a new spreadsheet enter the data and apply formatting as shown below:

	A	B	C	D	E
1			Fluffy Bakery		
2			Income Statement		
3			for the years 1999-2001		
4					
5			1999	2000	2001	
6	Revenues:				
7	Cookie Sales	$15,500	$16,896	$17,864	
8	Cake Sales	$27,589	$26,298	$25,982	
9	Bread Sales	$24,980	$25,298	$25,398	
10	Total Revenues:				
11	Expenses:				
12	Advertising	$5,000	$4,500	$4,500	
13	Baking Supplies	$2,000	$1,000	$2,750	
14	Ingredients	$13,275	$15,298	$16,490	
15	Salaries	$30,000	$30,000	$35,000	
16	Utilities	$6,570	$7,250	$8,090	
17	Total Expenses:				
18	Net Income/(Loss):				

b) Save the spreadsheet naming it Income Statement.

c) In row 10, enter formulas that uses a function to calculate the total revenues for each year.

d) In row 17, enter formulas that use a function to calculate the total expenses for each year.

e) In row 18, enter formulas that use cell references to calculate the net income or loss for each year. The net income/loss is calculated by subtracting total expenses from total revenues. Format the values as currency with 0 decimal places.

f) Create a header with your name right aligned.

g) Save the modified Income Statement and print a copy with gridlines and row and column headings.

h) Execute the appropriate action to display the formulas in the cells instead of values. Resize columns as necessary so that the formulas are completely displayed. Print a copy with gridlines and row and column headings.

A student wants to use a spreadsheet to create a budget for her fall semester.

a) In a new spreadsheet enter the data and apply formatting as shown below:

	A	B	C	D	E	F	G	H	I
1	**Personal Budget**								
2									
3		**Sep-01**		**Oct-01**		**Nov-01**		**Dec-01**	
4		Budgeted	*Actual*	Budgeted	*Actual*	Budgeted	*Actual*	Budgeted	*Actual*
5	**Income:**								
6	Loan	$4,000	$4,000	$0	$0	$0	$0	$0	$0
7	Job	$500	$425	$500	$465	$500	$485	$600	$725
8	Parents	$5,500	$5,500	$0	$0	$0	$0	$0	$0
9	*Totals:*								
10	**Expenses:**								
11	Tuition	$3,000	$2,943	$0	$0	$0	$0	$0	$0
12	Room/Board	$5,500	$5,575	$0	$0	$0	$0	$0	$0
13	Books	$200	$235	$0	$45	$0	$0	$0	$0
14	Food	$300	$315	$300	$325	$300	$320	$250	$375
15	Entertainment	$150	$175	$150	$165	$150	$180	$175	$200
16	Clothes	$50	$0	$50	$80	$50	$0	$100	$100
17	*Totals:*								

b) Save the spreadsheet naming it Budget.

c) In row 9, enter formulas that use a function to calculate the total budgeted and actual income for each month.

d) In row 17, enter formulas that use a function to calculate the total budgeted and actual expenses for each month.

e) In cell A18, enter the label Budgeted Savings: and right align it. Enter formulas that use cell references to calculate the budgeted savings for each month. Budgeted savings are calculated by subtracting the total budgeted expenses from the total budgeted income.

f) In cell A19, enter the label Actual Savings: and then right align it. Enter formulas that use cell references to calculate the actual savings for each month. Actual savings are calculated by subtracting the total actual expenses from the total actual income.

g) Italicize the titles in cells A18 and A19. Resize columns as necessary so that all the data is displayed entirely.

h) Create a header with your name right aligned.

i) Save the modified Budget and print a copy with gridlines and row and column headings.

j) Execute the appropriate action to display the formulas in the cells instead of values. Resize columns as necessary so that the formulas are completely displayed. Print a copy with gridlines and row and column headings.

A spreadsheet can be used to calculate the costs of producing brochures in different quantities. The cost of the brochure is made up of fixed costs and variable costs. Fixed costs remain the same no matter how many brochures are produced. Variable costs change depending on the number of brochures produced.

a) In a new spreadsheet enter the data and apply formatting as shown below:

	A	B	C	D	E	F
1	Brochure Costs					
2						
3	Number of Brochures:	100	250	500	750	1000
4						
5	Fixed Costs:					
6	Art work	$500.00	$500.00	$500.00	$500.00	$500.00
7	Salaries	$1,500.00	$1,500.00	$1,500.00	$1,500.00	$1,500.00
8	Initial setup fee	$1,000.00	$1,000.00	$1,000.00	$1,000.00	$1,000.00
9	Variable Costs:					
10	Paper					
11	Printing					
12	Labor					
13	Shipping					

b) Save the spreadsheet naming it Brochure Costs.

c) The breakdown of variable costs per brochure are:

Paper	$0.20
Printing	$0.12
Labor	$0.07
Shipping	$0.10

Variable costs are calculated by multiplying the variable cost per brochure by the number of brochures produced. In cells B10 through F13, enter formulas that use cell references to calculate the variable costs. Format the cells as currency with 2 decimal places.

d) In cell A14, enter the label Total Costs: and right align and bold it. Enter formulas that use a function to calculate the total cost of producing the different quantity of brochures. Total cost is calculated by adding the fixed costs plus the variable costs.

e) In cell A15, enter the label Cost per Brochure: and right align and bold it. Enter formulas that use cell references to calculate the cost per brochure of producing the different quantities of brochures. Cost per brochure is calculated by dividing the total costs by the number of brochures produced.

f) Create a header with your name right aligned.

g) Save the modified Brochure Costs and print a copy with gridlines and row and column headings.

h) Execute the appropriate action to display the formulas in the cells instead of values. Resize columns as necessary so that the formulas are completely displayed. Print a copy with gridlines and row and column headings.

Advanced
Exercise 16 ——————————————————— Club

Create a new spreadsheet that stores relevant numbers about a club or organization that you belong to. The spreadsheet should contain at least five columns and five rows of data. Include at least two formulas in the spreadsheet. Format the spreadsheet appropriately and include informative headers or footers. Save the spreadsheet naming it Club and print a copy with gridlines and row and column headings. Print a copy of the spreadsheet so that formulas are displayed in the cells instead of values.

Advanced
Exercise 17 ——————————————————— Vacation Costs

Create a new spreadsheet that stores estimated costs for vacations to at least three different countries you would like to visit. The spreadsheet should contain at least four columns and four rows of data. Include at least two formulas and one function in the spreadsheet. Format the spreadsheet appropriately and include informative headers or footers. Save the spreadsheet naming it Vacation Costs and print a copy with gridlines and row and column headings. Print a copy of the spreadsheet so that formulas are displayed in the cells instead of values.

Advanced
Exercise 18 ——————————————————— Fund-raiser Finances

Create a new spreadsheet that stores financial information about a fund-raiser you have participated in. The spreadsheet should contain at least six columns and six rows of data. Include at least three formulas and two functions in the spreadsheet. Format the spreadsheet appropriately and include informative headers or footers. Save the spreadsheet naming it Fund-raiser Finances and print a copy gridlines and row and column headings. Print a copy of the spreadsheet so that formulas are displayed in the cells instead of values.

A Guide to Microsoft Office 2000 Professional

Find

Replace

Insert Function

Rows

Columns

Delete

Page Setup

Page Break

Remove Page Break

Chapter Eight Objectives

After completing this chapter you will be able to:

1. Plan a large spreadsheet.
2. Locate cells containing specific data and replace the contents with specific data.
3. Copy and move labels, values, and formulas.
4. Use the MAX and MIN functions.
5. Enter functions using the Function command and Paste Function button.
6. Understand absolute cell references.
7. Insert and delete rows and columns.
8. Change the margins, print orientation, and page breaks of a spreadsheet.
9. Use the IF function and use text in the IF function.

$\mathbf{I}$n this chapter, planning and modifying a spreadsheet are explained and more functions are introduced. Commands for copying, moving, and locating cell contents are also introduced.

8.1 Planning a Spreadsheet

To be useful, a spreadsheet should be carefully planned by answering the following questions:

1. What new information should the spreadsheet produce?

2. What data must the spreadsheet store to produce the new information?

3. What calculations will be needed?

4. How should the data be organized and displayed on the screen?

For example, a company that wants to use a spreadsheet to calculate their weekly payroll would plan the spreadsheet by answering the questions as follows:

1. The spreadsheet should produce each employee's gross and net pay for the week. Gross pay is the amount earned before any deductions (such as taxes) are made. Net pay is the amount that the employee receives after deductions.

2. The spreadsheet needs to store the following data:

   • Employee name and pay rate per hour
   • Hours worked per day for each weekday
   • Social security and tax rates

3. Gross pay is calculated by multiplying the total number of hours worked by the employee's hourly pay rate. Net pay is calculated by subtracting social security and taxes from the gross pay. Social security and taxes are calculated by multiplying the gross pay by the social security rate or tax rate.

4. Determining how the data should be organized and displayed is best done by drawing a sketch of the spreadsheet that includes each label and the type of data stored:

Soc. Sec. Rate:										
Employee	Rate/hr	Mon	Tue	Wed	Thu	Fri	Total Hours	Gross Pay	Soc. Sec.	Taxes	Net Pay
text	currency	number with one decimal place					currency	currency	currency	currency	currency

Practice 1

In this practice you will plan a spreadsheet for Net Provider, a national Internet service provider that offers basic and premium internet service to all 50 states. Basic service is $17.95 and premium service is $19.95 per month. The owner of the company wants to know the monthly revenues from both the basic service and the premium service per state, as well as the total monthly revenue per state. Revenue is the money collected and is based on the monthly service price and the number of accounts using that service. Using paper and pencil, plan the spreadsheet by answering the four questions discussed in the previous section.

8.2 The Find and Replace Commands

The Find and Replace commands in the Edit menu are useful when working with a large spreadsheet. For example, a cell that contains a particular value, label, or formula can be located using the Find command. Selecting the Find command (Ctrl+F) displays a dialog box where the cell contents to be searched for is typed:

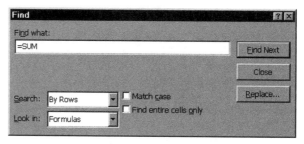

Search text is typed in the Find what entry box

In this example =SUM has been entered as the search text. The option selected in the Look in collapsible list indicates whether to search by Formulas (what is stored in the cell) or Values (what is displayed in the cell). Selecting the Find Next button initiates the search from the current cell.

Selecting cell A1 before executing the Find command will begin the search at the beginning of the spreadsheet. A dialog box is displayed if the search text is not found.

The Replace command (Ctrl+H) displays a dialog box similar to the Find dialog box. It is used to locate labels, formulas, and values, and then change them to data you supply.

The Go To Command

Selecting the Go To command from the File menu displays a dialog box with options that allow you to move the cell cursor to a specific cell quickly.

8.3 The Copy, Cut, and Paste Commands

Commands in the Edit menu are used to copy and move cell contents and formatting. These commands can help when the same label, value, or formula needs to be stored in a number of different cells.

The steps for copying a block of cells are:

1. Highlight the cells to be copied.

2. Select the Copy command (Ctrl+C). A copy of the cells' contents and formatting is placed on the Clipboard.

3. Select the first cell where the data is to appear.

4. Select the Paste command (Ctrl+V). The contents of the Clipboard are placed in the cells.

When the Copy command is selected, the highlighted cells are outlined with a moving dashed line to show what will be copied. After pasting the cells, the Esc key or Enter key is pressed to remove the dashed outline.

The Cut command (Ctrl+X) is used to move cell contents and formatting. Selecting the Cut command places a copy of the selected cells' contents and formatting on the Clipboard and outlines the cells to be moved. Selecting the Paste command places the contents of the Clipboard in the new location and removes the original, outlined cells on the spreadsheet.

When pasting cell contents, only the upper-left cell where the range of cells is to be pasted needs to be selected. Any existing cell contents at the new location are replaced by the Clipboard contents when the Paste command is selected.

    The Cut (), Copy (), and Paste () buttons on the Standard Toolbar can also be used to select the editing commands.

Practice 2

In this practice you will search the NET PROVIDER spreadsheet and copy labels and values.

1) OPEN NET PROVIDER

Open NET PROVIDER. This spreadsheet is based on the spreadsheet discussed in Practice 1.

2) SEARCH FOR THE TEXT "Vermont"

   a. Select cell A1 if it is not already selected.
   b. Select Edit → Find. A dialog box is displayed.
       1. In the Find what entry box, type Vermont.
       2. Select Find Next. Excel moves the cell cursor to cell A50 which contains the name Vermont. You may need to move the Find dialog box by dragging its Title bar to see cell A50.
       3. Select Close to remove the dialog box.
   c. Select cell B50 and enter 101 as the new number of basic accounts.

3) REPLACE "N." WITH "North"

   a. Select cell A1.
   b. Select Edit → Replace. A dialog box is displayed.
       1. In the Find what entry box, type N. (be sure to type the period).
       2. In the Replace with entry box, type North.
       3. Select Find Next. The cell cursor is moved to the cell containing "N. Carolina."
       4. Select the Replace button in the dialog box. The current text in the cell is replaced and the cell cursor moves to the next cell containing the search text.
       5. Select Replace. The current text in the cell is replaced and the cell cursor remains on the cell indicating there are no more occurrences of the search text.
       6. Select Close. The dialog box is removed.

4) MOVE CELL CONTENTS

   a. Select cells A56 through C56.
   b. Select Edit → Cut. A moving dashed line is placed around the cells.
   c. Select cell A16.
   d. On the Standard Toolbar, click on the Paste () button. The label and values in cells A56 through C56 are moved to cells A16 through C16.

5) SAVE THE MODIFIED NET PROVIDER

8.4 The MAX and MIN Functions

Excel includes two functions that determine the maximum or minimum value stored in a range of cells. The MAX function takes the form:

> MAX(<range of cells>)

For example, =MAX(C2:C9) displays the maximum (largest) of all the values in the range C2 to C9.

The MIN function takes the form:

> MIN(<range of cells>)

For example, =MIN(B2:F3) displays the minimum (smallest) of all the values in the range B2 to F3.

8.5 Inserting a Function into a Formula

Instead of typing a function's name into a formula, selecting the Function command from the Insert menu displays the Paste Function dialog box, which lists available functions:

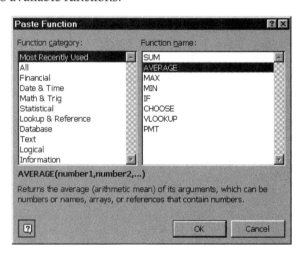

Selecting an option in the Function category list limits the functions that are displayed. Selecting the desired function in the Function name list and then OK displays the formula palette for the selected function. For example, selecting AVERAGE and then OK displays the following formula palette:

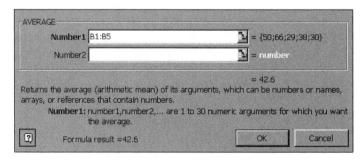

Formula palettes have entry boxes for cell references, ranges, and values for the selected function

---

Function Box

After typing an equal sign (=) in a cell, the Function box appears on the Formula bar. The Function box can be used as an alternative to typing a function name:

Clicking on the down arrow of the Function box and selecting the desired function displays its formula palette. If the function is not listed, selecting More Functions displays the Paste Function dialog box.

Excel automatically enters a range of cells in the Number1 entry box to be used in the function, in this case the cell range that is to be averaged. The cell range can be changed, if necessary, by typing or pointing to cells on the spreadsheet. Selecting OK removes the formula palette and the function is entered into the formula. Excel automatically precedes the function with an equal sign if it is not already part of a formula.

Sometimes the formula palette may be covering the cells of the spreadsheet that you need to select for a range. Dragging on the formula palette will move it.

 The Paste Function button () on the Standard Toolbar can also be used to display the Paste Function dialog box.

Practice 3

In this practice you will compute the maximum and minimum number of basic and premium accounts. Open NET PROVIDER if it is not already displayed.

1) DETERMINE THE HIGHEST NUMBER OF BASIC ACCOUNTS IN ANY STATE

   a. Select cell A56 and enter the label Max accounts: then right align and italicize the label.
   b. Select cell B56.
   c. Select Insert → Function. An equal sign is inserted into cell B56 and the Paste Function dialog box is displayed.
       1. Click on All in the Function category list.
       2. Scroll until MAX is visible in the Function name list and then select it.
       3. Select OK. The formula palette is displayed.
       4. Excel automatically enters the range B6:B55 in the Number1 entry box.
       5. Select OK to accept the range entered by Excel. Oklahoma's basic accounts, 7,787, is displayed as the maximum value in the cell range used in the function.

2) DETERMINE THE LOWEST NUMBER OF BASIC ACCOUNTS IN ANY STATE

   a. Select cell A57 and enter the label Min accounts: then right align and italicize the label.
   b. Select cell B57.
   c. Select Insert → Function. An equal sign is inserted into cell B57 and the Paste Function dialog box is displayed.
       1. Scroll until MIN is visible in the Function name list and then select it.
       2. Select OK. The formula palette is displayed. Note the range B6:B56 in the Number1 entry box, which is not the correct range.
           a. Modify the range to be B6:B55.
           b. Select OK. Georgia's Basic accounts, 2, is displayed as the minimum value in the cell range used in the function.

3) COPY THE MAX AND MIN FORMULAS

   a. Highlight cells B56 and B57.
   b. Select Edit → Copy.
   c. Select cell C56.
   d. Select Edit → Paste. The formulas are pasted into cells C56 and C57 with cell references automatically changed.
   e. Press the Esc key to remove the moving dashed outline.

4) SAVE THE MODIFIED NET PROVIDER

8.6 Absolute Cell References

As discussed in Chapter Seven, relative cell references automatically change when copied. However, there may be times when a cell reference should remain the same. A cell reference that does not change when copied is called an *absolute cell reference*. An absolute cell reference contains dollar signs in front of both the column letter and row number (e.g., $A$1).

For example, in the spreadsheet below, shipping charges are calculated using a shipping rate stored in cell B3. The shipping for the first item could be calculated using the formula =B6*B3 in cell C6. However, if this formula were copied to cells C7, C8, and C9, the cell reference B3 would become B4, B5, and B6 respectively. To prevent this, the formula was entered as =B6*$B$3 and then copied to cells C7 through C9:

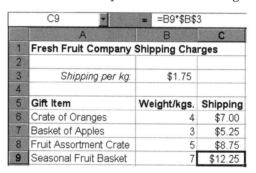

Note the formula in the Formula bar

The *F4 key* can be used to place dollar signs in front of a cell reference. For example, the shipping formula in cell C6 was entered by first typing =B6*. Next, cell B3 was clicked and then the F4 key pressed to create the absolute cell reference, $B$3, to cell B3.

Practice 4

In this practice you will use absolute copying to calculate revenues. Open NET PROVIDER if it is not already displayed.

1) ENTER FORMULAS TO CALCULATE REVENUES

Revenue is calculated by multiplying the service price per month by the number of accounts receiving that service.

a. Select cell D6.
b. Type an equal sign (=).
c. Click on cell B6 to enter it into the formula.
d. Type an asterisk (*).
e. Click on cell B3 and then press the F4 key once. The absolute reference $B$3 appears in the formula.
f. Click on the Enter button to enter the formula which calculates the revenue, $8,185.20.
g. In cell E6, enter the formula =C6*$C$3 to calculate the premium service revenue.
h. In cell F6, enter the formula =D6+E6 to total the revenues for each type of service.

2) COPY THE FORMULAS

a. Highlight cells D6 through F6.
b. Drag the Fill handle in cell F6 down to cell F55. The formulas are copied for each state.

3) SAVE, PRINT, AND THEN CLOSE THE MODIFIED NET PROVIDER

8.7 Inserting and Deleting Rows and Columns

Rows and columns can be inserted between data in a spreadsheet. A new row is inserted by clicking on the row number where the new row is to appear and then selecting the Rows command from the Insert menu. The selected row and all those below it move down to accommodate the newly inserted row. Columns can be inserted by clicking on the column letter and then selecting the Columns command from the Insert menu. The selected column and all those after it are moved to the right.

Newly inserted rows and columns are empty and contain no data or formulas. However, cells in the new row or column have the same formatting as the cells above or to the left of them respectively.

Rows and columns can also be deleted from a spreadsheet. A row is deleted by clicking on its row number and then selecting the Delete command from the Edit menu. All rows below the deleted row move up to fill its position. A column is deleted by clicking on its column letter and then selecting the Delete command. The columns to the right of the deleted column then move to the left.

Immediately selecting the Undo command or the Undo button on the Standard Toolbar restores a deleted row or column.

Rows and columns can also be inserted or deleted by right clicking on the row number or column letter, which displays a menu. Selecting the Insert command in this menu inserts a row or column similar to using the Rows and Columns commands. Selecting the Delete command in this menu removes the row or column.

When cells are inserted or deleted, Excel automatically changes the cell references in any affected formulas. For example, if row 3 is deleted, the formula =SUM(C1:C10) changes to =SUM(C1:C9). If a row is inserted between rows 1 and 10, the formula becomes =SUM(C1:C11).

Practice 5

In this practice you will add columns to the PAYROLL spreadsheet to calculate the social security, taxes, and net pay for each employee.

1) OPEN PAYROLL

The spreadsheet is based on the spreadsheet plan discussed in Section 8.1. Note that the spreadsheet already contains some formulas.

2) ENTER A FORMULA TO CALCULATE SOCIAL SECURITY

Social security is calculated by multiplying the gross pay by the social security rate, which is stored in cell B2.

a. Select cell J5.
b. Enter the formula =I5*$B$2 to calculate the social security deduction as 6.5% of the gross pay, $14.63.

3) ENTER A FORMULA TO CALCULATE NET PAY

In cell K5, enter the formula =I5–J5 to calculate the net pay (gross pay minus social security deduction). $210.38 is displayed.

4) COPY THE FORMULAS

Copy the formulas in cells J5 through K5 to cells J6 through K26.

5) CHANGE THE SOCIAL SECURITY RATE

In cell B2, enter the value 6.00%. Note that Excel automatically recalculates all the values in columns J and K.

6) DELETE THE ROW CONTAINING DATA FOR EMPLOYEE OTIS, H.

a. Select cell A1.
b. Select Edit → Find. A dialog box is displayed.
   1. In the Find what entry box, type Otis and then select Find Next. The cell cursor is moved to the cell containing the search text "Otis."
   2. Select Close. The dialog box is removed.
c. Click on the row number of the row containing H. Otis' data to select it.
d. Select Edit → Delete. The row is deleted and all rows below it move up to fill the space. All the cell references in the formulas are automatically updated.

7) INSERT A COLUMN FOR THE TAXES

a. Right-click on the column letter K. A menu is displayed.
b. Select the Insert command. A new column is inserted.
c. In cell K4, enter the label Taxes. Note that the label is automatically formatted.
d. In cell K5, enter the formula =I5*15% to calculate 15% of the gross pay.
e. Copy the new formula to cells K6 through K25.

8) MODIFY THE NET PAY FORMULA

a. In cell L5, modify the formula to be: =I5–J5–K5
b. Copy the new formula to cells L6 through L25.

9) SAVE THE MODIFIED PAYROLL

8.8 Printing a Large Spreadsheet

A spreadsheet that has many columns of data is often too wide to print on a single sheet of paper. When this happens, Excel prints the spreadsheet on consecutive sheets starting from the leftmost column and proceeding to the right. However, changing the print orientation, the margins, or adding page breaks before printing can help fit the spreadsheet onto the desired number of pages.

Changing the print orientation allows more columns to fit on a page. The Page Setup command from the File menu displays a dialog box that contains the Orientation options:

landscape orientation
portrait orientation

Selecting the Page tab and then the Landscape option prints the spreadsheet across the widest part of the page in *landscape orientation*. This allows more columns and fewer rows to fit on a page. *Portrait orientation* is the default and allows more rows to be printed on a page.

changing the margins

One way to fit more rows and columns on a printout is to decrease the margins. Selecting the Margins tab in the Page Setup dialog box displays options that affect the margins. Decreasing the Top and Bottom margins may allow more rows to fit on a page, and decreasing the Left and Right margins may allow more columns to fit on a page.

repeating labels on
multiple pages

One difficulty encountered when printing large spreadsheets is that the labels at the beginning of rows or columns of data are not printed on every page. Specific rows and columns can be printed on every page by selecting the Sheet tab in the Page Setup dialog box and specifying the appropriate rows and columns in the Rows to repeat at top and Columns to repeat at left entry boxes.

page break

A page break can be added to a spreadsheet to format the printout so it is easier to read. Page breaks are added by selecting the Page Break command from the Insert menu, which inserts a page break before the currently selected row or column. If a single cell is selected before executing the command, the page break is created above and to the left of that cell. The page break is indicated by a dashed line, and the effects of page breaks can be seen by previewing the spreadsheet. A page break is removed by selecting a cell in the row or column after the page break and executing the Remove Page Break command from the Insert menu.

8.9 The IF Function

Excel includes several built-in functions that make decisions based on the data stored in a spreadsheet. One of these functions is the IF function, which makes a decision based on a comparison. If the comparison is true, one value is displayed in the cell; if the comparison is false, a second value is displayed. The IF function takes the form:

IF(<comparison>, <true value>, <false value>)

For example, the formula

=IF(C4<E7,10,20)

displays a 10 if the value in C4 is less than the value in E4. If the value in C4 is greater than or equal to the value in E7, 20 is displayed. What will be displayed if C4 contains the value 35 and E7 contains 30?

relational operators

The comparison argument of the IF function can contain one of the following *relational operators*:

=	equal to
<	less than
>	greater than
<=	less than or equal to
>=	greater than or equal to
<>	not equal to

The arguments of an IF function can contain values, cell references, or calculations as shown in the following formulas:

=IF(N1<=25,50,100)
=IF(B2<K25,0,B2*15%)
=IF(C9>MIN(C2:C7),C11,C14)
=IF(D22<>F25,0,SUM(E1:E10))

an IF example

The IF function is used in a spreadsheet when a comparison is needed to make a calculation. An example of this is when a business needs to calculate an employee's gross pay that includes time and half for hours worked over 40 hours.

E2			=	=IF(D2>40,(40*B2)+((D2-40)*C2),D2*B2)	
	A	B	C	D	E
1	Employee	Rate/Hr	Overtime Rate/Hr	Hours Worked	Gross Pay
2	Foselum	$7.50	$11.25	42	$322.50
3	Kinzer	$9.00	$13.50	35	$315.00
4	Noakes	$8.50	$12.75	40	$340.00
5	Rincon	$10.00	$15.00	39	$390.00
6	Watson	$7.00	$10.50	45	$332.50

Using Large Numbers with the IF Function

When entering a large number in the comparison argument of the IF function, do not include commas as thousands separators. This causes an error because Excel expects each argument to be separated by a comma.

The formula in cell E2 checks if the number of hours worked is over 40. If this is true, the gross pay is calculated by multiplying 40 hours by the regular rate and all the hours over 40 by the overtime rate, and then adding the two values. If the hours worked is less than or equal to 40, then the hours worked is multiplied by the regular rate.

Practice 6

In this practice you will modify the PAYROLL spreadsheet to calculate gross pay that includes overtime pay. Open PAYROLL if it is not already displayed.

1) ENTER A NEW GROSS PAY FORMULA

a. In cell I5, modify the formula to be:

=IF(H5>40,(40*B5)+((H5–40)*(B5*1.5)),H5*B5)

Because the value in H5 is less than 40, the total hours worked is multiplied by the regular hourly rate and the gross pay does not change.

b. Copy the formula in cell I5 to cells I6 through I25.

A Guide to Microsoft Office 2000 Professional

2) VIEW THE SPREADSHEET AS IT WILL APPEAR WHEN PRINTED

    a. Select File → Print Preview. The print preview window is displayed

    b. Press the Page Down key. Note that the Soc. Sec., Taxes and Net Pay columns appear on page 2.

    c. Select Close to return to the spreadsheet window.

    d. Select File → Page Setup. A dialog box is displayed.

        1. Select the Page tab to display the orientation options if they are not already displayed.

        2. Select the Landscape option.

        3. Select OK. The dialog box is removed.

    e. Print preview the spreadsheet. Note how all the data fits on one page.

    f. Return to the spreadsheet window.

3) SAVE, PRINT, AND THEN CLOSE THE MODIFIED PAYROLL

8.10 Using Text in the IF Function

It can be useful to display text as a result of a comparison. For example, the formula

    =IF(B3>=70,"Plenty","Reorder")

displays Plenty if the value in cell B3 is greater than or equal to 70. Otherwise, Reorder is displayed. Notice that quotation marks must surround text in a function.

Cell references of a cell storing a label can also be used in the IF function. For example, if Plenty is stored in cell C1, and Reorder in cell C2, then the formula =IF(B3>=70,C1,C2) produces the same result as the formula above.

Text can also be used in the comparison part of the IF function. When compared, the alphabetical order of the text is determined. For example, the following formula displays True because apple comes before orange alphabetically:

    =IF("apple"<"orange","True","False")

Cells that store labels can also be compared. If apple is stored in cell B3 and orange stored in cell B5, the formula =IF(B3<B5,B3,B5) displays apple.

Practice 7

In this practice the Grades spreadsheet created in Chapter Seven will be modified to display each student's status.

1) OPEN GRADES

2) ENTER A LABEL AND FORMAT IT

    In cell G1, enter the label Status then center align the label.

3) ENTER FORMULAS TO DETERMINE THE STUDENTS' STATUS

    a. In cell G3, enter the formula:

        =IF(F3>=70,"Passing","Below Average")

    Since the value in cell F3 is greater than or equal to 70, Passing is displayed in cell G3.

    b. Center align the label in cell G3.

c. Copy the formula in cell G3 to cells G4 through G8. Note that since the value in cell F5 is less than 70, Below Average is displayed in cell G5.

d. Widen column G to display all the labels entirely.

<u>Check</u> – Your spreadsheet should look similar to:

	A	B	C	D	E	F	G
1	Name	Test 1	Test 2	Test 3	Test 4	Student Average	Status
2		9/12/2001	10/10/2001	11/14/2001	12/12/2001		
3	Demps, K.	85	73	88	92	84.5	Passing
4	McCallister, T.	92	88	85	91	89.0	Passing
5	Matos, A.	72	63	67	72	68.5	Below Average
6	Smith, L.	87	92	85	93	89.3	Passing
7	Sun, L.	94	91	93	84	90.5	Passing
8	Adams, V.	70	74	80	83	76.8	Passing
9	*Test Average*	83.33	80.17	83	85.83		

4) *SAVE, PRINT, AND THEN CLOSE THE MODIFIED GRADES*

5) *EXIT EXCEL*

Chapter Summary

planning a spreadsheet

This chapter covered planning and modifying large spreadsheets. Spreadsheets should be carefully planned before creating them in Excel by first deciding what new information the spreadsheet will produce, what data is needed to produce the new information, what calculations are needed, and what the spreadsheet should look like when finished. A sketch of the spreadsheet should be done to plan its format. The sketch should indicate labels and the type of data stored.

Cell contents can be searched using the <u>F</u>ind command from the <u>E</u>dit menu. The R<u>e</u>place command is used to locate labels, formulas, and values and then change them to data supplied by the user.

The Cu<u>t</u> command is used to move a cell's contents, while the <u>C</u>opy command is used to copy a cell's contents. The <u>P</u>aste command places the Clipboard contents into a selected cell. All three commands are found in the <u>E</u>dit menu.

MAX, MIN

The MAX and MIN functions display the maximum or minimum value stored in a specified range of cells, respectively.

An alternative to typing a function name is to use the <u>F</u>unction command from the <u>I</u>nsert menu or the Paste Function button on the Standard Toolbar.

Cell references are kept from changing when formulas are copied by placing dollar signs ($) in front of the column letter and row number ($A$3). These are called absolute cell references. The F4 key can be used to place dollar signs in a cell reference.

Rows or columns can be inserted into a spreadsheet using the <u>R</u>ows or <u>C</u>olumns commands from the <u>I</u>nsert menu, respectively. The <u>D</u>elete command from the <u>E</u>dit menu can be used to delete a row or column. The point of insertion or deletion is indicated by clicking on the appropriate row number or column letter. Excel automatically changes the ranges of any involved formulas when a column or row is inserted or deleted.

print orientation
The way a spreadsheet is printed can be changed by modifying the margins or print orientation using the Page Setup command from the File menu. Printing a spreadsheet in landscape orientation prints more columns and fewer rows on a single sheet of paper. Inserting page breaks using the Page Break command from the Insert menu also affects the spreadsheet's printout.

IF
A decision can be made based on the data in a spreadsheet by using the IF function. When a comparison is true, the second argument in the function is displayed in the current cell. When a comparison is false, the third argument is shown. For example, evaluating the formula =IF(A5>B4,30,15) displays 30 when the value in A5 is greater than the value in B4, and 15 when the value in A5 is less than or equal to the value in B4. The comparison argument of the IF function uses relational

relational operators
operators (=, <, <=, >, >=, <>).

Text can be used in the IF function. For example, the formula =IF(A5<30,"Cheap","Expensive") displays Cheap if A5 is less than 30 and Expensive if A5 is greater than or equal to 30. The cell reference of a cell storing a label can also be used in the IF function.

Relational operators can be used to compare text in the comparison part of the IF function. For example, if cell A5 contains George and B12 contains Andrews, then the formula =IF(A5<B12,"Yes","No") displays No since George is greater than Andrews.

Vocabulary

Absolute cell reference A cell references that does not change when copied because dollar signs have been used with the cell reference (i.e., $A$5).

F4 key Places dollar signs in front of the column letter and row number in a cell reference.

IF Function that makes a decision based on a comparison.

Landscape orientation A printing orientation that indicates a spreadsheet is to be printed across the widest part of the paper.

MAX Function that displays the largest value in a range of cells.

MIN Function that displays the smallest value in a range of cells.

Portrait orientation The default printing orientation that indicates a spreadsheet is to be printed across the narrowest part of the paper.

Relational operators Used to compare two values. Operators include =, <, >, <=, >=, <>.

Excel Commands and Buttons

Columns command Inserts a column to the left of the currently selected column. Found in the Insert menu.

Copy command Places a copy of the highlighted cells' contents and formatting on the Clipboard. Found in the Edit menu. The Copy button (⊞) on the Standard Toolbar can be used instead of the command.

Cut command Removes the highlighted cells' contents and formatting and places it on the Clipboard. Found in the Edit menu. The Cut button (✂) on the Standard Toolbar can be used instead of the command.

Delete command Removes a selected column or row from a spreadsheet. Found in the Edit menu.

Find command Displays a dialog box that allows the user to search a spreadsheet for labels, values, or formulas. Found in the Edit menu.

Function command Displays a dialog box where a function to insert into a cell can be selected. Found in the Insert menu. The Paste Function button (ƒ*) on the Standard Toolbar can be used instead of the command.

Insert command Inserts a row or column. Displayed by right-clicking on a row number or column letter.

Page Break command Inserts a page break into a spreadsheet. Found in the Insert menu.

Page Setup command Displays a dialog box where options for changing the margins and the print orientation can be selected. Found in the File menu.

Paste command Places the Clipboard contents in a spreadsheet starting at the selected cell. Found in the Edit menu. The Paste button (⊞) on the Standard Toolbar can be used instead of the command.

Remove Page Break command Removes a page break. Found in the Insert menu.

Replace command Displays a dialog box that allows the user to search a spreadsheet for labels, values, or formulas and replace it with other data. Found in the Edit menu.

Rows command Inserts a row above the currently selected row. Found in the Insert menu.

Review Questions

Sections 8.1 — 8.6

1. What four questions should be answered when planning a large spreadsheet?

2. Sketch the layout for a spreadsheet that will contain an automobile dealership's inventory. The spreadsheet should include model names, quantity in stock, and asking prices.

3. a) List the steps required to find each cell in a spreadsheet that contains the SUM function.
   b) List the steps required to find each cell in a spreadsheet that contains the label Jamie and replace it with the label Pat.

4. List the steps required to copy the contents of cell B4 into cell A9.

5. List the steps required to move the values stored in cells A1, A2, and A3 to cells T1, T2, and T3.

6. Write a formula that calculates:
   a) the maximum value stored in the range of cells D4 to Y5.
   b) the minimum value stored in the range of cells C1 to C9.

7. List the steps required to enter a function into a formula without typing the function.

8. List the steps required to include a cell reference to B5 in a formula so that when the formula is copied, the cell reference remains constant.

Sections 8.7 — 8.10

9. List the steps required to insert a column titled Tue that comes between columns titled Mon and Wed.

10. List the steps required to delete an employee's row in the PAYROLL spreadsheet.

11. a) The formula =SUM(C3:C22) is used to sum the values in cells C3 to C22. If a row is inserted directly above row 20, what must be done to include the new cell in the sum?
    b) If a row is inserted directly above row 24, what must be done to include the new cell in the sum?
    c) If row 20 is deleted, what must be done to the formula so that the deleted cell is no longer in the range?

12. List the steps required to print a spreadsheet across the widest part of the paper.

13. What will be displayed by the following formulas if cell D4 stores a value of 30 and cell E7 stores a value of −12?
    a) =IF(D4<=E7,10,20)
    b) =IF(E7*D4<-5,E7,D4)
    c) =IF(D4−42=E7,D4*2,E7*3)

14. Write a formula that:
    a) displays 50 if the value stored in D20 equals the value in C80, or 25 if they are not equal.
    b) displays the value in B40 if the sum of the range of cells C20 to C30 exceeds 1000, otherwise displays a 0.
    c) displays the value of R20*10 if R20 is less than 30, otherwise displays the value in R20.

15. Write formulas using the IF function for each of the following:
    a) If B3 is less than or equal to C12 display Low, if greater than display High.
    b) If A5 is equal to Z47 display Jonathan, if not equal to display Judith.
    c) If Great! is greater than Terrible! display True, otherwise display False.

Exercises

Exercise 1 ——————————————————————— MULTIPLICATION

An elementary school teacher wants to use a spreadsheet to create multiplication tables for her students. Open MULTIPLICATION and complete the following steps:

a) Copy the contents of cells A3 through E13 to cells A15 through E25.

b) In cell A15, type 1 to replace the 0. Note that the table now contains a multiplication table for 1.

c) In columns A through E, create multiplication tables for numbers 2 through 5 by copying and pasting the values and formulas in cell A3 through E13, replacing the bold number appropriately. Leave a blank row between each table.

d) In columns G through K, create multiplication tables for numbers 6 through 11 by copying and pasting the values and formulas in cell A3 through E13, replacing the bold number appropriately. Leave a blank row between each table.

e) Add a page break where appropriate so the multiplication table for each number is not on different pages when the spreadsheet is printed.

f) Create a header with your name right aligned.

g) Save the modified MULTIPLICATION and print a copy with gridlines and row and column headings.

Exercise 2 ——————————————————————— Squeaky Clean Cars

The budget created in Chapter Seven, Exercise 2 needs to be modified to include July's budgeted expenses. Open Squeaky Clean Cars and complete the following steps:

a) Copy the contents of cells B3 and B4 to cells F3 and F4. In cell F3, change June to July.

b) July's budgeted expenses are based on the differences between the budgeted and actual expenses for June stored in column D. July's budgeted expenses will be the same as those for June when the difference is greater than or equal to 0, otherwise they will be 5% more. In column F, enter formulas that use a function to calculate the budgeted expenses for July. Include appropriate labels and proper formatting.

c) Copy the formula in cell B10 to cell F10.

d) Save the modified Squeaky Clean Cars and print a copy with gridlines and row and column headings.

Exercise 3 ——————————————————————— Swim Meet

The swim meet spreadsheet created in Chapter Seven, Exercise 3 needs to be modified. Open Swim Meet and complete the following steps:

a) Pats's scores need to be added to the spreadsheet. The following are the times for Pat: 2:45:55, 3:12:07, 2:45:19, 3:02:00, 4:45:58, and 5:45:10. Insert a column between columns E and F, and then enter the values and an appropriate column heading.

A Guide to Microsoft Office 2000 Professional

b) In the next available columns, enter formulas that use functions to calculate the fastest time and slowest time for each event (remember the fastest time in swimming is the lowest time). Include appropriate column headings and right align the labels. Resize the columns as necessary so that all the data is displayed entirely.

c) Save the modified Swim Meet and print a copy in landscape orientation with gridlines and row and column headings.

Exercise 4 ☼ ——————————————————— Student Stats

The student statistics spreadsheet created in Chapter Seven, Exercise 4 needs to be modified. Open Student Stats and complete the following steps:

a) The Engineering and Nursing colleges need to be added to the spreadsheet. Insert the new data shown below into the spreadsheet so the colleges remain in alphabetical order:

College	Undergraduate	Graduate
Engineering	1,645	189
Nursing	876	45

b) In rows 11 and 12, enter formulas that use a function to calculate:

- the maximum number of undergraduate students and the maximum number of graduate students in a college
- the minimum number of undergraduate students and the minimum number of graduate students in a college

Include appropriate labels and proper formatting. Resize columns as necessary so that all the data is displayed entirely.

c) Save the modified Student Stats and print a copy with gridlines and row and column headings.

Exercise 5 ☼ ——————————————————— Coral Employees

The payroll spreadsheet created in Chapter Seven, Exercise 5 needs to be modified. Open Coral Employees and complete the following steps:

a) The comptroller has hired two more employees. Insert the new data shown below into the spreadsheet so that the employee names remain in alphabetical order by last name:

First Name	Last Name	Salary
Dedra	Roberts	$42,000
Philip	Jorge	$28,000

Copy the weekly pay formula for the new employees into cells D5 and D6.

b) Tax deductions are calculated by multiplying 15% by the weekly pay when the salary is less than $30,000, and 28% by the weekly pay when equal to or higher than $30,000. In column E, enter the label Taxes and then enter formulas that use a function and cell references to calculate the taxes.

c) Social security deductions also need to be calculated. Insert two blank rows at the top of the spreadsheet. In cell A1, enter the label Soc. Sec. Rate:. In cell C1, enter the value 6%. In column F, enter the label Soc. Sec. and then enter formulas that use absolute and relative cell references to calculate social security by multiplying the rate by the weekly pay.

d) Net pay is computed by making the necessary deductions from the weekly pay. In column G, enter the label Net Pay and then enter formulas that use cell references to deduct the taxes and social security from the weekly pay of each employee to get the net pay.

e) The employees of Coral County receive yearly bonuses based on the position they hold. Cho, Roberts, and White are managers. The rest of the employees are assistants. Insert a column after the salary column, enter the label Position. Enter the appropriate positions for each person, either Manager or Assistant.

f) Every year, managers receive a bonus of 20% of their weekly pay and assistants receive a bonus of 10% of their weekly pay. In column I, enter the label Bonus. Enter formulas that use a function and cell references to calculate the bonus amounts.

g) Format all the data appropriately. Resize columns as necessary so that all the data is displayed entirely.

h) Save the modified Coral Employees and print a copy with gridlines and row and column headings.

Exercise 6 — Dive Log

The dive log spreadsheet created in Chapter Seven, Exercise 6 needs to be modified. Open Dive Log and complete the following steps:

a) Two dives were not recorded. Insert the new data shown below into the spreadsheet so that the dates remain in chronological order:

Date	Depth	Duration	Water temp	Visibility
5/9/01	15	45	28	11
5/12/01	20	40	24	9

b) In rows 10 and 11, enter formulas that use a function to calculate:

- the maximum depth of the dives and the maximum duration of the dives
- the minimum depth of the dives and the minimum duration of the dives

Include appropriate labels and proper formatting. Resize columns as necessary so that all the data is displayed entirely.

c) Save the modified Dive Log and print a copy with gridlines and row and column headings.

A Guide to Microsoft Office 2000 Professional

The expense spreadsheet created in Chapter Seven, Exercise 7 needs to be modified. Open Pizza Palace and complete the following steps:

a) Pepperoni pizza needs to be added to the spreadsheet before the Everything pizza column. Enter an appropriate column heading and values for the pepperoni pizza. Copy the cost of pizza formula for the pepperoni pizza into cell D13.

b) Format the data appropriately. Resize the column as necessary so that all the data is displayed entirely.

c) The menu price for each pizza needs to be added to the spreadsheet in row 14. When the cost of pizza is less than or equal to $4.00 the price is one and a half (1½) times the cost, and it is two (2) times the cost when it is higher than $4.00. Enter formulas that use a function to calculate the menu price of the pizzas. Include an appropriate label and proper formatting.

d) Save the modified Pizza Palace and print a copy with gridlines and row and column headings.

The PROFIT spreadsheet contains income and expenses for a company. Open PROFIT and complete the following steps:

a) In row 6, enter formulas that use a function to calculate the total income for each year. Total income is calculated by summing the three type of sales.

b) In row 14, enter formulas that use a function to calculate the total expenses for each year. Total expenses are calculated by summing all the expense categories.

c) In row 15, enter formulas that use cell references to calculate the profit for each year. Profit is calculated by subtracting total expenses from the total income.

d) In rows 18 and 19, enter formulas that use functions to calculate the highest and lowest sales amounts of the three types of sales for each year.

e) Row 15 stores the profit and row 16 stores the profit that the company wanted to obtain. In row 20, enter formulas that use a function to display Yes if the profit goal was reached or No if the actual profit was less than the goal profit.

f) Center align the labels in cells B2 through E20.

g) Create a header with your name right aligned.

h) Save the modified PROFIT and print a copy with gridlines and row and column headings.

The DANCE spreadsheet contains information on the expected profit for a dance. The dance coordinator wants to know how much profit the dance will make depending on the number of people attending. Open DANCE and complete the following steps:

a) In rows 3, 4, and 5 enter formulas that use absolute and relative cell references to calculate expected income when 50, 100, 200, or 300 people attend the dance. Use the following information to create the formulas:

- The income from tickets is calculated by multiplying the number of people attending by the ticket price. Cell B3 contains the ticket price.
- The income from food is calculated by multiplying the number of people attending by the expected amount each person will spend on food. Cell B4 contains the expected amount each person will spend on food.
- The income from beverages is calculated by multiplying the number of people attending by the expected amount each person will spend on beverages. Cell B5 contains the expected amount each person will spend on beverages.

Note: If the values in cells B3, B4, or B5 are changed, the calculated income values in rows 3, 4, and 5 should reflect that change.

b) In rows 7, 8, and 9 enter formulas that use absolute and relative cell references to calculate the costs of the food and beverages when 50, 100, 200, or 300 people attend the dance. Use the following information to create the formulas:

- The expense for tickets is calculated by multiplying the number of people attending by the ticket printing price. Cell B7 contains the ticket printing price.
- The expense for food is calculated by multiplying the number of people attending by the cost of the food for each person attending the dance. Cell B8 contains the cost of the food for each person attending the dance.
- The expense for beverages is calculated by multiplying the number of people attending by the cost of the beverages for each person attending the dance. Cell B9 contains the cost of the beverages for each person attending the dance.

Note: If the values in cells B7, B8, or B9 are changed the expense values in rows 7, 8, and 9 should reflect that change.

c) In row 10, enter formulas that use functions to calculate the profit (total income less total expenses) for the different number of people attending the dance.

d) Resize columns as necessary so that all the data is displayed entirely.

e) Create a header with your name right aligned.

f) Save the modified DANCE and print a copy with gridlines and row and column headings.

The STOCKS spreadsheet contains stock information. Open STOCKS and complete the following steps:

a) Determine how much was originally paid for each stock. Insert a column between the purchase price and Jan columns. Enter the label Original Value and then enter formulas that use cell references to calculate the original value of each stock. The original value of each stock is calculated by multiplying the shares purchased by the purchase price.

b) Determine how much each stock is worth in March. In column H, enter the label March Value and then enter formulas that calculate the value of each stock in March. The value is calculated by multiplying the shares purchased by the price they are selling for in March.

c) Resize columns as necessary so that all the data is displayed entirely.

d) In rows 16 and 17, enter formulas that use a function to calculate:

- the maximum original price and the maximum final price
- the minimum original price and the minimum final price

Include appropriate labels in columns C and G and proper formatting. Resize columns as necessary so that all the data is displayed entirely.

e) It would be best to sell those stocks in March which have a value at least 25% higher than their original value. In column I, enter formulas that use a function to display Sell for stocks that should be sold or Retain for stocks that should be held. Include an appropriate column heading and proper formatting. Resize the column as necessary so that all the data is displayed entirely.

f) Center align the data in Column I.

g) Create a header with your name right aligned.

h) Save the modified STOCKS and print a copy in landscape orientation with gridlines and row and column headings.

The manager of an amphitheater wants to use a spreadsheet to calculate ticket prices. There are three types of tickets: Floor, Balcony, and General Admission. The price of the tickets are different for each act and the amphitheater charges a handling fee for all tickets.

a) In a new spreadsheet enter the following data starting in cell A1:

Act	Seats	Price
The Motherboards	Floor	$55
	Balcony	$40
	Gen. Adm.	$28
Blue Knights	Floor	$65
	Balcony	$55
	Gen. Adm.	$28
The Altairs	Floor	$85
	Balcony	$65
	Gen. Adm.	$28

b) Bold the labels in row 1, italicize the act titles, and right align the Price label. Resize columns as necessary so that all the data is displayed entirely. Save the spreadsheet naming it Tickets.

c) The handling fee is $5 when the price of the ticket is less than or equal to $50, and $10 when the ticket price is greater than $50. In the next available column, enter formulas that use a function to calculate the handling fee. Include an appropriate label and proper formatting.

d) The total price of the ticket is the price of the ticket plus the handling fee. In the next available column, enter formulas that use cell references to calculate the total price. Include an appropriate label and proper formatting.

e) Resize columns as necessary so that all the data is displayed entirely.

f) Create a header with your name right aligned.

g) Save the modified Tickets and print a copy with gridlines and row and column headings.

Exercise 12 ———————————————————— Track Progress

A track team coach wants to use a spreadsheet to keep track of the team's progress of the 100 meter and 200 meter runs. The spreadsheet should record the names of the members, the time in seconds, and the distance in meters for each month January through April.

a) At the top of a new spreadsheet in separate cells, include a label and value for the state record of 13.5 seconds for the 100 meter and 26.7 seconds for the 200 meter. Bold the labels.

b) Enter the following data into the spreadsheet.

Student	January	February	March	April	Meters
Hannah Otis	16.5	16.3	16.0	15.8	100
Russel Rosen	16.8	16.9	16.5	16.2	100
Rolanda Lopez	15.5	14.4	14.0	14.4	100
Paul Quinn	18.5	18.3	18.0	17.8	100
Hannah Otis	34.9	34.8	34.8	34.7	200
Emma Del Vecchio	32.5	32.4	32.0	31.8	200
Paul Quinn	35.5	35.3	35.0	34.8	200
Callie Ramis	30.7	30.3	30.3	30.2	200

c) Bold the labels in row 1 and right align the labels in columns B through F. Format all the times as number with 1 decimal place. Resize columns as necessary so that all the data is displayed entirely. Save the spreadsheet naming it Track Progress.

d) In columns G, H, and I, enter formulas that use a function to calculate:

- the fastest time during the four months for each student (remember the fastest time in running is the lowest time)
- the slowest time during the four months for each student
- the difference between the fastest time and the state record depending on the type of race. (Hint: You should do a comparison using the IF function with absolute and relative cell references to determine the type of race.)

Include appropriate labels and proper formatting. Format all the times as number with 1 decimal place. Resize columns as necessary so that all the data is displayed entirely.

e) Paul Quinn's February time for the 200 meter should be 35.8. Update the spreadsheet.

f) Create a header with your name right aligned.

g) Save the modified Track Progress and print a copy in landscape orientation with gridlines and row and column headings.

Exercise 13 ——————————————————————— Coins

A coin collector wants to use a spreadsheet to keep track of the value of each coin in the collection. The spreadsheet should record the coin name, year of coin, condition, and estimated value.

a) The condition of a coin is called its grade, and it is a major factor in determining a coin's worth. Coins are rated using the Mint State (MS) grade scale, which ranges from 70 (high) to 60 (low). In a new spreadsheet enter the following coin data starting in cell A1:

Coin	Year	Grade	Value
Half Dollar	1860	Mint State-63	$679
Half Dollar	1917	Mint State-63	$125
Half Dollar	1937	Mint State-63	$39
Half Dollar	1942	Mint State-64	$34
Half Dollar	1946	Mint State-65	$109
Quarter Eagle	1913	Mint State-62	$449
Eagle	1901	Mint State-62	$495

Bold the labels in row 1 and right align the Year and Value labels. Center align column C. Format the coin values as currency with 0 decimal places. Resize columns as necessary so that all the data is displayed entirely.

b) Save the spreadsheet naming it Coins.

c) Replace all occurrences of "Mint State" with MS.

d) In rows 9, 10, and 11, enter formulas that use a function to calculate:

- the maximum value of a single coin in the collection
- the minimum value of a single coin in the collection
- the total value of the collection

Include appropriate right aligned and bold labels in column C. Resize columns as necessary so that all the data is displayed entirely.

e) The collector has decided that it would be best to trade those coins which have a value less than or equal to $150. In the next available column, enter the label Status. Enter formulas that use a function to display Trade for the coins that should be traded or Keep for coins that should not be traded.

f) Center align the data in column E and bold the label.

g) Create a header with your name right aligned.

h) Save the modified Coins and print a copy with gridlines and row and column headings.

The Meteorology department at the local university wants to use a spreadsheet to record the average yearly temperatures for a city.

a) In a new spreadsheet, enter the data below starting in cell A1 with the years in column A and the temperatures in column B. To save typing, use a formula to calculate and display the year:

Year	Temp (Celsius)	Year	Temp (Celsius)
1982	18	1992	22
1983	14	1993	18
1984	19	1994	18
1985	20	1995	22
1986	22	1996	21
1987	23	1997	22
1988	19	1998	19
1989	22	1999	22
1990	23	2000	19
1991	19	2001	22

b) Bold the labels in row 1. Resize columns as necessary so that all the data is displayed entirely. Save the spreadsheet naming it City Temp.

c) In rows 22 and 23, enter formulas that use a function to calculate:

- the highest temperature within the 20 years
- the lowest temperature within the 20 years

Include appropriate labels and proper formatting. Resize columns as necessary so that all the data is displayed entirely.

d) Create a header with your name right aligned.

e) Save the modified City Temp and print a copy with gridlines and row and column headings.

The cost spreadsheet created in Chapter Seven, Exercise 15 needs to be modified. Open Brochure Costs and complete the following steps:

a) The spreadsheet would be more useful if the variable costs per brochure were stored in cells instead of in the formulas. Insert a column between columns A and B. Enter the variable costs for each of the items listed below:

Paper	$0.20
Printing	$0.12
Labor	$0.07
Shipping	$0.10

Format the data appropriately. Resize the column smaller.

b) In rows 10, 11, 12, and 13, modify the formulas to use absolute and relative cell references to calculate the variable costs (multiply the variable cost per brochure by the number of brochures). Note: the calculated variable costs should reflect changes if the values in cells B10, B11, B12, or B13 are changed.

c) The printing costs have increased to $0.15 per brochure printed. Make the necessary adjustment to cell B11.

d) Save the modified Brochure Costs and print a copy with gridlines and row and column headings.

Advanced
Exercise 16 ——————————————————————— My Finances

A spreadsheet is a good way to manage your personal finances. Plan a spreadsheet to record your income and expenses each month for a year. A number of categories such as food, movies, and clothing should be selected so that few of your expenses fall into a miscellaneous category. Include a savings category that uses an IF function to either display a zero if you spent more money than you had or display the percent of income you saved based on the amount of income and expenses for that month. The spreadsheet should also include formulas that use functions to total the income and expenses for each month and for each category for the year. Create the spreadsheet using Excel. Format all the data appropriately. Save the spreadsheet naming it My Finances and print a copy.

Advanced
Exercise 17 ——————————————————————My Checking Account

Plan a spreadsheet to keep track of your checking account. The spreadsheet should include a starting balance, transaction dates, check numbers, transaction amounts, and descriptions. It should also be able to handle deposits. The spreadsheet should use formulas that contain cell references to determine the new balance after each transaction. Create the spreadsheet using Excel. Format all the data appropriately. Save the spreadsheet naming it My Checking Account and print a copy.

Advanced
Exercise 18 ↻ ————————————————————————————————

Modify one of the spreadsheets created in Exercises 16, 17, or 18 in Chapter Seven to include four additional rows and one additional column of data. Also include at least one formula containing the IF function. Format the spreadsheet appropriately. Save the modified spreadsheet and print a copy.

A Guide to Microsoft Office 2000 Professional

Page Set<u>u</u>p

C<u>h</u>art

<u>A</u>ll

Chart <u>O</u>ptions

<u>S</u>ource Data

<u>A</u>dd Data

Chapter Nine Objectives

After completing this chapter you will be able to:

1. Use and print multiple sheets.
2. Copy and move data between sheets.
3. Refer to data in different sheets.
4. Create pie, bar, and line charts of spreadsheet data.
5. Modify, format, and print charts.

This chapter explains how to use the worksheets in a workbook. Creating charts using the data stored in a spreadsheet is also explained.

9.1 Using Multiple Sheets

An Excel spreadsheet is called a *workbook*, and each workbook contains three *worksheets*, also called sheets. *Sheets* are used to organize, store, and link related information in a workbook. In Chapters Seven and Eight, only the first sheet of a workbook was used in the practices and exercises.

displaying a sheet

A sheet is displayed, or made *active*, by clicking on the appropriate tab at the bottom of the Excel window:

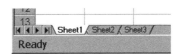

Sheet1 is the active sheet

renaming a sheet

Sheets are given the default names of Sheet1, Sheet2, Sheet3. A sheet can be renamed by double-clicking on its name to highlight it, typing a new name, and then pressing Enter. For example, a workbook (spreadsheet) named Clothing Sales could contain sheets named 1999 Sales, 2000 Sales, and 2001 Forecast Sales.

Copying and Moving Sheets

Sheet order can be changed by dragging a sheet's tab to a new location. Dragging a sheet tab displays a solid triangle indicating where the sheet is being moved to and the pointer changes to the ⌖ shape. When the mouse button is released, the sheet is moved.

Similarly, a sheet can be copied by dragging its tab to the desired location while holding down the Ctrl key.

9.2 Copying and Moving Data Between Sheets

The Copy, Cut, and Paste commands from the Edit menu can be used to copy or move data between sheets. The steps for copying or moving a block of cells between sheets are:

1. Highlight the cells to be copied or moved.

2. Select the Copy or Cut command. A copy of the cells' contents and formatting is placed on the Clipboard.

3. Using the sheet tabs, display the sheet to receive the new data.

4. Select the first cell where the data is to appear.

5. Select the Paste command. The contents of the Clipboard are placed in the cells.

The Cut, Copy, and Paste buttons on the Standard Toolbar can also be used to copy or move data.

Practice 1

In this practice you will modify a spreadsheet that contains three different sheets.

1) OPEN CAR SALES

Open CAR SALES. This spreadsheet (workbook) contains data in three different sheets: New Car Sales, Used Car Sales, and Sheet3. The Total Sales column contains formulas.

2) VIEW THE DIFFERENT SHEETS IN THE WORKBOOK

a. Click on the Used Car Sales tab at the bottom of the Excel window. The second sheet in the workbook is displayed.
b. Click on the Sheet3 tab. The third sheet in the workbook is displayed.

3) RENAME SHEET3

a. Double-click on the Sheet3 name. The sheet name is highlighted
b. Type Total Sales and then press Enter to replace the default name.

4) COPY LABELS TO SHEET3

a. Display the New Car Sales sheet.
b. Highlight cells A4 through A23.
c. Select Edit → Copy.
d. Display the Total Sales sheet.
e. Select cell A4.
f. Select Edit → Paste.
g. Display the New Car Sales sheet and then press Esc. The dashed lines are removed.
h. In the New Car Sales sheet, copy the labels in cells B3 through E3 to cells B3 through E3 in the Total Sales sheet. If the Office Clipboard appears, click on its Close button to remove it.

5) SAVE THE MODIFIED CAR SALES

9.3 Referring to Data in Different Sheets

When using multiple sheets, it is possible for a formula to contain a cell reference to a cell on another sheet. Referring to a cell on a different sheet takes the form:

'<sheet name>'!<cell reference>

For example, given the two spreadsheet fragments

A1		=	=Sheet2!B4
	A	B	C	D
1	45			
2				
3				
4				
5				

Sheet1 / Sheet2 / Sheet3 /

B4		=	=SUM(B1:B3)
	A	B	C	D
1		10		
2		15		
3		20		
4		45		
5				

Sheet1 \ Sheet2 / Sheet3 /

cell A1 in Sheet1 displays 45 because it contains a formula that references cell B4 in Sheet2, =Sheet2!B4. If the data in cell B1 in Sheet2 changes to 20 then cell A1 in Sheet1 will display 55.

> ### *Adding and Deleting Sheets*
>
> By default, each workbook contains three sheets. A new sheet is inserted in front of the active sheet by selecting the Worksheet command from the Insert menu. A sheet is deleted by right-clicking on its name and selecting the Delete command in the displayed menu.

Scrolling Sheets

Renaming sheets and adding sheets to a workbook may result in some of the sheet tabs not being displayed. Tab scrolling buttons are displayed to the left of the sheet tabs, and are used to scroll the sheet tabs:

9.4 Printing Sheets

All the sheets in a workbook are printed by selecting the Entire workbook option in the Print what section of the Print dialog box. Selecting the Active sheet(s) option and then OK in the Print dialog box prints only the active sheet. Selecting the Print button on the Standard Toolbar also prints only the active sheet.

Selecting the Page Setup command from the File menu displays the Page Setup dialog box. Options selected in this dialog box affect only the active sheet, making it possible for sheets to be printed differently. For example, Sheet1 can be printed in portrait orientation and Sheet2 in landscape orientation.

Practice 2

In this practice you will reference data between the three sheets in CAR SALES. Open CAR SALES if it is not already displayed.

1) TOTAL NEW AND USED CAR SALES

a. Display the Total Sales sheet if it is not already displayed.
b. Select cell B4 and type an equal sign (=).
c. Click on the New Car Sales tab to display the first sheet. Note that ='New Car Sales'! is displayed in the Formula bar.
d. Click on cell B4. Note how the Formula bar now displays ='New Car Sales'!B4.
e. Type a plus sign (+).
f. In the Used Car Sales sheet, click on cell B4. The formula bar should now display ='New Car Sales'!B4+'Used Car Sales'!B4.
g. Click on the Enter button to enter the formula and again display the Total Sales sheet. Cell B4 displays $156,217.
h. Copy the formula in cell B4 to cells C4 and D4. Employee Alfred's total new and used car sales for January, February, and March are displayed.
i. Copy the formulas in cells B4 through D4 to cells B5 through D23.

2) TOTAL SALES FOR ALL THREE MONTHS

a. Display the New Car Sales sheet.
b. Select cell E4. This cell stores a formula that totals the sales for the three months.
c. Select Edit → Copy.
d. Display the Total Sales sheet.
e. Select cell E4.
f. Select Edit → Paste. The formula is pasted into cell E4.
g. Copy the formula in cell E4 to cells E5 through E23.

3) SET PRINT OPTIONS FOR A SHEET

a. Display the Total Car Sales sheet if it is not already displayed.
b. Select File → Page Setup. A dialog box is displayed.
   1. Select the Sheet tab if the sheet options are not already displayed.
   2. Select the Gridlines option.
   3. Select the Row and column headings option.
   4. Select OK. The dialog box is removed.

4) SAVE, PRINT, AND THEN CLOSE THE MODIFIED CAR SALES

   a. Save the modified CAR SALES.
   b. Select File → Print. A dialog box is displayed.
      1. In the Print what section of the dialog box, select the Entire workbook option.
      2. Select OK. All three sheets in the workbook are printed. Note that only the Total Car Sales sheet contains gridlines and row and column headings.
   c. Close CAR SALES.

9.5 Charts

Studies show that people remember 10% of what they read, 20% of what they hear, 30% of what they see, and 70% of what they hear and see. For this reason, spreadsheet data is often presented in *chart*, which shows the relationship between data.

titles, labels, legend
data series

A chart contains titles, labels, a legend, and at least one data series. *Titles* and *labels* are used to describe what is charted. A *legend* contains labels that identify the different data series. A *data series* is a set of related data to be plotted on the chart. The data to be charted dictates what type of chart to use. The three most commonly used chart types are pie, bar, and line.

pie chart

A *pie chart* can include only one series of data, with each *slice* representing a value from the series. The size of a slice varies with its percentage of the total:

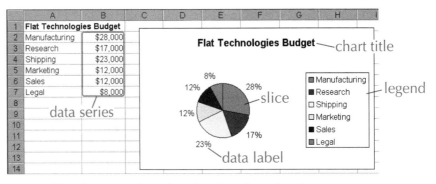

Pie charts are best for charting data that is a percentage of a whole

bar chart

A *bar chart* can include several series of data, with each bar representing a value. The height of the bar is proportional to the value it represents. Bar charts are therefore useful for comparing the differences between values. Excel can create bar charts with either vertical bars or horizontal bars. In Excel, a vertical bar chart is called a *column chart*. In the column chart on the next page, only one series is charted:

column chart

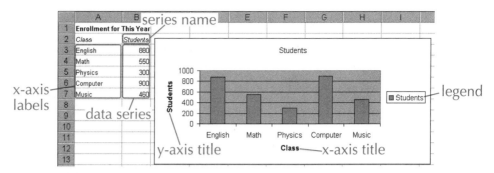

Bar charts are best for comparing the differences between values

line chart
A *line chart* can include several series of data with each line representing a series. The values in a series are represented by a point on the line. Line charts are therefore useful for displaying the differences of data over time:

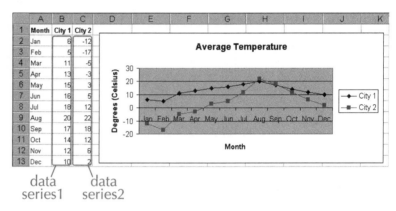

Line charts are best for charting data that changes over time

9.6 Creating a Pie Chart

planning a chart
Before creating a chart, it should be planned by answering the following questions:

1. What series should the chart contain?

2. What type of chart should be used?

3. What titles, labels, and legends will make the chart easier to read and understand?

Chart Wizard
In Excel, a chart can be created using the *Chart Wizard*, which provides dialog boxes for specifying how the data should be charted. The steps for using the Chart Wizard to create a pie chart are:

1. **Select the data to be charted.** Highlight the portion of the spreadsheet that contains the data to be charted, which is called the *data range*. The following spreadsheet data will be used as an example:

data range

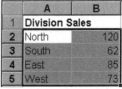

2. **Start the Chart Wizard.** Select the C<u>h</u>art command from the <u>I</u>nsert menu or click on the Chart Wizard button ( ) on the Standard Toolbar, which displays the first Chart Wizard dialog box.

3. **Select the Pie chart type.** From the Chart type list, click on Pie:

Chart Types

Note that for each **Chart type** there are different variations or sub-types to choose from.

The **Custom Types** tab in the first Chart Wizard dialog box contains predefined charts to choose from.

4. **Verify the source data and chart appearance.** Select the Next button to display the second Chart Wizard dialog box. Here, verify that the correct range of cells was selected and that the chart appears as desired. The Series in option is used to indicate whether each series of data is in a row or column. Note that the Data range entry box includes the name of the sheet:

Problems Creating a Chart?

If a chart does not appear as desired, check the data range that was highlighted. A chart's appearance can change significantly based on what data range is charted.

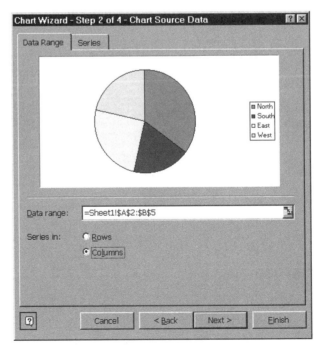

5. **Enter the chart title and select data labels.** Select the Next button to display the third Chart Wizard dialog box. Here, a descriptive title for the chart, such as This Month's Sales, is typed in the Chart title entry box:

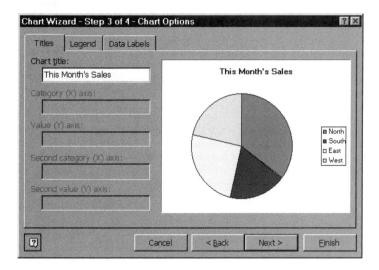

Because pie charts are useful for showing parts of a whole, the percentage each slice represents should be added to make the chart more descriptive. Selecting the Data Labels tab displays options for including percentages in a pie chart. In the example below, the Show percent option was selected to show the percentage of sales for each division:

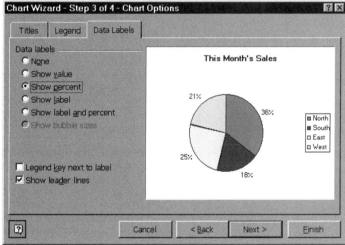

The Finish Button

After selecting the desired options in the third chart wizard dialog box, all the information needed to create a pie chart has been entered. Selecting the Finish button at this point creates the chart and displays it on the active sheet.

---

6. **Select the placement of the chart.** Selecting Next displays the last Chart Wizard dialog box. Here, the location of the chart is selected. The As new sheet option creates a new chart sheet in the spreadsheet, which contains only the chart. The As object in option places the chart in a specified sheet in the workbook:

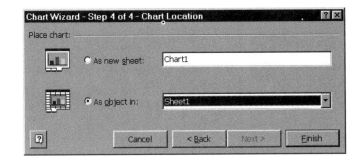

Where to Place a Chart?

A chart that is large and complex should usually be displayed on its own chart sheet. If you want to view the data in the spreadsheet and its associated chart at the same time, the chart should be displayed on the active sheet.

7. **Display the chart.** Select the Finish button to create the pie chart and display it.

updating a chart   Once created, a chart is linked to the spreadsheet data. Therefore, if a number is changed in the spreadsheet, the chart automatically changes to reflect the new data. When a spreadsheet is saved, any charts that were created are saved with it. Therefore, it is important to save a spreadsheet each time a chart is created or modified.

Practice 3

In this practice you will create a pie chart using the data stored in the CONTINENTS spreadsheet to show the percentage each continent is of the world's total land area.

1) OPEN CONTINENTS

The CONTINENTS spreadsheet contains the area in square kilometers of the seven continents.

2) CREATE A PIE CHART

a. Highlight cells A2 through B8. The data range is selected.
b. Select Insert → Chart. The first Chart Wizard dialog box is displayed.
1. In the Chart type list, click on the Pie option.
2. Select Next. The second Chart Wizard dialog box is displayed.
3. Verify that the correct range (=Sheet1!$A$2:$B$8) is displayed in the Data range entry box. An example of the pie chart is displayed in the dialog box.
4. Select Next. The third Chart Wizard dialog box is displayed.
5. In the Chart title entry box, type Area of Continents (sq km).
6. Select the Data Labels tab. The Data labels options are displayed.
7. Select the Show percent option. Note that the pie chart example now displays percentages next to each slice.
8. Select Next. The fourth Chart Wizard dialog box is displayed.
9. Select the As object in option if it is not already selected.
10. Select Finish to display the pie chart. The Chart Toolbar may also be displayed.

3) CHANGE A VALUE IN THE SPREADSHEET

a. Note the size of the Africa slice in the pie chart. It is 11% of the pie.
b. Select cell B2.
c. A mistake was made when recording the data for Africa. Type the correct value of 30,330,000 and then press. Notice how the Africa slice has increased to 20% of the pie.

Check – Your chart should look similar to:

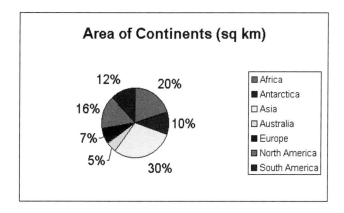

4) SAVE THE MODIFIED CONTINENTS

The chart is saved with the spreadsheet.

9.7 Moving, Sizing, and Deleting Charts

selecting a chart A chart is *selected* by clicking in the Chart Area. The *Chart Area* is the blank portion of the chart. When a chart is selected, it is displayed with

handles *handles,* and the corresponding data series and labels are outlined in color in the sheet:

Chart Toolbar

The Chart Toolbar can be used to change the appearance of a selected chart. The Chart Type collapsible list (▇) is used to change the active chart's type. The Format button (▣) is used to format whatever chart object is selected (formatting is discussed later in the chapter). The Legend button (▤) is used to display or hide the legend. The Chart Toolbar can be removed by clicking on its Close box.

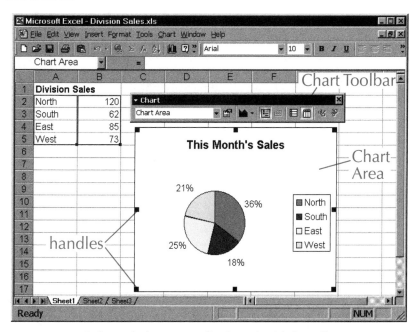

Selected charts are displayed with handles

moving a chart Dragging a chart by the Chart Area (not on a handle) moves it. This is often necessary to display data stored in cells located behind the chart.

resizing a chart Sometimes it is desirable to display a chart and its associated spreadsheet data on the screen at the same time. This may require resizing the chart, which may affect the appearance of its titles and labels. Dragging a handle changes the size of the chart:

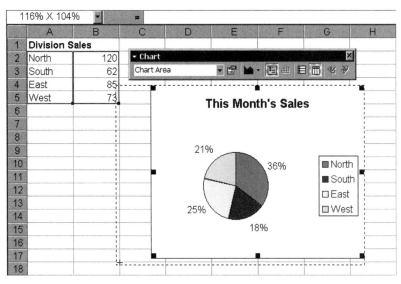

Dashed lines indicate the new size of a chart when dragging a handle

deleting a chart   A selected chart can be deleted by pressing the Delete key or selecting the All command from the Clear submenu in the Edit menu. If a chart is deleted by mistake, selecting the Undo command or the Undo button restores the chart.

9.8 Printing a Chart

A chart can be printed by printing the sheet that it appears in using the Print command from the File menu or the Print button on the Standard Toolbar. Before printing a chart, the Print Preview command from the File menu should be used to view the spreadsheet and determine if the chart will fit completely on a page.

Sizing or moving a chart may be necessary to fit it on a single sheet of paper. Changing the orientation to landscape or changing the margins may also help fit a spreadsheet with a chart onto a single sheet of paper.

Selecting a chart and then the Print command prints only the chart on a single sheet of paper in landscape orientation.

If a chart is in its own sheet, the chart sheet must first be made active and then the Print command selected to print the chart.

Practice 4

In this practice you will resize, move, and print the pie chart stored in the CONTINENTS spreadsheet. Open CONTINENTS if it is not already displayed.

1) RESIZE AND MOVE THE CHART

    a. If the chart's handles are not displayed, move the pointer into an empty portion of the chart until a screen tip with the words Chart Area is displayed. Click once to select it and display the handles.

    b. Move the pointer over the handle in the bottom-right corner of the chart. The pointer changes to a double-headed arrow shape.

    c. Drag the handle down and to the right a little. The chart is resized larger.

d. Move the pointer into the Chart Area so the screen tip with the words Chart Area is displayed.

e. Drag the chart so that it is below the spreadsheet data.

2) SAVE, PRINT, AND THEN CLOSE THE MODIFIED CONTINENTS

a. Make sure the chart is not selected and then print preview the spreadsheet. If necessary, resize and move the chart on the sheet so that all the data and chart fit on one page.

b. Save the modified CONTINENTS.

c. Make sure the chart is not selected and then click the Print button on the Standard Toolbar. The spreadsheet is printed with the chart.

d. Close CONTINENTS.

9.9 Creating Bar and Line Charts

The steps for creating a bar or line chart are:

1. **Select the data to be charted.** Highlight the portion of the spreadsheet that contains the data to be charted. The following spreadsheet data will be used as an example:

	A	B	C	D	E	F
1			T-Shirt Fund-raiser			
2	Color	Juan	Greta	Nan	Mick	Total
3	red	5	22	2	7	36
4	blue	12	8	3	12	35
5	green	4	12	10	18	44
6	pink	2	4	16	18	40
7	Total:	23	46	31	55	

2. **Start the Chart Wizard.** Select the Chart command or click on the Chart Wizard button (), which displays the first Chart Wizard dialog box.

3. **Select the desired chart type.** From the Chart type list, click on the desired chart type. In this example, Column is selected:

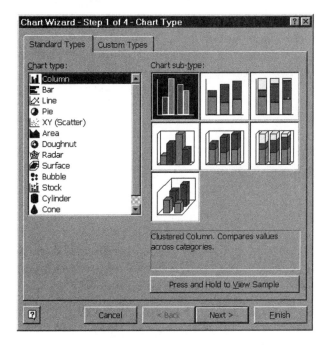

4. **Verify the source data and chart appearance.** Select the Next button to display the second Chart Wizard dialog box. Here, verify that the correct range of cells was selected and that the chart appears as desired. The Series in option is used to indicate whether each series of data is in a row or column. In this example, the series are in columns so the Columns option must be selected:

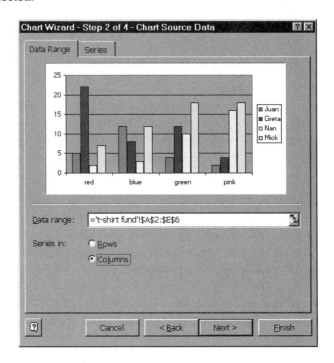

5. **Enter chart and axes titles.** Select the Next button to display the third Chart Wizard dialog box. Here, descriptive titles for the chart and each axis can be entered:

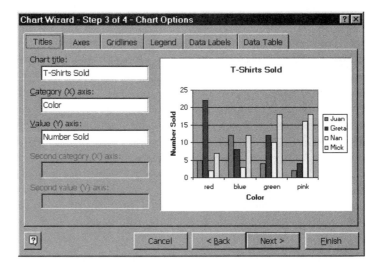

6. **Select the placement of the chart.** Select the Next button to display the last Chart Wizard dialog box. Here, the location of the chart is selected.

7. **Display the chart.** Select the Finish button to create the chart and display it.

Practice 5

In this practice you will create a line chart.

1) OPEN PLANT GROWTH

The PLANT GROWTH spreadsheet contains the results of a plant growth experiment.

2) CREATE A LINE CHART

a. Highlight cells A3 through E4. The results for the first four weeks of control group A are selected.

b. On the Standard Toolbar, click on the Chart Wizard button ( ). The first Chart Wizard dialog box is displayed.

　1. In the Chart type list, click on the Line option.

　2. Select Next. The second Chart Wizard dialog box is displayed.

　3. Verify that the correct range (=Sheet1!$A$3:$E$4) is displayed in the Data range entry box. An example of the line chart is displayed in the dialog box.

　4. Select Next. The third Chart Wizard dialog box is displayed. Select the Titles tab if the title options are not already displayed.

　5. In the Chart title entry box, modify the existing title to read Control Group A Growth Results.

　6. In the Category (X) axis entry box, type Period.

　7. Select Finish. The line chart is displayed.

Check – Your chart should look similar to:

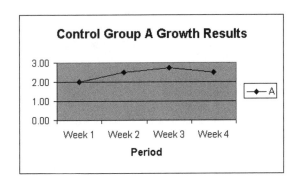

3) SAVE THE MODIFIED PLANT GROWTH

9.10 Modifying a Chart

The contents of a selected chart can be modified by selecting the Chart Options command from the Chart menu, which displays the Chart Options dialog box:

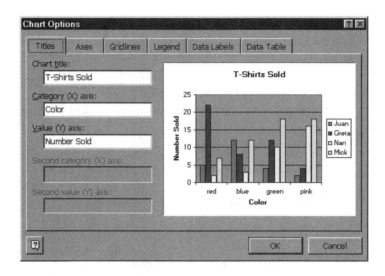

This dialog box is similar to the third Chart Wizard dialog box. Changes can be made to the chart using the options in the dialog box:

- Titles tab contains options for editing the chart title, x-axis title, and y-axis title.

- Axes tab contains options for hiding or displaying each axes.

- Gridlines tab contains options that affect the gridlines behind the chart. A chart may be easier to read if gridlines are displayed. Vertical and horizontal gridlines are displayed by selecting the Major gridlines option in the Category (X) axis and Value (Y) axis sections, respectively. When these options are selected, gridlines are shown both on the screen and when printed.

- Legend tab contains options for specifying the placement of the legend (bottom, corner, top, right, and left).

- Data Labels tab contains options for displaying the value or label at the top of the bar (similar to the data labels added to pie charts).

Selecting OK applies the changes to the chart.

9.11 Adding Adjacent Series and Labels

A series can be added to a selected chart by dragging on one of the colored handles of the original data to include the new series. This method can only be used if the new series is adjacent to the data already charted. For example, in the spreadsheet below the range A2:B6 has already been charted:

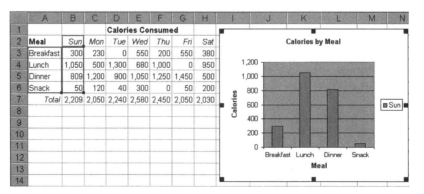

Modifying Chart Titles

A title can also be changed by first clicking once on it in the chart to select it. Next, typing new text and pressing Enter replaces the selected title.

Data Table

The Data Table tab in the Chart Options dialog box contains options for displaying the actual spreadsheet data within the chart.

A Guide to Microsoft Office 2000 Professional

The green outline around cell B2 indicates that the cell is used in the legend as a label for the data series. The purple outline around cells A3 to A6 indicate those cells are used for the x-axis labels. The blue outline around cells B3 to B6 indicate those cells are used for the data series. The data series and label in column C can be added to the chart by dragging the blue handle in the lower-right corner of cell B6 to include column C.

The Source Data command from the Chart menu can also be used to add an adjacent data series and label to an existing chart. The Source Data command displays a dialog box similar to the second chart wizard dialog box.

Practice 6

In this practice you will modify the chart stored in PLANT GROWTH. Open PLANT GROWTH if it is not already displayed.

1) MODIFY THE LINE CHART

    a. Note that there is no title for the y-axis values along the left side of the chart.

    b. Click on the Chart Area to select the chart if it is not already selected.

    c. Select Chart → Chart Options. A dialog box is displayed.

        1. Select the Titles tab if the title options are not already displayed.

        2. In the Value (Y) axis entry box, type Centimeters.

        3. Select the Axes tab. The axes options are displayed.

        4. Deselect the Value (Y) axis option.

        5. Select the Gridlines tab. The gridline options are displayed.

        6. In the Category (X) axis options, select the Major gridlines option.

        7. Select the Data Labels tab. The data labels options are displayed.

        8. Select the Show value option.

        9. Select OK to remove the dialog box. The chart is modified.

2) ADD DATA TO THE CHART

    a. Click on the line chart if it is not already selected. The corresponding data in the spreadsheet should have color outlines. Note that the last week of data for control group A is in cell F4 and its corresponding label is in cell F3.

    b. Drag the blue handle in the lower-right corner of cell E4 to the right until cells F3 and F4 are included in the color outlines. The new data is added to the chart.

3) ADD A NEW SERIES TO THE CHART

    a. Click on the line chart if it is not already selected. Note that only control group A is charted.

    b. Drag the blue handle in the lower-right corner of cell F4 down until cells A5 through F5 are included in the color outlines. The new series is added to the chart.

    c. Modify the chart title to be "Control Group A and B Growth Results."

4) SAVE THE MODIFIED PLANT GROWTH AND PRINT THE LINE CHART

    a. Save the modified PLANT GROWTH.

    b. Select the line chart if it is not already selected.

    c. On the Standard Toolbar, click the Print button. Only the chart is printed.

9.12 Adding Nonadjacent Series and Labels

It is possible to add a data series to an existing chart even if the data series is not contiguous, meaning it is not stored in cells adjacent to those already specified for the chart. A nonadjacent data series is added to a selected chart by executing the Add Data command from the Chart menu, which displays the Add Data dialog box:

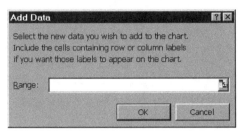

The range of cells containing the new data series is then entered into the Range entry box by placing the cursor in the entry box and then selecting the appropriate cells in the spreadsheet. Any cells containing labels for the chart legend should also be included in the range.

For example, the Friday and Saturday data series can be added to the Calories by Meal chart by entering the range of cells containing the new data series (G2:H6) in the Add Data dialog box and then selecting OK:

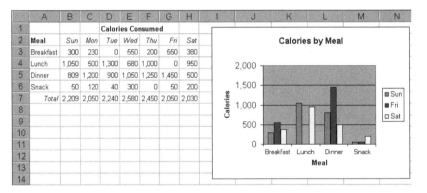

When labels are not adjacent to the series of data they are describing, they can be added to a selected chart by executing the Source Data command and then selecting the Series tab in the displayed dialog box. For example, when the total calories data in row 7 of the spreadsheet above is charted, the cells containing the days of the week need to be added as the x-axis labels to replace the default labels:

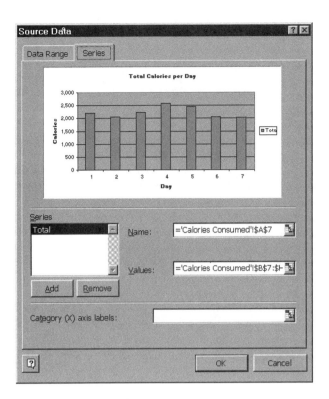

The labels are added by placing the cursor in the Category (X) axis labels entry box and then selecting the appropriate cells in the spreadsheet. Selecting OK removes the dialog box.

Nonadjacent labels for pie chart slices can be added to an existing pie chart using the Series tab similar to the method stated above, except the cell range is entered in the Category Labels entry box.

9.13 Formatting a Chart

There are many ways to modify the appearance of a chart. For example, the chart below has been formatted so that the chart title is in a different font, the y-axis title is vertical, the major x-axis gridlines are displayed, the data values are displayed, and the data series are in a different order (Greta now comes before Juan):

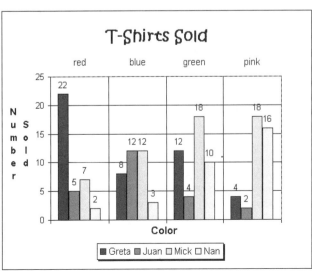

Double-clicking on any object in a chart displays a Format dialog box. For example, double-clicking on the legend of a chart displays the Format Legend dialog box. In this dialog box, options for the pattern, font, and placement of the legend can be changed.

Commands in the Format menu can also be used to display a Format dialog box. The Format menu is a smart menu. For example, clicking once on the chart title displays the Selected Chart Title command in the Format menu while clicking once on the legend displays the Selected Legend command. These methods can be used to format the y-axis, x-axis, titles, data series, gridlines, and Chart Area.

Practice 7

In this practice you will create a vertical bar chart and format it. Open PLANT GROWTH if it is not already displayed.

1) CREATE A BAR CHART

    a. If necessary, move the chart so that cells G3 through G10 are displayed.
    b. Highlight cells G3 through G10. The data for the total plant growth is highlighted.
    c. On the Standard Toolbar, click on the Chart Wizard button ( ). A dialog box is displayed.
        1. In the Chart type list, click on the Column option if it is not already selected.
        2. Select Next. The second Chart Wizard dialog box is displayed.
        3. Verify that the correct range (=Sheet1!$G$3:$G$10) is displayed in the Data range entry box.
        4. Select Next. The third Chart Wizard dialog box is displayed.
        5. Select the Titles tab if the title options are not already displayed.
        6. In the Chart title entry box, change the existing title to Experiment Results.
        7. In the Category (X) axis entry box, type Control Group.
        8. In the Value (Y) axis entry box, type Centimeters.
        9. Select Next. The fourth Chart Wizard dialog box is displayed.
        10. Select the As new sheet option and enter Total Growth Chart in the entry box.
        11. Select Finish. The chart is displayed in its own sheet.

Check – Your chart should look similar to:

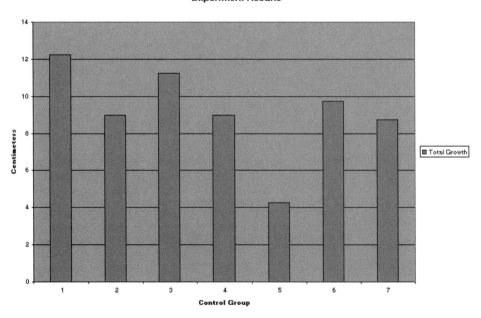

     A Guide to Microsoft Office 2000 Professional

2) ADD LABELS TO THE CHART

Notice how the control group letters are not displayed on the x-axis. The letters in cells A4 through A10 need to be added to the chart.

a. Display the chart sheet if it is not already displayed.
b. Select Chart → Source Data. A dialog box is displayed.
   1. Select the Series tab if the series options are not already displayed.
   2. Place the cursor in the Category (X) axis labels entry box.
   3. Display Sheet1 and then select cells A4 through A10 on the spreadsheet. Verify that the correct range (=Sheet1!$A$4:$A$10) is displayed in the dialog box.
   4. Select OK. The dialog box is removed. The control group letters are added as x-axis labels.

3) FORMAT THE BAR CHART

a. Double click on the chart title (Experiment Results). A dialog box is displayed.
   1. Select the Font tab. Font options are displayed.
   2. Change the Font, Font style, and Size.
   3. Select OK. The dialog box is removed and the chart title has been formatted.
b. Double click on the y-axis title (Centimeters). A dialog box is displayed.
   1. Select the Alignment tab. Alignment options are displayed.
   2. In the Degrees entry box, change the existing number to 0.
   3. Select OK. The dialog box is removed and the y-axes title is now displayed horizontally.
c. Click once on one of the bars to select the data series.
d. Select Format → Selected Data Series. A dialog box is displayed.
   1. Select the Patterns tab if the pattern options are not already displayed.
   2. In the Color collapsible list, select a different color.
   3. Select OK. The dialog box is removed. The data series has been formatted.

4) SAVE, PRINT, AND THEN CLOSE THE MODIFIED PLANT GROWTH

a. Save the modified PLANT GROWTH
b. Display the chart sheet if it is not already displayed.
c. On the Standard Toolbar, click on the Print button. The chart sheet is printed.
d. Close PLANT GROWTH.

5) EXIT EXCEL

Chapter Summary

This chapter covered how to use worksheets and how to create charts using data stored in a spreadsheet.

workbook
sheet

In Excel, spreadsheets are called workbooks, and each workbook contains worksheets. A sheet is displayed by clicking on its tab at the bottom of the Excel window. A sheet can be renamed by double-clicking on its name.

Data can be copied or moved between sheets using the Copy, Cut, and Paste commands from the Edit menu. Data can be used between sheets by referring to a cell in another sheet. For example, 'Sheet1'!A4 refers to cell A4 on Sheet1.

Options in the Print dialog box allow you to specify whether the entire workbook (spreadsheet) or the active sheet should be printed. Page options, such as gridlines or headers, need to be set for each sheet using the Page Setup command from the File menu.

pie chart

bar chart, line chart

Charts are used to show the relationship between data. A pie chart shows the percentage relationship between different parts of a whole quantity, a bar chart (column chart) compares different values, and a line chart tracks data over time. A new chart is created using the Chart command from the Insert menu or the Chart Wizard button ().

Before it can be moved, resized, deleted, or modified, an existing chart must first be selected by clicking in the Chart Area. The entire spreadsheet and any charts it contains can be printed by selecting the Print command or clicking on the Print button. A selected chart can be printed by itself on a single sheet of paper by selecting the Print command.

A chart can be modified by first selecting it and then selecting the Chart Options command from the Chart menu, which displays the Chart Options dialog box. Double-clicking on a chart also displays the Chart Options dialog box.

Commands from the Chart menu can be used to add adjacent and non-adjacent data to an existing chart. The Source Data command adds an adjacent data series and the Add Data command adds a nonadjacent data series to an existing chart. The Source Data command also adds labels that are not adjacent to the series of data they are describing to an existing chart.

Double-clicking on any object in a chart displays a Format dialog box where options can be selected to change the appearance of the chart.

Vocabulary

Active sheet The currently displayed sheet.

Bar chart Data graphed as a series of bars.

Chart A graphical representation of data stored in a spreadsheet.

Chart Area Blank portion of a chart.

Chart Wizard Displays dialog boxes where the user can select options to create a chart.

Column chart Data graphed as a series of vertical bars.

Data range The data to be charted.

Data series The set of related data points plotted on a chart.

Handles Used to resize a selected chart or data series.

Label Describes what is charted.

Legend Labels that identify the series in a chart.

Line chart Data graphed using a continuous line.

Pie chart Data graphed as segments of a circular pie.

Selected chart A chart that displays handles.

Sheet A spreadsheet in a workbook that is used to organize, store, and link related information.

Slice Part of a pie chart that represents one fractional part of a whole.

Title Describes what is charted.

Workbook An Excel spreadsheet.

Worksheet See sheet.

Excel Commands and Buttons

Add Data command Displays a dialog box where a nonadjacent series of data can be selected to add to an existing chart. Found in the Chart menu.

All command Deletes the active chart. Found in the Clear submenu in the Edit menu.

Chart command Displays the Chart Wizard dialog box used to create a chart. Found in the Insert menu. The Chart Wizard (■) button on the Standard Toolbar can be used instead of the command.

Chart Options command Displays a dialog box where options for changing the titles, axes, gridlines, legend, and data labels can be selected. Found in the Chart menu.

Copy command Places a duplicate of the highlighted cells' contents on the Clipboard. Found in the Edit menu. The Copy button (■) on the Standard Toolbar can be used instead of the command.

Cut command Removes the highlighted cells' contents and places it on the Clipboard. Found in the Edit menu. The Cut button (■) on the Standard Toolbar can be used instead of the command.

Page Setup command Displays a dialog box where options for changing page options can be selected for the active sheet. Found in the File menu.

Paste command Places the Clipboard contents in a spreadsheet starting at the selected cell. Found in the Edit menu. The Paste button (■) on the Standard Toolbar can be used instead of the command.

Print command Displays a dialog box where options for printing the entire workbook or the active sheet can be selected. Also used to print the charts on a spreadsheet. Found in the File menu.

Source Data command Displays a dialog box where the user can add an adjacent data series to an existing chart. Nonadjacent labels can also be added to an existing chart using this command. Found in the Chart menu.

Review Questions

Sections 9.1 — 9.4

1. a) What is a worksheet?
   b) How many sheets are in a workbook?
   c) How is a sheet displayed?

2. List the steps required to rename Sheet1 to Jan Sales.

3. Is it possible to copy or move data between sheets in a workbook?

4. Is it possible to reference cell B5 on Sheet1 in a formula stored in a cell on Sheet2? If so, how?

5. a) List the steps required to print all the sheets in a workbook at one time.
   b) List the steps required to print only the second sheet in a workbook.

6. List the steps required to print Sheet1 in landscape orientation and Sheet2 in portrait orientation.

Sections 9.5 — 9.9

7. What type of chart (bar, line, or pie) is best suited to display:
   a) a student's GPA over four years.
   b) the percentage each department spent of a company's total budget.
   c) the number of full-time, part-time, and temporary employees in a company.
   d) the number of books sold each day for a month at the college bookstore.

8. What happens to a chart when the data in the spreadsheet is changed?

9. List the steps required to resize and then move a chart.

10. a) List the steps required to print a chart that is stored on the same sheet as the charted data so that the chart and data are both printed.
    b) List the steps required to print a chart that is stored on the same sheet as the charted data so that only the chart is printed.

11. List the steps required to create a bar chart titled Employee Rates from the PAYROLL spreadsheet that displays each employee's rate/hr.

Sections 9.10 — 9.13

12. What command is used to edit an existing chart's title or legend?

13. List the steps required to modify a chart to include an additional adjacent series of data without using a command.

14. List the steps required to modify a chart to include an additional nonadjacent series of data.

15. List two ways to format a legend in a chart.

Exercises

When creating the charts in the exercises of this chapter, your charts may look different than those shown. It is the content of the chart (height and number of bars, labels, legend, title, etc.) that is important, not that its appearance exactly match that shown in the text. The font size of the labels in the chart may need to be changed in order to display all the labels clearly.

Exercise 1 ———————————————— Theater Attendance

A local theater wants to use a spreadsheet to keep track of the attendance for their performances for the last two years.

a) In a new spreadsheet enter the following data:

	Students	Adults	Senior Citizens
Romeo and Juliet	356	125	89
Othello	259	98	175
Bus Stop	289	125	112

Bold and right align the labels in row 1 and italicize the labels in column A. Resize columns as necessary so that all the data is displayed entirely.

b) Save the spreadsheet naming it Theater Attendance.

c) Rename Sheet1 to 2000 Attendance and Rename Sheet2 to 2001 Attendance.

d) Copy all the labels from the 2000 Attendance sheet into the 2001 Attendance sheet, pasting them into the same cell positions. Resize the columns as necessary so that all the data is displayed entirely.

e) Enter the attendance for 2001 into the second sheet:

	Students	Adults	Senior Citizens
Romeo and Juliet	389	255	110
Othello	188	145	175
Bus Stop	97	112	99

f) Rename Sheet3 to Total Attendance and copy the labels from the 2001 Attendance sheet into the Total Attendance sheet, pasting them into the same cell positions. Resize the columns as necessary so that all the data is displayed entirely.

g) In the Total Attendance sheet, enter formulas that use cell references to the first two sheets to calculate:

- the total number of students, adults, and senior citizens attending Romeo and Juliet
- the total number of students, adults, and senior citizens attending Othello
- the total number of students, adults, and senior citizens attending Bus Stop

h) Create a header on each sheet with your name right aligned.

i) Create a footer on each sheet with the name of the sheet center aligned.

j) Save the modified Theater Attendance and print a copy of all the sheets with gridlines and row and column headings.

Exercise 2 ———————————— Squeaky Clean Cars

The owner of Squeaky Clean Cars wants the data reorganized and charted for the budget spreadsheet modified in Chapter Eight, Exercise 2. Open Squeaky Clean Cars and complete the following steps:

a) Rename Sheet1 to June's Budget and rename Sheet2 to July's Budget.

b) Copy all the labels in column A from the June's Budget sheet into the July's Budget sheet, pasting them into the same cell positions. Resize the columns as necessary so that all the data is displayed entirely.

c) Move the labels and formulas in column F from the June's Budget sheet into the July's Budget sheet, pasting them into column B. Note that the formulas automatically update to refer to the cells on the first sheet.

d) Produce a pie chart on a new sheet named July's Expense Chart that displays the percentage of the budgeted expenses for July. Title the chart July's Budgeted Expenses:

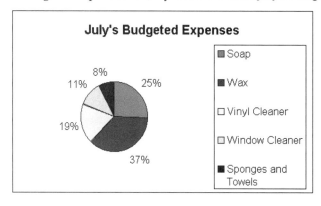

e) Create a header with your name right aligned in the July's Budget sheet and the July's Expense Chart sheet.

f) Save the modified Squeaky Clean Cars and print a copy of the July's Budget sheet with gridlines and row and column headings and the chart sheet.

Exercise 3 ——————————————————Swim Meet

The swim coach wants the data charted for the swim meet spreadsheet modified in Chapter Eight, Exercise 3. Open Swim Meet and complete the following steps:

a) Produce a bar (column) chart on the active sheet that displays the times for the first event. Title the chart 100 M Freestyle Results and include axes titles as shown:

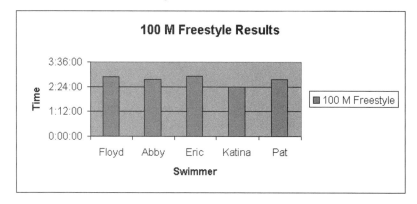

b) Modify the chart to include all six events. Edit the chart title appropriately.

c) Print preview the spreadsheet, then resize and move the chart so it and the data fit on one page in landscape orientation. Make sure the labels in the chart are displayed clearly. Save the modified Swim Meet and print a copy in landscape orientation with gridlines and row and column headings.

Exercise 4  Student Stats

The university wants the data charted for the student statistics spreadsheet modified in Chapter Eight, Exercise 4. Open Student Stats and complete the following steps:

a) Produce a pie chart on the active sheet that displays the percentage of undergraduate students in each college. Title the chart Undergraduate Students and format it as shown:

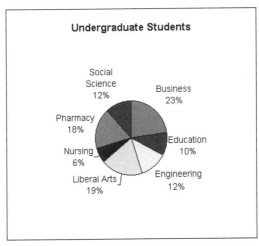

b) Produce a pie chart on the active sheet that displays the percentage of graduate students in each college (Hint: use the Series tab in the second Chart Wizard dialog box to include the labels for pie slices). Title the chart Graduate Students and format it as shown:

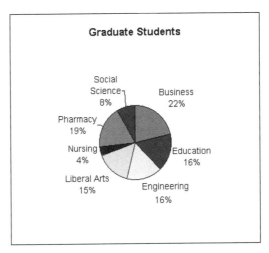

c) Print preview the spreadsheet, then resize and move the charts so that the charts and data fit on one page. Make sure the labels in the chart are displayed clearly. Save the modified Student Stats and print a copy with gridlines and row and column headings.

Exercise 5 —————————————————————————— AQUARIUM

The AQUARIUM spreadsheet contains the ammonia, nitrite, and nitrate levels for a new salt water aquarium. Open AQUARIUM and complete the following steps:

a) Produce a line chart on a new sheet named Water Cycle Chart that displays the ammonia, nitrite, and nitrate levels for each day since set-up (Hint: use the Series tab in the second Chart Wizard dialog box to include the days since set-up as the x-axis labels). Title the chart New Salt Water Aquarium Cycle and include axes titles as shown:

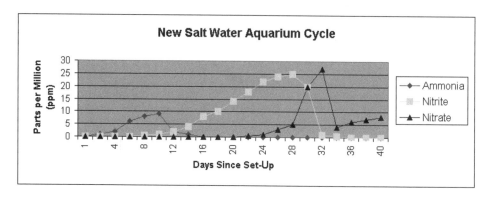

b) Create a header with your name right aligned in the Water Cycle Chart sheet.

c) Save the modified AQUARIUM and print the chart sheet.

Exercise 6 —————————————————————————— BREAK EVEN

In business, the break even point is when the sales revenue (money earned) equals the expenses (money paid out). A line chart can be used to determine the break even point. Open BREAK EVEN and complete the following steps:

a) Produce a line chart on the active sheet that displays the revenues and expenses per unit sold (Hint: use the Series tab in the second Chart Wizard dialog box to include the units sold as the x-axis labels). Title the chart Break Even Point and include axes titles as shown:

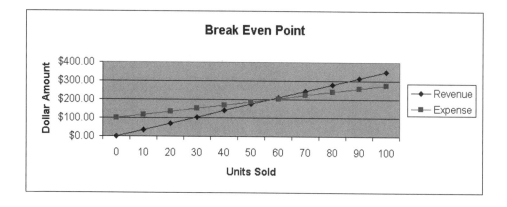

The chart shows that about 60 units must be sold for the company to break even.

b) Create a header with your name right aligned.

c) Print preview the spreadsheet, then resize and move the chart so that it and the data fit on one page in landscape orientation. Make sure the labels in the chart are displayed clearly. Save the modified BREAK EVEN and print a copy with gridlines and row and column headings.

Exercise 7 ⟳ ———————————————————————— Pizza Palace

The owner of Pizza Palace wants the data charted for the expense spreadsheet modified in Chapter Eight, Exercise 7. Open Pizza Palace and complete the following steps:

a) Produce a pie chart on the active sheet that displays the ingredients and the percentage of their costs for the Everything pizza (Hint: use the **Series** tab in the second Chart Wizard dialog box to include the labels for pie slices). Title the chart Ingredient Costs for the Everything Pizza and format it as shown:

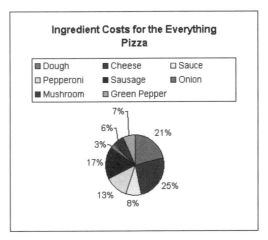

b) Print preview the spreadsheet, then resize and move the chart so that it and the data fit on one page. Make sure the labels in the chart are displayed clearly. Save the modified Pizza Palace and print a copy with gridlines and row and column headings.

Exercise 8 ⟳ ———————————————————————— Balance Sheet

The accountant wants data added to the balance sheet created in Chapter Seven, Exercise 8. Open Balance Sheet and complete the following steps:

a) Rename **Sheet1** to Jan 2001, rename **Sheet2** to Feb 2001 and rename **Sheet3** to March 2001.

b) Copy all the data from the **Jan 2001** sheet into the **Feb 2001** and **March 2001** sheets, pasting them into the same cell positions. Resize the columns as necessary so that all the data is displayed entirely.

c) Delete all the assets, liabilities, and stockholder's equity values in the second and third sheets (do not delete the formulas).

d) Edit the date in cell C3 in the second and third sheets appropriately. Note that there are 28 days in February 2001 and 31 days in March 2001.

e) Using the data below, enter the appropriate values into the Feb 2001 and March 2001 sheets:

	Feb	March
Cash	$12,250	$17,500
Accounts Receivable	$14,750	$8,500
Gym Equipment	$40,000	$38,900
Office Computers	$43,500	$42,750
Accounts Payable	$80,525	$79,525
Stockholder's Equity	$29,975	$28,125

f) Create a header with your name right aligned on the second and third sheets.

g) Save the modified Balance Sheet and print a copy of the second and third sheets with gridlines and row and column headings.

Exercise 9 — DANCE

The dance coordinator wants the data charted for the profit spreadsheet modified in Chapter Eight, Exercise 9. Open DANCE and complete the following steps:

a) Produce a bar (column) chart on the active sheet that displays the profit when 50, 100, 200, and 300 people attend the dance (Hint: use the Series tab in the second Chart Wizard dialog box to include the x-axis labels). Title the chart Dance Profit and format it as shown:

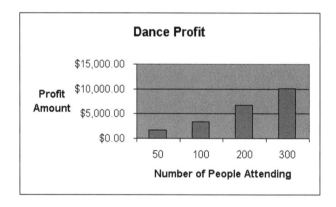

b) Print preview the spreadsheet, then resize and move the chart so that it and the data fit on one page. Make sure the labels in the chart are displayed clearly. Save the modified DANCE and print a copy with gridlines and row and column headings.

Exercise 10 ⚙ ———————————————————— STOCKS

The track coach wants the data charted for the spreadsheet modified in Chapter Eight, Exercise 10. Open STOCKS and complete the following steps:

a) Produce a bar (column) chart on a new sheet named Stock Value Chart that displays the original values of the stocks (Hint: use the Series tab in the second Chart Wizard dialog box to include the x-axis labels). Title the chart Stock Values and include axes titles as shown:

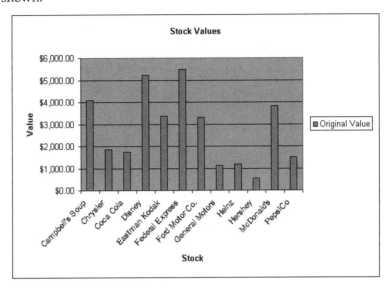

b) Create a header with your name right aligned in the Stock Value Chart sheet.

c) Modify the chart to include the March values of the stocks as a new data series.

d) Save the modified STOCKS and print the chart sheet.

Exercise 11 ⚙ ———————————————————— Tickets

The amphitheater manager wants the data reorganized for the spreadsheet created in Chapter Eight, Exercise 11. Open Tickets and complete the following steps:

a) Rename Sheet1 to The Motherboards, rename Sheet2 to Blue Knights and rename Sheet3 to The Altairs.

b) Move the appropriate data so that each act's data is in the appropriate sheet. Remember to also copy the labels in row 1 to the new sheets. Resize the columns as necessary so that all the data is displayed entirely.

c) Create a header with your name right aligned on the second and third sheets.

d) Create a footer on each sheet with the name of the sheet center aligned.

e) Save the modified Tickets and print a copy of all the sheets with gridlines and row and column headings.

The track coach wants the data charted for the progress spreadsheet created in Chapter Eight, Exercise 12. Open Track Progress and complete the following steps:

a) Produce a line chart on the active sheet that displays the students' progress in the 100 meter run over the four months. Title the chart Track Team's Progress in 100 Meter and include axes labels as shown:

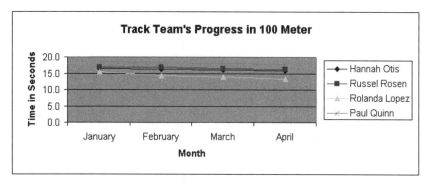

b) Produce a line chart on the active sheet that displays the students' progress in the 200 meter run over the four months (Hint: use the Series tab in the second Chart Wizard dialog box to include the x-axis labels). Title the chart Track Team's Progress in 200 Meter and include axes labels as shown:

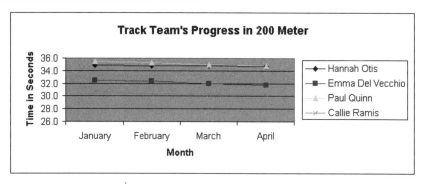

c) Print preview the spreadsheet, then resize and move the charts so that the charts and data fit on one page in landscape orientation. Make sure the labels in the chart are displayed clearly. Save the modified Track Progress and print a copy in landscape orientation with gridlines and row and column headings.

Exercise 13 ✑ —————————————————

The accountant want the data charted for the income statement created in Chapter Seven, Exercise 13. Open Income Statement and complete the following steps:

a) Produce a line chart on a new sheet named Income Chart that displays the net income/loss for 1999–2001 (Hint: use the Series tab in the second Chart Wizard dialog box to include the x-axis labels). Title the chart 1999-2001 Income and include axes titles and formatting as shown:

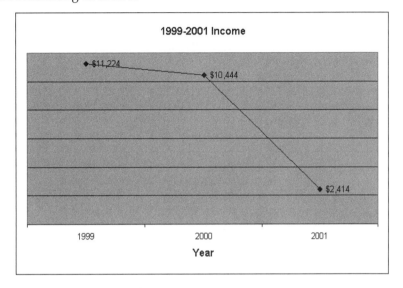

b) Create a header with your name right aligned on the Income Chart sheet.

c) Produce a line chart on the active sheet that charts the total revenues for 1999 and 2000 (Hint: use the Series tab in the second Chart Wizard dialog box to include the x-axis labels). Title the chart Revenues 1999–2000 and include axes titles as shown:

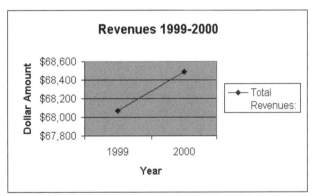

d) Modify the revenue chart to include all three years 1999–2001.

e) Modify the revenue chart to include the total expenses for all three years as a new data series. Edit the title appropriately.

f) Save the modified Income Statement and print each chart separately.

The Meteorology department wants the data modified to include Fahrenheit temperatures and charted for the spreadsheet modified in Chapter Eight, Exercise 14. Open City Temp and complete the following steps:

a) Rename Sheet1 to Celsius and Rename Sheet2 to Fahrenheit.

b) Copy all the data in column A from the Celsius sheet to the Fahrenheit sheet, pasting them into the same cell positions.

c) In the Fahrenheit sheet, enter formulas that use cell references to the Celsius sheet to convert the Celsius temperatures to Fahrenheit. The formula needed to convert from degrees Celsius to Fahrenheit is 9/5*(Celsius Temp)+32.

d) Title the column heading appropriately and include proper formatting. Resize columns as necessary so that all the data is displayed entirely.

e) In rows 22 and 23, enter formulas that use a function to calculate the highest temperature within the 20 years and the lowest temperature within the 20 years, respectively.

f) Create a line chart on the Celsius sheet that displays the temperature for the years 1982 to 1992 (Hint: use the Series tab in the second Chart Wizard dialog box to include the x-axis labels). Title the chart 1982-1992 Temperatures and include axes titles and formatting as shown:

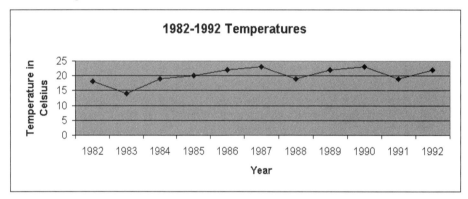

g) Create the same line chart for the Fahrenheit temperatures in the Fahrenheit sheet.

h) Modify both charts to include the data for all 20 years and edit the titles appropriately.

i) Create a header with your name right aligned in the Fahrenheit sheet.

j) Print preview both sheets, then resize and move the charts so that the charts and data fit on each sheet in landscape orientation. Make sure the labels in the charts are displayed clearly. Save the modified City Temp and print a copy of both sheets in landscape orientation with gridlines and row and column headings.

The printing company wants the data charted for the cost spreadsheet modified in Chapter Eight, Exercise 15. Open Brochure Costs and complete the following steps:

a) Produce a pie chart on the active sheet that displays the percentage of each type of fixed cost (Hint: use the **Series** tab in the second Chart Wizard dialog box to include labels for the pie slices). Title the chart Fixed Costs and format it as shown:

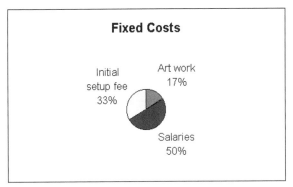

b) Create a bar (column) chart on the active sheet that shows the cost per brochure for the different number of brochures produced (Hint: use the **Series** tab in the second Chart Wizard dialog box to include the x-axis labels). Title the chart Cost Per Brochure and include axes titles and formatting as shown:

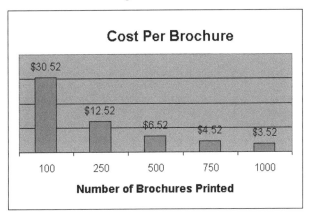

c) Print preview the spreadsheet, then resize and move the charts so that the charts and data fit on one page. Make sure the labels in the charts are displayed clearly. Save the modified Brochure Costs and print a copy with gridlines and row and column headings.

Advanced
Exercise 16 ⚙ ————————————————————————————— My Finances

Modify the My Finances spreadsheet created in Chapter Eight, Exercise 16 so that it contains a line chart of your savings. Save the modified spreadsheet and then print a copy of only the chart.

Advanced
Exercise 17 ————————————————————————————— New Charts

This chapter only discussed pie, line, and bar charts. Excel allows many different types of charts to be created. Enter data into a new spreadsheet so that it can be charted. Create three charts besides pie, line, or bar from the data. Save the spreadsheet naming it New Charts and then print a copy.

Advanced
Exercise 18 ⚙ ————————————————————————————————

Modify one of the spreadsheets created in Exercise 17 or 18 in Chapter Eight to include a chart on its own sheet. Save the modified spreadsheet and then print the chart sheet.

Chapter Ten
Advanced Spreadsheet Techniques

Sort

Freeze Panes

Unfreeze Panes

Set Print Area

Clear Print Area

Hyperlink

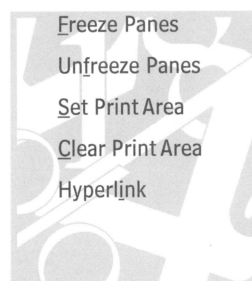

Chapter Ten Objectives

After completing this chapter you will be able to:

1. Answer What If? questions using a spreadsheet.
2. Sort the data in a spreadsheet.
3. Use the CHOOSE and VLOOKUP functions.
4. Freeze selected rows and columns.
6. Use text in CHOOSE and VLOOKUP functions.
7. Create an amortization table using the PMT function.
8. Print a selected spreadsheet area.
9. Create hyperlinks to the Internet.
10. E-mail a spreadsheet.

This chapter introduces advanced functions and explains how to use a spreadsheet to answer "What If?" questions. The chapter ends by discussing how to use Excel with the Internet.

10.1 Asking "What If ?"

A spreadsheet is often used to answer *What If?* questions. For example, a cookie manufacturer may ask: What if the price of sugar increases? How will this affect the cost of my cookies? These questions are easily answered by changing numbers in a spreadsheet.

model   A spreadsheet modified to answer What If? questions contains data relating to a particular situation and is called a *model*. For example, consider a cookie manufacturer's spreadsheet that includes the cost of the ingredients, packaging, and labor. If the cost of sugar were to increase, the new cost could be entered into the spreadsheet so that it could be used as a model to see how the overall cost of production is affected. A decision about raising the price of the cookies could then be made based on this model. Many businesses use this technique to help make decisions.

Practice 1

In this practice you will answer the "What If?" questions described in Section 10.1 for a cookie manufacturer.

1) OPEN COOKIE COSTS

The COOKIE COSTS spreadsheet contains the production costs per batch of cookies.

2) ENTER TITLES AND VALUES FOR THE NEW PRICES

a. In cell C3, enter the label Sugar Decrease then right align and bold the label.
b. In cell D3, enter the label Sugar Increase then right align and bold the label.
c. In cell C4, enter the price $1.00.
d. In cell D4, enter the price $2.50.

3) CALCULATE THE EXPENSES

a. Copy the values in cells B5 through B9 to cells C5 through D9.
b. The formula in cell B10 totals the expenses. Copy the formula in cell B10 to cells C10 through D10.

4) SAVE, PRINT, AND THEN CLOSE THE MODIFIED COOKIE SALES

10.2 Using Sort to Organize a Spreadsheet

ascending, descending

alphabetical, chronological

Placing rows of data in a specified order is called *sorting*. In Excel, rows can be sorted in either *ascending* (low to high) or *descending* (high to low) order based on the data in a specified column. Ascending order is also called *alphabetical* order when the data is text, and *chronological* order when the data is times or dates.

The Sort Ascending ( ) and Sort Descending ( ) buttons on the Standard Toolbar are used to sort highlighted rows of data. When the desired Sort button is clicked, the rows are ordered based on the values displayed in the first column of the highlighted data. For example, when the following cells are highlighted:

	A	B
1	**Item**	**Price**
2	Food	$429
3	Hotel	$650
4	Airfare	$1,025
5	Rental Car	$198
6	**Total:**	$2,302

Clicking the Sort Ascending button orders the rows so that they are in alphabetical order based on the values in column A (the first highlighted column):

	A	B
1	**Item**	**Price**
2	Airfare	$1,025
3	Food	$429
4	Hotel	$650
5	Rental Car	$198
6	**Total:**	$2,302

The highlighted block has been sorted by column A

Basing a Sort on More Than One Column

When a second column and order are specified in the **Then by** option in the Sort dialog box, rows that have the same data in the key sort column are sorted based on the data in the second column.

The *key sort column* is the column that contains the values that a sort is based on. The Sort Ascending or Sort Descending buttons always use the first highlighted column as the key sort column. A different column can be designated as the key sort column by using the <u>S</u>ort command from the <u>D</u>ata menu, which displays the Sort dialog box. This dialog box contains options for selecting the key sort column and the method of sort, such as ascending.

Practice 2

In this practice the Grades spreadsheet will be sorted.

1) OPEN GRADES

2) SORT ALL THE STUDENT DATA

    a. Point to the row number for row 3 and drag down to the row number for row 8 to highlight all the rows containing student data.

    b. On the Standard Toolbar, click on the Sort Ascending ( ) button. The highlighted rows are sorted in alphabetical order by column A.

    c. Click anywhere in the spreadsheet to remove the highlight.

3) SAVE AND CLOSE THE MODIFIED GRADES

10.3 The CHOOSE Function

The CHOOSE function is used to return a value from a list of many values. The CHOOSE function takes the form:

$$CHOOSE(\text{<choice>}, \text{<option}_1\text{>}, \text{<option}_2\text{>}, ..., \text{<option}_N\text{>})$$

<choice> is a number between 1 and N (the number of possible values) and <option1>, <option2>, ... store the possible values to return. CHOOSE returns the value in the list of arguments that corresponds to <choice>. If <choice> is 1, CHOOSE returns <option$_1$>; if <choice> is 2, then <option$_2$> is returned, and so on. For example, the formula

$$=CHOOSE(A1,55,44,66,22)$$

displays 55 if the value stored in cell A1 is 1, 44 if the value is 2, 66 if the value is 3, and 22 if it is 4. If <choice> is less than 1 or greater than N, #VALUE! is displayed, meaning that a corresponding value is not available.

Only the integer portion of <choice> is used to determine which value to return. For example, if A1 stores 1.6, 55 is displayed because only the integer portion of the value, 1, is used. The options (<option$_1$>, <option$_2$>, etc.) in the CHOOSE function can include values, formulas, or cell references.

Practice 3

In this practice you will modify the PAYROLL spreadsheet to calculate a contribution amount using the CHOOSE function.

1) OPEN PAYROLL

2) INSERT COLUMNS

    a. Select column L by clicking on its column letter.
    b. Select Insert → Columns. A new column is inserted. Repeat this procedure to insert a second new column. Net Pay is now in column N.

3) ENTER TITLES

    a. In cell L4, enter the title Contrib. Code.
    b. In cell M4, enter the title Contribution.
    c. Adjust the column widths to display the labels entirely.

4) ENTER THE CONTRIBUTION CODES

    a. There are four contribution codes numbered 1 through 4 which determine the percentage of gross pay that will be deducted for each employee. Enter the code numbers on the next page into the indicated cells in column L:

In cell	L5	enter	2		In cell	L16	enter	1
	L6		2			L17		2
	L7		1			L18		3
	L8		3			L19		3
	L9		1			L20		4
	L0		1			L21		1
	L11		1			L22		1
	L12		2			L23		1
	L13		2			L24		2
	L14		4			L25		1
	L15		1					

b. Format the values in column L as number with 0 decimal places.

5) ENTER THE FORMULA TO CALCULATE CONTRIBUTIONS

Each of the codes above corresponds to the following percentages which are used to calculate the contribution deduction:

Code	Percentage
1	0%
2	1%
3	2%
4	5%

a. In cell M5, enter the formula:

=CHOOSE(L5,0,I5*1%,I5*2%,I5*5%)

The CHOOSE function first looks in cell L5 to determine the value of <choice>. Because the value in cell L5 is 2, this corresponds to <option$_2$> and Excel calculates I5*1% to compute the contribution. Cell M5 displays $2.25, the result of $225.00*1%.

b. Copy the formula in cell M5 to cells M6 through M25.

6) RECALCULATE THE NET PAY

a. In cell N5, modify the existing formula to be:

=I5–J5–K5–M5

Net pay is now computed by subtracting social security, taxes, and contribution from the gross pay, and $175.50 is displayed in cell N5.

b. Copy the formula in cell N5 to cells N6 through N25.

7) SAVE THE MODIFIED IVY PAYROLL

Check – Your spreadsheet should look similar to:

I	J	K	L	M	N
Gross Pay	Soc. Sec.	Taxes	Contrib. Code	Contribution	Net Pay
$225.00	$13.50	$33.75	2	$2.25	$175.50
$236.00	$14.16	$35.40	2	$2.36	$184.08
$232.00	$13.92	$34.80	1	$0.00	$183.28
$100.75	$6.05	$15.11	3	$2.02	$77.58
$407.25	$24.44	$61.09	1	$0.00	$321.73
$294.50	$17.67	$44.18	1	$0.00	$232.66
$531.69	$31.90	$79.75	1	$0.00	$420.03
$171.00	$10.26	$25.65	2	$1.71	$133.38

10.4 The VLOOKUP Function

The VLOOKUP function is used to return a value from a table of values stored in the spreadsheet. The VLOOKUP function takes the form:

VLOOKUP(<value>, <range>, <column>)

<value> is a number and <range> is the cell range where the VLOOKUP table is stored. VLOOKUP finds the largest number in the first column of <range> which is less than or equal to <value>, and then returns the value stored in the same row in column <column> of the VLOOKUP table. The value of <column> is usually 2 to indicate that the second column in the VLOOKUP table stores the value to be returned.

For example, consider the spreadsheet below:

C2		=	=VLOOKUP(B2,$E$7:$F$11,2)		
	A	B	C	D	E	F
1	Customer	Purchase Amount	Shipping & Handling			
2	Graham	$39.75	$7.49			
3	McKenna	$100.00	$12.49			
4	Peterson	$52.50	$7.49			
5	Rizzo	$176.75	$14.99			
6					Shipping & Handling	
7					$0	$4.99
8					$30	$7.49
9					$60	$10.49
10					$100	$12.49
11					$150	$14.99

With the formula =VLOOKUP(B2,$E$7:$F$11,2) in cell C2, Excel looks in cell B2 for its value, which is $39.75. Excel then looks in the first column of the VLOOKUP table for the largest value which is less than or equal to $39.75, in this case $30 (stored in E8). The corresponding value in the second column of the table, in this case $7.49, is then displayed in cell C2. In a similar manner, the function displays $12.49 in cell C3 because cell E10 stores the largest value in the VLOOKUP table which is less than or equal to $100 (the value in B3).

The values in the first column of the VLOOKUP table must be in ascending order for VLOOKUP to work correctly. If <value> is less than the first value stored in the VLOOKUP table, #N/A! is displayed. For this reason, the first value stored in the VLOOKUP table must be less than any value that will be looked up.

VLOOKUP differs from CHOOSE in that <value> can be negative or zero as long as it falls within the values stored in the VLOOKUP table. Also, <value> can be a range of decimal numbers. One advantage of the VLOOKUP function is that the values to be returned are stored in cells in the spreadsheet, not in the function itself.

In the VLOOKUP function, absolute references should be used to define the VLOOKUP table so that the table range does not change if the formula containing the VLOOKUP function is copied.

An example of using VLOOKUP is when a business needs to calculate tax deductions for their payroll based on the following criteria:

Gross Pay	Tax Rate
under $51	0%
$51 – $524	15%
$525 – $1,124	28%
$1,125 and above	31%

The VLOOKUP table is created by first determining what the contents of the table must be in order to work with the VLOOKUP function. The table is then entered in the spreadsheet, and the necessary VLOOKUP function is placed in an appropriate formula:

	C2	▼	=	=B2*VLOOKUP(B2,$B$7:$C$10,2)		
	A	B	C	D	E	F
1	Employee	Gross Pay	Taxes			
2	Fetzer, R.	$356.88	$53.53			
3	Martinez, L.	$175.50	$26.33			
4	Nudelman, B.	$1,126.00	$349.06			
5						
6		Tax Rate Table				
7		$0.00	0%			
8		$51.00	15%			
9		$525.00	28%			
10		$1,125.00	31%			

Fetzer's gross pay is $356.88, therefore the VLOOKUP function returns 15% which is then multiplied by the value in cell B2 to display $53.53.

10.5 Freezing Cells

One difficulty encountered when working with a large spreadsheet is that rows and columns that contain descriptive labels may scroll off the screen. This makes it difficult to determine which columns or rows the displayed cells are in. Excel solves this problem by enabling you to *freeze* selected rows and columns so they cannot be scrolled.

Selecting the Freeze Panes command from the Window menu designates every row above the cell cursor and every column to the left of the cell cursor as frozen. For example, selecting cell B5 and then selecting Freeze Panes freezes the cells in column A and rows 1 through 4:

	A	B	C	D	E	F
1						
2	Soc. Sec. Rate:	6%				
3						
4	Employee	Rate/Hr	Mon	Tue	Wed	Thu
5	Alban, B.	$7.50	9.0	0.0	6.0	9.0
6	Angulo, M.	$8.00	0.0	9.5	7.0	8.0
7	Balto, Y.	$8.00	8.0	0.0	8.0	7.0
8	Cruz, S.	$7.75	5.0	5.0	3.0	0.0

Frozen cells are displayed with solid borders

When scrolling vertically, frozen rows remain on the screen. Frozen columns remain on the screen when scrolling horizontally. Selecting the Unfreeze Panes command again unfreezes all the frozen cells.

Freezing cells does not affect how the spreadsheet is printed.

Spreadsheet Templates

Rather than recreating a complex spreadsheet over and over again, it can be created once and then saved as a template enabling new, untitled duplicates to be created. Templates are previously created files that include only the basic elements.

Selecting the Save As command from the File menu and then selecting Template from the Save as type collapsible list saves the current spreadsheet as a template. A template is used by selecting it from the General tab in the New Office Document dialog box.

Excel supplies many previously created spreadsheet templates.

Practice 4

In this practice PAYROLL will be modified to allow for four tax rates. Cells will be frozen to keep the employee names and column titles on the screen. Open PAYROLL if it is not already displayed.

1) ADD A VLOOKUP TABLE TO THE SPREADSHEET

The following tax rates will be used in calculating taxes:

Salary	Tax Rate
under $51	0%
$51 – $524	15%
$525 – $1,124	28%
$1,125 and above	31%

a. In cell B27, enter the label Tax Rate Table then bold it.
b. Enter the following values into the indicated cells to create the tax VLOOKUP table:

In cell	B28	enter	$0	In cell	C28	enter	0%
	B29		$51		C29		15%
	B30		$525		C30		28%
	B31		$1,125		C31		31%

2) FREEZE TITLES

a. Select cell B5. Be sure that cell A1 is displayed on the screen as well.
b. Select Window → Freeze Panes. The frozen cells are indicated by solid borders.
c. Click on the right scroll arrow to scroll horizontally. Column A remains while other columns are scrolled off the screen.
d. Click on the down scroll arrow to scroll vertically. Rows 1 through 4 remain on the screen.

3) CALCULATE TAXES USING THE VLOOKUP FUNCTION

a. In cell K5, replace the existing formula with

=I5*VLOOKUP(I5,$B$28:$C$31,2)

The gross pay stored in cell I5 is $225.00, which is multiplied by 15% to compute the tax deduction of $33.75. Dollar signs ($) are needed in the function to keep the cell references for the VLOOKUP table from changing when the formula is copied.
b. Copy the formula in cell K5 to cells K6 through K25.

Check – Your spreadsheet should look similar to:

	A	H	I	J	K	L	M	N
1								
2	Soc. Sec. Rate:							
3								
4	Employee	Total Hours	Gross Pay	Soc. Sec.	Taxes	Contrib. Code	Contribution	Net Pay
5	Alban, B.	30.0	$225.00	$13.50	$33.75	2	$2.25	$175.50
6	Angulo, M.	29.5	$236.00	$14.16	$35.40	2	$2.36	$184.08
7	Balto, Y.	29.0	$232.00	$13.92	$34.80	1	$0.00	$183.28
8	Cruz, S.	13.0	$100.75	$6.05	$15.11	3	$2.02	$77.58

4) SAVE, PRINT, AND THEN CLOSE THE MODIFIED IVY PAYROLL

a. Select Window → Unfreeze Panes. The cells are no longer frozen.
b. Save the modified PAYROLL and print a copy.
c. Close PAYROLL.

10.6 Using Text in the CHOOSE and VLOOKUP Functions

As with the IF function, text can be used in both the CHOOSE and VLOOKUP functions. For example, the formula

=CHOOSE(C3,"Beginner","Intermediate","Advanced","Expert")

displays the word Beginner if the value stored in cell C3 is 1, Intermediate if C3 stores the value 2, etc. Cell references of a cell storing a label can also be used.

The VLOOKUP function can also be used to display text by storing labels in the VLOOKUP table. For example, the formula =VLOOKUP(B2,$B$9:$C$11,2) in cell C2 below displays High Normal because cell B10 stores the largest value in the VLOOKUP table less than or equal to the value in cell B2:

	C2		=	=VLOOKUP(B2,$B$9:$C$11,2)	
	A	B	C		D
1	Patient	Blood Pressure	Diagnosis		
2	Gershwin, E.	130	High Normal		
3	Baron, N.	128	Normal		
4	Hajdu, B.	150	High Blood Pressure		
5	Dean, D.	129	Normal		
6					
7					
8		Systolic Blood Pressure Table			
9		0	Normal		
10		130	High Normal		
11		140	High Blood Pressure		

Practice 5

In this practice the Grades spreadsheet will be modified to display each student's letter grade.

1) OPEN GRADES

2) ENTER AND FORMAT A LABEL

In cell H1, enter the label Grade then center align the label.

3) ADD A VLOOKUP TABLE

a. In cell B12, enter the label Letter Grade Table then bold it.
b. Enter the following data into the indicated cells to create the VLOOKUP table:

In cell	B13	enter	0	In cell	C13	enter	F
	B14		60		C14		D
	B15		70		C15		C
	B16		80		C16		B
	B17		90		C17		A

Note that the scores in the letter grade table are in ascending order so that the VLOOKUP function will work properly.

A Guide to Microsoft Office 2000 Professional

4) ENTER FORMULAS TO DETERMINE THE STUDENTS' GRADES

    a. In cell H3, enter the formula:

        =VLOOKUP(F3,$B$13:$C$17,2)

        Since 70 is the largest number less than or equal to the value in cell F3, C is displayed.

    b. Center align the letter grade in cell H3.

    c. Copy the formula in cell H3 to cells H4 through H8.

Check - Your spreadsheet should look similar to:

	H8			=	=VLOOKUP(F8,$B$13:$C$17,2)		
	A	B	C	D	E	F	G	H
1	Name	Test 1	Test 2	Test 3	Test 4	Student Average	Status	Grade
2		9/12/2001	10/10/2001	11/14/2001	12/12/2001			
3	Adams, V.	70	74	80	83	76.8	Passing	C
4	Demps, K.	85	73	88	92	84.5	Passing	B
5	Matos, A.	72	63	67	72	68.5	Below Average	D
6	McCallister, T.	92	88	85	91	89.0	Passing	B
7	Smith, L.	87	92	85	93	89.3	Passing	B
8	Sun, L.	94	91	93	84	90.5	Passing	A
9	Test Average	83.33	80.17	83	85.83			
10								
11								
12		Letter Grade Table						
13		0	F					
14		60	D					
15		70	C					
16		80	B					
17		90	A					

5) CHANGE SMITH'S SCORE ON TEST 3

    A mistake was made when Smith's Test 3 score was entered. Select cell D7 and enter 95, the correct score. Note how Excel automatically recalculates all formulas that refer to the cell containing the test score: Smith's average has been recalculated and the grade is now an A.

6) SAVE, PRINT, AND THEN CLOSE THE MODIFIED GRADES

    a. Save the modified Grades.

    b. Print a copy of the spreadsheet in landscape orientation.

    c. Save the modified Grades and then close Grades.

10.7 Amortization Tables and the PMT Function

installment loan

principal

A useful application of a spreadsheet is an amortization table. *Amortization* is a method for computing equal periodic payments for an *installment loan*. Car loans and mortgages are often installment loans. Each installment, or payment, is the same and consists of two parts: a portion to pay interest due on the principal for that period and the remainder which reduces the principal. The *principal* is the amount of money owed, and decreases with each payment made.

An *amortization table* displays the interest and principal amounts for each payment of an installment loan. For example, the monthly payment on a 30 year loan of $100,000 borrowed at 12% interest (1% per month) is $1,028.61. In the first payment, $1,000.00 pays the interest due (1% × $100,000) and $28.61 goes to reduce principal ($1,028.61 − $1,000). In the next payment, $999.71 pays the interest due and $28.90 goes to reduce

Set Print Area
Clear Print Area

principal. As payments are made, the interest due decreases because there is less principal to charge interest on. In the final payment, $10.18 pays the interest due and $1,018.43 pays off the principal.

The PMT function is used to calculate the equal periodic payment for an installment loan. The interest rate, the number of payments to be made, and the amount of the loan (principal) are the arguments needed by the PMT function. The PMT function takes the form:

PMT(<rate>, <term>, <principal>)

<rate> is the interest rate per period, <term> is the total number of payments to be made, and <principal> is the amount borrowed. For example, the PMT function would be used to determine the monthly payment on a mortgage. The formula below calculates the monthly payments on a 30-year, $100,000 loan with an annual interest rate of 12%:

=PMT(12%/12, 360, –100000)

Since the payments are made monthly, the interest rate must also be computed monthly by dividing the annual interest rate of 12% by 12. The number of payments is 360, 30 years × 12 months. The principal is negative because it is the amount borrowed. This formula computes the monthly payment as $1,028.61.

10.8 Printing a Selected Spreadsheet Area

At times, only part of a spreadsheet may need to be printed. The Set Print Area command from the Print Area submenu in the File menu is used to change the printable spreadsheet area. Highlighting the desired block of cells and then selecting the Set Print Area command designates the printable spreadsheet area. Selecting the Print command then prints only those cells in the range. Once the print area is set, only those cells will be displayed in print preview and included in a printout.

The entire spreadsheet can be set as the print range by selecting the Clear Print Area command from the Print Area submenu in the File menu.

Practice 6

In this practice you will complete an amortization table.

1) OPEN LOAN

The LOAN spreadsheet is a partially completed amortization table.

2) ENTER THE LOAN'S INFORMATION

   a. In cell B3, enter the yearly interest rate 12%.
   b. In cell B4, enter the number of payments 360 (30 years × 12 monthly payments).
   c. In cell B5, enter the principal $100,000.

3) CALCULATE THE MONTHLY PAYMENT

In cell B7, enter the formula:

=PMT(B3/12,B4,–B5)

The division by 12 is needed to convert the yearly interest rate in cell B3 to a monthly value. $1,028.61 is displayed.

4) CALCULATE TOTAL PAID AND TOTAL INTEREST

    a. In cell B9, enter the formula:

        =ROUND(B4*B7,2)

    This formula computes the total paid for the loan, $370,300.53, including principal and interest.

    b. In cell B10, enter the formula =B9–B5 to total interest paid over the 30 years, $270,300.53.

5) ENTER THE FIRST PAYMENT DATA

    a. In cell A13, enter 1.

    b. In cell B13, enter =B5.

    c. In cell C13, enter the formula

        =B13*($B$3/12)

    to calculate one month's interest on the loan. $1,000.00, which is 1% (12%/12) of the principal, is displayed. The cell reference B3 contains dollar signs because the interest rate will be the same for each payment.

    d. In cell D13, enter the formula

        =IF(C13<0.01,0,$B$7–C13)

    to calculate the amount of the payment which is applied to the principal, $28.61. If the value in cell C13 is less than 0.01 (less than a penny), then 0 is displayed.

    e. In cell E13, enter the formula =B13–D13 to calculate the new principal owed.

6) ENTER FORMULAS FOR THE SECOND PAYMENT

    a. In cell A14, enter the formula: =A13+1

    b. In cell B14, enter =E13 to display the new principal.

    c. Copy the formulas in cells C13 through E13 into cells C14 through E14. This completes the data for the second payment and the principal owed, $99,942.49 is displayed in cell E14.

7) COMPLETE THE TABLE

    Copy the formulas in cells A14 through E14 into cells A15 through E372. The principal owed is $0.00 which indicates the loan has been paid in full.

Check – Your spreadsheet should look similar to:

	A	B	C	D	E
1	Loan Amortization Table				
2					
3	Interest rate =	12%			
4	Number of payments =	360			
5	Principal =	$100,000.00			
6					
7	Monthly payment =	$1,028.61			
8					
9	Total paid =	$370,300.53			
10	Total interest =	$270,300.53			
11					
12		Payment	Principal	Pay to Interest	Pay to Principal	Principal Owed
13		1	$100,000.00	$1,000.00	$28.61	$99,971.39
14		2	$99,971.39	$999.71	$28.90	$99,942.49
15		3	$99,942.49	$999.42	$29.19	$99,913.30
16		4	$99,913.30	$999.13	$29.48	$99,883.82
17		5	$99,883.82	$998.84	$29.77	$99,854.05

8) *PRINT A PORTION OF THE SPREADSHEET*

a. Highlight cells A1 through E15.
b. Select <u>F</u>ile → Prin<u>t</u> Area → <u>S</u>et Print Area. Note the dashed lines around the cells indicating the print area.
c. Print preview the spreadsheet. Note that only the cells designated as the print area are displayed.
d. Save the modified LOAN and then print the spreadsheet.
e. Select <u>F</u>ile → Prin<u>t</u> Area → <u>C</u>lear Print Area. The print area is now set to the entire spreadsheet.
f. Click on any cell to remove the highlight.

9) *CREATE AN AUTO LOAN MODEL*

The present values in LOAN represent a house loan. Because the data is stored in cells, it is easy to answer What If? questions. Therefore, the spreadsheet can easily be used to produce the payments for a car loan.

a. In cell B3, enter the new yearly interest rate 10%.
b. The car loan is a 5 year loan; therefore, the number of monthly payments will be 5 × 12. In cell B4, enter the new number of payments 60.
c. In cell B5, enter the new principal $12,000.
d. Note how the spreadsheet has been recalculated. Scroll down to row 72 which contains the last payment. The spreadsheet can easily model loans with less than 360 payments.
e. Save the modified LOAN.

10) *ENTER YOUR OWN VALUES INTO THE LOAN SPREADSHEET*

a. Experiment by changing the rate, term, and principal of the LOAN spreadsheet to any values you like. Change the number of payments to see how that affects the interest paid.
b. Select <u>F</u>ile → <u>C</u>lose. Click on No in the dialog box when prompted to save the file.

10.9 Creating Hyperlinks to the Internet

In addition to numeric data and text, a spreadsheet can include hyperlinks to Web pages on the Internet. Clicking on a hyperlink in an Excel spreadsheet connects your computer to the Internet and displays the Web page. Note that the computer you are using needs to have Internet access in order to connect to the Internet.

A hyperlink is inserted into a selected cell by either selecting the Hyperl<u>i</u>nk command from the <u>I</u>nsert menu or clicking on the Insert Hyperlink button (⬛) on the Standard Toolbar to display the Insert Hyperlink dialog box:

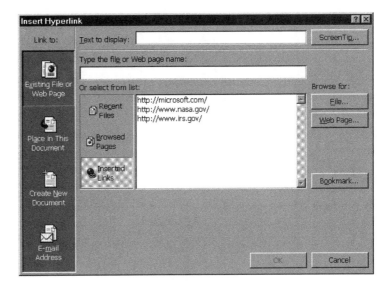

Entering a URL for the Web page in the Type the file or Web page name entry box and selecting OK inserts a hyperlink into the selected cell. The text http:// is automatically added to the beginning of the URL. Hyperlinks are automatically formatted as underlined blue text in an Excel spreadsheet.

On some occasions, you may want a description to appear in the spreadsheet as the hyperlink instead of the URL. Typing text in the Text to display entry box, in addition to entering a URL in the Type the file or Web page name entry box, will place the text in the spreadsheet and format it as a hyperlink to the specified URL.

After inserting a hyperlink, pointing to it changes the pointer to a hand shape () which indicates that you can click on the hyperlink to connect to the Web page.

Practice 7

In this practice you will insert a hyperlink in PAYROLL. This practice assumes you have access to the Internet.

1) OPEN PAYROLL

2) ADD A HYPERLINK

    a. In cell A32, enter the label For current tax rates visit the IRS Web site: then italicize it.
    b. Select cell A33.
    c. On the Standard Toolbar, click on the Insert Hyperlink button ( ). A dialog box is displayed.
        1. Click on the Existing File or Web Page button at the left side of the dialog box if it is not already selected.
        2. In the Text to display entry box, type IRS Web Site.
        3. In the Type the file or Web page name entry box, type www.irs.gov.
        4. Select OK. A hyperlink is displayed in cell A32.

3) DISPLAY THE IRS WEB SITE

    a. Move the mouse pointer over the hyperlink you just entered until the hand pointer () is displayed and click. If necessary, ask your instructor for help in connecting to the Internet. After connecting to the Internet, the IRS Web page is displayed.
    b. Explore the Web page. When done, close the Web page.

4) SAVE AND THEN PRINT THE MODIFIED PAYROLL

10.10 E-Mailing a Spreadsheet

A spreadsheet can be e-mailed from Excel. For example, an accountant could e-mail a payroll spreadsheet to the clerk who prepares the checks.

An open spreadsheet can be sent as an e-mail message by first clicking on the E-mail button () on the Standard Toolbar, which displays the address information entry boxes above the spreadsheet:

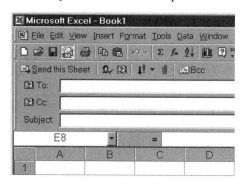

The e-mail address of each recipient is typed in the To entry box separated by semicolons, and a description is typed in the Subject entry box. Clicking on the Send this Sheet button (Send this Sheet) connects your computer to the Internet and sends the spreadsheet as an e-mail message. The address information is removed from the screen and the document remains open and displayed.

Practice 8

In this practice you will e-mail the PAYROLL spreadsheet. This practice assumes you have access to the Internet and an e-mail account. Open PAYROLL if it is not already displayed.

1) E-MAIL A SPREADSHEET FILE

a. On the Standard Toolbar, click on the E-mail button ( ). The address information entry boxes are displayed at the top of the window.

b. In the To entry box, type office@lvp.com or an address specified by your instructor. Note that the Subject entry box already contains the name of the file.

c. Click on the Send this Sheet button (Send this Sheet). If necessary, ask your instructor for help in connecting to the Internet. After connecting to the Internet, the message is sent and then the address information entry boxes are removed.

2) SAVE AND CLOSE THE MODIFIED PAYROLL

3) EXIT EXCEL

10.11 Where can you go from here?

The last four chapters have introduced you to the concepts of a spreadsheet: how one is designed, created on the computer, and used to produce calculations. Excel has many spreadsheet features not discussed in this text which you may want to explore using the online help.

Spreadsheets can be used to store laboratory data to produce scientific and statistical calculations as well as for financial calculations. There are many different spreadsheet programs available. Because you have learned how to use Excel, you will easily be able to learn and use other spreadsheets.

Chapter Summary

This chapter explained how spreadsheets can be used to answer "What If?" questions. By including factors that relate to a particular situation, a spreadsheet model can be produced and then used to make decisions.

 The Sort Ascending and Sort Descending buttons on the Standard Toolbar are used to organize the rows in a spreadsheet in alphabetical or numerical order.

CHOOSE The CHOOSE function can select one value from a list of many. When given a choice, 1 to *N*, the CHOOSE function returns the value in the position corresponding to choice. For example, if cell C3 stores the value 2, then the formula =CHOOSE(C3,"Red","Blue","Green") displays Blue.

VLOOKUP The VLOOKUP function selects values from a table that is stored in a range of cells. When given a numeric expression and the cell range where values are stored, VLOOKUP finds the largest number in the VLOOKUP table which is less than or equal to the numeric expression. It then returns the value stored in the specified column of the table. Both the CHOOSE and VLOOKUP functions can be used to display text.

Excel allows rows and columns to remain on the screen by using the Freeze Panes command from the Window menu. This feature is especially useful for keeping rows and columns containing labels from scrolling off the screen.

amortization table An amortization table displays how much interest and principal make
PMT up each payment of an installment loan. The PMT function is used to calculate the periodic payments of an installment loan.

The Set Print Area command from the Print Area submenu in the File menu is used to print only a portion of a spreadsheet. Selecting the Clear Print Area command from the Print Area submenu restores the print area to the entire spreadsheet.

 A hyperlink to a Web page on the Internet can be inserted into a cell using the Hyperlink command from the Insert menu or the Hyperlink button on the Standard Toolbar.

 A spreadsheet file can be e-mailed from Excel using the E-mail button on the Standard Toolbar.

Vocabulary

Alphabetical   Sorting text in ascending order form A to Z.

Amortization   A method for computing equal periodic payments for an installment loan.

Amortization table   Displays the interest and principal amounts for each payment of an installment loan.

Ascending   Increasing in value from low to high, such as alphabetical order.

CHOOSE   Function that returns a value from a list of many values.

Chronological   Sorting times or dates in ascending order.

Descending   Decreasing in value from high to low.

Installment loan   Loan that is repaid in a series of periodic payments.

Key sort column   The column that contains the values that a sort is based on.

Model   A spreadsheet containing data relating to a particular situation.

PMT   Function that calculates the periodic payment for an installment loan.

Principal   The amount of money owed.

Sorting   Placing rows of data in a specified order.

VLOOKUP   Function that returns a value from a table of values stored in the spreadsheet.

What If? question   A question that is answered using a spreadsheet model.

Excel Commands and Buttons

Clear Print Area **command**   Restores the print area to the entire spreadsheet. Found in the Print Area submenu in the File menu.

E-mail button   Displays options for e-mailing the current spreadsheet.

Freeze Panes **command**   Keeps rows and columns from scrolling off the screen. Found in the Window menu.

Hyperlink **command**   Inserts a hyperlink into a cell. Found in the Insert menu. The Hyperlink button ( ) on the Standard Toolbar can be used instead of the command.

Send this Sheet | **Send this Sheet button**   A button used to connect the computer to the Internet and send the open spreadsheet as an e-mail message. Displayed after selecting the E-mail button.

Set Print Area **command**   Designates a specific range of cells to be printed. Found in the Print Area submenu in the File menu.

Sort Ascending button   A button on the Standard Toolbar used to place selected rows of data in order from low to high based on the column that was highlighted first.

Sort **command**   Displays a dialog box where options to select the key sort column and sort order can be selected. Found in the Data menu.

Sort Descending button   A button on the Standard Toolbar used to place selected rows of data in order from high to low based on the column that was highlighted first.

Unfreeze Panes **command**   Unfreezes all the cells. Found in the Window menu.

Review Questions

1. How can a spreadsheet be used to answer "What If?" questions?

2. Make a list of five "What If?" questions that can be answered using the PAYROLL spreadsheet.

3. List the steps required to sort the data in the PAYROLL spreadsheet in descending order based on the employee's name.

4. List three situations in which the CHOOSE function could be used.

5. Write a CHOOSE function that displays 100 if cell B20 contains a value of 1, 500 if a 2, 900 if a 3, and 1200 if a 4.

6. List three situations in which a VLOOKUP table could be used.

7. The Lawrenceville Widget Company uses the following discount rates when large numbers of widgets are ordered:

Number of Widgets	Discount
100 - 149	10%
150 - 999	20%
1000 - 1999	30%
2000 and above	70%

   a) Convert this into a VLOOKUP table and make a sketch of the table.
   b) Write a formula that uses the VLOOKUP function to display the proper discount percent if cell C12 stores the number of widgets and cells A1 through B5 store the VLOOKUP table created in part (a).

8. List the steps required to keep the row containing the labels that identify the columns in PAYROLL from scrolling off the screen.

9. Write a CHOOSE function that displays the word Excellent if cell B20 contains a value of 1, Good if a 2, Fair if a 3, and Poor if a 4.

10. Briefly explain what an amortization table is.

11. a) How much interest is paid in the first month of a loan of $5,000 borrowed for 5 years at 12% per year interest?
    b) Show what PMT function is used to calculate the monthly payments on the above loan.

12. a) List the steps required to print only the values displayed in the cell range A3:D17.
    b) List the steps required to print the entire spreadsheet after a print area was previously set.

13. List the steps required to insert a hyperlink to the MTV Web page (www.mtv.com) in cell B5.

14. List the steps required to e-mail a spreadsheet.

Exercises

Exercise 1 ———————————————————————— FLORIDA FLIGHTS

A small commuter airline wants to use a spreadsheet to calculate revenue (money they collect). Open FLORIDA FLIGHTS and complete the following steps:

a) Revenue is based on the number of tickets purchased and the type of ticket. Column B contains the type of ticket, 1 for coach and 2 for first class. The price for tickets will be determined by the following scale:

Ticket Type	Ticket Price
1	$99
2	$150

Revenue is calculated by multiplying the ticket price by the number of tickets purchased. In column D, enter the label Revenue and right align it. Enter formulas that use the CHOOSE function to calculate and display the revenue earned for each route.

b) Format the revenue as currency with 0 decimal places. Resize the column as necessary so that all the data is displayed entirely.

c) Create a header with your name right aligned.

d) Save the modified FLORIDA FLIGHTS and print a copy with gridlines and row and column headings.

Exercise 2 ———————————————————————— Used Books

A university bookstore buys used textbooks based on their condition. A student wants to use a spreadsheet to determine how much the bookstore will pay for last semester's books.

a) In a new spreadsheet enter the following data starting in cell A1:

Book Title	Original Price	Condition
Introduction to Digital Logic Design	$75.80	1
A Guide to Computing Fundamentals	$125.25	1
Introduction to Arthurian Legend	$32.50	3
Fiction Writing Basics	$15.45	2

Bold the labels in row 1 and right align the Original Price and Condition labels. Resize columns as necessary so that all the data is displayed entirely.

b) Save the spreadsheet naming it Used Books.

c) The bookstore buys used textbooks at a percentage of the original price based on the condition of the book:

Condition	Percentage
1	40%
2	20%
3	10%

The used price is calculated by multiplying the original price by the appropriate percentage. In column D, enter the label Used Price. Enter formulas that use the CHOOSE function to calculate and display the used price for each book.

d) Bold and right align the label in cell D1. Format the values in column D as currency with 2 decimal places.

e) The student has decided that if the used price is over $20, it would be best to sell the book, otherwise it is best to donate the book to the library. In column E, enter the label What To Do. Enter formulas that use a function to display Sell for the books that will be sold or Donate for books that will be donated to the library.

f) Center align all the data in column E. Resize columns as necessary so that all the data is displayed entirely.

g) Create a header with your name right aligned.

h) Save the modified Used Books and print a copy with gridlines and row and column headings.

Exercise 3 ———————————————— Target Zone

A gym wants to use a spreadsheet to determine the target heart rate zone for its members.

a) In a new spreadsheet enter the following data starting in cell A1:

Gym Member	Age
Brian	25
Christine	20
Stephanie	32
Marchello	44

Bold the labels in row 1 and right align the Age label. Resize columns as necessary so that all the data is displayed entirely.

b) Save the spreadsheet naming it Target Zone.

c) The target heart rate is based on a person's age. In cell A8, enter the label Target Heart Rate Table and bold it. Starting in cell A9, create a VLOOKUP based on the following criteria:

Age	Target Zone
20 – 24	100 to 150
25 – 29	98 to 146
30 – 34	95 to 142
35 – 39	93 to 138
40 – 44	90 to 135
45 – 49	88 to 131
50 – 54	85 to 127
55 – 59	83 to 123
60 – 64	80 to 120
65 – 69	78 to 116
70 and older	75 to 113

d) In column C, enter the label Target Zone and bold it. Enter formulas that use the VLOOKUP function to display the target zone for each gym member.

e) Center align all the data in column C. Resize the column as necessary so that all the data is displayed entirely.

f) Insert a hyperlink to the American Heart Association Web page at www.amhrt.org in cell A21.

g) Create a header with your name right aligned.

h) Save the modified Target Zone and print a copy with gridlines and row and column headings.

Exercise 4 ———————————————————— MUSIC SALE

The MUSIC SALE spreadsheet contains an inventory of used musical instruments. Open MUSIC SALE and complete the following steps:

a) The spreadsheet would be better organized if the instruments in column A were in alphabetical order. Sort the spreadsheet so that the instruments and their corresponding information are in alphabetical order.

b) The selling price is a percentage of the original price based on the condition of the instrument:

Condition	Percentage
1	60%
2	50%
3	40%
4	30%
5	20%

The selling price is calculated by multiplying the original price by the appropriate percentage. In column D, enter the label Selling Price and bold and right align it. Enter formulas that use the CHOOSE function to calculate and display the selling price for each instrument. Format the values as currency with 2 decimal places.

c) Each instrument will either be sold, donated, or thrown away based on the selling price. In cell A12, enter the label What To Do Table. Starting in cell A13, create a VLOOKUP table based on the following criteria:

Sale Price	What to Do?
under $100	Throw Away
$100 – $499	Donate
$500 and above	Sell

d) In column E, enter the label What To Do and bold it. Enter formulas that use the VLOOKUP function to display what to do with each instrument.

e) Center align all the data in column E. Resize columns as necessary so that all the data is displayed entirely.

f) Create a header with your name right aligned.

g) Save the modified MUSIC SALE and print a copy with gridlines and row and column headings.

A Guide to Microsoft Office 2000 Professional

Exercise 5 ———————————————————— AQUARIUM

The AQUARIUM spreadsheet modified in Chapter Nine, Exercise 5 can be modified to evaluate the toxicity of the water to marine animals. Open AQUARIUM and complete the following steps.

a) The toxicity of water in a marine aquarium is based on the nitrite levels. In cell B27, enter the label Nitrite Table and bold it. Starting in cell B28, create a VLOOKUP table based on the following criteria:

ppm	Result
under 0.25	safe
0.25 – 0.49	OK
0.5 – 0.99	unsafe
1 – 1.99	very unsafe
2 – 3.99	toxic
4 and above	very toxic

b) In column E, enter the label Water is:. Enter formulas that use the VLOOKUP function to display the toxicity of the water. Center align all the data in column E.

c) Format all the data appropriately. Resize columns as necessary so that all the data is displayed entirely.

d) Create a header with your name right aligned.

e) Save the modified AQUARIUM and print a copy of the spreadsheet with gridlines and row and column headings.

Exercise 6 ———————————————————— BOOKSTORE PAYROLL

The BOOKSTORE PAYROLL spreadsheet contains the monthly payroll information for a bookstore's employees. Open BOOKSTORE PAYROLL and complete the following steps:

a) The spreadsheet would be better organized if the employees were listed in alphabetical order. Sort the spreadsheet so that the employees and their corresponding information are in alphabetical order.

b) The taxes for each employee need to be calculated. Tax deductions are based on the number of dependents each employee has:

Dependents	Percentage
1	8%
2	7%
3	6%

Taxes are calculated by multiplying the monthly gross pay by the appropriate percentage. In column D, enter the label Taxes and right align and bold it. Enter formulas that use the CHOOSE function to calculate and display the tax for each employee.

c) Social security is calculated by multiplying the social security rate in cell B3 by the monthly gross pay. In column E, enter the label Soc. Sec.. Enter formulas that use absolute and relative cell references to calculate the social security deductions.

d) The net pay for each employee is calculated by making the necessary deductions from the monthly gross pay. In column F, enter the label Net Pay. Enter formulas that use cell references to deduct the taxes and social security from the gross pay of each employee to get the net pay.

e) Format all data appropriately. Resize columns as necessary so the data is displayed entirely.

f) Create a header with your name right aligned.

g) Save the modified BOOKSTORE PAYROLL and print a copy with gridlines and row and column headings.

Exercise 7 ⚙ ———————————————————— Pizza Palace

Pizza Palace wants to use the expense spreadsheet modified in Chapter Nine, Exercise 7 to ask What If? questions. Open Pizza Palace and answer the following questions:

a) The owner of pizza palace wants to determine what affect switching suppliers would have on the cost of the pizzas. The new supplier has better quality items but the cost of dough would increase from $1.25 to $1.40, and the cost of cheese would increase for each pizza to $1.75. Update the spreadsheet to calculate the new cost of the pizzas.

b) The owner has decided to change the way the menu prices are calculated because of the higher costs. The menu price will now be calculated by multiplying the cost of pizza by 225%. Update the spreadsheet to calculate the new pizza prices.

c) Save the modified Pizza Palace. Print a copy of only the cells containing data (not the chart) with gridlines and row and column headings.

Exercise 8 ———————————————————— FLOWER STORE

The FLOWER STORE spreadsheet contains the items sold at a discount flower retailer. Open FLOWER STORE and complete the following steps:

a) The spreadsheet would be better organized if all the flowers in column A were in alphabetical order. Sort the spreadsheet so the flowers and their corresponding information are in alphabetical order.

b) The selling price of the flower arrangements are based on a percentage markup. In cell B14, enter the label Markup Table and bold it. Starting in cell A15, create a VLOOKUP table based on the following criteria:

Cost	Markup
$0 – $25	35%
$26 – $45	45%
$46 and above	35%

c) Insert a column between columns B and C, and enter the label Selling Price. The selling price is calculated by multiplying the cost by the markup percentage and then adding that total to the cost. Enter formulas in the new column that use the VLOOKUP function to display the selling price.

d) Frequent buyers receive discounts that vary depending on the flower. Column D contains the discount codes 1 through 4. The discount on the selling price is determined by the following percentages:

Discount Code	Percentage
1	20%
2	15%
3	10%
4	5%

The discount price is calculated by multiplying the selling price by the appropriate percentage and then subtracting all of that from the selling price. In column E, enter the label Discount Price. Enter formulas that use the CHOOSE function and cell references to calculate and display the discounted selling price for each item.

e) Format all the data appropriately. Resize columns as necessary so that all the data is displayed entirely.

f) Create a header with your name right aligned.

g) Save the modified FLOWER STORE and print a copy with gridlines and row and column headings.

Exercise 9 —————————————————————— SCHOOL LOAN

The SCHOOL LOAN spreadsheet contains a loan amortization table. Open SCHOOL LOAN and answer the following What If? questions about different school loans:

a) The tuition and room/board fees for one year at the local university are $8,250. The loan options are:

- 7% interest for a five year loan
- 8% interest for a three year loan
- 6% interest for a ten year loan

In cells B3, B4, and B5, enter the appropriate data for the first loan (7% for five years).

b) In cell B7, enter a formula that uses the PMT function with cell references to calculate the periodic payment for the five year loan option.

c) In cells C3, C4, and C5, enter the appropriate data for the three year loan option and calculate the monthly payment, total amount paid, and total interest paid.

d) In cells D3, D4, and D5, enter the appropriate data for the ten year loan option and calculate the monthly payment, total amount paid, and total interest paid.

e) Create a header with your name right aligned.

f) Save the modified SCHOOL LOAN and print a copy of cells A1 through E16 with gridlines and row and column headings.

The stock spreadsheet modified in Chapter Nine, Exercise 10 can be modified to evaluate the stock portfolio. Open STOCKS and complete the following steps:

a) A commission must be paid to a stockbroker when a stock is sold. The commission rate is based on the number of shares purchased. In cell G20, enter the label Commission Table and bold it. Starting in cell G21, create a VLOOKUP table based on the following criteria:

Number of Shares	Commission
0 – 29	5%
30 – 69	4%
70 – 99	2%
100 – 149	1%
150 and above	0.5%

b) The dollar amount of the commission is calculated by multiplying the March value of the stock by the appropriate commission percent. In column J, enter the label Commission. Enter formulas that use the VLOOKUP function to calculate and display the sales commission on each of the stocks.

c) Modify the formulas in column J to display N/A for stocks that are retained, and display the dollar amount of the commission otherwise.

d) Format all the data appropriately. Resize columns as necessary so that all the data is displayed entirely and fits on one page.

e) Insert a hyperlink to the New York Stock Exchange Web page at www.nyse.com in cell I19.

f) Save the modified STOCKS. Print a copy with gridlines and row and column headings.

Exercise 11  ————————————————————— Class Scores

The spreadsheet created in Chapter Seven, Exercise 11 can be modified to display your letter grade. Open Class Scores and complete the following steps:

a) Create a VLOOKUP table of percentages and their corresponding letter grade in the spreadsheet based on the grading scale at your school.

b) In cell C8, enter a formula that uses the VLOOKUP function to calculate and display your letter grade. Bold and italicize the letter grade.

c) Save the modified Class Scores and print a copy with gridlines and row and column headings.

A loan amortization table can be used for any kind of loan, including car loans. Amortization tables can also be combined with What If? questions to help make decisions when purchasing a new car.

a) In a new spreadsheet enter the data and apply formatting as shown below:

	A	B	C	D	E
1	New Car Loan Amortization Table				
2					
3		3 Year Loan	3 Year Loan	5 Year Loan	5 Year Loan
4	Interest rate =	7%	10%	7%	10%
5	Number of payments =	36	36	60	60
6	Principal =				
7					
8	Monthly payment =				
9					
10	Total paid =				
11	Total interest =				

b) Save the spreadsheet naming it Car Loan.

c) Using the Internet, find an ad for a new car.

d) Enter the price of the car in the ad as the principal of the car loan in row 6 of the spreadsheet.

e) In row 8, enter formulas that use the PMT function with cell references to calculate the periodic payment for the different loan interest rates and payment periods.

f) In row 10, enter formulas that use cell references to calculate the total amount paid (number of payments multiplied by the monthly payment).

g) In row 11, enter formulas that use cell references to calculate the total interest paid (total amount paid minus the principal).

h) Insert a hyperlink to the Web page were you found the ad in cell A13.

i) Create a header with your name right aligned.

j) Save the modified Car Loan and print a copy with gridlines and row and column headings.

Advanced
Exercise 13

Modify one of the spreadsheets created in Exercises 16, 17, or 18 in a previous spreadsheet chapter to include either the VLOOKUP or CHOOSE function. Format the spreadsheet appropriately. Save the modified spreadsheet and print a copy with gridlines and row and column headings.

Advanced
Exercise 14 _____ Credit

Credit cards can be used to borrow money. This is usually an expensive method of borrowing and best used for only short periods of time or not at all. Create a new spreadsheet that stores the amount of money to borrow, the number of months to pay back the borrowed money, and the annual interest rate. Include columns for annual interest rates ranging from 5% to 25% in increments of 5%. The spreadsheet should calculate the monthly payment, total amount paid, and total interest paid for each of the different interest rates. Experiment by changing the amount borrowed and the length of time. Save the spreadsheet naming it Credit and print a copy with gridlines and row and column headings. The spreadsheet model shows that borrowing at a low interest rate for a short period of time saves substantial amounts of money. Often credit card companies charge 20% or more to borrow money while banks usually charge considerably less.

Advanced
Exercise 15 _____ My Loan

Create an amortization table in a new spreadsheet to display the interest and principal amounts for an installment loan. Use Practice 6 from this chapter as a guide. Format the spreadsheet appropriately. Save the spreadsheet naming it My Loan and print a copy with gridlines and row and column headings.

Integrating the Word Processor and Spreadsheet

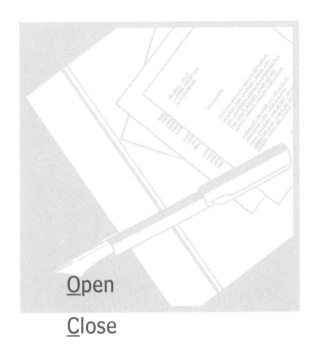

Open

Close

Copy

Paste

Hyperlink

Paste Special

Object

Chapter Eleven Objectives

After completing this chapter you will be able to:

1. Open multiple files in an application and switch between them.
2. Copy text between Word documents.
3. Copy data between Excel spreadsheets.
4. Open multiple files in different applications and switch between them.
5. Copy data between Excel spreadsheets and Word documents.
6. Copy data into a new file.
7. Copy a chart into a Word document.
8. Create hyperlinks to files.
9. Understand OLE.
10. Create embedded and linked objects in Excel spreadsheets and Word documents.

Microsoft Office allows data to be copied between files in the same application and files in different applications. In this chapter, a newsletter is created by integrating data from Word documents and Excel spreadsheets. Using OLE to integrate data is also introduced.

11.1 Working with Multiple Files in an Application

In Word and Excel, more than one file can be open at the same time. The Open command (Ctrl+O) from the File menu or the Open button ( ) on the Standard Toolbar can be used to open files in an application that is already running. For example, after opening a Word file, additional Word files are opened using the Open command or the Open button.

The Windows 98 Taskbar at the bottom of the screen displays a button for each open file. For example, if two Word documents are open, the Taskbar looks similar to:

The active file's button appears pushed in

An open file can be displayed by clicking on its button on the Taskbar.

The Window menu in Word and Excel can also be used to switch between open files. Clicking on the Window menu displays a list of open files in that application:

The *active file* is designated by a check mark and is the one currently displayed. A different file is displayed by selecting it from the Window menu.

An open file does not have to be saved until you have finished working with it. However, it is a good practice to save modified files from time to time as a precaution. Selecting the Save command from the File menu saves only the active file.

Why Work with Multiple Files?

The ability to have more than one file open at a time allows the data in each file to be viewed quickly. For example, while typing a Word document you may need to refer to a paragraph in another Word document. With both files open at the same time, you can view the paragraph in one and then switch to view the other document.

File Status

Each open file is maintained independently in its own window, including any changes to the file's window size or the cursor position. Therefore, you can work with one file, switch to another, and return to the first file exactly where you left off. Also note that an option set in one window has no effect on any other window.

11.2 Removing Files from Memory - Close

When work on an open file is complete, the file should be closed by selecting the <u>C</u>lose command from the <u>F</u>ile menu. Closing a file frees some of the computer's memory and avoids accidental changes to the file. When a file is closed, its window is removed from the screen, and the next open file is displayed and made active.

Closing a file that has been edited but has not yet been saved display a warning dialog box.

11.3 Copying Data Between Files

In previous chapters, data was copied using the <u>C</u>opy and <u>P</u>aste commands. This method can also be used to copy data from one file to another. Since there is only one Windows Clipboard, its contents remains the same regardless of which file is displayed. Therefore, making a different file active and then selecting the <u>P</u>aste command places a copy of the Clipboard contents into the active file.

11.4 Copying Text Between Word Documents

The ability to copy text from one Word document to another can save time typing and help to maintain consistency between documents. The steps for copying text from an open Word document to another are:

1. Highlight the text to be copied.

2. Select the <u>C</u>opy command.

3. From the <u>W</u>indow menu, select the document to receive the copied text.

4. Place the cursor where the text is to be inserted and select the <u>P</u>aste command.

Copying text places a copy of the highlighted block on the Clipboard and does not change the original document. However, pasting data into the receiving document modifies that document, and before it is closed it must be saved to retain the changes.

Paragraph formatting options can be retained when copying text by including the corresponding end of paragraph marker in the highlighted block and then copying the text. If the paragraph marker is not copied, the text will be given the format of the paragraph in the receiving document. Character formats are retained when text is copied.

Memory Limits

Although Office allows any combination of Word and Excel files to be open simultaneously, the number of open files is limited by the amount of memory your computer has available.

Office Clipboard

There is only one Office Clipboard. Therefore, the Office Clipboard can be used to copy up to 12 different items between different files.

Static Data

Using the <u>C</u>opy and <u>P</u>aste commands creates copied data that is static. That is, if data is copied from one file to another and then changed in the original file, the copied data remains unchanged.

A Guide to Microsoft Office 2000 Professional

Practice 1

In this practice you will copy text from multiple Word documents to another Word document.

1) OPEN THE GRETA LEE DOCUMENT

2) OPEN ANOTHER WORD DOCUMENT

On the Standard Toolbar, click on the Open button (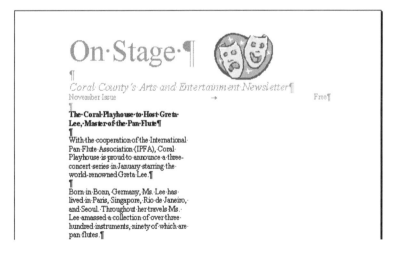). A dialog box is displayed.
1. In the Look in collapsible list, select the appropriate folder.
2. Click on ON STAGE and then select Open. ON STAGE, an empty newsletter, is displayed in its own window as the active document. Note the two document buttons on the Taskbar.

3) DISPLAY GRETA LEE

a. Display the Window menu. Note that there are two documents open.
b. From the Window menu, select GRETA LEE. The GRETA LEE document is now the active document.

4) COPY TEXT TO THE CLIPBOARD

a. Select Edit → Select All. All of the text in the GRETA LEE document is highlighted.
b. Select Edit → Copy. A copy of the highlighted text is placed on the Clipboard.
c. Select File → Close. The GRETA LEE document is removed and ON STAGE is displayed. Note on the Ruler that the newsletter is already formatted with two columns.

5) PASTE THE CLIPBOARD CONTENTS INTO THE ON STAGE NEWSLETTER

a. Place the cursor in the last blank paragraph of the document if it is not already there.
b. Select Edit → Paste. The Clipboard contents are placed at the current cursor position.

Check – Your document should look similar to:

6) COPY A STORY TO THE NEWSLETTER

a. Open ARTS COUNCIL MEMBERS.
b. Highlight all of the text in the ARTS COUNCIL MEMBERS document.
c. Select Edit → Copy.
d. Close ARTS COUNCIL MEMBERS because it is no longer needed. The ON STAGE newsletter is again displayed.

e. Place the cursor in the newsletter in the blank paragraph at the end of "The Coral Playhouse to Host Greta Lee…" story if it is not already there and press Enter once to create a blank line.

f. Select Edit ➜ Paste. The Clipboard contents are placed at the current cursor position.

7) COPY MORE TEXT TO THE NEWSLETTER

a. Open ART EXHIBITS.

b. Highlight all the text in the ART EXHIBITS document.

c. Select Edit ➜ Copy.

d. Close ART EXHIBITS. The ON STAGE newsletter is again displayed.

e. Place the cursor in the blank paragraph at the end of the "Coral Arts Council Membership Growing" story if it is not already there and press Enter once to create a blank line.

f. Select Edit ➜ Paste. The Clipboard contents are placed at the current cursor position.

8) SAVE AND CLOSE THE MODIFIED ON STAGE

9) EXIT WORD

11.5 Copying Data Between Excel Spreadsheets

Data can be copied from one Excel spreadsheet to another in the same way text is copied between Word documents. This can help avoid retyping data. The steps for copying data from an open Excel spreadsheet to another are:

1. Highlight the cells to be copied.

2. Select the Copy command.

3. From the Window menu, select the spreadsheet to receive the copied data.

4. Place the cell cursor where the data is to appear and select the Paste command.

Pasted cells include all formulas and formatting that they had in the original spreadsheet. However, if the spreadsheet containing the data to be copied is closed before the data is pasted, the pasted data will not contain formatting. Column widths do not copy.

When coping data, room must be made in the receiving spreadsheet. For example, to copy a row from one spreadsheet into the center of another you must first insert a blank row in the receiving spreadsheet. If blank space is not created in the receiving spreadsheet, the pasted data will overwrite existing data.

Practice 2

In this practice you will copy a range of cells from one Excel spreadsheet to another Excel spreadsheet.

1) OPEN TWO EXCEL SPREADSHEETS

a. Open GRODER.

b. Open EXHIBITS.

2) *INSERT AN EMPTY ROW IN THE EXHIBITS SPREADSHEET*

a. Highlight row 6 by clicking on its row number.
b. Select Insert → Rows. A new row is inserted above the one highlighted.

3) *COPY DATA TO THE CLIPBOARD*

a. On the Taskbar, click on the GRODER button. The GRODER spreadsheet is displayed.
b. Highlight the four cells containing data, cells A1 through D1.
c. Select Edit → Copy.
d. Close GRODER. The EXHIBITS spreadsheet is displayed.

4) *PASTE THE CLIPBOARD CONTENTS INTO THE EXHIBITS SPREADSHEET*

a. Select cell A6.
b. Select Edit → Paste. The Clipboard contents are placed in the empty cells.

Check – Your spreadsheet should look similar to:

	A	B	C	D
1	Douglas Powers Center for the Arts			
2				
3	Exhibit	Attendance	Cost of Exhibit	Donations
4	Local Sculptors	510	$380	$790
5	Jo Marten: Watercolors	200	$575	$438
6	The Groder Collection	450	$610	$532
7	Winter Photography	560	$420	$816

5) *SAVE THE MODIFIED EXHIBITS*

11.6 Working with Multiple Applications

More than one Office application can be running at the same time and have files open. The Open Office Document command from the Start menu on the Taskbar is used to open files in different applications.

The Taskbar is used to switch between open files, regardless of the application. For example, if two Word documents and two Excel spreadsheets are both open, the Taskbar looks similar to:

The active file's button appears pushed in

In the buttons on the Taskbar, the ⊠ symbol indicates a Word document and the ⊠ symbol indicates an Excel spreadsheet. An open file in a different application can be displayed by clicking on its button on the Taskbar.

An open file does not have to be saved until you have finished working with it. However, it is a good practice to save modified files from time to time as a precaution. Selecting the Save command from the File menu saves only the active file.

11.7 Copying Data Between Excel Spreadsheets and Word Documents

from Excel to Word

Businesses sometimes send memos or letters that contain the data from a spreadsheet. Using Office, you can copy Excel spreadsheet data into a Word document. The steps for copying data from an open Excel spreadsheet to an open Word document are:

1. Highlight the cells to be copied.

2. Select the Copy command.

3. From the Taskbar, select the Word document to receive the copied data.

4. Place the cursor where the data is to be inserted and select the Paste command.

When data is copied from an Excel spreadsheet to a Word document the data is automatically placed in a table structure.

from Word to Excel

Data from a Word document can also be copied into an Excel spreadsheet. This allows calculations to be performed on the data. The data being copied needs to be in a table, either separated by tabs or stored in a table structure.

The steps for copying data from a table in an open Word document to an open Excel spreadsheet are:

1. Highlight the data in the table to be copied.

2. Select the Copy command.

3. From the Taskbar, select the Excel spreadsheet to receive the copied data.

4. Place the cell cursor where the data is to appear and select the Paste command.

When data separated by tabs is copied into an Excel spreadsheet, each line in the table is placed in a row and each tab identifies a new column. When data in a table structure is copied into an Excel spreadsheet, each row of the table is placed in a row of the spreadsheet with each column corresponding to a column in the spreadsheet.

Copying a Word Table

When data is copied from a table structure to an Excel spreadsheet, the cells storing the copied data are formatted with borders. The borders can be removed using the **Border** options in the Format Cells dialog box.

Practice 3

In this practice you will copy data from an Excel spreadsheet to a Word document. Open EXHIBITS if it is not already displayed.

1) COPY DATA TO THE CLIPBOARD

    a. In the EXHIBITS spreadsheet, highlight cells A3 through B7.
    b. Select Edit → Copy.

2) OPEN A WORD DOCUMENT

    a. On the Taskbar, click on the Start button.
    b. Select the Open Office Document command. A dialog box is displayed.
        1. In the Look in collapsible list, select the appropriate folder.
        2. Click on ON STAGE and then select Open. Word is started and ON STAGE is displayed.

c. Display the <u>W</u>indow menu. Note that there is only one Word document open. However, there are two buttons on the Taskbar. One button is for the Word document and the other is for the Excel spreadsheet.

3) PASTE THE CLIPBOARD CONTENTS INTO THE ON STAGE DOCUMENT

a. In the middle of the second column, place the cursor in the blank paragraph after the paragraph that ends "…have drawn large crowds and donations:" in the "Art Exhibits Draw Crowds and Donations" story.

b. Press Enter once to create a blank line.

c. Select <u>E</u>dit → <u>P</u>aste. The Clipboard contents are placed at the current cursor position in a table structure.

<u>Check</u> – Your document should look similar to:

¶
Ms.·Lee·is·considered·to·be·the·world·
genius·on·pan·flutes,·partially·due·to·her·
travels·and·collection,·but·also·due·to·her·
skills.·Not·only·is·she·a·natural·musician,·
but·she·also·studied·under·the·pan·flute·
maser·Jean·Claude·Moll·for·several·
years.¶
¶
The·concerts·will·be·held·January·13,·14,·
and·15·in·the·auditorium.·Tickets·are·
available·at·the·box·office·and·prices·are·
as·follows:·$6.50·for·students·and·

Art·Exhibits·Draw·Crowds·and·Donations¶
¶
The·last·four·exhibits·at·the·Douglas·Powers·Center·for·the·Arts·have·drawn·large·crowds·and·donations:¶
¶

Exhibit¤	Attendance¤	¤
Local·Sculptors¤	510	¤
Jo·Marten·Watercolors¤	200	¤
The·Groder·Collection¤	450	¤
Winter·Photography¤	560	¤

¶

4) SAVE AND CLOSE THE MODIFIED ON STAGE

5) EXIT WORD

Exit Word. Excel is displayed with the EXHIBITS spreadsheet as the active document.

Office Clipboard

Multiple items can be copied between files in different applications using the Office Clipboard. For example, selecting the <u>C</u>opy command in Word and then selecting the <u>C</u>opy command in Excel results in two items being placed on the Office Clipboard:

11.8 Copying Data into a New File

So far, the <u>C</u>opy command has been used to copy data from a Word document or Excel spreadsheet into a previously created document. The <u>C</u>opy command can also be used to transfer data to a new document by creating a new document and then pasting the Clipboard contents into it.

The steps for coping data into a new document are:

1. Highlight the data to be copied.

2. Select the <u>C</u>opy command.

3. Create a new, empty Word document or Excel spreadsheet.

4. Place the cursor or select the cell where the data is to appear and select the <u>P</u>aste command.

Practice 4

In this practice you will create a new Excel spreadsheet named Donations using information from the EXHIBITS spreadsheet. Open EXHIBITS if it is not already displayed.

1) COPY DATA TO THE CLIPBOARD

a. Highlight cells A1 through D7.

b. Select <u>E</u>dit → <u>C</u>opy.

2) *PASTE THE CLIPBOARD CONTENTS INTO A NEW EXCEL SPREADSHEET*

a. On the Standard Toolbar, click on the New button (▢). A new, empty spreadsheet is displayed.
b. Select cell A3.
c. Select Edit → Paste. The Clipboard contents are placed starting at the selected cell.
d. Click anywhere to remove the highlight.

3) *MODIFY THE NEW SPREADSHEET*

a. Widen the columns until all the data is completely visible.
b. Select cell B3. Select Edit → Cut.
c. Select cell A3. Select Edit → Paste. The label is now in cell A3.
d. Highlight column B by clicking on its column letter.
e. Select Edit → Delete. Column B is deleted.
f. Highlight the new column B by clicking on its column letter if it is not already selected.
g. Select Edit → Delete. Column B is deleted.

4) *SAVE THE SPREADSHEET*

Save the new spreadsheet in the appropriate folder naming it Donations.

5) *CLOSE EXHIBITS*

a. On the Taskbar, click on the EXHIBITS button. The EXHIBITS spreadsheet is displayed.
b. Close EXHIBITS. Donations is again displayed.

11.9 Copying a Chart into a Word Document

Businesses sometimes include charts in letters and memos. Office allows an Excel spreadsheet chart to be copied to a Word document. The steps for copying a chart from an open Excel spreadsheet to an open Word document are:

1. Select the chart to be copied by clicking once on its Chart Area.

2. Select the Copy command.

3. From the Taskbar, select the Word document to receive the copied chart.

4. Place the cursor where the chart is to appear and select the Paste command.

inline graphic

floating graphic

The spreadsheet containing the chart to be copied must remain open until after the Paste command is executed so that the chart is pasted as an inline graphic. Paragraph alignment, indents, tabs, and tab stops can be used to position an *inline graphic* in a document. If the spreadsheet containing the chart to be copied is closed before Paste is executed, the chart is pasted as a floating graphic. A *floating graphic* is positioned in a document by dragging the graphic. Clicking once on a pasted chart selects it and displays handles, which can then be dragged to resize the chart.

Practice 5

In this practice you will copy a chart to a Word document. Open Donations if it is not already displayed.

1) CREATE A PIE CHART

    a. Highlight cells A6 through B9.
    b. Select Insert → Chart. The first Chart Wizard dialog box is displayed.
        1. In the Chart type list, click on the Pie option.
        2. Select Next. The second Chart Wizard dialog box is displayed.
        3. Verify that the correct range (=Sheet1!$A$6:$B$9) is displayed in the Data range entry box.
        4. Select Next. The third Chart Wizard dialog box is displayed.
        5. Select the Titles tab if the title options are not already displayed.
        6. In the Chart title entry box, type Exhibit Donations.
        7. Select the Data Labels tab. More options are displayed.
        8. Select the Show percent option.
        9. Select Finish. The pie chart is displayed.
    c. Resize the chart to about half its original size.

Check – Your chart should look similar to:

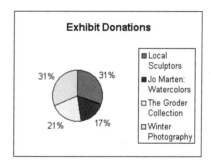

2) COPY THE CHART TO THE CLIPBOARD

    a. Save the modified Donations.
    b. Select the pie chart if it is not already selected.
    c. Select Edit → Copy.

3) PASTE THE CLIPBOARD CONTENTS INTO THE NEWSLETTER

    a. Open the ON STAGE Word document.
    b. Near the bottom of the second column, place the cursor in the blank paragraph after the spreadsheet data you previously pasted.
    c. Press Enter once to create a blank line below the spreadsheet data.
    d. Select Edit → Paste. The chart is placed at the cursor position.
    e. If necessary, resize the chart smaller so that it appears at the bottom of the second column on the first page of the newsletter.

4) SAVE THE MODIFIED ON STAGE

5) SAVE AND CLOSE DONATIONS

6) EXIT EXCEL

11.10 Creating Hyperlinks to Files

Online Documents

Hyperlinks are used for documents that are viewed on the computer.

Hyperlinks connect the user to a Web page. Additionally, hyperlinks can be used to display another Office file on your computer. For example, a Word document can have a hyperlink to an Excel spreadsheet. When the document is active, clicking on the hyperlink displays the spreadsheet.

The steps for creating a hyperlink from a Word or Excel file to another Word or Excel file are:

1. Place the cursor or select the cell where the hyperlink is to be inserted.

2. Select the Hyperlink command from the Insert menu or click on the Insert Hyperlink button ( ) on the Standard Toolbar, which displays a dialog box:

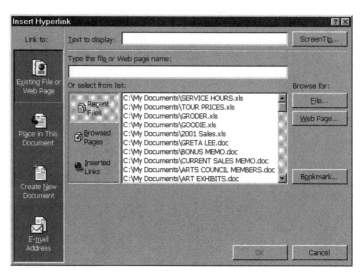

3. Enter the text that will be displayed as hyperlink in the Text to display entry box. If no text is entered, the file name becomes the hyperlink.

4. Select the Recent Files button to display a list of recently used files. If the desired file is not in the list, select the File button to display another dialog box similar to the Open dialog box.

5. Select the desired file.

6. Select OK to remove the dialog box and insert the hyperlink.

After inserting a hyperlink, pointing to it changes the pointer to a hand shape ( ) which indicates you can click on the hyperlink to display that file.

Practice 6

In this practice you will create a hyperlink from a Word document to an Excel spreadsheet. Open ON STAGE if it is not already displayed.

1) CREATE A HYPERLINK TO THE EXHIBITS SPREADSHEET FILE

a. Near the bottom of the second column, place the cursor after the pie chart and then press Enter twice.

b. Type the following sentence:

> Refer to for more information on the exhibits.

c. If necessary, resize the chart smaller so the document fits on one page.
d. Select File → Save.
e. Place the cursor after "to" in the sentence you just typed and press the spacebar.
f. On the Standard Toolbar, click on the Insert Hyperlink button (🔗). A dialog box is displayed.
   1. Select the Existing File or Web Page button if it is not already selected.
   2. In the Text to display entry box, type Exhibits.
   3. Click on the Recent Files button, a list of recent files is displayed.
   4. Click on EXHIBITS.
   5. Select OK. The hyperlink is inserted into the document.

2) SAVE THE MODIFIED ON STAGE

3) USE THE HYPERLINK TO DISPLAY THE SPREADSHEET

a. Move the mouse pointer over the hyperlink you just entered until the hand pointer (👆) is displayed.
b. Click once. The EXHIBITS spreadsheet is displayed.

4) CLOSE EXHIBITS

5) PRINT AND THEN CLOSE THE MODIFIED ON STAGE

a. Display the ON STAGE Word document.
b. Print the document.
c. Close ON STAGE.

11.11 OLE

OLE (pronounced o-lay) is an integration technology that allows an Office file to contain an object created by another Office application. An *object* is the information created by an application. For example, an Excel spreadsheet can contain an object that is a Word document:

A Word object was used to add text to this spreadsheet

Why Use OLE?

Previously, text or data was copied from a file and pasted into another file. Once pasted, the data has the same properties as the other data in the file. For example, data copied from an Excel spreadsheet and pasted into a Word document is no longer numeric data. The numbers are now simply text characters and can no longer be used in calculations. However, by using OLE the data may be added to a document without changing its type. In the Excel window shown on the right, the Word object contains hanging indents and superscript text. This kind of formatting is not possible in an Excel spreadsheet. Therefore, OLE can be used as a powerful form of integration.

An Excel spreadsheet object can also be placed in a Word document:

Excel's Menu bar
Excel's toolbars
Excel's Formula bar

active object

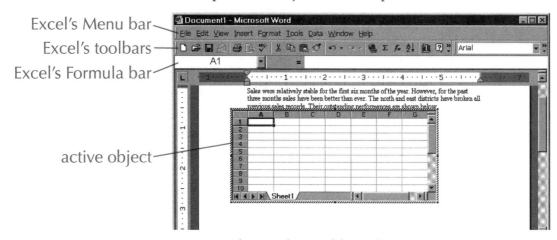

The Excel spreadsheet object is active

OLE allows an object to be modified from within the file where it is inserted. For example, in the Word window above, Excel's Menu bar, toolbars, and Formula bar are displayed because the Excel spreadsheet object is active.

11.12 Embedding Data from an Existing Excel Spreadsheet

One type of OLE object is called an embedded object. An *embedded object* is created by one application and inserted into another type of file, becoming part of that file. For example, when a spreadsheet created in Excel is inserted into a Word document as an embedded object, the spreadsheet object becomes part of the Word document and is no longer related to the original Excel file.

The steps for inserting an Excel spreadsheet into a Word document as an embedded object are:

1. Highlight the spreadsheet data to be embedded.

2. Select the Copy command.

3. Make the Word document active.

4. Place the cursor where the embedded object is to appear and select the Paste Special command from the Edit menu, which displays a dialog box:

Embedded Objects

Any changes made to an embedded object are not reflected in the file the data originally came from and vice versa. However, when a file that contains an embedded object is saved, the embedded object and any changes made to it are saved with that file.

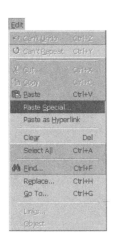

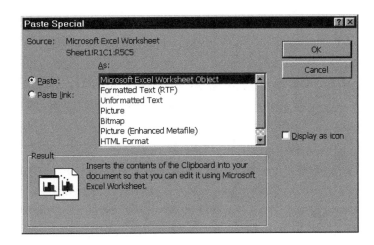

5. Select Microsoft Excel Worksheet Object from the list of options and select OK.

The file that an embedded object was created from must remain open until after the Paste Special command is executed.

selecting and moving an embedded object

When an Excel spreadsheet is embedded in a Word document, the spreadsheet object is inserted as a floating graphic. It can be selected by clicking once on it. A selected embedded object displays handles and can be moved by dragging the object. Clicking outside the object deselects it.

activating an embedded object

Double-clicking on an embedded object activates it. When an embedded spreadsheet object is activated in a Word document, Excel's menus and toolbars are displayed in the Word window, similar to the active spreadsheet object shown on the previous page. Dragging on a handle of an active spreadsheet object hides or displays other columns and rows. Clicking outside an embedded object deactivates it.

editing data in an embedded object

Data may be entered and edited in an embedded object while the data outside the object retains its properties. For example, the SUM function can be used in an embedded spreadsheet object while the Word document contains a bulleted list.

Practice 7

In this practice you will embed data from the 2000 SALES Excel spreadsheet into the PAST SALES MEMO Word document.

1) OPEN THE PAST SALES MEMO DOCUMENT

2) OPEN THE 2000 SALES SPREADSHEET AND COPY DATA

a. Open 2000 SALES.
b. Highlight cells A1 to E5.
c. Select Edit → Copy.

3) EMBED THE SPREADSHEET DATA

a. Display the PAST SALES MEMO document.
b. Place the cursor in the last blank paragraph of the document.
c. Select Edit → Paste Special. A dialog box is displayed.
   1. In the list, select Microsoft Excel Worksheet Object.

2. Select OK. The data is embedded in the Word document. Note that gridlines and row and column headings are displayed because the original spreadsheet file was formatted with those options.

4) MODIFY THE SPREADSHEET DATA

a. Double-click on the spreadsheet object to activate it. Note how Excel's menus, toolbars, and Formula bar are displayed even though you are in a Word document.
b. Drag the right handle to the right so column F is displayed.
c. In cell F1, enter the label Total.
d. In cell F2, enter the formula: =SUM(B2:E2)
e. Copy the formula in cell F2 to cells F3 through F5.
f. Click any place outside the spreadsheet object. The object is deactivated and Word's menus and toolbars are again displayed.

5) SAVE, PRINT, AND THEN CLOSE THE MODIFIED PAST SALES MEMO

6) DISPLAY THE 2000 SALES SPREADSHEET

a. Display the 2000 Sales spreadsheet. Note that column F contains no data even though data was added to the embedded spreadsheet object in the Word document.
b. Close 2000 Sales.

7) EXIT EXCEL

11.13 Embedding a New Excel Spreadsheet

A new Excel spreadsheet can be embedded into a Word document. The steps for embedding a new Excel spreadsheet into a Word document are:

1. Display the Word document.

2. Place the cursor where the embedded object is to appear and select the Object command from the Insert menu, which displays a dialog box:

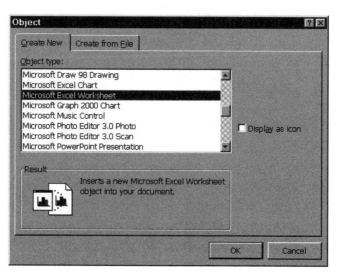

3. Select Microsoft Excel Worksheet from the Object type list and then select OK.

When a new spreadsheet is embedded into a Word document, the spreadsheet object is inserted as an inline graphic and is automatically activated. When the Word document is saved, the embedded spreadsheet object is saved with it.

Practice 8

In this practice you will embed a new Excel spreadsheet object into the BONUS MEMO Word document.

1) **OPEN THE BONUS MEMO DOCUMENT**

2) **EMBED A NEW SPREADSHEET OBJECT**
   a. Place the cursor in the last blank paragraph of the document.
   b. Select Insert → Object. A dialog box is displayed.
      1. Select the Create New tab if it is not already displayed.
      2. In the Object type list, select Microsoft Excel Worksheet.
      3. Select OK. A new spreadsheet object is embedded in the document and the object is active so that the data can be entered.

3) **ENTER DATA INTO THE SPREADSHEET OBJECT**
   a. In cell A1, enter the label 1st Quarter.
   b. In cell B1, enter the label 2nd Quarter.
   c. In cell C1, enter the label 3rd Quarter.
   d. In cell D1, enter the label 4th Quarter.
   e. In cell E1, enter the label Average.
   f. In cell F1, enter the label Bonus.
   g. Bold and right align all the labels in the spreadsheet object.
   h. Resize the columns as necessary so that all the data is displayed entirely.
   i. In cell E2, enter the formula =AVERAGE(A2:D2). #DIV/0! is displayed because data has not yet been entered in cells A2 through D2.
   j. In cell F2, enter the formula =E2*2% to calculate the bonus amount. #DIV/0! is displayed.
   k. Click any place outside the spreadsheet object. The object is deactivated.

4) **ENTER SALES AMOUNTS**

   When this memo is viewed online, each employee can enter their own data to figure out their bonus amounts.

   a. Double-click on the spreadsheet object. The object is activated.
   b. In cell A2, enter the value $45,000.
   c. In cell B2, enter the value $55,500.
   d. In cell C2, enter the value $42,750.
   e. In cell D2, enter the value $40,930.
   f. Format the cells with formulas as currency with 0 decimal places.
   g. Resize the object by dragging its handles so that only cells A1 through F2 are displayed.
   h. Click any place outside the spreadsheet object to deactivate it.

5) **SAVE, PRINT, AND THEN CLOSE THE MODIFIED BONUS MEMO**

11.14 Linking Data from an Existing Excel Spreadsheet

A second type of OLE object is called a linked object. A *linked object* is created in one application and inserted into another type of file while maintaining its relation to the original file. For example, when a spreadsheet created in Excel is inserted into a Word document as a linked object, the spreadsheet object is only a representation of the file it came from and only the link to that file is stored in the Word document. The linked object does not become part of the Word document.

The main difference between an embedded object and a linked object is that changes made to the file the object was created from are reflected in a linked object, but not reflected in an embedded object.

The steps for inserting an Excel spreadsheet into a Word document as a linked object are:

1. Highlight the spreadsheet data to be linked.

2. Select the Copy command.

3. Make the Word document active.

4. Place the cursor where the linked object is to appear and select the Paste Special command from the Edit menu, which displays a dialog box:

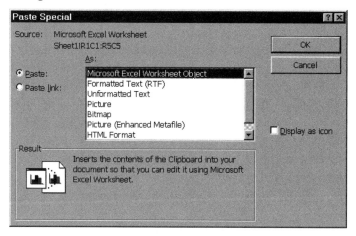

5. Select the Paste link option.

6. Select Microsoft Excel Worksheet Object from the list of options and select OK.

The file that a linked object was created from must remain open until after the Paste Special command is executed.

selecting and moving a linked object

When an Excel spreadsheet is linked to a Word document, the spreadsheet object is inserted as a floating graphic. It can be selected by clicking once on it. A selected linked object displays handles and can be moved by dragging the object. Clicking outside the linked object deselects it.

editing data in a linked object

Double-clicking on a linked spreadsheet object starts the Excel application and the file the linked object came from is displayed. Any changes saved in the original spreadsheet file are reflected in the linked object displayed in the Word document.

updating a linked object

A linked object is automatically updated when the file containing the linked object is opened or the linked object is double-clicked and edits are made to the original spreadsheet file. Selecting a linked object and then pressing the F9 key manually updates a linked object.

Practice 9

In this practice you will use the 2001 SALES Excel spreadsheet to insert a linked spreadsheet object into the CURRENT SALES MEMO Word document.

1) OPEN THE CURRENT SALES MEMO DOCUMENT

2) OPEN THE 2001 SALES SPREADSHEET AND COPY DATA

    a. Open 2001 SALES. If necessary, maximize the Excel window.
    b. Highlight cells A1 through C11.
    c. Select Edit → Copy.

3) LINK THE SPREADSHEET DATA

    a. Display the CURRENT SALES MEMO document.
    b. Place the cursor in the last blank paragraph of the document.
    c. Select Edit → Paste Special. A dialog box is displayed.
        1. Select the Paste link option.
        2. In the list, select Microsoft Excel Worksheet Object.
        3. Select OK. A linked spreadsheet object is inserted into the Word document.

4) CLOSE THE 2001 SALES SPREADSHEET AND EXIT EXCEL

5) MODIFY THE SPREADSHEET DATA

    a. Display the CURRENT SALES MEMO document if it is not already displayed.
    b. Double-click on the spreadsheet object. Excel is started and the linked file, 2001 SALES, is displayed. Note how it is displayed in an Excel window, unlike an embedded spreadsheet object. The Excel window may appear in front of the Word window.
    c. In cell C2, enter the value $25,000.
    d. Save the modified 2001 SALES spreadsheet.
    e. Close 2001 SALES.
    f. Display the CURRENT SALES MEMO document. Note that the spreadsheet object displays the new value because it is linked to the 2001 SALES spreadsheet file.

6) MODIFY THE SPREADSHEET DATA

    a. Display the Excel window.
    b. Open 2001 SALES from within Excel.
    c. In cell C3, enter the value $15,500.
    d. Save the modified 2001 SALES spreadsheet.
    e. Close 2001 SALES.

7) UPDATE THE LINKED OBJECT

    a. Display the CURRENT SALES MEMO document. Note that the new value is not displayed in the spreadsheet object. This is because the spreadsheet object has not yet been updated because the changes to the linked file were not made by first double-clicking on the linked object to display the file.
    b. Select the spreadsheet object by clicking once on it.
    c. Press the F9 key. The spreadsheet object reflects the new value in cell C3 because the file was manually updated.

11.15 Embedding or Linking Data from a Word Document

It is also possible to embed or link an existing Word document in an Excel spreadsheet using the Copy and Paste Special commands from the Edit menu.

The steps for inserting a Word document into an Excel spreadsheet as an embedded or linked object are:

1. Highlight the text to be embedded or linked.

2. Select the Copy command.

3. Make the Excel spreadsheet active.

4. Place the cell cursor near where the object is to be placed and select the Paste Special command from the Edit menu.

5. In the Paste Special dialog box, select the Paste option if embedding or the Paste link option if linking and then select Microsoft Word Document Object in the list, then select OK.

The file that an embedded or linked Word object was created from must remain open until after the Paste Special command is executed.

selecting and moving a Word object

When a Word document is embedded in or linked to an Excel spreadsheet, the Word object is placed as a floating graphic. It can be selected by clicking once on it. A selected Word object displays handles and can be moved by dragging the object. Clicking outside the object deselects it.

editing data in a Word object

Double-clicking on an embedded or linked Word object in an Excel spreadsheet has similar effects as double-clicking an Excel spreadsheet object, as discussed earlier in the chapter.

The Object command from the Insert menu can be used to embed a new Word document in an Excel spreadsheet by selecting the Microsoft Word Document option in the Create New section of the Object dialog box.

11.16 Embedding or Linking a Chart

When copying a chart using the Copy and Paste commands discussed in Section 11.9, the chart is embedded in the Word document.

The steps for inserting an Excel chart into a Word document as a linked object are:

1. Select the chart to be linked.

2. Select the Copy command.

3. Make the Word document active.

4. Place the cursor near where the chart is to appear and select the Paste Special command from the Edit menu.

5. In the Paste Special dialog box, select the Paste link option and then select Microsoft Excel Chart Object in the list, then select OK.

Embedding a New Chart in a Document

The Object command from the Insert menu can be used to embed a new Excel chart in a Word document. The charted data can be edited by activating the object.

The spreadsheet file that a linked chart was created from must remain open until after the Paste Special command is executed.

When an Excel chart is linked to a Word document, the chart object is inserted as a floating graphic. It can be selected by clicking once on it. A selected linked object displays handles and can be resized by dragging the handles and the object can be moved by dragging it. Clicking outside a linked chart object deselects it.

Double-clicking on a linked chart object starts the Excel application and the file the linked chart came from is displayed. Any changes saved in the original spreadsheet file are reflected in the linked chart object displayed in the Word document.

Practice 10

In this practice you will embed a Word object into the 2001 SALES Excel spreadsheet and link a chart to the CURRENT SALES MEMO Word document. CURRENT SALES MEMO should still be displayed from the last practice.

1) OPEN THE 2001 SALES SPREADSHEET AND EMBED A WORD OBJECT

    a. Open 2001 SALES. Maximize the window if it is not already maximized.

    b. Select cell A15.

    c. Select Insert → Object. A dialog box is displayed.

        1. Select the Create New tab is it is not already displayed.

        2. In the Object type list, select Microsoft Word Document.

        3. Select OK. A new Word object is embedded in the spreadsheet and the object is active so that the data can be entered.

    d. In the active Word object, enter the following text. Note that you may not see the previous line of text after pressing the Enter key at the end of each line:

> Quarter 1 sales are from 1/1/01 to 3/31/01
> Quarter 2 sales are from 4/1/01 to 6/30/01
> Quarter 3 sales are from 7/1/01 to 9/30/01
> Quarter 4 sales are from 10/1/01 to 12/31/01

    e. Resize the Word object so that all the text is displayed.

    f. Format the four paragraphs as a bulleted list.

    g. Click any place outside the Word object. The object is deactivated.

    h. If necessary, move the object so all the data in the spreadsheet is displayed entirely.

2) CREATE A BAR CHART

    a. Highlight cells A1 through B11.

    b. Select Insert → Chart. The first Chart Wizard dialog box is displayed.

        1. In the Chart type list, click on the Column option if it is not already selected.

        2. Select Next. The second Chart Wizard dialog box is displayed.

        3. Verify that the correct range (=Sheet1!$A$1:$B$11) is displayed in the Data range entry box.

        4. Select Next. The third Chart Wizard dialog box is displayed.

        5. Select the Titles tab if the title options are not already displayed.

        6. In the Chart title entry box, change the existing title to Quarter Sales.

        7. Select Finish. The chart is displayed.

    c. If necessary, resize and move the objects so that all the chart labels are displayed clearly, the objects are not covering any data, the spreadsheet fits on one page, and the object are below row 12.

3) COPY THE CHART TO THE CLIPBOARD

    a. Save the modified 2001 SALES.

    b. Select the chart if it is not already selected.

    c. Select Edit → Copy.

4) LINK THE CHART TO A WORD DOCUMENT

    a. Display the CURRENT SALES MEMO document.

    b. Place the cursor after the linked spreadsheet object.

    c. Select Edit → Paste Special. A dialog box is displayed.

        1. Select the Paste link option.

        2. In the list, select Microsoft Excel Chart Object if it is not already selected.

        3. Select OK. The chart is inserted into the Word document as a linked object.

    d. If the chart object is covering any text or the spreadsheet object, drag the chart object so all the text and the spreadsheet object are displayed entirely and fit on one page.

5) CLOSE THE 2001 SALES SPREADSHEET AND EXIT EXCEL

6) MODIFY THE SPREADSHEET DATA

    a. Display the CURRENT SALES MEMO document if it is not already displayed.

    b. Double click on the chart object. Excel is started and the linked file is displayed.

    c. In cell B2, enter the value $95,500. The chart in the spreadsheet reflects the new data.

    d. Save the modified 2001 SALES spreadsheet and print a copy.

    e. Close 2001 SALES and then exit Excel.

    f. Display the CURRENT SALES MEMO document if it is not already displayed. Note that the chart object displays the new value. However, the spreadsheet object does not display the new value.

7) UPDATE THE LINKED SPREADSHEET OBJECT

    a. Select the spreadsheet object.

    b. Press the F9 key. The spreadsheet object now reflects the new value.

8) SAVE, PRINT, AND THEN CLOSE THE MODIFIED CURRENT SALES MEMO

9) EXIT WORD

Chapter Summary

This chapter presented the commands necessary to integrate data between Word documents and Excel spreadsheets.

In an application, more than one file can be open at a time, each in its own window. The Window menu displays the names of open files. When work has been completed on a file, it should be saved and then closed.

More than one Office application can be running at one time and have files open. The Taskbar is used to switch between files in different applications.

This chapter explained how data can be copied between:

- two Word documents (Section 11.4)

- two Excel spreadsheets (Section 11.5)

- an Excel spreadsheet and a Word document (Section 11.7 and Section 11.9)

- an open file and a new document or spreadsheet (Section 11.8)

The steps for coping data between two open files are:

1. Highlight the data to be copied.

2. Select the Copy command.

3. Make the file receiving the data active.

4. Place the cursor where the data is to be inserted and then select the Paste command.

hyperlink

A hyperlink to a file can be created in a Word document or Excel spreadsheet. Clicking on a hyperlink displays that file.

OLE

embedded object

linked object

OLE is an integration technology used to embed an object in or link an object to a Word document or Excel spreadsheet. An embedded object is created by one application and inserted into another type of file, becoming part of that file. A linked object is created in one application and inserted into another type of file while maintaining its relation to the original file.

The Paste Special command from the Edit menu is used to embed or link an object from an existing file to a new type of file. The Object command from the Insert menu is used to embed a new object into a file.

Vocabulary

Active file   The file currently displayed.

Embedded object   An object that is created by one application and inserted into another type of file, becoming part of that file.

Floating graphic   An object inserted into a file that can be positioned by dragging the object.

Inline graphic   An object inserted into a file that can be positioned using paragraph alignment, indents, tabs, and tab stops.

Linked object   An object that is created in one application and inserted into another type of file while maintaining its relation to the original file.

Object   The information created by an Office application.

OLE   A technology that allows an Office document to contain an object created by another Office application.

Word and Excel Commands and Buttons

Close command   Removes the active document from the window and the computer's memory. Found in the File menu.

Copy command   Places a copy of the highlighted text, data, or chart on the Clipboard. Found in the Edit menu. The Copy button (🖹) on the Standard Toolbar can be used instead of the command.

Hyperlink command   Displays a dialog box that allows the user to insert a hyperlink to a file. Found in the Insert menu. The Insert Hyperlink button (🖹) on the Standard Toolbar can be used instead of the command.

Object command   Displays a dialog box that allows the user to insert a new embedded object into the file. Found in the Insert menu.

Open command   Displays a dialog box that allows the user to select the file to open in the current application. Found in the File menu. The Open button (📂) on the Standard Toolbar can be used instead of the command.

Open Office Document command   Opens a file in any Office application. Displayed by clicking on the Start button on the Windows 98 Taskbar.

Paste command   Places the Clipboard contents at the current cursor position. Found in the Edit menu. The Paste button (🖹) on the Standard Toolbar can be used instead of the command.

Paste Special command   Displays a dialog box that allows the user to paste the Clipboard contents as an embedded or linked object. Found in the Edit menu.

Window menu   Displays a list of open files in the current application.

Review Questions

1. List the steps required to open two Word documents.

2. What is an "active" file?

3. List two ways to switch from one open file to another open file in the same application.

4. Why should you close an open file after work on the file is complete?

5. The Word document NEWS contains a paragraph that describes the inauguration of a new president. List the steps required to copy this paragraph into a Word document named PRESIDENT.

6. List the steps required to copy two columns from an Excel spreadsheet named OWED and insert them between two existing columns in a spreadsheet named ASSETS.

Sections 11.6 — 11.10

7. List the steps required to open a Word document and then an Excel spreadsheet.

8. List the steps required to switch from an open Word document to an open Excel spreadsheet.

9. List the steps required to copy cells A1, A2, B1, and B2 from an Excel spreadsheet into a Word document.

10. How must the data being copied from a Word document to an Excel spreadsheet be organized?

11. List the steps required to copy text from a Word document into a new Word document.

12. List the steps required to copy an Excel chart into a Word document.

13. What is the difference between an inline graphic and a floating graphic?

14. List the steps required to create a hyperlink in a Word document to a file named Budget.

Sections 11.11 — 11.16

15. a) What is OLE?
    b) What is an object?

16. What is an embedded object?

17. What happens when an embedded spreadsheet object in a Word document is activated?

18. List the steps required for embedding a new Excel spreadsheet into a Word document.

19. What is the difference between an embedded object and a linked object?

20. A Word document that contains a linked spreadsheet object is opened. Then, Excel is started and the spreadsheet file that the linked object was created from is opened. Next, the spreadsheet is modified, and then saved. If the Word document is displayed, is the linked spreadsheet object updated? If not, how can it be updated?

21. What happens when a linked Word object in an Excel spreadsheet is double-clicked?

22. What happens to a linked chart in a Word document when the data charted in the original spreadsheet file is changed and the linked chart object is updated?

Exercises

Exercise 1 ———————————————— SUNPORT CAMPING

The CAMPING TIPS document last modified in Chapter Five, Exercise 5 contains a list of helpful camping tips. The SUNPORT CAMPING document modified in Chapter Five, Exercise 12 contains a short article on the Sunport Camping Symposium. The SUNPORT CAMPING article would be more informative if the CAMPING TIPS list was added to it. Open CAMPING TIPS and SUNPORT CAMPING and complete the following steps:

a) Insert two blank lines after the last paragraph in SUNPORT CAMPING and then enter the following sentence:

> To make your next camping trip easier, here are a few helpful tips:

b) Place a copy of the numbered list in the CAMPING TIPS document after the line you just entered. Do not copy the "Camping Tips" title. Include a blank line between the new sentence and the numbered list.

c) Delete the entire bulleted list from the first numbered camping tip.

d) Delete the sentence that begins "The following list..." at the end of the first numbered camping tip.

e) Save the modified SUNPORT CAMPING and print a copy.

Exercise 2 ———————————————— Student Stats

The Student Stats spreadsheet last modified in Chapter Nine, Exercise 4 contains statistics on the number of undergraduate and graduate students in each college at a university. The DOCTORATE STATS spreadsheet contains statistics on the number of doctoral students in each college at the university. The doctoral information needs to be added to the Student Stats spreadsheet. Open Student Stats and DOCTORATE STATS and complete the following steps:

a) The data stored in DOCTORATE STATS needs to be copied to Student Stats starting in cell D1. Move and resize the charts as necessary so column D is completely visible.

b) Place a copy of all the data in the DOCTORATE STATS spreadsheet in the Student Stats spreadsheet starting in cell D1. Resize the column as necessary so that all the data is displayed entirely.

c) Copy the total, average, maximum, and minimum formulas in column C to the new doctoral information in column D.

d) Save the modified Student Stats and print a copy with gridlines and row and column headings.

The CANDLE MEMO document contains sales figures which can be copied into a new spreadsheet to ask What If? questions. Open the CANDLE MEMO document and complete the following steps:

a) Create a new Excel spreadsheet.

b) Place a copy of the entire table containing the sales figures from the CANDLE MEMO document in the new spreadsheet starting in cell A1.

c) Change the font of the copied data to Arial 10 point, bold the labels in row 1, and right align the October, November, and December labels. Resize columns as necessary so that all the data is displayed entirely.

d) Save the spreadsheet naming it Estimated Candle Sales.

e) In cell A8, enter the label Total: and bold and right align it. In row 8, enter formulas that use a function to total the sales for each month.

f) In cell E1, enter the label Q4 Total. In column E, enter formulas that use a function to total the fourth quarter sales for each item. Fourth quarter sales are calculated by summing the October, November, and December sales.

g) Insert a row at the top of the spreadsheet. In cell F1, enter the label Expected Quarter 1 Sales and bold it.

h) In cell F2, enter the label Price Increase and in cell G2 enter the label No Price Increase.

i) The sales manager wants to know the expected sales for the first quarter of next year if the company raises prices so that the first quarter sales increase 3% from the fourth quarter totals. In column F, enter formulas that use cell references to calculate the expected first quarter sales for each item if there is a price increase.

j) The sales manager wants to know the expected sales for the first quarter of next year if the company does not raise prices so that the first quarter sales increase 8% from the fourth quarter totals. In column G, enter formulas that use cell references to calculate the expected first quarter sales for each item if there is no price increase.

k) Format the values in columns F and G as currency with 0 decimal places. Resize the columns as necessary so that all the data is displayed entirely.

l) In cell A11, insert a hyperlink to the CANDLE MEMO document.

m) Create a header with your name right aligned.

n) Save the modified Estimated Candle Sales and print a copy in landscape orientation with gridlines and row and column headings.

The data in the Upgrade Costs spreadsheet created in Chapter Seven, Exercise 10 needs to be added to a memo. Open Upgrade Costs and complete the following steps:

a) Create a pie chart that displays the hardware, software, and training costs for the year 2000. Title the chart 2000 Upgrade Costs and display percentage data labels.

b) In a new Word document create the following memorandum, substituting your name for Student Name and inserting tabs and setting tab stops where appropriate:

MEMORANDUM

TO: Melissa Kinzer, Controller

FROM: Student Name, Technology Coordinator

DATE: January 3, 2000

SUBJECT: Upgrade Costs

The technology department has finished its upgrade cost estimates. The chart below shows the expected hardware, software, and training upgrade cost percentages for this year:

The table below shows the expected hardware, software, and training upgrade costs for years 2000 through 2005:

c) Save the document naming it Upgrade Memo.

d) Place a copy of the chart in the Upgrade Costs spreadsheet after the second sentence in the memo. There should be a blank line between the pasted chart and the paragraphs.

e) Place a copy of the data in cells A1 through D7 in the Upgrade Costs spreadsheet at the end of the memo. There should be a blank line between the pasted spreadsheet data and the last sentence in the memo.

f) Save both files and print a copy of the Upgrade Memo document.

The BREAKFAST document contains a letter introducing a bakery's products to nearby stores. The GOODIE spreadsheet contains price information on the products. Open GOODIE and BREAKFAST and complete the following steps:

a) Place a copy of the data in cells A3 to B8 in the GOODIE spreadsheet into the letter after the paragraph that ends "...quite a variety:". There should be a blank line before and after the pasted spreadsheet data.

b) The chart in the GOODIE spreadsheet also needs to be added to the BREAKFAST letter. Place a copy of the chart into the letter after the paragraph that ends "...you a tidy profit:". There should be a single blank line before the pasted chart.

c) In the BREAKFAST letter, replace the text "To Whom It May Concern" with your name.

d) Resize and move the chart so that the letter fits on one page. Make sure the labels in the chart are displayed clearly. Save the modified BREAKFAST and print a copy.

The FRANKLIN TOURS document contains a partial newsletter. The TOURS document and the TOUR PRICES spreadsheet contain information for the newsletter. Open FRANKLIN TOURS, TOURS, and TOUR PRICES and complete the following steps:

a) Place a copy of all the text in the TOURS document in the FRANKLIN TOURS document in the blank paragraph at the end of the newsletter.

b) The data in cells A1 through B5 in the TOUR PRICES spreadsheet needs to be added to the FRANKLIN TOURS newsletter. Place a copy of the data into the newsletter in the blank paragraph at the end of the newsletter.

c) The chart in the TOUR PRICES spreadsheet also needs to be added to the FRANKLIN TOURS newsletter. Place a copy of the chart into the letter below the spreadsheet data. There should be a blank line between the pasted chart and the pasted spreadsheet data.

d) In the FRANKLIN TOURS document, create a footer with your name right aligned.

e) Save the modified FRANKLIN TOURS and print a copy.

Exercise 7   *OLE required* ———————————————————— Contest

A university is holding a community service contest. The college (i.e. College of Business, College of Nursing, etc.) whose students perform the most community service hours receives ten new computers. The SERVICE HOURS spreadsheet contains the number of community service hours completed so far. Open SERVICE HOURS and complete the following steps:

a) In a new Word document create a one page document that promotes the contest. The document should include a short description of the contest and a paragraph about why community service is important. It should also include the deadline, which is the end of the semester. The document will be e-mailed to each college.

b) Save the document naming it Contest.

c) Insert two blank lines after the last line of text in the document and enter the following sentence:

   To date, students have performed the following community service hours:

d) The document needs to display the number of community service hours completed for each college. Using all the data in the SERVICE HOURS spreadsheet, insert a linked spreadsheet object into the Contest document after the sentence you just entered. Move the spreadsheet object so there is a blank line between the spreadsheet object and the last paragraph.

e) In the Contest document, create a header with your name right aligned.

f) The undergraduate students in the College of Business have just completed a total of 2,500 hours of community service. Edit the spreadsheet appropriately. If necessary, update the linked spreadsheet object to reflect the new hours.

g) Save the modified Contest and print a copy.

Exercise 8 ✿ *OLE required* ———————————————— Pizza Palace

The owner of Pizza Palace wants to add some information to the expense spreadsheet created in Chapter Seven, Exercise 7. Open Pizza Palace and complete the following steps:

a) Change the page orientation to landscape.

b) In a new, embedded Word object, enter a sentence explaining how the menu prices were calculated and give an example in a bulleted list.

c) Resize and move the Word object so it starts in column F near the Menu Price row and the entire spreadsheet fits on one page in landscape orientation. You may need to clear the print area.

d) Save the modified Pizza Palace and print a copy in landscape orientation with gridlines and row and column headings.

Exercise 9 ✿ *OLE required* ———————————————— Grand Opening

The Grand Opening document last modified in Chapter Four, Exercise 9 needs to include the sale prices of some of the special items sold at the store. Open Grand Opening and complete the following steps:

a) Insert a new, embedded spreadsheet object into the document.

b) In cell A1 in the spreadsheet object, enter the label Item. In cell B1, enter the label Original Price. In cell C1, enter the label Sale Price. Bold the labels and right align the labels in columns B and C.

c) In columns A and B, enter at least 5 special items and their original prices.

d) In column C, enter formulas that use cell references to display the item's sale price. The sale price is 20% of the original price.

e) Format the numeric data as currency with 2 decimal places. Increase the size of the font in the spreadsheet object to match the rest of the flyer. Resize the spreadsheet columns as necessary so that all the data is displayed entirely. Resize the spreadsheet object so only the 3 columns of data are displayed.

f) Modify the flyer appropriately so that the special items are not listed twice. Move the spreadsheet object so that the flyer prints on one page.

g) Save the modified Grand Opening and print a copy.

Exercise 10 ☼ *OLE required* ———————————————— Track Memo

The Track Progress spreadsheet last modified in Chapter Nine, Exercise 12 contains information on the track team's progress for the season. The coach wants to include some of this information in a memo to the head of the athletics department. Open Track Progress and complete the following steps:

a) In a new Word document create a memo to the head of the athletics department summarizing how the track season went. The document should contain a separate paragraph about the progress of the students running the 100 Meter and a paragraph about the progress of the students running the 200 Meter. Format the memo appropriately and include your name in the **FROM:** line.

b) Save the document naming it Track Memo.

c) Insert two blank lines after the paragraph about the 100 Meter progress. Using the Track Team's Progress in 100 Meter chart in the Track Progress spreadsheet, insert a linked chart object into the memo after the paragraph. Move the chart object so there is a blank line before and after the chart object.

d) Insert two blank lines after the paragraph about the 200 Meter progress. Using the Track Team's Progress in 200 Meter chart in the Track Progress spreadsheet, insert a linked chart object into the memo after the paragraph. Move the chart object so there is a blank line before the chart object.

e) The coach realized that the Track Team's Progress in 200 Meter chart had a mistake. Callie Ramis' January time in the 200 Meter should be 32.0. Edit the spreadsheet appropriately. If necessary, update the linked chart to reflect the new time.

f) Save the modified Track Memo and print a copy.

Advanced

Exercise 11 ☼ *OLE required* ———————————————— Newsletter

The Newsletter document created in Chapter Five, Exercise 15 needs to be modified. Open Newsletter and complete the following steps:

a) In a new, embedded spreadsheet object enter data that is relevant to the newsletter. Remember that the newsletter has two columns so the spreadsheet object should be resized appropriately.

b) Format the spreadsheet data appropriately.

c) Save the modified Newsletter and print a copy.

Advanced

Exercise 12 ——————————————————————————————

Use the My Finances spreadsheet modified in Chapter Nine, Exercise 16 as a basis for a letter to a financial planner requesting his or her advice. You would like to invest the money you will be saving. Copy the chart of your savings information from the spreadsheet into the letter. Also include a hyperlink to the spreadsheet file.

A Guide to Microsoft Office 2000 Professional

Chapter Twelve
Introducing the Relational Database

Primary Key

Save

Print

Page Setup

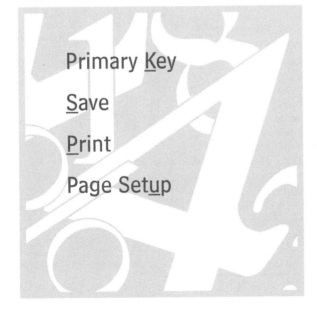

Chapter Twelve Objectives

After completing this chapter you will be able to:

1. Describe a relational database and its structure.
2. Define fields.
3. Design a relational database.
4. Create a relational database.
5. View tables in Design view and Datasheet view.
6. Create a form for a table.
7. Enter records using forms.
8. Format Datasheet view.
9. Print records.
10. Create and use filters to query a database table.
11. Save a filter.
12. Create and use a complex query.

The History of the Database

The broad category of data handling refers to the tools and techniques used to manipulate large amounts of data. One of the earliest significant achievements in data handling was the 1951-1952 Sort-Merge Generator developed by Betty Holberton for the UNIVAC 1, which initiated the development and widespread use of data processing tools. Early data processing environments used a flat-file system to maintain separate files of data for each application. For example, a company would maintain an employee file for payroll purposes and another employee file for job classification. However, maintaining duplicate data in separate files proved time-consuming and error-prone. The DBMS (Database Management System) model maintained data by combining files into a common framework. In 1971, CODASYL (Conference on Data Systems Language) set standards for the DBMS model. Oracle was among the first DBMS applications to implement this model which is still used today.

T his chapter introduces database terminology and describes a relational database management system. Microsoft Access is introduced for creating a relational database.

12.1 What is a Database?

The computer's fast retrieval and large storage capabilities make it an ideal tool for managing information in the form of a database. Many historians refer to our present time as the "Information Age" primarily because of the ability databases have given us to store and manipulate huge amounts of information.

A *database* is an application that is used to organize and store related data. For example, a company's inventory, customer information, and order information can all be organized into a database. A database stores digital information including text, numerical data, photos and graphics, sound files, e-mail addresses, and hyperlinks.

A database can store millions of pieces of data in the relatively small area of a hard disk. If paper forms were used to store this information, numerous file cabinets would be required. The data in a database can also be retrieved quickly. For example, in less than a second, a specific order from three months ago can be retrieved from a company's database. If paper forms had to be searched for this particular order, it could take hours. Additionally, a database can easily reorganize data and present it in many different ways for data analysis.

12.2 The Relational Database

The relational database is a type of database commonly used by companies and other organizations. In a *relational database*, data is separated into *tables* that consist of records. A *record* is a set of data about one item, where each piece of data corresponds to a *field*. For example, Pack Suppliers, Inc. uses a relational database that contains a table for inventory, another for customer information, and a third for transactions, as shown on the next page:

table, record
field

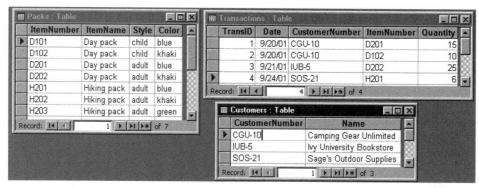

A relational database contains tables of data

A table can only contain unique records, meaning that no two records can be exactly the same. The Packs table below contains seven records:

ItemNumber	ItemName	Style	Color
D101	Day pack	child	blue
D102	Day pack	child	khaki
D201	Day pack	adult	blue
D202	Day pack	adult	khaki
H201	Hiking pack	adult	blue
H202	Hiking pack	adult	khaki
H203	Hiking pack	adult	green

a record — (pointing to D102 row)

an entry — (pointing to D202 khaki)

entry

The data stored in an individual field of a single record is called an *entry*. For example, blue is the Color field entry for the first record. The ItemNumber field contains only unique entries and is the primary key of the table. The *primary key* is a field designated to have unique entries in order to make each record of a table unique. The primary key may also be a combination of fields designated to have a unique combination of entries.

primary key

12.3 Defining Fields

A field is defined by its name, type, size, and format. A well designed database has fields that store one piece of data only. For example, a field named FullName that stores both a first and last name is considered poor design. A better design would include FirstName and LastName fields to separate name data.

field name

A field's name should be descriptive of its contents. The following guidelines should be followed when choosing field names:

- **Make field names within a table unique.** Access does not allow duplicate field names within a table. For example, two fields named Address in the same table is not permitted.

- **Choose the shortest possible name that accurately describes the contents of the field.** In Access, field names may be up to 64 characters. When multiple words are used for a field name, each word should begin with an uppercase letter and as a matter of good design, the field name should not contain spaces. For example, in the Packs table above ItemNumber is a field name that contains multiple words but no spaces.

- **Use complete words instead of numbers or abbreviations.** For example, FirstName is better than 1stName or FName.

field type   Fields are classified by the type of data they store:

- *text fields* store characters (letters, symbols, words, a combination of letters and numbers, etc.).
- *number fields* store only numeric values.
- *date/time fields* store a date or time.
- *currency fields* store dollar amounts.
- *memo fields* store several lines of text.
- *AutoNumber fields* are automatically given a numeric entry that is one greater than that in the last record added. An AutoNumber field is often used as the primary key for a table since each entry is automatically unique.

field size   The *size* of a field is the number of characters or the type of number it can store. Text fields can store up to 255 characters. A number field's size is defined by the type of value it stores. For fields that store a number with a decimal portion the field size *single* is used. Fields that store only whole numbers use the *long integer* field size. A size cannot be defined for date/time fields.

field format   The *format* of a field is the way in which its contents are displayed. Numeric field formats include:

- *general number* is the default and displays the number exactly as entered.
- *fixed* displays a field's entry to a specified number of decimal places.
- *percent* multiplies the value entered by 100 and displays it with a % sign.
- *standard* displays a field's entry with the thousands separator, usually a comma.

Date/time field formats include:

- *short form* (6/24/00; 10:12)
- *medium form* (24-June-00; 10:12 AM)
- *long form* (Saturday, June 24, 2000; 10:12:30 AM)

Text and memo fields usually have no format.

decimal places   Decimal places can be set as appropriate for numeric field types. A number field with the size long integer should have the number of decimal places set to 0. A number greater than 0 results in the entry being rounded.

12.4 Designing a Relational Database

A database should be created based on a design. Designing a database is a four step process:

1. **Determine what information should be stored.** This decision requires considering the purpose of the database.

   For example, Pack Suppliers, Inc. is a wholesaler of backpacks and needs a Backpacks database to keep track of inventory, customers, and transactions. Therefore, information such as item names, customer names, etc. should be stored.

2. **Divide information into named tables.** This should be done by grouping related information and then choosing a short descriptive name for each group. These named groups will be made into tables when the database is created.

   For example, the Backpacks database should contain inventory information (item number, item name, style, color), customer information (customer number, name), and transaction information (transaction ID, date, customer number, item number, and quantity). Appropriate names for each group are Packs, Customers, and Transactions, respectively.

3. **Determine the relationships among the tables.** When two tables contain the same field they are said to be "related" by this field. Each table of a relational database needs to be related to at least one other table in the database.

   For example, in the Backpacks database, the Packs table is related to the Transactions table by the ItemNumber field, and the Transactions table is related to the Customers table by the CustomerNumber field:

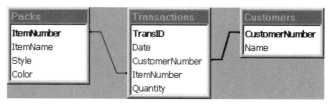

4. **Define the fields and determine the primary key for each table.** The guidelines in Section 12.3 should be used to define appropriate field names, types, sizes, and formats any. After defining the fields for a table, the primary key must also be designated.

   For example, the fields and primary key for the Packs table are:

   ItemNumber   text field, 4 characters (primary key)
   ItemName   text field, 15 characters
   Style   text field, 10 characters
   Color   text field, 30 characters

Foreign Key

A field is called a foreign key when that field is the primary key of another table. Two tables are said to be related when the primary key of a table is a foreign key in another table.

Practice 1

In this practice you will complete the Backpacks database design. Using paper and pencil, complete the following steps using the guidelines in Section 12.3:

1) *DEFINE FIELDS FOR THE TRANSACTIONS TABLE*

a. The Transactions table should contain the following information: transaction ID (a unique number automatically generated), date of transaction (similar to 6/24/00), customer number (a letter-number combination of up to six characters), item number (a letter-number combination of four characters), and quantity ordered. Write appropriate field names for the Transactions table information.

b. Next to each field name write down its type.

c. Next to each field type write down the field's size. Keep in mind that date/time fields do not have a size.

d. Next to each field size write down the field's format, if any. Keep in mind that text fields do not have a format.

e. Determine the primary key for the Transactions table. To do this, pick the field that will have a unique entry for each record. Write primary key next to this field.

Check – Your design should contain the following information:

TransID	AutoNumber field (primary key)
Date	date field, short form
CustomerNumber	text field, 6 characters
ItemNumber	text field, 4 characters
Quantity	number, long integer

2) *DEFINE FIELDS FOR THE CUSTOMERS TABLE*

The Customers table should contain the following information: customer number (a letter-number combination of up to six characters) and name.

Refer to step 1 to define the fields and determine the primary key for the Customers table. Write the field information below the Transactions table field information.

12.5 Creating a New Relational Database

Blank Database

Microsoft Access is the relational database application in the Microsoft Office package. Selecting the New Office Document command from the Start menu on the Windows Taskbar displays the New Office Document dialog box. Clicking on the Blank Database icon and then selecting the OK button displays the File New Database dialog box:

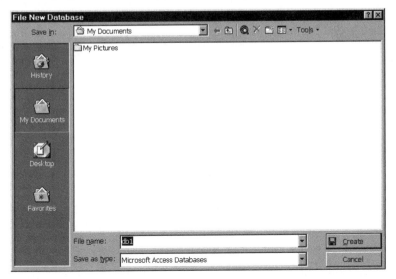

The name of the database must be typed in the File name entry box and the folder where the new database is to be stored is selected from the Save in collapsible list. Selecting the **Create** button removes the dialog box and creates the new database, with the Database window displayed:

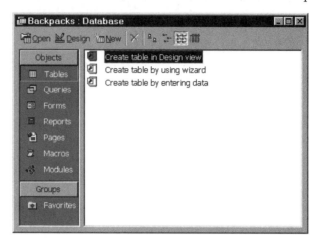

The Database window

saving a database

In Access there is no <u>S</u>ave command for saving an entire database. A database is automatically periodically saved to the folder and file specified when the database was created. Therefore, it is important that the appropriate folder be selected and a descriptive file name typed when the database is first created.

12.6 Creating a Table

Design view

A table is created in a relational database by first clicking on the **Tables** button in the **Objects** list in the Database window. Next, double-clicking on the Create table in Design view icon displays a new table in *Design view* where fields can be defined. In the table below, several fields have already been defined. The ItemNumber field currently contains the cursor and its field properties are shown at the bottom of the window:

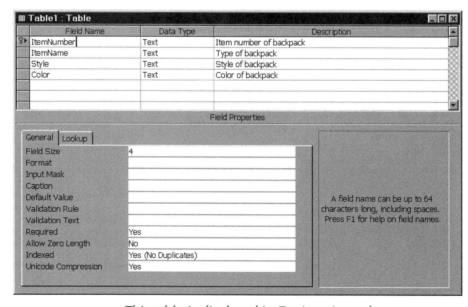

*This table is displayed in Design view where
fields are defined*

selecting the primary key
active field

Required option

The steps for defining a field in Design view are:

1. **Enter the field name.** In the first empty Field Name box, type the field's name.

2. **Select the field type.** In the corresponding Data Type box, select the appropriate type from the collapsible list.

3. **Enter a description.** In the corresponding Description box, type a description of the data expected in that field. A field's description is displayed when records are being entered, which helps the user understand what kind of entry is expected.

4. **Enter the field size.** In the Field Properties part of the window, enter the appropriate Field Size. (Be sure the General tab has been selected.) For a text field, type the greatest number of characters allowed in the field entry. For a number field, click in the Field Size box and from the collapsible list select either Long Integer or Single. A date/time field does not have a field size.

5. **Select a field format.** In the Field Properties part of the window, enter the appropriate Format. (Be sure the General tab has been selected.) For number and date/time fields, click in the Format box and from the collapsible list select the desired format. Text and memo fields do not have a format.

6. **Designate the number of decimal places.** In the Field Properties part of the window, enter the appropriate Decimal Places to be displayed. (Be sure the General tab has been selected.) Only single number and currency fields have decimal places.

To complete the table, a primary key must be selected. The primary key is designated by first making the desired field active. The *active field* contains the cursor and has the ▶ symbol to the left of its row. Next, the Primary Key button ( ) on the Toolbar is clicked or the Primary Key command from the Edit menu is selected. For the Packs table, ItemNumber was made the primary key, as indicated by the marker.

The primary key must have an entry for every record in the table in order to be unique. Therefore, the Required option in the Field Properties part of the table Design view window should be set to Yes.

Sometimes it is necessary to designate two fields as the primary key. The desired fields can be selected by clicking on the gray box to the left of the first field, holding down the Ctrl key, and then clicking on the gray box to the left of the second field. Next, clicking on the Primary Key button on the Toolbar selects both fields as the primary key.

12.7 Saving a Table

Access does not automatically save a new table or the modifications to an existing table. Therefore, the Save command (Ctrl+S) from the File menu or the Save button on the Toolbar ( ) must be used. The first time a table is saved, a dialog box is displayed so that a descriptive table name can be entered. After a table has been saved, its name appears in Tables of the Database window.

12.8 Datasheet View

The View button on the Toolbar is used to switch between Design view () and Datasheet view (). In *Datasheet view*, each row corresponds to a record, and each column corresponds to a field. For example, the Packs table in Datasheet view looks similar to:

	ItemNumber	ItemName	Style	Color
▶	D101	Day pack	child	blue
	D102	Day pack	child	khaki
*				

* The asterisk (*) that appears to the left of the last row in the table indicates where the next record entered will appear. It is not a blank record.

record selector
active record

The gray box to the left of each record is called the *record selector*. Clicking a record selector makes that record the *active record* and displays the ▶ symbol. Note that the first record in the datasheet above is the active record.

Practice 2

In this practice you will create the Backpacks relational database and its tables.

1) CREATE A NEW DATABASE

a. On the Taskbar, click on the Start button. A menu is displayed.

b. Select the New Office Document command. A dialog box is displayed.

    1. Click on the Blank Database icon to select it.

    2. Select OK. The Access application is started and the File New Database dialog box is displayed.

        a. In the File name entry box, type Backpacks.

        b. In the Save in collapsible list, select the appropriate folder for storing the database.

        c. Select the Create button. The Backpacks : Database window is displayed.

2) CREATE A NEW TABLE

a. In the Backpacks : Database window, click on the Tables button if it is not already selected.

b. Double-click on the Create table in Design view icon. A new table is displayed in Design view.

3) DEFINE THE FIELDS FOR THE TABLE

a. In the first Field Name box, type ItemNumber.

b. Press the Tab key to select the Data Type box. Text is the default type, which is appropriate for this field.

c. Press Tab to place the cursor in the Description box. Type Item number of backpack.

d. In the Field Properties part of the window, click in the Field Size box.

e. Delete the current field size number and type 4 which is the maximum number of characters allowed for an entry in this field.

f. In the next Field Name box, create a field named ItemName, of type Text, with description Type of backpack, and a field size of 15.

g. In the next Field Name box, create a field named Style, of type Text, with description Style of backpack, and a field size of 10.

h. In the next Field Name box, create a field named Color, of type Text, with description Color of backpack, and a field size of 30.

<u>Check</u> – Your table should look similar to:

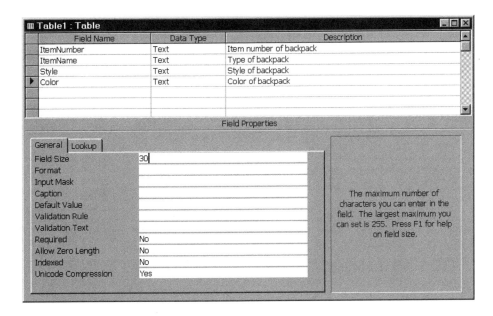

4) SELECT THE PRIMARY KEY FOR THE TABLE

The ItemNumber field is the primary key for this table because each ItemNumber is unique.

a. Click in the ItemNumber Field Name box to make it active.
b. On the Toolbar, click on the Primary Key button (⚷). A ⚷ symbol is displayed next to the ItemNumber field indicating that it is now the primary key for the table.
c. Every record should have an entry in the primary key field. In the Field Properties part of the window, click in the Required box and then select Yes from the collapsible list.

5) SAVE AND THEN VIEW THE TABLE IN DATASHEET VIEW

a. Select File → Save. A dialog box is displayed.
  1. In the Table Name entry box, type Packs.
  2. Select OK. The Packs table is saved with the relational database.
b. On the Toolbar, click on the View button (▦). The Packs table is displayed in Datasheet view. No records have been entered so the table is empty.
c. Click on the Close button (✖) of the Packs : Table window to remove it. The Backpacks : Database window should still be displayed. Note how Packs appears as a table name in the window.

6) CREATE THE TRANSACTIONS TABLE

The Transactions table has the following design:

TransID	AutoNumber field (primary key)
Date	date field, short form
CustomerNumber	text field, 6 characters
ItemNumber	text field, 4 characters
Quantity	number, long integer

a. Create a new table in Design view.
b. Click in the first Field Name box and type TransID.
c. In the TransID Data Type collapsible list, select AutoNumber.
d. In the TransID Description, type Transaction number.
e. In the Field Properties part of the window, select Long Integer for the Field Size if it is not already displayed.
f. Make TransID the primary key.

g. Click in the next Field Name box and type Date.

h. In the Date Data Type box, select Date/Time.

i. In the Date Description box, type Date of transaction.

j. In the Field Properties part of the window, select Short Date for the Format.

k. In the next Field Name box, create a field named CustomerNumber, of type Text, with description Customer number, and a field size of 6.

l. In the next Field Name box, create a field named ItemNumber, of type Text, with description Item number, and a field size of 4.

m. In the next Field Name box, create a field named Quantity, of type Number, with description Number of items ordered, and a field size of Long Integer. Set the number of decimal places to 0.

Check – Your table should look similar to:

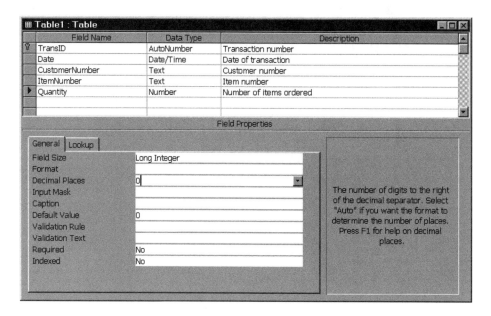

n. Select File ➔ Save. A dialog box is displayed.

    1. In the Table Name entry box, type Transactions.

    2. Select OK. The Transactions table is saved with the relational database.

o. Close the Transactions table.

7) CREATE THE CUSTOMERS TABLE

The Customers table has the following design:

        CustomerNumber   Text field, 6 characters (primary key)
        Name   Text field, 50 characters

a. Create a new table in Design view.

b. Define the CustomerNumber and Name fields using the design above. Enter appropriate descriptions for each of the fields.

c. Make CustomerNumber the primary key and in the Field Properties part of the window, select Yes in the Required collapsible list.

Check – Your table should look similar to:

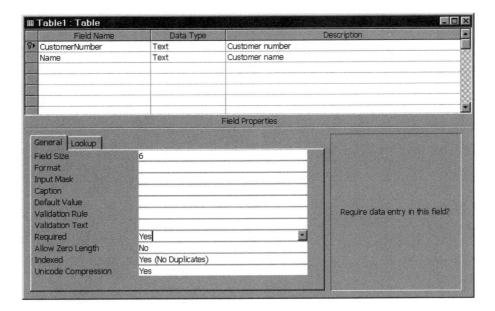

d. Select File → Save. A dialog box is displayed.
  1. In the Table Name entry box, type Customers.
  2. Select OK. The Customers table is saved with the relational database.
e. Close the Customers table.

12.9 The Relational Database Management System

A relational database consists of many objects that together are called a relational database management system (*RDBMS*). The core of any database is the data it stores. In an RDBMS, this data is the tables it contains. Other objects that make up the RDBMS are forms, queries, and reports.

form   A *form* is used for entering and viewing records. A form displays only one record at a time, making data entry less error-prone. It is similar to a paper form that an individual would fill out.

query   A *query* is used to limit the records displayed to those which meet certain criteria. Queries are a very useful tool for analyzing the data stored in a database.

report   A *report* is data formatted and organized for printing. Because reports can be used to print specified information, they are also a useful tool for analyzing data.

12.10 Creating a New Form

A form is a way to view one record of a table at a time. For example, a columnar form for the Packs table in the Backpacks database would look similar to:

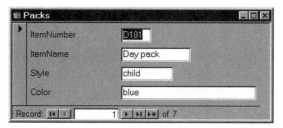

A form displays one record at a time

columnar form A *columnar form* displays a record with one field right after the other in a column. A form is usually the best way to enter records into a table because it makes data entry less error-prone.

Form Wizard In Access, a form can easily be created using the Form Wizard, which provides dialog boxes for selecting fields to be included in the form and form layout options. The steps for creating a form using the Form Wizard are:

1. **Start the Form Wizard.** Click the Forms button in the Objects list in the Database window and then double-click on the Create form by using wizard icon to display the Form Wizard dialog box:

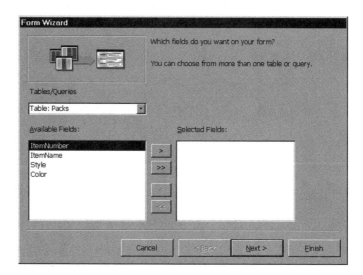

2. **Select the desired table and fields.** From the Tables/Queries collapsible list, select the desired table. The fields from that table are displayed in the Available Fields list. A form for a table usually includes all the fields of that table. Click on the >> button to move all the fields of the selected table to the Selected Fields list:

The New Button

When the Forms button in the Objects list of the Database window is selected, clicking the New button at the top of the Database Window displays the New Form dialog box. From this dialog box, several options, including Design view, are available for creating a new form. A specialized form can be created using form Design view, as discussed in Appendix A of this text.

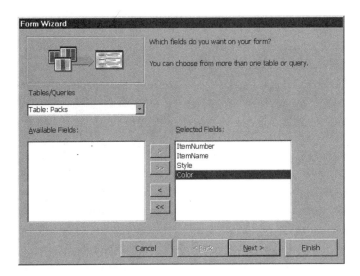

3. **Select the form layout.** Select the Next button to display layout options. Click on Columnar for a columnar form:

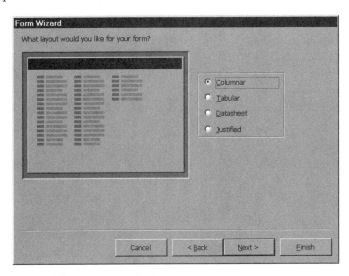

4. **Select the form style.** Select the Next button to display style options for the form background. Click on Standard for a plain gray background:

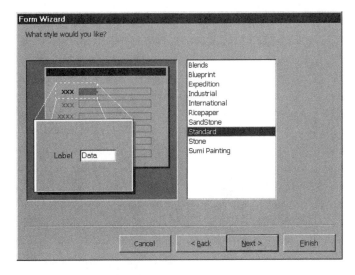

5. **Enter the form title.** Select the Next button to display the last Form Wizard dialog box where a form title can be entered and the option to open the form for data entry can be selected:

6. **Display the form.** Select the Finish button to display the new form.

12.11 Using Forms and Entering Records

record controls

Record controls are displayed at the bottom of a form. The number of the active record and the total number of records in the table are displayed next to controls that scroll records:

- displays the first record.
- displays the last record.
- displays the next record.
- displays the previous record.

If a table contains no data, then its corresponding form will display an empty record with empty entry boxes for all but number fields. A number field entry box automatically displays a 0 until it is replaced by another entry. AutoNumber field entries are not displayed until another entry of the record is entered.

A record is added to a database by typing entries into a form. The pointer can be clicked in the desired entry box to move the cursor to that box. However, data entry is usually faster when your hands are kept on the keyboard. In this case, the Enter key or the Tab key can be pressed to move the cursor from entry box to entry box. Pressing Shift+Tab moves the cursor to the previous field in the record. When the cursor is in the last field of a record, pressing Enter or Tab displays the next record in the table, if there is one, or an empty record otherwise.

To change an existing entry, the cursor must first be moved to that entry and then the entry edited.

When a form is active, the Status bar at the bottom of the Access window displays the description of the field containing the cursor. A field's description is the text entered in the Description box in table Design view.

Practice 3

In this practice you will add records to the Backpacks relational database. Open Backpacks if it is not already displayed.

1) CREATE A NEW FORM

    a. In the Backpacks : Database window, click on the Forms button.

    b. Double-click on the Create form by using wizard icon. A dialog box is displayed.

        1. In the Tables/Queries collapsible list, select Table : Packs. The fields of the Packs table are displayed in the Available Fields list.

        2. Click on the >> button. All the fields from the Available Fields list are moved to the Selected Fields list.

        3. Select the Next button. The form layout options are displayed.

        4. Select the Columnar option if it is not already selected.

        5. Select the Next button. The form style options are displayed.

        6. Select the Standard option if it is not already selected.

        7. Select the Next button. The dialog box displays an entry box for the form title and an option for viewing the form.

        8. In the What title do you want for your form? entry box, type Packs if it not already displayed.

        9. Select the Open the form to view or enter information option if it is not already selected.

        10. Select the Finish button. The Packs form is displayed with the first record's entries. Since there are no records in the Packs table the entry boxes are blank.

2) ADD A RECORD USING A FORM

    a. Place the cursor in the ItemNumber entry box if it is not already there. Note the text in the Status bar at the bottom of the Access window. It displays Item number of backpack, the description of the field.

    b. Type D101 and then press Enter. The cursor is moved to the next field.

    c. In the ItemName field, enter Day pack.

    d. In the Style field, enter child.

    e. In the Color field, type blue and then press Enter. A new, empty record in the table is displayed.

3) ADD SIX MORE RECORDS TO THE DATABASE

    Follow step 2 above to enter the next six records:

        D102, Day pack, child, khaki
        D201, Day pack, adult, blue
        D202, Day pack, adult, khaki
        H201, Hiking pack, adult, blue
        H202, Hiking pack, adult, khaki
        H203, Hiking pack, adult, green

4) SCROLL THE RECORDS OF THE PACKS TABLE

    a. Click on the ◄ record control to view the first record in the table.

    b. Click on the ► control to view the next record in the table.

    c. Click on the ►► control to view the last record in the table.

    d. Click on the form's Close button to remove it. The Backpacks : Database window should still be displayed. Note how Packs now appears as a form name in the window.

5) CREATE A FORM FOR THE CUSTOMERS TABLE

Use the Form Wizard to create a form for the Customers table. Refer to step 1 for the form options and name the form Customers.

6) ADD CUSTOMER RECORDS

a. Add the following records using the Customers form:

CGU-10, Camping Gear Unlimited
IUB-5, Ivy University Bookstore
SOS-21, Sage's Outdoor Supplies

b. Close the Customers form.

7) CREATE A FORM FOR THE TRANSACTIONS TABLE AND ADD TRANSACTION RECORDS

a. Use the Form Wizard to create a form for the Transactions table. Refer to step 1 for the form options and name the form Transactions.
b. Note the new form is displayed with (AutoNumber) highlighted in the TransID field. Press the Enter key. The cursor is moved to the Date field.
c. Type 9/20/01. The TransID entry changes to a 1 since this is the first record entered.
d. Enter CGU-10 in the CustomerNumber field, D201 in the ItemNumber field, and 15 in the Quantity field.
e. Add the remaining order records:

9/20/01, CGU-10, D102, 10
9/21/01, IUB-5, D202, 25
9/24/01, SOS-21, H201, 6

f. Close the Transactions form. Note that the Backpacks : Database window displays the names of three forms.

12.12 Formatting Datasheet View

When a table is created, the columns in Datasheet view have a default width that may or may not entirely display a field's name and entries. For example, the Customers table in Datasheet view looks similar to:

CustomerNum|	Name
▶ CGU-10	Camping Gear l
IUB-5	Ivy University B
SOS-21	Sage's Outdoor
✳	

*A column may not be wide enough to entirely display
its field name and entries*

The CustomerNumber column is not wide enough to display its field name.

changing column width

A column's width is changed by dragging the column's right boundary. Pointing to the *boundary*, the bar separating the column letters at the top of a table, changes the pointer shape to a double-headed arrow:

CustomerNum|	Name
▶ CGU-10	Camping Gear l
IUB-5	Ivy University B
SOS-21	Sage's Outdoor
✳	

Dragging the boundary to the right increases the width of the column. Columns that are unnecessarily wide should be narrowed by dragging the boundary to the left.

Another technique for resizing a column is to double-click on the column's right boundary. This method will resize a column so that it is just wide enough to display its field name and entries entirely.

changing field order

The order in which the fields appear in a table can be changed by dragging a selected field to the desired location. To select a field, the pointer is placed on the field name until the pointer shape changes to a solid arrow:

CustomerNumber	Name
▶ CGU-10	Camping Gear Unlimited
IUB-5	Ivy University Bookstore
SOS-21	Sage's Outdoor Supplies
✳	

Clicking the solid arrow pointer selects the field. The selected field can then be dragged to the desired position. Note the heavy dark line displayed when a field is dragged:

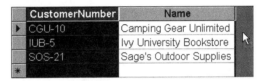

When the mouse button is released, the column is moved:

Name	CustomerNumber
▶ Camping Gear Unlimited	CGU-10
Ivy University Bookstore	IUB-5
Sage's Outdoor Supplies	SOS-21
✳	

After formatting Datasheet view, the table must be saved to retain the new layout.

12.13 Printing Records

printing a table

A table displayed in Datasheet view can be printed by selecting the Print command (Ctrl+P) from the File menu. If the table is too wide to fit on a single sheet of paper, columns are printed on consecutive sheets starting from the leftmost field and proceeding to the right. If the table is too long to fit on a single sheet, rows are printed on consecutive sheets starting from the first record and proceeding to the last.

landscape orientation

More columns can be printed on a sheet of paper by printing the table in landscape orientation. This can be useful for tables with many columns or very wide columns. The print orientation of a table is changed by selecting the Page Setup command from the File menu, which displays the Page Setup dialog box. Selecting the Page tab in this dialog box and then selecting the Landscape option and OK changes the print orientation. When the Print command is selected, the table is printed across the widest part of the paper allowing more columns, but fewer rows.

Select Record(s) option

The Select Record(s) option in the Print dialog box is used to indicate that only the active record should be printed. Multiple records can be selected for printing by holding down the Ctrl key and clicking in the record selector box to the left of the desired records.

printing records in a form

Selecting the Print command when a form is displayed prints all the records of the form, one right after the other, in a column. The Select Record(s) option in the Print dialog box is selected to print the displayed record only.

The Print button on the Toolbar () can be used to print one copy of a datasheet or a set of records in forms one after the other.

Practice 4 ⚙

In this practice you will format and print the tables in the Backpacks database. The Customers form will also be printed. Open Backpacks if it is not already displayed.

1) DISPLAY THE CUSTOMERS TABLE IN DATASHEET VIEW

a. In the Backpacks : Database window, click on the Tables button. The Customers, Packs, and Transactions table names are listed.
b. Double-click on the Customers table name. The Customers table is displayed in Datasheet view.

2) CHANGE THE WIDTH OF COLUMNS

a. Point to the boundary between the CustomerNumber and Name fields. The pointer changes to a double-headed arrow.
b. Drag the boundary to the right the width of about three characters. The CustomerNumber field name should now be entirely displayed. If not, continue to resize the field until its field name is entirely displayed.
c. Point to the boundary to the right of the Name field and then double-click the double-headed arrow pointer. The Name field column expands to a width that is just wide enough to display the field name and entries entirely.

Check – Your Customers table should look similar to:

CustomerNumber	Name
CGU-10	Camping Gear Unlimited
IUB-5	Ivy University Bookstore
SOS-21	Sage's Outdoor Supplies
*	

3) PRINT THE CUSTOMERS TABLE

a. Select File → Save. The modified table is saved.
b. Select File → Print. A dialog box is displayed.
   1. Select OK. The table is printed.
c. Close the Customers table.

4) FORMAT AND PRINT THE PACKS TABLE

a. Open the Packs table in Datasheet view.
b. Double-click on each field's right boundary. The fields are resized appropriately.
c. Save the modified Packs table.
d. Print and then close the Packs table.

5) FORMAT THE TRANSACTIONS TABLE

    a. Open the Transactions table in Datasheet view.
    b. Resize fields appropriately.
    c. Save, print, and then close the modified Transactions table.

6) PRINT THE TRANSACTIONS RECORDS

    a. In the Backpacks : Database window, click on the Forms button. The Customers, Packs, and Transactions form names are listed.
    b. Double-click on the Transactions form name. The Transactions form is displayed.
    c. Select File → Print. A dialog box is displayed.
         1. Select OK. The records are printed one after the other in a column.
    d. Close the Transactions form.

12.14 Filtering

query

A powerful feature of a relational database is the ability to perform queries. A *query* limits the records displayed to those which meet certain criteria. For example, for the Backpacks database, a query could be used to display the records of just blue packs. In Access, one way to query a database is to apply a *filter*.

criteria

The first step in filtering is to determine the criteria. The filter *criteria* is the data that a record must contain in order to be displayed. For example, the criteria when filtering for blue backpack records is "blue" in the Color field.

Filter by Form view

A filter can be applied to a displayed form or a table in Datasheet view by clicking the Filter By Form button () on the Toolbar, which displays the form or table in *Filter by Form view*. For example, the Packs form in Filter by Form view looks similar to:

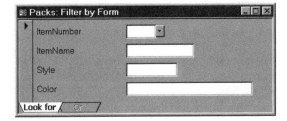

The Filter by Form view displays field entry boxes

Query criteria is specified by placing the cursor in the desired field's entry box and typing an entry or selecting an entry from the field's collapsible list. For example, clicking in the Color field and then clicking on the down arrow displays a list of all the entries made in the Color field:

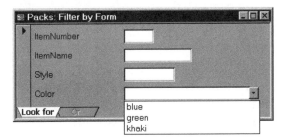

Clicking on blue enters it as the criteria.

After specifying the criteria, a filter is applied by clicking on the Apply Filter button () on the Toolbar. When the Packs filter is applied, there are three records that contain "blue" in the Color field. The records that do not meet filter criteria are filtered from view, and are said to be hidden. *Hidden records* have not been deleted, they are just no longer able to be displayed. The record controls at the bottom of the table or form indicate how many records meet the query criteria:

hidden records

three records meet the criteria

All the records in a form or table are again displayed by clicking on the Remove Filter button () on the Toolbar.

12.15 Using Saved Filters

Filters can be named and saved so that they can be applied again and again without having to reselect the criteria. A filter is saved by clicking on the Save As Query button () on the Toolbar, which displays the Save As Query dialog box:

Typing a descriptive name for the filter and selecting OK adds it to the database. A filter can only be saved before it is applied.

Selecting the Queries button in the Objects list in the Database window displays the names of saved filters. A saved filter is applied by double-clicking on the filter name, which displays the results in Datasheet view.

A saved filter is deleted by clicking once on its name in the Database window to highlight it and then pressing the Delete key.

Practice 5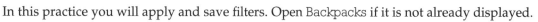

In this practice you will apply and save filters. Open Backpacks if it is not already displayed.

1) DISPLAY THE PACKS FORM

2) FILTER THE PACKS RECORDS

    a. On the Toolbar, click on the Filter By Form button (📋). The Packs form is displayed in Filter by Form view.

        1. Click in the Color field and then click on the down arrow. A list is displayed that contains all the entries made in the Color field.

        2. In the list, click on blue. The Color field displays "blue".

3. On the Toolbar, click on the Apply Filter button (). Note that the record controls indicate that three records meet the criteria.
   b. Use the record controls to scroll through the records of blue packs.
   c. On the Toolbar, click on the Remove Filter button (). All the Packs records are again available.

3) SAVE A FILTER

a. On the Toolbar, click on the Filter By Form button (). The Packs form is displayed in Filter by Form view.
   1. In the Style field, select the adult entry.
   2. In the Color field, delete the entry. Be sure to remove the quotation marks.
   3. On the Toolbar, select the Save As Query button (). A dialog box is displayed.
      a. Type Adult Packs.
      b. Select OK. The query is saved.
   4. On the Toolbar, click on the Apply Filter button (). The record controls indicate that five records meet the criteria.
   b. On the Toolbar, click on the Remove Filter button (). All the Packs records are again available.
   c. Close the Packs form.

4) APPLY AND PRINT A SAVED FILTER

a. In the Backpacks : Database window, click on the Queries button. The Adult Packs query name is displayed.
   b. Double-click on the Adult Packs query to run it. The filter results are displayed in a datasheet.
   c. Select File → Print. A dialog box is displayed.
      1. Select OK to print the filter results.
   d. Close the datasheet.

12.16 Advanced Filtering

complex query

Criteria can be entered for more than one field in Filter by Form view. This type of query is called a *complex query* because the records are checked for more than one entry. For example, the Packs records could be filtered to display only the records of adult day packs. The criteria for *and* this filter is "adult" in the Style field *and* "Day pack" in the ItemName field.

or
Or tab

Another type of complex query checks records for one entry or another. For example, the Packs records could be filtered to display the records of blue packs and green packs. The criteria for this filter is "blue" in the Color field *or* "green" in the Color field. This kind of criteria is entered by using the Or tab at the bottom of the Filter by Form view window:

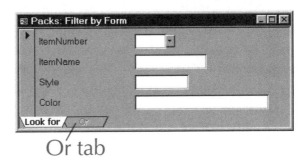

Or tab

The Or tab allows multiple filter criteria to be used

Clicking on the Or tab displays a blank Filter by Form view where additional criteria can be entered. Also, when the Or tab is clicked, a second Or tab appears making another Filter by Form view available, and so on. After the criteria is entered, the filter is applied as usual. For the Packs query, selecting blue in the Color field of the first Filter by Form view, clicking on the Or tab, selecting green in the Color field of the next Filter by Form view, and then applying the filter displays four records.

Practice 6

In this practice you will filter the Backpacks database. Open Backpacks if it is not already displayed.

1) DISPLAY THE PACKS FORM

2) APPLY A FILTER

    a. On the Toolbar, click on the Filter By Form button (⊞). The Packs form is displayed in Filter by Form view.

        1. In the ItemName field, select the Day pack entry.

        2. In the Style field, select the adult entry if it is not already displayed.

        3. On the Toolbar, click on the Apply Filter button (▽). Note that the record controls indicate that two records meet the criteria.

    b. Print the filter results.

    c. On the Toolbar, click on the Remove Filter button (▽). All the Packs records are again available.

3) FILTER THE PACKS FORM USING THE OR TAB

    a. On the Toolbar, click on the Filter By Form button. The Packs form is displayed in Filter by Form view.

        1. In the Color field, select the blue entry.

        2. Delete any other criteria on the form.

        3. At the bottom of the Filter by Form view window, click on the Or tab. A new, empty Filter by Form view is displayed.

        4. In the Color field, select the green entry.

        5. On the Toolbar, click on the Apply Filter button. Note that the record controls indicate that four records meet the criteria.

    b. Print the filter results.

    c. On the Toolbar, click on the Remove Filter button. All the Packs records are again available.

4) EXIT ACCESS

    Close the Packs form and then exit Access.

Chapter Summary

This chapter introduced relational databases for organizing and storing related data. The speed and storage capabilities of the computer make it an ideal tool for managing large amounts of information in the form of relational databases.

table, record field entry, primary key   Tables are the foundation of relational databases. Tables consist of records, where each record is a set of fields. Data in an individual field in a single record is called an entry. A primary key, which is a field with only unique entries, is designated for each table so that the records of a table are unique.

Each field is defined by its name, type, size, and format. A field name should describe its contents and must be unique to a table. Field types include text, number, date/time, currency, memo, and AutoNumber. The size of a field is the number of characters or type of number it can store. A field size of single stores a decimal number while a field size of long integer stores whole numbers only. Format refers to the way the field's contents are displayed. A number field can be formatted as fixed to display a specific number of decimal places, as a percent, or as standard to display commas to separate thousands. Formats for date/time fields include short form, medium form, and long form.

A database should be created based on a design. Designing a database is a four step process:

1. Determine what information should be stored.

2. Divide information into named tables.

3. Determine the relationships among the tables.

4. Define the fields and determine the primary key for each table.

When creating a new relational database, you must type a descriptive name for the database and select the folder where the database will be stored. Next, the tables from the database design are created. A table is created in Design view where each field's name, type, size, and if necessary the field's format including number of decimal places is defined. After the fields are defined, the primary key is selected and then the table saved using a descriptive name. The Save command from the File menu or the Save button on the Toolbar is used to save the table.

The View button on the Toolbar is used to switch between Design view and Datasheet view. In Datasheet view, each row corresponds to a record and each column corresponds to a field. The record selector is the gray box to the left of each record and is used to make a record active.

A Relational Database Management System includes tables, forms, queries, and reports. Forms are used to enter records. Queries are used to display records that contain specific information. Reports are printouts of formatted and organized data.

A form is a way to view one record of a table at a time. A columnar form displays a record as one field right after the other in a column. The record controls at the bottom of a form are used to display each record. The records entered into a form are added to the form's corresponding table. A form can be easily created using the Form Wizard.

record controls

To enter a record using a form, the cursor is placed in the desired field and then the field's entry typed. The cursor can be placed in a field by clicking in the entry box. Pressing the Enter or Tab key moves the cursor to the next entry box. Existing entries can be changed by placing the cursor in the entry box and then editing the entry. The record controls at the bottom of a form are used to display records.

In Datasheet view, a column's width is changed by dragging the column's right boundary. Double-clicking on a column's right boundary resizes the column so that it is just wide enough to display its entries entirely. A selected column is moved by dragging it to the desired position.

A table displayed in Datasheet view can be printed by selecting the Print command from the File menu or by clicking on the Print button on the Toolbar. Printing a table in landscape orientation allows more columns on a sheet of paper. Executing Print when a form is displayed prints the records one right after the other in a column. Only selected records are printed when the Select Record(s) option in the Print dialog box is selected.

query A query limits the records displayed to those which meet certain criteria. One way to query a database is to apply a filter. Filter criteria must be entered into Filter by Form view of the appropriate form or table. The Apply Filter button on the Toolbar is used to apply the filter. Records that do not contain the criteria are filtered out, or hidden from view. Clicking on the Remove Filter button displays all the records in the table.

 A filter is named and saved by clicking the Save As Query button on the Toolbar. A saved filter can be applied again and again with having to reselect the criteria.

Complex queries are used to display records with specific entries in two or more fields. Another type of complex query displays records with one of two or more entries in a single field. This type of complex query *Or tab* uses the Or tab at the bottom of a Filter by Form view window.

Vocabulary

Active field The field that contains the cursor and has the ▶ symbol to the left of its row in Design view.

Active record The record in Datasheet view that displays the ▶ symbol to the left of its row.

AutoNumber field A field type that automatically generates a numeric entry that is one greater than that in the last record added.

Boundary The bar separating the column letters at the top of a table.

Columnar form Displays a record with one field right after the other in a column.

Complex query A query that checks records for more than one entry.

Criteria The required data that a record must contain in order to be displayed by a query.

Currency field A field type that stores only dollar amounts.

Database A computer application that is used to organize and store related data.

Datasheet view A table displayed as rows and columns of data where each row corresponds to a record and each column corresponds to a field.

Date/time field A field type that stores only a date or time.

Design view The view used for defining the fields of a table.

Entry The data stored in an individual field of a single record.

Field Represents a piece of data in a record.

Filter A query method that displays specific records in a table.

Filter by Form view Used to enter query criteria.

Fixed A field format that displays a field's entry to a specific number of decimal places.

Form A way to view one record of a table at a time. Also used to add a record.

Format The way in which field contents are displayed.

General Number The default field format that displays a number exactly as entered.

Hidden records Records that do not meet query criteria and are therefore no longer displayed.

Long integer A field size that stores only whole numbers.

Memo field A field type that stores several lines of text.

Microsoft Access The relational database application in the Microsoft Office package.

Number field A field type that stores only numeric values.

Or tab Tab at the bottom of the Filter by Form view window that displays another Filter by Form view for entering additional query criteria.

Primary key A field or fields designated to have unique entries in order to make each record of a table unique.

Percent A field format that multiplies the value entered by 100 and displays it with a % sign.

Query Limits the records displayed to those which meet certain criteria.

Record A set of data about one item.

Record controls Provided at the bottom of a form to scroll records.

Record selector The gray box to the left of each record in Datasheet view that when clicked selects that record.

Relational database A database in which data is separated into tables of related records.

Relational Database Management System (RDBMS) The objects that make up the relational database, such as tables, forms, queries, and reports.

Report Data that is organized and formatted for printing.

Required Option in the Field Properties part of the table Design view window that should be set to Yes for the primary key.

Single A field size that can store numbers with a decimal portion.

Size The number of characters stored in a text field or type of numerical value stored in a number field.

Standard A number field format that displays a thousands separator, usually a comma.

Table Contains a set of records organized into rows and columns.

Text field A field type that stores characters (letters, symbols, word, a combination of letters and numbers).

Type The classification of a field based on the kind of data it stores.

Access Commands and Buttons

Page Set**up command** Displays a dialog box with options for changing the print orientation of a table.

Primary **key command** Designates the selected field as the primary key. Found in the Edit menu. The Primary Key button ( ) on the Toolbar can be used instead of the command.

Print **command** Displays a dialog box with options for printing a table that is in Datasheet view. Found in the File menu. The Print button ( ) on the Toolbar can be used instead of the command.

Save **command** Saves any changes to a table. Found in the File menu. The Save button ( ) on the Toolbar can be used instead of the command.

View Button Displays a table in Datasheet view.

Review Questions

Sections 12.1 — 12.4

1. What capabilities of the computer make it an ideal tool for managing information in the form of a database?

2. Why do historians refer to our present time as the "Information Age?"

3. a) What is a relational database?
   b) What is a table?
   c) What is a record?
   d) What is a field?
   e) What is an entry?

4. a) What is the primary key?
   b) Can a primary key consist of more than one field?

5. List the three guidelines for choosing a field name.

6. List the six field types discussed in the text and give an example of an entry for each.

7. a) When would you use single as the field size?
   b) When would you use long integer as the field size?

8. a) How does format affect a field?
   b) What is the fixed format used for?
   c) What is the difference between short form, medium form, and long form for date and time fields?

9. Determine appropriate field names, types, sizes, and formats for the following data:
   a) a person's first name
   b) a phone number
   c) an item's price
   d) the date a person was born
   e) the time of day a person was born
   f) a student's GPA
   g) an automatically calculated record number

10. a) What should be done before creating a database?
    b) List the four guidelines for designing a relational database.

Sections 12.5 — 12.8

11. Why is it important to select the appropriate folder when creating a database?

12. List the steps required to create a table in Design view.

13. List the steps required to designate a primary key.

14. What command is used to save a table with the relational database?

15. How are records displayed in Datasheet view?

16. What is the name of the gray box to the left of a record in Datasheet view and what is it used for?

Sections 12.9 — 12.13

17. What are the four objects found in a Relational Database Management System?

18. a) What is a columnar form?
    b) List the steps required to create a new columnar form named Pets that includes all the fields from a table named Pets.

19. What are the record controls used for?

20. List the steps required to add a record to a table using a form.

21. a) What does pressing the Tab key do in a form?
    b) What does pressing Shift+Tab do in a form?

22. List two ways to increase the width of a column in Datasheet view.

23. When should a column in Datasheet view be made narrower?

24. a) What effect does printing a table in Landscape orientation have on the number of columns printed?
    b) List the steps required to change the print orientation of a table to Landscape.

25. a) What is a query?
    b) What is a filter?
    c) What is criteria?
    d) What are hidden records?

26. What is the first step in applying a filter?

27. List the steps required to filter the Packs form for the records of child packs.

28. List the steps required to save a filter.

29. Can a filter be saved after it has been applied to a form?

30. List the steps required to apply a saved filter.

31. List the steps required to delete a saved filter.

32. What is a complex query?

33. a) List the steps required to filter the Packs form for records of adult day packs.
    b) List the steps required to filter the Packs form for records of khaki packs and blue packs.

Exercises

Exercise 1 ———————————————————————— FL COLLEGES

The FL COLLEGES database file contains one table with data about some of Florida's cities. An additional table is needed to complete the relational database. Open FL COLLEGES and complete the following steps:

a) Create a table that will store information on Florida colleges. After defining the fields below, save the table naming it Colleges:

Field Name	Type	Description	Size	Format	Decimals
Name ⚷	Text	Name of college	50		
City	Text	City location of college	25		
Enrollment	Number	Students attending	Single	Standard	0

b) Create a form named Colleges for the Colleges table and enter the following records:

University of Central Florida; Orlando; 29,821
University of Florida; Gainesville; 42,000
Florida Atlantic University; Boca Raton; 19,562
Florida International University; Miami; 30,092
Florida State University; Tallahassee; 31,193
University of South Florida; Tampa; 23,502
University of West Florida; Pensacola; 8,081

c) Format the Colleges table in Datasheet view appropriately.

d) Print the Colleges table.

e) Create and save a filter named Dade County that displays the records of cities in Dade county. Apply the query and then print the results.

f) Create and save a filter named South Florida Colleges that displays the records of colleges in Boca Raton and Miami. Apply the query and then print the results.

Exercise 2 ———————————————————————— Museum Exhibits

Sunport Science Museum wants to use a relational database to store information on its exhibits.

a) Using Access, create a relational database naming it Museum Exhibits.

b) Create a table that will store information on the different exhibits in the museum. After defining the fields below, save the table naming it Exhibits:

Field Name	Type	Description	Size	Format
ExhibitID ⚷	Text	ID of permanent exhibit	4	
Name	Text	Name of exhibit	30	
Department	Text	Department exhibit is in	30	
Updated	Date/Time	Date exhibit was last updated		Short Date

c) Create a table that will store information on the number of people attending each exhibit for years 2000 through 2002. After defining the fields below, save the table naming it Attendance:

Field Name	Type	Description	Size	Format	Decimals
ExhibitID 🔑	Text	ID of permanent exhibit	4		
Year 🔑	Text	Year of attendance	4		
Attendance	Number	Number of people	Long Integer	Standard	0

The primary key for the Attendance table is the ExhibitID and Year fields together. This is because there can only be one record for a specific exhibit in a specific year.

d) Create a form named Exhibits for the Exhibits table and enter the following eight records:

LWL1; Minerals and Rocks; Land We Live On; 1/5/01
LWL2; Earth's Interior; Land We Live On; 3/6/00
LWL3; Atmosphere and Weather; Land We Live On; 5/3/99
SWD1; Oceans; Secrets of Water Depths; 5/3/00
SWD2; Fresh Water; Secrets of Water Depths; 7/12/01
SWD3; Lakes, Rivers & Streams; Secrets of Water Depths; 1/1/98
WDH2; Earthquakes & Hurricanes; Why Does That Happen; 2/7/00
WDH3; Volcanoes; Why Does That Happen; 11/23/99

e) Create a form named Attendance for the Attendance table and enter the following 27 records:

LWL1; 2000; 1,560	LWL1; 2001; 1,540	LWL1; 2002; 1,494
LWL2; 2000; 1,298	LWL2; 2001; 1,600	LWL2; 2002; 1,678
LWL3; 2000; 1,364	LWL3; 2001; 1,467	LWL3; 2002; 1,645
SWD1; 2000; 1,254	SWD1; 2001; 1,374	SWD1; 2002; 1,575
SWD2; 2000; 1,156	SWD2; 2001; 1,245	SWD2; 2002; 1,312
SWD3; 2000; 1,324	SWD3; 2001; 1,437	SWD3; 2002; 1,545
WDH1; 2000; 1,256	WDH1; 2001; 1,345	WDH1; 2002; 1,512
WDH2; 2000; 1,224	WDH2; 2001; 1,435	WDH2; 2002; 1,442
WDH3; 2000; 1,381	WDH3; 2001; 1,483	WDH3; 2002; 1,547

f) Format the Exhibits and Attendance tables in Datasheet view appropriately.

g) Print both tables.

h) Create and save a filter named Attendance for 2000 that displays the attendance records for the year 2000. Apply the query and then print the results.

Exercise 3 ——————————————————————— Library

The local library wants to use a relational database to store information on its books.

a) Using Access, create a relational database naming it Library.

b) Create a table that will store information on the different books in the library. After defining the fields below, save the table naming it Books:

Field Name	Type	Description	Size
ISBN 🔑	Text	International Standard Book Number	13
Title	Text	Title of book	50
Type	Text	Type of book	10
AuthorID	Text	ID of author	4

c) Create a table that will store information on authors. After defining the fields below, save the table naming it Authors:

Field Name	Type	Description	Size	Format
AuthorID 🔑	Text	ID of author	4	
FirstName	Text	First name of author	15	
LastName	Text	Last name of author	30	
Birth	Date/Time	Birth date		Short Date
Death	Date/Time	Death date		Short Date

d) Create a form named Books for the Books table and enter the following 12 records:

1-879233-01-0; My Wedding - Your Wedding; Family; KW23
1-879233-39-8; All The Presidents' Wives; History; CB12
1-879233-42-8; The Complete College Guide; Reference; TB22
1-879233-44-4; Appeasement In The Republic; History; CB12
1-879233-51-7; Build Your Muscles; Health; SZ04
1-879233-56-8; The Orange Tide; Drama; KW23
1-879233-57-6; Effective Management Skills; Business; MS12
1-879233-59-0; The Dog Wore a Red Coat; Mystery; ZT19
1-879233-62-2; Asian Alliances; History; CB12
1-879233-82-7; Healthy Eating; Health; SZ04
1-879233-84-3; Reading the Butler's Writing; Mystery; ZT19
1-879233-92-4; The Gold Necklace; Mystery; ZT19

e) Create a form named Authors for the Authors table and enter the following six records:

CB12; Carrie; Brennan; 6/12/09; 12/3/96
KW23; Karen; Willamson; 10/23/74
MS12; Monica; Saliguero; 10/12/12; 3/16/90
SZ04; Slim; Zhorbyzki; 2/4/59; 11/11/93
TB22; Tomica; Broswell; 7/22/21; 9/6/92
ZT19; Zachery; Toening; 3/19/23; 6/20/89

f) Format the Books and Authors tables in Datasheet view appropriately.

g) Print both tables.

h) Create and save a filter named Mystery Novels that displays the records of books that are mystery novels. Apply the query and then print the results.

Exercise 4 ——————————————— Space Shuttle Missions

Orbiter vehicles, astronauts, and mission data can be maintained in a relational database.

a) Using Access, create a relational database naming it Space Shuttle Missions.

b) Create a table that will store orbiter vehicle data. After defining the fields below, save the table naming it Orbiter Vehicles:

Field Name	Type	Description	Size	Format
OrbiterID 🔑	Text	ID of vehicle	6	
Name	Text	name of vehicle	15	
RolloutDate	Date/Time	Date vehicle completed		Short Date

c) Create a table that will store astronaut information. After defining the fields below, save the table naming it Astronauts:

Field Name	Type	Description	Size	Format	Decimals
AstronautID ⚷	Text	ID of astronaut	4		
FirstName	Text	First name of astronaut	15		
LastName	Text	Last name of astronaut	30		
BirthYear	Number	Year born	Long Integer	Standard	0
TotalMissions	Number	Completed missions	Long Integer	Standard	0

d) Create a table that will store mission information. After defining the fields below, save the table naming it Missions:

Field Name	Type	Description	Size
MissionID ⚷	Text	ID of mission	6
CommanderID	Text	ID of commander	4
OrbiterID	Text	ID of vehicle	6
LaunchDate	Date/Time	Date of launch	Short Date

e) Create a form named OrbiterVehicles for the Orbiter Vehicles table and enter the following four records:

> OV-102; Columbia; 3/8/79
> OV-103; Discovery; 10/16/83
> OV-104; Atlantis; 3/6/85
> OV-105; Endeavour; 4/25/91

f) Create a form named Astronauts for the Astronauts table and enter the following four records:

> EC-1; Eileen; Collins; 1956; 3
> JC-1; John; Casper; 1943; 4
> LS-1; Loren; Shriver; 1944; 3
> RC-1; Robert; Cabana; 1949; 4

g) Create a form named Missions for the Missions table and enter the following eight records:

> STS-31; JC-1; OV-103; 4/24/90
> STS-46; LS-1; OV-104; 7/31/92
> STS-54; JC-1; OV-105; 1/13/93
> STS-62; JC-1; OV-102; 3/4/94
> STS-65; RC-1; OV-102; 7/8/94
> STS-77; JC-1; OV-105; 5/19/96
> STS-88; RC-1; OV-105; 12/4/98
> STS-93; EC-1; OV-102; 7/23/99

h) Format the tables in Datasheet view appropriately.

i) Print the tables.

j) Create and save a filter named OV-102 Missions that displays the missions of vehicle OV-102. Apply the query and print the results.

Exercise 5 ———————————————————————— Boat Storage

Sunport Boat Storage wants to use a relational database to store information on its business.

a) Using Access, create a relational database naming it Boat Storage.

b) Create a table that will store information on the employees. After defining the fields below, save the table naming it Employees:

Field Name	Type	Description	Size
EmployeeID ⸹	Text	ID of employee	4
FirstName	Text	First name of employee	15
LastName	Text	Last name of employee	30
Address	Text	Street address of employee	50
City	Text	City employee lives in	15
State	Text	State employee lives in	2
Zip	Text	Zip code of employee	10
Phone	Text	Phone number of employee	14

c) Create a table that will store information on the boats. After defining the fields below, save the table naming it Boats:

Field Name	Type	Description	Size	Decimals
Boat ⸹	Text	Name of boat	30	
SlotNumber	Number	Slot boat is stored	Long Integer	
EmployeeID	Text	Employee in charge of boat	4	
Fee	Currency	Monthly maintenance fee		0
OwnerID	Number	ID of boat's owner	Long Integer	

d) Create a table that will store information on boat owners. After defining the fields below, save the table naming it Boat Owners:

Field Name	Type	Description	Size
OwnerID ⸹	AutoNumber	ID of owner of a boat	Long Integer
FirstName	Text	First name of owner	15
LastName	Text	Last name of owner	30
Address	Text	Street address of owner	50
City	Text	City owner lives in	15
State	Text	State owner lives in	2
Zip	Text	Zip code of owner	10
Phone	Text	Phone number of owner	14

e) Create a form named Employees for the Employees table and enter the following five records:

DK86; Denita; Kilcullen; 86 Hampshire Road; Cody; WA; 12232; (617) 555-1229
HW28; Hillary; Walker; 1221 Rockledge Ave.; Cody; WA; 12232; (617) 555-9800
NG12; Nate; Gervin; NE 66th Plaza; Rostock; WA; 12241; (617) 555-9462
SM23; Sherman; MacGragor; 2334 12th Ave.; Cody; WA; 12232; (617) 555-0993
YA12; Yvette; Archibald; 13 Cypress Creed Rd.; Rostock; WA; 12241; (617) 555-7822

f) Create a form named Boats for the Boats table and enter the following 10 records:

Donned Upon You; 10; NG12; 70; 6
Jenny; 5; YA12; 62; 4
Just Desserts; 4; SM23; 50; 3
Monkey Business; 3; HW28; 86; 2
Shooting Star; 16; HW28; 77; 1
SteadyAsSheGoes; 13; DK86; 60; 5
The Sugar Queen; 12; NG12; 45; 4
Tidal Wave; 17; SM23; 55; 2
UR Behind Me; 9; DK86; 65; 5
Viking 5; 2; SM23; 55; 1

g) Create a form named Boat Owners for the Boat Owners table and enter the following six records:

> Rachell; Gundarssohn; 1671 Westchester Ave.; Poliney; WA; 12245; (232) 555-0912
> Pamela; Hogart; 12 Street; Monterey; WA; 12259; (232) 555-7021
> Dermont; Voss; 1087 67th Terrace; Monterey; WA; 12259; (232) 555-9000
> Zane; McCaffrey; 689 King Blvd.; Poliney; WA; 12245; (232) 555-7492
> Bethany; Mulberry; 8625 West View Drive Apt. 9; Rostock; WA; 12241; (617) 555-6524
> Damon; Deitrich; 4567 Sandalwood Ave.; Poliney; WA; 12245; (232) 555-2651

h) Format the Employees, Boats, and Boat Owners tables in Datasheet view appropriately.

i) Print all the tables in landscape orientation.

j) Create and save a filter named OwnerID 5 Boats that displays the boat records with OwnerID 5. Apply the query and then print the results.

Exercise 6 — Ivy U Athletics

Ivy University's Athletic department wants to use a relational database to store information on Ivy University's sports teams.

a) Using Access, create a relational database naming it Ivy U Athletics.

b) Create a table that will store information on the players. After defining the fields below, save the table naming it Players:

Field Name	Type	Description	Size
StudentID 🔑	Text	ID of student	5
FirstName	Text	First name of student	15
LastName	Text	Last name of student	30
Sport	Text	Sport the student plays	20
Position	Text	Position the student plays	20

c) Create a table that will store information on the different sports offered at Ivy University. After defining the fields below, save the table naming it Sports:

Field Name	Type	Description	Size	Decimals
Sport 🔑	Text	Name of sport	20	
Semester	Text	Semester sport is played	10	
Budget	Currency	Budget for sport		0

d) Create a table that will store information on the coaches at Ivy University. After defining the fields below, save the table naming it Coaches:

Field Name	Type	Description	Size	Decimals
CoachID 🔑	Text	ID of coach	5	
FirstName	Text	First name of coach	15	
LastName	Text	Last name of coach	30	
Sport	Text	Sport coached	20	
CoachTitle	Text	Title of coach	20	
Salary	Currency	Yearly salary for coach		0

e) Create a form named Players for the Players table and enter the following eight records:

> AS918; Adam; Schneider; Basketball; Shooting Guard
> AY245; Alyssa; Yaniv; Basketball; Center
> DM887; Derek; Mohatheny; Football; Linebacker
> EW265; Emilia; Watson; Softball; Pitcher
> JW387; Jody; Wainwright; Softball; First Base
> LP338; Lorenzo; Pearson; Football; Tailback

MD286; Myrna; Dixon; Softball; Centerfield
MS416; Matt; Silverstein; Basketball; Power Forward

f) Create a form named Sports for the Sports table and enter the following three records:

Basketball; Spring; 451,000
Football; Fall; 891,000
Softball; Spring; 256,000

g) Create a form named Coaches for the Coaches table and enter the following six records:

AR729; Alex; Rodriguez; Football; Head Coach; 102,000
BK122; Brian; Klitch; Basketball; Assistant Coach; 23,000
DW655; Diane; Whitman; Football; Defensive Coach; 41,000
JD113; Jeffrey; Dytko; Basketball; Head Coach; 86,000
MK541; Mary; Klinghoffer; Softball; Manager; 56,000
RB918; Regina; Baker; Softball; First Base Coach; 31,000

h) Format the Players, Sports, and Coaches tables in Datasheet view appropriately.

i) Print all the tables.

j) Create and save a filter named Softball Pitchers that displays the players records where softball is the sport and pitcher is the position. Apply the query and print the results.

Exercise 7 ———————————————— Second Ocean

Second Ocean specializes in relocating injured sea animals to facilities that can care for them.

a) Using Access, create a relational database naming it Second Ocean.

b) Create a table that will store information on the animals. After defining the fields below, save the table naming it Animals:

Field Name	Type	Description	Size	Format
AnimalID 🔑	AutoNumber	ID number of animal		
DateOfRescue	Date/Time	Date animal was rescued		short
Type	Text	Type of animal		
ApproxAge	Number	Approximate age of animal	Long Integer	
Gender	Text	Gender of animal - M/F	1	
Facility	Text	Facility animal relocated to	20	

c) Create a table that will store information on facilities. After defining the fields below, save the table naming it Facilities:

Field Name	Type	Description	Size
Facility 🔑	Text	Name of facility	20
State	Text	State facility is located	2
FirstName	Text	FIrst name of contact person	15
LastName	Text	Last name of contact person	30

d) Second Ocean checks on the progress of the animlas they have relocated. Create a table that will store information on facility checks. After defining the fields below, save the table naming it Facility Checks:

Field Name	Type	Description	Size	Format
CheckID 🔑	AutoNumber	ID of facility check		
Date	Date/Time	Date of check		Short
Facility	Text	Name of facility	20	
AnimalID	Number	ID number of animal checked	Long Integer	

e) Create a form named Animals for the Animals table and enter the following five records:

    8/11/00; Dolphin; 2; F; Ocean World
    6/5/00; Manatee; 3; M; Animal Help
    7/15/00; Manatee; 6; F; Animal Help
    2/1/00; Whale; 20; F; Ocean Care
    4/20/00; Dolphin; 10; M; Ocean World

f) Create a form named Facilities for the Facilities table and enter the following three records:

    Animal Help; FL; Mike; Gershberg
    Ocean Care; FL; Caitlin; Porter
    Ocean World; CA; Paula; Angelocci

g) Create a form named Facility Checks for the Facility Checks table and enter the following eight records:

    3/25/00; Ocean World; 1
    6/19/00; Animal Help; 2
    6/19/00; Animal Help; 3
    8/15/00; Ocean Care; 4
    10/14/00; Ocean World; 5
    10/14/00; Ocean World; 1
    11/12/00; Animal Help; 3
    12/22/00; Ocean Care; 4

h) Format the Animals, Facilities, and Facility Checks tables in Datasheet view appropriately.

i) Print all the tables.

j) Create and save a filter named Dolphins that displays the Animals records with dolphin as the animal type. Apply the query and print the results.

Exercise 8 ———————————————————— Green Thumb

Green Thumb is a plant nursery that wants to use a relational database to store information on its plants and sales.

a) Using Access, create a relational database naming it Green Thumb.

b) Create a table that will store information on the plants. After defining the fields below, save the table naming it Plants:

Field Name	Type	Description	Size	Decimals
PlantID ⚲	Text	ID of plant	3	
Plant	Text	Name of plant	15	
InStock	Number	Number of plants in stock	Long Integer	
Reorder	Number	When to reorder plants	Long Integer	
Cost	Currency	Price paid for plant		2
Retail	Currency	Selling price of plant		2
VendorID	Text	ID of vendor	2	

c) Create a table that will store information on the plant sales. After defining the fields below, save the table naming it Transactions:

Field Name	Type	Description	Size	Format
TransID ⚷	AutoNumber	ID of transaction		
Date	Date/Time	Date of transaction		Short Date
PlantID	Text	ID of plant purchased	3	
Quantity	Number	Number of plants purchased	Long Integer	

d) Create a table that will store information on the vendors from whom Green Thumb buys. After defining the fields below, save the table naming it Vendors:

Field Name	Type	Description	Size
VendorID ⚷	Text	ID of vendor	2
Name	Text	Name of vendor	30
Address	Text	Street address of vendor	50
City	Text	City where vendor is	15
State	Text	State where vendor is	2
Zip	Text	Zip code where vendor is	10
Phone	Text	Phone number of vendor	14
ContactFirstName	Text	First name of contact	15
ContactLastName	Text	Last name of contact	30

e) Create a form named Plants for the Plants table and enter the following five records:

Cac; Cactus; 60; 35; 4.99; 8.25; V2
Frn; Fern; 60; 50; 3.50; 5.75; V1
Hib; Hibiscus; 10; 40; 10.99; 25.00; V1
Tul; Tulip; 15; 25; 7.99; 10.50; V3
VF; Venus Flytrap; 45; 25; 7.99; 13.50; V2

f) Create a form named Transactions for the Transactions table and enter the following eleven records:

10/23/00; Frn; 10
10/25/00; Tul; 3
10/25/00; Cac; 12
11/3/00; Frn; 3
11/6/00; Hib; 2
11/7/00; Tul; 2
11/10/00; VF; 10
11/15/00; Cac; 2
11/17/00; Hib; 3
11/24/00; Tul; 5
11/29/00; VF; 6

g) Create a form named Vendors for the Vendors table and enter the following three records:

V1; Plantsalot; 1661 S. Yancy Ct.; Norman; OK; 44541; (617) 555-6122; Herbert; Mancini
V2; All Things Green; 30 Benton Dr.; Durango; CO; 89904; (912) 555-0265; Zeke; Mowatt
V3; Green Machines; 8429 W. 45th Ave.; Peducha; KY; 54426; (662) 555-2815; Abigail; Vanover

h) Format the Plants, Transactions, and Vendors tables in Datasheet view appropriately.

i) Print all the tables in landscape orientation.

j) Create and save a filter named Frn Transactions that displays the transactions records for PlantID Frn. Apply the query and then print the results.

The owner of Nudleman's Gym wants to use a relational database to store information on the progress of the gym members.

a) Using Access, create a relational database naming it Gym Members Progress.

b) Create a table that will store information on the members. After defining the fields below, save the table naming it Members:

Field Name	Type	Description	Size
MemberID 🔑	Text	ID of member	4
FirstName	Text	First name of member	15
LastName	Text	Last name of member	30
Address	Text	Street address of member	50
City	Text	City member lives in	15
State	Text	State member lives in	2
Zip	Text	Zip code of member	10
Phone	Text	Phone number of member	14

c) Create a table that will store information on the progress of the members. After defining the fields below, save the table naming it Progress:

Field Name	Type	Description	Size	Format
MemberID 🔑	Text	ID of member	4	
Date 🔑	Date/Time	Date member joined		Short Date
Weight	Number	Weight in kg	Long Integer	
PercentBodyFat	Number	Percent of body fat	Single	Percent
BenchPress	Number	Weight in kg	Long Integer	

The primary key for the Progress table is the MemberID and Date fields together. This is because there can only be one record for a specific member on a specific date.

d) Create a form named Members for the Members table and enter the following five records:

DAFU; David; Fulcher; 102 4th St. Box 10; Fenton; MN; 16542; (816) 555-1002
GEAC; George; Ackerman; 998 TonTon Blvd.; Reese; MN; 54421; (816) 555-2376
GEMO; Geraldine; Monesinos; 617 Drayton Dr.; Fenton; MN; 16542; (816) 555-1443
LICO; Lindsey; Colby; 772 Satin Fig Leaf Lane; Reese; MN; 54421; (816) 555-0525
LUWO; Lucinda; Wolfe; 1102 New Haven Dr.; Reese; MN; 54421; (816) 555-0099

e) Create a form named Progress for the Progress table and enter the following eight records:

DAFU; 4/5/00; 96; 27%; 76
DAFU; 5/1/00; 98; 25%; 85
GEAC; 10/23/00; 76; 13%; 55
GEAC; 11/22/00; 80; 15%; 65
GEMO; 5/22/00; 48; 14%; 20
LICO; 9/12/00; 60; 25%; 40
LUWO; 2/14/00; 60; 31%; 25
LUWO; 3/14/00; 62; 27%; 39

f) Format the Members and Progress tables in Datasheet view appropriately.

g) Print all the tables.

h) Create and save a filter named Progress of GEAC that displays the progress results for MemberID GEAC. Apply the query and print the results.

The owner of Pizza Palace wants to use a relational database to store information on the company's employees and payroll history.

a) Using Access, create a relational database naming it Pizza Payroll.

b) Create a table that will store information on the employees. After defining the fields below, save the table naming it Employees:

Field Name	Type	Description	Size
EmployeeID ⚷	Text	ID of employee	2
FirstName	Text	First name of employee	15
LastName	Text	Last name of employee	30
Address	Text	Street address of employee	50
City	Text	City employee lives in	15
State	Text	State employee lives in	2
Zip	Text	Zip code of employee	10
Phone	Text	Phone number of employee	14

c) Create a table that will store information on the payroll history. After defining the fields below, save the table naming it Payroll:

Field Name	Type	Description	Size	Format	Decimals
EmployeeID ⚷	Text	ID of employee	2		
Date ⚷	Date/Time	Date of paycheck		Short Date	
GrossPay	Currency	Employee's gross pay			2
Taxes	Currency	Tax deductions			2

The primary key for the Payroll table is the EmployeeID and Date fields together. This is because there can only be one record for a specific employee on a specific date.

d) Create a form named Employees for the Employees table and enter the following five records:

EI; Edna; Incahatoe; 254 20th St.; Armine; CT; 19154; (332) 555-1765
JF; Jess; Frank; 101 Red Villa Circle; Armine; CT; 19154; (332) 555-2792
RD; Rita; DiPasquale; 5672 56th Ct.; Weidner; CT; 77165; (332) 555-0276
TW; Thomas; Warner; 11 Roni Dr.; Weidner; CT; 77165; (332) 555-2665
WF; Wimberly; Franco; 86 Luther Ct.; Weidner; CT; 77165; (332) 555-1711

e) Create a form named Payroll for the Payroll table and enter the following ten records:

EI; 3/13/01; 244; 36.60
EI; 3/20/01; 254; 38.10
JF; 3/20/01; 191.67; 28.75
JF; 3/27/01; 210.75; 31.50
RD; 3/6/01; 175; 26.25
RD; 3/13/01; 180; 27
TW; 3/6/01; 210.24; 31.53
TW; 3/13/01; 225.64; 33.84
WF; 3/13/01; 187.82; 28.17
WF; 3/20/01; 195.25; 29.28

f) Format the Employees and Payroll tables in Datasheet view appropriately.

g) Print all the tables.

h) Create and save a filter named WF 3/13/01 Payroll that displays the payroll for the employee with ID WF for the pay date 3/13/01.

Exercise 11 ——————————————— Coral Research

The researchers who created the coral reef study proposal you edited in previous chapters want to create a relational database which will store their research findings.

a) Using Access, create a relational database naming it Coral Research.

b) Create a table that will store information on the kind of coral being studied and its location. After defining the fields below, save the table naming it Coral Sites:

Field Name	Type	Description	Size
SiteID ⚷	AutoNumber	ID of site location	Long Integer
CoralName	Text	Name of coral	20
Color	Text	Main color of coral	15
Description	Text	Identifying features	30

c) Create a table that will store information on the observed growth of the corals being studied. After defining the fields below, save the table naming it Growth Research:

Field Name	Type	Description	Size	Format	Decimals
Date ⚷	Date/Time	Date of observation		Short Date	
SiteID ⚷	Number	Location of the coral	Long Integer		
Time	Date/Time	Time of observation		Medium Time	
Size	Number	Coral's size in m	Single		3

The primary key for the Growth Research table is the Date and SiteID fields together. This is because there can only be one record for a specific site on a specific date.

d) Create a form named Coral Sites for the Coral Sites table and enter the following five records:

Slimy Sea Plume; violet; feather-like
Yellow Sea Whip; bright yellow; branched colonies
Knobby Brain Coral; tan; hemispherical heads
Scroll Coral; light gray; rounded, thin blades
Venus Sea Fan; lavender; network of branches

e) Create a form named Growth Research for the Growth Research table and enter the following six records:

5/8/00; 1; 6:10 AM; 0.8378
5/12/00; 2; 8:15 AM; 0.2045
5/25/00; 3; 7:25 AM; 0.144
6/2/00; 4; 6:35 AM; 1.387
5/11/01; 2; 8:15 AM; 0.205
6/4/01; 4; 6:35 AM; 1.389

f) Format the Coral Sites and Growth Research tables in Datasheet view appropriately.

g) Print both tables.

h) Create and save a filter named Growth Data for Site 2 that displays the growth research records for the site with ID 2. Apply the query and then print the results.

Exercise 12 ——————————————— Travel Agency

The Hot Spot travel agency wants to use a relational database to store information on its travel bookings.

a) Using Access, create a relational database naming it Travel Agency.

b) Create a table that will store information on Hot Spot's clients. After defining the fields below, save the table naming it Clients:

Field Name	Type	Description	Size
ClientID ⚷	Text	ID of client	2
FirstName	Text	First name of client	15
LastName	Text	Last name of client	30
Address	Text	Street address of client	50
City	Text	City client lives in	15
State	Text	State client lives in	2
Zip	Text	Zip code of client	10
Phone	Text	Phone number of client	14

c) Create a table that will store information on the vacation packages that Hot Spot offers. After defining the fields below, save the table naming it Vacations:

Field Name	Type	Description	Size	Decimals
Package ⚷	Text	Name of vacation package	20	
Cost	Currency	Cost of vacation		0
Nights	Number	Number of nights	Long Integer	
Location	Text	State/Country of vacation	30	
Type	Text	Type of vacation	15	

d) Create a table that will store information on the vacation packages that the clients have purchased. After defining the fields below, save the table naming it Booked Vacations:

Field Name	Type	Description	Size	Format
ClientID ⚷	Text	ID of client	2	
Date ⚷	Date/Time	Date vacation started		Short Date
Package	Text	Name of vacation package	20	

The primary key for the Booked Vacations table is the ClientID and Date fields together. This is because there can be only one record for a specific client on a specific date.

e) Create a form named Clients for the Clients table and enter the following six records:

DM; Diane; Mason; 8 Westchester Place; Bedrock; IL; 56224; (445) 555-1552
GM; Gail; Mintzer; 8891 SW 63rd Circle; Wilbraham; IL 76209; (298) 555-7392
HQ; Harvey; Quay; 33 Buren Blvd. Apt. 452; Wilbraham; IL 76209; (298) 555-7782
JU; Juan; Ulloa; 352 Eagle Trace Blvd.; Bedrock; IL; 56224; (445) 555-0287
RP; Richard; Pompeneur; 240 Keisha St.; Bedrock; IL; 56224; (445) 555-0208
SV; Sandy; Vanderhorn; 102 343th Terrace; Wilbraham; IL; 56624; (445) 555-8927

f) Create a form named Vacations for the Vacations table and enter the following seven records:

Beach Fun; 475; 7; Bahamas; Relaxing
City Dude; 725; 5; Texas; Adventure
French Getaway; 1,525; 7; France; Sightseeing
HighRiser Crusade; 823; 8; New York; Sightseeing
Honalulu Hideaway; 950; 3; Hawaii; Relaxing
Mountain Explorer; 420; 3; Vermont; Ski
Summit Skiing; 1,250; 5; Switzerland; Ski

g) Create a form named Booked Vacations for the Booked Vacations table and enter the following nine records:

DM; 4/21/01; HighRiser Crusade
GM; 1/5/01; Honalulu Hideaway
GM; 11/4/01; HighRiser Crusade
HQ; 2/16/01; Mountain Explorer
JU; 12/8/00; French Getaway
JU; 5/20/01; Beach Fun
JU; 12/13/01; Summit Skiing
RP; 11/23/01; Mountain Explorer
SV; 10/18/01; City Dude

h) Format the Clients, Vacations, and Booked Vacations tables in Datasheet view appropriately.

i) Print all the tables.

j) Create and save a filter named Adventure or Relaxing Vacations that displays the vacation records that are adventure or relaxing types. Apply the query and then print the results.

Advanced
Exercise 13 ———————————————————— Club

Design a relational database that organizes and stores information on a club or organization you belong to. Follow the four guidelines in Section 12.4 to design the database. Use Access to create the relational database naming it Club. Create a form for each table and enter at least five records in each table. Format the tables in Datasheet view appropriately. Print all the tables in your relational database in the appropriate orientation. Create and save a filter that queries one of the tables and print the results.

Advanced
Exercise 14 ———————————————————— Music

Design a relational database that organizes and stores information on past or upcoming music events and performers. Follow the four guidelines in Section 12.4 to design the database. Use Access to create the relational database naming it Music. Create a form for each table and enter at least five records in each table. Format the tables in Datasheet view appropriately. Print all the tables in your relational database in the appropriate orientation. Create and save a filter that queries one of the tables and print the results.

Advanced
Exercise 15 ———————————————————— Sports

Design a relational database that organizes and stores information on your favorite sports teams or sports event. Follow the four guidelines in Section 12.4 to design the database. Use Access to create the relational database naming it Sports. Create a form for each table and enter at least five records in each table. Format the tables in Datasheet view appropriately. Print all the tables in your relational database in the appropriate orientation. Create and save a filter that queries one of the tables and print the results.

Chapter Thirteen
Relational Database Techniques

Delete Rows

Sort Ascending

Sort Descending

Delete Record

Relationships

Show Table

Run

Save

Columns

Delete Columns

Save As

Chapter Thirteen Objectives

After completing this chapter you will be able to:

1. Add, rename, and delete a field.
2. Sort records.
3. Add, update, and delete a record.
4. Define relationships.
5. View a table's subdatasheets.
6. Create and use select queries.
7. Modify a select query.
8. Sort select query results.
9. Create range queries.
10. Create and use complex select queries.

$\mathbf{T}$his chapter describes the steps necessary to modify a table's design, modify the records in a table, and change the order of records in a table. A second way of querying, called select queries, is also explained.

13.1 Modifying a Table

A table can be modified by adding a new field, renaming a field, or deleting a field. Modifications to a table should be done in Design view.

displaying a table in Design view

A table is displayed in Design view by clicking on the Tables button in the Database window, clicking once on the desired table name, and then clicking on the Design button at the top of the Database window. A displayed table can be switched between Design view and Datasheet view by clicking the View button (▦) on the Toolbar.

renaming a field

A field is renamed by placing the cursor in the appropriate Field Name box in Design view, editing the existing text, and then pressing Enter.

adding a field

A field is added to a table by entering the field's name, type, and description in the first blank row after the last field in Design view. Next, the field's size, format, and decimal places, if necessary, are defined in the Field Properties part of the window.

deleting a field

A field is deleted by right-clicking on the desired field name in Design view and then selecting the Delete Rows command from the pop-up menu, which displays a warning dialog box:

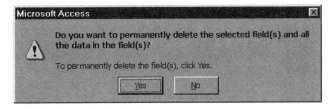

Access warns you when a field is about to be deleted

Selecting Yes removes the field and any data in that field from every record in the table. Selecting No retains the field.

updating a form

When the fields of a table have been modified, the table's corresponding form must be updated. The best way to update a form is to create a new one as explained in Section 12.10. After creating the new form it should be saved with the same name as the original, which will cause Access to display a message asking if you want to replace the existing form. Selecting Yes replaces the existing form with the new, updated form.

13.2 Sorting Records

alphabetical
chronological

Placing records in a specified order is called *sorting*. In Access, records can be sorted in either ascending or descending order based on the entries of a specified field. Ascending order is also called *alphabetical order* when the entries are text, and *chronological order* when the entries are times or dates.

  The Sort Ascending () and Sort Descending () buttons on the Toolbar are used to sort records. When the desired Sort button is clicked, records are ordered based on the entries of the field that contains the cursor. For example, to place the records in the Packs table in alphabetical order by color, an entry in the Color field is clicked to place the cursor in that field. Next, clicking the Sort Ascending button orders the records based on color.

Sorting the records of a table does not affect the order of records in a form. The records in a form are ordered by clicking on the desired entry and then clicking the appropriate Sort button.

The Sort <u>A</u>scending and Sort Des<u>c</u>ending commands in the <u>S</u>ort submenu from the <u>R</u>ecords menu can also be used to sort records.

Practice 1

In this practice you will modify the Customers table of the Backpacks database, update the Customers form, and sort the Customers table and form.

1) OPEN BACKPACKS

2) DISPLAY THE CUSTOMERS TABLE IN DESIGN VIEW

a. In the Backpacks : Database window, select the Tables button if it is not already selected.
b. Click on the Customers table name to select it.
c. At the top of the Database window, click on the Design button. The Customers table is displayed in Design view.

3) EDIT THE NAME FIELD

a. Click on the Name field name.
b. Edit the field name so that is appears as CustomerName.
c. Select <u>F</u>ile → <u>S</u>ave. The modified Customers table is saved.
d. On the Toolbar, click on the View button (). The Customers table is displayed in Datasheet view. Note the CustomerName field in place of the Name field.
e. Close the Customers table.

4) UPDATE THE CUSTOMERS FORM

a. In the Backpacks : Database window, select the Forms button.
b. Double-click on the Create form by using wizard icon. A dialog box is displayed.
   1. In the Tables/Queries list, select Table : Customers. The fields of the Customers table are displayed in the Available Fields list.
   2. Click on the >> button. All the fields from the Available Fields list are moved to the Selected Fields list.
   3. Select the Next button. The form layout options are displayed.
   4. Select the Columnar option if it is not already selected.
   5. Select the Next button. The form style options are displayed.
   6. Select the Standard option if it is not already selected.

7. Select the Next button. The dialog box displays an entry box for the form title and an option for viewing the form.
8. In the What title do you want for your form? entry box, type Customers.
9. Select the Open the form to view or enter information option if it is not already selected.
10. Select the Finish button. A dialog box is displayed.
   a. Select Yes. The new form replaced the existing form. Note the CustomerName field name.

5) SORT THE CUSTOMERS FORM

a. Place the cursor in the CustomerName field.
b. On the Toolbar, click on the Sort Descending button (⬛).
c. Use the record controls at the bottom of the form to scroll through the records. Note that the records are now in reverse alphabetical order by customer name.
d. Close the form.

6) SORT THE CUSTOMERS TABLE

a. Open the Customers table in Datasheet view.
b. Place the cursor in a CustomerName field entry.
c. On the Toolbar, click on the Sort Descending button (⬛). Note that the records are now in reverse alphabetical order by customer name.
d. Save and then close the table.

13.3 Modifying Records

Modifying records includes adding new records, changing the entries in existing records, and deleting records. Records should be modified using the appropriate form because a form displays only one record at a time, which may reduce errors.

adding a record

A new record is added by clicking the ⬛ record control at the bottom of a form to display a blank record. Next, the entries of the new record are typed.

updating

Changing the entries in an existing record is called *updating*. The record controls at the bottom of a form can be used to scroll the records until the record for updating is displayed. Alternatively, a filter may be applied to quickly find the record for updating. A displayed record is updated by double-clicking the desired entry and then typing to replace the existing entry. An entry can be edited by clicking once on the desired entry to place the cursor.

deleting a record

The Delete Record button (⬛) on the Toolbar is used to delete the record displayed by a form. The Delete Record command from the Edit menu may also be used. To display the appropriate record for deleting, the record controls at the bottom of a form are used to scroll the records. When Delete Record is executed, Access displays a warning dialog box:

Selecting Yes removes the active record. Selecting No retains the record.

Practice 2

In this practice you will modify records in the Backpacks database. Open Backpacks if it is not already displayed.

1) ADD A NEW TRANSACTIONS RECORD

a. Display the Transactions form.
b. At the bottom of the form, click on the ▶* record control to display an empty record.
c. Since the TransID field is type AutoNumber, there is no need to make an entry in that field. Starting with the Date field, enter the remaining field entries for the new transaction record:
9/24/01, SOS-21, H203, 15
d. Close the form.
e. Display the Transactions table. Note the new record.
f. Close the Transactions table.

2) UPDATE A PACKS RECORD

a. Display the Packs form.
b. On the Toolbar, click on the Filter By Form button. The Packs form is displayed in Filter by Form view.
    1. In the ItemNumber field, select the H202 entry.
    2. Delete any other criteria on the form.
    3. On the Toolbar, click on the Apply Filter button. The H202 pack record is displayed.
c. Double-click on the Color field entry to highlight it.
d. Type stone to replace the current color, khaki.
e. On the Toolbar, click on the Remove Filter button.
f. Close the Packs form.
g. Display the Packs table. Note the updated record.
h. Close the Packs table.

13.4 Defining Relationships

related

Two tables are *related* when the field in one table corresponds to a field in another table. Every table in a relational database must be related to at least one other table. For example, in the Backpacks database, the Transactions and Packs tables are related by the ItemNumber field and the Customers table is related to the Transactions table by the CustomerNumber field.

Access needs to know the relationships between tables so that data can be joined appropriately. For two fields to define a relationship, the type of data they store must be the same. Typically, the field names are also the same, but can be different.

Relationships are defined by clicking the Relationships button (⧉) on the Toolbar or by selecting the Relationships command from the Tools menu, which displays the Relationships window. If relationships have not yet been defined for a database, the Show Table dialog box is automatically displayed:

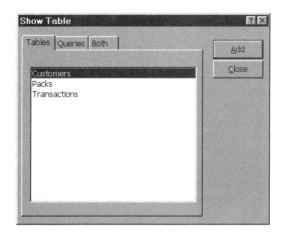

Clicking on a table name and then selecting the Add button adds that table to the Relationships window. When a database has not had any relationships defined, all of its tables must be added to the Relationships window so that their relationships can be defined. For the Backpacks database, the Relationships window with all the tables added looks similar to:

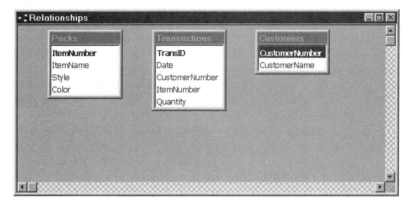

Relationships are defined in the Relationships window

To create a relationship, the field of one table is dragged to the field it relates to in the other table. When a field is dragged it appears like a small box. For the Backpacks database, the relationship between the Packs and Transactions tables is defined by dragging the ItemNumber field of the Packs table to the ItemNumber field of the Transactions table:

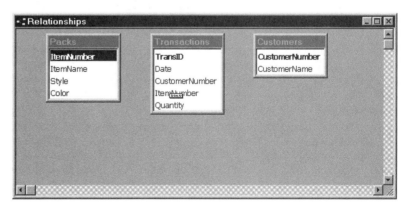

Releasing the mouse button displays the Edit Relationships dialog box:

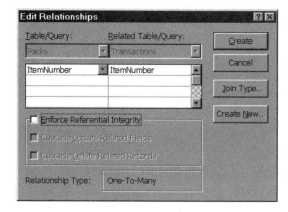

After verifying the related fields, Create is selected to create the relationship. A line is displayed between the two tables to indicate the relationship. When all the relationships in the Backpacks database are defined, the Relationships window looks similar to:

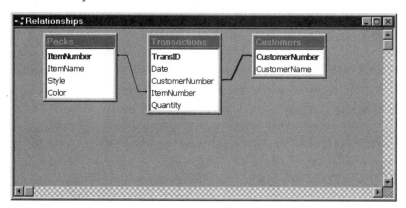

 Once the relationships for a database have been defined they need not be changed unless a table is added or a field defining a relationship changes. To add a table to the relationships window, the Show Table button ( ) from the Toolbar is clicked or the Show Table command from the Relationships menu is selected.

13.5 Using Subdatasheets

Subdatasheets are available in Datasheet view when relationships have been defined. A *subdatasheet* shows records related to a particular record.

expand indicator

An *expand indicator* ( ) is displayed next to each record of a table when subdatasheets are available. Clicking on this indicator displays the subdatasheet for that record. For example, in the Backpacks database, the Packs table is related to the Transactions table. Therefore, a subdatasheet in the Packs table shows a record's relation to the Transactions table:

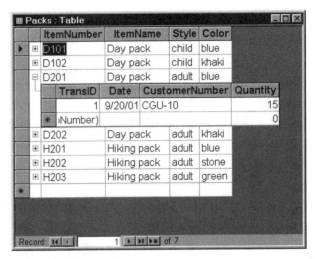

A subdatasheet is displayed by clicking on a record's expand indicator

contract indicator

In this case, the subdatasheet shows that customer CGU-10 ordered 15 of item D201. An expand indicator changes to a *contract indicator* (⊟) when a subdatasheet is displayed. Clicking on the contract indicator removes the subdatasheet.

Practice 3

In this practice you will define the relationships of the Backpacks database and then view subdatasheets. Open Backpacks if it is not already displayed.

1) DEFINE THE RELATIONSHIPS BETWEEN THE BACKPACKS TABLES

    a. On the Toolbar, click on the Relationships button ( ). The Relationships window is displayed with the Show Table dialog box on top.

        1. Click on Packs and then select **Add**. The Packs table is added to the window.

        2. Click on Transactions and then select **Add**. The Transactions table is added to the window.

        3. Click on Customers and then select **Add**. The Customers table is added to the window.

        4. Select the **Close** button to remove the Show Table dialog box.

    b. In the Packs table, drag the ItemNumber field to the ItemNumber field in the Transactions table. A dialog box is displayed:

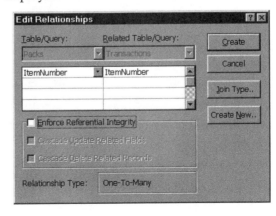

1. Verify that the ItemNumber field of the Packs table and the ItemNumber field of the Transactions table appear in the dialog box. If not, select Cancel and then drag the field again. If correct, select Create. A line is shown between the two fields indicating their relationship.

c. In the Customers table, drag the CustomerNumber field to the CustomerNumber field in the Transactions table. A dialog box is displayed:

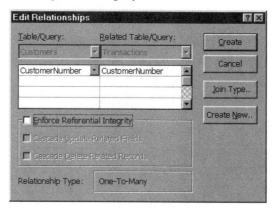

1. Verify that the CustomerNumber field of the Customers table and the CustomerNumber field of the Transactions table appear in the dialog box. If not, select Cancel and then drag the field again. If correct, select Create. A line is shown between the two fields indicating their relationship.

2) CLOSE THE RELATIONSHIPS WINDOW

Note that relationships exist between all the tables of the database. This is an important aspect of a relational database.

a. Select File → Save. The database relationships are saved.
b. Click on the Relationships window's Close button. The Relationships window is closed.

3) VIEW A SUBDATASHEET

a. Open the Packs table in Datasheet view. Note that each record displays an expand indicator.
b. Click on the expand indicator (⊞) for item D101. A subdatasheet is displayed. Note that there are no orders associated with this item.
c. Click on the expand indicator for item D102. A subdatasheet with one order record is displayed.
d. Click on the contract indicator (⊟) of the records to close the subdatasheets.
e. Close the Packs table.

13.6 Using Select Queries

In Chapter Twelve, filtering was used to limit the records displayed in a table. Another way to view data in a relational database is by applying a select query. A *select query* can include fields from any table and uses the relationships between tables to determine which data to display. The results of a select query are displayed in a datasheet.

The steps for creating a select query in Design view are listed on the next page. Throughout the steps, a query for adult pack sales for the Backpacks database is created.

1. **Display a new select query in Design view.** Click the Queries button in the Objects list in the Database window and then double-click on the Create query in Design view icon to display the Select Query window and the Show Table dialog box:

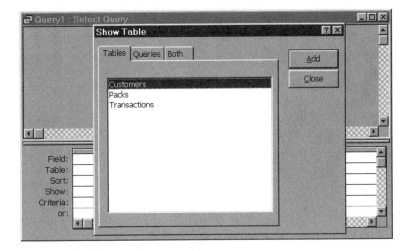

2. **Add the required tables to the select query.** In the Show Table dialog box, click on the appropriate table name and then select the Add button for each table needed by the query:

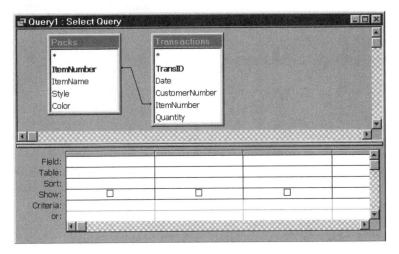

   Note the line indicating that the tables are related. The tables in a select query must be related for the query to work properly.

design grid 3. **Add fields to the design grid.** The *design grid* is where fields to be displayed by the select query must appear. To add a field to the design grid, drag it from the table to the desired Field box in the design grid, or click in the desired Field box and select the field from the collapsible list:

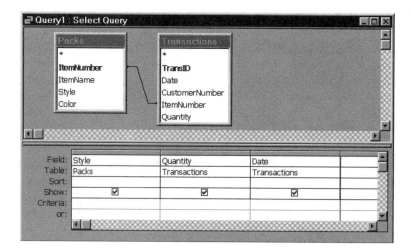

4. **Enter the criteria.** The Criteria line is where criteria is typed:

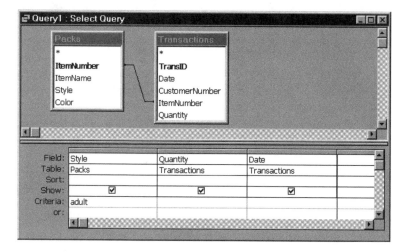

Numeric Query Criteria

Numeric criteria should be specified using only numbers and necessary decimal places. Including any other character such as a dollar sign, comma, or percent sign will result in an error.

5. **Display the query results.** Click the Run button () on the Toolbar or select the Run command from the Query menu. The select query results are shown in Datasheet view:

Style	Quantity	Date
adult	15	9/20/01
adult	25	9/21/01
adult	6	9/24/01
adult	15	9/24/01

6. **Save the select query.** With the query datasheet displayed, select the Save command from the File menu to display the Save As dialog box. Type a descriptive name in the Query Name entry box and select OK.

After saving a select query, it can be applied by clicking on the Queries button in the Objects list in the Database window and then double-clicking the desired select query name.

A Guide to Microsoft Office 2000 Professional

How a Select Query Works

When a select query is run, Access first *joins* the tables used in the query to form a new set of records. For example, the Packs and Transactions tables are shown below:

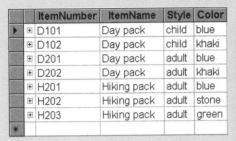

	ItemNumber	ItemName	Style	Color
⊞	D101	Day pack	child	blue
⊞	D102	Day pack	child	khaki
⊞	D201	Day pack	adult	blue
⊞	D202	Day pack	adult	khaki
⊞	H201	Hiking pack	adult	blue
⊞	H202	Hiking pack	adult	stone
⊞	H203	Hiking pack	adult	green
*				

	TransID	Date	CustomerNumber	ItemNumber	Quantity
	1	9/20/01	CGU-10	D201	15
	2	9/20/01	CGU-10	D102	10
	3	9/21/01	IUB-5	D202	25
	4	9/24/01	SOS-21	H201	6
	5	9/24/01	SOS-21	H203	15
*	Number)				0

To join the tables, Access compares the entries of the related fields for each table and joins records that have the same entries, resulting in one large table. The field relating Packs and Transactions is ItemNumber. A join results in the following:

Packs.ItemNumber	ItemName	Style	Color	TransID	Date	CustomerNumber	Transactions.ItemNumber	Quantity
D102	Day pack	child	khaki	2	9/20/01	CGU-10	D102	10
D201	Day pack	adult	blue	1	9/20/01	CGU-10	D201	15
D202	Day pack	adult	khaki	3	9/21/01	IUB-5	D202	25
H201	Hiking pack	adult	blue	4	9/24/01	SOS-21	H201	6
H203	Hiking pack	adult	green	5	9/24/01	SOS-21	H203	15

Access then filters the join table for the records that meet the query criteria defined in select query Design view. For the adult backpack sales query, the filtered join table looks similar to:

Packs.ItemNumber	ItemName	Style	Color	TransID	Date	CustomerNumber	Transactions.ItemNumber	Quantity
D201	Day pack	adult	blue	1	9/20/01	CGU-10	D201	15
D202	Day pack	adult	khaki	3	9/21/01	IUB-5	D202	25
H201	Hiking pack	adult	blue	4	9/24/01	SOS-21	H201	6
H203	Hiking pack	adult	green	5	9/24/01	SOS-21	H203	15

Access then displays the selected fields in Datasheet view. For the adult pack sales query, the Style, Quantity, and Date fields were selected which results in the following:

Query1 : Select Query

	Style	Quantity	Date
▶	adult	15	9/20/01
	adult	25	9/21/01
	adult	6	9/24/01
	adult	15	9/24/01
*			

Practice 4

In this practice you will create the adult pack sales select query. Open Backpacks if it is not already displayed.

1) ADD TABLES TO THE SELECT QUERY WINDOW

    a. In the Backpacks : Database window, select the Queries button.

    b. Double-click on the Create query in Design view icon. The Select Query window is displayed with the Show Table dialog box on top.

        1. Click on the Packs table name if it is not already selected and then select **Add**. The Packs table is added to the Select Query window.

        2. Click on the Transactions table name and then select **Add**. The Transactions table is added to the Select Query window.

        3. Select **Close**. The Show Table dialog box is removed.

2) ADD FIELDS TO THE DESIGN GRID

    a. Drag the Style field from the Packs table to the first Field box in the design grid.

    b. Drag the Quantity field from the Transactions table to the second Field box in the design grid.

    c. Drag the Date field from the Transactions table to the third Field box in the design grid. The design grid should look similar to:

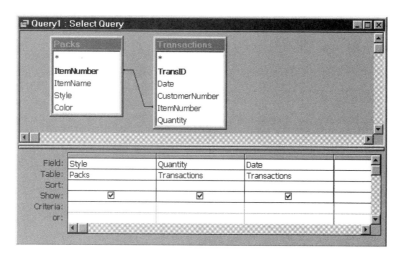

3) ADD CRITERIA TO THE DESIGN GRID

In the Criteria box of the first Field, type adult. The design grid should look similar to:

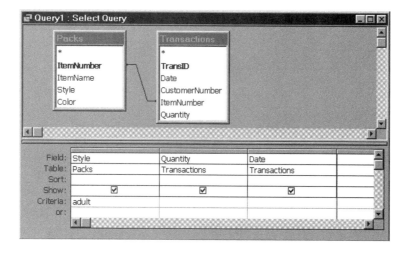

4) APPLY THE SELECT QUERY

    a. On the Toolbar, click the Run button (![]). The database is queried and the results shown in a datasheet. Note that four records are displayed:

Style	Quantity	Date
adult	15	9/20/01
adult	25	9/21/01
adult	6	9/24/01
adult	15	9/24/01

    b. Select File → Save. A dialog box is displayed.
        1. In the **Query Name** entry box, type Adult Pack Sales.
        2. Select OK. The query is saved.
    c. Select File → Print. A dialog box is displayed.
        1. Select OK. The datasheet is printed.
    d. Click on the Close button of the select query datasheet to remove the query results.

13.7 Modifying and Deleting a Select Query

A select query can be modified in Design view. If the select query datasheet is displayed, clicking on the View button (![]) on the Toolbar switches to Design view. A query saved with the database but not yet opened can be displayed in Design view by clicking on the **Queries** button of the Database window, clicking on the query name, and then clicking on the **Design** button at the top of the Database window.

removing and adding tables to select query Design view

A table is removed from select query Design view by clicking on it and then pressing the Delete key. When a table is removed, any of its fields in the design grid are also removed. A table is added using the Show Table dialog box, which is displayed by selecting the Show Table command from the Query menu or clicking on the Show Table button on the Toolbar (![]).

adding a column to the design grid

removing a column from the design grid

If a field needs to be added between existing fields in the design grid, a column must first be added to the design grid. A column is inserted into the design grid by selecting the Columns command from the Insert menu. The Columns command inserts a column to the left of the column containing the cursor. A column may also be deleted from the design grid by selecting the Delete Columns command from the Edit menu. The Delete Columns command removes the column containing the cursor and any field name and criteria it contains.

changing field order

The order in which fields are displayed by a select query is modified by reordering the fields in the design grid of the select query. To move a column in the design grid, it must be selected and then dragged to a new location, similar to moving a field in Datasheet view.

saving a query with a different name

A query can be saved under a different name by selecting the Save As command from the File menu. When Save As is selected, the Save As dialog box is displayed with an entry box for a new query name. For example, the Adult Pack Sales query could be modified to display child pack sales and then renamed using Save As:

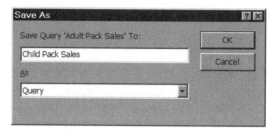

A modified query can be saved under a different name

deleting a query

A query is deleted by clicking on its name in the Database window and then pressing the Delete key. Access will display a warning dialog box. Selecting Yes removes the query.

13.8 Sorting Select Query Results

The results of the Adult Pack Sales select query would best be displayed in order by quantity. The order of a select query's records is designated by clicking in the Sort box of the desired field in the design grid and selecting an order from the Sort collapsible list. For example, Design view for the Adult Pack Sales query looks similar to the following after modifying it to display records in order by quantity:

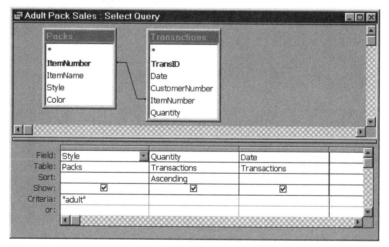

A Sort box is used to define a sort order for a select query datasheet

When the query is run, the records of the select query datasheet are sorted by quantity.

Practice 5

In this practice you will modify the Adult Pack Sales query and create a Child Pack Sales query. Open Backpacks if it is not already displayed.

1) MODIFY THE ADULT PACK SALES SELECT QUERY

   a. In the Backpacks : Database window, select the Queries button if query names are not already displayed.
   b. Click on Adult Pack Sales and then select the Design button at the top of the Database window. The Adult Pack Sales select query is displayed in Design view.
   c. In the Quantity column of the design grid, click in the Sort box. A down arrow is displayed in the box indicating a collapsible list is available.
   d. From the Sort collapsible list, select Ascending. The design grid should look similar to:

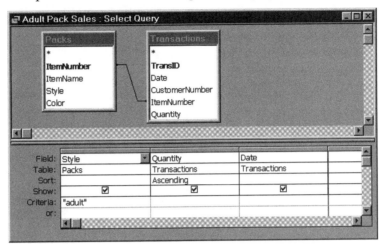

   e. Run the query. The Adult Pack Sales query results are displayed in order by quantity.
   f. Save the Adult Pack Sales select query.
   g. Print and then close the datasheet.

2) CREATE A CHILD PACK SALES SELECT QUERY

   a. Open the Adult Pack Sales query in Design view.
   b. Change the criteria of the Style field to child. The design grid should look similar to:

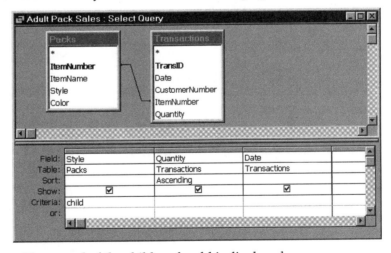

   c. Run the query. The record of the child pack sold is displayed.
   d. Select File → Save As. A dialog box is displayed.
       1. Type Child Pack Sales as the new query name.
       2. Select OK. The query is saved.
   e. Print and then close the datasheet.

3) CLOSE BACKPACKS

13.9 Range Queries

A *range query* has criteria that includes many different values. For example, a query that displays transactions that occurred after 9/20/01 has the criteria "a date later than 9/20/01" in the Date field. This kind of criteria is specified using relational operators:

relational operators

>   greater than
>=   greater than or equal to
<   less than
<=   less than or equal to
<>   is not equal to

For the transactions after 9/20/01 query, the criteria is ">9/20/01".

Similarly, relational operators can be used to query for a range of numbers. For example, to display the records of transactions in which 20 or more items were purchased, the criteria ">=20" in the Quantity field is used.

Relational operators can also be used to compare text. For example, the criteria for querying for customers with names that come before the letter M alphabetically is "<M" in the Name field.

Practice 6

In this practice you will use the PACK SUPPLIERS relational database, which has a structure similar to the Backpacks database.

1) OPEN PACK SUPPLIERS

2) DETERMINE WHICH TRANSACTIONS OCCURRED AFTER 9/28/01

  a. In the PACK SUPPLIERS : Database window, click on the Queries button.
  b. Double-click on the Create query in Design view icon. The Select Query window is displayed with the Show Table dialog box on top.
      1. Click on the Transactions table name and then select Add. The Transactions table is added to the Select Query window.
      2. Click on the Customers table name and then select Add. The Customers table is added to the Select Query window.
      3. Select Close. The Show Table dialog box is removed.
  c. Drag the TransID field from the Transactions table to the first Field box in the design grid.
  d. Drag the Date field from the Transactions table to the second Field box in the design grid.
  e. Drag the CustomerName field from the Customers table to the third Field box in the design grid.
  f. Drag the ItemNumber field from the Transactions table to the fourth Field box in the design grid.
  g. In the Criteria box of Date type >9/28/01. The design grid should look similar to:

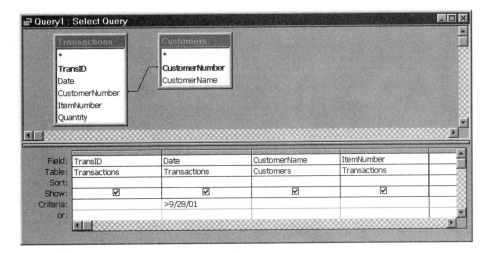

h. Run the query. The select query datasheet displays transactions that occurred on 9/29/01 and 9/30/01.
i. Save the query naming it Transactions after 9/28/01.
j. Print and then close the datasheet.

3) CREATE AND APPLY A TEXT RANGE QUERY

a. In the PACK SUPPLIERS : Database window, double-click on the Create query in Design view icon. The Select Query window is displayed with the Show Table dialog box on top.
   1. Add the Customers table to the Select Query window.
   2. Select Close. The Show Table dialog box is removed.
b. Drag the CustomerNumber field from the Customers table to the first Field box in the design grid.
c. Drag the CustomerName field from the Customers table to the second Field box in the design grid.
d. In the Criteria box of CustomerName type <=M.
e. In the CustomerName Sort box, select Ascending. The design grid should look similar to:

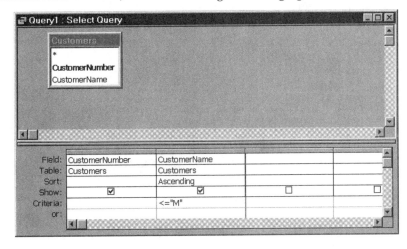

f. Run the query. The select query datasheet displays customers with names that start with a letter in the first half of the alphabet.
g. Save the query naming it A - M Customers.
h. Print and then close the datasheet.

13.10 Select Queries Involving And

Queries with *and* in the criteria require multiple entries in the Criteria row of a select query design grid. For example, the Pack Suppliers database could be queried to determine the items purchased in quantities greater than 15 by Graber National Park Store:

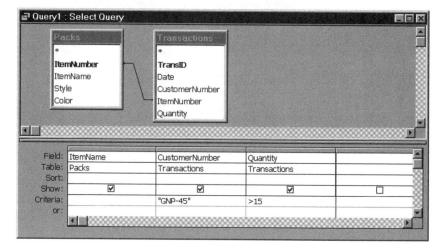

Practice 7

In this practice you will query the Pack Suppliers database. Open PACK SUPPLIERS if it is not already displayed.

1) DETERMINE THE ITEMS PURCHASED IN QUANTITIES GREATER THAN 15 BY GNP-45

   a. In the PACK SUPPLIERS : Database window, click on the Queries button if query names are not already displayed.
   b. Double-click on the Create query in Design view icon. The Select Query window is displayed with the Show Table dialog box on top.
      1. Add the Packs and Transactions tables to the Select Query window.
      2. Select **Close**. The Show Table dialog box is removed.
   c. Drag the ItemName field from the Packs table to the first Field box in the design grid.
   d. Drag the CustomerNumber and Quantity fields from the Transactions table to the second and third Field boxes in the design grid, respectively.
   e. In the Criteria box of CustomerNumber, type GNP-45.
   f. In the Criteria box of Quantity, type >15. The design grid should look similar to:

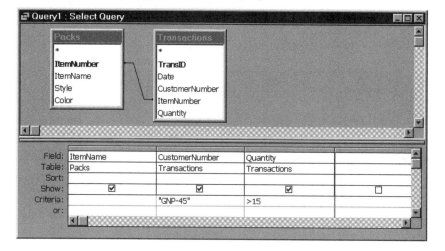

g. Run the query. The select query datasheet displays sales of items in quantities greater than 15 to Graber National Park Store.

h. Save the query naming it GNP-45 >15 Sales.

i. Print and then close the datasheet.

13.11 Select Queries Using Or

Just as the Or tab is used in filters for specifying complex query criteria, the or row of a select query design grid is used for complex select query criteria. For example, the PACK SUPPLIERS database could be queried to determine sales of 3 liter hydration packs. The criteria for this select query is "W204" in the ItemNumber field *or* "W205" in the ItemNumber field *or* "W206" in the ItemNumber field. The select query design grid for this query is:

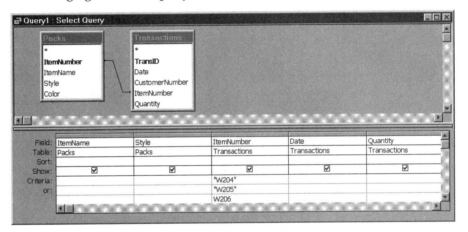

displaying additional rows for or criteria

The design grid of a select query may need to be expanded to accommodate multiple "or" criteria. Dragging the bottom of the select query Design view window expands the window to display more rows for or criteria.

As another example, the PACK SUPPLIERS database could be queried to determine sales of black packs and packs that sold in quantities greater than 75. The criteria for this select query is "black" in the Color field *or* ">75" in the Quantity field:

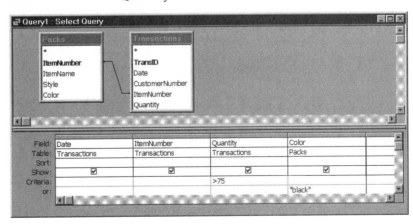

Practice 8

In this practice you will query the Pack Suppliers database. Open PACK SUPPLIERS if it is not already displayed.

1) DETERMINE THE SALES OF 3 L HYDRATION PACKS

    a. In the PACK SUPPLIERS : Database window, click on the Queries button if query names are not already displayed.

    b. Double-click on the Create query in Design view icon. The Select Query window is displayed with the Show Table dialog box on top.

        1. Add the Packs and Transactions tables to the Select Query window.

        2. Select Close. The Show Table dialog box is removed.

    c. Drag the ItemName and Style fields from the Packs table to the first and second Field boxes in the design grid, respectively.

    d. Drag the ItemNumber, Date, and Quantity fields from the Transactions table to the third, fourth, and fifth Field boxes in the design grid, respectively.

    e. In the Criteria box of ItemNumber, type W204.

    f. In the or box of ItemNumber, type W205.

    g. If necessary, drag the bottom of the Select Query window to expose another row for or criteria. In the second or box of ItemNumber, type W206. The design grid should look similar to:

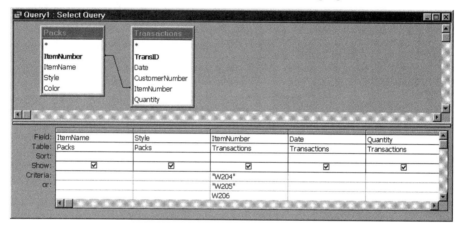

    h. Run the query. The select query datasheet displays four records.

    i. Save the query naming it 3 l Hydration Pack Sales.

    j. Print and then close the datasheet.

2) DETERMINE THE TRANSACTIONS OF TWO COMPANIES

    a. In the PACK SUPPLIERS : Database window, double-click on the Create query in Design view icon. The Select Query window is displayed with the Show Table dialog box on top.

        1. Add the Customers and Transactions tables to the Select Query window.

        2. Select Close. The Show Table dialog box is removed.

    b. Drag the CustomerName field from the Customers table to the first Field box in the design grid.

    c. Drag the Date, ItemNumber, and Quantity fields from the Transactions table to the second, third, and fourth Field boxes in the design grid, respectively.

    d. In the Criteria box of CustomerName, type Sage's Outdoor Supplies.

    e. In the or box of CustomerName, type ePacks Inc. The design grid should look similar to:

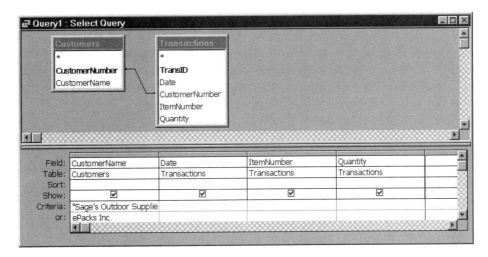

f. Run the query. The select query datasheet displays the transactions of two companies.

g. Save the query naming it SOS-21 and EPI-5 Sales.

h. Print and then close the datasheet.

3) DETERMINE THE SALES OF BLACK PACKS AND QUANTITIES GREATER THAN 75

a. In the PACK SUPPLIERS : Database window, double-click on the Create query in Design view icon. The Select Query window is displayed with the Show Table dialog box on top.

　1. Add the Packs and Transactions tables to the Select Query window.

　2. Select Close. The Show Table dialog box is removed.

b. Drag the Date, ItemNumber, and Quantity fields from the Transactions table to the first, second, and third Field boxes in the design grid, respectively.

c. Drag the Color field from the Packs table to the fourth Field box in the design grid.

d. In the or box of Color, type black.

e. In the Criteria box of Quantity, type >75. The design grid should look similar to:

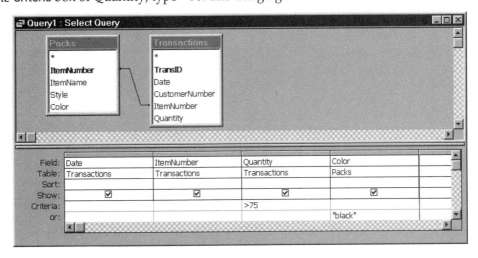

f. Run the query. The select query datasheet displays sales of black packs and the pack with sales in quantities greater than 75.

g. Save the query naming it Black Packs and >75 Packs.

h. Print and then close the datasheet.

4) CLOSE PACK SUPPLIERS

5) EXIT ACCESS

Chapter Summary

Modifications to a table should be done from Design view. After modifying a table, its corresponding form must be updated by creating a new form and saving it with the same name as the previous form.

The records of a table can be sorted to place them in a specified order. Records can be sorted in ascending or descending order using the Sort buttons on the Tool bar or the Sort submenu from the Records menu.

updating

Modifying records includes adding new records, changing the entries in existing records, and deleting records. Records are added using the record control. Changing the entries in an existing record is called updating. Records are deleted using the Delete Records button on the Toolbar or the Delete Record command from the Edit menu.

Modifications to records should be done using the appropriate form. The record controls at the bottom of a form can be used to locate the record to be modified. A filter may also be applied to display the record to be modified.

subdatasheets

In a relational database, each table must be related to another table by a field. Relationships between tables are defined using the Relationships button on the Toolbar or the Relationships command from the Tools menu. After relationships have been defined, subdatasheets are available in a table. A subdatasheet shows related records for a particular record.

select query

A select query is used to display field entries from any table in the database which match certain criteria. Access uses the relationships defined for the tables to determine which data to display. Select query results are displayed in a datasheet. There are six steps in creating a select query:

1. Display a new select query in Design view.
2. Add the required tables to the select query.
3. Add fields to the design grid.
4. Enter the criteria.
5. Display the query results.
6. Save the select query.

running a select query

An existing select query can be run by clicking on the Queries button in the Objects list in the Database window and then double-clicking on the desired select query name.

modifying a select query

A select query can be modified by first displaying the query in Design view. A table is removed by clicking on it and then pressing the Delete key. A table is added using the Show Table command from the Query menu. Fields can be added between existing fields by first inserting a column between the existing fields. A column is inserted by selecting the Insert Columns command from the Insert menu. Fields can be deleted from the design grid by deleting the column that contains the field. A column is deleted by selecting the Delete Columns command from the Edit menu.

Save As   A modified select query can be saved under a different name using the Save As command from the File menu. A select query is deleted by clicking on its name in the Database window and then pressing the Delete key.

sorting   Select query results can be sorted. The order of a select query's records is designated by clicking in the Sort box of the desired field in the design grid and selecting an order from the Sort collapsible list.

range query   A *range query* has criteria that includes many different entries. The criteria for this type of query is defined using relational operators (>, >=, <, <=, <>). Multiple entries can be entered in the Criteria row of the design
or row   grid for queries involving and. The or row in a select query's design grid is used for specifying complex criteria.

Vocabulary

Alphabetical order Sorting text in ascending order from A to Z.

Chronological order Sorting times and dates in ascending order.

Contract indicator Removes the subdatasheet for the active record.

Design grid Displayed in select query Design view and is where fields for the select query are added.

Expand indicator Displays the subdatasheet for the active record.

Range Query A query with criteria that includes many different entries.

Related Two tables with corresponding fields.

Select Query A query that includes fields from any table and uses the relationships between tables to determine which data to display.

Sorting Placing records in a specified order.

Subdatasheet Displays records related to a particular record. Available in Datasheet view when relationships have been defined

Updating Changing the entries in an existing record.

Access Commands and Buttons

Columns command Inserts a column in the design grid to the left of the column containing the cursor. Found in the Insert menu.

Delete Columns command Removes from the design grid the column containing the cursor and any field name and criteria it contains. Found in the Edit menu.

Delete Record command Deletes the record displayed by a form. Found in the Edit menu. The Delete Record button (⬚) on the Toolbar can be used instead of the command.

Delete Rows command Deletes the active field in a table displayed in Design view. Displayed by right-clicking on a field name.

Queries button Displays a list of queries in the database and is also used to create a select query. Found in the Objects list in the Database window.

Relationships command Displays the Relationships window where the relationships between the tables in the database can be defined. Found in the Tools menu. The Relationships button (⬚) on the Toolbar can be use instead of the command.

Run command Displays the select query results. Found in the Query menu. The Run button (⬚) on the Toolbar can be used instead of the command.

Save As command Displays a dialog box where a query can be saved under a different name. Found in the File menu.

Save command Used to save a select query. Found in the File menu.

Show Table command Displays a dialog box where the user can select a table to add to the Relationships window or select query Design view. Found in the Relationships menu or the Query menu. The Show Table button (⬚) on the Toolbar can be use instead of the command.

Sort Ascending command Sorts records in order from lowest to highest. Found in the Sort submenu from the Records menu. The Sort Ascending button (⬚) on the Toolbar can be used instead of the command.

Sort Descending command Sorts records in order from highest to lowest. Found in the Sort submenu from the Records menu. The Sort Descending button (⬚) on the Toolbar can be used instead of the command.

⬚ **View button** Switches the view between Datasheet view and Design view. Found on the Toolbar.

Review Questions

1. What view should a table be displayed in to modify its fields?

2. List the steps required to:
   a) rename a field.
   b) add a field.
   c) delete a field.

3. What must be updated after a field is added to an existing table?

4. a) What is sorting?
   b) List the steps required to sort a table by the FirstName field in descending order.

5. a) Why should a table's form be used to modify a record?
   b) How is a new, blank record displayed in a form?

6. a) What is updating?
   b) What should be applied to quickly display a record to be updated?

7. List the steps required to delete a record.

Sections 13.4 — 13.5

8. Is it necessary for the tables in a relational database to be related?

9. List the steps required to define a relationship between the two tables shown below:

CDs	Songs
CDNumber	SongNumber
Title	Title
Type	CDNumber
	SongLength

10. If a table is added to a database whose relationships have already been defined, how is the table added to the Relationships window?

11. a) What is a subdatasheet?
    b) When is a subdatasheet available?
    c) How is a subdatasheet viewed?
    d) How is a displayed subdatasheet removed from view?

Sections 13.6 — 13.11

12. a) What is a select query?
    b) What is a design grid?
    c) How are the results of a select query displayed?

13. List the steps required to create and run a select query.

14. What are the different ways an existing select query can be modified?

15. a) What command is used to add a column to the design grid of a select query?
    b) List the steps required to delete a table named Members from a select query Design view.

16. List the steps required to move the Date field of the Transactions table to the first column of the Adult Pack Sales select query created in the practices of this chapter.

17. List the steps required to save a select query under a different name.

18. Is it possible for the results of a select query to be displayed sorted? If so, how?

19. a) What is a range query?
    b) What are the relational operators that can be used in a range query?

20. How can a select query answer a question with "and" in the criteria?

21. What is the or row of a select query design grid used for?

Exercises

Exercise 1 ——————————————— FL COLLEGES

The FL COLLEGES relational database modified in Chapter Twelve, Exercise 1 needs to be updated and select queries applied to it. Open FL COLLEGES and complete the following steps:

a) In the Colleges table, change the Name field to CollegeName.

b) Update the Colleges form appropriately.

c) Add the following record to the Colleges table:

   Florida A&M University; Tallahassee; 10,702

d) Sort the Cities table by Population in descending order and then save and print the table.

e) The Cities and Colleges tables are related by the City field. Create the appropriate relationship between the Cities and Colleges tables.

f) Create a select query that displays the CollegeName, County, and Enrollment fields for those colleges located in Leon county. Save the select query naming it Leon County Colleges. Print the select query datasheet.

g) Create a select query that displays the CollegeName, City, Population, and Enrollment fields for those colleges that are in cities with a population greater than 300,000 and have an enrollment less than 30,000. Save the select query naming it Population > 300,000 and Enrollment < 30,000. Print the select query datasheet.

Exercise 2 ——————————————— Museum Exhibits

The Museum Exhibits relational database created in Chapter Twelve, Exercise 2 needs to be updated and queries applied. Open Museum Exhibits and complete the following steps:

a) In the Exhibits table, change the Name field to ExhibitName.

b) Update the Exhibits form appropriately.

c) Add the following record to the Exhibits table:

   WDH1; Physics; Why Does That Happen; 5/28/01

d) The attendance at the Earth's Interior exhibit (LWL2) in 2000 was recorded incorrectly. The correct attendance was 1,815. Update the appropriate record in the Attendance form.

e) Sort the Exhibits table by ExhibitName in ascending order and then save and print the table.

f) The Exhibits and Attendance tables are related by the ExhibitID field. Create the appropriate relationship between the Exhibits and Attendance tables.

g) Create a select query that displays the ExhibitID, ExhibitName, Attendance, and Year fields of exhibits with an attendance over 1,500 in 2002. The query results should be sorted in descending order by attendance. Save the select query naming it 2002 Attendance over 1,500. Print the select query datasheet.

h) Create a select query that displays the ExhibitName, Updated, Attendance, and Year fields of exhibits with an attendance over 1,500 in 2002 and last updated before 1/1/99. Save the select query naming it 2002 Attendance over 1,500 & Updated before 99. Print the select query datasheet.

Exercise 3 ✵ —————————————————————————— Library

The Library relational database created in Chapter Twelve, Exercise 3 needs to be updated and queries applied. Open Library and complete the following steps:

a) The ISBN for The College Guide was recorded incorrectly. The correct ISBN is 1-879233-03-7. Update the appropriate record in the Books form.

b) Add the following records to the Books table:

    1-879233-94-0; The Graduate College Guide; Reference; TB22
    1-879233-88-6; The Green Door; Drama; ZT19

c) Sort the Books table by Title in ascending order and then save and print the table.

d) The Books and Authors tables are related by the AuthorID field. Create the appropriate relationship between the Books and Authors tables.

e) Create a select query that displays the AuthorID, FirstName, LastName, and Title fields of books authored by TB22. Save the select query naming it Books by TB22. Print the select query datasheet.

f) Create a select query that displays the FirstName, LastName, Title, and Type fields of books that are of drama or mystery type. The query results should be sorted in ascending order by the author's last name. Save the select query naming it Drama or Mystery. Print the select query datasheet.

Exercise 4 ✵ ————————————————————— Space Shuttle Missions

The Space Shuttle Missions relational database created in Chapter Twelve, Exercise 4 needs to be updated and queries applied. Open Space Shuttle Missions and complete the following steps:

a) The Orbiter Vehicles and Missions tables are related by the OrbiterID fields. The Astronauts and Missions tables are related by the AstronautID and CommanderID fields. Create the appropriate relationships between the tables.

b) Create a select query that displays the FirstName, LastName, Name, and LaunchDate fields of all John Caspar's missions. Save the select query naming it Caspar Missions. Print the select query datasheet.

c) Create a select query that displays the FirstName, LastName, and LaunchDates of all missions after 1995. Save the select query naming it Missions After 1995. Print the select query datasheet.

d) Create a select query that displays the Name, FirstName, LastName, and LaunchDate fields of all missions in which the shuttle Columbia was used. Save the select query naming it Columbia Shuttle Missions. Print the select query datasheet.

Exercise 5 ———————————————————————— Boat Storage

The Boat Storage relational database was created in Chapter Twelve, Exercise 5. Open Boat Storage and then add a record and apply queries as follows:

a) Add the following record to the Boats table:

Sunshine; 1; NG12; 70; 4

b) The Employees and Boats tables are related by the EmployeeID field. The Boats table and Boat Owners table are related by the OwnerID field. Create the appropriate relationships between the Employees, Boats, and Boat Owners tables.

c) Create a select query that displays the Boat, OwnerID, FirstName of owner, LastName of owner, and Fee fields for those boats owned by OwnerID 2. Save the select query naming it OwnerID 2 Boats. Print the select query datasheet.

d) Create a select query that displays the Boat, Fee, FirstName of owner, and LastName of owner fields of those boats with a monthly fee greater than or equal to $70. The query should be sorted in ascending order by the owner's last name. Save the select query naming it Fees >= $70. Print the select query datasheet.

e) Create a select query that displays the FirstName of employee, LastName of employee, Boat, and SlotNumber fields of those boats stored in the first five slots. Save the select query naming Slots 1 through 5. Print the select query datasheet.

Exercise 6 ———————————————————————— Ivy U Athletics

The Ivy U Athletics relational database created in Chapter Twelve, Exercise 6 needs to be updated and queries applied. Open Ivy U Athletics and complete the following steps:

a) Add the following record to the Sports table:

Women's Basketball; Spring; 451,000

b) Add the following records to the Players table:

CS341; Clarissa; Sladek; Women's Basketball; Shooting Guard
MA276; Marie; Angulo; Women's Basketball; Power Forward

c) Add the following record to the Coaches table:

BS912; Barbara; Suppa; Women's Basketball; Head Coach; 86,000

d) Format all of the tables in Datasheet view appropriately.

e) Sort the Players table by LastName in ascending order and then save and print the table.

f) The Players and Sports tables are related by the Sport field. The Sports table and Coaches table are also related by the Sport field. Create the appropriate relationships between the Players, Sports, and Coaches tables.

g) Create a select query that displays the FirstName of player, LastName of player, Sport, and Semester fields of all those sports played in the Spring semester. The query results should be sorted in ascending order by the player's last name. Save the select query naming it Spring Sports. Print the select query datasheet.

h) Create a select query that displays the FirstName of coach, LastName of coach, Salary, Sport, and Budget fields of all those coaches with a salary less than $50,000 who have a sport's budget over $500,000. Save the select query naming it Salary < $50,000 & Budget > $500,000. Print the select query datasheet.

Exercise 7   ⚙ ———————————————————————— Second Ocean

The Second Ocean relational database created in Chapter Twelve, Exercise 7 needs to be updated and queries applied. Open Second Ocean and complete the following steps:

a) In the Facility Checks table, change the Date field to DateOfCheck.

b) Update the Facility Checks form appropriately.

c) Format the Facility Checks table in Datasheet view appropriately.

d) Add the following records to the Animals table:

> 8/13/00; Manatee; 5; F; Ocean Care
> 9/4/00; Manatee; 7; F; Ocean Care

e) The whale has recovered and been released back into the ocean. Delete her record from the Animals table.

f) The Animals and Facility Checks tables are related by the AnimalID field. The Facility Checks and Facilities tables are related by the Facility field. Create the appropriate relationships between the Animals, Facility Checks, and Facilities tables.

g) Create a select query to display the AnimalID, Type, Gender, DateOfRescue, Facility, and DateOfCheck fields for all the animals. Save the select query naming it Statistics on Animals. Print the select query datasheet.

h) Create a select query to display the Facility, DateOfCheck, AnimalID, and Type fields for facility Ocean World. Save the select query naming it Ocean World Facility Checks. Print the select query datasheet.

Exercise 8   ⚙ ———————————————————————— Green Thumb

The Green Thumb relational database was created in Chapter Twelve, Exercise 8. Open Green Thumb and apply the following queries:

a) The Transactions and Plants tables are related by the PlantID field. The Plants and Vendors table are related by the VendorID field. Create the appropriate relationships between the Transactions, Plants, and Vendors tables.

b) Create a select query that displays the Plant, Retail, Date, and Quantity fields of all ferns sold. Save the select query naming it Ferns Sold. Print the select query datasheet.

c) Create a select query that displays the Name, Plant, and Cost fields. Save the select query naming it Cost of Plants. Print the select query datasheet.

d) Create a select query that displays the Plant, InStock, Cost, and Name fields of those plants costing less than $10.00 and with less than 50 in stock. Save the select query naming it Plants < $10 and < 50 InStock. Print the select query datasheet.

e)   Create a select query that displays the Plant, Retail, Cost, Date, and Quantity fields of all plants sold in a quantity greater than or equal to 10. Save the select query naming it Plants Sold >= 10. Print the select query datasheet.

Exercise 9 ⚙ ——————————————— Gym Members Progress

The Gym Members Progress relational database was created in Chapter Twelve, Exercise 9. Open Gym Members Progress and apply the following queries:

a)   The Members and Progress tables are related by the MemberID field. Create the appropriate relationship between the Members and Progress tables.

b)   Create a select query that displays the FirstName, LastName, and BenchPress fields of those members who can bench press over 50 kilograms. Save the select query naming it Bench > 50. Print the select query datasheet.

c)   Create a select query that displays the MemberID, FirstName, LastName, Date, and PercentBodyFat fields for the member with ID LUWO. Save the select query naming it LUWO Progress. Print the select query datasheet.

d)   Create a select query that displays the FirstName, LastName, PercentBodyFat, and BenchPress fields for those members who can bench press over 70 kilograms and have less than 26% body fat (<0.26). Save the select query naming it Bench > 70 and Fat < 26%. Print the select query datasheet.

Exercise 10 ⚙ ——————————————————— Pizza Payroll

The Pizza Payroll relational database was created in Chapter Twelve, Exercise 10. Open Pizza Payroll and apply the following queries:

a)   The Employees and Payroll tables are related by the EmployeeID field. Create the appropriate relationship between the Employees and Payroll tables.

b)   Create a select query that displays the FirstName, LastName, Date, GrossPay, and Taxes fields of all those employees whose gross pay is less than $250 and taxes are less than $30. Save the select query naming it Gross Pay < $250 & Tax < $30. Print the select query datasheet.

c)   Create a select query that displays the EmployeeID, FirstName, LastName, Date, GrossPay, and Taxes fields for employee EI. Save the select query naming it Employee EI Payroll. Print the select query datasheet.

Exercise 11 ⚙ ——————————————————— Coral Research

The Coral Research relational database was created in Chapter Twelve, Exercise 11. Open Coral Research and apply the following queries:

a)   The Coral Sites and Growth Research tables are related by the SiteID field. Create the appropriate relationship between the Coral Sites and Growth Research tables.

b)   Create a select query that displays the CoralName, Color, Description, Date, and Size fields for the Knobby Brain Coral. Save the select query naming it Knobby Brain Coral. Print the select query datasheet.

c) Create a select query that displays the SiteID, CoralName, Date, and Size fields for all those corals larger than 1 meter in size. Save the select query naming it Size > 1. Print the select query datasheet.

d) Create a select query to display the Site ID, CoralName, and Date fields for all those corals in sites 1 or 2. Save the select query naming it Sites 1 or 2. Print the select query datasheet.

Exercise 12 ☯ ──────────────────────── Travel Agency

The Travel Agency relational database was created in Chapter Twelve, Exercise 12. Open Travel Agency and apply the following queries:

a) The Clients and Booked Vacations tables are related by the ClientID field. The Booked Vacations and Vacations tables are related by the Package field. Create the appropriate relationships between the Clients, Booked Vacations, and Vacations tables.

b) Create a select query that displays the FirstName, LastName, and Package fields for those clients who have booked a Mountain Explorer or Summit Skiing vacation package. Save the select query naming it Mountain Explorer/Summit Skiing. Print the select query datasheet.

c) Create a select query that displays the ClientID, Date, Package, and Cost fields of those vacations booked by client JU. Save the select query naming it Vacations Booked by JU. Print the select query datasheet.

d) Create a select query that displays the Package, Cost, and Date fields for all those vacations booked that are costing more than $500. Save the select query naming it Booked > $500. Print the select query datasheet.

e) Create a select query that displays the FirstName, LastName, Package, Cost, Location, Date, and Type fields for all those vacations booked which cost less than $1,000 and that are relaxing. Save the select query naming it Booked Relaxing < $1,000. Print the select query datasheet.

Exercise 13 ──────────────────────── VIDEO STORE

The VIDEO STORE relational database contains information on a video store's members, videos, and rentals. Open VIDEO STORE and complete the following steps:

a) The Members table should also include the Address, City, State, and Zip fields for each member. Add the appropriate text fields to the Members table.

b) Update the Members form appropriately and enter the following ten records:

        CS; 654 First St.; Sunport; FL; 33654
        JF; 274 Boca Lane; Medusa; FL; 33656
        JH; 9876 Dolphin St.; Medusa; FL; 33656
        JM; 985 Jefferson Ave.; Medusa; FL; 33656
        JS; 9898 Dolphin St.; Medusa; FL; 33656
        JS-2; 285 Boca Lane; Medusa; FL; 33656
        LP; 655 First St.; Sunport; FL; 33654
        NL; 983 Jefferson Ave.; Medusa; FL; 33656
        RG; 9821 Dolphin St.; Medusa; FL; 33656
        RG-2; 987 First St.; Sunport; FL; 33654

c) Add a record for yourself to the Members table.

d) Format the Members table in Datasheet view appropriately.

e) Sort the Members table by LastName in ascending order and print the table in landscape orientation.

f) Create a select query that displays the FirstName, LastName, and InDate fields of those members who have not returned a video. If a video has not been returned, the InDate field is blank. To display fields that are blank, Is Null is entered as the criteria. Save the select query naming it Not Returned. Print the select query datasheet.

g) Create a select query that displays the Name, Type, and OutDate fields for all those movies checked out before 2/7/00 that are Sci-Fi movies. Save the select query naming it Sci-Fi < 2/7/00. Print the select query datasheet.

Exercise 14 ———————————————— INVENTIONS

The INVENTIONS relational database contains information on inventions and inventors. Open INVENTIONS and complete the following steps:

a) In the Inventors table, rename the Country field BirthCountry.

b) Update the Inventors form appropriately.

c) Delete the Cash Register record from the Inventions table.

d) Sort the Inventions table by Inventor in ascending order and then save and print the table.

e) Sort the Inventors table by the year they were born in ascending order and then save and print the table.

f) Create a select query that displays the FirstName, LastName, BirthCountry, Invention, and Year fields of those inventions created after 1799 by inventors born in the United States. Save the select query naming it US > 1799. Print the select query datasheet.

g) Modify the US > 1799 query to display the FirstName, LastName, BirthCountry, Invention, and Year fields of those inventions created after 1799 by inventors born in England. Save the modified select query naming it England > 1799. Print the select query datasheet.

Advanced
Exercise 15 ⟳ ———————————————————— Club

Modify the Club database created in Chapter Twelve, Exercise 13 to include at least two select queries. Be sure that at least one of the queries is a range criteria. Another query should involve criteria with an "and" or an "or".

Advanced
Exercise 16 ——————————————————————— Music

Modify the Music database created in Chapter Twelve, Exercise 14 to include at least two select queries. Be sure that at least one of the queries is a range criteria. Another query should involve criteria with an "and" or an "or".

Advanced
Exercise 17 ——————————————————————— Sports

Modify the Sports database created in Chapter Twelve, Exercise 15 to include at least two select queries. Be sure that at least one of the queries is a range criteria. Another query should involve criteria with an "and" or an "or".

Chapter Fourteen
Relational Database Reports and Advanced Database Techniques

Chapter Fourteen Objectives

After completing this chapter you will be able to:

1. Create a report.
2. Create a report with a summary.
3. Use fields in select query criteria.
4. Create a calculation field.

One of the most powerful features of a relational database is its ability to present the information stored in a database as printed reports. In this chapter reports are introduced. Also explained is how to create calculation fields in a select query.

14.1 Reports

A *report* is used to print information from a relational database in an organized manner. A descriptive title and headings are also included on a report. For example, an informative sales report from the Pack Suppliers database looks similar to:

Sales Report			
ItemName	Style	Date	Quantity
Bike frame pack			
	large	9/27/01	55
	large	9/28/01	75
	small	9/25/01	25
	small	9/25/01	25
Bike handlebar pack			
	large	9/28/01	8
	large	9/28/01	75
	large	9/29/01	18
	small	9/25/01	60
	small	9/28/01	13
Bike seat pack			
	large	9/24/01	6
	large	9/29/01	35
	small	9/24/01	4
Biker backpack			
	adult	9/26/01	8
	adult	9/25/01	35
	adult	9/28/01	5
Child carrier frame pack			
	adult	9/26/01	7
Day pack			
	adult	9/20/01	15
	adult	9/29/01	80
	adult	9/21/01	25
	adult	9/27/01	70
	adult	9/29/01	30
	child	9/26/01	10
	child	9/20/01	10
Diaper day pack			
	adult	9/26/01	5
	adult	9/26/01	25

Wednesday, August 11, 1999

Page 1 of 3

Page 1 of Pack Suppliers sales report

A report can include any combination of fields because Access uses the relationships between tables to determine which entries to display. In addition, reports are useful for creating a formatted printout of a database table, and are also a good way to print the results of a select query. Any changes made to the tables or queries used in a report are automatically reflected the next time the report is displayed.

14.2 Creating a Report

Report Wizard

In Access, a report can easily be created using the *Report Wizard*, which provides dialog boxes for selecting fields to be included in the report and report formatting options. The steps for creating a report using the Report Wizard are listed below. Throughout the steps, the sales report for Pack Suppliers is created.

1. **Start the Report Wizard.** Click on the Reports button in the Objects list in the Database window and then double-click on the Create report by using wizard icon to display the Report Wizard dialog box:

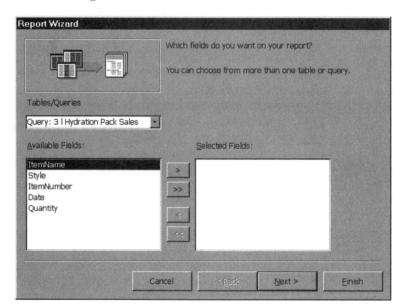

2. **Add the desired fields to the report.** Select the desired table or query from the Tables/Queries collapsible list. In the Available Fields list click on the desired field name and then click on the ⟩ button to move the field name to the Selected Fields list. Repeat this process to add each of the desired fields to the report. To add all the fields in the list, click on the ⟩⟩ button. For the Pack Suppliers sales report, the selected fields are:

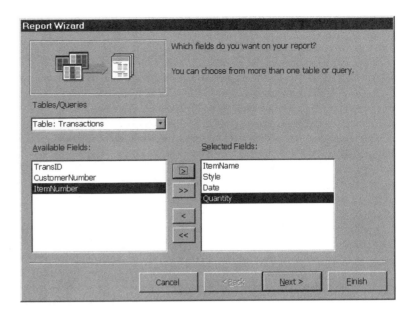

3. **Select a view.** Select the Next button to display the next Report Wizard dialog box. Here, clicking on a table name selects the way the report views the data. If there is only one table used in the report, then there is only one possible way to view the data and this dialog box is not displayed. However, when multiple tables are used in the report, the views correlate to the fields shown in each table's subdatasheet. For the Pack Suppliers report, the by Transactions view is selected. Because this table is related to more than one other table, it has no subdatasheets, and therefore only one level of data to view:

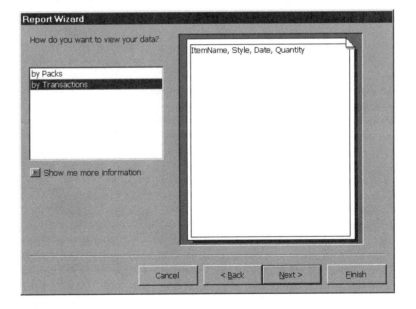

4. **Select the grouping of the data.** Select the Next button to display the next Report Wizard dialog box. Selecting a field and then the 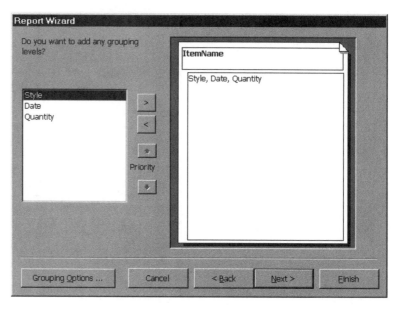 button groups the data in the report by this field's entries. For the Pack Suppliers report, the report is grouped on ItemName:

grouping data

Grouping data can eliminate displaying duplicate entries and make a report more readable. For example, the two reports below contain exactly the same data. However, the one on the left has been grouped on the ItemName field and the one on the right has no grouping:

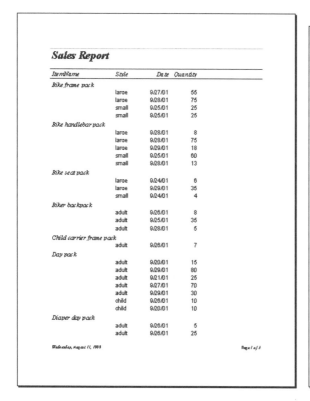

5. **Select the sort order.** Select the Next button to display the next Report Wizard dialog box. A report can be sorted based on a field's entries. For the Pack Suppliers report, the Style field is used to sort the report:

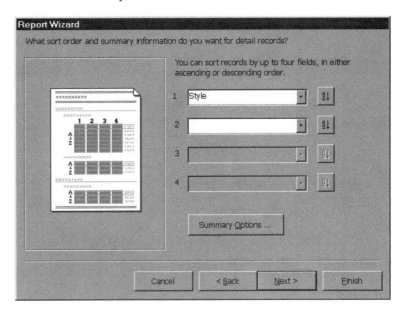

The button to the right of the sort field indicates the sort order. In this case, ascending. Clicking on this sort button reverses the sort order to descending.

Orientation

The **Orientation** options change the way the report will be printed. If many fields are included in the report, the **Landscape** option should be selected to display the report data across the widest part of the page. This will prevent data from being cutoff when printed.

6. **Select the layout.** Select the Next button to display the next Report Wizard dialog box. Clicking on a Layout option shows its corresponding layout in the left side of the dialog box. For the Pack Suppliers report, the default Stepped layout is selected:

7. **Select the report style.** Select the Next button to display the next Report Wizard dialog box. Here, the style of the report is chosen. For the Pack Suppliers report, the default Corporate style is selected:

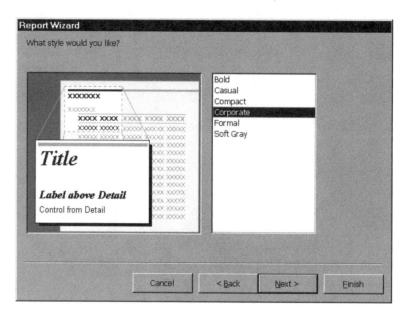

8. **Enter the report title.** Select the Next button to display the last Report Wizard dialog box where a report title is typed and the option to preview the report can be selected:

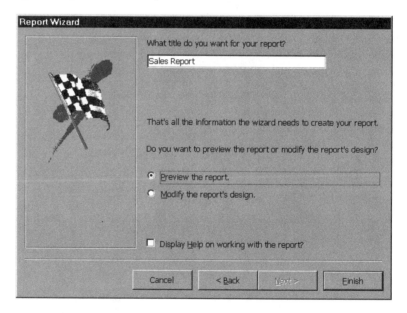

9. **Display the report.** Select the Finish button to display the new report. Clicking on the displayed report alternates between magnified and full-page views.

The Report Wizard is a simple, fast way to create a report. To determine the best presentation for your data, experiment with grouping, sorting, layouts, and styles.

Practice 1

In this practice you will create two reports for the PACK SUPPLIERS database.

1) OPEN PACK SUPPLIERS

2) CREATE A SALES REPORT

    a. In the PACK SUPPLIERS : Database window, click on the Reports button.

    b. Double-click on the Create report by using wizard icon. A dialog box is displayed.

        1. In the Tables/Queries collapsible list, select Table: Packs. The fields of the Packs table are displayed in the Available Fields list.

        2. Click on the ItemName field and then click on the [>] button. The ItemName field is moved to the Selected Fields list.

        3. Move the Style field to the Selected Fields list.

        4. In the Tables/Queries collapsible list, select Table: Transactions. The fields of the Transactions table are displayed in the Available Fields list.

        5. Move the Date and Quantity fields to the Selected Fields list.

        6. Select the Next button. Viewing options are displayed.

        7. Click on by Transactions.

        8. Select the Next button. Grouping level options are displayed.

        9. Click on the ItemName field if it is not already selected and then click on the [>] button. The sample report is shown grouped by ItemName.

        10. Select the Next button. Sorting options are displayed.

        11. In the first sort collapsible list, select Style.

        12. Select the Next button. Layout options are displayed.

        13. Select the Stepped layout option if it is not already selected.

        14. Select the Next button. Style options are displayed.

        15. Select the Corporate style option if it is not already selected.

        16. Select the Next button. The last dialog box is displayed.

        17. In the What title do you want for your report? entry box, type Sales Report.

        18. Select the Preview the report option if it is not already selected.

        19. Select the Finish button. The Sales Report is displayed.

    c. At the bottom of the report window, use the scroll buttons to view the pages of the report.

    d. Select File → Print. A dialog box is displayed.

        1. Select the Pages option. In the From entry box, type 1. In the To entry box, type 1.

        2. Select OK. The first page of the report is printed and looks similar to that shown on page 14-1.

3) CLOSE THE REPORT

    On the Sales Report window, click on the Close button ([X]). The report is closed. Note the report name displayed in the PACK SUPPLIERS : Database window.

4) CREATE A 3 L HYDRATION PACK SALES REPORT

    a. In the PACK SUPPLIERS : Database window, double-click on the Create report by using wizard icon. A dialog box is displayed.

        1. In the Tables/Queries collapsible list, select Query: 3 l Hydration Pack Sales. The fields of the hydration pack query are displayed in the Available Fields list.

        2. Click on the [>>] button. All the query fields are moved to the Selected Fields list.

        3. Select the Next button. Viewing options are displayed.

        4. Click on by Transactions.

        5. Select the Next button. Grouping level options are displayed.

        6. Click on the ItemNumber field and then click on the [>] button. The sample report is shown grouped by ItemNumber.

        7. Select the Next button. Sorting options are displayed.

        8. In the first sort collapsible list, select Quantity.

9. Select the Next button. Layout options are displayed.
10. Select the Stepped layout option if it is not already selected.
11. Select the Next button. Style options are displayed.
12. Select the Corporate style option if it is not already selected.
13. Select the Next button. The last dialog box is displayed.
14. In the What title do you want for your report? entry box, type 3 l Hydration Pack Sales Report.
15. Select the Preview the report option if it is not already selected.
16. Select the Finish button. The 3 l Hydration Pack Sales Report is displayed:

3 l Hydration Pack Sales Report

ItemNumber	Quantity	ItemName	Style	Date
W204				
	20	Hydration pack	3.0 l	9/25/01
W205				
	8	Hydration pack	3.0 l	9/26/01
W206				
	5	Hydration pack	3.0 l	9/27/01
	20	Hydration pack	3.0 l	9/26/01

b. Select File → Print. A dialog box is displayed.
1. Select OK. The report is printed.

5) CLOSE THE REPORT

Close the report. The report name is displayed in the Database window.

14.3 Report Summaries

Statistics on a number field can be displayed as a *summary* in a report. For example, the following Pack Suppliers report includes statistics about hydration pack sales:

3 l Hydration Pack Sales with Summary Report

ItemNumber	Quantity	ItemName	Style	Date
W204				
	20	Hydration pack	3.0 l	9/25/01
Summary for 'ItemNumber' = W204 (1 detail record)				
Sum	20			
W205				
	8	Hydration pack	3.0 l	9/26/01
Summary for 'ItemNumber' = W205 (1 detail record)				
Sum	8			
W206				
	5	Hydration pack	3.0 l	9/27/01
	20	Hydration pack	3.0 l	9/26/01
Summary for 'ItemNumber' = W206 (2 detail records)				
Sum	25			
Grand Total	53			

A Guide to Microsoft Office 2000 Professional

Note that the summary adds a total to the report for each ItemNumber's sales and a grand total for all the sales.

A summary is added to a report using the Summary Options button in the sorting options Report Wizard dialog box. The Summary Options button is available in the Report Wizard when the fields of a report are grouped and at least one of the fields in the report is a numeric field:

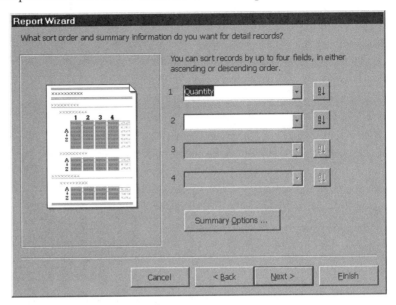

Selecting the Summary Options button displays the Summary Options dialog box with a list of the numeric fields included in the report. For the 3 l Hydration Pack Sales Report, the Summary Options dialog box lists the Quantity field, the only numeric field included in the report. The Sum option is selected to display total sales of each pack:

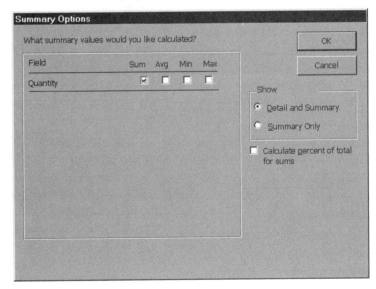

After selecting a summary checkbox, OK can be selected to remove the dialog box and continue with the other Report Wizard dialog boxes.

Practice 2

In this practice you will create a report with a summary. Open PACK SUPPLIERS if it is not already displayed.

1) CREATE A HYDRATION PACK REPORT WITH SUMMARY DATA

  a. In the PACK SUPPLIERS : Database window, click on the Reports button if report names are not already displayed.

  b. Double-click on the Create report by using wizard icon. A dialog box is displayed.

     1. In the Tables/Queries collapsible list, select Query: 3 l Hydration Pack Sales if it is not already displayed. The fields of the hydration pack query are displayed in the Available Fields list.

     2. Click on the ⏩ button. All the query fields are moved to the Selected Fields list.

     3. Select the Next button. Viewing options are displayed.

     4. Click on by Transactions.

     5. Select the Next button. Grouping level options are displayed.

     6. Click on the ItemNumber field and then click on the ▸ button. The sample report is shown grouped by ItemNumber.

     7. Select the Next button. Sorting options are displayed.

     8. In the first sort collapsible list, select Quantity.

     9. At the bottom of the dialog box, select the Summary Options button. A dialog box is displayed.

       a. Click on the checkbox below the Sum label.

       b. Select OK. Sorting options are again displayed.

     10. Select the Next button. Layout options are displayed.

     11. Select the Stepped layout option if it is not already selected.

     12. Select the Next button. Style options are displayed.

     13. Select the Corporate style option if it is not already selected.

     14. Select the Next button. The last dialog box is displayed.

     15. In the What title do you want for your report? entry box, type 3 l Hydration Pack Sales with Summary Report.

     16. Select the Preview the report option if it is not already selected.

     17. Select the Finish button. The 3 l Hydration Pack Sales with Summary Report is displayed. Note the summary after each group and at the bottom of the report.

2) PRINT AND THEN CLOSE THE REPORT

3) CLOSE PACK SUPPLIERS

14.4 Using Fields in Query Criteria

The criteria of a select query can refer to a field in the database. For example, Sage's Outdoor Supplies uses a database to maintain inventory information. A select query could be used to determine which products have a retail price that is more than twice the actual cost (a 100% markup). This query criteria is "greater than 2×Cost" in the Retail field:

Widening Columns

The columns of the query design grid can be widened by dragging the right boundary of the column or by double-clicking the right boundary. Widening a column is often necessary to entirely view long criteria.

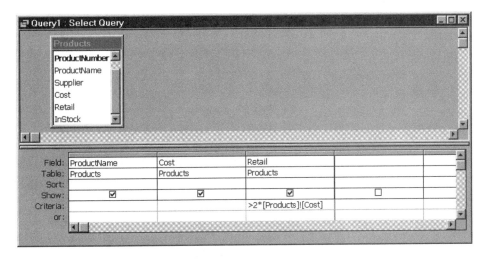

In the criteria, the format [Table Name]![Field Name] is used to refer to a field. An asterisk (*) is used to indicate multiplication. When run, the select query displays the following datasheet:

ProductName	Cost	Retail
▶ Compass	$28.00	$62.00
Wool cap	$6.50	$15.00
Sun hat	$3.00	$9.00
*	$0.00	$0.00

Practice 3

In this practice you will create a select query that uses a field in the criteria.

1) OPEN SAGE'S OUTDOOR SUPPLIES

2) QUERY FOR PRODUCTS WITH A MARKUP OVER 100%

 a. In the SAGE'S OUTDOOR SUPPLIES : Database window, click on the Queries button. Query names are displayed.

 b. Double-click on the Create query in Design view icon. The Select Query window is displayed with the Show Table dialog box on top.

  1. Add the Products table to the Select Query window.

  2. Select Close. The Show Table dialog box is removed.

 c. Drag the ProductName, Cost, and Retail fields from the Products table to the first, second, and third Field boxes in the design grid, respectively.

 d. In the Criteria box of Retail type >2*[Products]![Cost] similar to:

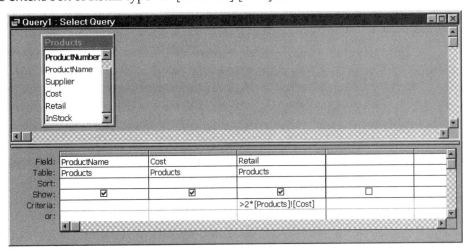

e. Run the query. The select query datasheet looks similar to that shown in Section 14.4. Note how each of the records have a retail price more than twice that of the cost.

f. Save the query naming it Over 100% Markup.

g. Print and then close the datasheet.

14.5 Calculation Fields

A *calculation field* is generated by a select query and can display the results of calculations based on data in other fields of the database. For example, a Sage's Outdoor Supply select query that displays the Product, Cost, and Retail fields can also include a calculation field that computes the profit for each item. A calculation field is created by typing a new field name followed by a colon and then an expression to calculate the values to be displayed in that field:

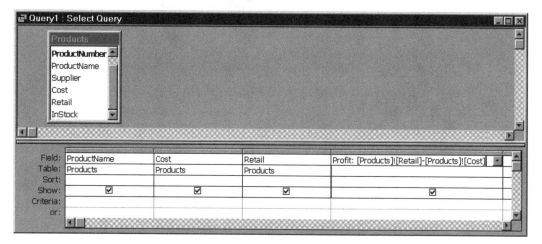

A field is referred to in an expression using the format [Table Name]![Field Name]. In the Profit calculation field above, the expression subtracts the Cost field value from the Retail field value to determine the value displayed in the new Profit field. To fully view the calculation field and its expression in the design grid, the column was widened by dragging its right boundary. Running the select query displays the following datasheet:

ProductName	Cost	Retail	Profit
Binoculars small	$35.00	$50.00	$15.00
Binoculars large	$50.00	$75.00	$25.00
Compass	$28.00	$62.00	$34.00
Hiking pack blue	$22.00	$35.00	$13.00
Rain hat	$4.00	$7.00	$3.00
Wool cap	$6.50	$15.00	$8.50
Sun hat	$3.00	$9.00	$6.00
Hydration pack red	$12.00	$20.00	$8.00
Hydration pack black	$12.00	$20.00	$8.00
*	$0.00	$0.00	

Note the Profit field is based on an expression entered in the select query, and is not a field in one of the database tables. Calculation fields are not stored in a table, their entries are calculated each time the query is run.

Formatting a Calculation Field

The data displayed by a calculation field may need to be formatted. A numeric format is selected by right-clicking on the calculation field in the design grid of the select query, selecting the Properties command, and then selecting the desired format from the **Format** collapsible list.

A Guide to Microsoft Office 2000 Professional

Practice 4

In this practice you will create a select query that includes a calculation field. Open SAGE'S OUTDOOR SUPPLIES if it is not already displayed.

1) CREATE A PROFIT CALCULATION FIELD

    a. In the SAGE'S OUTDOOR SUPPLIES : Database window, click on the Queries button if query names are not already displayed.

    b. Double-click on the Create query in Design view icon. The Select Query window is displayed with the Show Table dialog box on top.

        1. Add the Products table to the Select Query window.

        2. Select **Close**. The Show Table dialog box is removed.

    c. Drag the ProductName, Cost, and Retail fields from the Products table to the first, second, and third Field boxes in the design grid, respectively.

    d. In the fourth Field box, type the calculation field Profit:[Products]![Retail]-[Products]![Cost].

    e. Resize the design grid column so that the calculation field and its formula are displayed entirely. The design grid should look similar to:

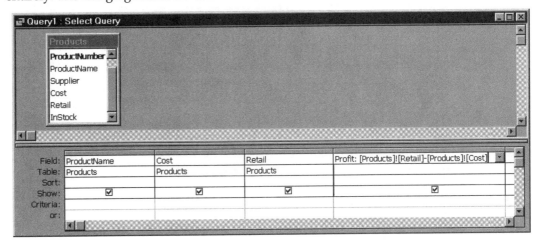

    f. Run the query. The select query datasheet looks similar to that shown in section 14.5.

    g. Save the query naming it Profit.

    h. Print and then close the datasheet.

2) CLOSE THE DATABASE.

3) EXIT ACCESS

14.6 Where can you go from here?

The last three chapters have introduced you to the concepts of relational databases. You can now create tables, forms, select queries, and reports in a relational database. The relational database has other options and applications not discussed in this text which you may want to explore using the Access online help.

A powerful feature of Access is its ability to integrate the information stored in a database with a Word document to produce personalized form letters. This process, called mail merge, is described in Chapter Fifteen. Chapter Seventeen describes how to mail merge a publication.

Reports and forms can be customized in Design view. Appendix B introduces creating forms and reports in Design view.

Because you have learned how to use Access, you will easily be able to learn to use other relational databases.

Chapter Summary

This chapter described how to produce reports. A report is used to print information from a relational database in an organized manner. Headings, a descriptive title, and any combination of fields are included in a report.

Report Wizard

A report is easily created using the Report Wizard, which provides dialog boxes for selecting fields to be included in the report as well as report formatting options. To create a report using the Report Wizard:

1. Start the Report Wizard.
2. Add the desired fields to the report.
3. Select a view.
4. Select the grouping of the data.
5. Select the sort order and summary options if desired.
6. Select the layout.
7. Select the report style.
8. Enter the report title and then display the report.

report summary

Statistics about a number field in a report can be displayed as a summary. The Summary Options button is available in the Report Wizard when the fields of a report are grouped and at least one of the fields in the report is a numeric field. The Summary Options button displays a dialog box where a summary option can be selected.

field names in criteria

Select queries can include fields in their criteria by using the format [Table Name]![Field Name] to refer to a field name.

calculation field

Calculation fields can be created in a select query to display the result of an expression. Calculation fields are not stored in a table, their entries are calculated each time the query is run.

Vocabulary

Calculation field   Displays the results of calculations based on data in other fields of the database. Generated by a select query.

Grouping data   Organizes the data in a report by a field's entries to eliminate displaying duplicate entries and makes a report more readable.

Report   Used to print information from a relational database in an organized manner.

Report Wizard   Provides dialog boxes for selecting fields to be included in a report and report formatting options.

Sort order   Determines the order in which records are listed in a report.

Summary   Displays statistics about a number field.

Review Questions

1. What is a report used for?

2. If a change is made to a table used in a report, is the change displayed the next time the report is viewed?

3. If a database contains five tables, fields from how many of the tables may be included in a report?

4. If four fields are displayed in the Available Fields list, how can all of them be moved at once to the Selected Fields list?

5. Explain how grouping data in a report can make the report more readable.

6. a) Explain what sort order is in a report.
   b) How can the sort order be changed from ascending to descending?

7. What does selecting a report style do to a report?

8. a) What is a report summary?
   b) List the steps required to add a report summary that averages the values in a number field.

Section 14.4 — 14.6

9. What is the format used to refer to a field name in the Criteria row of a design grid?

10. a) What is a calculation field?
    b) Can a calculation field be part of a table?

Exercises

Exercise 1 ——————————————— VIDEO STORE

The VIDEO STORE relational database contains information on a video store's members, videos, and rentals. Open VIDEO STORE and create the following reports and query:

a) Create a report that displays the FirstName, LastName, Phone, and Credit fields from the Members table. Group the report by the Credit field, and sort the report on the LastName field in ascending order. Select appropriate layout and style options. Title the report Members Report. Print the report.

b) Create a select query that displays the TapeID, Name, Year, and Type fields of movies that are of drama type. Save the select query naming it Drama Movies. Print the select query datasheet.

c) Create a report that displays the Name and Year fields from the Drama Movies query. Sort the report on the Name field in ascending order. Select appropriate layout and style options. Title the report Drama Movies Report. Print the report.

Exercise 2 ✑ ——————————————— Museum Exhibits

The Museum Exhibits database last modified in Chapter Thirteen, Exercise 2 contains information on exhibits and attendance. Open Museum Exhibits and create the following reports and query:

a) Create a report that displays the ExhibitID, ExhibitName, and Department fields from the Exhibits table and the Year and Attendance fields from the Attendance table. View the report by Exhibits, and group the report by the Department field. Sort the report on the Attendance field in descending order, and include a summary that averages the Attendance field. Select appropriate layout and style options. Title the report Exhibits Attendance Report. Print the report.

b) Create a report that displays the ExhibitID, ExhibitName, and Attendance fields from the 2002 Attendance over 1,500 query and the Department field from the Exhibits table. Group the report on the Attendance field and include a summary that totals the Attendance field. Select appropriate layout and style options. Title the report 2002 Attendance over 1,500 Report. Print the report.

c) Create a select query that displays the ExhibitID, ExhibitName, Department, Year, and Attendance fields for all exhibits in the year 2002 and includes a calculated field named Predicted2003Attendance. Sunport Science Museum predicts that the attendance in 2003 will be 10% higher than the attendance in 2002. Therefore, the predicted 2003 attendance is calculated by multiplying the Attendance field by 1.1. Format the calculated field by right-clicking on the formula in the design grid, selecting Properties, and then selecting Standard from the Format collapsible list. Save the select query naming it Predicted 2003 Attendance. Format the select query datasheet appropriately and print a copy in landscape orientation.

The Library database last modified in Chapter Thirteen, Exercise 3 contains information on books and authors. Open Library and create the following reports:

    a) Create a report that displays all the fields from the Books table. Group the report by the Type field. Select appropriate layout and style options. Title the report Books Report. Print the report.

    b) Create a report that displays the FirstName and LastName fields from the Authors table and the Title and Type fields from the Books table. View the report by Authors, and sort the report on the Title field in ascending order. Select appropriate layout and style options. Title the report Authors and Their Books. Print the report.

Exercise 4 ——————————————————————————— INVENTIONS

The INVENTIONS relational database contains information on inventions and inventors. Open INVENTIONS and create the following queries and reports:

    a) Create a select query that displays the Invention, Country, Year, FirstName, and LastName fields of all inventions created in the United States. Save the select query naming it United States Inventions. Print the select query datasheet.

    b) Create a report that displays the Invention, Year, FirstName, and LastName fields from the United States Inventions query. Sort the report on the Year field in ascending order. Select appropriate layout and style options. Title the report United States Inventions Report. Print the report.

    c) Create a select query that displays the FirstName, LastName, Country, and Born fields for all the inventors born in the 1800s. You will need to enter >=1800 And <=1899 as the criteria for the Born field. Save the select query naming it Inventors Born in the 1800s. Print the select query datasheet.

    d) Create a report that displays all of the fields from the Inventors Born in the 1800s query. Group the report by the Country field, and sort the report on the LastName field in ascending order. Select appropriate layout and style options. Title the report Inventors Born in the 1800s Report. Print the report.

Exercise 5 ——————————————————————— Boat Storage

The Boat Storage database last modified in Chapter Thirteen, Exercise 5 contains information on employees, boats, and boat owners. Open Boat Storage and create the following reports and query:

    a) Create a report that displays the FirstName, LastName and Phone fields from the Employees table. Sort the report on the LastName field in ascending order. Select appropriate layout and style options. Title the report Employee Phone List. Print the report.

    b) Create a report that displays the FirstName and LastName fields from the Boat Owners table and the Boat, SlotNumber, and Fee fields from the Boats table. View the report by Boat Owners. Include a summary that totals the Fee field. Select appropriate layout and style options. Title the report Boat Fees Report. Print the report.

c) Create a select query that displays the Boat, Fee, FirstName of boat owner, and LastName of boat owner fields for all boat owners and includes a calculated field named AnnualRenewal. The annual renewal charge is calculated by multiplying the Fee field by 30% (0.30). Format the calculated field by right-clicking on the formula in the design grid, selecting Properties, and then selecting Currency from the Format collapsible list. Save the select query naming it Annual Renewal Charges. Format the select query datasheet appropriately and print a copy.

Exercise 6 ✧ ——————————————————— Ivy U Athletics

The Ivy U Athletics database last modified in Chapter Thirteen, Exercise 6 contains information on players, sports, and coaches. Open Ivy U Athletics and create the following reports and queries:

a) Create a report that displays the FirstName, LastName, Sport, and Salary fields from the Coaches table. Group the report on the Sport field, and sort the report on the LastName field in ascending order. Include a summary that totals the Salary field. Select appropriate layout and style options. Title the report Coaches Salary Report. Print the report.

b) Create a report that displays the FirstName, LastName, and Sport fields from the Players table and the Semester field from the Sports table. View the report by Sports, and group the report on the Sport field. Sort the report on the LastName field in ascending order. Select appropriate layout and style options. Title the report Players Report. Print the report.

c) Create a select query that displays the FirstName of the coach, LastName of the coach, Sport, and Salary fields for all the coaches and includes a calculated field named Bonus. The bonus is calculated by multiplying the Salary field by 0.15. Format the calculated field by right-clicking on the formula in the design grid, selecting Properties, and then selecting Currency from the Format collapsible list. Save the select query naming it Coach Bonuses. Format the select query datasheet appropriately and print a copy.

d) Create a select query that displays the Sport, Semester, and Budget fields for all sports and includes a calculated field named BudgetProposal. The budget proposal is calculated by multiplying the Budget field by 1.15. Format the calculated field by right-clicking on the formula in the design grid, selecting Properties, and then selecting Currency from the Format collapsible list. Save the query naming it Budget Proposal. Format the select query datasheet appropriately and print a copy.

Exercise 7 ✧ ——————————————————— Second Ocean

The Second Ocean database last modified in Chapter Thirteen, Exercise 7 contains information on animals, facilities, and facility checks. Open Second Ocean and create the following reports:

a) Create a report that displays all the fields from the Statistics on Animals query. View the report by Facility Checks, and group the report by the Facility field. Sort the report on the DateOfCheck field in descending order. Select appropriate layout and style options. Title the report Animal Statistics Report. Print the report.

Exercise 8 ————————————————————— Green Thumb

The Green Thumb database last modified in Chapter Thirteen, Exercise 8 contains information on plants, transactions, and vendors. Open Green Thumb and create the following reports and queries:

a)   Create a report that displays the Plant, InStock, Cost, and Retail fields from the Plants table. Sort the report on the Plant field in ascending order. Select appropriate layout and style options. Title the report Plants Report. Print the report.

b)   Create a report that displays the Name, Address, City, State, and Zip fields from the Vendors table. Sort the report on the Name field in ascending order. Select appropriate layout and style options. Title the report Current Vendors. Print the report.

c)   Create a report that displays all the fields from the Cost of Plants query. View the report by Vendors and sort the report on the Plant field in ascending order. Select appropriate layout and style options. Title the report Cost of Plants. Print the report.

d)   Create a report that displays the Plant field from the Plants table and the Date and Quantity fields from the Transactions table. View the report by Plants and sort the report on the Date field in descending order. Include a summary that totals the Quantity field. Select appropriate layout and style options. Title the report Transactions Report. Print the report.

e)   Create a select query that displays the Name, Phone, Plant, InStock, and Reorder fields for all plants that have less stock than their reorder number. Save the select query naming it Plants to Reorder. Print the select query datasheet.

f)   Create a select query that displays the Plant, Cost, and Retail fields for all plants and includes a calculated field named Profit. The profit of a plant is calculated by subtracting the Cost field from the Retail field. Save the query naming it Plant Profit. Print the select query datasheet.

g)   Create a select query that displays the TransID, Date, PlantID, Quantity, and Retail fields for all transactions and includes a calculated field named Revenue. The revenue of a transaction is calculated by multiplying the Retail field by the Quantity field. Format the calculated field by right-clicking on the formula in the design grid, selecting Properties, and then selecting Currency from the Format collapsible list. Save the query naming it Transaction Revenues. Print the select query datasheet.

h)   Create a report that displays all the fields from the Transaction Revenues select query. Group the report on the PlantID field and sort the report on the TransID field in ascending order. Include a summary that totals the Quantity, Retail, and Revenue fields. Select appropriate layout and style options. Title the report Transaction Revenues Report. Print the report.

Exercise 9 ————————————————— Gym Members Progress

The Gym Members Progress database last modified in Chapter Thirteen, Exercise 9 contains information on members and progress. Open Gym Members Progress and create the following report:

a)   Create a report that displays the MemberID, PercentBodyFat, and BenchPress fields from the Progress table. Group the report on the MemberID field. Include a summary that displays the minimum of the PercentBodyFat field and the maximum of the BenchPress field. Select appropriate layout and style options. Save the query naming it Current Progress Report. Print the report.

Exercise 10 ⚙ ———————————————————————— Pizza Payroll

The Pizza Payroll database last modified in Chapter Thirteen, Exercise 10 contains information on employees and payroll. Open Pizza Payroll and create the following reports and queries:

a) Create a report that displays the LastName, FirstName, Address, City, State, and Zip fields from the Employees table. Sort the report on the LastName field in ascending order. Select appropriate layout and style options. Title the report Current Employees. Print the report.

b) Create a report that displays the EmployeeID, Date, GrossPay, and Taxes fields from the Employee EI Payroll query. View the report by Employees and sort the report on the Date field in descending order. Include a summary that averages the GrossPay and Taxes fields. Select appropriate layout and style options. Title the report Employee EI Report. Print the report.

c) Create a report that displays the FirstName and LastName fields from the Employees table and the Date, GrossPay, and Taxes fields from the Payroll table. View the report by Employees and sort the report on the Date field in descending order. Include a summary that totals the GrossPay and Taxes fields. Select appropriate layout and style options. Title the report Payroll Report. Print the report.

d) Create a select query that displays the EmployeeID, Date, GrossPay, and Taxes fields for all employees and includes a calculated field named NetPay. Net pay is calculated by subtracting the Taxes field from the GrossPay field. Save the query naming it Net Pay. Print the select query datasheet.

Exercise 11 ⚙ ———————————————————————— Coral Research

The Coral Research database last modified in Chapter Thirteen, Exercise 11 contains information on coral sites and growth research. Open Coral Research and create the following report:

a) Create a report that displays the CoralName field from the Coral Sites table and the Date and Size fields from the Growth Research table. View the report by CoralName. Sort the report on the Date field in ascending order. Select appropriate layout and style options. Title the report Coral Growth Report. Print the report.

Exercise 12 ⚙ ———————————————————————— Travel Agency

The Travel Agency database last modified in Chapter Thirteen, Exercise 12 contains information on clients, vacations, and booked vacations. Open Travel Agency and create the following report and query:

a) Create a report that displays the FirstName and LastName fields from the Clients table, the Package and Cost fields from the Vacations table, and the Date field from the Booked Vacations table. View the report by Clients. Sort the report on the Date field in ascending order. Include a summary that totals the Cost field. Select appropriate layout and style options. Title the report Booked Vacations Report. Print the report.

b) Create a select query that displays the Package and Cost fields for all vacations and includes a calculated field named Discount. The discount is calculated by multiplying the Cost field by 0.20 and then subtracting that amount from the Cost field. Save the query naming it Early Booking Discounts. Print the select query datasheet.

Advanced
Exercise 13 ☼ ———————————————————————— Club

Modify the Club database created in Chapter Twelve, Exercise 13 to include at least one report. Include a summary in one of the reports, if possible. Create a select query that uses either a field in the criteria or includes a calculated field.

Advanced
Exercise 14 ☼ ———————————————————————— Music

Modify the Music database created in Chapter Twelve, Exercise 14 to include at least one report. Include a summary in one of the reports, if possible. Create a select query that uses either a field in the criteria or includes a calculated field.

Advanced
Exercise 15 ☼ ———————————————————————— Sports

Modify the Sports database created in Chapter Twelve, Exercise 15 to include at least one report. Include a summary in one of the reports, if possible. Create a select query that uses either a field in the criteria or includes a calculated field.

Integrating the Database with the Word Processor and Spreadsheet

Copy

Paste

Select All Records

Rename

Mail Merge

Chapter Fifteen Objectives

After completing this chapter you will be able to:

1. Copy database entries to a Word document.
2. Copy database entries to an Excel spreadsheet.
3. Create an Access table from Excel spreadsheet data.
4. Create form letters with mail merge.
5. Create mailing labels with mail merge.

$\mathbf{A}$s discussed in Chapter Eleven, data can be copied between files of the same application and different applications. In this chapter, integrating data between Access, Word, and Excel is discussed. Mail merge, a special technique for merging a database with a Word document, is also introduced.

15.1 Copying Database Entries to a Word Document

The entries and records in an Access table or query displayed in Datasheet view can be copied to a Word document. Businesses sometimes use this feature to include data from databases in letters and memos. The steps for copying data from an Access table or query displayed in Datasheet view to an open Word document are:

1. Highlight the entries to be copied.

2. Select the Copy command from the Edit menu.

3. Make the Word document active.

4. Place the cursor where the data is to be inserted and select the Paste command from the Edit menu.

When data is copied from Access to Word, the data is automatically placed in a table structure. The first row of the table contains the field names, and the remaining rows contain the copied entries.

highlighting records

15.2 Techniques for Copying Database Entries

When copying database entries, a query should be applied so that only the desired data is displayed. If entries from a table are to be copied, a filter can be used to limit the records displayed. If entries from different tables are to be copied, a select query should be used to display the desired data in one datasheet.

In Datasheet view, an entire record is highlighted by clicking on its record selector. Dragging from one record selector down to another record selector highlights multiple records. All of the records can be highlighted by executing the Select All Records command from the Edit menu.

highlighting entries   A field entry is highlighted by placing the mouse pointer just to the left of the entry until the pointer changes to a plus sign (✛). Clicking the plus sign pointer selects that entry. Dragging the plus sign pointer selects multiple entries.

Practice 1

In this practice you will copy Access database entries to a Word document. A select query will be used to display only the desired data.

1) *OPEN THE CONCESSION STAND MEMO DOCUMENT*

2) *OPEN THE CONCESSION STAND DATABASE*

3) *APPLY A SELECT QUERY*

   Run the Reorder query. The ProductName and InStock fields for the products that have less than 100 in stock are displayed in a datasheet.

4) *HIGHLIGHT THE DATA TO BE COPIED*

   Select Edit ➡ Select All Records. All of the records are highlighted.

5) *COPY AND THEN PASTE DATA*

   a. With all the records highlighted, select Edit ➡ Copy. The records are copied to the Clipboard.
   b. Close the select query datasheet.
   c. On the Taskbar, click on the **CONCESSION STAND MEMO** button. The CONCESSION STAND MEMO document is displayed.
   d. Place the cursor in the blank paragraph after the sentence that begins "The following…" and press Enter once.
   e. Select Edit ➡ Paste. (The command name may be Paste Cells.) The entries on the Clipboard are placed in a table structure.

Check - Your memo should look similar to:

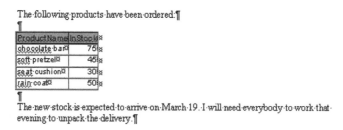

6) *SAVE, PRINT, AND THEN CLOSE THE MODIFIED CONCESSION STAND MEMO*

7) *EXIT WORD*

15.3 Copying Database Entries to an Excel Spreadsheet

What If? questions can be performed on data stored in a database by copying the entries to a spreadsheet. The steps for copying entries from a displayed Access datasheet to an open Excel spreadsheet are:

1. Highlight the entries to be copied.

2. Select the Copy command.

3. Make the Excel spreadsheet active.

4. Select the first cell where the data is to appear and then select the Paste command.

When data is copied from Access to Excel, the data is placed in rows and columns similar to a datasheet. This means that entries in the first field are placed in the first column, the entries in the second field in the second column, and so on. Field names are placed in the first row of the spreadsheet with special formatting applied:

	A	B
1	roductNam	InStock
2	bottled water	225
3	chocolate bar	75
4	cola	275
5	juice	119

Cell widths are not automatically widened to accommodate the copied entries. However, the row height of a cell does automatically increase so that text entries are displayed entirely, similar to word wrap. The entries can be displayed on one line by increasing the column width and then decreasing the row height by double-clicking on the row's bottom boundary, the line between the row numbers.

Cell Shading

In Excel, cell shading can be changed by selecting the Cells command from the Format menu to display a dialog box. Selecting the Patterns tab displays the Cell shading options.

Practice 2

In this practice you will copy Access database entries to a new Excel spreadsheet. Open the CONCESSION STAND database if it is not already displayed.

1) CREATE A NEW EXCEL SPREADSHEET

2) HIGHLIGHT THE DATA TO BE COPIED

    a. On the Taskbar, click on the CONCESSION STAND button. The CONCESSION STAND database is displayed.
    b. Open the Products table in Datasheet view.
    c. Point just to the left of the ProductName field entry of the first record until the pointer changes to a plus sign (✛).
    d. Drag the pointer until all ProductName and InStock entries are highlighted.

3) COPY AND THEN PASTE DATA

    a. Select Edit → Copy. If the Office Clipboard is displayed, close it.
    b. Close the Products table.

c. On the Taskbar, click on the Microsoft Excel button. The new, blank spreadsheet created in step 1 is displayed.

d. Select cell A1 if it is not already selected.

e. Select Edit → Paste. The entries on the Clipboard are pasted into the spreadsheet starting in cell A1.

f. Click anywhere to remove the highlight.

4) FORMAT THE SPREADSHEET

a. Widen column A until the product names are on one line.

b. Highlight rows 2 through 11 by dragging from row number 2 to row number 11.

c. Point to one of the row boundaries of the highlighted rows. The mouse pointer changes to a double-headed arrow (↨).

d. Double-click the double-headed arrow pointer. The rows are resized.

e. Click anywhere to remove the highlight.

5) ADD CALCULATIONS TO THE SPREADSHEET

a. In cell A13, type Units in Stock. If the row height increases, widen column A and then decrease the row height.

b. In cell B13, enter the formula for computing the sum of the stock:

=SUM(B2:B11)

Check – Your spreadsheet should look similar to:

	A	B
1	ProductName	InStock
2	bottled water	225
3	chocolate bar	75
4	cola	275
5	juice	119
6	popcorn	143
7	soft pretzel	45
8	potato chips	100
9	gum	175
10	seat cushion	30
11	rain coat	50
12		
13	Units in Stock	1237

6) SAVE, PRINT, AND THEN CLOSE THE SPREADSHEET

a. Save the spreadsheet in the appropriate folder naming it Concession Stand Stock.

b. Print a copy of the spreadsheet with gridlines and row and column headings.

c. Save Concession Stand Stock again and then close the spreadsheet.

15.4 Creating an Access Table from Excel Spreadsheet Data

Spreadsheets are often used to maintain rows and columns of data. For example, a company may use a spreadsheet to maintain hours worked be employees. In this spreadsheet, each row corresponds to an employee and has a format similar to a database record. The spreadsheet data can then be used to create a table in the company's relational database so that queries and reports can include the employee data.

A Guide to Microsoft Office 2000 Professional

The steps for using Excel data to create a table in an open Access database are:

1. Highlight the spreadsheet cells to be used to create a table.

2. Select the Copy command.

3. Make the database active. Only the Database window with the Tables button selected should be displayed.

4. Select the Paste command.

The spreadsheet must remain open until the copied data is pasted into a new table.

When the Paste command is selected, Access displays a dialog box asking if the first row of the copied data contains column headings:

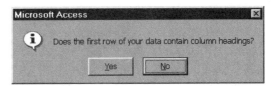

Selecting Yes uses the first row of data as field names. Selecting No uses the first row of data as a record. If No is selected, the table will need to be displayed in Design view so that appropriate field names can be defined.

renaming a table   When data from an Excel spreadsheet is pasted into an Access database, Access creates a table with a default name similar to Sheet1. The table name can be changed by right-clicking on it in the Database window and then selecting the Rename command in the displayed menu, which highlights that table name and displays a blinking cursor. The new name can then be typed and Enter pressed to rename the table.

After the table is renamed, it should be displayed in Design view to select the primary key and check the field types and formats. Descriptions should also be added for each of the fields. The new table's relationship to the other tables in the database must be defined before the new table can be used in a select query or report.

Practice 3 ——————————————————————————

In this practice you will create a new Access database table from Excel spreadsheet data. Open the CONCESSION STAND database if it is not already open.

1) OPEN THE CONCESSION STAND EMPLOYEES SPREADSHEET

2) COPY THE SPREADSHEET DATA

    a. Highlight cells A3 through C7.
    b. Select Edit → Copy. The employee data is copied to the Clipboard.

3) CREATE A NEW TABLE

    a. On the Taskbar, click on the CONCESSION STAND button. The CONCESSION STAND database is displayed.
    b. In the CONCESSION STAND : Database window, click on the Tables button if the table names are not already displayed. Be sure that there are no open tables, forms, or queries.
    c. Select Edit → Paste. A dialog box is displayed.
        1. Select Yes. A new table is created and a dialog box is displayed.
            a. Select OK. The dialog box is removed.

d. Right-click on the name of the new table, Sheet1. A menu is displayed.
e. Select the Rename command. The menu is removed and the table name is displayed highlighted with a blinking cursor.
f. Type Employees and then press Enter to replace the existing table name.

4) MODIFY THE NEW TABLE

a. Display the Employees table in Design view.
b. Click in the EmployeeID Field Name box to make it active if it is not already.
c. On the Toolbar, click on the Primary Key button.
d. From the Required collapsible list in the Field Properties part of the window, select Yes.
e. Enter appropriate descriptions for each field.
f. Change the Field Size to 4 for the EmployeeID field, 20 for the FirstName field, and 30 for the LastName field.
g. Save and close the modified table. If warning dialog boxes are displayed, select Yes in each one.

5) DEFINE THE RELATIONSHIP BETWEEN THE EMPLOYEES AND SALES TABLES

a. Select Tools → Relationships. The Relationships window is displayed.
b. On the Toolbar, click on the Show Table button ( ). A dialog box is displayed.
   1. Add the Employees table.
   2. Select Close. The dialog box is removed.
c. In the Employees table, drag the EmployeeID field to the EmployeeID field in the Sales table. A dialog box is displayed.
   1. Verify that the EmployeeID field of the Employees and Sales table appear in the dialog box.
   2. Select Create. The dialog box is removed.
d. Select File → Save.
e. Close the Relationships window.

6) QUERY THE DATABASE

a. Create a select query that displays bottled water sales and includes the FirstName and LastName fields from the Employees table, the ProductName field from the Products table, and the Quantity field from the Sales table.
b. Save the query naming it Bottled Water Sales and then print the query datasheet.

7) CLOSE CONCESSION STAND AND EXIT ACCESS

8) CLOSE CONCESSION STAND EMPLOYEES AND EXIT EXCEL

15.5 Mail Merge - Form Letters

Microsoft Office includes a feature called *mail merge* that integrates the information stored in an Access database with a Word document. Mail merge is commonly used to create personalized form letters. For example, businesses sometimes mail the same letter to thousands of recipients with each letter personalized.

merge field

A *form letter* is a Word document that includes *merge fields*, which are placeholders that indicate where data from an Access table or query should be inserted. When the data is merged, one copy of the form letter is printed for each record in the selected table or query with the appropriate field entries substituted for the merge fields.

Because mail merge documents will not usually be printed for every record in a table, a query should be used to limit the number of documents produced. For example, a department store preparing a form letter about a sale on electronic products might use a query that displays only previous Electronic Department customers. Each customer would receive the same letter, except the merge fields would be replaced by the name of that customer.

The steps for creating a mail merge form letter are:

1. **Create a new Word document.**

2. **Set up the document for mail merge.** Select the Mail Merge command from the Tools menu, which displays the Mail Merge Helper dialog box:

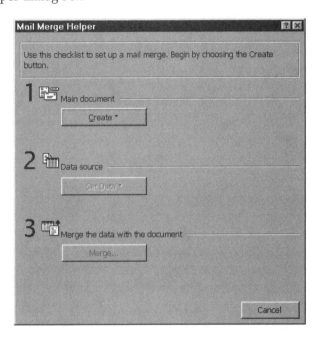

3. **Select the mail merge type.** In the Mail Merge Helper dialog box, click on the Create button and then select Form Letters from the list:

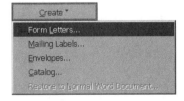

A dialog box is displayed:

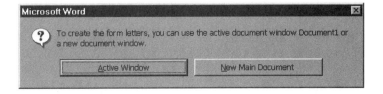

Select Active Window since the current document will be used.

4. **Select the database for merging.** In the Mail Merge Helper dialog box, select the Get Data button and then select Open Data Source from the list:

The Open Data Source dialog box is displayed, which is similar to the Open dialog box. In the Files of type collapsible list, select MS Access Databases. Select the desired database file from the appropriate folder and then select the Open button. Access is started, the selected database is opened, and a dialog box is displayed listing the tables and queries in the database.

5. **Select the table or query for merging.** In the dialog box displayed by Access, select the table or query that contains the fields to be used in the form letter:

Select OK. A dialog box is displayed with a message indicating that the main document must be edited:

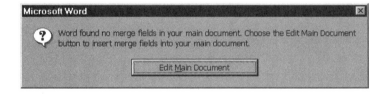

Select Edit Main Document. The dialog box with the message and the Mail Merge Helper dialog box are removed.

6. **Complete the form letter by typing the text and inserting merge fields.** To insert a merge field at the current cursor position, click on the Insert Merge Field button (Insert Merge Field ▾) on the Mail Merge Toolbar and then select the desired field name from the displayed list:

Mail Merge Toolbar—

merge fields

This form letter contains three merge fields

The merge field can be highlighted and formatted like any other text. Formatting applied to the marker will appear on the merged database entries.

7. **Print the letters.** On the Mail Merge Toolbar, click on the Merge to Printer button () to display the Print dialog box. Select OK to print a letter for each record in the database table or query, replacing the merge fields with the appropriate entry. To print a non-merged copy of the letter, select the Print command from the File menu.

The merged letters can be previewed by clicking on the View Merged Data button () on the Mail Merge Toolbar, which replaces the merge fields in the letter with the data from the selected table or query. Text surrounding the merged fields automatically adjusts to accommodate field entries of any length. The merged letters can be scrolled using the *mail merge record controls* on the Mail Merge Toolbar:

mail merge record controls

The mail merge record controls

Clicking on the button merges the first record with the form letter and displays it in the window. Clicking on the ▶| button merges the last record with the form letter. The other buttons are used to scroll each record of the table or query and merge them with the letter.

Clicking on the Mail Merge Helper button () on the Mail Merge Toolbar displays the Mail Merge Helper dialog box, where the mail merge options can be changed.

Practice 4

In this practice you will create and print mail merged letters.

1) CREATE A NEW WORD DOCUMENT

2) CREATE A FORM LETTER

a. Select Tools → Mail Merge. The Mail Merge Helper dialog box is displayed.
  1. Click on the Create button and then select Form Letters. A dialog box is displayed.
     a. Select the Active Window button. The dialog box is removed.
  2. Click on the Get Data button and then select Open Data Source. A dialog box is displayed.
     a. In the Files of type collapsible list, select MS Access Databases.
     b. In the Look in collapsible list, select the appropriate folder.
     c. Click on CONCESSION STAND and then select the Open button. The Microsoft Access dialog box is displayed.

        d. Select the Employees table and then OK. Another dialog box is displayed.

        e. Select the **Edit Main Document** button to remove the dialog box. The Mail Merge Helper dialog box is also removed and the Word document is displayed.

  b. Type today's date and then press Enter twice.

  c. Type Dear and a space.

  d. On the Mail Merge Toolbar, click on the Insert Merge Field button (Insert Merge Field ▾). A list of available fields is displayed.

  e. Click on the FirstName field. A merge field is inserted in the document.

  f. Type a space and then insert the LastName merge field.

  g. Type a colon (:) and then press Enter twice.

  h. Type the rest of the letter and insert the FirstName merge field as shown below. Type your name as the manager name in the closing:

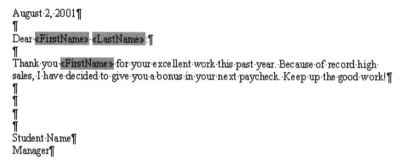

3) PRINT A NON-MERGED COPY OF THE FORM LETTER

  a. Save the form letter in the appropriate folder naming it Concession Stand Bonus.

  b. Select File → Print. A dialog box is displayed.

      1. Select OK to print a non-merged copy of the form letter. Note that the merge fields are displayed on the printout.

4) VIEW THE MERGED DATA

  a. On the Mail Merge Toolbar, click on the View Merged Data button (《》/ABC). The merge fields are replaced by field entries from the Employees table.

  b. On the Mail Merge Toolbar, click on the scroll arrows of the record controls to view the merged letters.

5) PRINT THE MAIL MERGED LETTERS AND THEN CLOSE THE DOCUMENT

  a. On the Mail Merge Toolbar, click on the Merge to Printer button (🖨). A dialog box is displayed.

      1. Select OK. Four letters are printed, with each personalized for the employees in the database.

  b. Save and close Concession Stand Bonus.

15.6 Mail Merge - Mailing Labels

Businesses often use labels to address letters or advertisements for mailing. In Office, mail merge can also be used to create *mailing labels.* Like a mail merge form letter, mailing labels are created in a document that includes merge fields. Selecting the appropriate command prints one label for each record in the table or query, substituting the appropriate field entries for the merge fields.

  A Guide to Microsoft Office 2000 Professional

When printing mailing labels, special adhesive paper with multiple labels to a page is used in the printer. The Avery© brand of adhesive labels is widely used, and the dimensions of many of its labels have been included in Word. Therefore, when using Avery labels, only the product number needs to be selected for Word to automatically print labels in the appropriate format.

The steps for creating mailing labels, similar to those for creating a mail merged letter, are:

1. **Create a new Word document.**

2. **Set up the document for mail merge.** Select the Mail Merge command from the Tools menu, which displays the Mail Merge Helper dialog box.

3. **Select the mail merge type.** In the Mail Merge Helper dialog box, click on the Create button and then select Mailing Labels from the list:

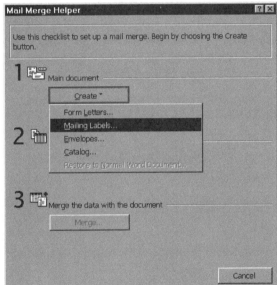

A dialog box is displayed:

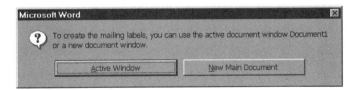

Select Active Window since the current document will be used.

4. **Select the database for merging.** In the Mail Merge Helper dialog box, select the Get Data button and then select Open Data Source from the list, which displays a dialog box. In the Open Data Source dialog box, select MS Access Databases from the Files of type collapsible list, the desired database file from the appropriate folder, and then the Open button. Access is started, the selected database is opened, and a dialog box is displayed listing the tables and queries in the database.

5. **Select the table or query for merging.** In the dialog box displayed by Access, select the table or query that contains the fields to be used in the mailing labels. Select OK. A dialog box is displayed with a message indicating that the main document must be set up:

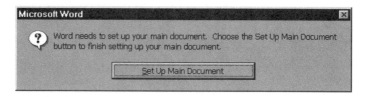

Select Set Up Main Document. The dialog box is removed and the Labels Options dialog box is displayed:

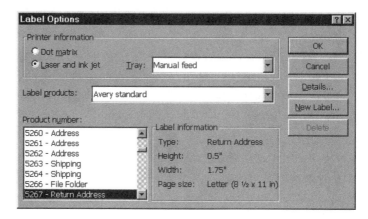

Select the appropriate Product number and any other desired options, and then select OK. Note that the product number is shown on the package containing the special adhesive labels.

6. **Complete the label by typing the text and inserting merge fields.** Select OK in the Label Options dialog box to display the Create Labels dialog box. Here, complete the labels by inserting merge fields and typing the text that should appear on every label. To insert a merge field, click on the Insert Merge Field button and then select the desired field name from the displayed list:

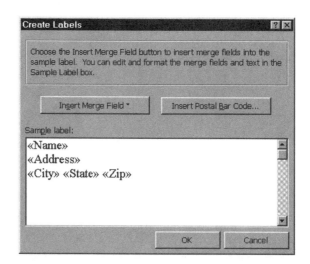

A Guide to Microsoft Office 2000 Professional

Select OK to remove the dialog box and display the Mail Merge Helper dialog box.

7. **Print the labels.** Select the Close button in the Mail Merge Helper dialog box to remove the dialog box. Next, insert the adhesive paper into the printer and then click on the Merge to Printer button ( ) on the Mail Merge Toolbar to display the Print dialog box. Select OK to print a label for each record in the database table or query, replacing the merge fields with the appropriate entry.

The mailing labels can be previewed by clicking on the View Merged Data button ( ) on the Mail Merge Toolbar. The merge fields are replaced by merged data in the document:

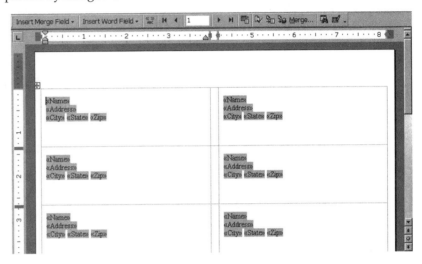

Practice 5

In this practice you will create mailing labels and print them on plain paper.

1) CREATE A NEW WORD DOCUMENT

2) CREATE MAILING LABELS

a. Select Tools → Mail Merge. The Mail Merge Helper dialog box is displayed.
　1. Click on the Create button and then select Mailing Labels. A dialog box is displayed.
　　a. Select the Active Window button. The dialog box is removed.
　2. Click on the Get Data button and then select Open Data Source. A dialog box is displayed.
　　a. In the Files of type collapsible list, select MS Access Databases.
　　b. In the Look in collapsible list, select the appropriate folder.
　　c. Click on CONCESSION STAND and then select the Open button. The Microsoft Access dialog box is displayed.
　　d. Select the Vendors table and then OK. Another dialog box is displayed.
　　e. Select the Set Up Main Document button to remove the dialog box. The Label Options dialog box is displayed.
　　f. In the Label products collapsible list, select Avery standard if it is not already selected.
　　g. In the Product number list, select 5160 - Address.
　　h. Select OK. The Label Options dialog box is removed and the Create Labels dialog box is displayed.
　　i. In the Create Labels dialog box, click on the Insert Merge Field button. A list of field names is displayed.

j. Click on the ContactFirstName field. A merge field is inserted into the dialog box.

k. Type a space and then insert the ContactLastName merge field.

l. Insert the rest of the merge fields as shown below:

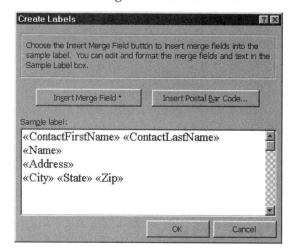

m. Select OK. The dialog box is removed.

3. In the Mail Merge Helper dialog box, select Close. The dialog box is removed. Note how the document is formatted to print multiple labels on one page.

3) VIEW THE MERGED DATA

On the Mail Merge Toolbar, click on the View Merged Data button (⟨⟨»⟩ABC). The merge fields are replaced by field entries from the Vendors table.

4) SAVE, PRINT, AND THEN CLOSE VENDOR LABELS

a. Save the labels document in the appropriate folder naming it Vendor Labels.

b. On the Mail Merge Toolbar, click on the Merge to Printer button (🖳). A dialog box is displayed.

1. Select OK to print a label for each vendor in the CONCESSION STAND database.

c. Save the modified Vendor Labels.

d. Close Vendor Labels.

5) EXIT WORD

Chapter Summary

This chapter presented the steps necessary to integrate an Access database with a Word document or Excel spreadsheet. Mail merge was also covered.

copying data from Access to Excel or Word

The steps for copying Access database entries from a displayed datasheet to an open Word document or Excel spreadsheet are:

1. Highlight the entries to be copied.

2. Select the Copy command.

3. Make the appropriate file active.

4. Place the cursor where the data is to appear and select the Paste command.

When copying entries, a query should first be applied so that only the desired data is displayed. The data copied to a Word document is automatically placed in a table structure. Data copied to an Excel spreadsheet can be used to ask What If? questions.

creating an Access table from Excel data

A new Access database table can be created from data stored in an Excel spreadsheet using the same steps above, except the <u>P</u>aste command is selected after the Tables button is selected in the Database window. The table should be renamed after it is created. The table should also be displayed in Design view so the primary key can be defined and any necessary changes can be made.

mail merge

Mail merge is the process of creating multiple copies of the same form letter while replacing the merge fields in the form letter with the corresponding Access database entries. The merge fields hold places for entries from a single table or a single query. Mail merge is also used to create mailing labels. The steps for creating a mail merge form letter or mailing labels are:

1. Create a new Word document.

2. Set up the document for mail merge by selecting the Mail Me<u>r</u>ge command from the <u>T</u>ools menu.

3. Select the mail merge type.

4. Select the Access database for merging.

5. Select the table or query for merging.

6. Complete the form letter or labels by typing the text and inserting merge fields.

 7. Print the letters or labels by selecting the Merge to Printer button on the Mail Merge Toolbar.

Before printing mailing labels, special adhesive paper needs to be inserted into the printer.

Vocabulary

Form letter The Word document that contains merge fields and text that will be printed on every page during mail merge.

Mail merge The integration of entries stored in an Access database table or query with a Word document.

Mailing labels A type of mail merge document used to print addresses on special adhesive paper.

Merge fields Indicates where the Access database table or query entries will appear when a form letter is merged.

Access and Word Commands and Buttons

Insert Merge Field | **Insert Merge Field button** Insert a merge field at the current cursor position. Found on the Mail Merge Toolbar.

Mail Merge command Displays a dialog box that allows the user to select options for creating a form letter or mailing labels. Found in the Tools menu.

Mail Merge Helper button Displays the Mail Merge Helper dialog box. Found on the Mail Merge Toolbar.

Mail merge record controls Used to scroll through mail merged letters. Found on the Mail Merge Toolbar.

Merge to Printer button Displays a dialog box where the user can select options for printing merged letters and mailing labels. Found on the Mail Merge Toolbar.

Rename command Used to rename an Access table. Displayed by right-clicking on a table name.

Select All Records command Highlights all the records in a datasheet. Found in the Edit menu.

View Merged Data button Used to preview merged letters and mailing labels. Found on the Mail Merge Toolbar.

Review Questions

Sections 15.1 — 15.4

1. List the steps required to copy the first two records in an Access database table to a Word document.

2. How do records copied from an Access database table appear in a Word document?

3. Why would you want to copy entries from an Access database table to an Excel spreadsheet?

4. List the steps required to copy records from an Access database table to an Excel spreadsheet.

5. Where do records copied from an Access database table appear in an Excel spreadsheet?

6. List the steps required to create an Access database table named Employees from data stored in an Excel spreadsheet.

Sections 15.5 — 15.6

7. What is mail merge?

8. What is a form letter?

9. What are merge fields?

10. List the steps required to create a mail merge document that uses the data stored in a query.

11. a) How do you preview a mail merge letter?
    b) What are the mail merge record controls used for?

12. What are mailing labels?

13. List the steps required to create mailing labels.

Exercises

Exercise 1 ——————————————— Vacation Prices

The owner of Hot Spot travel agency wants to ask What If? questions about the data stored in the Travel Agency database created in Chapter Twelve, Exercise 12. Open Travel Agency and complete the following steps:

a) Copy all the records in the Vacations table to a new Excel spreadsheet starting in cell A1. Resize columns and rows as necessary so that all the data in each cell fits on one line and is displayed entirely.

b) Insert two columns between columns C and D (Nights and Locations).

c) In cell D1, enter the label Cost per Night. In column D, enter formulas that use cell references to calculate the cost per night of the vacation packages. Cost per night is calculated by dividing the cost by the number of nights. Include appropriate formatting. Resize the column as necessary so that all the data is displayed entirely.

d) In cell E1, enter the label Price. The owner has decided that if the cost per night is less than $200, then the price of the vacation package is 20% more than the cost, otherwise the price of the vacation package is 50% more than the cost. In column E, enter formulas that use the IF function to calculate and display the price. Resize the column as necessary so that all the data is displayed entirely.

e) Format the spreadsheet appropriately.

f) Save the spreadsheet naming it Vacation Prices and print a copy with gridlines and row and column headings.

Exercise 2 ——————————————— Exhibits Memo

The board members of Sunport Science Museum want a list of the exhibits and the last time they were updated. The desired information is stored in the Museum Exhibits database created in Chapter Twelve, Exercise 2. Open Museum Exhibits and complete the following steps:

a) In a new Word document create the following memorandum, substituting your name for Student Name and allowing Word to wrap the text:

Memorandum

TO: Board Member

FROM: Student Name

DATE: February 1, 2001

RE: Exhibit List

The following list shows the exhibits currently showing at Sunport Science Museum, the department they are in, and the last time the exhibits have been updated:

b) Copy the ExhibitName, Department, and Updated entries in the Exhibits table to the memo after the last paragraph. Make sure there is a blank line between the paragraph and the copied data.

c) Save the memorandum naming it Exhibits Memo.

d) Open the BOARD MEMBERS spreadsheet that contains information on all the board members of Sunport Science Museum.

e) Create a new table in the Museum Exhibits database from the data stored in the BOARD MEMBERS spreadsheet.

f) Rename the new table Board Members.

g) Define the FirstName and LastName fields as the primary key. Add descriptions and modify the Field Properties for each field appropriately.

h) The Exhibits and Board Members tables are related by the Department and DepartmentHead fields. Create the appropriate relationship between the Exhibits and Board Members tables.

i) Using the Museum Exhibits database, modify the memorandum to mail merge the board members' first and last names in place of the word "Board Member."

j) Save the modified Exhibits Memo.

k) Print a non-mail merged copy of the memorandum and then print the mail merged memorandums.

Exercise 3 ⚙ —————————————— Plants, Green Thumb Vendor Labels

The owner of a plant nursery wants to ask What If? questions about the data stored in the Green Thumb database created in Chapter Twelve, Exercise 8. Open Green Thumb and complete the following steps:

a) Copy the Plant, InStock, Reorder, Cost, Retail, and VendorID entries in the Plants table to a new spreadsheet starting in cell A1. Resize columns and rows as necessary so that all the data in each cell fits on one line and is displayed entirely.

b) Insert one column between columns C and D (Reorder and Cost).

c) In cell D1, enter the label Reorder Now. Resize the column as necessary so that the label is displayed entirely. Plants need to be reordered when the amount in stock is less than the reorder number. In column D, enter formulas that use the IF function to display Reorder when more plants need to be reordered, or No Reorder if not. Include appropriate formatting.

d) Insert two columns between columns F and G (Retail and VendorID).

e) In cell G1, enter the label Profit. In column G, enter formulas that use cell references to calculate the profit made on each plant. The profit is calculated by subtracting the cost of the plant from the retail price of the plant. Resize the column as necessary.

f) In cell H1, enter the label Total Profit. In column H, enter formulas that use cell references to calculate the total profit made when all the plants are sold. The total profit is calculated by multiplying the profit per plant by the number of plants in stock. Resize the column as necessary.

g) Format the spreadsheet appropriately.

h) Save the spreadsheet naming it Plants and print a copy in landscape orientation with gridlines and row and column headings.

i) In a new Word document create mailing labels (5160 - Address) using the Vendors table in the Green Thumb database.

j) Save the document naming it Green Thumb Vendor Labels and then print the merged labels on plain paper.

Exercise 4 ————————————————————————Activity Letter

The COMPUTER CLONES CLUB relational database contains information on the history and activities of the Computer Clones club. The president of the club wants to send a letter to all the members informing them of the activities the club has done. Open COMPUTER CLONES CLUB and complete the following steps:

a) In a new Word document create the following letter, substituting your name for Student Name and allowing Word to wrap the text:

January 1, 2001

Dear Member:

This semester is going to be a great semester for the Computer Clones. With your help and dedication, I hope to increase our membership to 15 people. For the meeting on January 15, please look over the following activities we have done in the past and bring suggestions and ideas for new activities:

Sincerely,

Student Name
President

b) In the COMPUTER CLONES CLUB database, create a query that displays the Date, Activity, and Attendance fields from the Activities table. Save the query naming it List of Activities.

c) Copy all the records in the List of Activities select query to the letter after the last sentence in the body of the letter, which ends "…for new activities:". Be sure there is a blank line before and after the copied data.

d) Save the letter naming it Activity Letter.

e) Open the COMPUTER CLONES CLUB MEMBERS spreadsheet that contains information on the members of Computer Clones club.

f) Create a new table in the COMPUTER CLONES CLUB database from the data stored in cells A3 through E11 in the COMPUTER CLONES CLUB MEMBERS spreadsheet.

g) Rename the new table Members.

h) Define the StudentID field in the Members table as the primary key. Add descriptions and modify the Field Properties for each field appropriately.

i) The Activities and Members tables are related by the InCharge and StudentID fields. The Members and Club History tables are related by the StudentID field. Create the appropriate relationships between the Activities, Members, and Club History tables.

j) Create a query that displays the FirstName, LastName, and Status fields of the Members table of those members who are still active. Save the query naming it Active Members.

k) Using the Active Members query in the COMPUTER CLONES CLUB database, modify the letter to mail merge the active members' first and last names in place of the word "Member."

l) Scroll through the merged letter to make sure only active members will receive the letter. Make any necessary corrections.

m) Save the modified Activity Letter.

n) Print a non-mail merged copy of the letter and then print the mail merged letters.

Exercise 5 ——————————————————— Repair Request Letter

The ARCADE relational database contains information on the games owned by a local arcade. The owner of the arcade needs to send letters to all the manufacturers regarding broken games. Open ARCADE and complete the following steps:

a) Open the ARCADE MAINTENANCE RECORD spreadsheet that contains all the maintenance information on the games at the arcade.

b) Create a new table in the ARCADE database from the data stored in cells A3 through H13 of the ARCADE MAINTENANCE RECORD spreadsheet.

c) Rename the new table Maintenance.

d) Define the JobNumber field in the Maintenance table as the primary key. Add descriptions and modify the Field Properties for each field appropriately.

e) The Games and Maintenance tables are related by the Game field. Create the appropriate relationship between the Games and Maintenance tables.

f) Create a select query that displays the Name, ContactFirstName, ContactLastName, Game, Problem, Date, and Fixed fields of those games that have not been fixed. Save the select query naming it Broken Games.

g) In a new Word document create the following letter, substituting your name for Student Name, entering the merge fields as shown (using the Broken Games query in the ARCADE database), and allowing Word to wrap the text:

July 15, 2001

Dear <<ContactFirstName>> <<ContactLastName>>:

I own the <<Game>> game. However, the game is not working properly because of the following reason: <<Problem>>. It has been out of service since <<Date>>. Please send a maintenance representative from your company as soon as possible.

Thank you,

Student Name
Owner of Nickel and Dime Arcade

h) Scroll through the merged letter to make sure only the manufactures of the broken equipment will receive the letter. Make any necessary corrections.

i) Save the letter naming it Repair Request Letter.

j) Print a non-mail merged copy of the letter and then print the mail merged letters.

Advanced Exercise 6

Create an informative form letter based on Exercise 13, 14, or 15 in Chapter Twelve. The form letter should be merged based on a query resulting in less than five letters being printed. Also the form letter should contain information from the database that will be printed on every page. Save the form letter with an appropriate name. Print a non-mail merged copy of the letter and then print the mail merged letters.

Advanced Exercise 7

Create a database that contains a table that can be used as an address book. The table should contain at least 20 records of friends or family members. Create mailing labels that could be used to send holiday cards. Save the mailing labels with an appropriate name. Print the mail merged letters.

Making Presentations with PowerPoint

Vi̲ew Show

End S̲how

Slide N̲avigator

N̲ew Slide

D̲elete Slide

C̲lip Art

P̲rint

H̲eader and Footer

Select Al̲l

Appl̲y Design Template

S̲lide Master

Chapter Sixteen Objectives

After completing this chapter you will be able to:

1. Explain what a presentation is.
2. Create a new presentation based on a template.
3. Display a presentation in different views.
4. Display different slides.
5. View a presentation.
6. Edit text on a slide.
7. Add and delete slides, and change the order of slides.
8. Add a graphic to a slide.
9. Print a presentation.
10. Add footers to slides.
11. Add slide transitions and animation to slides.
12. Add a chart from an Excel spreadsheet to a slide.
13. Plan and design a presentation.
14. Use the Slide Master.
15. Create and print speaker notes.

The History of Presentations

In the past, visuals included slides, handwritten or typed overheads, chalkboards, and poster boards. Some slide presentations required teams of artists to spend days or weeks laying out the slides using special expensive equipment. Today, presentations are easily created electronically, which simplifies the preparation time and allows more time for refinement.

With advances in technology, it is becoming easier to use a computer to play the presentation, whether it is displayed on a large screen in an auditorium or on a monitor at eye level. One of the bestselling presentation software applications is Microsoft PowerPoint, with tens of millions of copies sold in the last few years.

$\mathbf{T}$his chapter describes how to make presentations that include text, charts, spreadsheet data, and clip art using Microsoft PowerPoint.

16.1 What is a Presentation?

Professionals and students all give presentations at one time or another. A *presentation* is an informative talk, such as a lecture or speech, that usually includes visuals. These *visuals* are often slides that are projected onto a screen while the speaker talks. For example, a sales representative for a clothes hanger company visits dry cleaners and gives a presentation on why their hangers are the best. The sales representative uses slides to outline and emphasize the most important points of the presentation. Some slides contain graphics and charts which convey information that would otherwise be difficult to describe in words.

visuals

In the past, the visuals for a presentation were overhead transparencies, paper flip charts, or slides in a slide projector. Producing these visuals was often complicated and costly. Now, professional-looking visuals can be produced quickly on a computer using a presentation application such as *Microsoft PowerPoint*, the presentation application in the Microsoft Office package. A *PowerPoint presentation* is a collection of slides stored in a file with each *slide* as an individual screen of the presentation. The presentation can be viewed on a screen by connecting the computer to a special projector or viewed on a large monitor.

PowerPoint presentation
slide

16.2 Creating a New PowerPoint Presentation

PowerPoint contains files called templates that are used for creating a presentation. A *PowerPoint template* is an already formatted presentation that can be modified to fit specific needs. Selecting the New Office Document command from the Start menu displays the New Office Document dialog box. Selecting the Presentations tab displays the templates:

PowerPoint template

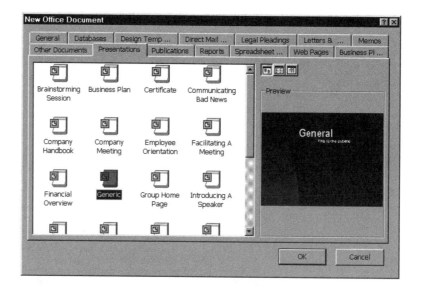

Selecting one of the templates and then OK starts PowerPoint and creates an untitled presentation that contains several slides. The presentation is displayed in Normal view, one of several views in PowerPoint. Normal view displays a presentation in a window divided into three separate *panes* sections called *panes*. For example, selecting the Generic template and then OK displays the following:

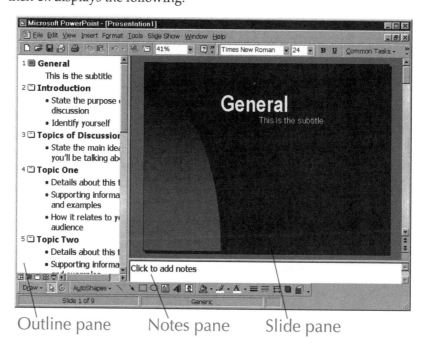

Outline pane   Notes pane   Slide pane

- **Outline pane** contains the text of all the slides in a format similar to Outline view in Word.

- **Slide pane** displays one slide at a time as it will appear in the presentation.

- **Notes pane** contains notes for the speaker that correspond to the displayed slide.

saving a presentation   A new presentation should be saved with a descriptive file name using the <u>S</u>ave command from the <u>F</u>ile menu.

16.3 PowerPoint Views

PowerPoint has five views that can be used to display slides. Each view is selected by clicking on one of the buttons in the lower-left corner of the PowerPoint window:

* **Normal view** displays a presentation in a window divided into three separate panes, which allows the slide, outline, and lecture notes to be edited without changing views.

* **Outline view** expands the Outline pane so that the text of the presentation can easily be edited.

* **Slide view** expands the slide pane.

* **Slide Sorter view** displays miniature slides that allow the order of slides in a presentation to be modified. Slide transitions and animations, discussed later, can be added in this view.

* **Slide Show view** displays the current slide in full-screen size as it appears during a presentation.

In any view that has panes, a pane can be resized by dragging on its top or right border.

Commands in the View menu can also be used to change the view.

16.4 Displaying Slides

Normal view, Outline view, and Slide view all include the Slide pane, where one slide is displayed at a time. The next or previous slide in the presentation can be displayed in this pane using several methods:

* clicking on the vertical scroll bar, box, or arrows

* clicking on the Previous Slide (⤴) or Next Slide (⤵) button, located below the vertical scroll bar

* pressing the Page Up or Page Down key

slide indicator

The *slide indicator* at the bottom of the window indicates the current slide and the total number of slides in the presentation:

slide indicator

active pane

The slide indicator is displayed when the Slide pane is active. A pane is made *active* by clicking in it.

16.5 Viewing a Presentation

Slide Show view is used to play a completed presentation. The presentation can be started at the currently displayed slide by selecting the Slide Show button () at the bottom of the window. Selecting the View Show command from the Slide Show menu starts the presentation from Slide 1, no matter what slide is currently displayed.

Once the presentation is started, the slides are displayed in full-screen size and the PowerPoint window is no longer visible. The keyboard and mouse are used during the presentation to control the slides:

- The next slide is displayed by either clicking the mouse button, pressing the N key, the Page Down key, or the spacebar.

- The previous slide is displayed by either pressing the P key or the Page Up key.

- The slide show is ended by pressing the Esc key, or by clicking the right mouse button and then selecting the End Show command from the displayed menu.

In Slide Show view you can quickly display a specific slide by clicking the right mouse button and then selecting the Slide Navigator command from the Go submenu, which displays a dialog box. Selecting the desired slide and then the Go To button displays that slide.

Practice 1

In this practice you will create a new PowerPoint presentation using a template.

1) CREATE THE PRESENTATION

    a. On the Taskbar, click on the Start button. A menu is displayed.

    b. Select the New Office Document command. A dialog box is displayed.

        1. Click on the Presentations tab to display the template icons.

        2. Click on the Generic icon and then select OK. PowerPoint is started and the first slide of a generic presentation is displayed in Normal view. Note the three panes.

2) VIEW THE SLIDE SHOW

    a. At the bottom of the PowerPoint window, click on the Slide Show button (). PowerPoint starts the presentation by filling the screen with the first slide:

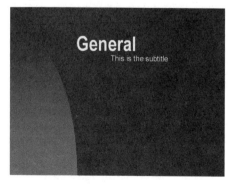

    b. Click the mouse button once. The show is advanced to the next slide, titled "Introduction."

    c. Press the N key. The next slide is displayed.

    d. Press the P key. The previous slide is displayed.

    e. Press the Esc key. The presentation is again displayed in Normal view.

3) **DISPLAY THE PRESENTATION IN DIFFERENT VIEWS**

 a. At the bottom of the PowerPoint window, click on the Outline view button (▤). The Outline pane is enlarged.

 b. Click on the Slide view button (▢). The Slide pane is enlarged.

 c. Click on the Normal view button (▣). The presentation is again displayed in Normal view.

4) **USE THE SLIDE INDICATOR**

 a. Click once on the text "Introduction" in the Outline pane. This pane is now active and the slide indicator displays "Outline."

 b. Click once on the slide in the Slide pane. This pane is now active and the slide indicator displays "Slide 2 of 9."

 c. Click once on the down scroll arrow in the Slide pane. The slide indicator now displays "Slide 3 of 9" and the "Topics of Discussion" slide is displayed.

 d. At the bottom of the vertical scroll bar, click on the Next Slide button (⬇). The slide indicator now displays "Slide 4 of 9."

 e. Press the Page Down key. Slide 5 of 9 is displayed.

 f. Press the Page Up key. Slide 4 of 9 is displayed again.

5) **SAVE THE FILE NAMING IT GEMSTONE**

Select File ➜ Save. A dialog box is displayed.

 1. In the File name entry box, type Gemstone to replace the existing text.

 2. In the Save in collapsible list, select the appropriate folder.

 3. Select Save. The presentation is saved with the name Gemstone.

16.6 Editing Text

The text in a slide may be edited in the Slide pane or in the Outline pane. Clicking once on the text in the Slide pane displays the outline of a *text object* and places the cursor in the box:

text object

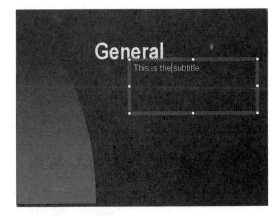

The text within the text object may then be edited. For example, the subtitle was clicked in the slide shown above to make its text object active. Note that the word "General" must be in a separate text object since it is not enclosed by the active text object. To edit the word "General," it must first by clicked to activate its text object.

In the Outline pane, clicking on text places the cursor and the text may then be edited.

Automatic Spell Checking

Text in text objects is automatically spell checked just as it is in Word. If a word is spelled incorrectly or is not in the dictionary file, a red wavy line appears below it. A misspelled word can be corrected by right-clicking on it to display a menu of suggested words, then clicking on the correct spelling.

16.7 Adding and Deleting Slides

When using a template, slides usually need to be deleted or added to the presentation.

A new slide can be added after the current slide by selecting the New Slide command (Ctrl+M) from the Insert menu, which displays a dialog box:

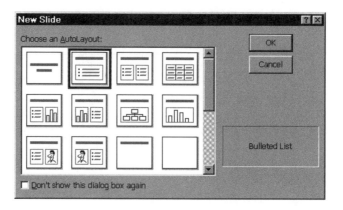

The appearance of the new slide is selected and then OK to insert a new slide after the current slide. The new slide can then be edited.

Individual slides can be deleted from a presentation by first displaying the slide in the Slide pane and then selecting the Delete Slide command from the Edit menu. The previous slide is then displayed and the slide indicator at the bottom of the window is updated. A slide can also  be deleted by selecting the slide's icon (▭) in the Outline pane and then selecting the Delete Slide command or pressing the Delete key.

Practice 2

In this practice you will add a slide, delete slides, and edit text in a presentation. Open Gemstone if it is not already displayed.

1) ADD A NEW SLIDE

    a. Display slide 6 of 9.

    b. Select Insert → New Slide. A dialog box is displayed.

          1. Select the third slide in the bottom row, then select OK. The new slide should look similar to:

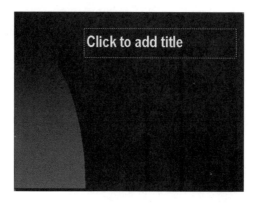

2) ENTER THE TITLE

a. In the Slide pane, click in the text "Click to add title." The outline of the text object is displayed, the text disappears, and the cursor is placed.

b. Type Mohs Hardness Scale, then click anywhere on the slide outside of the text object to deselect it. This slide will be added to in a later practice.

3) DELETE SLIDES

a. Display slide 3 of 10.

b. Select Edit → Delete Slide. The slide is deleted and slide 3 of 9 is now displayed.

c. Display slide 7 of 9.

d. Select Edit → Delete Slide. Slide 7 of 8 is now displayed.

4) DELETE A SLIDE USING THE OUTLINE PANE

a. In the Outline pane, point to the slide icon (▦) for slide 7 until the pointer shape changes to a cross hairs with arrows (✛), then click once. The entire slide's text is highlighted.

b. Press the Delete key. The slide is deleted.

5) ENTER TEXT FOR THE FIRST SLIDE

a. Display slide 1, then double-click on the word "General" in the Slide pane. The text object is made active and the word is highlighted.

b. Type Gemstone Lecture.

c. Click in the text "This is the subtitle." The cursor is placed.

d. Highlight the text "This is the subtitle."

e. Type By followed by your name.

6) ENTER THE REST OF THE TEXT

a. Click on the Outline view button (▤). The Outline pane is enlarged.

b. In the text for slide 2, edit the two bulleted items under "Introduction" to:

■ Gemstones are made of minerals
■ One type of mineral can form several types of gemstones

c. Change the Topic One, Topic Two, and Topic Three slides (slides 3, 4, and 5) to the following:

Quartz
■ Occurs in crystals
■ Very common mineral
■ Examples: amethyst, citrine

Corundum
■ Aluminum oxide material
■ Found in USA, India, South Africa
■ Examples: ruby, sapphire

Beryl
■ Very large crystals
■ Found in Colombia, Australia, Russia
■ Examples: emerald, aquamarine

d. Change the Next Steps slide (slide 7) to the following:

Summary
■ Quartz: amethyst, citrine
■ Corundum: ruby, sapphire

e. With the cursor at the end of the word sapphire, press Enter. A new bulleted item is added.

f. Type Beryl: emerald, aquamarine.

7) CHANGE VIEWS AND THEN SAVE THE MODIFIED GEMSTONE

   a. Display the presentation in Normal view.

   b. Save the modified Gemstone.

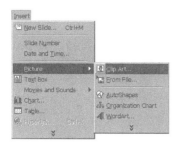

16.8 Adding Graphics to a Slide

Clip art graphics can be placed on a slide and then moved and resized as needed. Selecting the Clip Art command from the Picture submenu in the Insert menu displays the Microsoft Clip Gallery, and clicking on a category displays the clip art graphics in that category. Clicking on a graphic displays a pop-up menu, from which the Insert clip button (![icon]) can be selected to place a copy of the graphic on the current slide. The Back button (![icon]) in the dialog box can be used to display the categories again. Clicking on the Close button (✖) removes the dialog box.

A graphic can be dragged on a slide to move it, and resized by dragging one of its handles. The Cut, Copy, and Paste commands can be used to create copies or move a selected graphic to another slide. Pressing the Delete key deletes the selected graphic.

16.9 Changing the Order of Slides

Slide Sorter view allows you to get an overall view of the slides in a presentation. Clicking on the Slide Sorter View button (▦) at the bottom of the window displays the presentation as miniature slides:

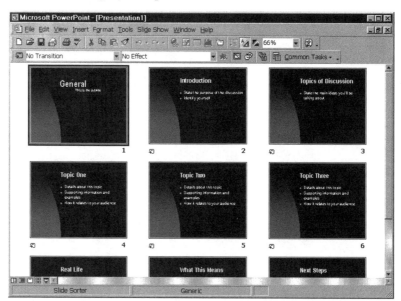

Slide Sorter view displays miniature slides

Viewing Slides in Slide Sorter View

The Scroll bars can be used to display slides not visible in the window.

Selecting Multiple Slides

In Slide Sorter view, multiple slides can be selected by holding down the Ctrl key and clicking on them.

The order of slides in a presentation can easily be changed in the Slide Sorter view. Clicking once on a slide selects it, indicated by a thick outline. For example, slide 1 is selected in the window above. A slide may then be dragged to another position in the window.

The order of slides can also be changed in other views in the Outline pane by dragging a slide's icon (▭) to another position in the outline.

16.10 Printing a Presentation

A presentation can be printed in several different arrangements by selecting the Print command from the File menu, which displays the Print dialog box. Options in the Print what collapsible list affect the contents of the printouts:

- The Slides option prints one slide per page.

- The Handouts option prints six miniature slides on each page. The number of slides on each page can be changed in the Slides per page option.

- The Outline View option prints the outline of the presentation as it appears in the Outline pane.

Options in the Print range section of the dialog box affect how much of the presentation is printed:

- The All option prints the entire presentation.

- The Current slide option prints only the displayed slide.

Practice 3

In this practice you will add a clip art graphic to the presentation and then print a copy. Open Gemstone if it is not already displayed.

1) ADD A CLIP ART GRAPHIC

a. Display slide 1 in Normal view.
b. Select Insert → Picture → Clip Art. A dialog box is displayed.
1. Click on the Shapes category. Graphics of different shapes are displayed.
2. Click on the first graphic, a star shape, to select it. A pop-up menu is displayed.
3. Click on the Insert clip button (![icon]). The graphic is placed on slide 1.
4. Click on the Close button of the dialog box. The dialog box is removed.

2) RESIZE AND MOVE THE GRAPHIC

a. If the graphic's handles are not displayed, click once on the graphic to select it.
b. Drag the lower-right handle of the graphic downwards and to the right. When the outline of the resized graphic is approximately twice the size, release the mouse button.
c. Drag the center of the graphic so that it is centered below the subtitle "By *your name*."

3) SAVE AND PRINT THE PRESENTATION

a. Save the modified Gemstone.
b. Select File → Print. A dialog box is displayed.
1. In the Print range section, select the All option if it is not already selected.
2. In the Print what collapsible list, select the Handouts option.
3. In the Handouts section, verify that the Slides per page option is 6.
4. Select OK. The Gemstone presentation is printed with six slides per page.

16.11 Adding Footers to Slides

Information about a presentation can be included at the bottom of each slide. Selecting the Header and Footer command from the View menu displays a dialog box, and selecting the Slide tab displays options for the footer:

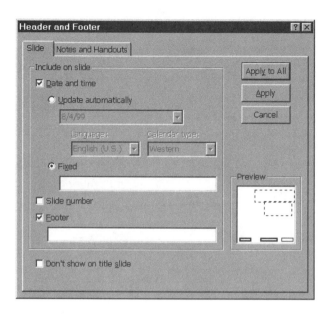

These options allow you to include the Date and time, the Slide number, and text in the Footer. Selecting Apply adds the selected options to the currently displayed slide, or selecting Apply to All adds them to every slide.

16.12 Slide Transitions

A *slide transition* is the way one slide changes to the next in Slide Show view. For example, the current slide can appear to fall off the screen to reveal the next slide, or it can dissolve into the next slide.

A slide transition is added in Slide Sorter view by first selecting the desired slide or slides and then selecting the transition from the Slide Transition Effects collapsible list on the Toolbar:

Except for special circumstances, all the slides in a presentation usually have the same transition and can be selected quickly by executing the Select All command (Ctrl+A) from the Edit menu.

 A transition icon (⬓) is displayed below each slide that has a transition applied to it. The transition can be previewed by clicking on the icon.

16.13 Animation

A slide can have animation added to it so that the separate items in the slide appear one by one in Slide Show view. *Animation* refers to the way items move onto a slide. For example, a slide with three bulleted items can first appear with just the slide's title. When the mouse button is clicked, the first item can appear by sliding in from the left side, or it can dissolve into place. The next click makes the next item appear in the same manner. After all the bulleted items are displayed, the next click displays the next slide.

Animation is added in Slide Sorter view by first selecting the desired slide or slides and then selecting the animation from the Preset Animation collapsible list on the Toolbar:

A Guide to Microsoft Office 2000 Professional

| No Effect | ▼ |

    ☰ᴵ   An animation icon (☰ᴵ) is displayed below each slide that has an animation applied to it. The transition and animation can be previewed at once by clicking on the animation icon.

Practice 4

In this practice you will add information to the bottom of each slide and then add slide transitions and animation. Open Gemstone if it is not already displayed.

1) ADD A FOOTER WITH THE SLIDE NUMBER AND TEXT

    a. Display slide 1 in Normal view.
    b. Select View → Header and Footer. A dialog box is displayed.
        1. Select the Slide tab if those options are not already displayed.
        2. Deselect the Date and time option.
        3. Select the Slide number option.
        4. Place the cursor in the Footer entry box and type Science Lecture Series.
        5. Select the Apply to All button. Slide 1 is displayed with the text and slide number at the bottom of the slide.
    c. Display slide 2. Note the footer information.

2) VIEW THE SLIDE SHOW

    a. Select Slide Show → View Show. The presentation starts with slide 1. Note the footer.
    b. Click the mouse button once. Slide 2 is displayed.
    c. Continue clicking the mouse button to view the entire slide show and return to Normal view.

3) ADD TRANSITIONS TO THE ENTIRE PRESENTATION

    a. Click on the Slide Sorter View button (⊞). The presentation is displayed in Slide Sorter view.
    b. Select Edit → Select All. All the slides in the presentation are selected.
    c. On the Toolbar, click on the down arrow of the Slide Transition Effects collapsible list, then scroll down and select Dissolve. The transition is applied to all of the slides.

4) ADD ANIMATION TO THE ENTIRE PRESENTATION

    a. All of the slides should still be selected from the previous step.
    b. On the Toolbar, click on the down arrow of the Preset Animation collapsible list, then select Fly From Left. The animation is applied to all of the slides.

5) VIEW THE SLIDE SHOW

    a. Select Slide Show → View Show. The presentation starts with slide 1. Notice the subtitle is not yet displayed.
    b. Click the mouse button once. The subtitle moves in from the left side of the screen.
    c. Click the mouse button again. Slide 1 "dissolves" in transition to slide 2. Note that only the title of slide 2, "Introduction," is displayed.
    d. Click the mouse button once. The first bulleted item moves in from the left side.
    e. Click the mouse button again. The second bulleted item moves onto the screen.
    f. Click the mouse button again. Slide 2 "dissolves" in transition to slide 3.
    g. Continue clicking the mouse button to view the entire slide show and return to Slide Sorter view.

6) SAVE THE MODIFIED GEMSTONE

16.14 Adding a Chart from an Excel Spreadsheet

Slides can include charts of data from an Excel spreadsheet. Charts can be added to any slide by copying and pasting. The steps for copying a chart from an open Excel spreadsheet onto a slide are:

1. Select the chart to be copied.

2. Select the Copy command.

3. Display the PowerPoint window.

4. Display the slide in Normal view or Slide view and select the Paste command.

On a slide, a chart can be moved and resized like a clip art graphic. Clicking on a chart selects it and displays handles for resizing.

Practice 5

In this practice you will add a chart to a slide. Open Gemstone if it is not already displayed.

1) ADD A CHART

a. Open the MOHS SCALE spreadsheet, which contains information on the Mohs hardness scale used to determine the strength of gemstones.
b. Click once on the Chart Area of the chart to select it if it is not already selected.
c. Select Edit → Copy. The chart is copied to the Clipboard.
d. Display the PowerPoint window. The Gemstone presentation is displayed.
e. Display slide 6 of 7 in Normal view.
f. Select Edit → Paste. The chart is pasted onto the slide.
g. Drag the chart until it is centered under the slide's title.
h. Display the spreadsheet.
i. Close MOHS SCALE and exit Excel without saving changes.

2) SAVE AND PRINT THE MODIFIED GEMSTONE

a. Save the modified Gemstone.
b. Print the presentation as Handouts with 6 slides per page.
c. Close Gemstone.

16.15 Planning a Presentation

A successful presentation is carefully planned before it is created. Even the most experienced lecturers spend time planning each detail of their presentation. Planning a presentation is a three step process:

1. **Carefully plan the lecture or speech** that will accompany the presentation, including what to say and how to say it:

   • Identify the purpose of the presentation. For example, will it be used to persuade opinions or present ideas?

   • Identify the audience so that appropriate language and speech styles can be determined. For example, a presentation for young children uses different vocabulary than one for lawyers.

A Guide to Microsoft Office 2000 Professional

- Keep remarks short and to the point. When the presentation is ended the audience should want to hear more, not be relieved it is over.

2. **Sketch the slides** using pencil and paper.

   - Make sure that the slides emphasize the key points to be made in the lecture.

   - Separate information over several slides to avoid putting too many concepts and ideas on one slide.

3. **Create the presentation using PowerPoint.**

   - Limit your design to two or three fonts. Also, avoid text that is all uppercase letters because it is more difficult to read.

   - Keep the text short and in a color different from the background color, preferably a light color on a dark background or vice versa.

16.16 Presentation Design

elements

layout

Any presentation can be made more effective if the elements on each slide reflect the presentation's purpose or subject matter. *Elements* are the objects and formatting on a slide, such as the text, graphics, colors, and fonts. The *layout* of the slide refers to the placement of text and graphics and is also part of the design. For example, a presentation on financial information could have a dark blue background and a plain font such as Times New Roman, which are more appropriate than a pink background and a script font.

The background and fonts of an entire presentation can be changed by selecting the Apply Design Template command from the Format menu which displays the Apply Design Template dialog box:

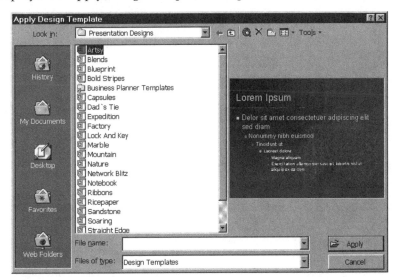

Selecting a design template in the list displays a sample of the design in the right side of the dialog box. Selecting Apply changes the background design and fonts of all the slides in the presentation.

Slide Master

Just the font can be changed on all the slides using the *Slide Master*. Selecting the Slide Master command from the Master submenu in the View menu displays a slide similar to:

Any formatting applied to text in the Slide Master is applied to all the slides in the presentation. Note that the text on the Slide Master need only be clicked on, not selected, to be formatted.

Practice 6

In this practice you will format a presentation.

1) OPEN FLORIDA GIFT SHOW

This presentation contains three slides.

2) VIEW THE SLIDE SHOW

a. Select Slide Show → View Show. The presentation starts with slide 1.
b. Click the mouse button once. Slide 2 is displayed.
c. Continue clicking the mouse button to view the entire slide show.

3) CHANGE THE DESIGN TEMPLATE

a. Display the presentation in Slide Sorter view.
b. Select Format → Apply Design Template. A dialog box is displayed.
    1. Select Soaring in the list. An example of this design is displayed in the dialog box.
    2. Select Apply. The Soaring design appears on all the slides in the presentation.

4) CHANGE THE TEXT FORMATTING

a. Select View → Master → Slide Master. The Slide Master slide is displayed.
b. At the top of the slide, click in the text "Click to edit Master title style."
c. On the Formatting Toolbar, in the Font collapsible list select Times New Roman. The font is changed from Arial to Times New Roman.
d. On the Formatting Toolbar, click on the Bold button. The text is now bold.
e. Click in the text "Click to edit Master text styles" in the first bulleted item.
f. On the Formatting Toolbar, in the Font collapsible list select Arial. The font is changed from Times New Roman to Arial.
g. Display slide 1 in Normal view. Note the fonts of the title and subtitle.

5) VIEW THE SLIDE SHOW

a. Select Slide Show → View Show. The presentation starts with slide 1.

A Guide to Microsoft Office 2000 Professional

b. Click the mouse button once. Slide 2 is displayed.

c. Continue clicking the mouse button to view the entire slide show.

6) *SAVE AND THEN PRINT THE MODIFIED FLORIDA GIFT SHOW*

a. Save the modified FLORIDA GIFT SHOW.

b. Print the presentation as Handouts with 6 slides per page. The three slides print on one page.

<table>
<tr><td>

Notes Page View

Selecting the Notes Page command from the View menu displays the presentation with each slide on a page with the notes below it.

</td><td>

16.17 Creating and Printing Speaker Notes

Notes for the speaker can be entered into the Notes pane for each slide. Clicking in the Notes pane places the cursor, which allows text to be typed. Dragging on the top boundary of the pane expands it.

The notes can be printed by selecting Notes Pages in the Print what collapsible list in the Print dialog box, which prints one slide and the corresponding notes on each page.

</td></tr>
</table>

Practice 7

In this practice you will create and print notes. Open FLORIDA GIFT SHOW if it is not already displayed.

1) *EXPAND THE NOTES PANE*

a. Display slide 1 in Normal view if it is not already displayed. The Notes pane is displayed below the Slide pane.

b. Drag upwards on the top boundary of the Notes pane until the Slide pane is half as tall.

2) *TYPE NOTES FOR EACH SLIDE*

a. Click in the text "Click to add notes" to place the cursor. The text is removed.

b. Type the following text, pressing Enter at the end of the first line:

At Ryder Resort in Orlando.
Biggest show to date.

c. Click once in the slide pane to activate it, then press the Page Down key to display slide 2.

d. Type the following text in the Notes pane, pressing Enter at the end of each line:

HOT: stuffed animals and bean bags.
Candles: scented were most popular.
Music boxes were expensive.

e. Click once in the slide pane to activate it, then press the Page Down key to display slide 3.

f. Type the following text in the Notes pane, pressing Enter at the end of each line:

Some companies offered free point-of-purchase displays.
Free with purchase promos were popular.
A hot topic was point systems.

3) *SAVE, PRINT, AND THEN CLOSE THE MODIFIED FLORIDA GIFT SHOW*

a. Save the modified FLORIDA GIFT SHOW.

b. Select File → Print. A dialog box is displayed.

1. In the Print range section, select the All option if it is not already selected.

2. In the Print what collapsible list, select the Notes Pages option.

3. Select OK. One slide and the corresponding notes are printed per page.

c. Close FLORIDA GIFT SHOW.

4) *EXIT POWERPOINT*

16.18 Where can you go from here?

This chapter introduced you to the concepts of a presentation application: how slides are created, edited, and modified to produce a professional-looking presentation. PowerPoint has other options not discussed in this text which you may want to explore using the online help.

Presentation applications are becoming more common in both academic and business environments. Because you have learned how to use PowerPoint, you will easily be able to learn and use other presentation applications.

Chapter Summary

This chapter introduced the Microsoft PowerPoint presentation application. A PowerPoint presentation is a collection of slides stored in a file with each slide as an individual screen of the presentation. A PowerPoint Template is an existing presentation that can be modified to fit specific needs.

PowerPoint presentation template

A new presentation is displayed in Normal view, which contains three panes. The Outline pane contains the text of all the slides, the Slide pane displays a slide as it will appear in the presentation, and the Notes pane contains speaker notes.

panes

A presentation can be viewed in five different views: Normal, Outline, Slide, Slide Sorter, and Slide Show. The buttons in the lower-left corner of the window can be selected to change views.

Normal view, Slide view, and Outline view all include the Slide pane, where one slide is displayed at a time. The next or previous slide in the presentation can be displayed using the vertical scroll bar, the Previous Slide (⬆) or Next Slide (⬇) button, or the Page Up or Page Down key. The slide indicator at the bottom of the window indicates the current slide and the total number of slides in the presentation.

slide indicator

A presentation can be viewed in Slide Show view starting at the currently displayed slide by selecting the Slide Show button (🖵). Selecting the <u>V</u>iew Show command from the Sli<u>d</u>e Show menu starts the presentation from Slide 1. The next slide is displayed by either clicking the mouse button, pressing the N key, the Page Down key, or the spacebar on the keyboard. The previous slide is displayed by either pressing the P key or the Page Up key. The slide show is ended by pressing the Esc key, or by clicking the right mouse button and then selecting the End <u>S</u>how command from the displayed menu.

In Slide Show view, clicking the right mouse button displays a menu. Selecting the Slide <u>N</u>avigator command from the <u>G</u>o submenu displays a dialog box that allows a specific slide to be displayed.

Clicking on text on a slide in the Slide pane displays the outline of a text object, allowing the text in that object to be edited. The text of slides may also be edited in the Outline pane.

text object

A new slide can be added after the current slide by selecting the New Slide command from the Insert menu. The current slide can be deleted by selecting the Delete Slide command from the Edit menu, or by selecting the slide's icon (⊟) in the Outline pane and then selecting the Delete Slide command or pressing the Delete key.

Clip art graphics can be placed on a slide using the Clip Art command from the Picture submenu in the Insert menu. The graphic can be dragged on the slide to move it, and resized by dragging one of its handles. Pressing the Delete key deletes the selected graphic.

Slide Sorter view displays the entire presentation in miniature slides, allowing the order of slides to be modified. The presentation can be printed with six miniature slides to a page by selecting the appropriate options in the Print dialog box.

Slides can be made more descriptive by including footers. The Header and Footer command from the View menu can be used to add the date, time, slide number, and text to the bottom of a slide.

Slide transitions and animation can be added to slides selected in Slide Sorter view by selecting the desired effects from the Slide Transition Effects and Preset Animation collapsible lists on the Toolbar. A transition icon (⟲) displayed below a slide allows the transition to be previewed by clicking on the icon. An animation icon (≡) is used similarly.

A chart from an Excel spreadsheet can be added to a slide by first selecting the chart in the spreadsheet and then selecting the Copy command. The slide that is to receive the chart is displayed and then the Paste command selected.

Presentations should be carefully planned using a three step process in order to have an effective presentation. The three steps include planning the lecture or speech, sketching the slides and their contents, and then creating the presentation using PowerPoint.

elements, layout   Each slide has many elements. The layout of a slide refers to the placement of text and graphics. The background and font of each slide in the presentation is changed using the Apply Design Template command from *Slide Master*   the Format menu. The Slide Master is used to change the font on all the slides.

Speaker notes can be entered into the Notes pane for each slide. The notes can be printed by selecting Notes Pages in the Print what collapsible list in the Print dialog box, which prints one slide and the corresponding notes on each page.

Vocabulary

Animation   The way items move onto a slide.

Elements   The objects and formatting on a slide, such as the text, graphics, colors, and fonts.

Layout   The placement of text and graphics on a slide.

Normal view   Displays a presentation in a window divided into three separate panes, which allows the slide, outline, and lecture notes to be edited.

Notes pane   Contains notes for the speaker that correspond to the displayed slide.

Outline pane   Contains the text of all the slides in a format similar to Outline view in Word.

Outline view   Expands the Outline pane so that the text of the presentation can easily be edited.

Pane   A section of a window.

PowerPoint presentation   A collection of slides stored in a file with each slide as an individual screen of the presentation.

PowerPoint template   An already formatted presentation which can be modified to fit specific needs.

Presentation   An informative talk, such as a lecture or speech, that usually includes visuals.

Slide   An individual screen of a presentation.

Slide indicator   Indicates the current slide and the total number of slides in a presentation.

Slide pane   Displays a slide as it will appear in the presentation.

Slide Show view   Displays the current slide in full-screen size as it appears during a presentation.

Slide Sorter view   Displays an overall view of the presentation in miniature slides.

Slide transition   The way one slide changes to the next in Slide Show view.

Slide view   Expands the Slide pane.

Visuals Overhead transparencies, paper flip charts, or slides projected on a screen while a speaker talks.

PowerPoint Commands and Buttons

Apply Design Template **command** Displays a dialog box that allows the user to change the background and fonts of an entire presentation. Found in the Format menu.

Clip Art **command** Displays a dialog box that allows the user to insert clip art into a slide. Found in the Picture submenu in the Insert menu.

Delete Slide **command** Deletes the currently displayed slide. Found in the Edit menu.

End Show **command** Ends the slide show. Found in the menu displayed by right clicking during a slide show.

Header and Footer **command** Displays a dialog box that allows the user to insert the date, time, slide number, and text in the footer of all the slides in a presentation. Found in the View menu.

New Slide **command** Displays a dialog box that allows the user to insert a slide after the currently displayed slide. Found in the Insert menu.

Next Slide button Displays the next slide. Located below the vertical scroll bar.

Normal View button Displays a presentation in Normal view. Found at the bottom of the window.

Outline View button Displays a presentation in Outline view. Found at the bottom of the window.

Previous Slide button Displays the previous slide. Located below the vertical scroll bar.

Slide Master **command** Displays the Slide Master slide, which allows the fonts on all the slides to be changed at once. Found in the Master submenu in the View menu

Slide Navigator **command** Displays a dialog box that allows the user to specify the number of the slide to display during a presentation. Found in the Go submenu in the menu displayed by right clicking during a slide show.

Slide Show button Starts the presentation from the currently displayed slide. Found at the bottom of the window.

Slide Sorter View button Displays a presentation in Slide Sorter view. Found at the bottom of the window.

Slide View button Displays a presentation in Slide view. Found at the bottom of the window.

View Show **command** Starts the presentation from Slide 1, no matter what slide is currently displayed. Found in the Slide Show menu.

Review Questions

Sections 16.1 — 16.7

1. a) What is a presentation?
    b) What are visuals?
    c) What is a slide?

2. a) What is a template?
    b) What is a pane?
    c) List the three different panes displayed in Normal view and what each pane displays.

3. List the steps required to create a new presentation in PowerPoint using the Generic template.

4. List the five different views that a presentation can be displayed in and describe what each view is used for.

5. a) List three different ways to display the next slide of a presentation in Normal view.
    b) How can you tell which slide is currently displayed in Normal view?

6. a) List four different ways to display the next slide in Slide Show view.
    b) How do you end a slide show?

7. List the steps required to quickly display slide 5 of a presentation when slide 1 of 26 is displayed in Slide Show view.

8. List the steps required to edit the text on a slide.

9. a) List the steps required to add a new slide after slide 4 in a presentation displayed in Normal view.
    b) How can a slide be selected in the Outline pane?
    c) List two different ways to delete the current slide in Normal view.

Sections 16.8 — 16.14

10. List the steps required to place a clip art graphic on slide 3 of a presentation displayed in Normal view.

11. a) What is displayed in Slide Sorter view?
    b) What is Slide Sorter view used for?

12. List the steps required to print a presentation with six slides on each page.

13. List the steps required to display the current date and time, slide number, and the text Marketing on the bottom of every slide in a presentation.

14. a) What is a slide transition?
    b) List the steps required to add a Box Out transition to all the slides in a presentation.
    c) Where is a transition icon displayed?
    d) What is a transition icon used for?

15. a) What is animation?
    b) List the steps required to add a Wipe Right animation to slide 2 in a presentation.
    d) Where is an animation icon displayed?
    c) What is an animation icon used for?

16. a) List the steps required to place a copy of a chart stored in an Excel spreadsheet onto slide 6 in a presentation.
    b) List the steps required to move and resize a chart on a slide.

Sections 16.15 — 16.18

17. Describe the three step process used in planning a presentation.

18. a) What are elements?
    b) List two examples of elements.
    c) What is the layout of a slide?

19. List the steps required to change the background and font on all the slides to the Marble design template.

20. List the steps required to change the font on all the slides to 22 point Arial.

21. a) List the steps required to enter speaker notes on slides 2 and 4 of a presentation.
    b) List the steps required to print the speaker notes of a presentation.

Exercises

Exercise 1 —————————————————————— Catsharks

Create a new presentation based on the Generic template. Save the presentation naming it Catsharks and complete the following steps:

a) Modify the presentation so that it contains five slides with the following text:

Catsharks
  A Brief Introduction

Characteristics
  ■ bottom-dwellers
  ■ small, up to 1 meter long

Coral Catshark
  ■ found in the Pacific Ocean
  ■ white spots on dark body

Swellshark
  ■ found in the Pacific Ocean
  ■ dark brown mottled color

Striped Catshark
  ■ found in the Atlantic Ocean
  ■ dark horizontal stripes

b) Apply the Capsules design template to the presentation.

c) Add the slide number and your name in the footer of each slide.

d) Add the Dissolve transition and Peek From Bottom animation to each slide.

e) Save the modified Catsharks.

f) Print the presentation so that all the slides are printed on one page.

Exercise 2 —————————————————————— Maple Trees

Create a new presentation based on the Generic template. Save the presentation naming it Maple Trees and complete the following steps:

a) Modify the presentation so that it contains five slides with the following text:

Maple Trees
  Broadleafed Tree Series

Sugar Maple
  ■ sap is used for maple syrup
  ■ height - 24 meters

Silver Maple
  ■ leaves have large teeth
  ■ height - 15 meters

Red Maple
- bright red flowers and buds
- height - 30 meters

Tree Heights

b) In a new Excel spreadsheet, enter the tree names and their height data, and create a bar chart titled Maple Trees. Save the spreadsheet naming it Maples.

c) Place a copy of the chart on slide 5, the slide with the title "Tree Heights." Resize and move the chart appropriately.

d) Apply the Expedition design template to the presentation.

e) Add the slide number and your name in the footer of each slide.

f) Add the Cover Left transition and Spiral animation to each slide.

e) Save the modified Maple Trees.

f) Print the presentation so that all the slides are printed on one page.

Exercise 3 ☼ ———————————————— Volcano Presentation

The VOLCANOES document modified in the practices of Chapter Six can be used as the basis for a presentation. Print a copy of the VOLCANOES report and complete the following steps:

a) Using paper and pencil, sketch five slides for the presentation.

b) Using PowerPoint, create a new presentation based on the Generic template. Save the presentation naming it Volcano Presentation.

c) Modify the existing slides so that the presentation contains the following:

- five slides containing the appropriate text
- an appropriate design template applied to the slides
- the slide number and your name in the footer of each slide
- the Box Out transition and Fly From Right animation added to each slide
- Arial font on each slide
- at least one clip art graphic
- an increased font size on the title slide

d) Save the modified Volcano Presentation.

e) Print the presentation so that all the slides are printed on one page.

Exercise 4 ☼ ———————————————Track Team Performance

Create a new presentation based on the Generic template. Save the presentation naming it Track Team Performance and complete the following steps:

a) Modify the presentation so that it contains four slides with the following text:

Track Team 2001
    Performance Plan

Team Progress - 100 Meter

Team Progress - 200 Meter

Improving our Performance
- nutrition
- cross training
- attitude seminar

b) On slide 1, add a clip art graphic. Resize and move the graphic appropriately.

c) Open the Track Progress spreadsheet last modified in Chapter Nine, Exercise 12. Place a copy of the "Track Team's Progress in 100 Meter" chart on slide 2. Resize and move the chart appropriately.

d) Place a copy of the "Track Team's Progress in 200 Meter" chart on slide 3. Resize and move the chart appropriately.

e) Close Track Progress.

d) Apply the Network Blitz design template to the presentation.

e) Add the slide number and your name in the footer of each slide.

f) Add the Split Vertical In transition and Swivel animation to each slide.

g) Save the modified Track Team Performance.

h) Print the presentation so that all the slides are printed on one page.

Advanced Exercise 5 ——————————— Computer History Presentation

Plan a presentation on the history of computers using the information in Chapter One, sections 1.1 through 1.10. Using paper and pencil, sketch the slides of the presentation. Using PowerPoint, create a new presentation based on the Generic template. Save the new presentation naming it Computer History Presentation. Include appropriate clip art, footer text, slide transitions, and animation. Create speaker notes for each slide. Print the presentation so that all the slides are printed six slides to a page and then print all the slide notes.

Advanced Exercise 6 ——————————— Environmental Presentation

Plan a presentation on an environmental issue of your choice. Using paper and pencil, sketch the slides of the presentation. Using PowerPoint, create a new presentation based on the Generic template. Save the new presentation naming it Environmental Presentation. Include appropriate clip art, footer text, slide transitions, animation, and a chart. Create speaker notes for each slide. Print the presentation so that all the slides are printed six slides to a page and then print all the slide notes.

Plan a presentation in which you propose a business plan for a company you wish to start. Using PowerPoint, create a new presentation based on the Generic template. Save the presentation naming it Persuade Investors. Include appropriate clip art, footer text, slide transitions, animation, and a chart. Create speaker notes for each slide. Print the presentation so that all the slides are printed six slides to a page and then print the slide notes.

Delete Object

Delete Text

Zoom

Whole Page

Page Width

Clip Art

Go to Background, Go to Foreground

Send to Background, Send to Foreground

Page

Delete Page

Layout Guides

Text File

Open Data Source

Merge

Show Merge Results

Print Merge

Chapter Seventeen Objectives

After completing this chapter you will be able to:

1. Explain what desktop publishing is.
2. Create a new publication and use the Quick Publication Wizard to change its appearance.
3. Create text frames and enter text.
4. Select, position, and resize text frames.
5. View a publication at different magnifications.
6. Add a graphic to a publication.
7. Resize and move the graphic.
8. Move objects to the background or foreground, and display the background or foreground.
9. Print a publication.
10. Create folded greeting cards.
11. Display different pages.
12. Understand layout guides, and create and move ruler guides.
13. Add and delete pages.
14. Change margins and add guides for columns.
15. Insert text from a Word document into a text frame.
16. Connect text frames and display text in overflow.
17. Use mail merge to personalize a publication.

The History of Desktop Publishing

In the past, publications were created manually by using sticky wax to affix pieces of paper onto a board. The sticky wax allowed the designer to rearrange the text and graphics before they sent the board, called a mock-up, to the printer. Written specifications had to be included with the mock-up, including the point sizes, fonts, the distances between each graphic and paragraph, and many other measurements. The printer then interpreted all this and painstakingly created the final publication.

With desktop publishing applications, anyone can quickly create a publication that includes graphics and text, many fonts, and elaborate formatting. With a click of the mouse, the publication is printed quickly. Many changes and printouts can easily be made.

T his chapter discusses desktop publishing and how to use text and graphics to produce professional-looking documents. The Microsoft Publisher application is introduced.

17.1 What is Desktop Publishing?

publication

Desktop publishing is the process of combining text and graphics into one file, called a *publication*. Publications can include brochures, greeting cards, and newsletters. A desktop publishing application such as Microsoft Publisher, included in the Microsoft Office package, has tools and features that make creating a publication easy.

17.2 Creating a New Publication

Blank
Publication

A new publication is created by first selecting the New Office Document command from the Start menu, which displays the New Office Document dialog box. Clicking on the Blank Publication icon and then selecting OK starts Publisher and displays the Catalog dialog box. Selecting the Blank Publications tab displays the following options:

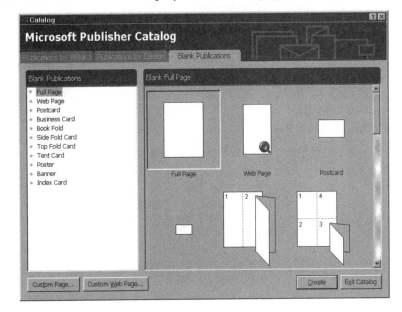

thumbnail

Different types of publications are listed in the left side of the dialog box, and a small picture, called a *thumbnail*, of each type is displayed in the right side. Selecting a publication type and then the **Create** button displays the Publisher window with a blank publication:

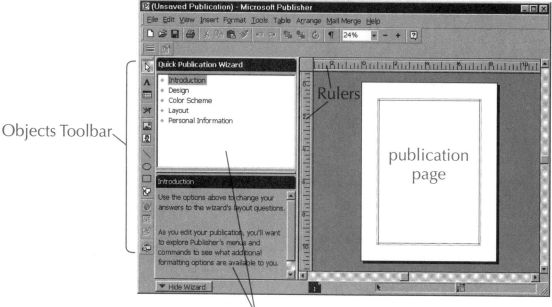

Objects Toolbar

Rulers

Quick Publication Wizard panes

- **Objects Toolbar** contains buttons for creating objects on the publication page.

- **Quick Publication Wizard** has two panes and is used to format a publication.

- **Publication page** is the page as it will appear when printed.

- **Rulers** contain markings for measuring and are used to create guides, which are discussed later.

If Publisher is already running, a new publication can be created by selecting the <u>N</u>ew command from the <u>F</u>ile menu, which displays the Catalog dialog box.

saving a publication

A new publication should be saved with a descriptive file name using the <u>S</u>ave command from the <u>F</u>ile menu. When working in Publisher, if an open publication has not been saved in the past fifteen minutes, a dialog box appears prompting you to save your work.

opening a publication

An existing publication can be opened by selecting the <u>O</u>pen command from the <u>F</u>ile menu.

17.3 The Quick Publication Wizard

The *Quick Publication Wizard* is a tool that helps the user select design and color options for a publication. The wizard is displayed in two panes next to the publication page, with a list of options in the top pane. The bottom pane displays the choices available depending on the option selected in the top pane.

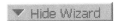

The Quick Publication Wizard can be removed from the window by clicking on the Hide Wizard button (▼ Hide Wizard) at the bottom of the window. This expands the publication page to the entire window and changes the button to the Show Wizard button (▲ Show Wizard), which can be clicked to again display the wizard.

Practice 1

In this practice you will create a new publication and use the Quick Publication Wizard.

1) CREATE THE PUBLICATION

    a. On the Taskbar, click on the Start button. A menu is displayed.
    b. Select the New Office Document command. A dialog box is displayed.
        1. Click on the General tab to display those icons if they are not already displayed.
        2. Click on the Blank Publication icon and then select OK. Publisher is started and the Catalog dialog box is displayed.
            a. Select the Blank Publications tab to display those options.
            b. In the list, select the Full page publication type if it is not already selected.
            c. Select Create to display the new publication in the Publisher window. Note the Quick Publication Wizard panes.

2) USE THE QUICK PUBLICATION WIZARD TO CHANGE THE DESIGN

    a. In the top pane of the Quick Publication Wizard, click on the Design option. Choices for this option are displayed in the bottom pane.
    b. In the bottom pane of the wizard, click on the Butterfly option. Graphics are added to the publication page.
    c. In the bottom pane of the wizard, click on Pinwheel. The graphics on the publication page are changed.
    d. In the bottom pane of the wizard, click on Corner Art. The graphics on the publication page are changed again.

3) USE THE WIZARD TO CHANGE THE COLOR SCHEME

    a. In the top pane of the wizard, click on the Color Scheme option. Choices for this option are displayed in the bottom pane.
    b. In the bottom pane of the wizard, click on the Clay option. The colors of the graphics on the publication page are changed.
    c. In the bottom pane of the wizard, click on Lagoon. The colors of the graphics on the publication page are changed again.

4) HIDE THE WIZARD

At the bottom of the window, click on the Hide Wizard button (▼ Hide Wizard). The wizard's panes are removed from the window.

5) SAVE THE PUBLICATION NAMING IT PICNIC FLYER

Select File → Save. A dialog box is displayed.
    1. In the File name entry box, type Picnic Flyer.
    2. In the Save in collapsible list, select the appropriate folder.
    3. Select Save. The publication is saved with the name Picnic Flyer.

17.4 Text Frames

The Text Frame Tool (A) on the Objects Toolbar is used to create an object on a publication page called a *text frame*. A *frame* is a gray outline that defines the edges of an object. Text cannot be typed directly onto a publication page, a text frame must first be created and then text typed into the frame. Selecting the Text Frame Tool and then dragging the cross hairs pointer (+) on the publication page creates a text frame with the cursor already placed in it, ready for text to be typed.

editing and formatting text in a frame

Once text is typed into a frame, it can be edited and formatted in the same manner as in Word. The text must first be highlighted, and then formats applied using the Formatting Toolbar or commands in the Format menu.

moving and resizing a text frame

A text frame can be resized and moved on the publication page. Clicking once on text selects its frame, and pointing to a handle changes the pointer to the RESIZE shape ( ). Dragging then resizes the frame, changing the flow of the text in it. A text frame is moved by first pointing to the gray frame, not on a handle, which changes the pointer to the MOVE shape ( ). Dragging then moves the frame.

Right clicking in a text frame displays a menu:

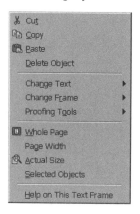

| Cut |
| Copy |
| Paste |
| Delete Object |
| Change Text ▶ |
| Change Frame ▶ |
| Proofing Tools ▶ |
| Whole Page |
| Page Width |
| Actual Size |
| Selected Objects |
| Help on This Text Frame |

The Cut, Copy, and Paste commands can be used to edit text and text frames. If text is highlighted in the frame, these three commands manipulate the highlighted text. If no text is highlighted, the entire frame is cut or copied. Selecting the Delete Object command deletes the frame, and selecting the Delete Text command deletes highlighted text in the frame.

Creating a Text Frame

A text frame can be created quickly by selecting the Text Frame Tool on the objects Toolbar and then clicking once on the publication page.

Automatic Spell Checking

Text in text frames is automatically spell checked just as it is in Word. If a word is spelled incorrectly or is not in the dictionary file, a red wavy line appears below it. A misspelled word can be corrected by right-clicking on it to display a menu of suggested words, then clicking on the correct spelling.

17.5 Viewing a Publication

Commands in the Zoom submenu in the View menu can be used to change the magnification of the publication page in the window. The Whole Page command (Ctrl+Shift+L) displays the entire page, and the Page Width command displays the page as wide as possible. Specific percentages of magnification can also be selected from the Zoom submenu.

In any magnification, the scroll bars are used to display hidden parts of the page. The Page Up and Page Down keys can also be used to vertically scroll a publication.

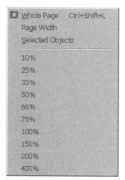

A Guide to Microsoft Office 2000 Professional

The Zoom Out ( ) and Zoom In (+) buttons on the Standard Toolbar can be used to change the magnification of the publication page. The Zoom collapsible list on the Standard Toolbar can also be used to change magnification.

The F9 key can be used to zoom into a selected object. For example, selecting a text frame and pressing F9 zooms into the text frame, no matter where it is on the publication page. Pressing F9 again zooms back out to the previous magnification.

Practice 2

In this practice you will change the magnification, create text frames, and format text. Open Picnic Flyer if it is not already displayed.

1) CHANGE VIEWS

a. Select <u>V</u>iew → <u>Z</u>oom → Page Width. The publication page is displayed as wide as possible.
b. Press the Page Down key. The lower part of the publication page is displayed.
c. Select <u>V</u>iew → <u>Z</u>oom → <u>W</u>hole Page. The entire publication page is displayed.

2) CREATE A TEXT FRAME

a. On the Objects Toolbar, click on the Text Frame Tool (**A**).
b. Move the pointer to the publication page. Note that the pointer has changed to a cross hairs shape (+).
c. Inside the border design, drag from the upper-left corner of the page to the bottom right corner. A text frame is created and the cursor is in the upper-left corner of the frame.

3) ZOOM INTO THE TEXT FRAME AND ENTER TEXT

a. Press the F9 key. The view is zoomed into the top of the text frame.
b. Type the following text, pressing Enter at the end of each line:

    The 2001
    McCallister
    Family Picnic!
    Food!
    Fun!
    Swimming!

c. Highlight all of the text and format it as 48 point, bold, and center aligned.
d. Press the F9 key. The entire publication page is displayed.

4) RESIZE THE TEXT FRAME

a. Click once on the text to select the text frame. Handles and the gray frame are displayed.
b. Point to the center handle at the bottom of the text frame. The pointer changes to the RESIZE shape ( ).
c. Drag upwards until the bottom of the frame is just below the bottom of the "Swimming!" text. The frame is resized.

5) CREATE ANOTHER TEXT FRAME AND ENTER TEXT

a. On the Objects Toolbar, click on the Text Frame Tool (**A**).
b. Inside the border design, drag to create a text frame that fills the space below the text frame that was just resized.
c. Press the F9 key. The view is zoomed into the new text frame.

d. Type the following text, pressing Enter at the end of each line:

> Saturday, July 21
> 10 a.m. to 4 p.m.
> Heron Park

e. Highlight all of the text and format it as 28 point and italic.
f. Press the F9 key. The entire publication page is displayed.

Check – Your publication page should look similar to:

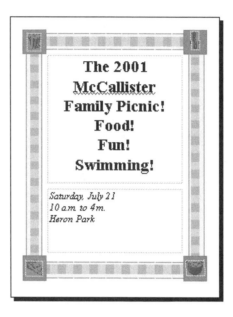

6) SAVE THE MODIFIED PICNIC FLYER

17.6 Adding Graphics

Clip art graphics can be placed on a publication page and then moved and resized as needed. Selecting the Clip Art command from the Picture submenu in the Insert menu displays the Microsoft Clip Gallery, and clicking on a category displays the clip art graphics in that category. Clicking on a graphic displays a pop-up menu, from which the Insert clip button () can be selected to place a copy of the graphic on the current publication page. The Back button (⇐) in the dialog box can be used to display the categories again. Clicking on the Close button (✕) removes the dialog box.

moving and resizing a graphic

A graphic placed on a publication page has a frame just like a text frame. Clicking once on a graphic selects its frame, and pointing to a handle changes the pointer to the RESIZE shape (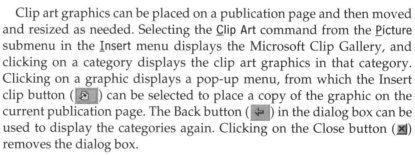). Dragging a corner handle resizes the graphic proportionally, and dragging a side, top, or bottom handle stretches the graphic. Pointing to anywhere on a graphic, except a handle, changes the pointer to the MOVE shape ( ). Dragging then moves the graphic.

17.7 The Background and Foreground

Objects can be placed either on the background or foreground of a publication. The *background* and *foreground* are two separate parts of a publication, and only one can be accessed at a time using the Go to Background and Go to Foreground (Ctrl+M) commands in the View menu. For example, a graphic placed on the background can only be resized and moved when the Go to Background command has been selected, making the background active. Note that viewing the background displays only objects on the background. Viewing the foreground displays all objects, but only the objects on the foreground can be selected and edited.

headers and footers

Objects are usually placed on the foreground, except for objects that do not need to be edited frequently. Any object on the background appears on every page in a publication. For example, headers and footers are created on the background in text frames. The Send to Foreground and Send to Background commands in the Arrange menu are used to move a selected object to the desired part of the publication.

17.8 Printing and Closing a Publication

A publication can be printed by selecting the Print command from the File menu, which displays the Print dialog box. Selecting OK prints a copy of the publication using the default settings. The Print button on the Standard Toolbar may be used to print a publication without displaying the Print dialog box.

A publication should be closed when you are finished working on it by selecting the Close command from the File menu. When a publication is closed, a new, blank publication is automatically displayed.

exiting Publisher

Publisher can be exited by selecting the Exit command from the File menu.

Practice 3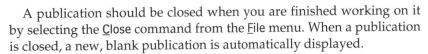

In this practice you will move objects to the background, add a footer, and add clip art. Open Picnic Flyer if it is not already displayed.

1) CHANGE VIEWS

   a. Select View → Go to Background. The background of the publication is displayed. Note that there are no objects on the background.
   b. Select View → Go to Foreground. The foreground of the publication is again displayed.

2) MOVE AN OBJECT TO THE BACKGROUND AND VIEW IT

   a. Click once on the border that was added using the wizard in Practice 1. The border is selected.
   b. Select Arrange → Send to Background. A dialog box is displayed with a message.
      1. Select OK. The border is still visible but is now on the background.
   c. Click once on the border to try to select it. Note that it cannot be selected.
   d. Select View → Go to Background. The background of the publication is displayed, now with the border. Note that the text frames are not displayed.
   e. Click once on the border to try to select it. The border is selected.

3) CREATE A FOOTER

    a. On the Objects Toolbar, click on the Text Frame Tool (**A**).

    b. At the bottom of the page, below the border design, drag to create a small text frame in the center:

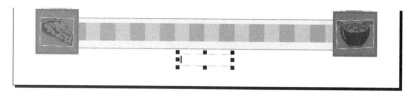

    c. Press the F9 key. The view is zoomed into the new text frame.

    d. Type your name, then resize the text frame so that just your name is visible.

    e. Move the text frame so that it is approximately centered below the border.

    f. Select View → Zoom → Whole Page. The entire publication page is displayed.

    g. Select View → Go to Foreground. The foreground of the publication is again displayed, and both the border, the footer, and the other text frames are visible.

4) PLACE A GRAPHIC

Select Insert → Picture → Clip Art. A dialog box is displayed.

    1. Click on the Seasons category. Graphics are displayed.

    2. Click on the fourth graphic, a sun wearing sunglasses, to select it. A pop-up menu is displayed.

    3. Click on the Insert clip button (🗗). The graphic is placed on the publication page.

    4. Click on the Close button of the dialog box to remove it.

5) MOVE THE GRAPHIC

    a. If the graphic's handles are not displayed, click once on the graphic to select it.

    b. Point to the graphic. The pointer changes to the MOVE shape (🖓).

    c. Drag the graphic so that it is in the right half of the bottom text frame.

    d. Click anywhere in the publication to deselect the graphic.

Check – Your publication page should look similar to:

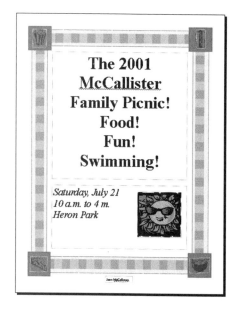

6) SAVE, PRINT, AND THEN CLOSE THE MODIFIED PICNIC FLYER

    a. Save the modified Picnic Flyer.

    b. Select File → Print. A dialog box is displayed.

        1. Select OK to print the publication.

    c. Select File → Close. A new, blank publication is displayed.

17.9 Creating Folded Greeting Cards

In addition to one-page flyers like that created in Practices 1 and 2, greeting cards can be created using Publisher. A greeting card is made by folding an 8.5" x 11" piece of paper twice, which results in a front "page," two inside "pages," and a back "page:"

A new publication for a greeting card is created by selecting the Side Fold Card publication type in the Blank Publications tab in the Catalog dialog box, which displays the following dialog box:

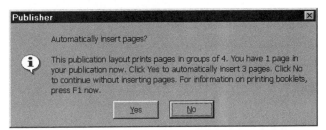

Selecting Yes creates a new publication with four pages, which correspond to the front, inside, and back "pages" of folded piece of paper.

The card is completed in Publisher by placing text and graphics on the appropriate pages in the publication and formatting as desired. The publication is then printed and folded to make the greeting card.

17.10 Working with Multiple Pages

Many publications have more than one page. Each page is represented by a page icon at the bottom of the publication window:

This publication has four pages, with page 2 currently displayed as indicated by the highlighted icon

Clicking on a page icon highlights the icon and displays that page in the window.

Displaying Pages Using the Keyboard

Pressing Ctrl+F5 displays the next page in the publication, and pressing Shift+F5 displays the previous page.

17.11 Using Guides

layout guides

Publications have colored lines called *guides* that help to precisely arrange objects on a page. The pink and blue guides are *layout guides*. The pink guides indicate the margins, and the blue guides are automatically created one-tenth of an inch inside the margins to help avoid placing objects directly on the margin. *Ruler guides* are green and can be added anywhere on a page and moved around. A ruler guide is added by holding down the Shift key, pointing to one of the Rulers until the pointer changes to the ADJUST shape (⬍), and then dragging off the Ruler to the desired location:

ruler guides

The Snap to Guides Command

The Snap to Guides command (Ctrl+W) from the Tools menu allows you to turn on and off the snap to guides feature.

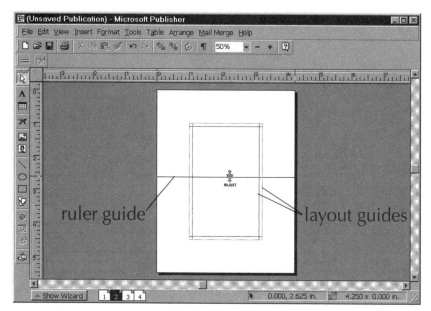

Any object that is moved near a guide "snaps" or "jumps" exactly to the guide. This helps to precisely line up objects on a page.

moving a ruler guide

A ruler guide can be moved by holding down the Shift key, pointing to the ruler guide until the pointer changes to the ADJUST shape (⬍), and then dragging the guide to a new position. Dragging a ruler guide off the publication page deletes the guide.

deleting a ruler guide

Practice 4

In this practice you will create a new greeting card publication, format it, and work with multiple pages.

1) CREATE THE PUBLICATION

Select File → New. A dialog box is displayed.
1. Select the Blank Publications tab to display those options.
2. In the list, select the Side Fold Card publication type.
3. Select Create. A dialog box is displayed.
   a. Select Yes create the new publication with four pages.

2) CHANGE THE DESIGN AND COLOR SCHEME

a. In the top pane of the Quick Publication Wizard, click on the Design option.
b. In the bottom pane of the wizard, click on the Birthday option. Graphics are added to the publication page.

c. In the top pane of the wizard, click on the Color Scheme option.

d. In the bottom pane of the wizard, click on the Prairie option. The colors are changed.

e. At the bottom of the window, click on the Hide Wizard button (▼ Hide Wizard). The wizard's panes are removed from the window.

3) DISPLAY PAGE 3 AND ENTER TEXT

a. At the bottom of the window, click on the page 3 icon (3). Page 3 is displayed. Note that the design and color scheme are not applied to this page, just page 1.

b. Create a text frame on page 3, as large as possible inside the blue layout guides.

c. Zoom in and type the following text, pressing Enter at the end of each line:

> Join us at the Zoo for
> Timmy's Birthday!
> 11 a.m. to 1 p.m.
> Meet us by the lions!

d. Highlight all of the text and format it as 14 point and italic.

4) POSITION THE TEXT FRAME

a. Drag the text frame so that the upper-left corner of the frame moves toward the layout guides in the upper-left corner of the page. Note how the frame snaps to a guide as it gets near it.

b. Position the text frame so that its upper-left corner is against the blue layout guides in the upper-left corner of the page.

5) CREATE A RULER GUIDE

a. Press and hold down the Shift key. Do not release it yet.

b. Point to the horizontal Ruler above the publication page. The pointer changes to the ADJUST ⬍ shape.

c. Drag down off the Ruler, creating a ruler guide, and keep dragging until the guide is at the 2.25" mark on the vertical Ruler.

d. Release the Shift key.

e. Resize the text frame so that its bottom right corner is against the ruler guide and the blue layout guide.

6) PLACE A GRAPHIC

a. Click once anywhere outside the text frame to deselect it.

b. Select Insert → Picture → Clip Art. A dialog box is displayed.

  1. Click on the Animals category. Graphics are displayed.

  2. Click on the first graphic, a lion, to select it. A pop-up menu is displayed.

  3. Click on the Insert clip button (🖼). The graphic is placed on the publication page.

  4. Click on the Close button of the dialog box to remove it.

c. Move the graphic so that its bottom-right corner is against the blue layout guides in the bottom-right corner of the page.

d. Click anywhere in the publication to deselect the graphic.

Check – Your publication page should look similar to:

7) SAVE, PRINT, AND THEN CLOSE THE PUBLICATION

    a. Save the publication in the appropriate folder naming it Zoo Party.

    b. Print a copy of Zoo Party.

    c. Close Zoo Party. A new, blank publication is displayed.

8) FOLD THE GREETING CARD

With the printed side down, fold the printout in half so that pages 1 and 4 are visible on one side, and pages 2 and 3 are visible on the other side. Fold the paper again in half, with the birthday cake graphic on the outside and the lion graphic on the inside.

17.12 Adding and Deleting Pages

Pages can be added to a publication by selecting the **Page** command (Ctrl+Shift+N) from the <u>I</u>nsert menu, which displays the Insert Page dialog box:

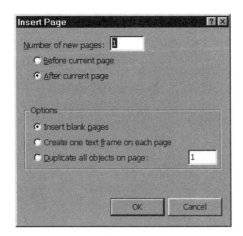

Typing the **Number of new pages** desired in the entry box and then selecting the **Before current page** or **After current page** option indicates how many pages are to be inserted and where they will go with respect to the currently displayed page. Selecting OK adds the pages to the publication.

The currently displayed page can be deleted from a publication by selecting the **Delete Page** command from the <u>E</u>dit menu.

A Guide to Microsoft Office 2000 Professional

17.13 Changing Margins and Adding Guides for Columns and Rows

The margins of a publication can be changed by selecting the Layout Guides command from the Arrange menu, which displays the Layout Guides dialog box:

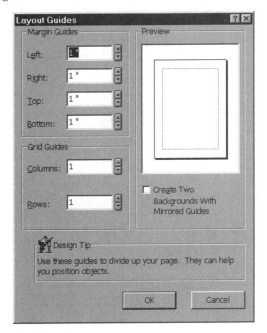

Typing values into the Left, Right, Top, and Bottom entry boxes and then selecting OK changes the layout guides on all pages in the publication.

Guides that separate the page into rows and columns can be added to a publication using the Columns and Rows entry boxes in the dialog box shown above. For example, typing 3 in the Columns entry box, 2 in the Rows entry box, and selecting OK places guides on all pages as follows:

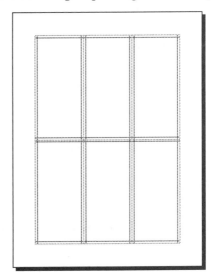

Practice 5 ———————————————————————————

In this practice you will open a publication, add and delete pages, change the margins, and add guides for columns.

1) OPEN THE PUBLICATION

Select File → Open. A dialog box is displayed.

1. In the Look in collapsible list, select the appropriate folder.
2. Click on SOS QUARTERLY.
3. Select Open. The SOS QUARTERLY publication is displayed, which contains a text frame, two graphics, and a ruler guide.

2) ADD PAGES

Select Insert → Page. A dialog box is displayed.

1. In the Number of new pages entry box, type 2.
2. Select OK. Two new pages are added to the publication after page 1, and page 2 is displayed.

3) DELETE A PAGE

Select Edit → Delete Page. The current page is deleted, leaving two pages in the publication.

4) CHANGE THE MARGINS

a. Select Arrange → Layout Guides. A dialog box is displayed.

1. In the Left entry box, type 0.5.
2. In each of the Right, Top, and Bottom entry boxes, type 0.5.
3. Select OK. The margins are changed from 1" to 0.5", and the layout guides on the publication page are also changed.

b. At the bottom of the window, click on the page 1 icon. Page 1 is displayed. Note that the layout guides have also been changed on this page.

5) ADD GUIDES FOR COLUMNS

Select Arrange → Layout Guides. A dialog box is displayed.

1. In the Columns entry box, type 3.
2. Select OK. Guides are added for three columns on both pages.

6) MOVE THE TEXT FRAME AND THE GRAPHICS

a. Move the text frame so that its upper-right corner is against the blue layout guides in the upper-right corner of the page.
b. Move the tree graphic so that its upper-left corner is against the blue layout guides in the upper-left corner of the page.
c. Move the mountain graphic so that its bottom-right corner is against the blue layout guides in the bottom-right corner of the page.

7) SAVE THE MODIFIED SOS QUARTERLY

17.14 Inserting Text from a Word Document

Word documents can be inserted into an existing text frame in a publication, allowing the text to be created and edited in the word processor before it is placed in Publisher.

A Guide to Microsoft Office 2000 Professional

The steps for inserting text from a Word document into an open publication are:

1. Create a text frame and select it.

2. Select the T**e**xt File command from the **I**nsert menu, which displays a dialog box similar to the Open New Document dialog box.

3. Select the desired Word document in the dialog box.

4. Select OK to insert the text from the document into the selected text frame.

If a text frame is not large enough to fit all of the inserted text, a dialog box is displayed:

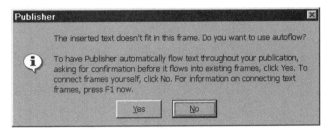

overflow
A ▪▪▪

Selecting No places all of the text into the frame, with some of the text hidden. The hidden text is said to be in *overflow*. The Text In Overflow indicator (A ▪▪▪) is displayed at the bottom of any text frame that has text in overflow.

One way to display the text in overflow is by resizing the text frame larger, which increases the amount of text that can be displayed. Another way to display the text in overflow is by connecting text frames, described in the next section.

17.15 Connecting Text Frames

flowed

Text in overflow can be continued, or *flowed*, into another text frame by connecting the frames. Connecting text frames does not mean that the frames are physically connected or touch each other. The separate frames are linked to each other in the publication so that as text is added or deleted to one frame, it can flow into or out of the next connected frame.

The steps for connecting a text frame to a text frame that has text in overflow are:

1. Create a new text frame.

2. Select the text frame that has text in overflow.

3. Click on the Connect Text Frames button (⊜) on the Toolbar. The pointer changes to a pitcher shape 🜨.

4. Move the pitcher over the second text frame until the pointer changes to a pouring pitcher shape 🜨, and click once to flow the text and connect the frames.

Selecting a connected frame displays the Go To Previous Frame button (⬅️⌨️), the Go to Next Frame button (⌨️➡️), or both buttons:

Go To Previous Frame button

| This is an example of three linked frames. The first frame contains some text, the sec- | ond frame has more, and the third frame contains the rest of the text. Note the Go To Previous Frame | button at the top of the middle frame and the Go To Next Frame button at the bottom of the middle frame. |

Go To Next Frame button

Clicking one of the buttons selects the previous or next connected frame.

Practice 6

In this practice you will insert text from Word documents and connect text frames. Open SOS Quarterly if it is not already displayed.

1) CREATE A TEXT FRAME

    a. Display page 1 if it is not already displayed.
    b. Create a text frame in the first column.
    c. Resize the text frame so that it fits across the first column, between the blue layout guides.
    d. Move the text frame so that its top is against the green ruler guide.
    e. Resize the text frame so that its bottom is against the blue layout guide at the bottom of the page.

2) INSERT TEXT

    a. Select the text frame if it is not already selected.
    b. Select Insert → Text File. A dialog box is displayed.
        1. In the Look in collapsible list, select the appropriate folder.
        2. Click on PEACE RIVER.
        3. Select OK. A dialog box is displayed.
            a. Select No. The PEACE RIVER document is inserted into the text frame. Note the Text In Overflow indicator (🅰️•••) at the bottom of the text frame, indicating that there is text in the frame that is not displayed.

3) CONNECT TEXT FRAMES

    a. Create a text frame in the second column.
    b. Resize and move the text frame so that it fits across the second column, between the blue layout guides, and its top is against the green ruler guide.
    c. Resize the text frame so that its bottom is against the blue layout guide at the bottom of the page.
    d. In the first column, select the text frame, which already has text in it.
    e. On the Toolbar, click on the Connect Text Frames button (🔗).
    f. Move the pointer to the text frame in the second column. The pointer changes to the pouring pitcher shape 🫗.
    g. Click once. The text is flowed into the text frame in the second column. Note the Go To Previous Frame button at the top of this frame.

4) INSERT MORE TEXT

    a. Create a text frame in the third column.

    b. Resize and move the text frame so that it fits across the third column, between the blue layout guides, and its top is against the green ruler guide.

    c. Resize the text frame so that its bottom is about 2" above the mountain graphic. Use the markings on the vertical Ruler for measuring.

    d. Select the text frame if it is not already selected.

    e. Select Insert → Text File. A dialog box is displayed.

        1. In the Look in collapsible list, select the appropriate folder.

        2. Click on BINOCULARS.

        3. Select OK. A dialog box is displayed.

            a. Select No. The BINOCULARS document is inserted into the text frame. Note the Text In Overflow indicator, indicating that there is text that is not displayed.

    f. Resize the text frame so that its bottom is just above the mountain graphic. The Text In Overflow indicator is no longer at the bottom of the text frame because all text is displayed.

5) SAVE THE MODIFIED SOS QUARTERLY

17.16 Using Mail Merge in a Publication

Microsoft Office includes a feature called *mail merge* that integrates the information stored in an Access database with a publication.

The steps for creating a mail merge publication are:

1. **Select a text frame.** Select a text frame in the publication and move the cursor to where the merge fields are to be placed.

2. **Select the database for mail merge.** Select the Open Data Source command from the Mail Merge menu. The Open Data Source dialog box is displayed:

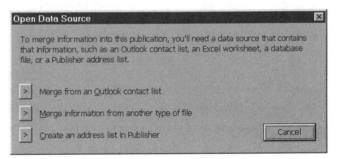

In the Open Data Source dialog box, select the Merge information from another type of file button. A dialog box similar to the Open Document dialog box is displayed:

> ### More on Mail Merge
>
> Creating form letters and mailing labels using mail merge is discussed in Chapter Fifteen.

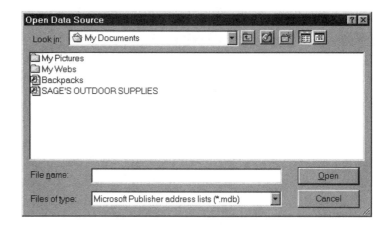

Select the desired database and then Open. The Choose Table dialog box is displayed:

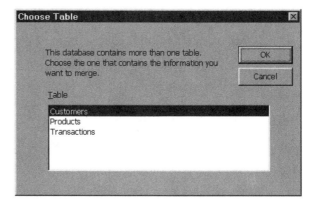

3. **Select the table that contains the desired fields.** In the Choose Table dialog box, select the desired table and then OK. The Insert Fields dialog box is displayed:

4. **Select the desired fields.** In the Insert Fields dialog box, select a field and then Insert. A merge field is placed at the current cursor position. Repeat this process for each desired field. After placing all the desired merge fields, select Close to remove the dialog box. In the publication, the merge fields are displayed in the text frame and can be formatted as desired.

5. **Merge the data.** Select the Merge command from the Mail Merge menu. The data is merged into the publication and the Preview Data dialog box is displayed:

Clicking on the ⏮ button displays data from the first record, and the ⏭ button displays data from the last record. The other buttons are used to scroll each record of the table. Select Close to remove the dialog box and display the merge fields. The Preview Data dialog box can again be displayed by selecting the Show Merge Results command from the Mail Merge menu.

6. **Print the merged publications.** Select the Print Merge command from the File menu. One copy of the publication is printed for each record.

Practice 7

In this practice you will complete the newsletter by adding text on page 2 and printing the mail merged newsletters. Open SOS Quarterly if it is not already displayed.

1) ADD TEXT TO PAGE 2

a. Display page 2.
b. Create a text frame that fits across all three columns, between the blue layout guides on the far left and far right edges of the page.
c. Move the text frame so that its top is against the blue layout guides at the top of the page.
d. Place a horizontal ruler guide at 5.5" on the vertical Ruler.
e. Resize the text frame so that its bottom is a little above the ruler guide you just placed.
f. Zoom in and type the following text, pressing Enter at the end of each line:

> Sage's Outdoor Supplies
> Announces the first annual
> Fall Clearance Sale
> Saturday and Sunday
> September 8 and 9
> 10 a.m. to 6 p.m.

g. Highlight all of the text and format it as 36 point, bold, italic, and center aligned.
h. Press the F9 key. The entire publication page is displayed.
i. Click in a blank area outside the text frame. The frame is deselected.

2) CREATE A TEXT FRAME

a. Place a horizontal ruler guide at 8" on the vertical Ruler.
b. Below the ruler guide, create a text frame that fits across the second and third columns, between the blue layout guides.
c. Move the text frame so that its top is against the ruler guide at 8".
d. Resize the text frame so that its bottom is against the blue layout guides at the bottom of the page.

3) ADD MERGE FIELDS

 a. Make sure the text frame you just created is selected.

 b. Select Mail Merge → Open Data Source. A dialog box is displayed.

  1. Click on the Merge information from another type of file button. A dialog box is displayed.

   a. In the Look in collapsible list, select the appropriate folder.

   b. Click on SAGE'S OUTDOOR SUPPLIES.

   c. Select Open. A dialog box is displayed.

   d. Select the Customers table if it is not already displayed.

   e. Select OK. A dialog box is displayed.

   f. Select the FirstName field if it is not already displayed.

   g. Select Insert. A merge field for the FirstName field is inserted in the text frame.

   h. Insert the LastName field, Address field, and the City, State, and Zip fields.

   i. Select Close. The dialog box is removed and a merge field for each field is in the selected text frame.

 c. Zoom into the text frame.

 d. Highlight all of the merge fields and format them as 18 point.

 e. Add spaces and paragraph markers so that the merge fields look similar to:

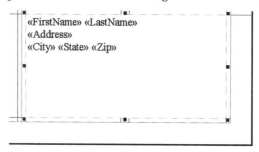

4) MERGE THE DATA

Select Mail Merge → Merge. A dialog box is displayed.

  1. Clicking on the ⏩ button. The data from the last record is displayed.

  2. Scroll through the records using the buttons.

  3. Select Close when you are finished. The dialog box is removed and the merge fields are again displayed.

5) SAVE AND PRINT THE MERGED PUBLICATIONS

 a. Save the modified SOS QUARTERLY.

 b. Select File → Print Merge. A dialog box is displayed.

  1. Select OK. Four copies are printed, each personalized for the customers in the database.

6) CLOSE THE MODIFIED SOS QUARTERLY

7) EXIT PUBLISHER

17.17 Where can you go from here?

This chapter introduced you to the basics of using Publisher for desktop publishing. Publisher has many other features not discussed in this text which you may want to explore using the online help.

Applications such as Publisher are widely used in academic, home, and business environments. Because you have learned how to use Publisher, you will easily be able to learn and use other desktop publishing applications.

Chapter Summary

publication

Blank
Publication

This chapter introduced desktop publishing and the Microsoft Publisher application. A new publication is created by selecting the Blank Publication icon in the New Office Document dialog box and then OK, which displays the Catalog dialog box. Selecting the Blank Publications tab, a publication type, and then the Create button creates a new publication.

The Objects Toolbar contains buttons for creating objects. The Standard and Formatting Toolbars contain shortcuts for commonly used actions. The Quick Publication Wizard is used to format a publication.

A new publication should be saved with a descriptive file name using the Save command. An existing publication can be opened by selecting the Open command.

The Quick Publication Wizard is displayed in two panes next to the publication page. The bottom pane displays the choices available depending on the option selected in the top pane. The wizard can be removed from the window by clicking on the Hide Wizard button. The Show Wizard button can be clicked to again display the wizard.

The Text Frame Tool on the Objects Toolbar is used to create a text frame object. Text can be typed into a text frame and then edited and formatted in the same manner as in Word.

RESIZE

A selected text frame can be resized and moved on the publication page by pointing to a handle until the pointer changes to the RESIZE shape and then dragging. A text frame is moved by pointing to the gray frame until the pointer changes to the MOVE shape and then dragging.

Right clicking in a text frame displays a menu with the Cut, Copy, and Paste commands. The Delete Object command from this menu deletes the frame, and Delete Text deletes highlighted text in the frame.

24%

F9

The Whole Page command in the Zoom submenu in the View menu displays the entire page, and the Page Width command displays the page as wide as possible. The Zoom Out and Zoom In buttons and the Zoom collapsible list are also used to change the magnification of the publication page. Pressing F9 zooms into a selected object, and pressing F9 again zooms back out to the previous magnification.

Clip art graphics can be placed on a publication page by selecting the Clip Art command from the Picture submenu in the Insert menu. Dragging the handle of a selected graphic resizes it. Pointing to anywhere on a graphic, except a handle, changes the pointer to the MOVE shape, allowing the graphic to be moved.

The background and foreground are two separate parts of a publication and can be accessed using the Go to Background and Go to Foreground commands in the View menu. Objects on the background appear on every page, for example, text frames used as headers and footers. The Send to Foreground and Send to Background commands in the Arrange menu are used to move a selected object to the foreground or background.

A publication can be printed by selecting the Print command or the Print button. A publication is closed by selecting the Close command. Publisher can be exited by selecting the Exit command.

Greeting cards can be created using Publisher by creating a new publication using the Side Fold Card publication type. Text and graphics are placed on the appropriate pages and the publication is printed and folded to make the greeting card.

Each page in a publication is represented by a page icon at the bottom of the publication window. Clicking on a page icon highlights the icon and displays that page in the window.

layout guides
ruler guides

The pink and blue guides in a publication page are layout guides. A green ruler guide is added by holding down the Shift key, pointing to a Ruler until the pointer changes to the ADJUST shape, and then dragging. Holding down the Shift key, pointing to a ruler guide until the pointer changes to the ADJUST shape, and dragging moves the guide. Dragging a ruler guide off the page deletes the guide.

Pages are added by selecting the Page command from the Insert menu. The currently displayed page is deleted by selecting the Delete Page command from the Edit menu. The margins can be changed and guides added for rows and columns by selecting the Layout Guides command from the Arrange menu.

Word documents can be inserted into a text frame using the Text File command from the Insert menu. The Text In Overflow indicator is displayed at the bottom of a text frame that has hidden text. Text frames can be connected using the Text Frames button on the Toolbar. Selecting a connected text frame displays the Go To Previous Frame button, the Go to Next Frame button, or both buttons.

A mail merge publication can be created using the Open Data Source command from the Mail Merge menu. The Merge command from the Mail Merge menu is used to merge data into the publication, and selecting the Print Merge command from the File menu prints the publication.

Vocabulary

Desktop publishing The process of combining text and graphics into one file.

F9 key Zooms into or out of a selected object.

Frame A gray outline that defines the edges of an object.

Mail merge A feature included in Microsoft Office that integrates the information stored in an Access database with a publication.

Objects Toolbar Contains buttons for creating objects on the publication page.

Publication A desktop publishing file.

Publication page The page as it will appear when printed.

Quick Publication Wizard A tool that helps the user select design and color options for a publication.

Text frame An object that contains text.

Text Frame Tool Used to create a text frame. Found on the Objects Toolbar.

Text In Overflow indicator Indicates that some text is hidden. Displayed at the bottom of a text frame that has text in overflow.

Thumbnail A small picture.

Publisher Commands and Buttons

<u>Cl</u>ip Art **command** Displays a dialog box that allows the user to insert clip art onto a publication page. Found in the <u>P</u>icture submenu in the <u>I</u>nsert menu.

Connect Text Frames button Used to connect text frames.

<u>D</u>elete Object **command** Deletes the selected text frame. Found in the menu displayed by right clicking on a text frame.

Delete <u>P</u>age **command** Deletes the currently displayed page. Found in the <u>E</u>dit menu.

Delete Te<u>x</u>t **command** Deletes the highlighted text in the text frame. Found in the menu displayed by right clicking on a text frame.

G<u>o</u> to Background **command** Displays the background of the publication page. Found in the <u>V</u>iew menu.

G<u>o</u> to Foreground **command** Displays the foreground of the publication page. Found in the <u>V</u>iew menu.

Go to Next Frame button Selects the next connected text frame. Displayed on a connected text frame.

Go To Previous Frame button Selects the previous connected text frame. Displayed on a connected text frame.

Hide Wizard button Removes the Quick Publication Wizard from the window. Found at the bottom of the window.

<u>L</u>ayout Guides **command** Displays a dialog box that allows the user to change the margins of a publication. Found in the A<u>r</u>range menu.

<u>M</u>erge **command** Merges data into the publication and displays the Preview Data dialog box. Found in the <u>M</u>ail Merge menu.

<u>O</u>pen Data Source **command** Used to select a database for mail merge. Found in the <u>M</u>ail Merge menu.

Pa<u>g</u>e **command** Displays a dialog box that allows the user to add pages to a publication. Found in the <u>I</u>nsert menu.

Pa<u>g</u>e Width **command** Displays the page as wide as possible. Found in the <u>Z</u>oom submenu in the <u>V</u>iew menu.

<u>P</u>rint Merge **command** Prints one copy of the publication for each record. Found in the <u>F</u>ile menu.

Send to Back<u>gr</u>ound **command** Moves a selected object to the background of the publication. Found in the A<u>r</u>range menu.

Send to Fore<u>gr</u>ound **command** Moves a selected object to the foreground of the publication. Found in the A<u>r</u>range menu.

Show Merge <u>R</u>esults **command** Displays the Preview Data dialog box. Found in the <u>M</u>ail Merge menu.

Show Wizard button Displays the Quick Publication Wizard. Found at the bottom of the window.

T<u>e</u>xt File **command** Displays a dialog box that allows the user to insert text from a Word document into a text frame. Found in the <u>I</u>nsert menu.

<u>W</u>hole Page **command** Displays the entire page. Found in the <u>Z</u>oom submenu in the <u>V</u>iew menu.

Zoom In button Increases the magnification of the publication page. Found on the Standard Toolbar.

Zoom Out button Decreases the magnification of the publication page. Found on the Standard Toolbar.

Review Questions

1. What is desktop publishing?

2. What is a thumbnail?

3. a) What is the Quick Publication Wizard?
   b) How can the Quick Publication Wizard be removed from the window?
   c) How can the wizard be redisplayed?

4. a) What is a text frame used for?
   b) List the steps required to create a text frame and enter your name.
   c) List the steps required to resize a text frame.
   d) List the steps required to move a text frame.

5. List the steps required to zoom into a selected text frame and then zoom back out again.

6. a) List the steps required to place a clip art graphic on a publication page.
   b) List the steps required to resize the graphic.

7. a) What kind of objects are usually placed on the background?
   b) List the steps required to move an object from the foreground to the background.
   c) List the steps required to select an object that is on the background.

Sections 17.9 — 17.17

8. List the steps required to create a greeting card.

9. How can you display page 3 in a publication that has 4 pages?

10. a) What are layout guides?
    b) What are ruler guides?

11. a) List the steps required to create a vertical ruler guide at 3" on the horizontal Ruler.
    b) List the steps required to delete a ruler guide.

12. a) List the steps required to add three pages to a publication that currently has one page.
    b) How is the currently displayed page deleted from a publication?

13. List the steps required to change the top and bottom margins in a publication to 1".

14. List the steps required to format a publication with three columns.

15. List the steps required to insert text from a Word document named Badminton into a new, blank publication.

16. a) What is overflow text?
    b) List two ways to display text in overflow.

17. a) List the steps required to connect two text frames, one with text in overflow and one empty text frame.
    b) What is the Go To Next Frame button used for?

18. What is mail merge?

Exercises

Exercise 1 ——————————————— Cantina Flyer

Create a new publication based on the Full Page publication type. Save the publication naming it Cantina Flyer and complete the following steps:

a) Change the design to the Maze design.

b) Change the color scheme to Tropics.

c) Create a text frame and type the following text, pressing Enter at the end of each line:

CORNER CANTINA
FRIDAY
LUNCH
SPECIALS!

Burritos $2
Tacos $1
Taco Salad $2

d) Format all of the text as bold and center aligned.

e) Format the text "FRIDAY LUNCH SPECIALS!" as 48 point, and the rest of the text as 36 point.

f) Resize and move the text frame if necessary so that it fits inside the border.

g) Save the modified Cantina Flyer and print a copy.

Exercise 2 ——————————————— Fingerpaint Flyer

Create a new publication based on the Full Page publication type. Save the publication naming it Fingerpaint Flyer and complete the following steps:

a) Change the design to the Handprint design.

b) Change the color scheme to Iris.

c) Create a text frame and type the following text, pressing Enter at the end of each line:

Wee One Art School
presents
ADVANCED
FINGERPAINTING

Sunday, November 11
2 p.m. to 4 p.m.
$5 per Child

Call for reservations
555-MESS

d) Format all of the text as bold, italic, and center aligned.

e) Format the text "Call for reservations 555-MESS" as 24 point, and the rest of the text as 36 point.

f) Resize and move the text frame if necessary so that it fits inside the border.

g) Save the modified Fingerpaint Flyer and print a copy.

Exercise 3 —————————————————————————— Thank You Card

Create a new publication based on the Side Fold Card publication type. Save the publication naming it Thank You Card and complete the following steps:

a) On page 1, change the design to the Linear Accent design and the color scheme to Reef.

b) Display the background, create a text frame and type Thanks so much!

c) Format the text as 12 point, bold, and center aligned.

d) Resize and move the text frame so that its top is against the blue layout guide at the top of the page and the frame fits from the left blue layout guide to the right.

e) Display the foreground, then on page 1 create a text frame and type Many Thanks.

f) Format the text as 24 point, bold, italic, and center aligned.

g) Add a horizontal ruler guide at 2.5" on the vertical Ruler.

h) Resize and move the text frame so that its top is against the ruler guide and the frame fits from the left blue layout guide to the right.

i) On page 3, create a text frame and type What a wonderful gift!

j) Format the text as 18 point, italic, and center aligned.

k) Add a horizontal ruler guide at 1.5" on the vertical Ruler.

l) Resize and move the text frame so that its top is against the ruler guide and the frame fits from the left blue layout guide to the right.

m) On page 3, add a clip art graphic that represents the gift you received. Move the graphic so that its bottom-right corner is against the bottom and right blue layout guides. Resize the graphic if necessary so that it is completely inside the layout guides on the page.

n) Save the modified Thank You Card.

o) Print a copy and fold the paper to make a greeting card.

Exercise 4 —————————————————————————— Pool Party

Create a new publication based on the Side Fold Card publication type. Save the publication naming it Pool Party and complete the following steps:

a) On page 1, change the design to the Tilt design and the color scheme to Berry.

b) Display the background, create a text frame and type Swimming! Swimming!

c) Format the text as 12 point, italic, and center aligned.

d) Resize and move the text frame so that its bottom is against the blue layout guide at the bottom of the page and the frame fits from the left blue layout guide to the right.

e) Add an appropriate clip art graphic. Move the graphic so that the its top is against the blue layout guide at the top of the page, and the graphic is approximately centered between the left and right layout guides. Resize the graphic if necessary so that it is completely inside the layout guides on the page.

f) Display the foreground, then on page 1 create a text frame and type the following text, pressing enter at the end of each line:

POOL
PARTY!

g) Format the text as 48 point, bold, and center aligned.

h) Add a horizontal ruler guide at 1" on the vertical Ruler.

i) Resize and move the text frame so that its top is against the ruler guide and the frame fits from the left blue layout guide to the right.

j) On page 3, create a text frame and type the following text, pressing enter at the end of each line:

Farrah's House
13 Shoe Lane
Rydale, NY
Sunday July 15
Noon to dusk

Food! Splashing!
Water Volleyball!

RSVP 555-8768

k) Format the text as 16 point and italic.

l) Resize and move the text frame so that its top is against the blue layout guide at the top of the page and the frame fits from the left blue layout guide to the right.

m) Save the modified Pool Party.

n) Print a copy and fold the paper to make a greeting card.

Exercise 5 ——————————————————— Music Monthly

Create a new publication based on the Full Page publication type. Save the publication naming it Music Monthly and complete the following steps:

a) Change all the margins to 0.5" and format the publication for two columns.

b) Add a horizontal ruler guide at 2.5" on the vertical Ruler.

c) Create a text frame and type the following text, pressing Enter at the end of each line:

MUSIC MONTHLY
Distributed FREE at all Mockingbird Music Locations
Volume 10, October 2001

d) Format the text "MUSIC MONTHLY" as 48 point, bold, and center aligned.

e) Format the rest of the text as 18 point, bold, italic, and center aligned.

f) Resize and move the text frame so that its top is against the blue layout guide at the top of the page, its bottom is above the ruler guide, and the frame fits from the far left blue layout guide to the far right.

g) Create a text frame in the first column and insert the text from the MUSIC LESSONS Word document. There will be text in autoflow.

h) Resize and move the text frame so that its top is against the ruler guide, its bottom is against the blue layout guide at the bottom of the page, and the frame fits between the blue layout guides in the first column.

i) Create a text frame in the second column and connect it to the first text frame, flowing the text into it.

j) Resize and move the text frame so that its top is against the ruler guide, its bottom is against the blue layout guide at the bottom of the page, and the frame fits between the blue layout guides in the second column. There should no longer be any text in overflow.

k) Add a new page after page 1.

l) On page 2, add a horizontal ruler guide at 8" on the vertical Ruler.

m) On page 2, create a text frame in the first column and insert the text from the INSTRUMENTS Word document. Resize and move the text frame so that its top is against the blue layout guide at the top of the page, its bottom is against the ruler guide, and the frame fits between the blue layout guides in the first column. There should not be any text in overflow.

n) On page 2, create a text frame in the second column and insert the text from the MUSIC LIST Word document. Resize and move the text frame so that its top is against the blue layout guide at the top of the page, its bottom is against the blue layout guide at the bottom of the page, and the frame fits between the blue layout guides in the second column. There should not be any text in overflow.

o) On page 2, add an appropriate clip art graphic. Move the graphic so that the bottom of its frame is against the blue layout guide at the bottom of the first column, and the left side is against the blue layout guide at the left of the first column. Resize the graphic using the upper-right corner handle so that it is completely inside the first column.

p) Save the modified Music Monthly and print a copy.

Advanced Exercise 6 ———————————————————— Leisure News

Using Publisher, create a two-page newsletter that contains information about local recreational activities. Save the publication naming it Leisure News. Change the design and color scheme of the publication, format it with three columns, and include at least one clip art graphic. Save the modified publication and print a copy.

A Guide to Microsoft Office 2000 Professional

The Internet and the Social and Ethical Implications of Computers

Close

Source

Print

Chapter Eighteen Objectives

After completing this chapter you will be able to:

1. Describe Web pages.
2. Use Internet Explorer to access a Web page with a known URL.
3. Describe HTML.
4. Search for Web pages that match criteria using search engines.
5. Display previously accessed Web pages in the History list.
6. Store the address of a Web page so it can be accessed later using the Favorites list.
7. Print Web pages.
8. Refine search criteria.
9. Evaluate Web sources.
10. Cite Web pages for research papers.
11. Describe how computers are used at home.
12. Describe different computer related careers and their educational requirements.
13. Understand the social and ethical implications of computer use and programming.
14. Understand right to privacy issues and data protection.

This chapter explains how to use a Web browser to access information on the Internet. Gathering appropriate information for academic research, evaluating it, and citing the sources are also discussed. The social and ethical implications of living in a computerized society as well as career possibilities related to computers are described.

18.1 Why use the Internet?

Chapter One briefly introduced the Internet, a worldwide network of computers. What makes the Internet so incredibly powerful is that these millions of computers store an extraordinary amount of information which is accessible from any computer connected to the Internet.

Information accessed through the Internet is different from that stored in books in two ways. First, all of the information is stored, transmitted, and received digitally which means that it can be accessed in a number of different forms including text, video, and audio. Second, the Internet is interactive which means that the information you receive is a result of the selections you make. For example, in accessing a news source you could be asked to select the type of news you are interested in—sports, financial, political, movie reviews, etc. After making a selection you would then be shown a list of stories within that category. Selecting a specific title might then display text and show a short video clip.

18.2 Web Pages

As discussed in Chapter One, the Web is a popular feature of the Internet. Most Web sites are divided into Web pages with one page designated as the *home page*. The home page usually serves as a base for the rest of the pages at that Web site. For example, the home page for Pack Suppliers, Inc. provides access to other pages that have information about the company:

A hypothetical home page

Web pages can contain hyperlinks that appear as text or as graphics. As the mouse pointer is moved across a page its shape changes to a hand shape (🖑) when it moves over a hyperlink. For example, the Products button is a hyperlink in the home page shown above. Clicking on the Products button takes you from Pack Supplier's home page to another Web page containing product information and hyperlinks. Clicking on *surfing* hyperlinks to go from Web page to Web page is called *surfing* or *browsing*, as the name Web browser suggests.

Information about a Web site is usually included at the bottom of its home page. The date that the home page was last modified may be included, as well as the number of hits the home page has received. One *hit* *hit* is recorded each time that Web page is accessed. Other information found at the bottom of home pages can include the names of the Web site's designers, the company that provides the server where the Web site exists, and small advertisements for any sponsors that help pay for it. Also usually included is a hyperlink used to send e-mail to the *Webmaster*, which is the person in charge of the Web site.

18.3 Using Internet Explorer

starting Internet Explorer A Web browser is needed to view Web pages. In this text, the *Microsoft Internet Explorer* Web browser is discussed. Selecting the Programs command from the Start menu on the Windows Taskbar displays a submenu. Clicking on Microsoft Internet Explorer in the submenu starts the browser, connects the computer to the Internet, and displays a preselected home page:

Displaying Toolbars

If the Address bar or the Toolbar is not displayed, commands from the Toolbars' submenu in the View menu can be selected to display them.

AutoComplete

As a URL is typed in the Address bar, a list of previously used URLs that match it are displayed:

The arrow keys can be used to scroll through the list and then the Enter key pressed to select the URL.

Changing the Preselected Home Page

The home page initially displayed when Internet Explorer is first started can be changed by selecting the Internet Options command from the Tools menu, which displays a dialog box. Selecting the General tab and then typing a URL in the Address entry box changes the home page.

accessing a Web page

Address bar —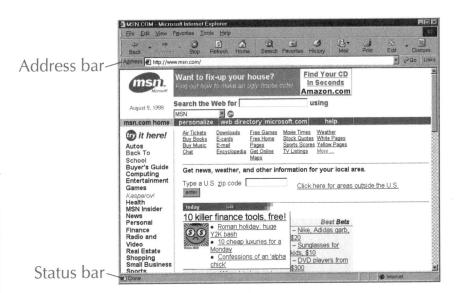

Status bar —

The Microsoft home page

There are numerous features in Internet Explorer:

- **Address bar** displays the URL for the displayed Web page, in this case http://www.msn.com. Also used to enter the URL of a Web page in order to display the page.

- **Title bar** displays the name of the displayed Web page, in this case MSN.COM.

- **Scroll bar** used to view parts of a page not currently displayed.

- **Back button** ( ) displays the previously selected Web page.

- **Forward button** ( ) displays the next Web page from the previously selected pages.

- **Stop button** ( ) turns red when Internet Explorer is loading a Web page. Used to stop a transmission.

- **Refresh button** ( ) updates the displayed Web page. Used to update the information on a page that changes frequently (e.g. stock prices) or when graphics did not load properly.

- **Home button** ( ) displays a preselected Web page, which is the Web page that is displayed when Internet Explorer is first started.

- **Status bar** displays the progress of loading a Web page.

Typing a URL in the Address bar and then clicking on the Go button ( ) or pressing Enter accesses that Web page. Note that with Internet Explorer and most other browsers, it is not usually necessary to type the http:// of a URL because the browser will automatically add it. For example, the URL of CNN's home page is http://www.cnn.com, but it is only necessary to type www.cnn.com in the Address bar.

After entering a URL in the Address bar or clicking on a hyperlink, the status bar displays messages on the progress of opening the Web page, such as Web site found... or Opening page.... When the transmission is complete the Stop button is dimmed and the status bar displays Done. If a transmission or transfer is taking too long, clicking on the Stop button will end the attempted transmission. Another URL can then be entered or a hyperlink selected.

Selecting the Close command from the File menu exits Internet Explorer and closes the Internet Explorer window.

Practice 1

In this practice you will view a preselected home page and then CNN's home page. The practices in this chapter assume that you have Microsoft Internet Explorer and access to the Internet.

1) START INTERNET EXPLORER

Select Start → Programs → Internet Explorer. Internet Explorer is started and the computer is connected to the Internet. Note that it may take a few seconds for the preselected home page to load.

2) MOVE AROUND A WEB PAGE

a. Click on a hyperlink that interests you. A new page is transmitted and then displayed.
b. Click on another hyperlink that interests you.

3) RETURN TO THE PREVIOUS PAGES

a. You have now accessed three pages, including the preselected home page. At the top of the window, click on the Back button ([Back]) once to return to the previous page.
b. Click on the Back button again to return to the first page that was displayed.
c. At the top of the window, click on the Forward button ([Forward]) until it is dimmed, indicating that there are no more pages.

4) GO TO CNN's HOME PAGE

a. In the Address bar, replace the existing URL with www.cnn.com, the URL for CNN's home page.
b. Press Enter. The Web page is transmitted, note the messages on the Status bar. Use the scroll bar to scroll through CNN's home page.

5) VIEW CNN STORIES

a. Click on a story hyperlink that interests you.
b. Continue to surf CNN's Web pages. Realize that a hyperlink may display a Web page at a site other than CNN. You can easily return to CNN's site by using the Back button.

6) EXIT INTERNET EXPLORER

Select File → Close. Internet Explorer is closed.

18.4 HTML

hypertext

tags

source code

Web pages are written in a language called *HTML* (HyperText Markup Language). *Hypertext* is text that contains links to other text. HTML documents can be created using any word processor. In an HTML document, special codes, called *tags*, are placed inside brackets. Web browsers use these tags to determine how the Web page should be displayed. The tags and the rest of the information for the Web page are called the *source code*. Some of the source code for Pack Supplier's home page looks similar to that shown on the next page:

```
<html>

<head>
<title>PSI Home Page</title>
<meta name="GENERATOR" content="Microsoft FrontPage 4.0">
<meta name="ProgId" content="FrontPage.Editor.Document">
<meta name="Microsoft Theme" content="expeditn 011, default">
<meta name="Microsoft Border" content="tl">
</head>

<body>
<p align="center"><font size="4">Welcome to PSIs site on the
WWW.</font></p>
<p align="left">PSI produces quality packs for every occasion in a
variety of styles and colors for children and adults.</p>
<p align="center"><img border="0" src="images/psilogo.gif"
width="170" height="171"></p>
<p align="center">E-mail the <a
href="mailto:webmaster@psi.fake.com">webmaster</a></p>
<p align="center">last modified on <!—webbot bot="Timestamp"
S-Type="EDITED"
S-Format="%B %d, %Y" —>
</body>

</html>
. . .
```

viewing source code

In Internet Explorer, the source code of the displayed Web page can be viewed by selecting the Source command from the View menu. This displays the source code in a new window, with the URL of the Web page in the Title bar. Clicking on its Close button closes the new window.

There are many tags that can be used in the source code of an HTML document. Tags control every aspect of the Web page including text formatting, graphics, and links. In the source code shown above, the <p align= "center"> tag indicates that the text after it should be center aligned. A slash in the tag indicates the end of that formatting, for example </p> indicates the end of the paragraph formatting. The <a href= tag tells the Web browser that a hyperlink is to follow, in this case a hyperlink that sends e-mail to webmaster@psi.fake.com when the user clicks on the text webmaster.

Practice 2

In this practice you will view the source code of a Web page.

1) START INTERNET EXPLORER

2) VIEW THE SOURCE CODE

    a. Select View → Source. A new window is displayed with the source code for your preselected home page.

    b. Scroll down to view the different tags used to create the Web page. Can you identify any?

    c. Click on the window's Close button when you are finished viewing the source code.

18.5 Searching the Web

In previous sections you learned how to access a Web page using its URL, but with millions of Web pages available how do you find pages when you do not know the URL? To solve this problem search engines have been developed. A *search engine* is a program that searches a database of Web pages for words that you supply and then lists the hyperlinks to pages that contain those words.

search engine

search criteria

When using a search engine, search criteria is entered. *Search criteria* can include single words or phrases that are then used by the engine to determine a match. A *match* is a Web page that contains the search criteria. For example, if you are going to travel to the Acropolis in Athens, Greece and need information about it, you could use a search engine and enter the criteria acropolis. The search engine will then display hyperlinks to pages in its database that contain the word acropolis. You could also search on the words athens or greece, but the more specific the search criteria, the better the chance you'll find the information you are looking for.

Clicking on the Search button on the Toolbar displays the Search pane in the left side of the window:

Searching Using the Address Bar

Entering go, find, or ? followed by the search criteria in the Address bar, searches for Web pages that match the criteria using a preselected search engine.

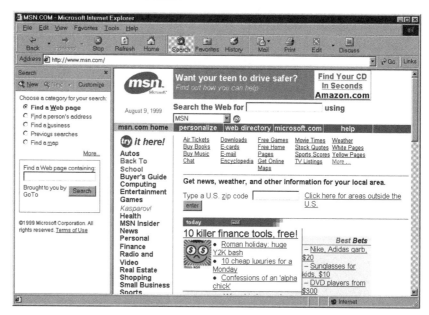

In the Search pane, typing the search criteria in the entry box and then selecting the Search button displays the search results from a preselected search engine in the form of hyperlinks. Clicking on a hyperlink displays its Web page in the right pane, leaving the search results displayed in the left pane:

The Web page selected in the Search pane is displayed in the right pane of the Internet Explorer window

searching using a different search engine

Clicking on the down arrow of the Next button in the Search pane displays a list of search engines:

The currently selected search engine is displayed with a dot next to its name. Selecting a different search engine displays the results of the search criteria using that search engine. Different search engines will display different results.

initiating a new search
closing the Search pane

The New button (New) in the Search pane is used to initiate a new search with new search criteria. Clicking on the Close button (✕) in the Search pane closes the Search pane and the Web page in the right pane is expanded to fill the space.

problems with searching

There are two common problems in searching the Web. First, search engines usually return many more hyperlinks than it is possible to access. For example, the search criteria acropolis found more than 10,000 matches. The second problem is that different search engines find different pages because each engine has its own database of hyperlinks and its own method of determining a match. Solutions to both of these problems is discussed later in the chapter.

subject tree

Some search engines also provide a *subject tree* which is a list of sites separated into categories. The term subject tree comes from many of the categories "branching" off into subcategories. These subcategories allow you to narrow down the subject and display a list of appropriate hyperlinks, which are at the lowest level of the tree. One popular search engine is Yahoo. Entering the Yahoo URL (www.yahoo.com) in the Address bar displays the Yahoo home page which contains a subject tree:

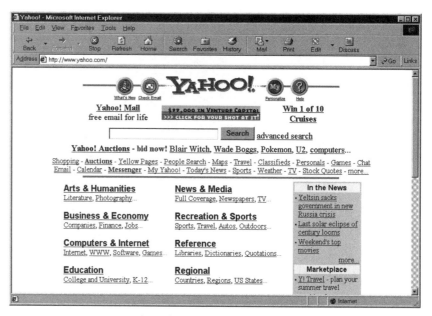

Yahoo lists categories of sites

Clicking on a category hyperlink produces a large list of subcategories. As you continue making selections, the list is narrowed until Yahoo finally displays a list of appropriate sites including descriptions and hyperlinks to the sites. Note that for any subject tree a staff of editors has determined which sites to include, a list which is far from all inclusive.

There are many search engines available. The search engines listed below also contain hyperlinks to information on structuring search criteria for use with their sites. The home page URLs are:

Lycos www.lycos.com   **Northern Light** www.northernlight.com
GoTo www.goto.com   **HotBot** www.hotbot.com
AltaVista www.altavista.com   **Webcrawler** www.webcrawler.com

Practice 3

In this practice you will search the Web using search engines. Start Internet Explorer if it is not already displayed.

1) SEARCH THE WEB

    a. On the Toolbar, click on the Search button (![Search]). The Search pane is displayed in the left side of the window. Locate the entry box in the Search pane.

    b. In the entry box, type stonehenge.

    c. Press Enter to start the search. After a few moments a list of hyperlinks to pages that contain the search criteria is displayed. How many matches are there?

    d. Scroll down to display the results of the search, then click on one of the hyperlinks that interests you to go to its Web page. A new page is transmitted and displayed in the right pane. If a page takes too long to access, click on the Stop button to cancel the search.

2) SELECT OTHER WEB PAGES

    a. In the Search pane, click on one of the hyperlinks to another Web page.

    b. Continue this process to access additional pages.

3) SEARCH THE WEB USING A DIFFERENT SEARCH ENGINE

    a. In the Search pane, click on the down-arrow of the Next button (Next). A list of search engines is displayed.

    b. Select a different search engine. New matches are displayed using the selected search engine. How many matches are there? Note the difference in the number of matches produced by the different search engines.

    c. In the Search pane, click on the Close button (✖) to close the pane.

4) GO TO THE YAHOO SEARCH ENGINE

    a. In the Address bar, type www.yahoo.com, the URL for Yahoo's home page.

    b. Click on the Go button (Go). The Yahoo home page is displayed.

5) FIND A UNIVERSITY USING A SUBJECT TREE

    a. Click on the <u>Education</u> hyperlink in the list of Yahoo categories. More hyperlinks to education subcategories are displayed.

    b. Scroll down if necessary and click on the <u>Higher Education</u> link.

    c. In the new subcategories list, scroll down if necessary and click on the <u>Colleges and Universities</u> link. A list of country subcategories is displayed.

    d. Scroll down if necessary and click on the <u>United States</u> link. A list of subcategories is displayed.

    e. Scroll down if necessary and click on the <u>Public by State</u> link. A list of state subcategories is displayed.

    f. Click on the <u>Florida</u> link. A list of public universities in Florida is displayed.

    g. Click on the <u>Florida Atlantic University@</u> link and then in the new list click on the <u>Florida Atlantic University</u> link. The Florida Atlantic University home page is displayed after a few seconds.

6) ENTER YOUR OWN CRITERIA

    a. Using Yahoo, enter your own search criteria. How many matches are there?

    b. Access several of the Web pages listed.

18.6 History List

As you browse from Web page to Web page on the Internet it is helpful to be able to return to a previously visited page. One method is to continue clicking on the Back button until the page is reached. Another method is to access the *History list*, a list of the pages you have been to in the last 20 days. Clicking on the History button on the Toolbar displays the History list in a pane in the left side of the Internet Explorer window:

Go To Command

Selecting the Go To command from the View menu displays a submenu that contains URLs of Web pages visited that session.

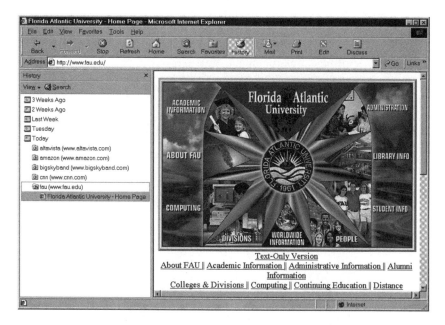

The View button can be used to specify how the History list is displayed. When viewing the History list By Site, clicking on one of the sites in the list displays a sublist of that Web site's pages. Clicking on a page displays that page in the right pane. When viewing the History list By Date, as shown above, clicking on a day displays the URLs for the Web sites accessed that day. Viewing the History list By Most Visited or By Order Visited Today displays the most viewed pages and the pages accessed that day, respectively.

18.7 Favorites List

Your *Favorites list* can be used to quickly view Web pages you frequently access or return to pages many months after visiting them. Clicking on the Favorites button on the Toolbar displays the Favorites pane in the left side of the window:

The Favorites pane displays your Favorites list

Selecting any of the Web pages in the list will access that page and display it in the pane in the right side of the window. Your Favorites list can be organized using folders, as shown on the previous page. Clicking on a folder displays the Web pages stored in that folder.

adding a Web page to your Favorites list

The currently displayed Web page can be added to your Favorites list by clicking on the Add button (Add...) in the Favorites pane, which displays a dialog box:

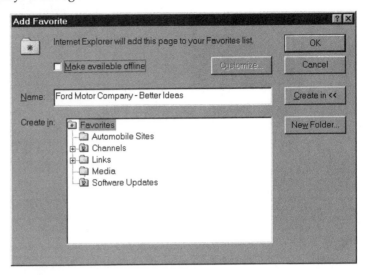

Clicking on a folder in the Create in list and then selecting OK adds the URL to the list in that folder. Clicking on the New Folder button creates a new folder in your Favorites list.

The Organize button (Organize...) in the Favorites pane is used to display a dialog box where you can create folders and rename, move, or delete a folder or Web page. Commands from the Favorites menu can also be used to view and organize your Favorites list.

18.8 Printing Web Pages

Often you will want a printed copy of a Web page. The contents of the currently displayed page can be printed by selecting the Print command (Ctrl+P) from the File menu, which displays a dialog box. Selecting the OK button in the displayed dialog box prints the current page. The Print button on the Toolbar can also be used to print the displayed Web page using the default print settings.

Practice 4

In this practice you will access a number of Web pages and then return to selected pages using the History list. Favorites will be saved for several Web pages and then a page will be printed. Start Internet Explorer if it is not already displayed.

1) SURF THE WEB USING YAHOO

    a. In the Address bar, type www.yahoo.com, the URL for Yahoo's home page, and then press Enter. Yahoo's home page is displayed.

    b. Enter the search criteria automobile and then click on the Search button.

    c. Go to at least five Web pages.

2) RETURN TO THE SECOND WEB PAGE

a. On the Toolbar, click on the History button (History). The History pane is displayed in the left side of the window.

b. From the View button, select the **By Order Visited Today** option.

c. Click on the name of the second automobile site visited. This will probably be the fourth site from the top. If a sublist of the pages at that site is displayed, click on one of the pages in the sublist. The page is displayed in the right pane.

3) ADD WEB PAGES TO THE FAVORITES LIST

a. On the Toolbar, click on the Favorites button (Favorites). The Favorites pane is displayed in the left side of the window.

b. In the Favorites pane, click on the Add button (Add...). A dialog box is displayed.

    1. Select the **New Folder** button. Another dialog box is displayed.

        a. In the entry box, type Automobile Sites.

        b. Select OK. The dialog box is removed.

    2. Select OK. The dialog box is removed and the current page is added to the Automobile Sites folder in the Favorites list.

c. Go to two more Web pages you found interesting and add them to the favorites list in the Automobile Sites folder.

4) RETURN TO A FAVORITE WEB PAGE

a. In the Favorites pane, click on the Automobile Sites folder to displays the pages you added.

b. Click on one of the Web page names. The selected page is displayed in the right pane.

5) DELETE WEB PAGES FROM YOUR FAVORITES LIST

In the Favorites pane, click on the **Organize** button (Organize...). A dialog box is displayed.

    1. Click on the Automobile Sites folder to select it.

    2. Click on the **Delete** button. A warning is displayed. Select Yes to delete the folder and the Web page URLs in it.

    3. Select **Close**. The dialog box is removed.

6) PRINT A WEB PAGE

a. Use the History list to return to one of the sites you visited.

b. Select File → Print. A dialog box is displayed.

    1. Select the **Pages** option.

    2. In the from entry box, type 1 if it is not already displayed.

    3. In the to entry box, type 1 if it is not already displayed.

    4. Click on the OK button. The first page of the Web page is printed.

18.9 Refining Web Searches

After performing the practices it should be obvious that most searches yield far too many matches to be useful. Limiting the number of matches to a reasonable number can usually be accomplished by refining the words used to form the search criteria. For example, entering hawaii as the criteria using the AltaVista search engine returns more than 2,000,000 matches, but the criteria hawaii +resort lowers the number to around 300,000 matches.

+ (plus sign)   The + (plus sign) can be used in search criteria to limit a search to only those Web pages containing two or more specified words. For example, a search for florida +hotel returns only hyperlinks to pages containing both words. It is possible to use more than one + to refine a search, for

example the criteria florida +hotel +pool returns only hyperlinks to pages containing all three words. Note that there should not be a space between the plus sign and the next word.

spaces　Separating words with just a space broadens the search to find pages that contain any of the words in the criteria. For example, a search for dive scuba returns hyperlinks to pages containing either of the words dive or scuba. The pages listed first contain both dive and scuba, then pages with either of the words are listed. One common search technique is to use several synonyms for a word as the search criteria. For example, house cottage bungalow. Spaces are also useful for searching with different spellings of a word, for example, color colour.

– (minus sign)　The – (minus sign) is used to exclude unwanted Web pages. For example, the search for shakespeare –play returns hyperlinks to pages containing the word Shakespeare, but eliminates pages that also contain the word play. As with the plus sign, there should not be a space between the minus sign and the next word.

The +, –, and space can be combined to produce more precise criteria. For example:

horse +buggy –carriage

tuna salmon –salad

recipe chicken –soup

university +connecticut –yale

" " (quotation marks)　Phrases can be used as search criteria by surrounding them with quotation marks. For example, a search for "space shuttle" or "product liability" will only return Web pages that contain the entire phrase. Phrases in quotes are the only occasion that uppercase letters (capitalization) should be used. In most cases, lowercase letters should be used in search criteria.

You will discover that not all search engines make use of plus signs, spaces, minus signs, and quotation marks in quite the way we have described here. Before you use a search engine, first determine how the search criteria should be structured.

18.10 Evaluating Sources

Information from the Internet, like most information, should be evaluated for accuracy. Anyone can post information on the Internet and there are no rules as to the accuracy or reliability of the information. This means that you must discriminate, read carefully, and check sources.

A few questions to answer when considering the reliability of a source are:

1. **Date.** On what date was the Web page last updated? Is the information current?

2. **Fact or opinion.** Is the information factual or just the author's opinion? If factual, where did the facts come from?

3. **Source.** What is the primary source of the information? Information posted by NASA or the University of Chicago is more likely to be factual than information posted by a high school student who cites no sources.

4. **Author.** Does the author present his or her credentials? A well established authority in the field you are researching is probably a trustworthy source.

copyright   A *copyright* protects a piece of work (artwork, documents, etc.) from reproduction without permission from the work's author. This includes material in an electronic format, such as information found on the Internet. Therefore it is necessary to cite the sources. Material found on the Internet may be protected by copyright laws even if a copyright notice is not displayed.

18.11 Citing Web Pages in a Research Paper

The primary purpose of a citation is to give credit to the original author and allow the reader to locate the cited information. A widely accepted form for citation is published by the Modern Language Association (MLA) in its publication *MLA Handbook for Writers of Research Papers, Fourth Edition*. The guidelines for referencing electronic material are similar to the MLA guidelines for printed material, with the addition of a few items. Referencing material accessed through the Internet should include the publication medium (Online), name of the network (Internet), the date it was accessed, and the URL (optional) preceded by the word Available:

> Author's Last Name, First Name MI. "Title of the Material." <u>Title of periodical, newsletter, or something similar</u> Volume number or similar (date of publication): Number of pages or paragraphs or n. page for no pagination. Online. Internet. Access date. Available http:URL.

For example:

> Harrison, Sally W. "Effects of Tourism on Australian Resources." <u>Hudson Economy Journal</u> 120 (10 June 1996): 24 pars. Online. Internet. 2 Feb. 2000. Available http: www.Austcham.com.Au.

Practice 5

In this practice you will refine your search criteria in order to limit the number of matches. You will begin by performing the research for a paper on the reconstruction of Shakespeare's Globe Theatre in London. Start Internet Explorer if it is not already displayed.

1) USE NORTHERN LIGHT

In the Address bar, type www.northernlight.com, the URL for Northern Light's home page, and press Enter. Northern Light's home page is displayed.

2) ENTER AND REFINE THE SEARCH CRITERIA

a. Perform a search using the criteria shakespeare. How many matches are there?
b. Refine the criteria to shakespeare +"Globe Theatre" and see how many matches there are.

    c. Refine the criteria to shakespeare +"Globe Theatre" +reconstruction and see how many matches there are.

    d. Further refine the criteria to shakespeare +"Globe Theatre" +reconstruction –usa and see how many matches there are.

    e. Click on a few of the hyperlinks to determine if their Web pages include the type of information that would be helpful in writing the research paper.

3) CREATE REFERENCES FOR THE WEB PAGES YOU VISITED

    a. Pick three Web pages from the ones you just visited to create citations for them.

    b. Start Word.

    c. In a numbered list, answer the questions in Section 18.10 to determine if the pages are reliable.

    d. Create citations for the three pages.

    e. Format the citations appropriately.

    f. Create hyperlinks to each of the pages.

    g. Save the document naming it Shakespeare Sources and print a copy.

    h. Exit Word.

4) EXIT INTERNET EXPLORER

18.12 Computers at Home

Personal computers are so inexpensive that many homes include at least one. Much of the software created in recent years has been specifically designed for the home user.

Internet   The fastest growing use of home computing is Internet access. With Internet access, home users can shop online, make travel arrangements, do research, and take educational courses, among many other things.

entertainment   A popular use for home computers is in the field of entertainment. For example, there are thousands of different types of computer games available. Educational software for children are often in the form of a game. The Internet has also become a form of entertainment, allowing users to chat online and play games with other people who are online.

fax/modem   A fax/modem is also standard in many home systems. A *fax/modem* can operate as both a modem for telecommunications and as a fax machine that can receive and send files.

productivity software   Home users often make use of productivity software. Commonly used packages include financial software for maintaining bank accounts and investments, desktop publishing software for creating newsletters, and specialized software packages for creating cards, banners, and family trees. For example, software is now available that edits home videos and produces graphics that can be added to the video. This allows the home user to produce professional-looking home videos that include titles and animation.

multimedia   *Multimedia* is the integration of computer animation, graphics, video, and audio. Commonly used multimedia applications are encyclopedias, games, and trip planners.

18.13 Computer Related Careers

As computers have become more powerful they play an ever increasing role in the world we live in. Consequently many people, no matter what field they are employed in, use computers in some way.

data processing

The area of computing that employs the largest number of people is data processing. *Data processing* involves the electronic entry, storage, manipulation, and retrieval of data. Businesses, governments, educational institutions—almost any organization—require the management of large amounts of data and therefore need employees capable of data processing. Careers in data processing are usually divided into five categories: data-entry operator, system analyst, system developer (programmer), system manager, and computer scientist.

data-entry operator

A *data-entry operator* types data into a computer. Data-entry operators may work for banks entering cancelled checks, department stores entering inventory figures, or educational institutions entering student records. A data-entry operator should possess a high school diploma and the ability to type quickly and accurately.

system analyst

Before a data processing system can be set up a *system analyst* must first analyze and design the system. The analyst must determine how an organization will use the computer system, what data will be stored, how it will be accessed, and how the system is expected to grow in the future. A system analyst should possess a comprehensive knowledge of data-processing methods, software, hardware, and programming languages. Most system analysts are college graduates who have majored in computer science or information systems or both.

programmer

After the system analyst has determined what type of system should be installed, the *programmer* creates the necessary software. A programmer should possess a detailed knowledge of the programming language or languages being used as well as an ability to reason analytically and pay close attention to details. Many businesses employ programmers who have graduated from a technical school or community college with a degree in programming. Large or specialized companies, which need highly sophisticated programming, usually require employees with a four-year college degree.

system manager

Companies with large data processing requirements usually employ a manager who is responsible for running the Management Information Systems department (MIS). The *MIS manager* must organize the computer and human resources of the department in order to best achieve the organization's goals. A system manager should possess a detailed understanding of data-processing methods, hardware, and software. A college degree in business administration with a concentration in information systems is usually required.

computer scientist

The study of computer science is a very broad field involving many disciplines including science, electronics, and mathematics. A *computer scientist* often works in research at a university or computer manufacturer developing new computer applications software and hardware. It is computer scientists who design and develop robots, natural language processors, and the many applications that we have mentioned. A computer scientist usually has both undergraduate and graduate degrees in computer science.

A Guide to Microsoft Office 2000 Professional

The computer industry careers discussed on the previous page are directed at data processing. There are many computing careers with concentrations in other fields, such as those described below.

computer engineer

Computer engineers design and manufacture computers. This field is broad and includes engineers who develop new computer applications. Other engineers translate ideas produced by researchers into manufactured products. A computer engineer usually possesses both undergraduate and graduate degrees in engineering.

manufacturing worker

The people who help build computer systems need to possess the ability to work well with tools. *Manufacturing workers* usually have earned a high school diploma or community college degree. Good preparation for such a career includes taking courses in mechanical arts as well as science and mathematics.

technical support technician

Working mainly over the phone, *technical support technicians* assist customers of both hardware and software companies. Customers that have questions or problems with any aspect of the company's products, including installation and compatibility call the technical support phone number and speak with a technician who then identifies the problem and offers a solution. A technical support technician is usually a graduate of a technical school or community college.

computer sales representative

A large number of people sell computers either as representatives who travel and visit clients or as salespeople in computer stores. It is important that they possess a thorough knowledge of the computer equipment they sell and be able to explain how it may be used. The level of education required for this job will depend on the sophistication of the equipment being sold. Often a high school or community college degree is sufficient. To sell large computer systems, a sales representative may be required to have a four-year college degree.

computer teacher

Employees currently working in a computer-related field are often there because of *computer teachers*. In high schools and colleges, teachers and professors do research and teach all aspects of computing from computer science to ethics. For teaching at the high school level, a four-year college degree in a computer field is the minimum. At the college level, a graduate degree is the minimum requirement.

technology coordinator

At most educational institutions, it is the job of the *technology coordinator* to plan and oversee the acquisition, distribution, and utilization of computer technology. Schools require such a person to insure that they have working facilities and are keeping up with new advancements in technology. A graduate degree in a computer field is often required.

Webmaster

With the rapid increase in the use of the World Wide Web, there is now a need for Webmasters. A *Webmaster* does everything from designing and creating Web pages to creating graphics for the site to maintaining the site. A Webmaster possesses extensive Internet knowledge, including programming skills, as well as design experience.

18.14 The Social and Ethical Implications of Computers

information age

The society in which we live has been so profoundly affected by computers that historians refer to the present time as the *information age*. This is due to the computer's ability to store and manipulate large amounts of information (data). Because of computers, we are evolving out of an industrial and into an information society. Such fundamental societal changes cause disruptions which must be planned for. For this reason it is crucial that we consider both the social and ethical implications of our increasing dependence on computers. By ethical questions we mean asking what are the morally right and wrong ways to use computers.

right to privacy

Probably the most serious problem associated with computers is the possibility of invading our privacy. Because computers can store vast amounts of data we must decide what information is proper to store, what is improper, and who should have access to the information. Every time you use a credit card, make a phone call, withdraw money, reserve a flight, or register at school a computer records the transaction. These records can be used to learn a great deal about you—where you have been, when you were there, and how much money was spent. Should this information be available to everyone?

Computers are also used to store information about your credit rating, which determines your ability to borrow money. If you want to buy a car and finance it at a bank, the bank first checks your credit records on a computer to determine if you have a good credit rating. If you purchase the car and then apply for automobile insurance, another computer will check to determine if you have traffic violations. How do you know if the information being used is accurate? To protect both your privacy and the accuracy of data stored about you, a number of laws have been passed.

The **Fair Credit Reporting Act of 1970** deals with data collected for use by credit, insurance, and employment agencies. The act gives individuals the right to see information maintained about them. If a person is denied credit they are allowed to see the files used to make the credit determination. If any of the information is incorrect, the person has the right to have it changed. The act also restricts who may access credit files to only those with a court order or the written permission of the individual whose credit is being checked.

The **Privacy Act of 1974** restricts the way in which personal data can be used by federal agencies. Individuals must be permitted access to information stored about them and may correct any information that is incorrect. Agencies must insure both the security and confidentiality of any sensitive information. Although this law applies only to federal agencies, many states have adopted similar laws.

The **Financial Privacy Act of 1978** requires that a government authority have a subpoena, summons, or search warrant to access an individual's financial records. When such records are released, the financial institution must notify the individual of who has had access to them.

The **Electronic Communications Privacy Act of 1986** (ECPA) makes it a crime to access electronic data without authorization. It also prohibits unauthorized release of such data.

The NII

Living in the information age requires access to information stored on computers all over the world. To help make this information available to every school, hospital, business, and library, a U.S. government initiative called the National Information Infrastructure (NII) is working to develop and integrate hardware, software, telecommunications, network standards and much more.

Laws such as these help to insure that the right to privacy is not infringed by the improper use of data stored in computer files. Although implementing privacy laws has proven expensive and difficult, most people would agree that they are needed.

18.15 Protecting Computer Software and Data

piracy

Because computer software can be copied electronically, it is easy to duplicate. Such duplication is usually illegal because the company producing the software is not paid for the copy. This has become an increasingly serious problem as the number of illegal software copies distributed through *piracy* has grown. Developing, testing, marketing, and supporting software is an expensive process. If the software developer is then denied rightful compensation, the future development of all software is jeopardized.

Software companies are increasingly vigilant in detecting and prosecuting those who illegally copy their software. Persons found guilty of using illegally copied software can be fined, and their reputation damaged. Therefore, when using software it is important to use only legally acquired copies, and to not make illegal copies for others.

cracker

Another problem that is growing as computer use increases is the willful interference with or destruction of computer data. Because computers can transfer and erase data at high speeds, it makes them especially vulnerable to acts of vandalism. Newspapers have carried numerous reports of computer users gaining access to large computer databases. Sometimes these *crackers* change or erase stored data. These acts are usually illegal and can cause very serious and expensive damage. The Electronic Communications Privacy Act of 1986 specifically makes it a federal offense to access electronic data without authorization.

virus

One especially harmful act is the planting of a virus into computer software. A *virus* is a series of instructions buried into a program that cause the computer to destroy data when given a certain signal. For example, the instructions to destroy data might check the computer's clock and then destroy data when a certain time is reached. Because the virus is duplicated each time the software is copied, it spreads to other computers, hence the name virus. This practice is illegal and can result in considerable damage. Computer viruses have become so widespread that anti-virus programs have been created to detect and erase viruses before they can damage data.

Contaminated diskettes are one way that viruses are spread from computer to computer

The willful destruction of computer data is no different than any other vandalization of property. Since the damage is done electronically the result is often not as obvious as destroying physical property, but the consequences are much the same. It is estimated that computer crimes cost the nation billions of dollars each year.

18.16 The Ethical Responsibilities of the Programmer

It is extremely difficult, if not impossible, for a computer programmer to guarantee that a program will always operate properly. The programs used to control complicated devices contain millions of instructions, and as programs grow longer the likelihood of errors increases. A special cause for concern is the increased use of computers to control potentially dangerous devices such as aircraft, nuclear reactors, or sensitive medical equipment. This places a strong ethical burden on the programmer to insure, as best as he or she can, the reliability of the computer software.

The Department of Defense (DOD) is supporting research aimed at detecting and correcting programming errors. Because it spends billions of dollars annually developing software, much of it for use in situations which can be life threatening, the DOD is especially interested in having reliable programs.

As capable as computers have proven to be, we must be cautious when allowing them to replace human beings in areas where judgement is crucial. As intelligent beings, we can often detect that something out of the ordinary has occurred which has not been previously anticipated and then take appropriate actions. Computers will only do what they have been programmed to do, even if it is to perform a dangerous act.

Chapter Summary

This chapter briefly introduced how to use Internet Explorer to find, evaluate, and cite information on the Internet. The most popular way to interact with the Internet is through the World Wide Web. To view Web pages, both a Web browser and a URL are needed.

Web sites are divided into Web pages with one page designated as the home page. Web pages contain links to other pages. These hyperlinks can be text or graphics. Clicking on hyperlinks to go from Web page to Web page is called surfing.

Microsoft Internet Explorer is the Web browser discussed in this chapter. The Address bar at the top of the window is used to access a Web page. As the mouse pointer moves across a Web page, it turns into a hand shape (🖑) when placed on a hyperlink. Clicking on a hyperlink displays the Web page for that link. The Back and Forward buttons can be used to back and forward through previously visited pages. The Stop button is used to stop a search in progress.

HTML tags

HTML (HyperText Markup Language) is the language that Web pages are written in. HTML uses special codes called tags to determine what the Web page looks like. These tags and other programming code for a

Web page can be viewed by displaying the Web page and then selecting the Sour<u>c</u>e command from the <u>V</u>iew menu.

search engines
subject tree

The Web can be searched using search engines. Some search engines also provide a subject tree. A subject tree lists Web pages by category and subject. A match is a Web page that contains the search criteria.

History list

The History list is created by Internet Explorer to keep track of all the Web pages recently visited. The History list is displayed by selecting the History button on the Toolbar.

Favorites list

The Favorites list allows you to store the name and URL of a selected Web page in a file so that it can be accessed at a later time. The Favorites pane is used to add a Web page to your Favorites list and can also be used to organize the folders and Web pages in your Favorites list.

The currently displayed Web page can be printed by selecting the <u>P</u>rint command from the <u>F</u>ile menu.

+

spaces

-

" "

The number of matches in a search can be limited to a reasonable number by refining the words used in the search criteria. Using a plus sign limits the search to pages containing two or more specified words, for example cat +dog. Separating words with spaces broadens a search to pages containing any of the words in the criteria, for example cat dog horse. The minus sign excludes unwanted pages, for example cat -dog. A phrase enclosed in quotation marks may also be used as the search criteria, for example "rip tide."

citing Web pages

The reliability of a source should be considered when using information found on the Internet. Information found on a Web page should always be cited in a research paper.

computers at home

The use of personal computers in the home has become popular and will grow with the increased availability of telecommunications and networks. Home computers are often used to play games, entertain, and help users be more productive.

computer related careers

Computer related careers and the educational requirements needed to pursue them are discussed in this chapter. Careers which require only a high school education as well as those requiring a college education are presented.

information age

Historians refer to the present time as the information age due to the computer's ability to store and manipulate large amounts of data. As the use of computers increases they will profoundly affect society. Therefore, it is important to analyze the social and ethical implications of computer use.

right to privacy

piracy

cracker, virus

A problem created by computers is their potential for invading our right to privacy. Laws have been passed to protect us from the misuse of data stored in computers. Because computer software is easy to copy, illegal copies are often made. This denies software manufacturers their rightful compensation. Another problem has been the willful destruction of computer files by crackers erasing data or planting virus programs.

As computers are increasingly used to make decisions in situations which can impact human life, it becomes the responsibility of programmers to do their best to insure the reliability of the software they have developed. We must continue to be cautious not to replace human beings with computers in areas where judgement is crucial.

Vocabulary

Address bar Displays the URL for the displayed Web page and also used to enter the URL of a Web page in order to display the page.

Browsing See surfing.

Copyright Protects a piece of work from reproduction without permission from the work's author.

Cracker Person who enters a computer system without authorization.

Data processing Entry, storage, manipulation, and retrieval of information using a computer.

Favorites list The name and URL of selected Web pages that can be accessed at a later time.

Fax/modem A device that operates as both a modem and a fax.

History list A list of the Web pages visited in the last 20 days.

Hit When a Web page is accessed.

Home page The page designated as the first page in a Web site.

HTML (HyperText Markup Language) The language that Web pages are written in.

Hypertext Text that contains links to other text.

Information age Current time characterized by increasing dependence on the computer's ability to store and manipulate large amounts of information.

Match A Web page that contains the search criteria.

Microsoft Internet Explorer A Web browser.

Multimedia The integration of computer animation, graphics, video, and audio.

Piracy Illegally copying or distributing software.

Search criteria Words or phrases used by a search engine to determine if a Web page is a match.

Search engine A program that searches a database of Web page for words that you supply and then lists the hyperlinks to pages that contain those words.

Source code The HTML code for a Web page.

Subject tree A list of Web pages separated into categories which allow you to narrow down the subject.

Surfing Clicking on hyperlinks to go from Web page to Web page.

Tag A special code in HTML that is used to determine how the Web page should be displayed.

Virus Series of instructions in a program that causes a computer to destroy data when given a certain signal.

Internet Explorer Commands and Buttons

Back button Displays the previously selected Web page. Found on the Toolbar.

<u>C</u>lose **command** Used to exit Internet Explorer. Found in the <u>F</u>ile menu.

Favorites button Displays the Favorites list. Found on the Toolbar.

Forward button Displays the next Web page from a series of previously selected pages. Found on the Toolbar.

History button Displays the History list. Found on the Toolbar.

Home button Displays a preselected home page. Found on the Toolbar.

<u>P</u>rint **command** Prints the currently displayed Web page. Found in the <u>F</u>ile menu. The Print button ( ) on the Toolbar can be used instead of the command.

Refresh button Updates the currently displayed page. Found on the Toolbar.

Search button Displays the Search pane where search criteria can be entered into a search engine to search the Web. Found on the Toolbar.

Sour<u>c</u>e **command** Displays the source code for the displayed Web page. Found in the <u>V</u>iew menu.

Stop button Stops a transmission. Turns red when Internet Explorer is loading a Web page. Found on the Toolbar.

Review Questions

1. How is the information accessed through the Internet different from that stored in books?

2. What is a home page?

3. What does it mean to surf the Web?

4. When does the mouse pointer change to a hand shape?

5. How do you move backwards and forwards through Web pages that you have previously accessed?

6. How can you tell when Internet Explorer is in the process of transmitting or receiving information?

7. List the steps required to access a Web page with the URL http://www.pbs.org.

8. a) What is HTML?
   b) List the step(s) required to view the source code of the currently displayed Web page.

Sections 18.5 — 18.8

9. What would you need to do to research a topic on the Web, for example automobiles, if you do not know the appropriate URLs?

10. a) What is a search engine?
    b) What is a match?
    c) List the steps required to use a search engine to search for Web pages that contain the word kayak.

11. What is a subject tree?

12. Explain how to directly return to a previously visited Web page without using the Back or Forward buttons.

13. List the steps required to:
    a) add a URL to the Favorites list.
    b) access a Web page from the Favorites list.
    c) delete a Web page from the Favorites list.

14. List the step(s) required to print the currently displayed Web page.

Sections 18.9 — 18.11

15. Write search criteria to locate Web pages that contain the following information:
    a) restaurants in Los Angeles
    b) art museums in Boston
    c) auto repair jobs in Montreal, Canada
    d) mosquitos and bees, but not ants
    e) the English author Jane Austen
    f) the phrase *to each his own*
    g) George Washington and John Adams, but not Thomas Jefferson
    h) travel to Ireland, but not Dublin

16. Why is it difficult to determine if information on the Web is accurate?

17. How can you attempt to determine the accuracy of information on a Web page?

18. On May 4, 2001 Tara Perez placed her 26-page master's degree thesis titled *Bird Watching in South Florida's Soccer Fields* on a Web page at http://www.tarap.ufl.edu. Write a citation for a research paper that quotes Tara's thesis.

Sections 18.12 — 18.16

19. List two ways computers are used in the home.

20. List three careers in the computer field and describe them.

21. What is meant by the information age?

22. a) How do you believe society is benefitting from the information age?
    b) What are some of the negative aspects of the information age?

23. How can computers be used to invade your privacy?

24. What can you do if you are turned down for credit at a bank and believe that the data used to deny credit is inaccurate?

25. a) What is necessary for a federal government authority to access an individual's financial records?
    b) What must an authority do after accessing the records?

26. a) What is computer piracy?
    b) What is a computer cracker?
    c) What is a computer virus?

27. a) What ethical responsibilities does a programmer have when writing a program that will impact human lives?
    b) Can a programmer absolutely guarantee that a program will operate properly? Why?

Exercises

Exercise 1 ——————————————————— Job Search

You are interested in finding a job in San Francisco, California and are skilled in television production, including editing, camera work, etc. A full-time position with a local TV or cable access channel would be ideal.

a) Conduct a search on the Internet using at least two search engines to find two possible positions.

b) In a new Word document, insert hyperlinks to the Web pages of the two positions and give a brief description of each of the positions that you found.

c) Save the document naming it Job Search.

d) Once you have found the position of your choice you need information on making the move to San Francisco. First, you will want to rent an apartment, and can't afford more than $1,200 a month. Conduct a search on the Internet to come up with brief descriptions of three apartments in San Francisco that rent for $1,200 or less.

e) In the Job Search document add a paragraph that describes all three apartments, including number of bedrooms and bathrooms and rent per month. Insert hyperlinks to the three URLs after the paragraph.

f) Create a header with the text San Francisco center aligned.

g) Create a footer with your name right aligned.

h) Check the document on screen for errors and misspellings and make any corrections.

i) Save the modified Job Search and print a copy.

Exercise 2 ——————————————————— American Authors

Your English instructor has assigned a report on the American authors Kurt Vonnegut, Jr. and Ernest Hemingway. Keep in mind that knowledge of information like the titles of their books might help in your search. Because people maintain Web pages as homages to their favorite authors, but are not obligated to check their facts for accuracy, it is a good idea to double check the information you find with more than one Web page.

a) Conduct a search on the Internet using at least two search engines to find biographical data on each author.

b) In a new Word document, write a paragraph of biographical information for each author. Insert hyperlinks to the Web pages in the space below the paragraph.

c) Save the document naming it American Authors.

d) Create a header with the text Two American Authors center aligned.

e) Create a footer with your name right aligned.

f) Check the document on screen for errors and misspellings and make any corrections.

g) Save the modified American Authors and print a copy.

Exercise 3 ——————————————— Car Purchase

You have decided to purchase an automobile that costs $15,000 or less. A used car will probably give you the best value.

    a) Conduct a search on the Internet using at least two search engines to find four used cars in your price range.

    b) In a new Word document, list each car's specifications and price, and insert hyperlinks to the Web pages where the information came from.

    c) Save the document naming it Car Purchase.

    d) Select one of the four cars for purchase and explain your choice in a paragraph.

    e) You will need automobile insurance for your used car. Search the Internet and find two insurance companies that offer automobile insurance. In the Car Purchase document, insert hyperlinks to the URLs for the two pages.

    f) Create a header with the text Used Cars center aligned.

    g) Create a footer with your name right aligned.

    h) Check the document on screen for errors and misspellings and make any corrections.

    i) Save the modified Car Purchase and print a copy.

Exercise 4 ——————————————— Tennis Elbow

A good friend has just injured her elbow playing tennis and would like you to find out as much as you can about her injury.

    a) Conduct a search on the Internet using at least two search engines to find four Web pages that have information about tennis elbow injuries.

    b) In a new Word document, write a one-paragraph description of the injury.

    c) Save the document naming it Tennis Elbow.

    d) In a second paragraph, write about possible treatments for the injury, then below the paragraph insert hyperlinks to the Web pages where the information came from.

    e) Create a header with the text Tennis Injury Research center aligned.

    f) Create a footer with your name right aligned.

    g) Check the document on screen for errors and misspellings and make any corrections.

    h) Save the modified Tennis Elbow and print a copy.

Exercise 5 ———————————————————— New Zealand

You and a friend have decided to take a trip to New Zealand. Before you go you should find out about airfare, hotels, climate, travel documents, and restaurants. Information about New Zealand's museums and tourist attractions would also be helpful in planning your trip.

a) Conduct a search on the Internet using at least two search engines to find six Web pages that have information about New Zealand.

b) In a new Word document, write a one-paragraph description of the country.

c) Save the document naming it New Zealand.

d) In a second paragraph, write about the places that you might visit, then below the paragraph insert hyperlinks to the Web pages where the information came from.

e) Create a header with the text Vacation center aligned.

f) Create a footer with your name right aligned.

g) Check the document on screen for errors and misspellings and make any corrections.

h) Save the modified New Zealand and print a copy.

Exercise 6 ———————————————————— Pyramids

Your history instructor has assigned a research paper on the building of the pyramids in Egypt.

a) Conduct a search on the Internet using at least two search engines to find six Web pages that have information about the pyramids in Egypt.

b) In a new Word document, write a detailed description of the pyramids.

c) Insert hyperlinks to the Web pages where the information came from.

d) Create a header with the text The Great Pyramids center aligned.

e) Create a footer with your name right aligned.

f) Check the document on screen for errors and misspellings and make any corrections.

g) Save the document naming it Pyramids and print a copy.

Exercise 7 ———————————————————— Graduate Programs

You have decided to change careers and become a marine biologist.

a) Conduct a search on the Internet using at least two search engines to find six graduate degree programs in marine biology.

b) In a new Word document, list each programs' location (college name), the degree (M.S., Ph.D., etc.), and the number of credits required to finish a degree, and insert hyperlinks to the Web pages where the information came from.

c) Create a header with the text Marine Biology center aligned.

d) Create a footer with your name right aligned.

e) Check the document on screen for errors and misspellings and make any corrections.

f) Save the document naming it Graduate Programs and print a copy.

Advanced Exercise 8 ——————————————————Artist

Each of the following people has made a major contribution to the world of art or music. Select one of the six artists listed below and then find a minimum of five Web pages that provide information about the artist, including pictures of his or her works. Using the information you find, write a two-page report in a new Word document. Be sure to cite each source. Save the document naming it Artist and print a copy.

- Mary Cassatt
- Frederic Remington
- Georgia O'Keeffe
- Pablo Picasso
- Maxfield Parrish
- Annie Leibovitz

Advanced Exercise 9 ————————————— Earth Science Project

Select one of the six topics listed below and then find a minimum of five Web pages that provide information on your topic. Using the information you find, write a two-page report in a new Word document. Be sure to cite each source. Save the document naming it Earth Science Project and print a copy.

- hurricanes
- tornadoes
- the ocean floor
- the ozone layer
- earthquakes
- solar energy

Advanced Exercise 10 ————————————— Technology

Select one of the six topics listed below and then find a minimum of five Web pages that provide information on your topic. Using the information you find, write a two-page report in a new Word document. Be sure to cite each source. Save the document naming it Technology and print a copy.

- fuzzy logic
- virtual reality
- artificial intelligence
- neural networks
- speech recognition software
- computer viruses

Microsoft Office Keyboard Shortcuts and Functions

The following keyboard shortcuts are grouped by application. A list of functions that may be used in Excel and Access is also included.

Office Keyboard Shortcuts

The following keyboard shortcuts can be executed when using Word, Excel, Access, PowerPoint, and Publisher.

Files
Ctrl+N   Creates a new blank document, spreadsheet, database, presentation, or publication
Ctrl+O   Displays the Open dialog box
Ctrl+S   Saves the current document, spreadsheet, database object, presentation, or publication
F12   Displays the Save As dialog box
Ctrl+P   Displays the Print dialog box
Ctrl+W   Closes the current file
Alt+F4   Exits the application

Editing
Ctrl+Z   Reverses an action
Ctrl+Y   Repeats an action (Word and Excel only)
Ctrl+X   Cuts the highlighted block
Ctrl+C   Copies the highlighted block
Ctrl+V   Pastes a cut or copied block
Ctrl+A   Selects all
Ctrl+F   Displays a dialog box with the Find options displayed
Ctrl+H   Displays a dialog box with the Replace options displayed
Ctrl+G   Displays a dialog box with the Go To options displayed (Word and Excel only)
Ctrl+K   Inserts a hyperlinks at the current cursor position
F7   Starts the spelling checker

Help
F1   Displays the Assistant
Shift+F1   Displays the What's This pointer

Word Keyboard Shortcuts

The following keyboard shortcuts can be executed when using Word.

Views
Ctrl+F2   Print previews the document
Alt+Ctrl+P   Switches to Print Layout view
Alt+Ctrl+O   Switches to Outline view
Alt+Ctrl+N   Switches to Normal view

Windows
Ctrl+F5   Restores the document's window
Ctrl+F10   Maximizes the document's window
Alt+F5   Restores the Word window
Alt+F10   Maximizes the Word window
Ctrl+F6   Displays the next open document's window
Ctrl+Shift+F6   Displays the previous open document's window

Selection
F8 (once)   Starts highlighting (pressing an arrow key extends highlight)
F8 (twice)   Highlights a word
F8 (three times)   Highlights a sentence
F8 (four times)   Highlights a paragraph
F8 (five times)   Highlights the entire document
Shift+F8   Reduces highlight to previous level
Esc   Ends highlighting
Shift+Arrow key   Highlights in direction of arrow
Shift+End   Highlights to the end of the line
Shift+Home   Highlights to the beginning of the line
Shift+PgDn   Highlights one screen down
Shift+PgUp   Highlights one screen up
Ctrl+Shift+Right arrow   Highlights to the end of a word
Ctrl+Shift+Left arrow   Highlights to the beginning of a word
Ctrl+Shift+Down arrow   Highlights to the end of the paragraph
Ctrl+Shift+Up arrow   Highlights the beginning of the paragraph

Cursor Movement
Ctrl+Left arrow   Moves the cursor left one word
Ctrl+Right arrow   Moves the cursor right one word
Ctrl+Up arrow   Moves the cursor up one paragraph
Ctrl+Down arrow   Moves the cursor down one paragraph
Ctrl+PgUp   Moves the cursor to the top of the previous page
Ctrl+PgDn   Moves the cursor to the top of the next page
Ctrl+Home   Moves the cursor to the beginning of the document
Ctrl+End   Moves the cursor to the end of the document

Text Formatting
Ctrl+Shift+Plus sign   Makes highlighted text superscript
Ctrl+Equal sign   Makes highlighted text subscript
Ctrl+B   Bolds or removes bolding from highlighted text
Ctrl+I   Italicizes or removes italics from highlighted text
Ctrl+U   Underlines or removes underlines from highlighted text
Ctrl+Shift+A   Makes highlighted text all capital letters
Ctrl+Shift+F   Highlights the font in the Font list on the Tool bar
Ctrl+Shift+P   Highlights the size in the Font Size list on the Tool bar
Ctrl+D   Displays the Font dialog box with the Font options displayed
Ctrl+Shift+>   Increases the font size
Ctrl+Shift+<   Decreases the font size
Shift+F3   Changes the capitalization of highlighted text
Ctrl+Spacebar   Removes all character formatting

Paragraph Formatting
Ctrl+1   Single spaces the selected paragraph
Ctrl+2   Double spaces the selected paragraph
Ctrl+E   Centers the selected paragraph
Ctrl+J   Justifies the selected paragraph
Ctrl+L   Left aligns the selected paragraph
Ctrl+R   Right aligns the selected paragraph
Ctrl+M   Indents paragraph from the left
Ctrl+Shift+M   Removes left indented paragraph
Ctrl+T   Creates hanging indent

A Guide to Microsoft Office 2000 Professional

Ctrl+Shift+T   Removes hanging indent
Ctrl+Q   Removes all paragraph formatting

Editing   Ctrl+Enter   Inserts a manual page break
Alt+Shift+D   Inserts a date stamp
Alt+Shift+T   Inserts a time stamp
Alt+Shift+P   Inserts a page number
Ctrl+Backspace   Deletes one word to the left
Ctrl+Delete   Deletes one word to the right
F7   Starts the Spelling and Grammar Checker
Shift+F7   Starts the Thesaurus

Table   Alt+Home   Moves to the first cell in a row
Alt+End   Moves to the last cell in a row
Alt+PgUp   Moves to the first cell in a column
Alt+PgDn   Moves to the last cell in a column
Ctrl+Tab   Inserts a tab character in a cell
Shift+Enter   Starts a new paragraph in the cell

Style   Ctrl+Shift+N   Applies the Normal style
Alt+Ctrl+1   Applies the Heading 1 style
Alt+Ctrl+2   Applies the Heading 2 style
Alt+Ctrl+3   Applies the Heading 3 style

Outline View   Alt+Shift+Plus sign   Expands text under a heading
Alt+Shift+Minus sign   Collapses text under a heading
Alt+Shift+A   Expands or Collapses all text or headings
Alt+Shift+1   Displays all heading 1 paragraphs
Alt+Shift+n Displays all headings up to heading level n
Alt+Shift+Left arrow   Formats a heading one level up
Alt+Shift+Right arrow   Formats a heading one level down

Excel Keyboard Shortcuts

The following keyboard shortcuts can be executed when using Excel.

Window   Ctrl+F5   Restores the document's window
Ctrl+F9   Minimizes the document's window
Ctrl+F10   Maximizes the document's window
Ctrl+F6   Displays the next open document's window
Ctrl+Shift+F6   Displays the previous open document's window

Cell Cursor Movement   Ctrl+End   Moves the cell cursor to the end of document
Ctrl+Home   Moves the cell cursor to the beginning of document
Home   Moves the cell cursor to the first cell in that current row
Tab   Moves the cell cursor right one cell in the current row
Shift+Tab   Moves the cell cursor left one cell in the current row

Selection   F8   Starts a highlight block
Ctrl+A   Highlights the entire spreadsheet
Shift+Arrow key   Highlights in direction of arrow
Shift+Spacebar   Highlights a row
Ctrl+Spacebar   Highlights a column

Formatting   Ctrl+Shift+$ Applies Currency format
Ctrl+Shift+%   Applies Percent format
Ctrl+Shift+!   Applies Number format with two decimal places
Ctrl+Shift+~   Applies General number format
Ctrl+Shift+^   Applies Scientific number format
Ctrl+Shift+#   Applies Date format
Ctrl+Shift+@   Applies Time format
Ctrl+B   Applies and removes Bold style
Ctrl+I   Applies and removes Italic style
Ctrl+U   Applies and removes Underline style
Ctrl+9   Hides rows
Ctrl+Shift+(Displays hidden rows
Ctrl+0   Hides columns
Ctrl+Shift+)   Displays hidden columns
Alt+' (apostrophe)   Displays the Style dialog box
Ctrl+1   Displays the Format Cells dialog box
Shift+F3   Displays the Paste Function dialog box

Editing   F2   Edits the current cell
F11   Creates a chart
Alt+Enter   Starts a new line in the same cell
Ctrl+Delete   Deletes text to the end of the line
Ctrl+Shift+" (quote)   Copies contents of above cell
Ctrl+Shift+: (colon)   Inserts current time into cell
Ctrl+; (semicolon)   Inserts current date into cell
Ctrl+' (apostrophe)   Copies the formula from the cell above into the current cell
Ctrl+` (single left quotation mark)   alternates between displaying cell values and cell formulas
F4   Changes a cell's referencing methods (absolute or relative)
F9   Recalculate now

Access Keyboard Shortcuts

The following keyboard shortcuts can be executed when using Access.

Window   Ctrl+F6   Cycles between open windows
F11   Brings database window to the front
Alt+F1   Brings database window to the front

Cursor Movement   Tab   Moves the cursor to the next field
Shift+Tab   Moves the cursor to the previous field
End   Moves the cursor to the last entry in a record
Home   Moves the cursor to the first entry in a record

Selection   Ctrl+R   Selects a form or report
F8   Starts highlight (in Datasheet and Form View only)
Ctrl+PgDn   Highlights first field in record (in Datasheet View)
Ctrl+PgUp   Highlights last field in record (in Datasheet View)
Ctrl+A   Highlights the entire table
Shift+Right arrow   Highlights on character to the right
Shift+Left arrow   Highlights on character to the left
Shift+Up arrow   Highlights extends to previous record
Shift+Down arrow   Highlights extends to following record
F8 (once)   Highlights current entry (in Datasheet and Form View)

F8 (twice)   Highlights field (in Datasheet and Form View)
F8 (three times)   Highlights record (in Datasheet and Form View)

Editing   F5   Highlights current record number in Record Controls
Ctrl+Enter   Inserts a new line
Ctrl+' (quote)   Copies contents of same field from previous record
Ctrl+Shift+: (colon)   Inserts current time into field
Ctrl+; (semicolon)   Inserts current date into field
Ctrl+Plus sign   Adds a new record
Ctrl+Minus sign   Deletes the current record
F9   Recalculates the fields in a window

PowerPoint Keyboard Shortcuts

Working with Presentations   Ctrl+M   Inserts a new slide
Ctrl+D   Makes a copy of the selected slide
F6   Switch to the next pane (clockwise)
Shift+F6   Switch to the previous pane (counterclockwise)

Slide Show Controls   N, Enter, Page Down, Right arrow, Down arrow, Spacebar, P   Performs the next animation or advances to the next slide
Page Up, Left arrow, Up arrow, Backspace   Performs the previous animation or returns to the previous slide
B, Period   Displays a black screen or returns to the slide show from a black screen
W, Comma   Displays a white screen or returns to the slide show from a white screen
S, Plus sign   Stops or restarts an automatic slide show
Esc, Ctrl+Break, Hyphen   Ends a slide show
Both mouse buttons for 2 seconds   Returns to the first slide
Shift+F10 or right-click   Displays the shortcut menu
F1   Displays a list of controls

Publisher Keyboard Shortcuts

Adding and Viewing Pages   Ctrl+Shift+N   adds a page after the current page
F9   Moves between the current page view and actual size view
Ctrl+M   Moves between the background and the foreground page
F5   Go to page...
Shift+F5   Highlights the next page in the page navigation control
Page Up   Moves up within a page
Page Down   Moves down within a page
Ctrl+Page Down   Scrolls to the right
Ctrl+Page Up   Scrolls to the left
Ctrl+Shift+Y   Hides or shows special characters

Mail Merge   Ctrl+Shift+I   Display the Insert Fields dialog box

Internet Explorer Keyboard Shortcuts

Viewing and Exploring Web pages

Tab   Moves forward through the items on a Web page, the Address bar, and the Links bar

Shift+Tab   Moves back through the items on a Web page, the Address bar, and the Links bar

Alt+Home Displays the preselected Web page

Alt+Right arrow   Displays the next page

Alt+Left arrow, Backspace   Displays the previous page

Home   Moves to the beginning of a document

End   Moves to the end of a document

Ctrl+E   Displays Search pane

Ctrl+I   Displays Favorites pane

Ctrl+H   Displays History pane

Ctrl+click   In History or Favorites panes, opens multiple folders

Using the Address bar

Alt+D   Selects the text in the Address bar

F4   Displays the Address bar history

Ctrl+Enter   Adds "www." to the beginning and ".com" to the end of the text typed in the address bar

Functions

The following is a partial list of functions that may be used in Excel.

In the list of functions that follows:

<value> may be replaced by:
  a single value (such as 10)
  a cell reference (such as C5)
  an expression that evaluates to a single value (such as C5*2)
  a field reference (such as GPA)

<range> may be replaced by:
  a list of cells separated by commas (such as A1, B12, D5)
  a continuous range (A1:A10)
  a mixture of both separated by commas (A1, B1:B5, C3, C5:C7)
  a field reference (such as GPA)

Mathematical Functions

ABS(<value>)   Returns the absolute value of <value>: ABS(10) returns 10, ABS(–10) returns 10.

INT(<value>)   Returns <value> rounded down to the nearest integer: INT(1.9) returns 1. INT(–1.9) returns –2.

MOD(<value>, <divisor>)   Returns the remainder of <value> divided by <divisor>. <divisor> may not be 0.

PI()   Returns the constant 3.14159265358979, (pi), accurate to 15 digits. No argument is used.

RAND()   Returns a random number greater than or equal to 0 and less than 1. No argument is used. To generate a number between <low> and <high> use the formula =RAND()*(<high> – <low>) + <low>.

A Guide to Microsoft Office 2000 Professional

ROUND(<value>, <decimals>)   Returns <value> rounded up to <decimals> decimal places. When <decimals> is 0, <value> is rounded to the nearest integer.

ROUNDDOWN(<value>, <decimals>)   Returns <value> rounded down to <decimals> decimal places. When <decimals> is 0, <value> is rounded to the nearest integer.

ROUNDUP(<value>, <decimals>)   Returns <value> rounded up to <decimals> decimal places. When <decimals> is 0, <value> is rounded to the nearest integer.

SQRT(<value>)   Returns the square root of <value>. <value> must be positive.

SUM(<range>)   Returns the total of the values in <range>.

Statistical Functions

AVERAGE(<range>)   Returns the average of the values in <range>. Cells which are empty or contain text are not included.

COUNT(<range>)   Returns the number of cells in <range> that contain numbers, date, or text representation of numbers.

MAX(<range>)   Returns the largest value in <range>. Cells which contains text are not included.

MEDIAN(<range>)   Returns the middle number in <range>.

MIN(<range>)   Returns the smallest value in <range>. Cells which contains text are not included.

MODE(<range>)   Returns the most frequently occuring value in <range>. Cells which are empty or contain text are ignored.

STDEV(<range>)   Returns the standard deviation of the values in <range>.

VAR(<range>)   Returns the variance of the values in <range>.

Trigonometric Functions

ACOS(<value>)   Returns the arccosine of <value> in radians. <value> must be between –1 and +1.

ASIN(<value>)   Returns the arcsine of <value> in radians. <value> must be between –1 and +1.

ATAN(<value>)   Returns the arctangent of <value> in radians.

ATAN2(<Xvalue>, <Yvalue>)   Returns the arctangent in radians of an angle defined by the coordinates <Xvalue>, <Yvalue>.

COS(<value>)   Returns the cosine of <value> where <value> is an angle measured in radians.

DEGREES(<value>)   Returns <value> converted from radians to degrees.

RADIANS(<value>)   Returns <value> converted from degrees to radians.

SIN(<value>)   Returns the sine of <value> where <value> is an angle measured in radians.

TAN(<value>)   Returns the tangent of <value> where <value> is an angle measured in radians.

Logical & Exponential Functions ─────────────

EXP(<value>)   Returns *e* (natural logarithim) raised to the <value> power.

LN(<value>)   Returns the natural logarithm (base *e*) of <value>. <value> must be positive.

LOG(<value>, <base>)   Returns the logarithm of <value> to the base <base>. <value> must be positive.

LOG10(<value>)   Returns the base-10 logarithm of <value>. <value> must be positive.

Logical Functions ──────────────────────

AND(<range>)   Returns TRUE if every value in <range> evaluates to TRUE, and FALSE if any value in <range> evaluates to FALSE. If range stores values, 0 represents FALSE, and nonzero values are TRUE.

IF(<condition>, <true value>, <false value>)   Returns the <true value> if <condition> is true, <false value> if false. Both <true value> and <false value> may be text.

NOT(<value>)   Returns the reverse of <value>. Returns TRUE if <value> is 0, and FALSE if <value> is nonzero: NOT(1+1=3) evaluates to TRUE. <value> must be numeric.

OR(<range>)   Returns TRUE if any value in <range> evaluates to TRUE, FALSE if all values in <range> evaluate to FALSE. If range stores values, 0 represents FALSE, and nonzero values are TRUE.

Date / Time Functions ───────────────────

SECOND(<Time>)   Returns the seconds portion of a time. The time must be in quotes (").

MINUTE(<Time>)   Returns the minutes portion of a time. The time must be in quotes (").

HOUR(<Time>)   Returns the hours portion of a time. The time must be in quotes (").

DAY(<Date>)   Returns the day portion of a date. The date must be in quotes (").

MONTH(<Date>) Returns the month portion of a date. The date must be in quotes (").

YEAR(<Date>)   Returns the year portion of a date. The date must be in quotes (").

DAYS360(<Start Date>, <End Date>)   Returns the number of days between <Start Date> and <End Date>. <Start Date> and <End Date> must be in quotes(").

NOW()   Returns the current date and time. No argument is used.

TODAY()   Returns the current date. No argument is used.

Lookup Functions

CHOOSE(<choice>, <option$_0$>, <option$_1$>, ...)   Returns <option$_0$> if <choice> is 0, <option$_1$> if <choice> is 1, and so on. <options> may be text.

HLOOKUP(<value>, <range>, <row>)   Locates cell in first row of <range> that contains the largest value less than or equal to <value> and returns the corresponding cell's contents in row <rows>.

VLOOKUP(<value>, <range>, <column>)   Locates cell in first column of <range> that contains the largest value less than or equal to <value> and returns the corresponding cell's contents in column <column>.

Financial Functions

In the list of functions that follows:

<rate> is replaced with the interest rate per period
<nper> is replaced with the total number of payment periods
<per> is replaced with the period for which you want to find the interest and must be in the range 1 to nper
<pmt> is replaced with the amount of the periodic payment
<pv> is replaced with the present value of the principal
<fv> is replaced with the future value you want to obtain
<type> is replaced with the timing of payment: payment at the beginning of the period = 1; payment at the end = 0 or are omitted

FV(<rate>, <nper>, <pmt>, <pv>, <type>)   Returns the future value of an investment based on periodic, constant payments and a constant interest rate.

IPMT(<rate>, <per>, <nper>, <pv>, <fv>, <type>)   Returns the interest payment for a given period for an investment, based on periodic, constant payments and a constant interest rate.

NPER(<rate>, <pmt>, <pv>, <fv>, <type>)   Returns the number of total payment periods required to turn payments into the future value based on periodic, constant payments and a constant interest rate.

PMT(<rate>, <nper>, <pv>, <fv>, <type>)   Returns the payment for a loan based on constant payments and a constant interest rate.

PPMT(<rate>, <per>, <nper>, <pv>, <fv>, <type>)   Returns the payment on the principal for a given investment based on periodic, constant payments and a constant interest rate.

PV(<rate>, <nper>, <pmt>, <fv>, <type>)   Returns the present value of an investment.

RATE(<nper>, <pmt>, <pv>, <fv>, <type>)   Returns the interest rate per period of a loan.

Creating Customized Forms and Reports

In Chapters Twelve and Fourteen you created database forms and reports using the Form and Report Wizards. This appendix includes a brief introduction on how to create and modify forms and reports in Design view.

Form Layout

The forms created in the database chapters arranged fields using the columnar layout. However, a form may be easier to read when related fields are grouped together (like parts of an address) and more important and frequently used fields placed first.

The first step in creating a customized form is to plan the form's layout in a sketch. The *layout* is the arrangement of the fields. For example, a form for the Packs table in the Backpacks database could have the following layout:

Packs

Item Number ____
　　Item Name _____
　　Style _____
　　Color _____

A sketch of the Packs form—note how the information is grouped

label　　When sketching a form's layout, an appropriately sized line for each entry should be included. Labels should also be considered when designing the form. *Labels* are text that identify the form or give added information about a field. For example, on the sketch above, Packs is a label describing the form.

Creating Forms in Design View

Forms were created in Chapter Twelve using the Form Wizard, but can also be created and modified in *Design view*. A form can be created in Design view by first selecting the Forms button in the Objects list of the Database window and then clicking on the New button ( ) at the top of the Database window, which displays the New Form dialog box:

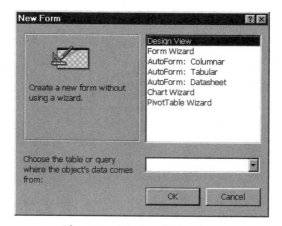

The New Form dialog box

Selecting Design View from the list of options, the desired table from the collapsible list, and then OK displays a new, blank form in Design view:

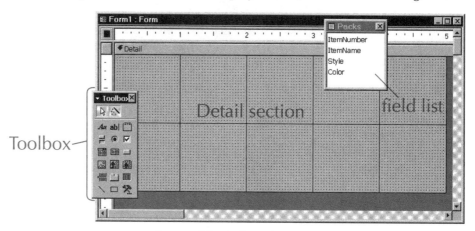

A new, blank form in Design view

- **Toolbox** contains tools that are used to place objects on the form, such as a label.

- **Detail section** is where objects are placed to represent their location on a form.

- **Field list** displays a list of available fields from the previously selected table.

adding fields

Fields can be added to the new form by dragging the field name from the field list to the Detail section, which inserts a field name box and field entry box:

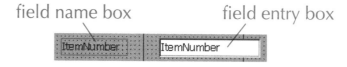

field name box

field entry box

The *field name box* is a label that stores the name of the field. The *field entry box* represents where the entry for a record will be entered, displayed, or updated.

Instead of repeating the same steps to add each field to the Detail section, all the fields can be added at once by first double-clicking on the field list's Title bar to highlight all the fields in the list. Then, dragging any of the highlighted fields to the Detail section inserts all of the fields aligned in a column.

Customizing Forms in Design View

New and existing forms can be customized in Design view to match a sketched layout. A previously created form is displayed in Design view by selecting the form name in the Database window and then clicking on the Design button () at the top of the Database window.

resizing field boxes

Access automatically formats the field entry box length and formats the length of the field name box so that it is just long enough to display the field name entirely. Both the field name and field entry box widths can be changed. Clicking on a box displays square *handles*:

move handle ⎯  ⎯ resizing handles

The selected field entry box displays handles

These handles indicate that it is *selected*. Dragging one of the resizing handles changes the width of the box.

When resizing fields, keep in mind that the length of the field name and field entry boxes determines the number of characters displayed on the screen, not the number of characters actually stored. For example, the ItemNumber entry will display D10 if the field entry box is sized to display 3 characters and D102 if it is sized to display 4 characters.

moving field boxes

A selected field name or field entry box is moved by pointing to the move handle, the large handle in the upper-left corner of the box, until the pointer changes to an upward-pointing hand:

An object can be moved by dragging the move handle with the upward-pointing hand pointer

Dragging while the ☝ shape is displayed moves the field name or field entry box.

Both the field name and field entry boxes can be moved together by pointing to either selected box until the pointer changes to an open hand shape:

Both field name and field entry boxes are moved by dragging with the open hand pointer

Dragging while the ✋ shape is displayed moves the field name and field entry box at the same time.

selecting multiple field boxes

Moving boxes as a group maintains the original spacing. A group of field name and field entry boxes can be moved at one time by first selecting them and then dragging. More than one box can be selected by holding down the Shift key and clicking on each desired box. An individual box in a group can be deselected by holding down the Shift key and clicking on the selected box. Clicking the mouse in an empty part of the Detail section deselects any selected field boxes.

adding labels

Labels can be added to the form to describe its contents and supply information about fields. A label is added by first selecting the Label tool on the Toolbox (Aa), which changes the pointer to the $^{+}$A shape. Next, clicking the pointer on the form places the cursor. Typing the label and then pressing Enter creates the label. A label can be moved by first clicking on it to select it and then dragging. A selected label can be deleted by pressing the Delete key.

resizing the Work area

When adding, moving, or deleting fields from a form, it may be necessary to change the size of the Detail section by dragging the black line separating the Detail section from the dark gray area.

formatting

The appearance of the form as well as the text in it can be formatted. Field names, entries, or labels are formatted by selecting the desired boxes and then selecting the desired options on the Formatting Toolbar. The background color of the form can be changed by clicking on an empty portion of the Detail section and then selecting the desired color from the Fill/Back Color button (⬥▾) on the Formatting Toolbar.

Creating Reports in Design View

Reports were created in Chapter Fourteen using the Report Wizard, but can also be created and modified in Design view. The first step in creating a report is to plan the report's layout in a sketch. If fields from different tables are to be included in the report, the report should be based on a select query. Once the report is planned, the report can be created in Design view by first selecting the Reports button in the Objects list of the Database window and then clicking on the New button (New) at the top of the Database window, which displays the New Report dialog box:

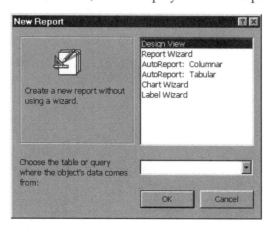

Selecting Design View from the list of options, the desired table or query from the collapsible list, and then OK displays a new, blank report in Design view:

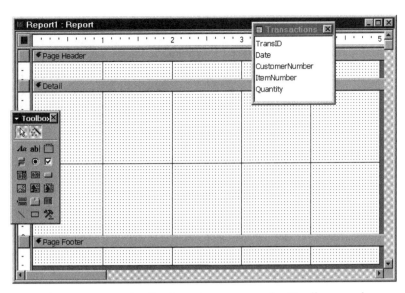

A new report in Design view—note the Toolbox and field list

In Design view, a new report is divided into three sections called Page Header, Detail, and Page Footer. These sections indicate where the information will be printed on the report. The *Detail* section usually contains the field entry boxes which indicate where the entries of each record will appear. The field name boxes are usually placed in the *Page Header* or *Page Footer* sections because anything in these sections appears on every page of the report.

After a new report is displayed, the field name and field entry boxes need to be added. The steps for adding a field name and its corresponding field entry box to the report are:

1. Drag the field from the field list to the Detail section of the report. A field name box and field entry box are inserted.

2. Click on the field name box to select it and then select the Cut command from the Edit menu.

3. Click once in the Page Header section and then select the Paste command from the Edit menu to place the field name box in the Page Header section.

4. Line up the field name box and field entry box by dragging.

Customizing Reports in Design View

New and existing reports can be customized in Design view to match a sketched layout. A previously created report can be displayed in Design view by selecting the report in the Database window and then clicking on the Design button ( ) at the top of the Database window.

resizing and moving field boxes

Customizing reports in Design view is very similar to customizing forms in Design view. The field name and field entry boxes in a report can be resized, moved, and formatted just as they were in the Design view of a form. However, it is not possible to move boxes between different sections of the report by dragging. Boxes can be moved between different sections using the Cut and Paste commands from the Edit menu or the Cut and Paste buttons on the Standard Toolbar.

headers and footers

Adding information in the Page Header or Page Footer section displays the information on every page of the report. Headers and footers can also be created so they are displayed only on the first page of the report and the last page of the report. Selecting the Report Header/Footer command from the View menu adds the Report Header and Report Footer sections to the report. The report header often contain the title of the report and the report footer often contains summaries.

Reports can be sorted and grouped by fields. Selecting the Sorting and Grouping command from the View menu or the Sorting and Grouping button (![icon]) on the Toolbar displays the following dialog box:

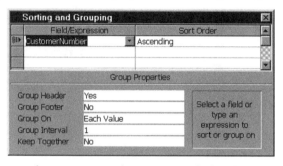

The Sorting and Grouping dialog box

sorting fields

Fields in a report are sorted by first clicking the pointer in a blank row under the Field/Expression section and then selecting the desired key sort field from the collapsible list. The sort order can be changed by selecting Ascending or Descending in the Sort Order section of the dialog box.

grouping fields

The report can be grouped by a field by first clicking in the row with the field name to select it, and then selecting Yes in either the Group Header or Group Footer options in the Group Properties section of the dialog box. Additional sections appear when a report is grouped by a specific field. For example, in the Transactions report there is a CustomerNumber Header section because the report was grouped by the CustomerNumber field:

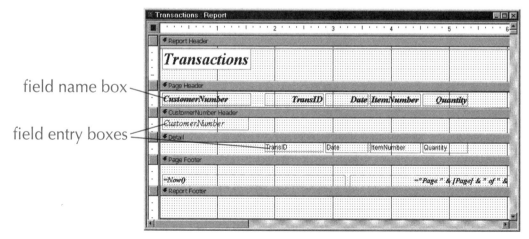

The Transactions report is grouped by
CustomerNumber

After the new Header or Footer section is added to the report, the field entry box for that field needs to be moved to the new section, as shown above.

Adding Summaries and Subsummaries to a Report

Summaries display statistics about fields and can be added to a report to make it more informative. A summary is added to a report by creating a box that contains a formula in the Report Footer section of the report. For example, to display the number of records in the Transactions report:

[ab]

1. Select the Text Box tool ([ab]) on the Toolbox. The pointer shape changes to ⁺[ab].

2. Click the ⁺[ab] pointer once in the Report Footer section to place two new boxes. The left box stores the label, and the right box stores the formula.

3. Select the label box, click again to place the cursor, and type the text Total Transactions.

4. Place the cursor in the box that will store the formula and type =COUNT([TransID]).

5. Drag both boxes until they are aligned as desired.

When the report is previewed or printed, the text Total Transactions and the total number of transactions are displayed on the last page of the report.

A report can also include a subsummary that displays statistics about each group of records. The report must be sorted and grouped by a field before a subsummary can be added. For example, to display the number of records for each CustomerNumber in the Transactions report:

1. Select the Grouping and Sorting button from the Toolbar, click on the row containing CustomerNumber, then select Yes in the Group Footer option to display the CustomerNumber Footer section.

2. Select the Text Box tool ([ab]) on the Toolbox. The pointer shape changes to ⁺[ab].

3. Click the ⁺[ab] pointer once in the CustomerNumber Footer section to place the boxes.

4. Select the label box, click again to place the cursor, and type the text Total Customer Orders.

5. Place the cursor in the second box and type the formula =COUNT([TransID]).

6. Drag both boxes until they are aligned as desired.

The SUM, AVERAGE, MAX, and MIN functions you used in the spreadsheet chapters can also be used in a formula to create summaries and subsummaries. These functions, respectively, are used to sum or average the values in a specified field, or find the maximum or minimum value in a specified field.

This appendix contains lessons for learning how to *touch type*. Timed practices are also included that will help develop speed and accuracy.

Learning to Touch Type

When touch typing, your hands are positioned on the keyboard so that you can strike any of the keys without looking down at the keyboard. The advantage of this is that your eyes are on the material you are typing. With touch typing, you will be able to type with greater accuracy and speed than you can using the "hunt and peck" method.

Before you begin to type your hands and body need to be in the proper positions. Your hands should be placed lightly on the keyboard with slightly curved fingers. The left pinky is placed on the **A** key and the rest of the left hand on the **SDF** keys. The right pinky is placed on the semicolon (;) key and the rest of the right hand on the **LKJ** keys. The right thumb is placed on the spacebar. With the fingers placed as just described, this is called the "home" position.

Place the chair you are sitting in so that your arms reach out and your elbows are loosely at your side. Sit in a relaxed but upright position with both feet flat on the floor. Maintaining proper posture will help to keep your body from tensing. Try not to slouch or bend over the keyboard.

In touch typing, the location of each of the keys on the keyboard needs to be memorized. This is accomplished by learning a few keys at a time in each of the following lessons. Developing a smooth rhythm as you type is important. Strike each of the keys with the same pressure. In the timed practices, you will keep track of how many words per minute you type and the number of mistakes made.

Each of the keyboarding lessons makes use of the Microsoft Word word processor. Therefore, you will begin by learning how to use the word processor. Read pages 3-1 through 3-10 and complete Practices 1, 2, and 3 in Chapter Three to learn how to use the word processor.

Lesson 1 - The Home Row: ASDF JKL;

Create a new word procesor document as described in Chapter Three. You will perform each of the typing lessons in a new document. Note the blinking cursor in the upper-left corner of the window, indicating where a typed character will appear.

Place your hands on the keyboard in the *home position* or on the *home row* described previously with the left hand on the keys **ASDF** and the right hand on the keys **JKL;**. The right thumb is placed on the spacebar.

Type the following letters and when you finish each line, press the Enter key with your right pinky. The cursor will move down one line and to the left side of the window. Note that the semicolon (;) is normally followed by a space when typing actual material. Do not look at your hands while you type, refer only to the picture of the keyboard below.

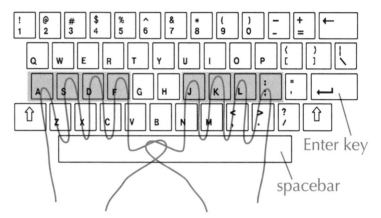

Place your fingers on the home row when beginning to type

Practice 1.1

```
1    aaa ;;; aaa ;;; sss lll sss lll ddd kkk ddd kkk fff jjj fjf
2    aaa sss sas asa sss aaa sas aaa sss sas aaa sss sas sss a;a
3    ddd ada ddd daa dss dad dsd ddd sss aaa ads asd asd dad sls
4    sss aaa ddd ddd ssa dad dsd dsa dsa dss daa aaa sss dda dkd
5    fff fff faf fss fss fas fas fad ffd faa fsa ffs fsa fad fjf
6    fss saf fad sfa fss fad fsa sda fad aff fsd sff ffa sss fjf
7    jjj jjj jja jaf jfj jdj jfs jja jad jsf jja jda jaf jjj jfj
8    jad daj fja das saj jjs jsa daf sfj jad faj jjj jad jaa dkd
9    kkk kka kkk kak kjk kss kkj kak ksa ksk kfk kkf kkk kjj kdk
10   kad dak sak adk sak akk kak jak jak dak ask sak kkk kjk ala
11   lll lll lff llk lak las lad lfl lld lll lsk lfl lkl ljl lal
12   lsl sal fal dsl lsl llf jal all sal lsa fal lll lkl lal a;a
13   ; ; ; ; fa; da; sa; da; fj; sa; da; jl; ; ; ; sa; lad; jak;
14   dad dad lad lad sad sad add add lad ask dad fall fall falls
15   ask ask fad fad ads ads dad lass lass sass sass salad salad
```

Practice 1.2

```
 1   ;;; aaa lll sss kkk ddd jjj fff ;a; a;a lsl sls kdk dkd jfj
 2   sas saa asa asa dfd fdf ffd dfd das sad sad das las das ad;
 3   jjkk kkjj jkjk kjkj jkkj l; l; jkl kjl; dakl kald jakl jakl
 4   jjk jjl jj; jaj ksk lal las las kad kad laf laf la; ja; la;
 5   aad aas aaf aaj aak aal aa; fad fad dad dad lad lad sad sad
 6   dask jljl fafa fajk ddl; jadl lads lads dads dads sads jakl
 7   asks asks dads fall lass fads lask fads lads ffjj kkll fkf;
 8   sass salad asks; dads jass as hass lass fall alls lads ;gas
 9   has; fall aaj k;j sas ask adds sad; jjkl fall alls lads ssl
10   jass dads has all gas adds lass fall alls lads ask as sad;;
```

Repeat the practices above until you can type the characters without referring to the keyboard diagram.

When you have completed the lesson and want to leave Word select the Exit command from the File menu as described in Section 3.12. You will then be asked if you wish to save the file. Click on the No button.

Lesson 2 - RTYU

In this lesson you will learn the **RTYU** keys.

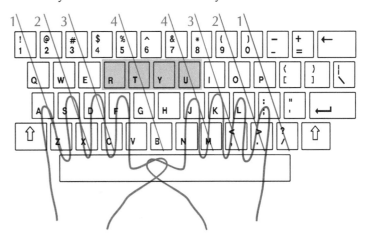

*Press **R** and **T** with the left hand, and **Y** and **U** with the right*

The letters **RT** are typed using the pointer finger of your left hand and **YU** with the pointer finger of your right hand. Note the lines that show which finger is used to type which keys: "1" for the pinky, "2" for the ring finger, "3" for the index and "4" for the pointer.

From this point on, each lesson will begin with a review of the previous lesson. Before proceeding to the new letters, practice this review several times until you feel comfortable. **Remember to press the Enter key with your right pinky at the end of each line.**

Review

```
1   aaa ;;; aaa ;;; sss lll sss lll ddd kkk ddd kkk fff jjj fjf
2   aaa sss lll sas asa ddd das kkk jjj lkl fff fjf jfj klk jas
3   ljl kfk ldf klj kjk ljk fsd sda jkl fsd sad sad lad lad fad
4   dada fada sads jass klas fas; dad; fkal dasd jjkk jaka fada
5   asks lads lass daj; jakl kfkf ladf klds adas fjl; dads lads
```

Practice 2.1

```
1    fff ffr frf frr frr rrr frr frf rrr frf frr rrr fff frf rrr
2    fff fft ftf ftt ftt ttt ttt ftf ttf ftf ttt ttt fff tff ftt
3    frt frt frt frt fra rta rat rat jar jar far far tar tar far
4    jjj jju juj juu juj jju juj juj uuu juu juj jjj uuu juj juu
5    jjj jjy jyj jyy jyy yyy jyj jyy jyy jyj yyy jyy jyj jyj yyy
6    juu juy jju juy jyu juy jyu jyu jyy juu uuu yyy uyu yuy yuy
7    fujy furt fryt juty rfrt sats fats jakd dar; rats rats sats
8    krad jury safy last last jury tars tars star star duty duty
9    yard jury duty fast just dark dust data klas jars furs yard
10   ruts says lass tar; hats sats rats yard dull tart last dad;
11   tars tar; hats sats rats yard dull tart last furt fryt juty
12   yard duty fast lads sad; ruts tar; hats sats dull tart last
13   dull tart last dad; ruts says lass tar; hats sats rats yard
14   kart dust sass furs just task task fast rats yard dull tart
15   asks just last fur dark ruts says lass tar; tart tars darts
```

A Guide to Microsoft Office 2000 Professional

```
 1   juts furs dust suds dart rats sats just just task task fast
 2   rats ruts daft rays sats lark jars salt suds suds lads furs
 3   yard duty fast lads sad; lass tars hats data tart last dust
 4   jar ask fry lad fat dad add sad rut dad add say say far tar
 5   dart dull rut; ruts furs asks lass rust just fall star rays
 6   dusk last fast lads kart dust sass furs furs just task salt
 7   dull darts suds jars lark dusts rust data data rats salt as
 8   asks just last fur dark dart says jury task tart tars darts
 9   tar rat sally sally last yard dark try; fats lark dark data
10   ruts rudy trudy rust dart just salt dark furs say; dust tad
```

Repeat the practices above until you can type the keys without refer-ring to the keyboard diagram. When you are finished, exit Word.

Lesson 3 - EGHI

In this lesson you will learn the keys **EGHI**. Rather than pressing the Enter key at the end of each line we are now going to allow the computer to determine where the end of each line is. If there is not sufficient room for a word at the end of a line the word will automatically be moved to the beginning of the next line in a process called *word wrap*. Where your computer breaks a line will differ from what is shown in this text since the break is determined by where the margin is set. Just keep typing the lines on the next page without ever pressing Enter:

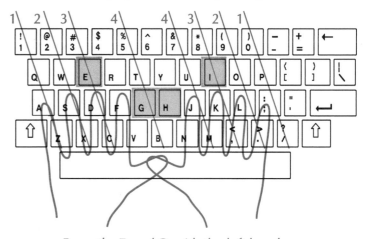

*Press the **E** and **G** with the left hand,*
*and the **H** and **I** with the right*

Review

```
1   fff frr frf frf fft ftf ftt ftf ttt juu juj jju jju juu juj
2   jyy jyy jyj jyj fuy fuy frt fju juy jyy ftt frr jyy juy juy
3   asks jury yard jars arts judy lark rust dust just fast dark
4   trudy dark sally yard daffy salt rat tar fur rays tall fall
5   darts fats sat; us all task lad; salt dust trust last fault
```

Practice 3.1

```
1    ddd ded ded dee dde ded ded ded ddd ded dee dee dee eee ded
2    fff fgf fgf fgg fgf fgf fgg fgf fgg ggg fgg fgf fgg ggg fgf
3    fgd deg fed def fgd deg fed def deg def feg dfe eee ggg ege
4    jjj jhj jhj jhh jhj jjj hhh jhj jhh jhj jhj jjh jjh hhh jhj
5    kkk kik kik kik kii kii kik iii iii kii kik kii kii iii kik
6    jhki jhik kiik kijh kijh khij jhik kihj jhki jhki jhki jjkk
7    did tug lad the she hid set age red red did ask let age the
8    did lug tug hit age yet ask rut elk gas she she did did use
9    rake dirt sake high dirt rail jail kiss jilt hale side said
10   saddle kettle us huddle jerry jail dirt yet little rut side
11   ask rail; kiss jilt hale said elks gas hers juggle rid teds
12   the fights hight fester justify sights satisfy deride kitty
13   hale aisle federal drill salt kitty kite hats dred egg said
14   did fight justify sight little dirt yet little she kit uses
15   hight sight fester deride just sight father fifth kettle a;
```

```
 1   did lag elk yes age let rug kiss rake that said; sail hills
 2   her; dig a rut age is hill high hear set sail satisfy there
 3   erase refer defer agree reset sir differ legal degrees tell
 4   satisfy father egret fifes fifth fly leg hedge sell his her
 5   gail harsh heart thigh yalta light irish alight; ideal star
 6   last jelly judge high kelly jail; kay jest hail to thee jet
 7   halts the digs highest eight three furs halt judge judge as
 8   lilly ladle legal aisle drill salt the these as; highest to
 9   drudge tusk halt fudge last jest hail has gall deak salt as
10   hark yak said sail the less; fastest highest edge all halts
```

Timed Practice 3.3

The next few lessons end with a timed practice which allows you to check your speed. Type for 1 minute and then calculate your speed in words per minute by counting the words typed. Each line contains the equivalent of 12 words (one word is five typed characters). Words in a partial line are calculated using the scale below the lines.

```
 1   did yes let rug age rut set ted ask elk yet dad sad lads hit  12
 2   sake rail jail dirt side said jails kiss rake that tug; dull  24
 3   jilt just fads fife flag fall digs ages rail tell star kills  36
 4   fight sight deride just father fifth kettle jelly judge ask;  48
          1    2    3    4    5    6    7    8    9    |    1    2
```

Lesson 4 - CVB MNO

In this lesson the letters **CVB MNO** are added as well as capital letters. Use the finger lines in the diagram to determine which finger is used to type the new letters. To type capital letters use either your left or right pinky to depress one of the Shift keys and type the letter. If the capital letter is typed with the right hand the left pinky is used to depress the Shift key. If it is typed with the left hand the right pinky is used. As in Lesson 3, allow the computer to determine where the end of each line is by not pressing the Enter key.

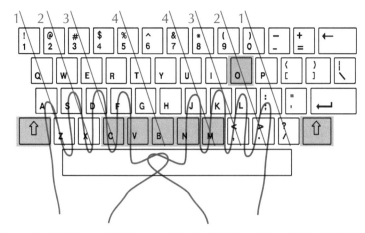

Press the **C**, **V**, and **B** keys with the left hand, and the **M**, **N**, and **O** keys with the right. Use the pinky to press Shift.

Review

1   ded eee fgf ggg jhj hhh kik iii fge fgf jhj fgh jhi dek deg

2   digs ruts ages hill high sats fads sake rail dirt side said

3   all irish thigh gale takes legal aisle salt eight that flag

4   hail thee; fastest gail sledge haste tasks jet get hail art

Practice 4.1

1   ddd dcd dcc dcd ddc dcc dcc dcc ccc dcc dcd ccc dcc dcc dcd

2   fff fvf fvf fvv fvv vvv fvv fvv fvf vvv fvf fvv fvv fvv fvf

3   fff fbf fbf fbb ffb bbb fbb fbf fbb bbb fbf fbb fbb bbb fbf

4   dcv dcv cfv fvb fvb fbv fbf fvv vdc bdc bbd ccc vvv bbb bvc

5   jjj jmj jmj jmm jjm mmm jmm jmj jmm mmm mmm jmm jmj jmm jmj

6   jjj jnj jnj jnn jnn nnn jnn jnj jnj nnn jnn jnj jnj jnn jnj

7   lll lol lol loo ooo loo loo lol lol ooo loo lol lol loo lol

8   jmn jnm jnm jml jno loj ojn ooj jmn jno loj mno mno bcv bcv

9   Bill odd nod boy Bob night vent Sam avoids mad bite buried;

10 dock mint convert common bimini money none bongo volume vat

11 convince civic conic occur yucca bulb blurb member mayor to

12 ninth linen noun announce mono minds vocation victim vacate

13 kitty Gerry highly Eighty saddle kettle monies Tony convert

14 Jimmy Miami Thomas Fast Kludge Doll Rest Ernest Joan Laurie

15 Satisfy small Father; fight federal Jail tuggle yet Law Jim

A Guide to Microsoft Office 2000 Professional

Practice 4.2

1 Lara Nina monkey said Gray is art color Has Harry come home

2 Janet will not be at school today It is too late to make up

3 Let us make haste before school starts This is not the time

4 Should you be very good or not This is the universal Return

5 George Ferrit was raised in Iowa John Smith in Rhode Island

6 You need to make some money; to be able to go to the movies

7 Bob Cindy Virginia Monica Nina Ollie Barbara Veronica Bruce

8 This is the time for to be verbal Robert is a very nice guy

9 Miami New York Chicago Cleveland Boston Houston Dallas Dent

10 The gain made by becoming a good typist may be considerable

Timed Practice 4.3

Type for 1 minute and then calculate your speed in words per minute by counting the words typed. Each line contains 12 words. The words in a partial line are calculated using the scale below the lines.

1 Come to my house if you need to sell a vacuum cleaner today; 12

2 This is not a good time to help you with cooking the turkeys 24

3 Bill Crane is the secretary at our local offices of the club 36

4 Virginia is a beautiful state; Its capitol city is Richmond 48

       1   2   3   4   5   6   7   8   9 | 1   2

Lesson 5 - WQZX P,.?

In this lesson the letters **WQZX P** are added along with the comma (,), period (.), and question mark (?). The question mark is typed by pressing the left Shift key with the left pinky and the ? key with the right. Note the finger lines for determining which finger to use for each key.

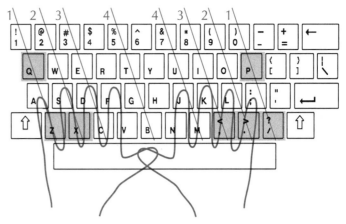

*Press the **Q**, **Z**, and **X** keys with the left hand, and the*
***P**, comma, period, and question mark with the right*

Review

1 dcdc fvvf fbfb jmmj jnjn Jmnj jnlo loon fvcd Fcvf jmnl Lojn

2 very task dark volt None vast many salt belt bolt none cold

3 Verbal Bimini Bahamas vacuum Nina member announce mist mold

4 members linen Venice Bob Vermont San Antonio convert Melvin

Practice 5.1

1   sss sws sww sww sws sww www sws ssw sww sws sws www sws sws

2   aaa aqa aqa aqq aqq qqq aaq aqa aqq aqq aqq aqa qqq aqa aqa

3   aaa aza azz azz zzz azz azz aza azz azz azz azz zzz azz aza

4   ;;p ;;p ;p; ;p; ;p; pp; pp; ll. ll. l.l lo. lo. la. ll. l.l

5   sss sxs sxx sxx xxx sxs sxx sxs xxx xxx ssx sxx sxs sxx sxs

6   kk, kk, kk, k, kkk, k, k, kk, ; ? ; ? ; ? ; ; ? ; ? ; ? la?

7   aqua, zap? Zeus, want; aqua. quart, extra, quilt. Zoe quill

8   quick query equip quilt quits quote Queen quality paper top

9   apple panel support append popular profess quota quail pops

10 Rudy Penn Paul, plastics proof quart quit? Walter Thomas at

11 Aztec zero, unzip. fuzzy gauze sizes Inez epitomize Prizes?

12 exact axiom vexed Felix, Exxon. Xerox, mixed index exciting

13 dozen Zeke. Brazil, William, hertz gauze dozes? lazy Zurich

14 zonal zooms seize quilt quick prime power opera? allow. Zak

15 Oprah robot Boone, Texas, Portland, Zeus Zola extremely fax

Practice 5.2

1 Jake quit his jobs. What do you want? Exit from the west.

2 Zinc is not really that pretty. Would you please be quiet?

3 I would like to go to Zurich, Brazil, Texas and Queensland.

4 Robert Roodez is a fine person whose qualities are special.

5 In which Texas cities would you like to stay at Quality Inn?

6 The Aztecs had an advanced civilization which disappeared.

7 What equipment would you like to have added to a gymnasium?

8 I have visited Washington, Texas, Arizona, Utah, Vermont.

9 Inez Zola has the qualities that will make her quite famous.

10 Do you have zebras, polar bears, and turtles at your zoo?

Timed Practice 5.3

Type for 1 minute and then calculate your speed in words per minute by counting the words typed. Each line contains 12 words. The words in a partial line are calculated using the scale below the lines. To test your accuracy count the number of letters and spaces missed.

1 There are qualities which are required to become successful. 12

2 The following will come to the front; Bob, Zelda, and Betty. 24

3 Would you please; ask your parents to allow you to visit me? 36

4 Twelve quiet students sat on the wall waiting for the twins. 48

      1   2   3   4   5   6   7   8   9 | 1   2

Lesson 6 - :"/

In this lesson the colon (:), quote marks ("), and slash or division sign (/) are added. The colon is typed by pressing the left Shift key with the left pinky and typing the key containing the semicolon and colon. A space always follows a colon. Quote marks are typed by pressing the left Shift key with the left pinky and the key to the right of the colon key using the right pinky. The slash is typed using the right pinky.

Review

1 dozen unzip zesty gauze amaze wants excite explain exhausts

2 prop Perhaps? personal, profit, operator. Quality qualify

3 equip quest quicken, proud supports puppy Zanadu? Exciting

4 quit extra Paul Zak? Extra qualify pest apple quart quick.

Practice 6.1

1 : : "abcd" l: "What is that?" "This is a quote from Jane."

2 "John is the best." The team is: Zeke, Jake, Rob and Quent.

3 ; / / ; / ; abc/de x/y; words/minute nt/m miles/hr, xyz/abc

4 These states are in the west: Utah, Oregon, and California.

5 What person said: "We have nothing to fear but fear itself"?

Lesson 7

The two practices in this lesson are *timed practices*. In the first, type for one minute and then calculate your speed in words per minute by counting the words typed. Each line contains 12 words. The words in a partial line are calculated using the scale below the lines. To test your accuracy, count the number of letters and spaces missed. Record both your speed in words per minute and the number of errors per minute. Repeat the practice a few times recording the results of each attempt. Your speed and accuracy should improve each time. Note the specific letters which appear as errors and repeat the lesson for that letter. For example, if you often type the letter R instead of T by mistake, go back and repeat Lesson 2. Note that this material is fairly difficult; you should perform all the previous lessons before attempting this one.

Timed Practice 7.1

1 dale rail flight word, solve draft general; writers rough at 12

2 Important: work orders going ahead; instead rise part, taken 24

3 gift week disaster creates advantage been skill oral success 36

4 sharpen your smile coal miners desire: insure achieve smiles 48

5 Press exit Zack; suspend flowers: beginning strokes reunite, 60

6 carriage blooms crowd works quite document fashion computer: 72

7 having options print transfer undo; Marcia, Melvin, Samantha 84

```
   1    2    3    4    5    6    7    8    9   |   1    2
```

Timed Practice 7.2

The **Tab** key is located on the upper left of the keyboard, next to the Q key. Rather than using spaces, Tab is used to indent paragraphs and to begin lines which do not start at the left margin. In the practices below, you will press Tab once with the left pinky to indent each paragraph.

In this practice type for five minutes and then calculate your speed in words per minute by counting the words typed and dividing by 5. The total of words is given at the end of each line. Test your accuracy by counting the number of letters and spaces missed. Repeat the practice typing for ten minutes and then calculate your speed and accuracy. Repeat this practice several times, over several days. You should note an increase in both your speed and your accuracy.

1   Many of the advances made by science and technology are   12
dependent upon the ability to perform complex mathematical   23
calculations and to process large amounts of data. It is   34
therefore not surprising that for thousands of years   44
mathematicians, scientists and business people have   54
searched for "computing" machines that could perform   65
calculations and analyze data quickly and accurately.   76

2   As civilizations began to develop, they created both   87
written languages and number systems. These number systems   99
were not originally meant to be used in mathematical   109
calculations, but rather were designed to record   119
measurements. Roman numerals are a good example of this.   130
Few of us would want to carry out even the simplest   140
arithmetic operations using Roman numerals. How then were   151
calculations performed thousands of years ago?   162

3   Calculations were carried out with a device known as   173
an abacus which was used in ancient Babylon, China and   186
Europe until the late middle-ages. Many parts of the   196
world, especially in the Orient, still make use of the   207
abacus. The abacus works by sliding beads back and   217
forth on a frame with the beads on the top of the frame   228
representing fives and on the bottom ones. After a   239
calculation is made the result is written down.   249

     1   2   3   4   5   6   7   8   9 | 1   2

Lesson 8

In this lesson you will make use of the top row of keys that contains both numbers and symbols. Note which finger is used to press each key. The right Shift key is used to type the symbols at the top of the keys 1 through 5 and the left Shift key for the symbols on the top of keys 6 through =.

Practice 8.1

```
1    aqa aq1 aq1 aq1 a1a a1a a11 sws sw2 sw2 sw2 s2s s2s s22 ss2

2    ded de3 de3 de3 d3d d3d d33 de3 frf fr4 fr4 f4f f4f ff4 fr4

3    fr5 fr5 fr5 f5f f5f f55 ff5 juj ju7 ju7 ju7 j7j j7j ju7 j77

4    jyj jy6 jy6 jy6 j6j j6j jy6 j66 kik ki8 ki8 k8k k8k ki8 k88

5    lol lo9 lo9 l9l l9l lo9 l99 ;p; ;p0 ;p0 ;p0 ;0; ;0; ;;0 ;p0

6    aq1! aq1! aq1! aq!! sw2@ sw2@ s2s@ Sw@@ s@@s de3# de3# d#3d

7    fr4$ fr4$ fr$$ fr$f f$4r fr5% fr5% f5%% f5%5 f%f% jy6^ jy6^

8    ju7& ju7& ju7& j&j& ju&j ki8* ki8* k**k k*8* k8*8 lo9( lo9(

9    L(990); : L( ; 0) ; )0 )) (9923) : ; 00) 19(00)  ; - - __ ;

10   ; + +567 - 342 =$45.60 + ; " ' ;+ ; + = - ; ___ -- +1895.00

11   $435.00; = 389* (873) &23 $35.89@ 380.23! 89 + 78 = $382.00

12   Mary has bought a dress that costs $145.67 plus 6.0(%) tax.

13   (A) 3^2 = 9 & $12@ for 5 items = $60.00. 89 * 34 = 3026 47%

14   If I win the Florida $10,000,000.00 lottery I must pay tax.

15   Jack & Jill went up the 3,450 m hill to fetch 12# of water.

16   23 & 79 are odd numbers! (34 + 78) / (245 * 12.8) = 0.00035
```

Timed Practice 8.2

In this practice type for five minutes and then calculate your speed in words per minute by counting the words typed and dividing by 5. The total of words is given at the end of each line. The words in a partial line are calculated using the scale below the lines. To test your accuracy count the number of letters and spaces missed.

1   Hortense Bargain has decided to reduce the price of   11
stock items #3485 (paint), #7431 (electric saws) and #2945   23
(lawn furniture) by 45%. The new prices will be $38.50@,   35
$72.95@ and $14.98@.   39

2   Ivy University is having a book fair and charging the   51
following for books and supplies: pens $0.45@, note books   62
$3.78@, and boxes of paper clips $0.67@. The text "A Guide   74
to Microsoft Office Professional" is specially priced   85
with a 10% reduction (plus 6% sales tax). The stock number   97
of this text is #015-7 (for paperback) and #016-5   108
(hardcover). Henri Camri's new novel "Old Houses in New   119
Jersey" is specially priced at $12.45 after a 25% discount.   131

3   Please be advised of the addition of the following   142
courses to the Ivy University catalog: #126 Advanced   153
Computing (2 credits), #365 Very Advanced Computing (7   164
credits), #782 Computing for the Exceptionally Intelligent   176
(12 credits). The tuition for each course is $45.00@.   187
What a bargain!   190

        1   2   3   4   5   6   7   8   9 | 1   2

Lesson 9

In this lesson type for five minutes and then calculate your speed in words per minute by counting the words typed and dividing by 5. The total of words is given at the end of each line. The words in a partial line are calculated using the scale below the lines. To test your accuracy count the number of letters and spaces missed. Repeat the practice typing for ten minutes and then calculating your speed and accuracy.

1   One of the most important advances made in computing   11

has been in the field of "telecommunications." By   21

telecommunications we mean the sending of computer data   32

over telephone lines. To do this an additional piece of   43

hardware called a "modem" is required to translate the   54

binary data of the computer into waves which can then be   65

transmitted over phone lines. To receive data a modem   76

must also have the capability of translating the waves back   88

into binary form.   92

2   With a modem a microcomputer is capable of transmitting 104

and receiving data between any two locations connected   115

by telephone lines. The rate at which the data is sent   126

over the phone lines is measured in bits per second   136

(bps), where eight bits are equivalent to one character.   147

Older modems transmit at the rate 28800, 33600, and   157

56600 bits per second. However, current modems are being   168

developed with the capability of communicating at even   179

higher speeds.   182

3   In a recent newspaper article the Internal Revenue   193

Service (IRS) defined artificial intelligence as "the   204

science of making machines do things that would require   215

intelligence if done by man." As an example, there are   226

currently computers which can play chess so well that they 238

can beat all but the best players. Universities actually   250

challenge each other's computers to play chess to determine 262

which has the best chess playing program. Are these   272

computers really intelligent? Most computer scientists   283

would say no. They are simply programmed to make a series 295

of decisions in response to the moves made by their   305

opponents. It is merely their speed and ability to access 317

huge amounts of stored data which make them appear to be   329

intelligent.   331

    1   2   3   4   5   6   7   8   9 | 1   2

Index

D

F

G

H

K

L

M

Q

R

S

Z